I0200040

Duffy's Tavern

A History
of
Ed Gardner's
Radio Program

Martin Grams, Jr.

BearManor
Media

Albany, Georgia

Duffy's Tavern: A History of Ed Gardner's Radio Program
© 2014 Martin Grams, Jr. All Rights Reserved.

No part of this book may be reproduced in any form or by any means, electronic, mechanical, digital, photocopying or recording, except for the inclusion in a review, without permission in writing from the publisher.

BearManor Media
PO Box 71426
Albany, GA 31708
www.BearManorMedia.com

Layout and design by Allan Duffin, duffincreative.com

ISBN 978-1-62933-358-8

Printed in the United States of America

Dedicated to
Ed Gardner, Jr.

I hope I did justice by immortalizing your father, one of the
funniest comedians of the 20th Century.

Table of Contents

Introduction

EARLY RADIO BROADCASTING REQUIRED FINE-TUNING — and not the kind that came from twiddling the dials. Case in point: June 26, 1931. NBC presented "The Fearful Seven," the tale of Merton Moth and his noiseless glider, Michael Mosquito — brief glimpses into the home lives of Fanny Fly, Frankie Flea, Grand Roach and their friends. The NBC offering was promised to be a comedy and newspaper columnists were assured that the comedy element would predominate the production. There was nothing funny with the story and radio, had it not already established itself as a medium of music, news, prayer and commentary, might have been doomed as a result of this disastrous broadcast. If radio audiences wanted authentic laughter from a weekly half-hour program, what they needed was Ed Gardner. Ten years after Merton Moth had flown away into the ether, *Duffy's Tavern* would usher in a new form of comedy entertainment.

Like the genially sarcastic, ever-hopeful Archie, Ed Gardner was a product of New York's lower East Side along Third Avenue and was noted for his stupendous misuse of the English language. He would sling words and phrases around with blissful disregard for grammar and he showed a definite knack for handling malapropisms. His weakness tended towards gullibility in succumbing to any money making schemes... and beautiful women... especially rich ones. In real life, Ed Gardner was a brilliant and shrewd businessman. His insistence on adding comedy to an hour-long infomercial helped save M-G-M studios from a financial disaster. Gardner quickly established himself as a successful producer for a variety of radio programs spotlighting Rudy Vallee and Robert L. Ripley. He often trusted his instincts and learned all about radio programming from experience, working his way up the ladder of success. What little he didn't know about the craft he made up for in shrewd business deals. Towards the end of eleven successful years of *Duffy's Tavern*, Ed Gardner proved himself so valuable that NBC signed a contract to retain his services knowing well enough in advance that they would take a loss of more than $100,000.

On *Duffy's Tavern*, Archie defined the cynical second-generation Irishman at the outer fringe of New York's social order. The program quickly developed a following that crossed social, economic and geographical boundaries. According to popularity polls, *Duffy's Tavern* ranked with Fred Allen's program as the goofiest slapstick comedies on the air. Archie was the pivot of the establishment but he was not alone. Always on hand were the absent proprietor's gabby, man-hungry daughter, known simply as Miss Duffy, who spoke in pure Brooklynese, and the waiter, Eddie, a shrewd black menial who obeyed with "Yazzuh" but always got the better of his boss in their verbal exchanges. Habitués included Clifton Finnegan, a moron with occasional flashes of brilliance whose every line began with "Duhhh," and radio veteran Colonel Stoopnagle, the rotund inventor of such useful devices as the 10-foot pole, "for guys who wouldn't touch with one," and the gun with two barrels, one to shoot ducks with and the other, which didn't work, to not shoot other hunters.

Crackpot O'Toole, forger and poet who wrote mostly bum

checks and sonnets "in pure cubic centimeter," was another Duffy's regular. Not heard but often discussed in the early years was Two-Top Gruskin, a two-headed baseball player whose value to his team was that he could watch first and third at the same time. Two-Top (whose real name was Athos and Porthos Gruskin) once went to a masquerade ball as a pair of bookends and won the affections of a pretty girl because he was a tall blond and brunette. "There was just something different about him," she explained. Officer Clancy made frequent visits, usually threatening to close the place for some petty violation, ever thwarted by Archie's logical argument: "You can't close us up. We ain't got a license."

Archie wasn't otherwise so successful with his unceasing efforts to con or exploit his guests. When smooth-talking Slippery McGuire, seeking to beat his bar tab, suggested to Archie how he could make a fortune by patenting electricity, Archie paid him $10 to register the patent. After coughing up another $3 to print stock certificates and $5 more to include DC along with AC, he believes himself the King of Kilowatts, even though Eddie is doubtful ("I always connected you more with natural gas"). The plans fall through when Archie learns that Benjamin Franklin had beaten him to the patent, but Slippery launches him on a new career by informing him that Franklin had carelessly forgotten to take one out on the kite.

Today, anyone looking back on *Duffy's Tavern* realizes that Ed Gardner insulted most of Hollywood through professional ribbing approved in advance and typed into script form. This was perhaps the show's greatest asset and the reason why cinephiles today often seek out episodes. From Oscar winners to the bobbysoxer idols, many celebrities loved accepting and delivering one-liners as a change of pace. Others demanded changes in the script. When Rudy Vallee was introduced as a radio star of the old silent days, Archie told Duffy, "… he is sort of a prehistory Perry Como. Remember the time you bought a crystal set and thought there was something wrong with it? Well, Vallee was the guy."

When Mickey Rooney made an appearance on the show, Archie described the Hollywood star to Duffy on the phone. "Yeah, that's the guy. Short, freckles, blond hair, pug nose… sort of a Van Johnson at half mast. Yeah, a little bit of a guy. In fact, they tell me when two grasshoppers meet, one says to the other, 'I haven't seen you since you was knee-high to Mickey Rooney.' His size is a bit of a problem, too… especially in Hollywood… You know, he's too short to be a lover and too tall to be a producer."

Archie defined Lauren Bacall as "the dame with a husky, throaty voice, like Tallulah Bankhead on a clear day. She inspired the 'Lauren' in 'laurengitis'." Of Arthur Treacher, Archie remarked: "Some guys go around looking as though they smelled something bad but Treacher looks like he found it." Of Frank Sinatra: "There's a thin line between singing and crooning, and that thin line is known as Sinatra. He makes the bobby-soxers swoon because his voice sounds better when the listener is unconscious. How can they dare say every week that this guy is so round, so firm and so fully packed?"

When Archie told actress Gertrude Lawrence that he was her new Noel Coward, she replied: "You're half right." Archie dubbed singer Hildegarde as "the rich man's Cass Daley," and Marlene Dietrich as "the baritone Margaret Truman." "Actually," said Archie, "I'm very fond of Marlene. With them legs, she's made more successful crossings than the Matson Line. They've earned her a couple of million bucks and you've gotta admit that's pretty good pin money."

Some stars, however, put one over on Archie. When the barkeep asked Dinah Shore how long she had been away from *Duffy's Tavern*, she answered: "Two years, eleven months, three weeks, two days, seven hours and twenty-two minutes." When he chided her for counting, she quipped, "I always count my blessings."

Humphrey Bogart, making his only appearance at the tavern, remarked: "I've experienced many killings in my movie career, but this is the first time I've watched a guy bump off a language."

In 1949, the long-running radio program moved production to Puerto Rico to take advantage of a tax exemption the island gave to new industries, although the New York Third Avenue setting of the fictional tavern remained the same. The stellar guests who had once regularly visited Duffy's, however, didn't care to travel so far for a broadcast. The program's ratings fell precipitously.

To this date, the mainstream public knows *Duffy's Tavern* only as a Trivial Pursuit question as the possible forerunner for the popular television series *Cheers*, which also had a long and successful run in broadcast history. The television program was credited by James Burrows, son of Abe Burrows. Ed Gardner was also godfather to James. In the past two decades, the radio program has received very little coverage except for a few magazine articles and entries in encyclopedias. In 2001, I submitted a lengthy article and broadcast log for SPERDVAC's *Radiogram*. The editor at the time cut sections out pertaining to the 1945 motion picture and the later television program since the magazine was devoted solely to old-time radio. Even as a three-part article in their February, March and April issues, I wanted people to know all they could about the program. To accomplish the task, I independently published the entire work, spiral bound, charging ten bucks to reimburse the expense of printing and binding. About 200 copies sold over a period of two years.

Afterwards, I never gave *Duffy's Tavern* much thought until 2007, when I discovered the log I had created was available on the internet with authorship credited to someone else. After making a hasty inquiry, I discovered the person who claimed they "authored" the log confessed that their primary source of material was a three-part article that appeared in *Radiogram*. No surprise there. Then I compared it word for word and realized it was their only source — they copied my log word for word. If there was any variation between the two, I could not find it. Thankfully, the website provider removed the log when he discovered someone was committing an act of plagiarism. But the problem was not resolved. Following sage advice from a friend who once told me, "publish or perish," I decided it was time to commit to a book about *Duffy's Tavern*. After a decade of gathering and filing away information about *Duffy's Tavern*, it was clear my prior compilation warranted an update. What you hold in your hands is the greatly expanded version. Rather than document the program in the form of an encyclopedia (meaning you can only digest it page by page over a period of months), I chose a different route, one with tongue-in-cheek humor and an enjoyable narrative from first page to last.

A book of this size could not exist without the assistance of a number of individuals, listed in no particular order: Fred Berney, Michael Hayde, Neal Ellis, Larry Kiner, Ken Stockinger, Frank Stockinger, Douglas Due, Frank Bresee, Sid Caesar, Esther Williams, Doug Hopkinson, Allan Duffin, Ben Ohmart, Scott Bailey, Hazel Shermet, Barb Davies and Dave Davies. Folks who granted me permission to reprint excerpts from prior publications or contributed to the preservation of *Duffy's Tavern* with magazine articles and encyclopedia entries of their own include Patrick Lucanio of SPERDVAC's *Radiogram*, Bob Burchett, Gary Yoggy, Jim Cox, John Dunning and Jay Hickerson. Research assistance provided by Rene Thompson, Roger Hill, John Macmillan, Michael Biel, the staff of the Charles E. Young Research Library at UCLA Film and Television Archive, the staff at the Recorded Sound Reference Center at the Library of Congress, the staff of the Archives of the Wisconsin Historical Society, the staff of the American Radio Archives of the Thousand Oaks Library, the staff of the American Heritage Center of the University of Wyoming, and the staff of the Billy Rose Theatre Collection of the Performing Arts Library. Special thanks to Derek Tague who spent many hours with me at Billy Rose taking down notes from the Abe Burrows Papers. Helping to verify small bits of trivia and factoids: Laura Leff, Michael Biel, and J. David Goldin. Recordings supplied by Terry Salomonson, David Siegel, Carl Amari, Randy Watts, Alex Daoundakis, Mark Tepper of Radio Spirits, Matthew Terlecky, Nick Hulbert, Jim Cooper, Mark Gross, and Steve Kelez. Proofreaders include Melanie Altman, Steve Thompson and Jo Bagwell. Photographs provided by Bryan Hendrickson, Jim Hathaway, Rick Payne, Bob Daniel, Graham Newton, David Lennick and Chun Hiller. Valued suggestions from Roy Bright, Rodney Bowcock, Walden Hughes, and Jack French. If there is anyone I forgot to mention, please forgive me and do not mistake my absent-mindedness as anything intentional.

I have to thank four individuals who deserve special recognition for going above and beyond: Dan Riedstra, who helped supply factoids, rare recordings and guidance for this book. Dan is probably the only person who shares a love for *Duffy's Tavern* more than myself. Terry Salomonson who, after learning of an individual who was holding back recordings because they chose pride over preservation, came to bat at the last minute to help with the completion of this book. Michelle, my wife, for her patience. Ed Gardner, Jr., who invited me to his home and graciously allowed me access to the family archives and deserves credit for more than half of the photographs in this book.

And now, as Archie himself would say, "Leave us look back at a time gone by..."

Martin Grams, Jr.
July 2013

CHAPTER ONE
ED GARDNER'S
EARLY RADIO CAREER

IN JULY OF 1954, ED GARDNER TOLD a newspaper columnist that he decided to hang up his hat for good. "I'm quitting as an actor and comedian. I've had it," he said. "Fifteen years is long enough to be a clown. I'd rather do something else now." Fourteen years prior, no one, not even Gardner, could have predicted a career that would rival in the ratings such luminaries as Jack Benny, Bob Hope, Eddie Cantor, Bing Crosby, Edgar Bergen and Charlie McCarthy, and Al Jolson. His portrayal of Archie, the barkeep for the fictional *Duffy's Tavern*, often typecast him as a poor man's comedian and a "master of malaprop." Unlike most other radio comedians, Gardner never had a career in vaudeville. He climbed the ladder of success by learning the business and the craft of radio itself.

Ed Gardner was born Edward Francis Poggenburg on June 29, 1901, in Astoria, Long Island. At the age of 14, he secured his first after-school job as a pianist at O'Bryan's Café, a colorful neighborhood bistro that later served partly as a model for Duffy's.* Had the young man suspected the significance of this position, the future course of events might have been different. As it was, his stay there was short-lived. His mother happened to walk by one afternoon, caught a fleeting glimpse through the swinging door of her son at the piano, and promptly ended his musical career. He would later remark that the piano playing gig was one of the few jobs he had ever left without being fired.

Poggenburg had dropped out of school at the age of 16, after his second year at Bryant High School, to begin what was to become a wild decade of odd jobs. "If Public School #4 was good enough for Archie, then why should I complain?" Gardner recalled in 1943. "The only degrees I'm interested in are Fahrenheit and Centigrade." The six-foot-two Irish-German-American used to boss a rough, tough street gang named One Ol' Cats out in Astoria, Long Island. At the time, further exposure to knowledge was not deemed necessary. "The family," he said, "thought I was pretty well-educated and by that time and judging by the standards of the neighborhood, I was."

---

* This statement has been in print for decades. Recent evidence, however, suggests otherwise. Steven and Rene Thompson, searching the New York State Archives: Albany, New York: State Population Census Schedules, 1925; Election District 70; Assembly District: 04; City: New York; County: Queens; Page 41, Within the household of Fred Poggenburg, found no "Edward Francis" in the early censuses but there is a "Frederick Poggenburg, Jr." listed with the correct age for Ed. The name "Edward Francis Poggenburg" first shows up in the state census in 1925 – no earlier. A census-taker's oversight was not uncommon in New York at the time because of varying factors including thick-tongue translation complications with foreign immigrants and complicated dialects. If the suggested evidence can be verified, his birth name was probably Frederick Poggenburg (no middle name), later changed to Edward Francis Poggenburg, and later changed again to Edward Gardner.

Ed Gardner as a youth.

At the age of 16, Poggenburg got a job selling pianos, a momentary success. Other jobs followed in rapid succession. He designed and built a miniature golf course. As a fight manager, he lasted through two minutes of the third round of his protégé's maiden bout. Then he was a typewriter salesman and a paint salesman – during one of these jobs he acquired a lisp. This, he explained once, was because receptionists and secretaries, who ordinarily threw salesmen out, would listen to his lisp, fascinated. Before they came out of their trance, Ed would be selling the boss a bill of goods. Always a quick thinker, he also told of the time when he was arrested for speeding while going through a

3

Pennsylvania town. Before he left, he sold the city fathers an order for repainting the jail!

In late 1928 or early 1929, Ed Poggenburg met a stage actress, Shirley Booth, who convinced him to change his name from Poggenburg to Gardner. She too had dropped out of public school, and this, among other common denominators, led to their mutual attraction. Having come from a middle-class family, Booth sought New York's theater district and a distinguished career behind the footlights — much to her family's disappointment. Supposedly the two met at a party put on by a producer of Broadway stage plays, J. Augustus Pitou. Gardner, known for being a ladies' man and possessing the gift of gab, flirted. They spent time together but Shirley apparently held back accepting his proposal until she felt she had established herself professionally. Gardner ultimately gave up a career as a salesman to learn more about the stage. Producer Hal Kanter recalled in his book, *So Far, So Funny* (1999, McFarland Publishing): "On their first night at sea, Shirley caught Ed stealing out of another woman's stateroom. 'Now you know the truth,' he said. 'I'm an international jewel thief.'" The lovebirds were married on the morning of November 23, 1929, hours before the final performance of *Claire Adams*, in which Shirley Booth (now Shirley Gardner) was performing. The play had lasted only one week at the Biltmore; the management killed any chance the show had.

Influenced by his wife, Ed Gardner chose a career in theater when he produced shows for the Works Progress Administration (WPA). Prior to this, he first found himself involved in the theater business as a promoter in the publicity department of Crosby Gaige. This led to a position in the New York office of Jennie Jacobs where he promoted stock companies, signed actors, rented theaters, handled hotels and theatrical transportation, painted scenery, typed scripts, directed shows, acted as stand-in and understudy and was casting director. (This experience would later come in handy when he took over the producing reins of many radio programs including *Duffy's Tavern*.) His first job as a theatrical producer was *Collitch*, a skit about college life. Then came another, *Coast-Wise Annie*, which lasted eight weeks at the Belmont. He acted alongside his wife in *The Mask and the Face*

4

(1933). Then, Gardner's supreme effort came as director for *After Such Pleasures*, adapted from the works of Dorothy Parker. "I was the guy who gave radio actors the brush-off," Gardner later recalled. *After Such Pleasures* was an independent feature which the Gardners produced out of their own pocket, mostly from handshakes, promises and giving away percentages of the profits. The play, however, was not profitable.

Shirley Booth and Ed Gardner

Having graduated from the WPA in the depths of the Depression of the thirties, his theatrical knowledge helped him establish a good reputation in radio broadcasting, which by now was earning him $30 a week as an actor. After appearing (unbilled) in dozens of radio programs originating from the New York studios, Ed Gardner accepted a job at the J. Walter

Thompson advertising agency, writing, producing and directing some of the higher-rated radio programs on the air. (The March 6, 1935, issue of *Broadcasting* magazine reported "Ed Gardner, who produced *Robinson Crusoe Jr.* serial for N.W. Ayer is now with the J. Walter Thompson radio department.) His employment with J. Walter Thompson required a move to California, where many of the agency's programs originated. Shirley Booth remained in New York City to perform on stage. Among Gardner's first major contributions were *The Shell Chateau* (January 2, 1937, to June 26, 1937) with series regular Joe Cook, and *The Joe Penner Show* (October 4, 1936, to June 27, 1937) featuring the comedian along with cartoonist Robert L. Ripley as series regulars. It was on the latter that Ed Gardner first met Ozzie Nelson and Harriet Hilliard, who would become good friends.

Gardner established such a notable reputation that in July 1937 his name was included among the rumors spreading of Ed Gardner and Tony Stanford, both employed at J. Walter Thompson, placing bids for *Hollywood Hotel.* The program was considered the most prestigious radio program to originate out of Hollywood, tapping screen talent that would otherwise not have considered radio. This proved to be only a rumor for the tabloids, because of assertions from L. Ward Wheelock of the F. Wallis Armstrong agency that the present setup would not be disturbed.

During the summer of 1937, Ed Gardner and Shirley Booth spent three weeks in Hawaii. Beginning October 9, 1937, Gardner co-produced with John Christ *The Baker's Broadcast* for a second season, again featuring the talented Feg Murray, again sponsored by Fleischmann. This time, Shirley Booth decided to accompany her husband to California. The first episode of the season had Richard Arlen appearing in a dramatization of how he got his motion picture start by breaking a leg. Walt Disney was in the interview spot. This type of variety, Gardner believed, was radio entertainment at its best.

Good News of 1938

Announced as the most spectacular radio show ever launched, with much hype and promotion, the *Good News* program cost

General Foods a reported $25,000 a week to sponsor an hour-long extravaganza featuring every Hollywood star under contract to Metro-Goldwyn-Mayer (MGM), "except Garbo." On October 21, 1937, the production staff at MGM for the Maxwell House-sponsored program was augmented by the addition of two seasoned producers who assisted Bill Bacher on the series: Ed Gardner, production executive at J. Walter Thompson, and Sam Moore, former producer of *The Camel Caravan*. (The unusual title *Good News of 1938* was decided on after several others had been earlier discarded.) The premiere broadcast from the El Capitan theater was a dress affair, with an invited audience to occupy the 1,572 seats. Bacher insisted on old Broadway stage favorites in a memory lane routine. Gardner worked with the comedy talent while Sam Moore scripted the comedy section of the show, preparing it for Bacher. Harry Kronman was in complete charge of the writers.

Myrna Loy and Ed Gardner during rehearsals of the Good News *radio program.*

By the end of October, Ed Gardner resigned from *The Baker's Broadcast* and Bob Brewster was transferred from New York to Hollywood to replace him. Gardner discovered his duties for the MGM-Maxwell program required more time than initially expected, even though he only handled the comedy part of the program. The premiere broadcast on November 7, 1937, was truly spectacular. Jeanette MacDonald and Allan Jones sang selections from *Firefly*, the host was Robert Leonard, the director of the film of the same name that opened the next day, and featured Hollywood stars George Murphy, Buddy Ebsen, Sophie Tucker, Eleanor Powell and Judy Garland, introduced as being 14 years old (she was already 15 by that time). Louis B. Mayer stepped before the microphone, as did C.M. Chester, president of General Foods. The sponsor was not disappointed, receiving more air time to promote Maxwell House Coffee than the usual hour-long radio broadcast. According to reviews, radio listeners were not disappointed either, but critics felt otherwise. MGM's primary interest seemed to be self-promotion, and that didn't play well on radio.

Back in New York, in mid-November, after the curtain fell on the opening night of *Too Many Heroes*, Shirley Booth immediately put in a long-distance phone call to her husband. She asked to have the charges reversed. Whereupon, Gardner cracked back, "What's the matter, honey? Didn't the show go over tonight?"

In late November 1937, after three weeks on the air, fiery, wild-eyed, autocratic production chief Bill Bacher, claiming that MGM wasn't giving him the cooperation necessary, resigned as producer of *Good News of 1938*. The veteran air producer asked to be relieved of his seven-year contract with the studio. Gardner, who happened to be Bacher's assistant at the time, moved into the post, with George Jessel in the capacity of advisory producer. Under Gardner's control, the entire *Good News* program underwent a major overhaul. The previewing of MGM motion pictures was cut down to ten minutes. As a new production twist to avoid similarity to other programs, special emphasis on the program would go towards original sketches. Casts would be drawn from players on the movie lot. One or two stellar names would top each week's offerings. George Jessel was hired to edit each script and write material for the emcee. Gardner managed to cut the budget. When Ted Healy demanded $30,000 for 10 weeks on the show, Gardner thumbed it down.

Gardner's position was supposed to be temporary. He proved so reliable, though, that, in mid-December, he was officially signed by MGM as a permanent writer, supervisor and producer of the program. When *Too Many Heroes* closed in December, Shirley Booth went to Hollywood to stay with her husband and accept any movie offers that might come her way. To say the marriage was a perfect union was an exaggeration. Relations were strained between husband and wife, with 3,000 miles separating their ambitions. Ed Gardner proved to be the breadwinner in the home and Shirley Booth, having made the move to California, agreed to stay and play the role of a housewife. It was no secret that Ed Gardner was a womanizer but on the West Coast the rumors were no different than those back East.

Any radio listener who heard the MGM show since its inception knew that it underwent quite a change during the first two months. Under Gardner's leadership, more comedy was added to the program. This was partially thanks to the presence of Fanny Brice and Frank Morgan who joined the program in late December and were zooming in fan favor. Bacher, Gardner explained, offered a fine show for the people who watched his broadcasts from the studio but the unseen audience couldn't appreciate them. One thing that Gardner wanted to develop was a working nucleus of personalities such as Brice, Morgan and Judy Garland, plus a top male star who would be a regular master-of-ceremonies; these ultimately included James Stewart, Robert Taylor and Robert Young. In January of 1938, Gardner talked to MGM to convince them to use Robert Taylor as a permanent emcee to build him up as an air name and at the same time numb the recent injurious publicity that had adversely affected the star's pull at the box office. Under Gardner's guidance, Taylor was given a "pretty boy" image and the campaign later proved successful.

In April, there was talk about Ed Gardner possibly producing the *Guess Where* program for Philip Morris. Shirley was a regular member of the program, which also featured Budd Hulick and, for a short time, future *Duffy's Tavern* alumnus Charles Cantor.

During his radio days, Ed Gardner collected autograph photos from actors and actresses including Gloria DeHaven and W.C. Fields.

Accepting the position would have meant moving back to New York. He turned down the offer to remain in California. He enjoyed his salary for the *Good News* program. In May 1938, the Gardners began looking for a house, eventually renting one on North Vermont Avenue in Los Angeles.

Over the summer, the *Good News* program was renewed for a second season with Gardner as the supervising director who made sure the successful formula of the prior season remained untouched for the second. Meredith Willson and his orchestra supplied the music. Fanny Brice and Hanley Stafford reprised their recurring roles as Baby Snooks and her father. Spencer Tracy and Mickey Rooney performed scenes from *Boys Town* (1938). Father Flanagan, founder of the real Boys Town in Nebraska, spoke. Alice Faye stretched her vocal chords. Louis B. Mayer was a guest speaker. With such a promising start, no one — not even Ed Gardner — predicted what would come from the following week's broadcast.

On the evening of September 8, Hunt Stromberg and Norma Shearer, the producer and actress of *Marie Antoinette*, made guest appearances on *Good News of 1939* (now re-titled for the new season) to promote their motion picture then playing in theaters across the country. As with *Boys Town* the week before, the movie studio hoped to use the weekly radio broadcasts to promote their latest movies and boost ticket sales. In his hilarious book, *There I Stood With My Piccolo* (1948), Meredith Willson recalled what happened behind the scenes. "Many times picture people don't understand how important the inflexible seconds are in the radio business, and at the rehearsal she sort of did everything her own way, so this young producer didn't have a chance to get any kind of an accurate timing. The unfortunate result was that we had to go on the air b'guess and b'God." The show was aired "live" and during the final fourth of the program, Shearer participated in an dramatization of a scene from *Marie Antoinette*, followed by a musical presentation of "The Peanut Vendor." This musical deluge ultimately threatened the program to go past its allotted time limit. The actress was in the midst of conversation with emcee Robert Young, making reference to the entire broadcast being dedicated to Norma Shearer, when the network attaché ordered

11

the announcer to sign off. When inquiries were made by both the movie studio and the advertising agency, Ed Gardner accepted full responsibility when he failed to wind up the proceedings on time. Had Gardner scrapped the musical feature, "The Peanut Vendor," the program would have wrapped up on time.*

Over the next two weeks, tabloids began reporting "several tiffs" between the principals and four weeks later, after the broadcast of October 6, Ed Gardner was asked to make way for a new producer, Donald Cope. Before Christmas, Ed Gardner and Shirley Booth packed their bags and moved back to their home in Westport.

This is New York

For many years a story circulated of how the character of 'Archie' was born; more or less by accident. Gardner was director of *This is New York* and, in one segment, needed the voice of a "typical New York mug" and couldn't find an actor to fill the bill. "There was a radio program called *This is New York*," Ed recalled for a newspaper columnist. "We wanted a guy to talk New Yorkese, but all we could get was voices that sounded like Dodger fans in the left-field bleachers. There is as much difference between New Yorkese and Kings County English as there is between Oxford and Choctaw." Gardner later explained in a 1943 magazine interview that a New Yorker, for instance, would say: "Laertes poisinned the point uf his foil." In Brooklyn he says it would be: "Layoytees purzind the pernt of his ferl." Gardner auditioned a number of actors for the role and was disappointed. The solution was supposedly found by a CBS program director who told Gardner he should play the role himself.

"He had Deems Taylor, who was a very well-known music critic at that time," recalled Simone Hegeman, Gardner's second wife, to Carl Amari in a radio interview. "And he had Deems Taylor playing the gentleman and talking very high brow musical stuff. And Ed wanted someone who was sort of the bum. The

---

* Meredith Willson's recollection was inaccurate in his autobiography that the dramatization of *Marie Antoinette* was cut in the middle of a scene.

counterpoint to Deems Taylor's gentleman. And he kept auditioning people and he was never happy. The New York accent wasn't right or the timing was off. So someone in the control booth pushed the button down and said, 'Hey Ed, why don't you do it? And by golly, he did. He was started doing Archie and was absolutely terrified. He was not an actor but his timing was good. He filled a picture of the character with his timing and his voice. But people had a completely different picture of what he was, physically. A lady came up to him one day and said, 'But you're not Archie. Archie is a little tiny fellow.' And Ed was 6 foot 2. He was very tall for those days."

Another story claims that 28 minutes before airtime, he was still auditioning actors for the part. In frustration, he took the mike himself, to demonstrate how the lines should be read. Out of his mouth popped Archie. "But," Gardner explained, "as I was sayin', one guy after the other gets up in front of the microphone and talks Brooklyn. Finally, I went out in front of the mike myself, because I have one guy who shows promise. He is only half-breed Brooklyn, on the distaff side. While I was demonstrating how it should sound, the gang in the control room is having hysterics."

"Why bother with an actor?" George Faulkner and others suggested, "Read it yourself."

"So who am I to argue with the fates? I went ahead and did it."

One of the "guys" in the control room in hysterics was his J. Walter Thompson colleague, George Faulkner, who, by most accounts, was the first to see a character in that voice and may have been the one who even named him Archie. Faulkner insisted the character remain a permanent fixture for *This is New York*. And to help cross-promote the program, Archie would make guest appearances on other variety programs managed by the same agency.

A third story reports that when Ed Gardner planned a show designed to contrast the cultural side of New York with the seamy side, he had set Deems Taylor as the protagonist for culture. When he listened to the playback of Taylor's audition record, for which Gardner himself had cued Taylor's lines, he suddenly realized that his own voice was just the one he had been looking for to play the other side of the coin. "That," he says gloomily, "is what comes of bein' born in Astoria."

Regardless of which story is accurate, there remains a more probable factoid: Ed Gardner no doubt had intentions from the beginning to have Archie among the cast of *This is New York*.

Ever since Major Edward Bowes staged his amateur hour in the Sunday night time slot in March of 1935, America was glued to its radio tubes for a talent show that on any given evening presented a man who could whistle two separate songs at the same time, church choirs, cowboy comics, blind accordion players... and still managed to hawk Chase and Sanborn Coffee to faithful radio listeners. In the spring of 1937, Chase and Sanborn took a gamble on a wooden dummy, Charlie McCarthy, who enlivened the same airwaves with his own unique brand of entertainment. The Sunday night time slot was regarded as the most valuable (and most expensive). Then came Orson Welles who boldly selected that hour to win an audience. That thousands were listening to him was indicated by the "Martian scare" in October of 1938 but the radio surveys estimated that a comparatively small percentage of the nation's radio audience was actually tuned in to Welles; the majority, they reported, were listening to the impish Charlie, and that was said to have averted "a major disaster" when the "hordes from Mars rocketed to Earth."

Orson Welles had forsaken the Sunday witching hour shortly after the panic broadcast when he secured a sponsor, Campbell Soups. The name of the program switched from *The Mercury Theater on the Air* to *The Campbell Playhouse* and made the move to Friday nights. This left the showmen of that hook-up with the old riddle again of finding a program to compete with Charlie McCarthy. Enter stage left, Ed Gardner. Having credits to his name with some of the most popular radio variety programs, CBS banked on *This is New York*, a variety program that stood very little chance of success against NBC's high-rated and ever-popular *Chase and Sanborn Hour* featuring Bergen and McCarthy. The program premiered on the evening of December 11, 1938. The plan, as described by a CBS Press release, was as follows: "Only that which has well-rooted origin in some of the many varied elements that give New York its fascinating personality will find a place on this diversified program of comedy, drama, music and lively human interest. Beginning with an example in point, the first master-of-ceremonies is to be James Montgomery Flagg, noted illustrator. He will introduce, among the guests, Alexander Woollcott, author and critic, and Louis Armstrong, whose trumpet probably speaks best for him. Leith Stevens' orchestra and a chorus led by Lyn Murray abetted by soloists will present the vast pattern of entertainment typical of New York. Take a dynamo, two high tension wires, a scoop full of TNT, mix thoroughly, add bushy eyebrows, a voice that sounds like the blend of a buzz saw and an irate cab driver – and there's Ed Gardner. He confounds most success formulas. He keeps terrible hours, never goes to the office unless he can't help it, parks his feet anywhere below the ceiling level and has boundless energy. He talks fast and acts faster."

Alexander Woollcott and Ed Gardner

Besides *This is New York*, CBS also had the option of another radio program, *Hollywood Café*, created by Ed Gardner and George McCall. This unproduced program was similar to *This is New York*, but with the appeal of Hollywood, California, instead of New York City. To protect his unsold proposal, Gardner filed for Federal copyright protection in December 1938.

The CBS revue successfully gave radio listeners a collage of the city landscape. "The sidewalks of New York and the people, famous and obscure, who tread them," as described by *Radio Guide*. CBS hoped a potential sponsor might hear the program and consider sponsorship. With no band interludes, the program cost CBS a weekly tab of $2,500. Each guest performed a substantial chore for the little sum paid to them. $375 went to Ed Gardner, a pittance compared to the money he was paid in Hollywood when producing the MGM-Maxwell House program. *This is New York* was said to have commercial nibbles, but no takers. Shirley wasn't getting any significant stage roles and to help offset some of the expenses, Gardner convinced his wife to guest as straight woman for George Jessel in one episode. Together they dramatized a cross-section of the Broadway heartbreak. With no commercial interest, however, CBS cancelled the program after the broadcast of March 19, 1939.

One thing that came from *This is New York* was Ed Gardner's introduction to Abe Burrows, who would ultimately become the head scriptwriter for *Duffy's Tavern*.* "When I met Ed Gardner, he was producing a radio show for CBS called *This is New York*," recalled Abe Burrows. "We met him because *This is New York* wanted Eddie Garr for a guest shot, and Frank Galen and I were told to go over to meet with Ed Gardner and find out what kind of material we should write for Garr's appearance on the show... He asked about what we had been doing, what our experience was. We admitted a few fairly funny lines, and then he finally said to us, 'Look, I haven't got room for Garr on this week's show, but I might be able to use you two guys as writers.' Well, we were thrilled, but we felt guilty because we had come there for Eddie Garr, and we said so. Gardner said he'd use Garr later on, but he needed writing help now. He said he would try us out for a week and pay us twenty-five dollars apiece. Well, to us this seemed like a terrific deal and we solemnly accepted his offer. Actually, we would have accepted this tryout for nothing."

---

* For a detailed explanation of Abe Burrows' duties as head scriptwriter, see Appendix K.

Ed Gardner and Abe Burrows

"We listened as Gardner began talking to the rest of his staff about their show for the coming week," Burrows continued. "And we were fascinated. This wasn't a matter of loose jokes; this was a whole show. At one point Gardner said something that made me think of an idea that might help, and I opened my mouth and said it. He looked at me, a long look, and he said, 'Tell you what, I'll raise it to thirty bucks a week.' When Frank and I left the office,

17

we were almost sick with joy. We had a job at CBS and we had already received our first raise. It was marvelous."

The Texaco Star Theater

The Texaco Star Theater started in October 1938 with an hour-long variety program originating from both coasts; the dramatic half from New York and the comedy/musical half from California. By the end of the first season, the sponsors expressed displeasure in the time slot which went up against Fred Allen. In May and June of 1939, Texaco put up a bid for Al Pearce to replace *Texaco Star Theater*, but lost. Bill Bacher, who served as ringmaster for 39 weeks, having taken it in hand from its inception, pulled out as producer. Outside interference by the agency and Texaco officials prompted Bacher to withdraw. Bacher had long resented meddling in his production affairs, and was disgusted when sponsor influence eliminated the drama spot and replaced it with Alexander Woollcott piped in from the East Coast for the final three broadcasts of the season. Texaco was not sure about the second season: the dramatic spot would be dropped from next season's hour opus, with Alexander Woollcott to continue on the show if the sponsor was impressed with his three-week trial starting next week.

Thus, before the first season of *Texaco Star Theater* concluded, in early June Gardner signed to take over for Bacher for the second season. He told the press that he would do his Archie character in addition to his duties as ringmaster. The intention of doing 'Archie' was dropped by request of the sponsor, days after Gardner made his intentions public. If Archie couldn't succeed in convincing a sponsor on *This is New York*, the sponsor concluded, the character should not appear on their program. In late August, Gardner flew back to California "for an indefinite stay for business" as he described it, to take over the variety half of the hour-long *Texaco Star Theater*. (The dramatic half was still being done in New York). The scripting staff for the West Coast included Frank Galen, Keith Fowler, Abe Burrows and Tom Langan. Langan had worked with Gardner on *This is New York*. Again, Gardner's wife remained in New York, this time with a successful run as Elizabeth Imbrie,

18

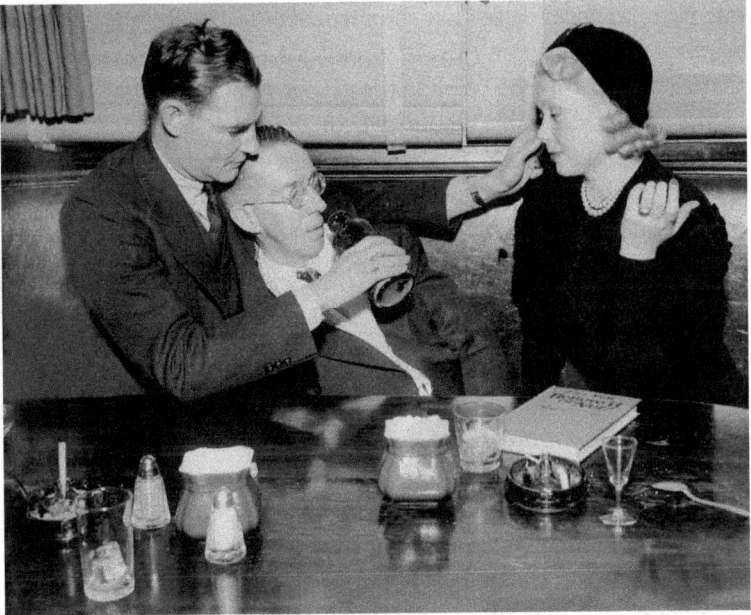

Ed Gardner clowns around with Robert Ripley.

a society magazine columnist, in Phillip Barry's new stage play, *The Philadelphia Story.*

In August, Texaco was reported to be dickering with Robert Ripley and Jack Pearl as permanent additions to the new program. Because Gardner formerly handled Ripley's *Believe it or Not* program, his influence was a no-brainer. Neither Ripley nor Pearl became regulars. Two weeks after the new season premiere, Ken Dolan submitted a comic to producer Ed Gardner for a spot on the Texaco program.

"On what premise?" Gardner wanted to know.

"He's gotta eat," shot back Dolan.

Good News Guest Appearance

Taking a leaf from the notebook of copyright ownership, the answer to the question of whether or not a radio broadcast of the past remains copyrighted today lies in the formation of the program itself. Special attention is paid when ownership is transferred from one party to another, so that the owners of today are not the same as during the program's initial broadcast run. The general rule is that the creator of the work is the owner of all copyright interests in the work. However, where two or more parties create a work together, copyright ownership becomes a more difficult issue, often requiring clarification in the form of a written agreement. In addition, copyright ownership is more difficult to determine when the creator of a work is being paid by a third-party to create the work, often known as "work for hire." Throughout the twenties, radio broadcasts consisted mainly of music, news and social commentary. Dramas were few and sometimes at the expense of the radio station. When the broadcasting moguls discovered that advertising was a means of counteracting production costs, and make a profit at the same time, the networks founded a working relationship with a number of advertising agencies. Among the notables were the J. Walter Thompson Agency, the Batten, Barton, Durstine & Osborn Agency, McCann-Erickson, the Leo Burnett Company, and Young & Rubicam. When a company sought interest in sponsoring a radio program, the advertising agency had a staff whose job was to create a number of programs, demonstrate the benefits to their clients through proposals, and hope the client would sign a contract. The agency was responsible for producing the entire program, hiring the cast and writers, and oftentimes the producer and/or director was a staff member of the agency, overseeing the entire production. The networks, such as NBC and CBS, were merely companies that sold the scheduled airtime for a fee — dependent on the time and day of the week chosen by the agency.

Under this scenario, the sponsor usually owned the program. Therefore, General Mills, which sponsored *Jack Armstrong, the All-American Boy* beginning with the first broadcast of the series in 1933, still retains ownership of that show to this date. Kraft Foods Inc. still retains ownership of *The Great Gildersleeve*, which they sponsored from 1941 to 1954.

In 1938, the Blackett, Sample and Hummert Agency in Chicago, Illinois, developed a children's program for the Skelly Oil Company. *Captain Midnight* was syndicated across the country for two years until the sponsor decided the program was not selling their product. In 1940, the Wander Company purchased the program from the Agency, in the hopes of pitching their product, Ovaltine, to the impressionable juvenile audience. Years later, in 1955 or 1956, after sponsoring 39 television episodes of *Captain Midnight*, the Wander Company decided not to renew production of an additional 39. Screen Gems decided to syndicate the program with a different sponsor. When officials at Wander learned of this through trade papers, they alerted Screen Gems that they owned the copyright to the Captain Midnight character, and forbid the studio from re-airing the episodes. Screen Gems was forced to change the name of *Captain Midnight* to *Jet Jackson, Flying Commando*, and syndicated the series with poorly dubbed dialogue substituting all references of Captain Midnight to Jet Jackson, proving that the sponsors often held the rights to the fictional character, name and image.

When Ed Gardner created the character of Archie, the fictional character was not the property of the advertising agency or the sponsor, even though Gardner was under employment with the agency and his creation would have normally been considered a "work for hire." Gardner's character was improvised out of necessity and many radio listeners, as well as sentimental columnists, could not tell the two apart. Gardner was Archie, and often headlined as Ed "Archie" Gardner.

Since executives at Texaco instituted an official stance against the use of Archie on their program, Ed Gardner approached the producer of the *Good News* program and succeeded. Thanks to a script by Abe Burrows (who was then assisting Gardner with the comic sketches for *Texaco Star Theater*), on the broadcast of November 9, 1939, Ed Gardner appeared as a guest in the role of Archie, describing in comedic fashion how he lived in a place called "Duffy's Bar and Grill." Archie, retaining his Brooklyn accent, describes how much he enjoys sunny California, where the radio broadcast originated. He explained to actor Edward Arnold (the emcee for the evening), how Gorilla Hogan visited California for the fights... and a battle between him and Slugface Sullivan.

Months later, the *Good News* program changed format beginning with the broadcast of March 7, 1940, when the series shrunk to a 30 minute time slot and eliminated weekly guests.

Singer Mary Martin was added to the series as well as Dick Powell to serve as master of ceremonies. Fanny Brice remained in the spotlight due to her popularity which the radio audience associated with more than the name of *Good News*. In an ironic twist of fate, Hollywood came knocking in 1943, offering a pretty purse for the screen rights to *Duffy's Tavern*. The studio was MGM.

When *The Philadelphia Story*, playing at the Shubert in New York City, decided to lay off during the week of Christmas, Katharine Hepburn spent her vacation at her parents' home in Hartford, Connecticut. Shirley Booth flew to Hollywood to visit her husband, Ed Gardner. When the comedy went on tour in February 1940, Shirley again flew to the Coast to join her husband. At that time, the *Texaco Star Theater* was enjoying its highest rating in two years. The Gardners sought a cook for their house. It seemed everything was going well for them, including a number of potential prospects for reviving Ed's Archie character on a weekly basis. In mid-April, Gardner resigned as producer of the West Coast section of *Texaco Star Theater* and Jack Runyon, radio director for the Buchanan agency, took over the show for the remaining 11 weeks of the current season. Runyon was a veteran of West Coast radio, having been with Lord & Thomas for 13 years before switching over to Buchanan in 1939. Runyon has been credited for originating the so-called Hollywood formula and was the first to use film stars in guest spots.

Forecast

In late April of 1940, Ed Gardner attempted to convince executives at Benton & Bowles to do his Archie characterization as a regular spot on the *Good News* program. When all attempts failed by early May, Gardner and his wife flew back to New York where Shirley signed on to co-star on a weekly radio drama, *Strictly Business*. Ed, meanwhile, approached CBS, which was then considering a number of radio packages for the summer. W. B. Lewis, CBS program chief, was currently in Hollywood tying up the West Coast ends for a new program tentatively titled *Opening Nights*, through which would parade stars of stage, radio and current audition programs. In essence, Columbia called up all the available new programs and personality shows that passed the preliminary stage and were deemed ripe for a single public airing so that audience and sponsor reaction could be better obtained. The idea had been in preparation since midwinter and was so thoroughly charted that all Lewis and his aides had to do was obtain the actual signatures of the artists and fill in the required writers. CBS deemed the program "the most pretentious alignment of name programs that has ever been associated with a network on a sustaining basis."

Personalities due to appear through the summer were Joe Cook and Jimmy Durante in a minstrel show surrounded by orchestral and vocal talent; Walter Huston in a radio drama; Edna Mae Oliver in a program built to reveal her versatility; Elmer Davis in a traditionalized news novelty; Paul Robeson and Eddie Green in a Negro stanza; George McCall, with a new twist on people who live in Hollywood; Fredric March and Florence Eldridge in a dramatic stint; *Battle of Music*, a swing vs. classics musical program with Albert Spalding and the Raymond Paige orchestra*; and various dramatic series to be topped by Maurice Evans, Franchot Tone, Raymond Massey, Thomas Mitchell and Judith Anderson. Included among the potential lineup was Ed Gardner with "a guest star revue."

In May, Gardner remarked to friends in the trade that he was considering giving up producing altogether so that he could concentrate on the sale of his 'Archie' character, something he had already enacted on several programs. Young & Rubicam represented Ed Gardner and his new proposal, originally titled "Archie's Tavern" for Pall Mall cigarettes, a subsidiary of the American Tobacco Company, which expressed interest and agreed to listen to the July broadcast and give it serious consideration.

---

* The Andre Kostelanetz-Albert Spalding program was successfully taken by Coca-Cola, with some modification from *Battle of Music*, retaining producer George Zachary and scripter George Faulkner but not including Raymond Paige or the classics-versus-swing idea.

Later titled *Forecast*, every production of the summer series featured two half-hour presentations (with an occasional hour-long presentation). W.B. Lewis and George Faulkner handled the East Coast presentations, Charles Vanda and Norman Corwin handled the West Coast productions. *Forecast* was created with the hope that potential sponsors would buy what they liked. But no matter under what general title the product presented, top shows were seldom put on display. *Forecast* was a notable exception. Even if an advertiser liked a showcased program he seldom bought it — unless after being displayed it received a network test run. Such was the intention of the Columbia Broadcasting System, which arranged for every episode to be recorded so potential sponsors, in the months to come, had an opportunity to listen to the presentations.

The result was illuminating. A few of the proposed programs came to fruition such as *Jubilee*, *Suspense**, *Hopalong Cassidy*, *Leave it to Jeeves*, *Mischa the Magnificent*, and *The Country Lawyer* which later had their own prime-time success. *Jubilee* ultimately became an AFRS production for black GIs. *Hopalong Cassidy* made a second attempt in the spring of 1942 on the West Coast but would become a regular series many years later under the ownership of William Boyd (the *Forecast* production had no involvement or connection to the later 1950-52 series). On the evening of July 29, 1940 (the third broadcast of the series), after the half-hour True Boardman presentation of *Angel* with Loretta Young and Elliott Lewis concluded, Ed Gardner introduced *Duffy's Tavern* to the radio audience for the first time, with guests Colonel Stoopnagle and Gertrude Niesen.

---

* It should be noted that the *Suspense* broadcast on *Forecast* was not the pilot program many associate with the long-running radio program of the same name, even though William Spier once claimed so in a magazine article. On *Forecast*, the *Suspense* proposal centered on adaptations of Alfred Hitchcock's movies, with the British director as the weekly host. It was certainly a different type of mystery anthology than the 1942 counterpart. (And that's Joseph Kearns playing the role of the British director. Hitchcock merely granted permission to the producer to use his name.)

This page and following three pages:
Promotional press release for the Forecast *broadcast.*
(Photos courtesy of Rick Payne.)

People are going to have fun at [

THEY'RE going to feel right at home there, whether their usual "hangout" is a cross-roads general store or New York's *21*. The all-embracing bigness of the place — the hilarity, music, and madness that echo from its doors and windows — the oddly-assorted yet friendly crowd that's always gathered there — these are the qualities that will make *Duffy's Tavern* America's favorite club. These ... and "Archie."

Gardner ... to stardom

For "Duffy's Tavern" is the long-awaited vehicle that will, we are confident, lift ED GARDNER to radio stardom. As "Archie" in *This Is New York*, Ed Gardner was the spark-plug that ignited audience enthusiasm from Manhattan to the Coast. As "Archie" in "Duffy's Tavern," he will be a comic Billingsley in a poor man's Stork Club — a Runyon-Lardner-Saroyan Mr.

Duffy's Tavern!

Dooley in a national bar and grill. Anybody can show up at Duffy's Tavern, from Ethel Merman and Bert Lahr to John Gunther and Dorothy Thompson, all seeking refreshment, repartee, and raisons d'etre from "Archie."

Grand Opening tonight

Tonight's Grand Opening will feature an assortment of musical specialties by John Kirby's Orchestra — some sizzling songs served up by Gertrude Niesen — an organ recital and other antics by Col. Lemuel Q. Stoopnagle — a breath-taking demonstration of skill and respiratory stamina by the world's greatest harmonica player, Larry Adler — and a grand finale built around song and good fellowship. "Archie" is going to have a busy evening. But who cares? Everybody else is going to have a wonderful time.

Ed Gardner will not only head the ever-changing cast at Duffy's Tavern, but will also direct the show. In this, he reverts to his original forte in radio, having directed such major network programs as Believe It Or Not, Shell Chateau, Texaco Star Theatre, the Rudy Vallee Hour, and Good News of 1938. In addition to *Frank Galen* and *Abe Burrows*, veteran gag men who have worked with him for two years, Gardner has also enlisted the talent of *Keith Fowler* and *John Whedon* to write his scripts.

To a V. P. in charge of sales

If putting people in good humor is an adjunct to successful selling (and it is) then Ed Gardner & Company should be immediately engaged by some manufacturer's vice-president in charge of sales. Purchase of the proprietorship of Duffy's Tavern, in other words, should be a profitable venture.

27

LARRY ADLER

JOHN KIRBY

ED GARDNER

GERTRUDE NIESEN

COLONEL LEMUEL Q. STOOPNAGLE

Colonel Stoopnagle would ultimately become a major player with *Duffy's Tavern* in the years to come. F. Chase Taylor, who had made the mistake of going into the stock brokerage business in 1929, then decided to try out as a production man for radio station WMAK in Buffalo, New York. One day in October 1930, a storm disrupted the CBS wires to the station and, on short notice, Budd Hulick, the announcer of the Buffalo station, found himself with a spot to fill. There being no other talent available, Taylor, scriptwriter in an adjoining office, was called upon to help out with the ad-libbing. It was probably one of the maddest japes ever heard on the air. To the tune of "I Love Coffee - I Love Tea," played by the studio organ, the two uncorked a radio bedlam that Buffalo never forgot. Within a few minutes, listeners were telephoning their approval. Stoopnagle answered the calls in front of the studio microphone, a stunt he enjoyed doing "live" on the air. Fan letters followed, and for the next year "Stoopnagle and Budd" were a nightly feature on the Buffalo station. After Buffalo came New York, network programs and stage appearances. Between 1931 and 1937 the pair were heard over three networks. In 1936-37, they were on *Town Hall Tonight* and *The Minute Men*. The Taylor-Hulick partnership dissolved in 1937.

Stoopnagle did much to introduce a type of comedy described only as "zany." He invented impossible things; he twisted words and phrases; he created many another word or term that wouldn't get even footnote room in any dictionary. Considered one of the pioneers in the development of radio humor, he was perfect for *Duffy's Tavern* and while he was not a weekly regular throughout the forties, the character of Finnegan would ultimately be molded in the image of Colonel Stoopnagle.

"Now Duffy, I can't brandy words with you now," Archie says.

In September of 1943, when Bristol-Myers released a 48 page book titled *Duffy's First Reader*, Abe Burrows wrote his own take on how Ed Gardner created *Duffy's Tavern*. This should not be considered a first-hand account of the creation of the radio program. There are a few errors in print, including Burrows remarking how *This is New York* was originally a presentation of *Forecast*.

"We're just goin' to go on the air for a broadcast." Duffy, the fictional owner of a tavern named after him, apparently tuned in to his radio to hear the broadcast and every few minutes would phone Archie to criticize the vocal talents, insisting what the tavern needed was an Irish tenor. Amidst the music and comedy, Archie tells the Colonel a story of "Two-Top Gruskin." The local cop on the beat, Clancy, eventually comes in and threatens to shut down the tavern. "You can't close us up," Archie debates. "We ain't got a license!" Realizing Clancy is Irish, Gertrude Niesen and Archie convince the lawman to belt a rendition of "When Irish Eyes Are Smiling" (which, incidentally, would later become the series theme song). The feature closes with Mel Allen explaining to the audience that the evening's presentation of *Duffy's Tavern* was intended as an "illustration of what you may expect from *Duffy's Tavern* if it eventually becomes a weekly feature." Allen encouraged listeners to write to CBS and express their enjoyment.

CBS felt the *Forecast* series was a success and for the summer of 1941 began offering another batch of proposed presentations. The series would have been heard over a third summer run in 1942 but the network's program department was too busy with current and forthcoming war shows.

In their August 7, 1940, issue, *Variety* reviewed the audition: "Columbia must have had a tobacconist in mind when it sprung this see-what-the-boys-in-the-back-room-will-have type of offering for sponsorial approbation. It's rowdy and rough and reeks of sawdust and brass rails. Withal, it's quite okay for male ears but hardly palatable for the dainty slippers. That sets it apart in its niche and shoppers after that type of program will know just where to look... The character has endless possibilities with Gardner's deft handling and could be integrated into any program for a solid sock. Duffy still wanting an Irish tenor on the program and the time getting short, it was not totally unexpected when Clancy, the cop, burst into *Irish Eyes*. That brought the tears to Duffy's eyes for a crying finish, which, if nothing else, is a novel denouement for a comedy show."

James F. Burke, manager of CBS program sales, was also the director of new program ideas and assistant director of program research. It was Burke who worked on the development and sale of such shows as *Duffy's Tavern*, *I Hear America Singing* and *Forecast*. Under the guidance of Burke, promotional material circulated in advance promoting *Duffy's Tavern* in the hopes of luring potential sponsors. CBS thought highly of the proposed series before it was aired, because *Duffy's* was promoted far more than any other pilot during the summer. Certainly the mention of a celebrity guest each week helped lure potential sponsors and, oddly, all of the CBS press releases centered on singer Gertrude Niesen far more than the program itself, causing most advertisements and news blurbs to herald her as the star, not Ed Gardner or Colonel Stoopnagle. One has to wonder if the network considered Niesen more popular than Gardner.

It didn't take long for the American Tobacco Company to place a non-favorable decision. CBS also transcribed every broadcast for later playback. Potential sponsors in the weeks to come might have expressed interest and offering the recordings for private review at their convenience was a high mark in salesmanship. A total of 49 favorable letters arrived at CBS in New York, according to CBS interoffice memos; excerpts from those letters were used as part of the network's marketing campaign. But no sale.

Thankfully, about the same time the *Duffy's Tavern* audition aired over CBS, Ed Gardner accepted a producer-director assignment for the Rudy Vallee program under sponsorship of Sealtest. Gardner replaced Vic Knight who was slated to handle the Eddie Cantor series debuting in the fall. Over lunch, Gardner met with J. A. McFadden of the McKee-Albright agency, who had been huddling with various directors in New York. The assignment was initially offered to Norman Corwin, but he had an RKO scripting deal and was not available. Martin Gabel reportedly declined an offer, along with Ed Gardner, but after *Duffy's Tavern* failed to sell to the tobacco firm, Ed Gardner accepted the job. Gardner's first call of duty was to replace boxer-turned-actor Max Rosenbloom, who was a weekly regular on Rudy Vallee's radio program, with his 'Archie' character. In October, Ed Gardner hit upon a stroke of brilliance by signing John Barrymore for a series of appearances on *The Rudy Vallee Sealtest Show*. Gardner had read in the papers of Barrymore's financial woes, resolved by bankruptcy, which minimized his total earnings until the debt was paid. His weekly appearances on the radio program helped settle a percentage of that debt. His initial appearances, contracted for eight consecutive weeks, brought him $2,750 per broadcast. His salary called for a rising scale after each eight-week period, and for a brief time, Jimmy Durante was considered his replacement. Barrymore's popularity was weighed against the sponsor, who agreed to renew the contract in 13-week increments for $3,000 a week — and no rise in salary. Barrymore agreed.

By 1941, Rudy Vallee's program very much needed a boost. Formerly a vagabond celebrity with one of the highest rated radio programs during the mid-thirties, Vallee agreed to do anything Gardner proposed. With John Barrymore added to the cast, involving self-mocking skits that lampooned his heavy drinking and subsequent career backslide, the ratings improved.

"When the pilot was finished, everyone who listened to the recording thought it was a very funny show, but nobody fought to sponsor it," recalled Abe Burrows. "People were saying it was too New Yorkish, too sophisticated. We heard all the old bromides: 'How will it go with the people in Kansas City?' 'The rest of the country doesn't care about New York.' So for a while we had to put *Duffy's Tavern* on hold. In 1941, a sponsor finally got interested in *Duffy's Tavern*. After a few weeks of negotiation the Schick Injector Razor people bought it. The show was Ed Gardner's dream. He and I left the Vallee show and went back to New York."

In the last week of January 1941, Ed Gardner signed to produce *Duffy's Tavern* over CBS for Rainbow, Inc., the company responsible for producing the Schick Injector Razor. The deal was closed on January 28, 1941, in New York, through the J.M. Mathes agency and Gardner left for the East Coast after the February 20 broadcast. Armand Deutsch was the East Coast head of the McKee-Albright agency and contact for the program. Since *Duffy's Tavern* would have to be done from New York, Gardner gave up his assignment of producer on *The Rudy Vallee Sealtest Show*, which originated from Hollywood. The choice for his replacement would fall on a combination producer-comedy writer due to the nature of the show. Abe Burrows, chief comedy writer on the Sealtest program, declined the offer. Burrows wanted to make the shift with Gardner. Under the terms of the contract with Rainbow,

Ed Gardner and Abe Burrows

Inc., Shirley Booth, now starring on Broadway in *My Sister Eileen*, would have a featured part. Gardner received a total of $4,000 a week on the package deal and as producer had to divide the costs between the scriptwriters and cast. Because *My Sister Eileen* was performing at the Biltmore in New York, the curtain had to be held for her at the Saturday night performance. Less than two weeks before Gardner's departure, Dick Mack was named writer and producer for the Rudy Vallee program. Mack for years was Edgar Bergen's scriptwriter. He quickly hired a staff of five writers.

"Shirley had a problem because the show was broadcast on Saturday night and she was then playing in *My Sister Eileen* on Broadway," recalled Abe Burrows. "That day she had a matinee and an evening show. Our show ran till 8:55 and the producers of *My Sister Eileen* used to hold the curtain for her. We'd have a car waiting outside and as soon as she said her last line on the air, she dashed out of the studio into the car and was onstage about ten minutes later."

Ed Gardner acquired the name of *Duffy's* from Duffy's Radio Tavern on West 40th Street in New York City. The late Bernard C. Duffy, proprietor, once told Gardner that the first Duffy's was established back in 1795. The inn was in Pennsylvania, run by two women, on the stagecoach route from Williamsport to Pittsburgh. Gardner once joked that he couldn't understand why the book in which the first *Duffy's* is described makes no reference to a 1795 Archie.

CHAPTER TWO
THE CBS YEARS
(1941-1942)

"It ain't that Duffy's cheap," Archie said of his boss' exploits, "It's just that he knows the value of money. He don't think money is used for feedin' pigeons. Duffy will buy a drink occasionally, usually on St. Patrick's Day or when he's under terrific emotional stress." Duffy, the proprietor, was non-existent – or rather, you know him only as the other party to those telephone conversations with Archie, the presiding genius. As much as the radio audience knew Duffy was a fictional character, the same audience believed Archie was real. Archie, whose voice was a cross between that of an aroused cop and a buzz saw was, like his creator, tall and lanky with a nervous manner. "Archie is just Gardner," was his own explanation, "an easy-going guy with tolerance and a terrific respect for knowledge. He's not a dummy, but he looks up to informed people and has a regard for culture that is almost reverence. But Archie sees right through phonies."

To begin with a touch of understatement, *Duffy's Tavern* was a wonderful place. It was so fine that when the phone rang every week, Archie the bartender answered with *Duffy's Tavern* – "where the elite meet to eat," and the audience knew a moment of paradoxical regret: You would like to find a place like *Duffy's Tavern*, at the same time that you were aware that, alas, it was too good to be true. There were plenty of acceptable bar-and-grills in New York City, but none that measured up to *Duffy's* for the fairly simple reason that it represented the finest entertainment — even if it was for only thirty minutes a week.

Season One

Although the July 1940 broadcast of *Forecast* failed to gain a cigarette sponsor, a transcription of the audition performance helped convince the Magazine Repeating Razor Company to pick up the tab, thanks to the efforts of the J.M. Mathes Advertising Agency (who wanted to hawk their product, Schick Razors, on the radio). In September 1940, two transcription discs were cut from *Forecast*. Executives at Mathes circulated one recording to potential sponsors while retaining the duplicate as a master backup for another, unnamed, potential sponsor.

The initial contract between the sponsor and the network stipulated a sixteen week sponsorship from March 1, 1941, to June 14, 1941, which was a bit unusual since most contracts with the network were placed on a thirteen week schedule (13 times 4 equals 52). Since it was proven that listenership was at the lowest during what was generally considered vacation time, 13 weeks in the summer were usually dedicated to a different radio program, paid for by the same sponsor, but for a cheaper price.

To attract new listeners, at the suggestion of the network the first season featured at least one celebrity guest every week. Under the same contract, CBS had the option of approval when choosing the celebrities. Obviously, the network made sure that no celebrity appearing on *Duffy's Tavern* would cross-promote a radio program presently heard over a competing network. Celebrities included Parks Johnson and Wally Butterworth, hosts of *Vox Pop*; Colonel Stoopnagle was the weekly host of *Quixie Doodles*. Both programs aired over CBS. At the time Paul Lukas, Hildegarde, Milton Berle and Orson Welles were making their guest appearances they were not presently committed to a radio program on the rival networks. For the broadcast of June 7, 1941, certainly a major influence on CBS, Ilka Chase, actress and novelist whose radio program, *Luncheon at the Waldorf*, had recently concluded, paid a visit to the tavern. Her appearance on *Duffy's* was designed to promote her new radio program, which premiered on June 6. The announcer, John Reed King, closed the episode with the following mention: "Archie wants me to thank Ilka Chase for coming here tonight and to announce that he will be her guest next Friday night on her new program for Camel Cigarettes... *Penthouse Party*."

The first season introduced listeners to two regulars: Shirley Booth and Eddie Green. Miss Duffy was the proprietor's daughter who, when she moved, sent a change of address form to her Peeping Toms. It was she who handled the cash register and acted like a magnet to every man who walked into the tavern. She often referred to her friend, Vera Fogerty, who was also man hungry. As Archie once put it, "Miss Duffy hasn't been in the arms of the armed forces as often as she would like." Adding a female element to the program provided an open door for jokes about matrimony, romance, dating and other similar topics. "In matrimony, you marry an armful and wind up with a roomful," Archie quipped in one early episode. "It takes two to make a marriage — a single girl and an anxious mother," Miss Duffy explained in another. After Miss Duffy described her cosmetic affairs to Archie, the barkeep turned to Eddie who added: "What with lipstick on their lips, rouge on their cheeks, mascara on their eyes, polish on their nails and now paint on their legs, the dames sure take a shellacking."

Shirley Booth was known primarily as a Broadway actress, who, up to the time *Duffy's Tavern* premiered, won critical praise for her role of Ruth Sherwood in the 1940 production of *My Sister Eileen*. During her tenure on *Duffy's*, the first three seasons, she received top billing at the opening of every broadcast, always billed as "the star of *My Sister Eileen*."*

It is assumed that Shirley Booth was selected for the role at the request of her husband, Ed Gardner, but publicity in newspapers

John Reed King was the first announcer for the series, who welcomed the studio audience by explaining the evening's proceedings and performed the commercials.

---

* More than one reference guide incorrectly claims Ed Gardner was the only person to receive on-air billing, while the other cast members remained un-credited. A review of the scripts in Ed Gardner Jr.'s personal collection, the Abe Burrows collection at the Billy Rose Theater Collection, and the Parke Levy papers at the University of Wyoming (Laramie) all verify otherwise.

and press releases often quoted Gardner as saying she was hired primarily because she was the only person who could do a perfect Brooklyn accent. Perhaps both are correct but it should be noted that until the age of seven, Shirley Booth grew up in Brooklyn. In January 1925, she made her Broadway debut in *Hell's Bells*, a Barry Conner play. Booth played the role of Nan Winchester, one of two unconcerned sisters, going through an about face when they believe their adventurer brother is now prosperous. Her love interest was Jimmy Todhunter, played by a then-unknown actor named Humphrey Bogart. Many years later, after Bogart established his screen persona courtesy of Warner Brothers, he would make a guest appearance on *Duffy's Tavern*. By then, Shirley Booth was no longer on the program and a cast reunion was not feasible. (When Shirley Booth was on the program, her lines were credited as "Booth" and "Shirley" in the scripts. When she parted ways, the role was credited in the script as "Miss Duffy.")

BOOTH: (to Ilka Chase) Your friends are always so classy, ain't they? They're all raconteuses, chanteuses, danseuses... it's a wonder you never bring down any hippopotamotuses.

When Booth left the series in 1943, actresses playing the role of Miss Duffy never received such limelight, downgraded to simply name mention like the rest of the cast.

Eddie Green, a well-known Negro comedian who would later find greater fame as Stonewall, the fix-it-all lawyer on *Amos n' Andy*, played Eddie the Negro waiter-extraordinaire and glorified handyman who also advised Archie on his various ventures. Apart from show business, the actor was also in the food business (ironically), the proud owner of a chain of Harlem restaurants for a couple decades. The character of Eddie was the equivalent of Jack Benny's Rochester who often had the best comeback lines for his employer.

ARCHIE: With a dame like Elsa Maxwell coming here, you think this tablecloth is high class enough?
EDDIE: Well, I tell you what you can do with it.
ARCHIE: What?

EDDIE: Tear one more hole in the corner and tell her it's
Italian lace.

The listening audience often dismissed reality because
orchestras like John Kirby's did not play in taverns like *Duffy's*
and sooner or later it would occur to the listeners that although
Archie was a bartender, no one ever seemed to take a drink. But no
one noticed it at the time, which said something about one of the
most original and consistently entertaining radio programs. With
the aid of John Kirby's famed Negro band, the music somehow
fit the Brooklyn Tavern. Kirby was an alumnus of the Fletcher
Henderson and Chick Webb bands and had even started his own
in 1937 at New York's Onyx Club. He was once married to actress
Maxine Sullivan.

John Kirby and his orchestra supplied the music for a full
calendar year, until General Foods took up sponsorship. Kirby, like
most orchestras that performed on the radio, spent a considerable
amount of time performing for hotels. During the summer break
between seasons, Kirby's orchestra performed at the Ambassador
East Hotel's Pump Room. When his tenure on *Duffy's Tavern*
concluded, he returned to the Ambassador for a three-week
engagement.

In the premiere episode of the series, in an effort to introduce
the weekly regulars to the radio audience, very little happens except
to establish Miss Duffy and Eddie's positions at the tavern. Duffy
wants Archie to hire Irish Tenors for musical accompaniment in
the tavern and visitor Colonel Stoopnagle, having heard the news,
tries to get hired for the job.

STOOP: Well, I have one new thing here I've just invented.
ARCHIE: What is it Colonel? To me it looks just like a door.
STOOP: It is a door. It's a bathroom door that you don't have to
wait outside of because it opens into a closet.
ARCHIE: Gee, Colonel – you certainly have a furtive mind.
I wish you could invent an Irish Tenor.
STOOP: Why, Archie?

(Photo courtesy of Bryan Hendrickson.)

ARCHIE: Well, Duffy says either I get an Irish Tenor or I'm fired.

STOOP: My boy, never despair. I, Lemuel Q. Stoopnagle, <u>am</u> an Irish Tenor.

ARCHIE: But Duffy only likes Irish Irish Tenors.

To prove his worth, Stoopnagle, with the assistance of the John Kirby orchestra, sings "Come Back to Erin." Stoopnagle fails to get the job, but his position on *Duffy's Tavern* would, ten years later, become more influential than anyone predicted in 1941. *Billboard* magazine reviewed the series premiere: "*Duffy's Tavern*, one of the better program ideas showcased in Columbia's *Forecast* series last summer, comes back with Ed Gardner and a sponsor. Gardner, a director of note on other radio programs, plays Archie, a harried bartender in Duffy's Tavern. Archie is Duffy's languid man-of-all work and is afflicted with a remarkable Hell's Kitchen dialect completely devoid of grammar and full of engaging malapropisms. Duffy is a mythical figure, his influence being indirect but very substantial. His presence becomes known when he telephones Archie to squawk about the music and demand an Irish Tenor. These conversations are one-way affairs. Archie answers to Duffy explaining everything. Program did not score as well as the original *Forecast* show, but was plenty good. Everything will depend upon script and how consistently Gardner can perform. Session as it stands is certainly a novel comedy set-up. Band is John Kirby's, a restrained though swingy orchestra. Series' first guest was Colonel Stoopnagle, strictly terrific in a lunatic impersonation of an Irish Tenor. Some of the plugs for Schick Razor were cleverly worked into the script."

The March 5, 1941, issue of *Variety* reviewed the series premiere: "J.M. Mathes, which had good luck buying another network-built program, *Information, Please*, for Canada Dry, had now contracted on behalf of Schick for this program that was unveiled last summer as on....Is a whacky idea, not easily classified. Its response, as with all comedy on the ga-ga side, either strikes the funny bone or deepens the so-what crevice between arched eyebrows. One the whole, it seems a promising entertainment, adapted to Saturday night and disarmingly hokey... The program may develop material trouble fast and seriously. But its starting premise of effortless somewhat meandering, whopper-telling double talk is painless diversion if the listener isn't thinking comparatively, and if Saturday dinner has been a success. Gardner's 'Archie' has not gotten a unanimous press. On the other hand, it has gotten this far — a CBS network."

Variety changed its tone weeks later, after listening to the

May 10 broadcast. "Elsa Maxwell and the duo-pianists Fray and Braggiotti provided a passable show... Gimmick of Miss Maxwell's performance was a theoretical party to celebrate the Duffys' 25th anniversary. It had a few chuckles and was finally built into a mild laugh climax. Miss Maxwell is still an amateur microphone performer. Fray and Braggiotti uncorked a single number — quite peppery."

ANNOUNCER: Some men will like one feature more than another, but whatever feature appeals to you most, the result is always the same. You get better shaves with a Schick Injector Razor. And this razor, with twelve double-thick Schick Blades, in a pigskin grain case, costs only one dollar. One dollar everywhere in the United States and Canada.

SEASON ONE
March 1, 1941, to June 14, 1941
Originates from the New York studios of the Columbia Broadcasting System
Sponsor: Rainbow, Inc., a.k.a. The Magazine Repeating Razor Company (Schick Razors)
East Coast Broadcast: Saturday, 8:30 to 8:55 p.m.*
Repeat for West Coast: 11:30 p.m. to 12 midnight for the West Coast
(Times listed above are performance times.
For West Coast time slot, subtract three hours.)
Music: John Kirby and his Orchestra
Announcer: John Reed King

Cast
Shirley Booth as Miss Duffy
Eddie Green as Eddie
Alan Reed as Clancy the Cop**

---

* Yes, the radio program was five minutes shorter in length for the East Coast.

** The character of Clancy the Cop was in many episodes, but not all of them.

Episode #1 — Broadcast Saturday, March 1, 1941
Guest: Col. Stoopnagle
Plot: See pages 40 and 42

Episode #2 — Broadcast Saturday, March 8, 1941
Guest: Deems Taylor
Plot: Still seeking musical night life for the tavern in reference to Duffy's request last week, Archie tries to figure out where he can hire musicians until Deems Taylor happens to drop by. Taylor kindly invites Archie and Miss Duffy to be his guests tomorrow at the Philharmonic. When Archie explains the tavern needs a little musical addition, Taylor gets them a calypso singer. John Kirby's Orchestra performs "Dance of the Sugar Plum Fairies" during the intermission.

Memorable Lines
ARCHIE: Eddie... what is a calypso?
EDDIE: Why, er, that's when the sun gets blotted out.
ARCHIE: Eddie, that's an eclipso... you see that, Mr. Taylor, and he's twice as smart as Duffy – and it's three to one you didn't know what a calypso was until you got on "Information Please."

Episode #3 — Broadcast Saturday, March 15, 1941
Guest: Orson Welles
Plot: Discussions about the bard and Francis Bacon are the order of the day due to the fact that Orson Welles is dropping by. Welles happens to be in New York City to do a play called *Native Son*, written by Richard Wright, which Welles and John Houseman are producing. Taking advantage of the opportunity, Archie tries to get Welles to participate as the feature attraction for the tavern's St. Patrick's Day pig roast since it's the right kind of job for a ham actor. Joan Edwards, who would later become a semi-regular on the program, is the musical guest and sings "Do I Worry?"

Memorable Lines
SHIRLEY: Mr. Welles, you're my idea of the perfect

Shakespeare actor. I will never forget you in that picture, "Romeo and Juliet."

WELLES: I was never in the picture, "Romeo and Juliet."

SHIRLEY: You see, Archie... it <u>was</u> Norma Shearer.

ARCHIE: Well, you're lookin' great. How's things in the drama?

WELLES: Well, Archie. My theatrical activities have been somewhat curtailed since my Hollywood peregrination.

ARCHIE: Oh, well, of course that's up to the individual.

WELLES: Well, naturally.

ARCHIE: So you were in Hollywood, hah? They keep you busy out there?

WELLES: Well, kind of.

ARCHIE: What were you doing?

WELLES: Same old thing – writing, directing, producing, and acting.

ARCHIE: Boy, you sound like a one-man Preston Sturges...

Episode #4 — Broadcast Saturday, March 22, 1941
Guests: Bill "Bojangles" Robinson and Sherman Billingsley
Plot: An income tax inspector arrives to look over the books while Archie attempts to lure Bill "Bojangles" Robinson to perform at Duffy's under an exclusive contract. Distracted because of the audit, Archie ultimately makes an error. While entertaining a man in the tavern named Sherman, Archie is unaware that the new guest is a spy for the Stork Club. Without Archie being aware of it, Robinson signs an exclusive to the Club and promptly leaves for new pursuits. John Kirby and his Orchestra perform "Why Cry Baby?" and "Hot Time in the Old Town." (Guest Sherman Billingsley was the proprietor of New York's famous celebrity center, The Stork Club.)

Episode #5 — Broadcast Saturday, March 29, 1941
Guests: Hildegarde and Arthur Treacher
Plot: Treacher is billed as "Hollywood's favorite screen butler" and steals the limelight from the entire radio cast in this script. Treacher goes from a gentleman's gentleman to a bum's bum when he is hired by Archie to become his assistant, who in turn

also answers the phone for Archie. Treacher's dreams of how to improve the tavern do not work, however, and Archie is forced to reduce the overhead. Hildegarde, who received top billing above Treacher in the opening of the broadcast, is constrained to a few lines of dialogue and singing "Sweet Petite."

Episode #6 — Broadcast Saturday, April 5, 1941
Guests: Morton Downey and the Vox Pop Boys
Plot: Miss Duffy tries to convince the Vox Pop Boys (Parks Johnson and Wally Butterworth) to allow her to audition for their program and she sings "You Walked By." Morton Downey shows up and sings "Molly Malone." Eddie gets mistaken as a contestant for the *Vox Pop* program. John Kirby and his Orchestra performs "Keep an Eye on Your Heart," and "The Dance of the Sugar Plum Fairies," the latter of which he performed in the first broadcast of the series.

Memorable Lines
WALLY: Well, the first question is: When waiting on tables should you serve from the left or from the right?
EDDIE: Well, that depends on which side of the customer is closest to the kitchen.
WALLY: Sorry, Eddie, you should always serve from the left.
EDDIE: From the left, eh?
WALLY: Yes.
EDDIE: Well, personally, I ain't superstitious.

Episode #7 — Broadcast Saturday, April 12, 1941
Guests: Arthur Murray and Larry Adler
Plot: Dance expert Arthur Murray gives some of the tavern's guests, including Miss Duffy, some dancing lessons and Larry Adler, the world-famous harmonica player (now appearing at the Roxy in New York City), performs three variations on a theme by Paganini. Duffy, meanwhile, spends his time stuck in a phone booth at the tailor shop without any pants, and is unable to come to the tavern and meet Murray in person. Archie pays Francis McCabe five bucks for dancing lessons. In order for Sam the

Tailor to accept Duffy's check, he needs proof Duffy is who he says he is, so Archie has Adler perform a song live on the radio by request of "Sam the Tailor."

Episode #8 — Broadcast Saturday, April 19, 1941
Guests: Colonel Stoopnagle and Joan Edwards
Plot: Archie thinks the tavern needs a hostess to help bring customers in, so Archie hereby calls to order the Board of Directors of Duffy's Tavern, Limited, consisting of Archie, Eddie and Miss Duffy. Stoopnagle, making an idiot's delight in assuming the tavern is no longer around, decides to buy a band and a bar and call it a tavern – Duffy's Tavern – "what a name!" When Stoop discovers that there is already such a place, he decides to sue them for plagiarism. This is the first episode to make reference to Clancy the Cop. Joan Edwards returns to sing another song.

Memorable Lines
ARCHIE: Oh, Colonel Stoopnagle... how are you?
STOOP: Shhh, I'm traveling incognito.
ARCHIE: Incognito, huh?
STOOP: Yes, I don't want you to know that I've been here...
  Don't refer to me by name.
ARCHIE: What'll I call you?
STOOP: Colonel Stoopnagle.
ARCHIE: I wish I were an idiot so I could enjoy this
  conversation.

Episode #9 — Broadcast Saturday, April 26, 1941
Guest: Tallulah Bankhead
Plot: By way of adding class to the tavern, Archie tries to teach Eddie the proper way to introduce a woman of Bankhead's stature. Eddie even fixes up the table with wax bananas. Bankhead, however, won't eat at the tavern when she learns that beer and pig knuckles are on the menu. Archie happens to be away for a moment when Bankhead arrives and when he returns, he mistakes her for a normal customer and makes embarrassing remarks about the tavern while talking up the great Tallulah Bankhead – unaware

she is standing in front of him the entire time. Bankhead closes the broadcast reciting a dramatic poem, "Abe Lincoln Walks at Midnight." John Kirby's orchestra performs "Arabian Nightmare."

Trivia, etc. The poem Bankhead recites originated from Burton Egbert Stevenson's *The Home Book of Verse* (1879).

"One of the great actresses who came off the perch for *Duffy's Tavern* was Tallulah Bankhead. Tallulah wasn't just an actress, she was a force. The first time I met her, I found her intimidating," recalled Abe Burrows. "Before the show started, I was left alone with her backstage. I didn't know what to say; I was still a new kid then. Tallulah broke the ice by talking about, of all things, baseball. I was startled to find out that she was a baseball fan. She was American, of course, but she had spent years in England and that colored her speech. Her baseball chatter had some odd phrases, like 'Mr. Burrows, I just heard Camilli knocked a homer.' Knocked a homer? Nobody ever says that. But with that voice of hers, Tallulah could say anything."

Episode #10 — Broadcast Saturday, May 3, 1941
Guests: Hildegarde and "Slapsie" Maxie Rosenbloom
Plot: When "Slapsie" Maxie Rosenbloom stops by the tavern, he accidentally crushes Miss Duffy's hand because of his strength. Hildegarde stops by and the prize fighter finds her "vivacious." Because Archie is in love with the singer, he gets jealous and makes an attempt to woo her after referring to her as "Mademoiselle Hildegarde, from the Savoy Plaza - the chanteuse." Hildegarde gives him a prompt rejection and proves to Archie, who was in disagreement with Rosenbloom, that a big handsome mass of muscle is what women really want.

Trivia, etc. *Variety* reviewed this episode, commenting: "Material was lively and Hildegarde's vocals were a shimmering addition to the proceedings, but the two visitors booted their dialog assignments all over the studio. Ed Gardner, as Archie, seemed to become rattled but Shirley Booth, the dimwit Miss Duffy, cracked every one of her laughs for a bullseye. Comedy bit between

Hildegarde, Rosenbloom and Gardner was ingeniously contrived for a solid tag."

Memorable Lines
SHIRLEY: Why did you give up fighting to go on the radio?
MAXIE: Well, all the time when I was a fighter, my ambition was to talk on the radio, but, at the end of every fight, they gave the other guy the microphone and he would say, "Hello, mom, I'll be right home."
SHIRLEY: Well, why didn't *you* say "Hello mom, I'll be right home," too?
ARCHIE: What, in his condition?

Episode #11 — Broadcast Saturday, May 10, 1941
Guest: Elsa Maxwell
Plot: To celebrate Duffy's 25th anniversary, Archie hires Elsa Maxwell, social set worker, to give a party at the tavern. He attempts to impress Maxwell with suggestions on party games, but Miss Duffy insists on playing Post Office and Spin the Bottle. Duffy, meanwhile, is beaten with a baseball bat and unable to attend the tavern to celebrate. Jacques Fray and Mario Braggiotti, a famed piano duo who performed on radio as early as 1932, supply musical entertainment using their two pianos.

Memorable Lines
ARCHIE: Oh, hello, Duffy. Congratulations on your twenty-fifth wedding. Mrs. Duffy kissed you how many times? No kiddin', twenty-five?… Oh, with a baseball bat.

Episode #12 — Broadcast Saturday, May 17, 1941
Guest: Milton Berle
Plot: Comedian Milton Berle pays a visit to the tavern, having grown up in the neighborhood but not having seen the place since he was a kid. He is shocked to see how the condition of the tavern has worn down. Archie attempts to convince Berle to emcee a floor show, suggesting it would improve the tavern's clientele. When Duffy is disillusioned, Berle relents and performs a comedy monologue.

Memorable Lines
ARCHIE: Say, Duffy, guess who's coming here tonight? Milton
Berle. That little noisy kid who used to hang around here all
the time. Milton Berle... Duffy, remember the kid who used
to buy joke books, memorize the jokes and then say he made
them up himself?... Well, that's Milton. Sure, he's been in
Hollywood...yeah, done pretty good, too. Yeah, I know you
always said he was a smart kid. Remember — he was the only
kid on the block who could explain the funny papers to you.

Trivia, etc. Orson Welles was scheduled make a return to the
program for the May 17 broadcast, but he took ill on the West
Coast and was unable to fly to New York, so Milton Berle
substituted.

Episode #13 — Broadcast Saturday, May 24, 1941
Guest: Paul Lukas
Plot: Paul Lukas, recent winner of the NY Drama Critics Award,
stops by the tavern as a guest. Miss Duffy assumes Lukas won the
Nobel prize. Archie proposes to singer Peg LaCentra, after she
performs "A Romantic Guy, I." She is swept off her feet when she
meets Paul Lukas and Archie's chances drop to zero.

Episode #14 — Broadcast Saturday, May 31, 1941
Guest: James J. Walker
Plot: James J. Walker, former mayor of New York City, is an old
friend of Duffy's and stops by to check out the tavern and the
people working hard behind the counter. Duffy apparently used
to be an old election district captain and helped Walker get 600
votes in the district. Walker has ulterior motives, however, when
he explains to Archie that he is here to help save the relationship
between Duffy and his wife. Miss Duffy mistakes Walker as
the new bartender and gives him tips on how not to overflow
the glasses, and how they all have fake bottoms. This is the first
appearance of Crudface and Dugan, Archie's lawyers.

Trivia, etc. To publicize this episode, CBS issued the following
press release:

It is going to cost the proprietors of the establishment something extra to entertain the former Mayor. The dapper Jimmy sent a wire to Ed Gardner, who plays Archie, the host of the joint, which read: "Just bought a new pair of shoes; be sure you have new sawdust on the floor of Duffy's place when I get there."

"Duffy will probably get sore, but what are you going to do when a guy goes to the expense of new shoes," lamented Archie. "Besides, that sawdust ain't been changed since repeal."

Memorable Lines
DUGAN: Don't answer that, Archie.
CRUDFACE: I object.
ARCHIE: Objection sustained.
DUGAN: Hey Crudface, what's that sustained?
CRUDFACE: That's a radio program without a sponsor.

Episode #15 — Broadcast Saturday, June 7, 1941
Guest: Ilka Chase
Plot: Ilka Chase, actress and novelist, pays a visit to the tavern. Archie wants her to do for the tavern what she did at the Waldorf and suggests calling the new radio program "Dinner at Duffy's." Such a stunt might keep the tavern open over the summer but when the question of salary comes along, she says no dice. Chase adds: "Is this to be 'Dinner at Duffy's' or 'Supper at Sing Sing?'" Chase leaves when the food is too rich at the tavern, having heard Archie explain what they serve, claiming she's going back to the Waldorf for some good old-fashioned corned beef and cabbage.

Trivia, etc. In the beginning of this episode, Archie makes a mention that next week is the last night for *Duffy's Tavern*, because Duffy plans to close the tavern for the summer. Ilka Chase's radio program, which was broadcast in the afternoon time slot, concluded just a couple weeks before her appearance on *Duffy's Tavern*.

Episode #16 — Broadcast Saturday, June 14, 1941
Guest: Miss June Nevin
Plot: Miss June Nevin of the Moore-McCormack Steamship

Lines, the one that hires entertainers and bands for the boats that go to South America, is guest in this episode and when Archie finds out who is planning to pay a visit, not only does this prompt a Carmen Miranda joke, but he attempts to get Eddie Green, "the singing waiter," booked for the coming season. Crudface and Dugan, Archie's lawyers, show up towards the end of the broadcast and create a fiasco that messes up the entire affair.

Trivia, etc. At the conclusion of this episode, the announcer informs the radio audience that *Duffy's Tavern* will return in the middle of September and to pay attention to local newspaper listings for details.

CHAPTER THREE
SCHICK AND SANKA
(1942 - 1943)

SALES RESULTS FROM ADVERTISEMENTS on *Duffy's Tavern* might have been enough to convince the Schick manufacturer to continue sponsorship after a brief summer hiatus but behind the scenes it appears the sponsor was on the fence. A favorable decision was considered based on a move from CBS to NBC. The J.M. Mathes Agency didn't like the Saturday night spot the show had for the first season but was unable to get a suitable time on CBS. It was understood there were open spots on both the Red and Blue networks of NBC, with the latter one said to be somewhat more advantageous. Executives at Rainbow, Inc., began looking towards greener pastures. Meanwhile, Ed Gardner and Shirley Booth spent their summer on a South American cruise, followed by a month at Nantucket and Cape Cod. In early August, while Gardner was still on vacation, a report was distributed that Rainbow, Inc. might revise its plans for reassuming the sponsorship of *Duffy's*

Tavern in the fall, on CBS, with the assistance of the Music Corp of America, the program's new agent. Gardner returned from vacation and, learning of Rainbow's indecision, started to look around for another sponsor.

The snag which loomed between Rainbow, Inc. and Ed Gardner had to do with material priorities. The Knapp-Monarch Company, which was also in the razor business, withdrew from the Blue Network early in 1942 because other time slots appeared more favorable. CBS recently reserved the Thursday, 8:30-8:55 p.m. period for the account and now that it was open Ed Gardner struck a deal and lined up his cast for the new season with the new time slot. Both CBS and Gardner were concerned about the program because even if Rainbow, Inc. did renew sponsorship, contractually in 13-week increments, the series would only last for 13 weeks. Gardner knew this would mean a strict deadline to find a substitute advertiser that would carry it for at least 26 weeks following.

CBS Press Release Dated September 11, 1941

"*Duffy's Tavern*, closed all summer for the want of a microphone, gets a CBS go-ahead on Thursday night at 8:30 p.m. This is a change from last year's Saturday schedule. Archie, the boss' hired man also returns in the off-the-air personage of Ed Gardner, but there won't be any opening night guest stars."

In the same manner as the first season, the Magazine Repeating Razor Company continued to sponsor *Duffy's Tavern* for a second season, in 13-week increments, with a contractual option to cancel at the end of any given 13 week period. Sponsorship ran longer than Ed Gardner anticipated, 26 broadcasts. Even with the move from Saturday to Thursday, retaining the same time slot, the radio audience noticed a number of changes when compared to the first season. Most notable was the lack of celebrity guests. Executives at the advertising agency representing the razor company expressed disappointment. The budget allotted for celebrity guests but Gardner insisted that he and his cast could carry the entire 30 minutes without screen or stage appeal. This is not to say that there were no celebrities during the second season — but their appearances were limited in number. As the producer for the comedy, Gardner pocketed the difference. This would prove to be a costly mistake.*

According to a press release issued by CBS, dated September 11, 1941, the reason for the premiere broadcast of the season not having any celebrities was explained by Gardner in the character of Archie. "To have a guest star you gotta push his feet into some wet cement on the sidewalk in front of the place where the show is goin' on. We have spent all our extra money washin' the windows... and besides, the cement won't set in time to let the crowd get into Duffy's place. Suppose all the customers get stuck in the cement. That ain't no way to stick people inside... if they are all stuck outside." A greater explanation was also explained in the same press release that "Archie (alias creator Ed Gardner) is of the opinion that the Schick Magazine Razor Company hired him, Miss Duffy, John Kirby's Orchestra, Eddie Green and John Reed King to entertain the audiences."

The greatest of these, of course, was Archie. He held the show together not only as a bartender, but because he was a fellow capable of handling practically any given situation. During the season, he had some pretty close escapes, because he was not the brightest guy in the world, but he was the brightest guy in *Duffy's Tavern*, and even when he failed he saw to it that no one else was aware of it. All right, he was taken in by Mme. Cacciatore,

---

* The Magazine Repeating Razor Company chose to sponsor a variety of programs following *Duffy's Tavern*. In late 1942, the company sponsored two short-run musical programs and, on the afternoon of November 27, 1943, through the agency of J.M. Mathes, Inc., the razor company sponsored the Army-Navy football game broadcast from West Point simultaneously on three networks (NBC Red, CBS and Mutual).

the opera singer with the Greenpernt accent (Greenpoint section of Brooklyn) and her manager, the Duke, but who was it who installed the pinball game in a corner of the Tavern where the floor slanted and thus made it impossible for anyone to win? Archie.

Added to the cast, beginning with the season opener, were tavern regulars Crudface Clifford (a safecracker) and Pat Dugan (a shortstop).* Beginning with the second episode, Clancy the Cop, who was referred to only by name during the first season broadcast of April 19, was now making weekly appearances at the tavern. For the broadcast of October 16, 1941, Archie got a new pinball machine for the tavern and Finnegan, a new tavern regular, was duped into wasting nickels in it. Regardless of what printed reference guides claim, the character of Finnegan (played by Charlie Cantor, an old vaudevillian and radio bit player who reportedly set a record of playing 125 different characters in a week and before that pounded the piano as "Pianistic Pete, the Barrel House Marvel") was not heard until the second season of *Duffy's Tavern*. Originally, Finnegan was just mentioned by name as one of the tavern regulars but he would quickly become a long-standing cast member. In fact, before the second season concluded, Finnegan replaced the characters of Crudface Clifford and Dugan the shortstop. (In the first season, Crudface and Dugan were Archie's lawyers. Their professions changed beginning with the second season.) Finnegan usually made his entrance to *Duffy's Tavern* every week when someone (usually Archie) made a crack of ignorance or stupidity, a trademark that became more of a running joke on the series. As Archie once remarked, "Finnegan, with a face like yours you shouldn't sneak up on people." In real life, Charles Cantor was regarded as a professional of the King's English.

Clifton Finnegan had the intellect of Lennie in *Of Mice and Men*, but was comical enough to stand out as a fixture of the tavern

---

* The character of Crudface Clifford originated from a comedy sketch on the July 24, 1939, radio script of *The Magic Key of RCA*, where Ed Gardner was a guest. The sketch, however, was deleted during rehearsals and never broadcast.

with his trademark "Duuuuh... Hiya, Arch!" A New Yorker by heart, New Englander Charlie Cantor was short-legged and long-faced. He played Socrates Mulligan on Fred Allen's program, and was a heavy on *Gang Busters*. He also played odds and ends parts in as many as 22 radio shows a week (according to columnist Bill Henry of the *Los Angeles Times*). "They say he has more money put away than most of the big name stars and he certainly gets more laughs than most of them. In a pinch he sings — he often does it on Allen's program — and plays a fair piano."

"A guy can be a great comedian, but he won't stay on top in

radio if he doesn't know comedy," Cantor once remarked. "Frank Fay's a great comedian, but he doesn't know radio comedy. Ed Gardner is a great comedian. Don't sell him short." Cantor recalled, "In our home, he would tell a dialect joke and he'd use three different dialect voices. He was wonderful. He was a little worried that Finnegan was a moronic character and he thought that maybe people might think he was in real life. [Gardner] went for psychology and taught that on the side in some college." He added, "As for the show, the characters may be earthy but the comedy is high class." Some of Cantor's best lines on the program centered on his late arrival to the tavern and Archie asking where he's been. "I was at the income tax bureau," Finnegan answers. Archie asks how much he paid and Finnegan responds, "Six hundred dollars... but I cheated a little. I copied from the guy next to me."

When *Hope for a Harvest* opened at the Guild Theater in New York City, Alan Reed feared he would have to bow out of many radio commitments. Actors were paid more money for stage duty compared to radio, but the producer held the play 20 minutes to permit Reed, one of the leads of the show, to double on the Fred Allen radio program. Reed had, for several seasons, played a comic character in support of Allen. Because he wasn't featured in the first act of *Harvest*, he was able to make his second-act entrance within the 20-minute delay. During the tryout tour of *Harvest*, in November of 1941, Reed was replaced on both the Fred Allen show by Ward Wilson, and by Ed Latimer on *Duffy's Tavern*.

Added to the musical talent was "Fats" Waller, a jazz pianist, composer and singer who worked with Ed Gardner previously on *This is New York*. Among his many accomplishments were a number of songs he wrote, including "I've Got a Feeling I'm Falling" and "Ain't Misbehavin'," both written in 1929; the latter of which he performed on *Duffy's Tavern* on at least one broadcast. Following Waller was Bob Howard, billed as "Radio's Ambassador of Rhythm" during his tenure on *Duffy's Tavern*. Howard knew how to make the audience his own with fast, sparkling music and a patter routine that never let up. He was famous for his parody of *My Sister and I*, which went over big with critics, but was never featured on the *Duffy's Tavern* program.

Variety reviewed the premiere broadcast: "'Archie' is one of the nicest things that has happened to network radio in the past couple years. He's a bona fide character and Mrs. Gardner (Shirley Booth) is a lady-sock in all her lines. They jibe and jell big."

Beginning with the broadcast of December 11, 1941, Dave Hossinger, a con man who claimed to represent a number of Hollywood celebrities, began making infrequent appearances. Archie often bragged that he could smell a con man a block away and yet he often fell victim to Hossinger's schemes. The *New York Times*, unobservant when reviewing studio press releases, on rare occasion would list the character of Hossinger among the cast and/or celebrity appearance among newspaper listings, failing to recognize the character was pure fiction and not a real person. (*Variety* once reviewed *Duffy's Tavern* listing both John Brown and Dave Hossinger among the cast, unaware that Brown played the role of Hossinger.)

When they were not working on *Duffy's Tavern*, John Brown and Eddie Green, two semi-name actors of radio, teamed to form that almost unheard of combination, a white and colored comedy act. As part of a regular spot on *Saturday Vaudeville*, both men delivered a comedic style closely resembling the patter often associated with Abbott and Costello. Green played the blundering and beguiling comic. Brown was the straight man with snappy one-liners. In one particular broadcast, Brown was a department store employee and Green the customer who wanted to return various purchases. His reasons were invariably balmy, but in each case his exasperating explanation drove Brown to frantic acquiescence.

Also added to the cast of rotating characters was Mrs. Cornelia Piddleton* and her Lord Byron Ladies' Literary Society, beginning with the broadcast of November 13, 1941. Mrs. Piddleton, for reasons unknown other than to establish a comical situation for

---

* The exact spelling of her name is not official. Piddleton switches back and forth to "Pittleton" depending on which scripts you consult. For the broadcast of May 26, 1942, her full name is not Cornelia, but Eustacia Hyancinty Pittleton. In almost all other scripts, she is referenced only by her last name.

the scriptwriters, was determined to use the tavern as a meeting hall for her society's monthly meetings. Archie dedicated himself to supplying the evening's entertainment, always failing in his mission and, in an act of desperation, usually convincing Finnegan to play the role of the guest speaker — disappointing the women but not the radio audience. For the broadcast of November 13th, Archie invited the members of the Lord Byron Ladies' Literary Society to convene at the tavern, where they were to hear Quincy Polk, a literary critic, who didn't appear. Instead they were treated to a thirty-second review by Finnegan of "Inside Latin America," with a copy of the World Almanac resting on the bar.

John K. Hutchens of the *New York Times* was an avid listener and fan of the program. In his November 23, 1941 column, he commented that "the tavern had its liveliest day when Gloria Swanson, in person, dropped by for a visit...Miss Swanson regarded him with little approval. How the panic-stricken Archie was rescued from his own bravado was a stirring epic, to be sure."

But it is no slight upon Gloria Swanson and such other guests such as Tallulah Bankhead, Joe E. Brown, Frank Fay, Deems Taylor and Bill Robinson to say that the Tavern was at its best when only the regulars were there and expressing themselves freely. The decision was left to the radio listeners – and the sponsor – who expressed disappointment and threatened to drop sponsorship in mid-season. As they used to say of the old-time saloon, it was the poor man's club. "How can we add some class to the joint?" Archie asked in one second season episode. The thirty-five cent dinner failed to draw clients away from the Rainbow Room. "Get these people outa here," says Eddie the waiter, referring to the usual clientele.

"It's a funny thing about the comedians; when they assume this dubious status professionally, sooner or later it begins to overlap into their everyday living," quoted R.W. Stewart of the *New York Times*. "No exception is Ed Gardner, animator of Archie, well-meaning but ill-starred man-of-all-work at WABC's make-believe *Duffy's Tavern*. If you are numbered among his friends or family, you might have been 'treated' to one of these impromptu gems the other night out. While being entertained by four singing waiters the gentleman in question took occasion to remark critically, 'They

sound like the invisible Inkspots.' Even Mr. Gardner admits —
after a while — that the gags on his program are much better."

Abe Burrows

The success of *Duffy's Tavern* was largely dependent on the gag
writers for the program. The first two seasons consisted of three
writers: Mac Benoff, Parke Levy and Abe Burrows. The latter
of whom, by his own admission, might have been a doctor if
his mother's determination had held out. Burrows' pre-medical
studies at City College depressed him, though. He switched to
accountancy at New York University. He worked on Wall Street
as a runner, board man, customer's man; rode out the Depression
in his father's paint and wallpaper business; sold maple syrup and
woven labels; and spent summers on the borscht circuit for bed
and board. In 1938, he sold his first radio material and went by
varying steps, some forward, some back, ultimately to the post of
head writer on *Duffy's Tavern*. Burrows and Levy wrote the first
few scripts to help establish the format of the program. Benoff and
Levy were promptly hired to add their own contributions.

*Ed Gardner, Mac Benoff, Parke Levy and Abe Burrows at the table
sharing a laugh at Gardner's expense – literally.*

"We sweated it out week after week," recalled Abe Burrows. "Our office was a suite in the Hotel Royalton. It was an old hotel, a few steps from the Lambs Club on Forty-fourth Street, and across the street from the Algonquin. The Royalton was known as the Poor Man's Algonquin. It offered a sort of frayed elegance; it had seen better days, but a lot of interesting people stubbornly remained there. George Jean Nathan had a beautiful baroque suite on the floor above us, and Robert Benchley lived in a suite that was — unfortunately for him — right next to ours. Three guys writing a radio comedy show make a lot of noise. We laughed aloud at our own jokes; then twice a week Gardner would join us and there would be a lot of hollering. The noise would go on far into the night. One day there was a knock at the door. I opened it and it was Benchley. He stood there with two suitcases beside him and I said something like, 'Good to see you, Mr. Benchley,' and he said, 'Abe, I just wanted to tell you that you can stop making noise now. I'm leaving.' He smiled, picked up his suitcases and went to California."

Decades later, Mac Benoff claimed that his first program on CBS led to the creation of *Duffy's Tavern*. Benoff wrote for *This is New York*, so his claim may be validated. Benoff did write a script for *Forecast* titled *Class of '41*, described as "a revue of newcomers to showbiz." The pilot, broadcast August 11, 1941, was produced by his friend Abe Burrows, in the hope the series would be picked up by a sponsor in the same manner as *Duffy's Tavern*. It never was.

Parke Levy was not a newcomer to radio comedy. Throughout the thirties, his contributions included writing material for Joe Penner, Ed Wynn, Jack Pearl and Ben Bernie. Levy later claimed he helped mentor Benoff but all three individuals were instrumental in reading each other's scripts and improving the scenarios by replacing boring dialogue with comedic lines and revising the deliveries. Benoff's major contributions include three consecutive episodes during the first season, May 3, 10 and 17, 1941; followed by a steady contribution (with the assistance of Parke Levy) to every episode from the second season (1941-1942) and less than half of the episodes from the third season (1942-1943), after which he attempted to leave the program when the season concluded in June of 1943. Parke Levy wrote the majority of the scripts for the third season. Keep in mind that all three scriptwriters looked over each other's scripts with Burrows having the final say as head writer for the series.*

"Ed taught me something about style and (although he would never have used the word) grace. His teaching method consisted of certain painfully pithy phrases. When I would come up with a 'bad' line, he would say, 'That's lousy.' Or 'That stinks.' Or sometimes he would be more polite. He would say, 'Hey Burrows, you can do better than that.' I remember at one of our early sessions everybody was sitting around trying to find an interesting entrance for some guest star — I think it was Walter Huston. The other writers were coming up with tricky ideas of how to bring him out. I didn't know what they were shooting for and I finally came up with a dazzling suggesting. I said (I really did say it), 'Why don't we just say 'Here comes Walter Huston now'?' The other writers all stared at me and Gardner said quietly, 'Abe, that's really rotten.' And I asked 'Why?' And he snapped back, 'I don't know why. It's just really really rotten.' That may not seem to be much help, but it started me thinking about clichés."

"Ed was actually the first person who made me feel that what I was doing was writing," Burrows explained. "Before that I thought of myself as a guy who made up jokes. A gagman. As I worked with him, I slowly and gingerly began to think of myself as a writer."

In the Abe Burrows script collection at the New York Public Library, a script for the premiere episode of the series featured Ed Gardner's penciled notation on the bottom right of the front page of the script: "To Abe – Without whose loyalty this wouldn't have been possible. Arch"

---

* Because all three individuals contributed to the scripts, listing the primary scriptwriter can be a nightmare of a chore — and still no verification of who deserves primary credit. The paragraph above pretty much sums up in general the authorship for the first three seasons.

SEASON TWO (The Schick Episodes)
September 18, 1941, to March 12, 1942
Originates from Studio 22 at the Columbia Broadcasting System
(New York City)
Sponsor: Rainbow, Inc., a.k.a. Magazine Repeating Razor
Company (Schick Razors)
East Coast Broadcast: Thursday, 8:30 to 8:55 p.m.
Repeat for West Coast: 11:00 to 11:25 p.m.
(September 18 and 25)
Repeat for West Coast: 12:00 midnight to 12:25 a.m.
(October 2 to March 12)
(Times listed above are performance times.)
Music: John Kirby and his Orchestra
Announcer: John Reed King

Guest Musicians
"Fats" Waller (pianist and singer, December 18, 1941, and
January 1 to 15, 1942)
Bob Howard (pianist, January 22, 1942, to March 12, 1942)

Cast
Shirley Booth as Miss Duffy
Eddie Green as Eddie
Charles Cantor as Finnegan
John Brown as Dave Hossinger and Crudface Clifford*
Alan Reed as Clancy the Cop*

Episode #17 — Broadcast Thursday, September 18, 1941
Plot: Duffy confesses he did not miss Archie during the past
thirteen weeks, much to Archie's disappointment, even when
expressing that if you don't see a dog for thirteen weeks, you still
miss it. Archie spends Duffy's money to spruce up the joint, such
as a new chromium bar-rail, painting the phone booth, and, as
Archie explains to Eddie, "show me another place where they
have an individual fly swatter on every table." When Duffy makes

---

* The characters of Clancy the Cop and Dave Hossinger were in
many episodes, not all of them.

mention that he plans to come down to visit the Tavern, Archie, fearing exposure of spending the money, attempts to find the worst acts to perform, including having Miss Duffy sing for tavern patrons. Archie stages a floor show featuring the vocal styling of Miss Duffy (who sings "Amapola") and some stale vaudeville jokes exchanged between tavern regulars Crudface Clifford and shortstop Pat Dugan. Throughout this season, Crudface Clifford and Dugan are regulars at the tavern, with Dugan demoted from a lawyer to a shortstop.

Trivia, etc. The first two episodes of the season were recorded off the line and a West Coast broadcast was presented via recording, not a live repeat performance. James C. Petrillo, president of the American Federation of Musicians (AFM), upon learning of this, reinforced a strict ban on the rebroadcasting of network commercial programs from records. When the U.S. Government consulted about the *Tavern* repeat, because this violated the anti-trust action against AFM, the AFM's New York local rep replied that he saw nothing objectionable. An apology was made and the Government was reassured that future broadcasts would consist of "live" repeats. This is why the first two episodes aired on the West Coast at a different time than the rest of the season. (Local stations recording the program for a delay was accepted and utilized in Michigan for the 1942-43 season, which aired the program two days after *Duffy's Tavern* was heard over the rest of the country.)

Episode #18 — Broadcast Thursday, September 25, 1941
Guest: Joe E. Brown
Plot: Duffy's Tavern announces a big Joe E. Brown imitation contest with a first prize of three dollars. Archie asks Joe to be the judge, and before the contest begins, the comedian tells one of his own inimitable stvories entitled the "MOUSIE." Contestants Crudface Clifford, Dugan the Shortstop and announcer John Reed King try to have the biggest mouths, causing Clancy the Cop to come in and threaten to close the joint for making too much noise. When Clancy raises his voice to them regarding his orders from the Sergeant, he wins the contest and the prize money. John Kirby and his Orchestra perform "Maria Elena."

Trivia, etc. For this script, all of Joe E. Brown's lines are in caps. This acknowledged his screen persona as a loud mouth with an enormous smile. Brown was originally scheduled to appear in the September 18 broadcast, but his appearance was postponed a week. Brown was the first of only three Hollywood celebrities to make guest appearances on *Duffy's Tavern* during the program's second season.

Memorable Lines
SHIRLEY: Oh, Mr. Brown, it's sure a pleasure to meet you in person… You know, most girls rave about Tyrone Power and Robert Taylor, but you're my favorite.
BROWN: Does she mean it Archie?
SHIRLEY: Oh, don't ask him – he always says I have no taste.*

KING: Er… Pardon me, Mr. Brown… I'm John Reed King.
BROWN: Well I can't help that.

Episode #19 — Broadcast Thursday, October 2, 1941
Guest: Frank Fay
Plot: Frank Fay, the famed vaudevillian and a singer who used to be on the Rudy Vallee radio program, visits the tavern and Archie and Miss Duffy attempt to convince him to emcee and sing for the tavern's… yes, you guessed it, another floor show. Fay isn't convinced the job is worth it. Archie explains that he'll have Eddie carry the food across the floor so Fay can follow a juggler. When Fay learns that Archie used to take piano lessons, and Archie stretches the truth about his talent, he convinces Archie to try out. Fay is tricked into performing and Duffy, having overheard the performance, phones Archie and tells him it won't work out. Fay appeared on the program plugging his current appearance at the Martinique in New York and his forthcoming radio series.

---

* During the years Shirley Booth was playing the role of Miss Duffy, her lines were acknowledged with "Shirley." Following the actress' departure from the series, the role was cited as "Miss Duffy."

Memorable Lines
ARCHIE: Listen Duffy, I'll call you back later. I've got to
straighten out the joint on account of Fay coming down
here tonight. No, not Alice Faye... this is Frank... He's
much older.

Episode #20 — Broadcast Thursday, October 9, 1941
Guest: Gloria Swanson
Plot: Knowing Gloria Swanson is coming to the tavern, and
learning that the actress is considered one of the ten best-dressed
women in the world, Archie hopes her visit will add "a little more
éclat and de tropp" to the *Tavern*. Eddie and Archie contemplate
what they can do to add class to the place. Eddie proposes throwing
out the people they have inside. Meanwhile, Miss Duffy is having
problems with her boyfriend, Ernest, who doesn't share the same
affection. Miss Duffy asks Gloria Swanson for advice, since the
actress is the "glamour type." Swanson suggests Miss Duffy have
herself psychoanalyzed.

Trivia, etc. *Variety* reviewed: "Gloria Swanson slipped into *Duffy's
Tavern* last Thursday night for a few minutes of fluffy chatter that's
carried off nicely. As posed by the script, Archie confounded his
cronies by 'proving' that Miss Swanson was not only a visitor to his
bierstube, but that she was that way about him."

Memorable Lines
ARCHIE: Take our Miss Duffy, for instance. Her idea of attire
is to do her hair up in curlers. You and I know that is the
kind of stuff you wear to an early morning fire... and a dame
like Miss Swanson wouldn't go to a fire in the first place.
She would have the fire brought to her on a tray. That's what
I call a joey-de-viverr... which is French for always let the
other guy hit you first. Then you are a gent, and can plead self
defense when the cops come.

Episode #21 — Broadcast Thursday, October 16, 1941
Plot: Archie gets a new pinball machine for the tavern and
Finnegan, a new tavern regular, is duped into wasting nickels in

the machine. Miss Duffy is planning on going out dancing with her boyfriend Ernest, along with her friend Vera Fogarty and Vera's boyfriend. When Vera discovers her boyfriend is breaking up with her, Miss Duffy attempts to convince Archie to date Vera. Archie protests: "I don't say that every dame I go out with has to be from Hollywood... but she don't have to be from hunger neither. That Vera is a professional blind date." Archie tries to line up Finnegan for the job, but he fails in his attempt. Miss Duffy tries to convince Crudface to go on a date with Vera, but he too has become obsessed with winning two dollars by attaining the highest score on the new pinball machine.

Memorable Lines
ARCHIE: Miss Duffy, did you ever hear Gracie Allen on the radio?
SHIRLEY: Yes, I think she's a very clever woman.
ARCHIE: I thought so.

Episode #22 — Broadcast Thursday, October 23, 1941
Plot: Archie hires a sandwich man to walk up and down in front of the place with a sign saying free lunch. Archie's scheme backfires, however, because the tavern's customers cannot read and, thinking it was a strike, are staying away. The crew contemplates hiring celebrities to attract customers, proposing Orson Welles as a candidate for the kitchen. With the opera season opening soon, Archie has Eddie slip money to socialites in the hope they will drop by and add a little class... but no one shows up.

Episode #23 — Broadcast Thursday, October 30, 1941
Guest: Joan Edwards
Plot: Miss Duffy introduces her boyfriend, Ernest, a vacuum cleaner salesman, to the crew at *Duffy's Tavern*. Singer Joan Edwards drops by the tavern, having appeared a few times last season to supply musical vocals. Archie, meanwhile, has been invited to a Halloween party but has no costume and no girl to bring along. This somehow makes Archie contemplate marriage. Clancy the Cop stops by and makes a wager with Archie that he won't be able to get a date from Joan Edwards. The tavern,

meanwhile, is pretty crowded to hear Edwards perform, proving a floor show is what the tavern needs to attract business. Miss Duffy's boyfriend, Ernest, shows up at the tavern but has his eyes set on Joan Edwards, and Archie quickly loses the bet.

Trivia, etc. Towards the end of this broadcast, Martin Lewis of *Movie-Radio Guide* magazine appears in person to present a bronze statue, the *Movie-Radio Guide* magazine's Award of Merit, for being the "outstanding new-comer in the comedy field of radio." Ed Gardner thanks the cast, the announcer, the sponsor, the musician and his three writers, Abe Burrows, Parke Levy and Mac Benoff.

Memorable Lines
ARCHIE: Hello, Duffy's Tavern. Where the elite meet to eat. Archie speaking, Duffy ain't here. Oh, hello Duffy... Duffy, I got something for you tonight... you know who's going to sing here? A dish! That's Joan Edwards... uh huh... uh huh... uh huh... nice voice, too.

Episode #24 — Broadcast Thursday, November 6, 1941
Plot: While the tavern is freezing, relationships are heating up. The tavern is freezing because the stock of coal is very low and the next delivery is not scheduled for a few more days. Miss Duffy, meanwhile, is having trouble with her boyfriend again, Ernest Diefendorffer, and asks for advice from Clancy the Cop. Archie sarcastically explains that all Ernest would have to do is "make a noise like a vacuum cleaner, and she'd be on his neck like a carbuncle." Eddie's ex, Sonia Jones, shows up at the tavern, furious. In desperation, she hired someone to pretend to be her new boyfriend to make Eddie jealous. When she proposes and he rejects, she beats him up as he refers to her as "shoo shoo la femme."

Trivia, etc. In this episode, Eddie's full name is revealed to be Edward Pluribus Green.

Memorable Lines

ARCHIE: Oh, hello, Duffy... Pretty good crowd... Moriarity was just here. And whadda'ya think? He kissed his wife! ... No, it wasn't an election bet! He was kissin' her goodbye... Well, the coal strike is over and he's sendin' her back to the mines.

Episode #25 — Broadcast Thursday, November 13, 1941

Supporting Cast: Arlene Francis (Cornelia Piddleton)

Plot: Mrs. Cornelia Piddleton and her Lord Byron Ladies' Literary Society are having their next meeting at the tavern to hear an author speak about "Inside Latin America." When the author doesn't show up, Archie, in desperation, convinces Finnegan to deliver the lecture. Posing as the literary critic, Quincy Polk, the ever clueless Finnegan finds himself up against the odds until Archie feeds him the answers. When Finnegan is asked by Mrs. Piddleton, "Mr. Polk, what are the most interesting places you saw in South America?" Archie feeds Finnegan the answer.

Memorable Lines

ARCHIE: (whispers) The Amazon and the Andes... (loudly) Do you mind repeating that question, Mrs. Piddleton?

PITTLETON: Mr. Polk, what are the most interesting places you saw in South America?

FINNEGAN: Amos and Andy.

Episode #26 — Broadcast Thursday, November 20, 1941

Plot: Duffy is offering a free meal in full Thanksgiving tradition. While the tavern members enjoy soup and nuts, the turkey has yet to arrive. Duffy himself is supposed to come down to the tavern to deliver the bird. Eddie, hungry, tells Archie he is suffering from vitamin deficiency. Vitamins T-U-R-K-E and Y. As time passes, Archie is looking worse for wear in front of his friends, and tempers start to rise, but he continues to promise his employer will pull through. Eddie sings to pass the time. Miss Duffy cracks jokes. Archie sweats every time someone explains how they gave up their Thanksgiving with family on the promise of the turkey

70

to end all turkeys and it has not yet arrived. While Duffy doesn't put in an appearance, the turkey eventually arrives and everyone is thankful for friendship.

Episode #27 — Broadcast Thursday, November 27, 1941
Supporting Cast: Arlene Francis (Madame Sicklesby)
Plot: After saving heiress Pamela Stafford from being hurt at a horse race, Archie figures she would naturally want to marry her rescuer. For $8 million dollars, he'd marry a race horse but he'll settle for the beautiful Stafford. Trying to impress the woman, Archie makes mistakes by claiming he enjoys Carnegie's Hall for music "divertissement." When asked if he is a Philharmonic subscriber, he claims he gets all the high-class magazines. When informed that she will not marry anyone without rich blood, Archie hires a genealogist, Madame Sicklesby, to trace his family history. Hoping to prove his pedigree, Archie's family ends up being populated with horse thieves and panhandlers. When he asks if his family tree can be traced back further, she determines he is descended from Adam.

Episode #28 — Broadcast Thursday, December 4, 1941
Plot: Archie is considering becoming a prize fight manager and asks Duffy for a cut in hours so he can run his little business off the side. Seeking investors, Archie tries to get a few partners involved, including Finnegan. His client? Eddie. Even Clancy the Cop won't buy it. Clancy accepts an offer to feel Eddie's muscles but he first has to put on his glasses before doing so. Eddie backs out when he learns Archie wants him to fight Killer Logan and, discovering he carelessly sold a 200 percent interest in him, Archie convinces Finnegan to become the Masked Marvel and fight Eddie. But his attempts to rig the fight don't go over too well with tavern members.

Episode #29 — Broadcast Thursday, December 11, 1941
Plot: An old pal of Archie's, Dave Hossinger, is paying the tavern a visit. Formerly known as "crooked little Davey," the con man attempts to pass off bad goods, jewelry, at a sixty percent discount. Since Christmas is coming up, Archie doesn't want to pass up

a good deal. Archie buys what he thinks are diamonds only to discover, upon Clancy's inspection, that he has been swindled.

Episode #30 — Broadcast Thursday, December 18, 1941
Plot: Duffy won't buy a Christmas tree for the tavern. Miss Duffy is making a list of the items she intends to buy for her friends before going Christmas shopping. Fats Waller, the new piano player, introduces himself and becomes a regular staple at the tavern. When he learns that Ernest is dropping by the tavern, Archie attempts to unload the fake diamonds he bought last week, hoping Ernest will give them as a present to his girl, Miss Duffy. Archie fails in his scheme because he convinces Finnegan to pretend to be a diamond appraiser who "happened" to be at the tavern at the time Archie tries to sell the goods.

Trivia, etc. Fats Waller, the famed piano player, makes the first of his multiple appearances on *Duffy's Tavern* in this episode, playing "Ain't Misbehavin'."

Episode #31 — Broadcast Thursday, December 25, 1941
Plot: As Archie sits around watching all of his friends display their gifts, he wonders why Duffy never mailed him *his* gift. Clancy the Cop even wonders why Archie hasn't gotten a gift, especially since Archie has been employed for seven years. Duffy calls to keep tabs on the tavern throughout the episode and Archie continues to keep his peace. After Walter Gross performs at the piano and we hear a chorus of "Jingle Bells," a package arrives for Archie. When he discovers it's a new bar rag, he loses his patience over the phone and shouts at Duffy until Eddie reminds him it's Christmas and Archie changes the tone of his voice.

Episode #32 — Broadcast Thursday, January 1, 1942
Guest: Joan Edwards
Plot: Eddie promises a number of New Year's resolutions... including making as much money as Rochester and having a mansion on Park Avenue. Resolving to stop daydreaming, Eddie grabs a broom. Archie, meanwhile, has no resolutions and Eddie proposes one for his employer: Archie stops tormenting the truth.

Archie tries but no matter what he keeps telling fibs, especially when a woman named Rosa Rita shows up, claiming the night before he told her that he was the head man at Duffy's. It seems Archie was so drunk he cannot remember the party last night and apparently promised her a job at the tavern. Rosa wants to perform the floor show with her bird calls and Archie realizes if he doesn't get rid of her, he himself will be a dead pigeon. Angry because his girl won't get the job, a man named Charlie pulls a gun and shoots Archie — then the tavern breaks out in laughter and Clancy explains that the whole scam was to convince Archie to stop stretching the truth.

Trivia, etc. At the time this book was completed, none of the CBS broadcasts were known to exist in recorded form. The scripts did not indicate the titles of all the songs performed, but on occasion, a song title was listed. When known, song titles are listed under their respective episode entries. Joan Edwards sings in this episode, songs remain unknown.

Episode #33 — Broadcast Thursday, January 8, 1942
Plot: Duffy is sending someone down to the tavern to inspect the books. Fearing the accountant will discover the $20 dollar shortage, Archie devises ways of making a quick $20. Finnegan ran up a tab of 75 cents and Archie tries to convince him that interest amounts to $19.25. When he fails, Archie, desperate, tries to get Eddie involved with another harebrained scheme. The solution is provided through a horse race and when the wrong horse is bet, Archie suspects he is in trouble until it turns out to be a blessing in disguise. The "wrong" horse was the winner and Archie wins $100. The orchestra performs "St. Louis Blues."

Episode #34 — Broadcast Thursday, January 15, 1942
Plot: Archie wonders what he is going to do with the leftover money he won on a horse last week. After spending half on Defense Bonds, he contemplates what to do with the rest of his new-found money. Eddie suggests putting the money into a bank, but Archie insists on investing the money in stocks with an unscrupulous investor. Discovering the scheme, Archie tries the

same by trying to convince Finnegan to buy stock he doesn't know is worthless. Naturally, the plan backfires when Archie loses his $50 and Finnegan gains $75.

Episode #35 — Broadcast Thursday, January 22, 1942

Plot: Determined to get Finnegan's $75 from the week prior, Archie explains that if Joe Leech can make legitimate money with his E.Z. Loans, he can do the same. After explaining collateral and interest to Finnegan, Archie tries to make him cough up an investment with the business. The Finn 'n Archie Corporation is quickly in business and their first client is Miss Duffy's friend, Tessie Mummler, who wants to buy a cheap mink. Only when Archie discovers he doesn't have the money to loan out, on account of he can't balance the books, Finnegan once again profits.

Memorable Lines

ARCHIE: Finnegan, whom would you say makes the most money in this neighborhood?
FINNEGAN: Legitimate?
ARCHIE: Yeah, legitimate.
FINNEGAN: Crudface Clifford. The safe cracker.

Episode #36 — Broadcast Thursday, January 29, 1942

Supporting Cast: Arlene Francis (Cornelia Piddleton)
Plot: A woman who is filthy rich from both culture and money, Mrs. Piddleton, president of the Lord Byron Ladies' Literary Society, is once again hosting an event at Duffy's Tavern. Archie wrote a play and pretends to be a Harvard professor, hoping the wealthy ladies will pay him to put the play on Broadway. Eddie knows this scheme is certain to fail for two reasons: One, Archie is no actor. Two, vaudeville is dead and rigor mortis sets in the drama minutes after he watches the opening scene of Crackpot O'Toole's "Eternal Death and Hollow Misery."

Episode #37 — Broadcast Thursday, February 5, 1942

Plot: Archie may not have been able to sell Mrs. Piddleton the idea of a Broadway play last week, but he receives a letter this week from a guy who wants to make a movie out of it, and Archie the star. The barkeep contemplates whether he or Lana Turner gets top billing. Miss Duffy, meanwhile, attempts to help Archie get into society by telling a little white lie to an influential person and the newspapers end up reporting: "It is rumored that Duffy's Tavern earnings last year have put Archie into the upper income brackets, which makes him the best catch in our neighborhood." This is what apparently attracted the fake producer, Mr. Yannuck of 19th Century Fox, into signing Archie, but Clancy the Cop sees through the scheme and takes the con man in.

Memorable Lines
ARCHIE: By the way, Mr. Yannuck, what picture company are you connected with?
YANNUCK: Young man, I am proud to say I am connected with the biggest company in the picture business, 19th Century Fox.
ARCHIE: 19th Century Fox... gee that name sounds familiar.
YANNUCK: I know what you're thinking but we started before they did.

Episode #38 — Broadcast Thursday, February 12, 1942
Plot: John Reed King congratulates Archie on his appearance on the Fred Allen show last night. "I don't like to brag," Archie replies, "but as they say in radio, I thought I laid quite an egg." As a result of the radio broadcast, Archie receives a telegram signed by Wilfred Benson asking him to make no moves without him. Miss Duffy, meanwhile, is once again upset at her vacuum cleaner salesman boyfriend, Ernest. When Wilfred Benson arrives, he wants to sign Archie for his own radio program called... get this... Duffy's Tavern. A tryout isn't convincing and the idea flops. Archie has second thoughts about a career on radio and believes it won't ever work.

Episode #39 — Broadcast Thursday, February 19, 1942
Supporting Cast: Arlene Francis (Sonia Jones)
Plot: With Archie's living expenses going up, he asks Duffy for a raise and gets turned down. Eddie finds himself avoiding engagement with Sonia Jones and Archie proposes ideas to help

him avoid matrimony. Taking matters into his own hands, without Eddie's approval, Archie tells Sonia that his staff came down with a rare tropical sickness called papayrakosus. Convincing Finnegan to play doctor was easy but convincing Sonia that Finnegan is on the level is another matter altogether.

Episode #40 — Broadcast Thursday, February 26, 1942
Plot: Archie brushes off Duffy's phone calls so he can play gin rummy with the boys. After discovering the hard way that Finnegan and Eddie are pros with the cards, Archie convinces the boys to con Mr. Hartzempfelder, a wealthy tavern guest, into losing some money in a high-stakes poker game. But it turns out that Hartz happens to be a pro at the game and cleans the house.

Episode #41 — Broadcast Thursday, March 5, 1942
Plot: Archie is writing his autobiography for Mr. Cromwell, a publisher who promises to put his name in his next book, "Tycoons of the Twentieth Century." Once again, Archie is unable to see past the con game and falls victim to another scheme devised by someone smarter than he.

Episode #42 — Broadcast Thursday, March 12, 1942
Supporting Cast: Arlene Francis (Millie Smith)
Plot: Millie Smith, the first girl Archie ever went out with and from whom he stole his first kiss, is going to drop by the tavern. Archie believes they'll be together again like Orpheus and his flute, "if I may use a nautical term," quotes Archie. Boy is he surprised when she shows up and he discovers she gained a lot of weight.

Memorable Lines
ARCHIE: Eddie, go ahead and wait on the dame.
(WHISTLES) Boy, is she a blimp!
MILLIE: I don't want to eat, I'm lookin' for Archie.
ARCHIE: I'm Archie.
MILLIE: Kewpie! Remember me? Dumpling? (GIGGLES)
ARCHIE: Dumpling!
EDDIE: That dumpling is sure full of yeast.

General Foods

Almost one year to the day that the Magazine Repeating Razor Company began funding *Duffy's Tavern*, the sponsor optioned a clause in their contract which stipulated that they could cease sponsorship after any given 13-week schedule, provided they give advance notice within a specific number of weeks, so the network would have time to sell the program to another sponsor without interruption of the time slot. The reason was because of a promotion on the broadcast of September 25, 1941, offering a special shaving kit with eight double-thick Schick blades for 69 cents. This was the advertiser's shrewd way of determining the size of the listening audience. The giveaway never reached the company's expectation level. This forced Ed Gardner to seek out executives he knew from his prior employment at the J. Walter Thompson Agency and he ultimately convinced General Foods to pitch Sanka Coffee for 26 weeks. Influenced by the sponsor, the network was forced to move the program to a new time slot (30 minutes later on the same day) and insert product placement. On a new night, a new time and with a new sponsor, *Duffy's Tavern* took the spot formerly occupied by *We, The People*, also sponsored by Sanka. According to CBS, the future of *We, The People* was not yet established at the time but it was certain the series would return to the air. Just a few weeks later, on the evening of April 26, it returned under sponsorship of Gulf Oil.

ANNOUNCER: Good evening and welcome to Duffy's Tavern's gala St. Patrick's Day reopening. From now on, every Tuesday night, you'll find the Tavern doors swung wide open for you. If any of you are strangers, come on in, and meet Shirley Booth, star of *My Sister Eileen*, as Miss Duffy, Eddie Green, Charlie Cantor, Ted Wilson and his café society orchestra... and starring Ed Gardner as Archie!... brought to you now under a new sponsorship... that of Sanka Coffee, the coffee that's 97 percent caffeine-free! And that freedom from caffeine makes Sanka an important coffee for all of you who are kept awake at night by the caffeine in ordinary coffee. It means that you can now enjoy the grand flavor and aroma... the deep, rich satisfaction of a real, honest-to-goodness coffee — without the penalty of a sleepless night. For you can drink Sanka Coffee as often as you wish… as late as you wish… you can always drink Sanka Coffee and sleep!

Eddie now served Sanka coffee in the tavern (evident at the beginning of each episode that opened with a babble of voices and Eddie shouting "One cup of Sanka comin' up!" before the phone rang). Ed Gardner protested against the product placement but relented as a result of sponsorship necessity. John Kirby and his Orchestra were replaced with Teddy Wilson and his Café Society Orchestra. Will Roland, manager of Benny Goodman, was handling Teddy Wilson and was responsible for Wilson's booking on *Duffy's Tavern*. The orchestra supposedly replaced John Kirby at the request of Ed Gardner, during negotiations with Sanka, because weeks prior he discovered that Kirby was making more money than he. From the very beginning of the negotiations, Sanka insisted on product placement and Gardner agreed — provided he be given a raise in pay. To help justify the expenses, the suggestion of Teddy Wilson was merely an economical decision. Harry Von Zell, under employment with Young & Rubicam, replaced the familiar John Reed King. Walter Gross and his Orchestra took over musical duties beginning April 14. Gross' big studio band was heard on several CBS sustaining programs and he had recently formed a new sextet for the program. This marked the first time that the bandleader appeared on a sponsored show.

It was a very useful coincidence that the new series, sponsored by Sanka beginning with the broadcast of March 17, 1942, began on the evening of St. Patrick's Day. Thus, the episode was proclaimed in the opening scene as "the Duffy's Tavern gala St. Patrick's Day reopening."

Variety reviewed the premiere Sanka broadcast: "Like the third draft is crowded with fat men, Tuesday night on the networks is crowded with funny men. Ed Gardner enters the congestion of Burns & Allen, Fibber McGee & Molly, Bob Hope, Red Skelton, Milton Berle and Bob Burns. It's pretty sure to be a peak night through the gloomy months ahead when folks are gonna want to escape from the headlines into the surcease of humor. The amiable illiterates of the imaginary Ninth avenue Tavern are little changed

Ed Gardner, Harry Von Zell and Shirley Booth.

since moving under the sponsorship of Sanka. Harry Von Zell is there to talk up the product; Teddy Wilson from Café Society Downtown (nitery) gets in some scattered hot click; Shirley Booth, Eddie Green, Charley Cantor, all reveal unpretentious I.Q.s. It ended with the irate Mr. Duffy bawling at the other end of the phone when an Irish Tenor named Sam Bush really gave out in true high Olcott. So it was all quite amusing period."

In the same capacity as Bill Goodwin on *The George Burns and Gracie Allen Show*, it was the original intention to have Harry Von Zell's appearance on the program be among the usual tavern regulars; standing alongside Eddie, Finnegan and Miss Duffy. In addition to *Duffy's Tavern*, Harry Von Zell was presently the announcer-spokesman for Eddie Cantor (Ipana, Sal Hepatica); William L. Shirer (Sanka); *The Aldrich Family* (Postum) and Dinah Shore (Ipana). Moreover, in the past listeners heard him as both announcer and stooge with such major stars as Fred Allen and Jack Benny for more than ten years, during which time he had built a considerable reputation as both a fluent salesman and an accomplished stooge.

According to the March 17, 1942, issue of *PM Magazine*, the stooging career started innocently enough a few years prior when Von Zell was with Fred Allen. Allen needed someone to play the voice of a well-decorated Christmas tree. Von Zell volunteered and from then on Allen made sure Von Zell was written in for all sorts of strange parts – dopes, monkeys (a Von Zell specialty), horses, cows, a talking fireplace and other inspired creations of the Allen imagination. There was nothing in his background to indicate a theatrical career. He was a Hoosier (Indianapolis), 35, of German-Irish stock (half approval from Archie, no doubt), and, except for some voice training, never thought the part-time radio job he got in California as an announcer fifteen years before would have led to anything much. He got the announcing job to augment his salary as a railroad clerk.

By the time Harry Von Zell made his debut on *Duffy's Tavern*, he had been married sixteen years and had a 13-year-old son, Kenneth, but his busy six-day radio schedule gave him little time to be home. Earlier in the calendar year he got home in time for a bawling out. It seems Von Zell had to do a commercial with a treble-voiced boy who was introduced on the air as Harry's son. The next morning his real-life son collared him. "For crying out loud," he complained, "who was that sissy I heard you with last night?"

Harry Von Zell was highly capable of hosting a program as well as serving as announcer. When Ralph Edwards, host of *Truth or Consequences*, entered the Army during WWII, it was Von Zell who was chosen as the new master of ceremonies until Edwards returned. Von Zell was on *Duffy's Tavern* only until late April. When Eddie Cantor arranged for his program to originate from the West Coast so he could perform and broadcast from several Army camps, most of his crew — announcer included — went to Hollywood. Replacing Von Zell on *Duffy's Tavern* was Jimmy Wallington, who remained on post for the remainder of the season. On the first two broadcasts to feature Wallington as an announcer, he told Archie that he received a postcard from Harry Von Zell, apparently "enjoying his vacation."

After four weeks under the new sponsorship, executives at Sanka notified the advertising agency and the network that they wanted to exercise their option to drop sponsorship after the contracted season concluded. Sanka did not believe the series was beneficial in promoting their product. According to an inter-office memo at General Foods, Ed Gardner and his writers agreed to incorporate Sanka Coffee into the scripts via product placement. However, neither would allow Sanka further intrusion within the comedy, disappointing the coffee company. "To the dismay of all right-thinking citizens, *Duffy's Tavern* retires with the performance of June 30, once more a victim of priorities," quoted the *New York Times* (June 14). "But, as its admirers hopefully point out, there is always a chance of another sponsor." This terminology was apparently fed to the network via a press release because the *Los Angeles Times* broke the news before citing: "Ed Gardner and his *Duffy's Tavern* show fade from the air after the next four shows because of priorities."

Gone this season was Clancy the Cop (the reason why he was no longer featured on the program remains unknown). A new character was added to the program on the broadcast of April 7, 1942. On that evening, Archie figures he has a better chance of inheriting an Alaskan gold mine from his visiting Uncle Homer Whimple if he can prove that he is a settled-down family man. In order to succeed he gets Miss Duffy to pretend to be his wife. Finnegan's 11-year-old brother, Wilfrid, poses as Archie's young son and Archie apologizes for the little boy not looking like anybody in the family — he was born out of town, Archie explains. The brainy Wilfrid, however, spots inconsistencies in the old man's background because the boy asks intelligent questions about the gold mine that Uncle Homer prefers not to answer, which ultimately exposes Archie as a fraud. As Uncle Homer explains, no one in the family could have given birth to someone that intelligent. This marked the first of many appearances of Wilfrid Finnegan. According to the script, Wilfrid is the proper spelling, not the expected "Wilfred." Among the actors to play the role was Dick Van Patten, who fondly recalled how Shirley Booth taught him how to play gin rummy. "Ed Gardner had a short fuse," he recalled. "When she missed a line or did not pronounce a word properly, he raised his voice and yelled at her — in front of everybody. She always remained calm and obeyed his every word."

The brief Sanka run lasted a mere 16 broadcasts instead of the minimum of 26 called for in the contract. The advertising agency representing the sponsor exercised a clause to cancel the intervening term of the deal in the event the contract was not renewed.

SEASON TWO (The Sanka Episodes)
March 17, 1942, to June 30, 1942
Originates from Studio 22 at the Columbia Broadcasting System
(New York City)
Sponsor: General Foods (Sanka Coffee)
East Coast Broadcast: Tuesday, 9:00 to 9:30 p.m., EST
Repeat for West Coast: 12:00 midnight to 12:25 a.m.
for the West Coast
Director: Sam Fuller
Music: Ted Wilson and his Café Society Orchestra
(March 17 to April 7, 1942)
Music: Walter Gross and his Orchestra
(April 14 to June 30, 1942)
Announcer: Harry Von Zell (March 17 to April 28, 1942)
Announcer: Jimmy Wallington (May 5 to June 30, 1942)

Cast
Shirley Booth as Miss Duffy
Eddie Green as Eddie
Charles Cantor as Finnegan

Episode #43 — Broadcast Tuesday, March 17, 1942
Guest: Sam Bush
Plot: It's the Duffy's Tavern gala St. Patrick's Day reopening. Harry Von Zell makes his introduction to the tavern as the new announcer, and to impress Archie, he arranges for some entertainment. Did he bring Jack Benny? Fred Allen? No, he brought Sam Bush. The tavern is packed and Archie won't allow Bush to perform because he's not a known talent. Instead, Archie roots around for a poet and allows Pete Bogg to recite his famous Irish poem, "Hi-O'Watha." Before the poem could finish with the

nursing of little Hiawatha, Duffy calls and says to either get rid of the poet or burn down the joint.

Episode #44 — Broadcast Tuesday, March 24, 1942
Plot: Archie is lovesick because he has no girl. Miss Duffy offers to hook him up with one of her friends but Archie rejects the idea. Duffy calls to say his wife's niece is coming down to meet Archie. Katie Brady is clumsy, ugly and stupid, but she has character. The matchmaking doesn't work out so well. Archie, however, attempts to make a fast buck with a man named Reynolds who is trying to sell black market meat without concern for rationing.

Episode #45 — Broadcast Tuesday, March 31, 1942
Plot: Archie is busy writing a song. A big-time song publisher, interested in hearing the composition, is coming down to hear a tryout. Archie claims the meeting was arranged because he had connections (he answered an ad). When Sam Washburn arrives and hears "My Blue Platonic Love," (pronounced *Play-tonic* by Archie) he makes a steady exit which turns out for the best for Archie since the publisher was actually a con man.

Episode #46 — Broadcast Tuesday, April 7, 1942
Plot: See page 81.

Memorable Lines
ARCHIE: How's your gold mine?

HOMER: Gold mine? Oh yes, my gold mine in — er, —

ARCHIE: Alaska.

HOMER: Oh yeah, Alaska. It's a wonderful gold mine. I'm making a fortune out of it — it's a regular gold mine. Matter of fact, I think I'll open a whole chain of them... Got three thousand Eskimos digging gold with their teeth.

ARCHIE: Three thousand Eskimos, eh?

HOMER: I pay them thirty-five dollars a day. Of course, the days are six months long... let's have another shot of that medicine, I got a touch of Aurora Borealis.

Episode #47 — Broadcast Tuesday, April 14, 1942
Plot: For the benefit of Mrs. Piddleton and her Lord Byron Ladies' Literary Society, Archie decides to add some class to the tavern by inviting the Metropolitan Opera to visit and perform. When the opera rejects Archie's invite, in favor of performing at the Fulton Fish Market, Archie gets Miss Duffy and Finnegan to pose as opera stars Gertrude Dammerung and Clifton Figaro.

Memorable Lines
ARCHIE: Hithertoforth, Duffy's Tavern is gonna become the meeting place of the intelligentsia, a place where artists can come to woo the moose.

Episode #48 — Broadcast Tuesday, April 21, 1942
Plot: After Miss Duffy gets bad boyfriend advice from a fortune-telling carnival swami, Archie uses her experience as inspiration to help Eddie dump his marriage-happy girlfriend Sonia Jones, by having Eddie dress up as Swami Letoh Rotsa (Hotel Astor spelled backward) in order to discourage Sonia. In an attempt to tongue-tie the cast, the scriptwriters began creating complicated names to pronounce for Miss Duffy's boyfriends. In this episode, Ernest Deifendorfer and Breckinridge Hartzempfeloer are referenced by name more than a couple of times.

Episode #49 — Broadcast Tuesday, April 28, 1942
Plot: Duffy breaks his arm and cannot sign the new lease for the tavern so he phones Archie to ask that he sign the contract in Duffy's place. After reading (and misinterpreting) the legal terms, Archie believes the entire contract is crooked. Archie then attempts to get the rent lowered before signing, causing more problems than could be imagined, proving it would have been simple enough to sign the contract like Duffy asked.

Memorable Lines
ARCHIE: Oh nothin' new. Moriarity's in jail. Traffic violation. He ran into a cop... Well, he pleaded not guilty. He said he was color blind and thought it was a pedestrian... Mmm,

it's bad too, it's his second offense. Well, his first offense was stealin' the car...

Episode #50 — Broadcast Tuesday, May 5, 1942
Plot: A music school offering free violin lessons convinces Archie he has the makings of a violin concert virtuoso. Mr. Cahill, however, turns out to be a con artist and goes so far as to sell Archie a phony Stradivarius for $25 bucks. Eddie warns Archie but to no avail and Archie is now stuck with a worthless forgery.

Episode #51 — Broadcast Tuesday, May 12, 1942
Plot: When a newspaper ad doesn't generate a sale, Archie tries to dump his phony Stradivarius on Finnegan and succeeds until he discovers he can sell it for more money to Breckinridge Hartzempfeloer, Miss Duffy's on-again/off-again fiancé. Archie spends a bit of time trying to buy it back from Finnegan, even paying more than he sold it for, but when the battleship painter isn't fooled, Archie learns a valuable (and expensive) lesson.

Trivia, etc. The opening commercial promoting Sanka Coffee is dramatized by the cast of the show, instead of Jimmy Wallington. Archie is angry at Duffy and will not answer the phone when Duffy calls. The cast not only answers the phone, but also does the commercial.

Episode #52 — Broadcast Tuesday, May 19, 1942
Plot: Convincing Miss Duffy's vocal teacher, Prof. Yasha Panyaslovnik, that he can be the proud possessor of a priceless Stradivarius, Archie uses the violin as a bargaining chip and offers to give it to Yasha if he agrees to get Miss Duffy to cease taking singing lessons.

Trivia, etc. A recording doesn't exist of this program and surviving scripts give no indication that actor Bert Gordon, already associated with Eddie Cantor as "The Mad Russian," was involved in any way. Gordon would later play the role of "Yasha Panyaslovnik" on *Duffy's Tavern*, but since the character name was used a number of times on the series before the confirmed Gordon cast credits, the actor playing the role of Yasha in this episode remains unknown.

Episode #53 — Broadcast Tuesday, May 26, 1942
Supporting Cast: Arlene Francis (Mrs. Piddleton)
Plot: An evening of poetry at the tavern causes conflict when Archie phones for a plumber to come figure out why there is no hot water in the tavern. Meanwhile, Mrs. Eustacia Hyancinty Piddleton and her Lord Byron Ladies' Literary Society are sponsoring a poetry night at Duffy's Tavern. When Archie's plan to have Miss Duffy pose as Edgar Allan Poe's "widow" fall through, he enlists the help of an unlikely ally — a plumber named Stevenson Browning, whose ode to burst pipes proves quite a success for all.

Episode #54 — Broadcast Tuesday, June 2, 1942
Guest: Gertrude Niesen
Plot: Miss Duffy's new boyfriend, Homer Prackleberry, a letter carrier, ends up falling for Archie's new squeeze, guest Gertrude Niesen, who ultimately dumps Archie for Homer. Miss Duffy, realizing her love life also came to an abrupt end, goes back to her former boyfriend, Breckinridge.

Episode #55 — Broadcast Tuesday, June 9, 1942
Plot: When Archie is anticipating a newspaper restaurant critic, he mixes the reporter up with a process-server looking for Duffy (for non-payment of his rental fees on a moose head). Naturally, Archie creates a mix-up and the lousy food is served to the reporter while the best in the house is served to the court official.

Memorable Lines
ARCHIE: Say Duffy, I'm glad you called — I'm sendin' the tablecloths out to be washed and the laundry man wants to know what the original color was… so he can know when they're done…

Episode #56 — Broadcast Tuesday, June 16, 1942
Guest: Harry McNaughton
Plot: When Archie discovers that the competition, Gilligan's, is

planning on having a vaudeville act to attract tavern members, Archie hires a British comedian named Hilarious Hawkins to perform impersonations of Englishmen such as Noel Coward, Charles Laughton and The Duke of Windsor.

Trivia, etc. This script was originally scheduled for broadcast on June 9. The first draft of this script features slight differences, especially Archie's motivation for hiring Hilarious Hawkins. Instead of competing against another tavern, he was convinced that vaudeville was making a comeback. Hilarious Hawkins was played by Harry McNaughton.

Episode #57 — Broadcast Tuesday, June 23, 1942
Guests: Gertrude Niesen and Harry McNaughton
Plot: Archie demotes Hilarious Hawkins from floor performer to dish washer and acts like a British aristocrat to impress his sweetie, Gertrude Niesen, who makes another return to the tavern. Niesen, instead, ends up falling for Hawkins, who turns out to be her long-lost vaudeville partner.

Memorable Lines
BOOTH: Just a second, Archie, I know more about women than you'll ever know.
Don't forget, I belong to the same sex as all girls do...
ARCHIE: So what?
BOOTH: So you're a man. You're only an ignorant bystander.

Episode #58 — Broadcast Tuesday, June 30, 1942
Plot: Archie's improbable history is highlighted in true patriotic fashion. Finnegan returns after failing his draft physical — it seems he has the mentality of a six-year-old. But this bad news comes just in time for Finnegan to join in the fun in Archie's War Bond Rally and Historical Pageant of America, featuring the entire gang in comical skits about American history. Archie wrote the pageant himself but was unable to spell the word "pageant." The non-speaking Duffy shows up at the tavern to give Archie a signed pledge for a $4,000 investment in War Bonds.

Archie in costume for the pageant.

CHAPTER FOUR
ENTER BRISTOL-MYERS
(1942 - 1943)

As CONCEIVED BY GARDNER HIMSELF, *Duffy's Tavern* was an old-fashioned, mirrored, and saw-dusty place that attracted "mostly ordinary people but a few of the hoi polloi." Duffy himself was never around, but while he was the little man who wasn't there, he had a definite character nevertheless. "Duffy," Gardner explained, "is a thick-hearted old gent who might have started as a bartender and built up the place that I'm now running for him."

By the end of the first season, the radio audience seemed to have appreciated the movie stars' patronage as much as Archie. Letters kept coming in asking the location of *Duffy's Tavern*. Gardner and company supposedly acquired the name of *Duffy's* from Duffy's Radio Tavern on West 40th Street in New York City. The late Bernard C. Duffy, proprietor, granted permission for the use of the name, understanding the need for free radio publicity. Whether this was true or not, the mental image Gardner created

89

of the tavern was, in fact, not based on Duffy's, but rather a tavern he remembered as a child. "When I was a kid out in Astoria there was an old-fashioned place like it. My Uncle Henry, who was a carpenter, used to hang out there most of the time and I used to work there occasionally. They'd have pig roasts on Saturday nights and I used to play the piano, a fellow named Fredy Vopat (on) drums and a guy called Theodore Smith, the violin. We were the band and we were rotten. It was a nice place, though, and everybody had a good time."

Ed Gardner, Edgar Bergen, Jose Iturbi, Dinah Shore and Don Ameche during rehearsals of What's New? *in 1943.*

The popularity of the comedy program was evident as people from all walks of life, across the country, began talking like a "New Yorker." Convicts at San Quentin voted *Duffy's Tavern* as their favorite radio program. *Duffy's Tavern* was awarded the Award of Merit in 1942 to Ed Gardner by one radio magazine. "*Duffy's Tavern*, like the *Fibber McGee and Molly* show, is not so much a variety bill as a running story about people whom you have come to know very well," quoted a columnist in the October 11, 1942, issue of the *New York Times*.

The third season underwent two noticeable changes. Ed Gardner, with controlled ownership of the program, offered *Duffy's Tavern* to the National Broadcasting Company — provided the network could find a new sponsor and a satisfactory time slot. Enter stage left the advertising agency, Young & Rubicam, which was instrumental in convincing Bristol-Myers to ink a deal whereby the company could hawk their most popular product, Ipana toothpaste.* The pharmaceutical company was already sponsoring *Mr. District Attorney* and agreed to fund an additional time slot for 52 weeks, adding *Duffy's Tavern* and a varying short-run summer program in a 52-week contract basis with sponsor option to renew with each year. In short, the sponsor owned the time slot.

Prior to the Blue Network contract deal, J.S. Davidson at the Pedlar & Ryan Advertising Agency represented Bristol-Myers, creating less-than-memorable programs such as *Ingram Shavers* (January 30, 1929, to April 21, 1930), featuring a barbershop trio alternating with the Ipana Troubadours; *Phil Cook and the Ingram Shavers* (April 3 to July 17, 1933); and *The Ipana Troubadors* (sic) (October 4, 1933, to March 14, 1934). During the Depression and the years that followed, the marketer's ad focus remained on two bestsellers; the company's slogan was "Ipana for the smile of beauty... Sal Hepatica for the smile of health." This same slogan, now a decade old, was heard on the *Duffy's Tavern* program. Right before the contract was drawn up, Bristol-Myers sponsored *Minit-Rub News* (February 17 to October 27, 1941), a weekly program providing... well, news of the week. (By 1939, Bristol-Myers was spending $1.4 million in network radio and was the 19th-largest network advertiser.)

---

* Other products promoted on *Duffy's Tavern* included Vitalis Hair Oil, Minit-Rub and Ingram Shaving Cream. Many reference guides and internet websites incorrectly claim Ipana Toothpaste as the sponsor of the program. (There should be a clarification regarding the difference between the name of the sponsor and the name of the product.)

The other noticeable change, of course, was the network itself. No longer of CBS, *Duffy's Tavern* was now heard over the Blue Network. The deal was inked in late June, within days of the season finale, and confirmed by two tabloids. According to the August 16, 1942, issue of the *New York Times*, "*Duffy's Tavern* has been salvaged from among the priority casualties, and, with Ed Gardner and his wife, Shirley Booth, in their accustomed roles, will be heard under new sponsorship beginning the first week of October, probably on Tuesday evenings." The program would also return to the same time slot it controlled earlier in the season, pushed back a half-hour. The reason for the move was the radio package, over which the network wanted to exercise full control. Gardner wanted the freedom of choice for guest celebrities. The network would not grant him the freedom so the radio star hoisted up anchor and took the program to NBC Blue. An executive at CBS would later publicly state that *they* developed the program and claim partial ownership but Gardner quickly straightened them out. (Bristol-Myers had originally wanted Friday at 9 p.m., but that time slot was already blocked off by Sloan's Liniment for the return of *Gang Busters*.)

Behind the scenes, all was not well with the scriptwriters. Ed Gardner negotiated a raise in salary for his work on the program. The scriptwriters never received a raise. Gardner was caught remarking in a magazine, "John Kirby's music is good and he gets more money than we did." This might explain why Kirby had been replaced with other bands and orchestras during the second season that were, according to inter-office memos, paid less than Kirby. With the third season, musical performers were almost non-existent. The guest singer had disappeared and the vacated solo spot had reverted to Miss Duffy, who reached for the high ones in an adenoidal shriek that, columnist John K. Hutchens remarked, "Shirley Booth must have been at some pains to cultivate." One third of the writing staff, Mac Benoff, was not afraid to express his desire to be paid more for his services. When his request was rejected, he walked away from the program in January 1943, seeking better employment. Three months later, he was rehired with a raise and returned to the series. One of the stipulations of his new employment was that he be required to turn in a treatment for a motion picture based on *Duffy's Tavern*. (The treatment was completed and dated November 22, 1943. See Appendix C.) Benoff did not remain with the program long afterwards, offering very little in the way of contributions, and made a permanent exit before the end of the calendar year. He was known behind-the-scenes for being more interested in how much other people were getting paid and comparing their salary with his. Benoff's radio career ultimately climbed after he left *Duffy's Tavern*. In January 1945, a trade column reported: "Mac Benoff has replaced Everett Freeman as head scribbler on the Fanny Brice show. He formerly scripted *Duffy's Tavern* and is now getting paid more money."

The New York Times reviewed: "The delightful half-hour at Duffy's each week is rapidly becoming one of radio's best comedy programs. One bad feature, however, is the applause after each character finishes his chore. Let Hope, Benny, Allen and the rest continue with this routine; perhaps it compensates their players, but please, Archie, in situation comedy let the unseen audience remember that the scene is at Duffy's on Thoid Avenue and not Studio 6B. For the guest star it's all right. It 'flatters them with flattery,' as Miss Duffy might say, and also pays for their transportation from and back to Hollywood. But when our real friends, Eddie the waiter, Finnegan, Clancy the Cop and the rest start taking bows – look out!"

The October 14, 1942, issue of *Variety* reviewed the season opener: "As before, Archie (Ed Gardner) struggles with the aggravations of conducting a drinking dive with pretensions to class that never quite comes off. His unhappy conversations with his boss, Duffy, occur over the telephone. The great Duffy never appears. His daughter, Miss Duffy, the would-be singer and would-be-date played by Shirley Booth (the former Mrs. Gardner), was heard every week. The Negro porter and the neighborhood boob are other characters of the tavern setting. The comic grief, consternation and naïve aspirations of the bartender-manager and the cross-play of characters add up to first-rate diversion in which the writers and directors do well by the several performers and vice versa. For the commercials: 'When you need a liniment – remember Minit-Rub – when you need a laxative, remember, Sal Hepatica.' Tiny Ruffner is back on big-time radio to read the copy. If the Bristol-Myers copy continues as inoffensive as on the first broadcast there will be no complaints."

By way of an explanation of the "former Mrs. Gardner" statement: Both Ed Gardner and Shirley Booth flew to Reno, Nevada, during the summer of 1942. Gardner became a Nevada resident for six weeks to dissolve his marital partnership with Shirley Booth. After the split, Booth went back to New York and Gardner stopped off in California long enough to play 'Archie' on *The Kraft Music Hall* on the evening of September 17 before flying back to New York to prepare for the new season of *Duffy's Tavern*. Shirley Booth had already achieved a toehold for herself in the theater, having appeared on Broadway as early as 1925. Her star fame rose faster than Gardner's and perhaps this might have become a problem with the two. Booth loved the New York stage and Gardner, the California radio stations. Shirley Booth still remained on the program throughout the 1942-43 season playing Miss Duffy, and the relationship during rehearsals and the actual broadcasts remained professional... strictly professional.

The October 17, 1942, issue of *Billboard* reviewed: "*Duffy's Tavern* comes back on a new net, with a new sponsor, new announcer and new orchestra. But the same crew of dimwits and illiterates that graced the 'poor man's Stork Club' last season is back to make the Tavern one of the more amusing places to be on a Tuesday evening. Altho the success of the show depends greatly on the quality of the script, which hit some high spots on the opening show, the pathetic dopiness of the characters is a pretty sure thing for the laughs. Ed Gardner, as Archie, manager of the café, continues to be effective in his numerous and harassed telephone conversations with the ever-absent Duffy, his mental arithmetic, his mispronunciations and malapropisms. But Archie sounds comparatively rational next to the ravings of Finnegan, the prize but not-so-bright customer, played by Charlie Cantor, and Miss Duffy, the boss' slightly moronic daughter, played by Shirley Booth. An unnecessary and annoying rendition of 'Smoke Gets In Your Eyes' and a foolish crying scene at the end of the program where everyone joins in for 'Auld Lang Syne' were the only sour parts of an otherwise entertaining comedy show. Peter Van Steeden's Ork and Tiny Ruffner, doing the announcing, were the newcomers and fit into the proceedings well. End commercial for Sal Hepatica is woven neatly into script."

The cast of Duffy's Tavern *circa December 1942 with Eddie Green, Shirley Booth, Charles Cantor, Dan Seymour and Mary Martin.*

Well-established as a program bent to murder the English language with verbal abuse and un-intelligent stooges, it was with the third season that *Duffy's Tavern* also established its reputation for insulting the celebrity guests. Gardner and his crew stirred up some of the hottest arguments this side of Marconi. However, despite the arguments engendered by his butchering of the mother tongue, the "biggies" of show business seemed to delight in appearing on *Duffy's Tavern.* Maybe they enjoyed being the butt of his "naïve" japery (and the checks, too, of course). Erudite Clifton Fadiman was introduced as "A sort of grown-up quiz kid." Vera Zorina as "the terpsicorpse from the ballet." Foppish Adolphe Menjou as the "guy who presses his trousers up to his chin."

For example, there was a notable call paid by Clifton Fadiman of *Information, Please* — introduced by Archie as "not one of the guys with the brains; he just asks the questions" — followed a week of so later by, of all people, Jane Cowl. Both of them could take it. They could also dish it out. But the Duffy fans will likely remember with particular pleasure the visit of Giovanni Martinelli, whose singing services Archie sought to obtain for the Tavern under a salary arrangement whereby Mr. Martinelli would have kept half of all the money thrown at him.

"The guy has a throat like a horse," Archie had reported admiringly on the phone to his employer. "When he lets out, you can hear him on Staten's Island."

When the audience heard a guest star on *Duffy's Tavern*, they were sure that he had proved his ability to "take it." It was practically the only requirement but on that point he was adamant. His best insults remained reserved for his phantom boss, Duffy. As Archie once told Miss Duffy, "I ain't never said a thing to his face that I wouldn't say behind his back. Besides, in regard to him firin' me, I have me own philofosy. If he fires me, I ain't got a job. If I ain't got a job, I don't eat. When I don't eat, I get skinny and emancipated-lookin'. And when that happens, I'd be so changed that Duffy could pass me on the street without even recognizin' me. So what? So you think I'm goin' to worry about a guy that won't even speak to me when he passes me on the street?"

A Spotlight on Eddie Green

Eddie Green was the waiter, handyman and foil for Ed Gardner's Archie. Unlike Rochester on the Jack Benny program, he was not prone to the excited approach and he took a more leisurely course in the subtle knifing of Archie. He succeeded on one broadcast in this manner:

ARCHIE: I suppose I wouldn't be no good as a producer?
EDDIE: Sure you would... after all, you wasn't no good as an actor and you ain't no good as a writer... so why shouldn't you be no good as a producer?

Green was a native of Baltimore, Maryland. He started his career as a boy magician and played in burlesque as Billy Minksy for eleven years. He was the original Ko-Ko in *The Hot Mikado* on Broadway, and won instantaneous fame for his written-and-acted burlesques of historical and classical heroes for Rudy Vallee's *Fleischmann* program, on which he made more than 20 appearances.* His first appearance was on the evening of April 9, 1936, billed as "the best in Harlem entertainment." On April 16, 1936, Green told an all-Negro story about King Arthur and the round table. On January 28, 1937, he performed a comical skit involving his failure to send a telegram. On August 5, 1937, he performed an all-Negro version of *Hamlet*. On June 30, 1938, he appeared in "a chocolate flavored version" of *Robin Hood*. (Green was also billed on that same broadcast as "the lovable little colored comedian.") He also made several appearances in Columbia's *Pursuit to Happiness* series, in the same manner, offering renditions such as the colored version of "Christopher Columbus." On the April 27, 1941, broadcast of *The Columbia Workshop*, Eddie Green recounted the legend of Jason and the Golden Fleece from a black viewpoint and with an all-Negro cast.

Green was heard weekly as a cast member of Lanny Ross' *Show Boat*, playing the role of Hattie McDaniel's husband, from August 19 to October 21, 1937. *Show Boat* was one of NBC's most popular and highest-rated programs. He reprised his stage role from *The Hot Mikado* on the April 23, 1939, broadcast of *The Magic Key*. On June 4, he presented his own version of "Anthony and Cleopatra" on the same program.

After co-starring with Louis Armstrong and Paul Robeson on radio, Green wrote numerous skits for his own radio program and is also credited for creating the role of "Sweeney the Jockey" for the Ben Bernie radio program. His hobby was that of an amateur radio operator, the call letters of his station once having been W2AKM, for which he held a license for more than 15 years. During his tenure on *Duffy's Tavern*, Green continued to work on stage. Beginning in March of 1943, Eddie Green could be seen playing a lead in Vinton Freedley's *Dancing in the Streets* on

---

* Green participated in a radio audition of "All God's Children," on CBS' *Forecast* series, offering a comical historical drama with an almost all-Negro cast.

Broadway. In late 1944, Green was performing at the Orpheum in Los Angeles, billed as "the waiter from *Duffy's Tavern*," performing a monologue that furnished the comedy relief for the bill. His delivery was deadpan, with laughs garnered from his continual flow of chatter about "Grandpa." He finished with a pantomime poker gang routine that reportedly stole the evening.*

In 1945, Eddie Green contributed his talents for many broadcasts of *Jubilee*, a morale-building service for Negro troops stationed overseas, first produced by the War Department, then by the Armed Forces Radio Service. Green was among the many celebrities who performed jazz, black-oriented swing and comedy sketches. Various episodes featured such highlights as a comedy sketch with Eddie Green preparing for a visit from his horrifying mother-in-law; Green and Ernie Whitman singing a duet, "One Meatball"; Eddie Green performing his "Jonah and the Whale" routine; and Eddie Green, Ernie Whitman and Lillian Randolph performing their own rendition of "The Courtship of Miles Standish."

As early as the summer of 1945, Bristol-Myers considered creating a radio program built around Eddie Green. Nothing ever came about it. On May 14, 1946, a CBS audition disk was recorded for a situation comedy titled *The Folks on Fourth Street*. Produced by Ken Dolan, the situation comedy concerned a schemer living with his sister, and his Negro handyman. Jess Kirkpatrick, Eric Rolfe, Lurene Tuttle and Ruth Perrott were featured. Eddie Green played the handyman. The audition never sold. On August 26, Ken Dolan and Charles Vanda produced another audition program with Eddie Green in the cast. *The Beulah Show*, with Bob Corley (a white male) playing the title role, replacing the late Marlin Hurt, was a success and the program aired over ABC beginning in February 1947. Eddie Green's schedule did not permit him to be

---

* Anyone wanting to hear Eddie Green's genuine vaudeville patter needs to look no further than a recording of the August 17, 1942, broadcast of *The Columbia Workshop*, presenting "An Old Fashioned Vaudeville Show" with The Delta Rhythm Boys, Pinky Lee and Eddie Green.

among the cast for the weekly program. Green was successful in securing a number of supporting roles on *Amos n' Andy*.

A Spotlight on Charlie Cantor

Poor Finnegan never quite understood anything and operated in a world of his own. By contrast, life in *Duffy's Tavern* seemed almost normal until Finnegan pierced the orthodox with an oblique observation. To wit:

ARCHIE: We was talkin' about splittin' the atom.
FINNEGAN: Oh, it's a big mistake Arch.
ARCHIE: [slowly] Expostulate.
FINNEGAN: Well, look what happened in the Garden of Eden. They split an Adam and look what came of it — dames!

In real life, Charles Cantor was a graduate of New York University who discovered additional income during the Depression by touring the country as a blackface comedian and later in musical comedy in stock. Radio offered lucrative income for stage actors because of their dialects and Cantor's specialty was playing a variety of characters in the same mold as Paul Frees and Mel Blanc. Radio fans today know Cantor also as Uncle Louie to Fanny Brice's immortal Baby Snooks.

Cantor built a solid reputation, resulting in a demand by numerous radio producers. From October 8, 1937, to April 15, 1938, he played a supporting role in each of the *Grand Central Station* broadcasts. From September 4, 1939, to March 25, 1940, he played comedic roles on *Quaker Party with Tommy Riggs*. In the spring of 1940, he made four appearances on *The Revuers* and 17 appearances on *Johnny Presents* before he made his first appearance as Finnegan on *Duffy's Tavern*. (He was also a talented piano player and on occasion supplied piano music on *Duffy's*.) *

---

* On the afternoon of October 6, 1940, Charles Cantor was a guest on *Behind The Mike* and was interviewed about his then 11-year-old radio career, his prior work on vaudeville and then demonstrated the various dialects he was able to perform.

During his tenure on *Duffy's Tavern*, Cantor kept busy on other radio programs, playing the role of Solomon Levy on Proctor & Gamble's *Abie's Irish Rose* from May of 1943 to June 26, 1943, and reprising his role in the Brooklyn portion of a skit from same on the September 11, 1943, broadcast of *Battle of New York*. In the spring of 1943, he created the recurring role of Socrates Mulligan on *The Texaco Star Theater*, starring Fred Allen. He played Eddie Cantor's brother-in-law on *Time to Smile* for five broadcasts from October 13 to November 24, 1943. He played Zero, Alan Young's best friend, on *The Alan Young Show* from September 20, 1946, to June 6, 1947. (These latter two programs were also sponsored by Bristol-Myers.)

In the spring of 1948, as soon as Rudy Vallee finished his role in the Preston Sturges film, *Unfaithfully Yours*, the crooner filmed a 23-minute television pilot at his Vallee-Video studios, entitled *College Life*. Charles Cantor was among the cast. Vallee produced, directed and starred in the pilot, an effort to break into the new medium of television. The pilot never sold, even though it was screened in New York for a number of prospective sponsors. Late that same year, Charles Cantor was hired to play a supporting role for *Just Outside Hollywood*, an audition recording for a proposed situation comedy about KOOK, a small radio station "just outside Hollywood," teetering on the brink of insolvency. Frank Nelson, Hanley Stafford and John Brown were also among the cast. The celebrity guest was Veronica Lake. The radio program never sold.

During the first week of April, 1947, Charles Cantor lectured at Beverly Hills High on — this will kill you — English.

According to the October 11, 1942, issue of the *New York Times*, the weekly cost of *Duffy's Tavern* was $3,500, a meager amount when compared to George Burns and Gracie Allen's $7,500, Fibber McGee and Molly's $6,500, Edgar Bergen's $11,000, Bob Hope's $10,000, Fred Allen's $15,000, and Jack Benny's astronomical $25,000!

Dropping the Tavern

Now on the Blue Network and under sponsorship of Bristol-Myers, *Duffy's Tavern* underwent a third noticeable change. The word "tavern" was dropped from the title. Columnist Jack Gould phrased it best, and accurately, in his October 18, 1942, column: "Effective with Tuesday's broadcast over WJZ and the Blue Network, *Duffy's Tavern* will no longer be called by that name. Hereafter it will be known simply as *Duffy's*, presumably to eliminate any alcoholic connotation. The change will be a disappointment to numerous tavern keepers throughout the country who had adopted the program's name in hopes of stimulating trade."

Indeed, a student of history once discovered that the first Duffy's Tavern was established in 1795, about 15 miles west of Williamsport, Pennsylvania. Since *Duffy's Tavern* went on the air in 1941, a whole crop of Duffyless Duffy's Taverns had sprouted up. It was reported that by 1942 tavern owners across the country had begun changing the name of their locale in an effort to cash in on the popularity of the radio program. In January 1946, Mike Romano, owner of Yankee Doodle and Elmer's Lounge, the latter being where Dorothy Donegan got her start a few years prior, opened a new tavern in Chicago, advertising itself as the joint "where the elite meet to eat," among other gimmicks from the Ed Gardner radio show.

Newspaper Advertisement. Cleveland, Ohio, February 15, 1947

101

The first two broadcasts of the new season were still called *Duffy's Tavern*. The title change began with the third broadcast on October 20. For years, verifying the exact date was difficult because the title change was not reflected on the front page of both first and revised drafts of the radio scripts until February 2, 1943. But information contained within pages of original radio scripts is never considered reflective to what was truly broadcast. Consulting recordings of radio broadcasts from December 15, 1942, and January 5, 1943, verifies Jack Gould's column, proving scripts should not be taken as verity.* Reflecting the change in the beginning of each episode, Ed Gardner answers the phone (sans "Tavern") with, "Hello, Duffy's, where the elite meet to eat..." According to historian Jim Cox, Ed Gardner proffered the term "Duffy's Variety" and the alteration was applied for a few installments, but none of the existing recordings or scripts substantiate this. But radio historians know that Gardner's suggestion could have been applied and, at a later date, be verified and the exact date or dates verified.

So why the change? It turns out an employee working for Bristol-Myers felt the "saloon" connection was unsavory and, with a little persuasion, convinced the heads at both Bristol-Myers and Young & Rubicam to demand the word "tavern" be dropped from the title. A press release explained in more detail that "some listeners — the majority being Catholics — had started public protests in an attempt to have the word 'tavern' dropped from the title. The protestors' excuse was that the word 'tavern' was partly advertising the hobby of drinking and should not be used over the radio." Fans, however, went on referring to the show as "Duffy's Tavern," as they had before. Gardner even suggested the title *Duffy's Variety*, which might actually have been used for a few episodes although that can't be substantiated.

The title change lasted only a year and a half, however, as

---

* When recordings of *Duffy's Tavern* were re-edited and played back for troops overseas, the AFRS announcer referred to the program as "Duffy's Tavern," not "Duffy's."

evident by the March 5, 1944, issue of *The New York Times* which reported: "The sponsor of *Duffy's* apparently has come to the conclusion that the citizenry was not greatly outraged by the alcoholic connotation in the word 'tavern.' In any event, the Ed Gardner show is reverting to its original title, *Duffy's Tavern.*" Coinciding with the movie studio's recent purchase of screen rights, it also remains possible that the sponsor was influenced by Paramount Studios, who was already making plans to release a motion picture of the same title.

Further digging reveals an interesting factoid: There was very little to support the statements of the employee working at Bristol-Myers. There were no apparent protests whatsoever regarding the title. A handful of letters maybe but no protests and no petitions. Beginning with the March 5, 1944, broadcast, with full title, *Duffy's Tavern* was here to stay. To celebrate, Colonel Stoopnagle, who was guest on both the *Forecast* broadcast and the March 1941 premiere, paid a return visit to *Duffy's Tavern.*

Duffy's Tavern, having shortened its name to *Duffy's*, chose to stray farther from its appointed course, due to sponsor influence. The omnipresent guest star and a regular singer were not present in the first four broadcasts — leaving it up to the supporting cast to carry most of the 30 minutes. Peter Van Steeden had a band of seven men that supplied the necessary music. Ed Gardner insisted that the second season worked well without celebrity guests but the advertising agency expressed disappointment. A full-fledged orchestra – Peter Van Steeden's – remained a good orchestra to be sure but even with a singer adding to the musical entertainment, celebrities gave ratings a boost, verified through a number of polls taken by the network, the sponsors and the trade columns. This was evident by the sponsor's decision to add more zing to the episode, and the threat of canceling sponsorship after the first 13 weeks. Gardner relented and, beginning with the broadcast of November 3, 1942, Peter Van Steeden's orchestra now played a more prominent part in the program, increased in number from seven men to fourteen. Guest personalities were also re-added to the lineup, changing the program substantially to a "revue." With the new "guest policy" (as described by inter-office memos), Madeleine Carroll, Monty Woolley and Clifton Fadiman (of radio's *Information, Please*) were first to visit the tavern during this period.

In the December 6, 1942, issue of *The New York Times*, John K. Hutchens offered a favorable review: "In a time of excessive uncertainty it is agreeable to find that life at *Duffy's* is still wonderful. *Duffy's Tavern*, that is. With some reason the admirers of that entertainment, who include all right-thinking citizens, were slightly alarmed a while ago when someone or other went into executive session and decided to delete the 'Tavern' from the title, presumably because it suggested an unholy alliance between levity and the evils of alcoholism. Was the joint about to get classy? The old admirers were worried and not less so when it acquired a feminine singer who sings well enough for other kinds of shows, but whose style was not for this one. And there was a full-fledged orchestra in place of the six-piece band or whatever it was that used to assault the Tavern's atmosphere with a fine, brassy ring. What, the old admirers asked, was going on here? Generally speaking, though, things are all right again... Indeed, though it verges on the extreme to say so, they may even discover that Archie and *Duffy's* in general are currently in better form than they have ever been. This conservative habitué of the Tavern is not ready to say so without reservation, because there have been some great nights there where 'the elite meet to eat.' But it could be, thanks to a policy *Duffy's* has lately adopted in regard to guest stars... At *Duffy's* a guest is a person who gets a good deal of pushing around — but with hilarity and no pain — as distinguished from the shoddy air of certain audience participation shows in which the visitor is rendered merely ridiculous. For at *Duffy's* the invited droppers-in are prominent and talented folk who can take care of themselves when the insults are flying and, the more rarefied the atmosphere from which they come to spend an evening at the Tavern, the better the time they have."

Street and Smith, publishers of pulp magazines including *The Shadow* and *Doc Savage,* adapted their most popular features to the then-burgeoning field of comic books in the early forties. Beginning in 1943, a regular back-up feature in *Doc Savage Comics* presented comic strip biographies of radio personalities including Jack Benny, Fanny Brice, Lon Clark and Burns and Allen. The July 1943 issue, on the stands in May of that year, cover-featured an eight-page bio-strip on Ed Gardner.

Highlights of the Season

During the 1942-43 season, rehearsals for *Duffy's Tavern* were an in-house highlight at Radio City. Every Tuesday afternoon the dress rehearsals featured about 100 assorted producers, office boys, salesmen, musicians, actors and agency people. Before Fred Allen moved to Sunday nights on CBS, the ex-vaudevillian once held the same affection for radio people. The audience gathered for belly laughs and was never discouraged since Gardner and his cast used this opportunity to test the laughs, mark where potential pauses might be needed for lengthier laughs, and eliminate or replace jokes that did not provoke a laugh. Gardner held this space with the added twist that he also played to the radio audience during the rehearsals. On one given afternoon he apologized for starting the dress rehearsal without the usual tomfoolery to soften up the studio audience. Then, when a company of stenographers had to hustle back to their office, he quipped, "Try us again next week, girls. We'll be better."

On the afternoon of March 25, 1943, during rehearsals for *Duffy's Tavern*, New Yorkers learned that the place to be caught during a blackout was a radio studio. Instead of turning their guests loose to wait in the corridors, which was standard procedure, the radio stars put on a show for the benefit of the guests. George Burns and Gracie Allen, the cast of *Duffy's Tavern* and members of *The Aldrich Family* gave what one member of the NBC tour described as "a superb extemporaneous show while the sirens screamed."

Throughout late December 1942 and early January 1943, Phil Baker, host of radio's *Take It or Leave It*, had to spend some time recovering from an operation. Having gotten out of the hospital recently after an appendectomy, Baker not only resumed his role on the radio quiz program but made numerous guest appearances on radio comedies including Jack Benny and *Duffy's Tavern*. On the evening of January 19, 1943, Phil Baker stopped by the tavern for a little relaxation (admitting the operation took a little toll on him) and played the piano. Archie strikes a bargain with him. If Baker puts on a *Take It or Leave It* quiz in the tavern, he'll let him play the piano. After Baker plays "Believe Me if All Those Enduring Young Charms," (Baker really plays the piano), the gang plays their own version of *Take It or Leave It* with hilarious answers to questions, including Finnegan mistaking the game show for *Information, Please*.

Memorable Lines

BAKER: The nicest place I've been in the last four weeks.
ARCHIE: Where you been in the last four weeks?
BAKER: In the hospital.

On the evening of February 9, 1943, Duffy asks Archie to hire George Jessel, one of America's biggest after dinner speakers, with a salary below Jessel's usual standards. While Miss Duffy reads silly limericks from her valentine, Jessel gives one of the great toasts for which he is famous. The attraction builds as Jessel seriously contemplates teaming with Miss Duffy on the stage. Archie finds himself engaged to Jessel's sister, Anna. When Duffy tells Jessel by phone that it will be a double wedding, Jessel discovers his mistake and confesses that he won't marry Miss Duffy, after which he leaves the tavern in a hurry.

George Jessel was in a high spot that week with three guest shots which, combined with *Showtime*, probably gave him his all-time salary high for any single week in his 30 years of show business. His first was on February 7 with Jack Benny. On February 10, he appeared on *Old Gold Tonight* and in all the comedian was pitching his forthcoming autobiography, *So Help Me*, then due out in stores shortly. Jessel had already turned down two commercial programs for March 4 and 15 due to prior plans to go on tour with *Showtime*, in which he co-starred.

"I appeared 30 times on almost as many different radio programs as a guest and this, my fellow artists, is no mean feat, for the method of procedure and format on each of these programs resemble each other as much as my aunt looks like Rita Hayworth," Jessel later recalled. "Each advertising company has a list of idiosyncrasies that must be majestically saluted. For example, on one program you must not mention anything about swimming, as the advertising company also handles a beer account and swimming reminds the people of water and that might hurt the beer business. On another program you must tell no jokes about a man who is little, as the client's wife has a father who is only five feet tall and therefore is very sensitive about such remarks. Yet on another you must write in jokes for the announcer to tell, even though he tells them lousy, but the client likes to hear him talk, and so on and so on."

"On *Duffy's Tavern*, be prepared to stand in the middle and take it," George Jessel continued. "Archie talks at you for three minutes, then you say. 'Oh is that so?' and then Shirley Booth takes care of you for the rest of the program. With Jack Benny, you learn an entire new sense of timing. If he asks you a question, wait three minutes and then after he goes hmmmm four times, you answer, but very slowly.

With Orson Welles, you listen to your introduction, then say thank you and sit down for 25 minutes, then say, 'Good night, Mr. Welles and good night everybody.' With Al Jolson, be prepared to be awed for you know that beneath that ragged shirt, there's $5,000,000 worth of Tel. & Tel. With Sammy Kaye, be prepared to rehearse on the fly because you've got to get him between the fifth and sixth show as he is always doubling in a theater and not only do you have to help carry the instruments but, in the bus going over, he beats you in Gin Rummy. With *Ellery Queen*, you listen to the evidence and when they ask you so seriously, 'Who done it?,' you're afraid to answer because by that time you think you did it. On *Double or Nothing*, you leave the studio fully realizing that your little nephew could have done much better. On Fred Allen's program, you have nothing to worry about. He respects your judgment and ability or he wouldn't have engaged you in the first place and, at the first rehearsal, he complains so much himself about conditions and his health and besides that you're ashamed to squawk about anything even if Falstaff is standing on your foot."

Variety reports: February 9, 1943. Albany, New York. Gardner Radio Productions, Inc., was chaptered to conduct a business in New York, Capital stock was 200 shares, no par value. A. Walter Socolow was the filing attorney. The Incorporation concerned Ed Gardner, owner of the *Duffy's Tavern* radio program on the Blue Network, made for the usual business purposes.

On the evening of March 2, 1943, Tito Guizar, described as "a real Latin lover" who plays the guitar, visits the tavern and Archie attempts to impress him with Spanish.

ARCHIE: Well, Tito Guizar... Welcome Sinior.
TITO: Hello Junior... You speak Spanish?
ARCHIE: Oh mucho, mucho.
TITO: We better talk English.
ARCHIE: O.K. if you prefer... You know I'm quite familiar with Panama-Namerica. I had an uncle down there – married a very wealthy Hacienda.
TITO: But Archie, a hacienda is a house.
ARCHIE: Well he liked them built that way.

Archie soon realizes that the tavern needs a musical highlight, with a Mexican atmosphere, and attempts to hire Guizar as musical accompaniment for the tavern. When Guizar makes verbal love to Miss Duffy, she decides to elope and when Duffy learns of this, he fires Archie.

TITO: Do not be frightened my little kitten. I adore you. Look, here is my guitar... has anyone ever made love to you on a guitar?
BOOTH: Oh, how can we both sit on that?

Breckenbridge, Miss Duffy's boyfriend, is shocked when he learns of the news and, together, the two plot to get rid of Guizar – for both their sakes – and do so by convincing Miss Duffy to sing which causes Guizar to run south for the border. With Guizar gone, Archie's job is safe and secure.

Having made a guest appearance on *Duffy's Tavern* on the evening of March 2, 1943, Tito Guizar was approached to be a weekly regular on the series. Beginning with the broadcast of April 20, Guizar helped cement the Good Neighbor bond of friendship with his unique guitar playing and singing as a new regular on *Duffy's Tavern*. Once billed on the radio program as "Mexico's answer to the Andrews Sisters," Guizar spent his off time playing at the Waldorf-Astoria in New York, by popular demand, billed by the hotel as the "Latin American Ambassador of Good Will." He served as musical entertainment until the end of the season. (Gardner and the cast had plans to move to California, Guizar went to Mexico to appear in a movie.)

For the broadcast of May 4, 1943, Archie agrees to a blind date but, after trying to spruce the tavern up, discovers his efforts were in vain when he sees the woman, Millie Smith, and discovers that she is more of a blimp than a date. After exchanging wisecracks with Eddie such as "hoarding helium" and "hipperino," Archie is saved by the bell when a friend in the tavern thinks Millie is "petite" and the two love birds get romantically entangled. The role of Millie Smith was played by actress Hope Emerson, known for towering over her male leads at 6' 2" and 230 pounds. At the time this book was completed, a recording of this episode was not known to exist. If the information contained in two radio scripts found at various archives are correct, Hope Emerson never received on-air credit and the character of Millie Smith is treated in the usual fashion as a weekly guest. During the same week Emerson appeared on *Duffy's*, she did her regular bit on the *Joe and Ethel Turp* radio series, rehearsed for a summer replacement at the Young & Rubicam agency, made an appearance on WHN's (New York) *Gloom Dodgers*, stooged on the Jimmy Durante-Garry Moore *Camel Comedy Caravan* program, played a part on *The Phillip Morris Playhouse*, did an audition for a new stanza under production at Trans-American and dickered with 20th Century-

Fox for a part in a Gregory Ratoff production (*Something to Shout About*, a 1943 musical) slated to start rolling June 15. In her spare moments, Miss Emerson scanned the "help wanted" columns.

Variety reports: June 9, 1943. "Duffy's Tavern" is the new moniker applied to San Quentin prison by cons. Name was taken from the radio program because warden at San Quentin was Clinton T. Duffy.

SEASON THREE
October 6, 1942, to June 29, 1943
Originates from the New York Studios of the Blue Network
Sponsor: Bristol-Myers (Ipana Toothpaste)
East Coast Broadcast: Tuesday, 8:30 to 9:00 p.m., EST
Repeat for West Coast: Tuesday, 9:00 to 9:30 p.m.
(not broadcast on October 6, 1942)
Director: Sam Fuller
Commercial Spokesman: Mark Hawley
(October 6, 1942, to May 1943)
Commercial Spokesman: Roland Winters
(May to June 29, 1943)
Announcer: Dan Seymour
Music: Peter Van Steeden and his Orchestra
Announcer: Tiny Ruffner
(October 6, 1942, to October 27, 1942)
Announcer: Dan Seymour
(November 3, 1942, to June 29, 1943)
Singer: Marie Green (November 3, 1942)
Singer: Clark Dennis (January 5, 1943, to February 16, 1943)
Singer: Joan Edwards (February 23, 1943)
Singer: Tito Guizar
(March 2, 1943, and April 20, 1943, to June 29, 1943)
Singer: Tessie Mummler (April 6, 1943, to April 13, 1943)

110

Cast
Shirley Booth as Miss Duffy
Eddie Green as Eddie
Charles Cantor as Finnegan
Alan Reed as Clancy the Cop*

Episode #59 — Broadcast Tuesday, October 6, 1942

Plot: Archie fights with Duffy about wanting a raise and when he doesn't get what he wants, Archie answers an ad for a restaurant manager, under the name Jack McBenny. Miss Duffy solicits her singing talents to Mr. Van Steeden, the band leader for this episode. While Miss Duffy sings, Archie makes cracks such as: "Frightening, ain't it?"
"This should only happen to Hitler."
"Eddie, take a note to Leon Henderson. Have a ceiling dropped on Miss Duffy."
"Eddie, make it the roof."
"There must be some way that voice can be used in the war effort."
Peter Van Steeden and his orchestra perform "Digga, Digga Doo."

Episode #60 — Broadcast Tuesday, October 13, 1942

Plot: Wanting to boost the society clientele of the tavern, Archie hires Professor Grayson to add culture. As a result, Miss Duffy is educated about the evils of the magazine she is reading called "True Trash" and Eddie is pressured to read books without pictures. Archie hopes to marry a society woman named Cartwright and Eddie insists every time Archie gets bitten by the love bug, he must have a tapeworm.

Memorable Lines
ARCHIE: Eddie, come here. Let's try it again... Miss Cartwright, allow me to welcome you to Duffy's. It is certainly a delight.
EDDIE: [mimics a female customer] Oh, thank you.

---

* The character of Clancy the Cop appeared in most of the episodes, not all of them.

ARCHIE: I can't tell you what an honor it is to have your midst among us... May I have your genuine mink coat?
EDDIE: If you don't mind, I'll wear it.
ARCHIE: But, Miss Cartwright, it ain't cold here.
EDDIE: It ain't safe neither.
ARCHIE: Look, Eddie, let's forget about it. Give me back the earrings.

Episode #61 — Broadcast Tuesday, October 20, 1942
Plot: The literary society pays the tavern another visit and since Mrs. Piddleton and her friends are real upper crusts, the same wax banana jokes from the Tallulah Bankhead broadcast of April 26, 1941, are used. Guest debater Major George Fielding Elliott is supposed to stop by the tavern and debate with Archie about military affairs, much to the liking of Piddleton. When Elliott cannot make it – having just been called up – Finnegan assumes the role of Elliott... with disastrous results.

Episode #62 — Broadcast Tuesday, October 27, 1942
Plot: Archie is running as a candidate for State Treasurer. Slippery McQuire acts as Archie's campaign manager, while Archie practices signing his name so it'll look nice on all the dollar bills that will be printed. In order to gain popularity votes, he is putting on a big election pageant, dramatizing highlights of his life, titled, "The Rise of Archie or, It Could Happen to Anybody." Peter Van Steeden and his Orchestra performs "Pennsylvania Polka."

Episode #63 — Broadcast Tuesday, November 3, 1942
Guest: Madeleine Carroll
Plot: Archie is in love with Madeleine Carroll and to everyone's surprise, she has feelings for the barkeep. But when she puts in an appearance at the tavern and tries to woo Archie, she is unaware that Miss Duffy pre-arranged Archie for a date with Katrina Yarbotz, a girl from downtown. When Carroll proposes they go out on the town with a friend of hers, Archie believes their date will lead to something serious — until it happens that Carroll's friend is the same Katrina.

Trivia, etc. It remains unclear if Peter Van Steeden was featured on this broadcast or if someone else conducted the orchestra. Steeden's mother passed away on November 2 and Steeden may have had to take a leave of absence from radio broadcasting for a few days, including *Mr. District Attorney*, beginning November 3.

Memorable Lines
CARROLL: Why don't we sit down and talk?
ARCHIE: About what?
CARROLL: (Romantically) Anything.
ARCHIE: Mmmm – Do you think Branch Rickey will help with the Dodgers? Gee, it's hot here...
CARROLL: Archie.
ARCHIE: Yeah?
CARROLL: C-mere – come a little closer.
ARCHIE: Yeah?
CARROLL: Closer, Archie.
ARCHIE: I can't – you're in my way.

Episode #64 — Broadcast Tuesday, November 10, 1942
Guest: Clifton Fadiman
Plot: Clifton Fadiman, moderator of the popular quiz program, *Information Please*, drops by the tavern and the boys attempt to sound real intelligent. While Clifton Finnegan wonders if he and Clifton Fadiman are related (seeing that you can be related by the first names – Louis the fifteenth and Louis the sixteenth), Fadiman tries to explain to the crew that reports of his intelligence are greatly exaggerated. The boys eventually play their own version of "Duffymation Please" but, as the questions are tossed around, the answers are twisted around until Fadiman finds himself answering the questions himself.

Memorable Lines
ARCHIE: Er – er – what do you say we have some brilliant conversation.
FADIMAN: Yes, that would be fun. Er... do you enjoy conversation, Miss Duffy?

SHIRLEY: Oh yes – er – very much – it's such an interesting topic.

ARCHIE: Well, what are we waiting for? Leave us converse... What's new, Mr. Fadiman?

FADIMAN: Oh not much. What's new with you?

ARCHIE: Not much. How's tricks?

FADIMAN: So-so. What's new with you, Miss Duffy?

SHIRLEY: Oh – not much. You know how it is.

FADIMAN: Er... how have you been, Archie?

ARCHIE: Oh... can't complain. And you?

FADIMAN: Oh – can't complain.

Episode #65 — Broadcast Tuesday, November 17, 1942
Guest: Jane Cowl
Plot: Archie wants to go on stage as an actor and Jane Cowl, one of the great ladies of American Theater, happens to drop in. Archie, wanting to get in good with Cowl, gives her a copy of "My Brother Eileen," a farce written by Crackpot O'Toole. When she learns she's to play the role of an Indian, she remembers that she promised the deceased Shakespeare that she owes him a play and promptly leaves.

Memorable Lines
ARCHIE: You've been around a long time. And yet where are you... Why ain't you in the movies?

COWL: Because I don't look good with my hair combed over one eye.

Episode #66 — Broadcast Tuesday, November 24, 1942
Guest: Giovanni Martinelli
Plot: Giovanni Martinelli, the celebrated Italian operatic tenor, stops by the Tavern and Miss Duffy wants him to get her a job singing at the Metropolitan. When Miss Duffy sings a quick bar, Archie tries to cover her mistake by claiming the sound from her throat was really a leak in the radiator. While singing "Kiss Me Again," Archie starts making cracks again such as "Somebody should kiss her with a brick" and "Eddie, you think that turkey's tough, listen to this." When his attempts fail, Archie tries to

convince Martinelli to come work for the tavern on a full-time basis.

Episode #67 — Broadcast Tuesday, December 1, 1942
Guests: Ethel Merman and Elsa Maxwell
Plot: Actress Ethel Merman pays a visit to the tavern and tries to convince Archie to put on a party to raise money for Christmas packages for servicemen stationed overseas. Archie uses a little assistance from Elsa Maxwell to get the ball rolling, which includes Archie telling ration jokes, Finnegan offering a kiss for a dollar and a musical trio from Maxwell, Merman and Archie. But the only money they raised is eleven dollars and one of them came from Merman, having made a donation for kissing Finnegan. Peter Van Steeden and his Orchestra perform "Marching Thru Berlin."

Memorable Lines
MERMAN: Hello, Archie. Nice place you got here – who desecrated it?
ARCHIE: Oh, we didn't call in any outside desecrater – we did it ourselves.
MERMAN: Quite a shambles you've made out of it.
ARCHIE: Yeah – we like it.
MERMAN: Is that Duffy over there?
ARCHIE: Where?
MERMAN: Oh, no. It's a moose head.

Episode #68 — Broadcast Tuesday, December 8, 1942
Guest: Mary Martin
Plot: Miss Duffy reads a love letter from a serviceman overseas, but can't marry him because he doesn't have enough money. Mary Martin drops by the tavern and Archie tries to impress her by claiming he's from Texas. When Finnegan tries to impress Martin by claiming his name is Dead Eye Finnegan and that he killed nine Nazis, Martin finds him a little "cowpunchy." Peter Van Steeden and his orchestra perform the "Pennsylvania Polka."

Trivia, etc. Mary Martin was very busy at the time she made her appearance on *Duffy's Tavern*. Three evenings before this *Duffy's*

Mary Martin on Duffy's Tavern.

Tavern broadcast, Mary Martin also appeared on the radio program, *Hobby Lobby*. Two days later, on Thursday, she appeared as a guest on *Stage Door Canteen*. On stage, she was playing the lead of Mary Hastings in Vinton Freedley's Broadway musical, *Dancing in the Streets*, which also featured Eddie Green. Her guest appearances were made courtesy of Paramount Pictures, producer of her latest picture, *Star Spangled Rhythm* (1942), and *Happy Go Lucky* (1943).

Memorable Line
ARCHIE: Duffy, you know who's coming down here tonight? Mary Martin, the Paramount picture star. She's coming all the way from California. Is California what? Duffy, California's even further than Los Angeles — and by the way, the word is farther, not further… Whoever heard of "Life with Further?" Look Duffy, you got an old map handy? No, I don't mean Mrs. Duffy. I mean jerography. You see, the United States is surrounded by two coasts. California is the West Coast and Coney Island is the East Coast… Look, Duffy, think of the United States as a horse. Florida is the right leg and California is the left leg. What about the other two legs? Think of it as a two-legged horse. What if the horse opens his mouth is that the Grand Canyon? No Duffy, that's you talkin'. Goodbye.

Episode #69 — Broadcast Tuesday, December 15, 1942
Guests: Kate Smith and Ted Collins (Smith's manager)
Plot: Four evenings before this broadcast, Ed "Archie" Gardner was a guest on *The Kate Smith Show*. Kate Smith returns the favor by appearing as a guest on this broadcast. Archie plans on getting Kate Smith to sign an exclusive contract whereupon she would sing at the tavern, but only after Duffy listens to her singing first (which doesn't go over very well). Her manager, Ted Collins, is too cunning for the boys and tries to interfere. Archie proposes a radio mystery, "Young Editor Archie," with roles for both Kate Smith and Ted Collins. Archie thinks he has the upper hand when Kate is convinced and signs the contract. Only after the guests leave does he realize he's been gypped – she signed "Kate Hancock." Peter Van Steeden and his Orchestra performs "For Me and My Gal". Kate Smith sings "Everything I've Got."

Trivia, etc. Archie's proposed radio drama, "Young Editor Archie," involves a crime reporter who investigates the murder of Ted Collins' entire family, including an infant in a crib where it was suggested that Collins "whack him over the head with a shovel." During the sketch, Kate Smith pre-maturely delivers part of her line before she was supposed to.

Episode #70 — Broadcast Tuesday, December 22, 1942
Guest: Robert L. Ripley
Plot: With Robert L. Ripley appearing as a guest, Archie, Eddie and Finnegan read many of Ripley's comic columns. Archie gets the brainstorm idea that if he can convince Ripley that Duffy's Tavern should be made into a cartoon, the name of the joint will be advertised in over 300 newspapers. Trying to impress Ripley with one silly stunt after another, including having Eddie eat six fresh rubber bands, the boys fail until the very last minute of the episode when Ripley is amazed at a sight coming through the door and faints – Duffy himself. (Note: Duffy never speaks a word in the script.)

At the end of this episode, Archie pitches next week's guest to Duffy over the phone:
ARCHIE: "Duffy's . . . where the elite meet to eat. Oh, hello Duffy. Yeah that's right, Duffy. Rochester. You know the guy who says "Hello there, Madame Queen." Yeah, for the Jack Benny Show."

Episode #71 — Broadcast Tuesday, December 29, 1942
Guest: Eddie "Rochester" Anderson
Plot: Archie gets a brain storm of an idea. He wants to start his own radio program, nationwide, "so that the name of Duffy's will be smirched from Coney Island to the Bronx." Since Eddie "Rochester" Anderson is going to stop by, Archie believes if he can get the comedian to appear in the new show, he could take the place of Jack Benny. In an effort to impress Rochester, Archie writes a comedy radio script and the crew performs their own version of *The Jack Benny Program*.

Memorable Lines
ARCHIE: Welcome to Duffy's, Rochester... great place we got here, ain't it?

ROCHESTER: Well, I been to a lotta night clubs but this is the Maxwell of them all...

ARCHIE: Rochester, how would you like to leave Benny and work with the best comedian in America?
ROCHESTER: Uh-uh... another offer from Fred Allen!

Episode #72 — Broadcast Tuesday, January 5, 1943
Guest: Milton Berle
Plot: After cracking jokes about what the word "Follies" means, the cast of Duffy's Tavern receive a visit from Milton Berle. Archie attempts to convince the comedian to put a dame into the Follies – a beautiful French dame who is, in reality, Miss Duffy. After putting on one act after another, Miss Duffy goes from murder to massacre and spoofing French accents and the gang fails to impress Berle who closes with "Ho-hum. Anuzzer day, anuzzer suicide." Clark Dennis is the new singer and sings "Why Don't You Fall in Love With Me?"

Memorable Lines
ARCHIE: "Duffy, you know who's coming down here tonight? Milton Berle – the star of the new Ziegfield Follies. What? Has he got nice legs? No, Duffy – you remember Milton – the kid that used to steal the joke books."

ARCHIE: "There is a well known Golden Rule. True the ages it's been true. Always be good to your neighbor – he may live next door to you."

Episode #73 — Broadcast Tuesday, January 12, 1943
Guest: Deems Taylor
Plot: Deems Taylor of the Philharmonic Orchestra pays a return visit to the tavern. Mrs. Piddleton, the upper crust society lady, pays a visit to the tavern and, having heard that Deems Taylor is on the lineup for the evening, is impressed. Archie and Taylor attempt to carry on an intelligent conversation only to have Archie mess up the whole affair. Clark Dennis sings "Please Think of Me."

Episode #74 — Broadcast Tuesday, January 19, 1943
Guest: Phil Baker
Plot: See page 106. Clark Dennis sings "Brazil."

Episode #75 — Broadcast Tuesday, January 26, 1943
Guest: Billie Burke
Plot: While Archie hires a French chef to do the cooking at the tavern, Clancy the Cop is walking the beat (punishment for leaving his horse in front of the butcher shop). Billie Burke drops by the tavern, cracks jokes about astrology and astro-numerology, and when Clancy later overhears Burke talking about lucky numbers, he mistakes her as an illegal bookie and arrests her.

Ed Gardner and Brace Beemer (Photo courtesy of Bob Daniel.)

Ed Gardner and Brace Beemer (Photo courtesy of Bob Daniel.)

Episode #76 — Broadcast Tuesday, February 2, 1943
Guest: The Lone Ranger (played by Brace Beemer)
Plot: When it's known that The Lone Ranger will be dropping by, Archie wants to do a favor for a friend who owns the local movie house by convincing their guest to make a personal appearance. Miss Duffy tries romancing The Masked Man, Eddie refers to him as "the Lone and Only Ranger" and Archie refers to him by first name basis, "Lone." When they succeed, though, the theater manager thinks The Lone Ranger is a crackpot and, after realizing his error, the manager is forced to don the mask himself for the benefit of the children.

Trivia, etc. There is a mention during this broadcast that *The Lone Ranger* cliffhanger serial, 15 chapters, was brought back to the screen and playing at the Tivoli in New York. To help promote the theatrical re-release of the 1938 serial, Brace Beemer made the first of four guest appearances on other radio programs throughout the spring of 1943: *Breakfast Club* (April 27, 1943), *The Quiz Kids* (May 2, 1943), *Meet Your Navy* (May 5, 1943).

Episode #77 — Broadcast Tuesday, February 9, 1943
Guest: George Jessel
Plot: See page 106.

Archie in costume.

Episode #78 — Broadcast Tuesday, February 16, 1943
Guest: Jane Cowl (an older actress known for her crying roles)
Plot: A touching and funny episode with a subtle moral. When Miss Duffy learns that Archie is putting on a pageant, with Jane

Cowl as the star, she isn't happy because she is not involved — until she learns that the pageant was designed to raise money for the troops overseas. In a humorous skit with Archie playing George Washington and Jane Cowl as Martha Washington, which shifts to General Custer and the Indians, Cowl decides to leave until she learns Archie's true motives for the skits. Clark Dennis sings "So Nice to Come Home To."

Episode #79 — Broadcast Tuesday, February 23, 1943
Guest: Dale Carnegie
Plot: Having fallen in love with Joan Edwards, the singer, Archie asks Dale Carnegie, author of *How to Win Friends and Influence People*, for advice on women. Carnegie suggests Archie try the "You attitude" but when he does he gets the opposite results. As for Carnegie, Joan finds an interest in him and the two leave hand in hand. Joan Edwards sings "I've Heard That Song Before."

Episode #80 — Broadcast Tuesday, March 2, 1943
Guest: Tito Guizar
Plot: See page 108.

Episode #81 — Broadcast Tuesday, March 9, 1943
Guest: Colonel Stoopnagle
Plot: Col. Stoopnagle makes a return visit to the tavern to talk to the Lord Byron Ladies' Literary Society on taxes. But giving the ladies of the society hard copy tax forms that don't have room for a name or address (in case you make any errors, the government can't trace you) proves successful to the ladies who, for once, leave the tavern very happy. It remains unclear why Stoopnagle appeared on this broadcast. He certainly wasn't promoting his weekly radio program, which expired this week.

Memorable Lines
ARCHIE: Duffy, what does March 15th mean to you? Two days before St. Patrick's Day! Listen Duffy, you better worry about March 15th or the next parade you march in you'll have your hand on the shoulder of the guy in front of you.

Episode #82 — Broadcast Tuesday, March 16, 1943
Guest: Morton Downey
Plot: Duffy is paying singer Morton Downey a thousand bucks for tomorrow's pig roast and Clancy the Cop reminds Archie that last year's roast started fights. If there turns out to be more fighting this year, he'll shut the tavern down. When Downey discovers that Duffy plans to pay him only a hundred dollars instead, he tries to back out. Archie tries his best to make everybody happy. During the broadcast, Downey sings "Danny Boy."

Trivia, etc. Morton Downey had a five-a-week 15-minute musical program on the Blue Network and his appearance helped promote his daily radio appearance.

Episode #83 — Broadcast Tuesday, March 23, 1943
Guests: Frank Buck and Susan Hayward
Plot: Guests include explorer Frank Buck who brings 'em back alive and actress Susan Hayward who is a reason for living. While Buck recounts a couple adventures in brief summary, Archie attempts to tell his own tall tales — doubling his efforts in an effort to impress Susan Hayward, hoping she will fall in love with him. Archie's tales, however, turn Hayward's attention toward Buck. Miss Duffy also sings a song which makes Archie start blasting his negative comments again including "No wonder Tarzan's always screaming" and "I would never bring her back alive."

Episode #84 — Broadcast Tuesday, March 30, 1943
Guests: Ilona Massey and Oscar Levant
Plot: Archie attempts to woo Hungarian-born actress Ilona Massey after seeing her gorgeous legs. When his attempt fails, he offers her an opportunity to sign at Duffy's with an exclusive contract. While she ponders the offer, funny man Oscar Levant arrives and remarks, "I've been to many places but this is the 4-F of them all." After joking about who is smarter, because Levant is a regular panelist on the quiz program, *Information Please*, Archie discovers Levant won't stay long because he finds the tavern difficult to take.

Memorable Lines
ARCHIE: Now, Miss Massey you'll see… when we're
    making love…
MASSEY: When we're making love?
ARCHIE: You don't think we're just gonna stand here and talk?
MASSEY: What is it about you that makes me feel like little
    Red Riding Hood?

Episode #85 — Broadcast Tuesday, April 6, 1943
Guest: Leo Durocher
Plot: Archie gets an opportunity to join the New York Giants and
when Dodgers Manager Leo Durocher shows up at the tavern the
wisecracks start flying. When Archie learns by phone of Giants
Manager Mel Ott's terms, he decides to quit the Giants. This was
the second of two broadcasts in which Miss Duffy was not heard
because Shirley Booth was needed for rehearsals of Broadway's
Tomorrow, the World. It was explained to the audience that Miss
Duffy was on vacation.

Episode #86 — Broadcast Tuesday, April 13, 1943
Guest: Ralph Bellamy
Plot: Archie and the gang are planning a surprise party for Miss
Duffy who is returning from her vacation. Finnegan, Eddie, singer
Tessie Mummler, Clancy the Cop, and the Ten Jolly Girls A.C.
(Athletic Club) help decorate the tavern. Miss Duffy is surprised
to see the party in her honor and as a token of her esteem, Miss
Duffy introduces them to actor Ralph Bellamy. Archie tries to
impress Bellamy by bragging he was once in pictures, until he
got a bad break. "Ruined by Technicolor," Archie explains. "Too
healthy, I photographed like an Indian." Bellamy thinks Archie
has possibilities — if he was two feet shorter, he'd be another
Mickey Rooney. Peter Van Steeden and his Orchestra perform "It
Can't Be Wrong."

Memorable Lines
EDDIE: Ralph Bellamy?
ARCHIE: Yeah, you know him, the guy that always saves the
    girl from the gangsters, gets her brother out of jail, rescues

her old man from a burning building... and then she marries somebody else.

Episode #87 — Broadcast Tuesday, April 20, 1943
Guests: Leo Durocher and Mel Ott
Plot: When Mel Ott receives a letter tipping him off that Leo Durocher is interested in Archie for the Dodgers, and Durocher receives a telegram saying that Ott is after him for the Giants, both baseball managers agree to visit the tavern to straighten the matter out. It is obvious that Archie wrote the letters. Tito Guizar returns to the program, having made a guest appearance on March 2. Guizar is now the weekly musical entertainment for the remainder of the season.

Memorable Lines
ARCHIE: Well Tito, how long you been playing that guitar?
TITO: Ten years.
ARCHIE: Didja ever drop it?
TITO: No.
ARCHIE: You'll make a great waiter.

ARCHIE: [on the phone] "What? No, Duffy. I'm sorry, I cannot consider that. Slugging your wife is not a pastime."

Episode #88 — Broadcast Tuesday, April 27, 1943
Guest: Ilka Chase
Plot: Actress Ilka Chase (whose autobiography, *Past Imperfect Vol. 1*, had then just recently been released) visits the tavern and Archie tries to push his friend Crackpot O'Toole's book, *Future Perfect*, to her. As Archie reads to her section by section from the book, (the Reader's Digest version, naturally), she starts getting drowsy and eventually needs to leave, feeling she wasted her time. Tito Guizar sings "Amapola."

Episode #89 — Broadcast Tuesday, May 4, 1943
Guest: Millie Smith, a fictional person (played by Hope Emerson)
Plot: See page 109. Peter Van Steeden and his orchestra perform "Wait for Me, Mary." Tito Guizar sings "As Time Goes By."

Red Skelton, Leo Durocher and Ed Gardner

Trivia, etc. Obviously recycling material, the same plot for this episode was used on the evening of March 12, 1942.

Episode #90 — Broadcast Tuesday, May 11, 1943
Guest: Akim Tamiroff
Plot: Archie wants to hire character actor Akim Tamiroff to be the singing doorman for Duffy's Tavern and to do so he has to make everyone in the tavern act like a Russian. When Duffy wants to hear Tamiroff sing, he is shocked to learn that Tamiroff takes a disliking to Russians. Tamiroff decides to sing Irish and this is enough to have Archie escort him to the door which he then slams, locking Tamiroff out.

Trivia, etc. Akim Tamiroff was originally scheduled for May 4, with this same script. When Tamiroff was forced to rescheduled for the week after, the script was pushed ahead a week. Although actually an Armenian, Tamiroff's oft-played Russian characterization has been said to be the inspiration for Paul Frees' voice as "Boris Badenov" on Jay Ward's *Rocky and His Friends*.

Episode #91 — Broadcast Tuesday, May 18, 1943
Guest: Herbert Marshall
Plot: When refined actor Herbert Marshall stops by the tavern, Archie makes fun of his English. "You borry the language from us and then you louse it up," quotes Archie, before asking the actor what his secret is for picking up dames West of the Mississippi. When Marshall steps out for a brief spell, a woman named Henrietta shows up at the tavern. Archie attempts to pass himself off as the actor in an effort to pick her up. Moments before Archie convinces the woman to screen test her kissing features in the phone booth, Marshall returns and Archie fails to impress her by calling the actor by another name.

Trivia, etc. During this broadcast, Archie makes reference that his picture appears in this week's issue of *Look* Magazine.

A year later Herbert Marshall would begin his own long-running radio series, *The Man Called X*.

Episode #92 — Broadcast Tuesday, May 25, 1943
Guest: Vera Zorina
Plot: Famed ballet dancer Vera Zorina drops by the tavern and Archie envisions opening night at Duffy's ballet. While Archie hopes to convince her to perform the "Dance of the Dying Swan," in which the swan dies at the end of the dance, Eddie proposes serving Swan A La King the next day. Finnegan, reading the sign outside that says "Special Tonight - Zorina," tells Archie he'll try a plate. Archie fails to convince Vera Zorina to quit the Metropolitan and come work for Duffy. He explains that, "at the Met you work yourself to death — fifteen, sixteen encores. You work here, it'll never happen."

Episode #93 — Broadcast Tuesday, June 1, 1943
Guest: Tallulah Bankhead
Plot: The great stage actress Tallulah Bankhead makes an appearance at the tavern, answering the phone for a momentarily-absent Archie. When the barkeep returns, he mistakes Bankhead for a common drifter and recites a welcome poem written by Crackpot O'Toole and then pretends to be an actor waiting for Bankhead's appearance so he can impress her with his talents. After introducing herself as Tallulah Bankhead, the actress proves her worth by reading a letter from the *The Last Days of Sevastopol* by Boris Voyetekhov.

Trivia, etc. Bankhead appeared on this episode of *Duffy's Tavern* by special arrangement with producer Sol Lesser under the condition that it was mentioned that she was among the many stars of *Stage Door Canteen*. Mention of the movie was overlooked unintentionally and Sol Lesser was upset, expressing his disappointment in a letter to Ed Gardner. To make up for the mistake, the motion picture was mentioned at the end of next week's broadcast, with Archie, over the telephone, endorsing the film to Duffy.

Episode #94 — Broadcast Tuesday, June 8, 1943
Guest: Roland Young
Plot: The tavern is falling apart, evident when the building

inspector cites a violation and the chef in the kitchen is hit by falling plaster. Rather than pay for the maintenance, Duffy strikes a deal with Archie, offering a percentage if the barkeep can sell the tavern. When English character actor Roland Young pays a visit to the tavern, Archie points out the cracks in the walls, the busted windows, the holes in the ceiling... "Why, this place is cryin' to be a sidewalk café," Archie explains. Archie convinces Finnegan to bid on the tavern when he commences with an auction. Roland Young, motivated, bids up to $11,000, but dopey Finnegan bids $12,000 and Duffy himself bids $13,000 and wins his own tavern.

Trivia, etc. Actress Carole Landis, then known for her work entertaining the troops overseas, was originally slated for this broadcast date but was not able to appear.

Memorable Lines
ARCHIE: Mm, I presume you will pay in advance?
O'TOOLE: Yeah – here's a check... you'll take it, of course?
ARCHIE: Mr. O'Toole, your check is as good as Rockefeller's.
O'TOOLE: It is Rockefeller's.
ARCHIE: Lemme see... Holy Cats, it is!
O'TOOLE: Certainly! I didn't do ten years for nothin'.

Episode #95 — Broadcast Tuesday, June 15, 1943
Guest: Clifton Fadiman
Plot: Clifton Fadiman is at the tavern to do a lecture written by Archie, to be delivered to the Lord Byron Ladies' Literary Society, holding their latest meeting at the tavern. The subject is about Contemporary Literature but when Fadiman realizes there are some incorrect parts, including mistakes such as claiming Ivan Hoe is a Russian, and how cavemen carried stone books, Fadiman tries to wash his hands of the whole matter. Peter Van Steeden and his orchestra play "Anything Goes." Tito Guizar sings "Siboney."

Episode #96 — Broadcast Tuesday, June 22, 1943
Guest: Monty Woolley
Plot: Archie receives a telegram from "Yarryl Danuck" (a play on Fox studio chief Darryl Zanuck) promising to visit the tavern

today with motion picture contracts, believing Archie is a potential Gary Cooper. Meanwhile, Miss Duffy is holding a dance and puts Archie down for two tickets, against his protests. When actor Monty Woolley - remembered today for his beard - shows up, Archie asks for advice before Danuck arrives. Woolley suggests Archie turn his back to the camera and modulate his voice, "but not too loud," explains Woolley. "Remember, a lot of people in the balcony didn't come to see the picture." Archie suspects something wrong when Danuck arrives and immediately mistakes Finnegan for him!

Episode #97 — Broadcast Tuesday, June 29, 1943
Guests: Ray Milland and Lee Bristol
Plot: Paramount star Ray Milland arrives from Hollywood and almost immediately begins to exchange jokes with Archie about the West Coast. Archie attempts to weasel his way into Hollywood by asking Milland to make arrangements with casting directors. Knowing Milland is a heart-throb for women, Archie gives the actor a bit of advice: "Don't go around with a married woman unless you can go two rounds with her husband." When Lee Bristol, the sponsor, shows up at the tavern, Archie tries to sell him a real advertising campaign... radio.

From July 6 to August 24, 1943, Colonel Stoopnagle starred in his own comedy program, *Meet the Colonel*. He was assisted by Eddie Green, the *Duffy's Tavern* waiter, Jeri Sullavan (or Sullivan, depending on which newspaper, magazine or movie screen credit you consult) who sang songs as well as provided comedy, and Florence Halop who, according to one newspaper columnist, was "a young lady who is not Shirley Booth but who sounds so much like her that Miss Booth should be getting royalties." Add a double-talk butler and the music of Paul Baron and his Orchestra, and you have a recipe for a successful comedy along the vein of *Duffy's Tavern*. The series was short-lived (pre-empted twice during those dates), lasting a mere six broadcasts.

131

CHAPTER FIVE
BRISTOL-MYERS
(1943 - 1944)

FROM THE PROGRAM'S INCEPTION TO 1948, *Duffy's Tavern* was performed twice in the same evening, first for the East Coast, and then for the West. At the early show, the studio was jammed with spectators, filling most of the empty seats. When the program originated from New York, the later performance did not feature an audience, and the seats remained empty so that the midnight repeat show could be closed down in a faster and efficient manner. (Today, fans of old-time radio who collect recordings dated between 1941 and 1948, can tell the difference between the East and West Coast version simply by listening for laughter from the audience.) But although it was part of the radio life of New York, people talked about it as if it were around the corner, which, in a sense, it was.

Before each East Coast broadcast, the warm-up for the studio audience involved Ed Gardner interviewing a stooge from the audience who would say that he lived in Eagle Rock. "How do you spend your time in Eagle Rock?" Ed would ask. "Mostly," the guy would say, "rocking eagles."

Postcard of NBC Studios, circa 1940, Hollywood and Vine Street

Preparations aside, the technicals involved during the fourth season were almost as complex as keeping track of who played Miss Duffy. After an initial broadcast at the new Blue Network Playhouse, Ed Gardner moved *Duffy's Tavern* to the old Warner Brothers lot and took over one of their sound stages for the show. Soon after, the program originated from the NBC studios at the corner of Sunset Boulevard and Vine Street. With a full season consisting of 39 broadcasts, the second batch of thirteen originated from New York, before returning to California. This involved changes in cast, characters, musical talents and even directors. Throughout the season, Ed Gardner continued to preside over the whole thing with the poise of the magnificently dumb and with that accent which thus far had defied students of local dialects from darkest Queens to the far reaches of upper Manhattan. The old admirers, who had followed him from his Columbia *Forecast* debut in 1940 through a stormy career that had included three sponsorships, could still tune in and laugh every week without fail.

And through it all, Gardner managed to turn a tidy profit, secure a new relationship in the bonds of matrimony and prepare for the biggest screen test of his career — a motion picture produced on the Paramount lot.

On the evening of April 10, 1943, a special 90-minute broadcast on the Blue Network, a gesture to welcome the chain's new director of music, Paul Whiteman, was broadcast nationally, embracing the talents of those whose careers stemmed from the Whiteman band. The event was certainly star-studded with Gracie Fields, Dinah Shore, Bing Crosby, Chester Lauck and Norris Goff (radio's *Lum and Abner*), Tom Breneman, Johnny Mercer, Don McNeil, Morton Downey, Tommy Dorsey, Matty Malneck and a score of others lending their talents. Ed Gardner was originally sought as emcee for the event because he was one of the few headliners in radio who never worked with or for Whiteman. Gardner declined but did participate with a brief *Duffy's Tavern* sketch. Rudy Vallee was the host. The President of the Blue Network delivered a speech. The event was so successful that it ran overtime an extra 15 minutes.

Inspired by the events of that evening, Ed Gardner approached Paul Whiteman throughout the summer of 1943 to negotiate the possibility of having Whiteman conduct the weekly orchestra on *Duffy's Tavern* when the comedy returned to the air on October 5. The contract called for Whiteman to swing the baton for the first thirteen weeks. Whiteman wanted more money and Gardner stood firm on the offer, explaining that thirteen weeks of guaranteed employment ensured more money than a single broadcast at higher fare. During the final week of August, Whiteman and his wife flew to the East Coast to spend vacation on their farm at Rosemont, New Jersey. Shortly before Whiteman left on vacation, his final stance on salary held firm and Gardner, realizing negotiations were at a standstill, hired Paul Weston as music director, the deal negotiated by Ken Dolan. According to one columnist, "Whiteman declined it, figuring that the spot wasn't quite the thing for him."

When Whiteman returned to the West Coast, Gardner approached the band leader about the possibility of being a guest on the season premiere. Whiteman again asked for too much

money. Instead, Paramount Pictures star Veronica Lake agreed to make a guest appearance, promoting *Hold Back the Dawn*, released theatrically in New York four weeks prior. Archie tries to impress Veronica with a new book he's written called *Duffy's First Reader*, dramatizing various pages and hoping to sell it to Hollywood as a motion picture. Veronica ends up falling for Duffy's new weekly crooner, Johnny Johnston.

One of the ironies of the radio trade was that Paul Whiteman wound up his services on an outstanding summer series, *Paul Whiteman Presents*, sponsored by Chase & Sanborn, without even the prospect of a commercial program for the new fall season. The program not only got a healthy rating for a vacation filler, but gathered plenty of newsprint comment. On the other hand, Whiteman's co-star on the series, Dinah Shore, emerged from the 13-week run with a program of her own. She went from Standard Brands, which hawked Chase and Sanborn coffee, to a competitor, General Foods, to plug the Bird's Eye brand on CBS Thursday nights. The celebrity guest for her first broadcast? Ed Gardner.

On the evening of August 29, Ed Gardner was a guest on *Paul Whiteman Presents*, an appearance under special arrangement. Standard Brands had the money to pay Gardner the standard fee but Gardner, showing no hard feelings for Whiteman's decision not to wave the baton on *Duffy's Tavern*, offered to appear on the program at a discount — provided the band leader would return the favor for a guest spot on *Duffy's*. Later in the season, for the January 25, 1944, broadcast, it appeared Gardner made a second attempt to have Whiteman as a guest. When Whiteman backed out, the script was modified to feature Deems Taylor.

Duffy's First Reader

Now a collectible premium, *Duffy's First Reader*, published in September of 1943, written by Gardner himself, borrowed jokes that had been used in prior radio scripts, with a foreword by Abe Burrows. The book sold for twenty cents and was available in bookstores beginning October 20. Early episodes in this season featured an announcement on how the radio audience could submit ten cents to Duffy's First Reader, P.O. Box 67, New York City, and receive a copy in the mail. It featured more than thirty pages of Duffy lore, a biography of Archie, limericks, jokes and brief sketches of American history. The book was promoted in the season premiere and every consecutive episode following for many weeks. What we consider today as product placement, broadcasting moguls considered a clever ploy to convince advertisers how lucrative and popular the program was. Sales figures (and giveaways) often convinced a skeptical sponsor to retain sponsorship for a longer period of time. It's possible that Abe Burrows wrote much of the content for *Duffy's First Reader*. At the conclusion of the November 23, 1943, broadcast, announcer Harry Von Zell told the radio audience that *Duffy's First Reader* was completely sold out. "We can't print any more copies because of the paper shortage," he explained, "so please don't send in any more dimes. To those who wanted a book but put off sending for it, we are sincerely sorry we have no more. To those who have their Duffy's Readers, we hope you will find this permanent souvenir of Duffy's a very pleasant reminder of our many Tuesdays together."

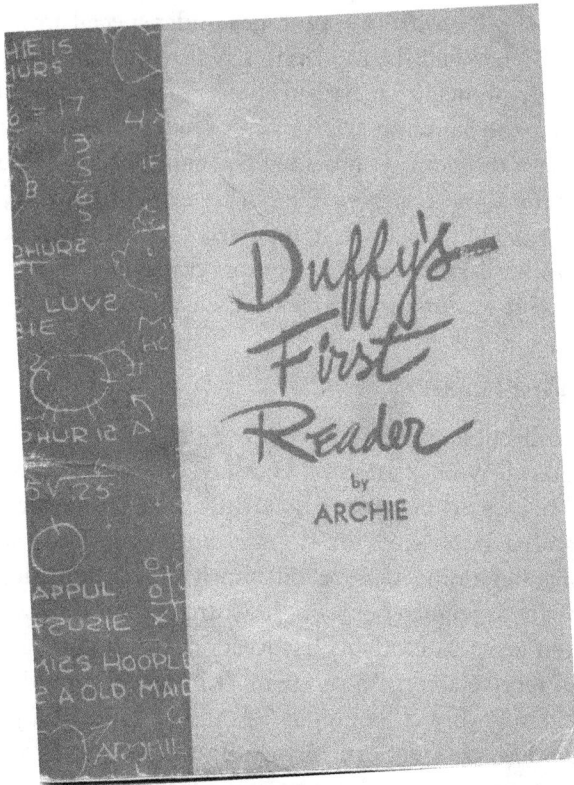

In the fall of 1945, Ed Gardner began work on a second tome, similar to *Duffy's First Reader*, "with a Pacific war flavor," according to *Variety*. Nothing ever came about from the intended sequel. Burrows, meanwhile, now in Hollywood, was still the head man on the scripting of *Duffy's Tavern* and was schooling a class of raw recruits in the art of scriptwriting. Among the assignments he gave them was 12 weeks to develop the men who put the funny sayings into the mouths of comics. Many of those jokes slipped into *Duffy's Tavern* radio scripts for the 1943-44 season (under contract he had first rights of use without requiring payment), and a couple of the writers eventually joined the script writing troupe under employment of Ed Gardner.

"In 1943, everybody decided we ought to move the show to California," recalled Abe Burrows. "By 'everybody' I mean the sponsor. Gardner and I were worried about this. The locale of our show was New York. The characters were all pure New York characters, mostly muggs. We felt it would be a little strange to have all these guys talking New Yorkese among the palm trees. However, in those days the sponsor was the boss."

Hoping to finalize a movie deal, Ed Gardner agreed to follow the old Horace Greeley "go west" bit, hence the program broadcast from Hollywood. The first broadcast of the season originated from Studio A in San Francisco, designed for programs which were performed in front of a studio audience. The radio network gave Gardner the temporary location because of crowded conditions in Los Angeles. Executives at NBC Blue were presently looking around for outside studio space and, beginning with the second broadcast of the season, *Duffy's Tavern* originated from station KFWB in Los Angeles (known as Warner Brothers Radio Studio). Gardner required a Monday night audience preview to test audience reaction to jokes, while at the same time requiring a Tuesday afternoon rehearsal and Tuesday night broadcast (twice - once for each coast). The Blue Network was especially hard put because of the prevailing audience shows ganging up at the network on Tuesday, Thursday and Sunday evenings. The chain had its own studio at Sunset and Highland, but soon required other remote sites as NBC moved in on all the available space at West Coast Radio City. The spaces most in demand were the two studios on the KFWB lot, certain to house other network shows before the year was out. Beginning with the broadcast of November 9, *Duffy's Tavern* moved to the Blue Network Radio Playhouse at Sunset and Highland. Nothing has been found to explain the move, but it is believed that Gardner was dissatisfied with the small quarters at the new playhouse and wanted a larger spot so as to play before a bigger studio audience. The Blue network honored his request

139

but later asked Ed Gardner to return to New York after the first thirteen-week cycle.

The October 2, 1943, issue of *Billboard* reported: "Third floor NBC studios getting a break at last. Secretaries who used to flock to eighth floor for Fred Allen and sixth for Archie of *Duffy's Tavern* now stream up to third to sigh for Tommy Taylor and his *Taylor Made Songs*."

The October 13, 1943, issue of *Variety* reviewed: "As the delight of that type of listener who likes his comedy on the rowdy-dowdy side, Gardner deals profusely as ever in broad malapropisms, wields the bladder lustily at silk hats and hustles and contrives to make good-humored muggery a sound, negotiable security in radio. The script for the seasonal opening did not make for a particularly hilarious performance. Florence Halop as the new 'Miss Duffy' passed her entry exams with high marks and proved that she's got the makings of a crack comedy trouper if only Gardner will give her something substantial to do. Gardner has surrounded himself with an able, gag-bouncing cast what with Miss Halop, Charley Cantor as 'Finnegan' and Eddie Green as the porter, but he (Gardner) seems inclined during most of the proceedings to go in for long monologs and assign but the leavings to his conferees. Veronica Lake would have been a happy booking if she likewise had been given an opportunity to participate in the crossfire on a broader scale. As it happened she had little else to do but act as a listening post to Gardner's monologs and to intersperse an occasional giggle. What little singing that Johnston was permitted to do seemed to fall pleasantly on the ear, while Paul Weston's orchestral hot clicks injected the right quality of lift to the program."

Florence Halop

The October 16, 1943, issue of *Billboard* offered a favorable review: "Sal Hepatica and Minit-Rub returned a favorite ether bistro to the air with Ed Gardner once more harried by the demands of the mythical Mr. Duffy and murdering the thesaurus in his best Hell's Kitchen form. Pattern is same as heretofore. Archie emcees and manages the joint with the same type of malapropic quips. Dimwit Finnegan, *Tavern's* star customer, is back, as is also Eddie the waiter, with Charlie Cantor and Eddie Green still playing the laugh combo. The unseen and unheard Mr. Duffy crabs about the talent and, as usual, matters are enlivened by the appearance of a guest celeb. Preem featured visit by Veronica Lake, with fun stemming from Archie's efforts to have program's new chanter, Johnny Johnston, make her do a swoonatra. Johnny didn't succeed, but his own chirping was definitely off the top shelf, and he is a welcome addition to the *Duffy* gang. Paul Weston and his band boys replace Peter Van Steeden in latest series and furnish creditable music background. Scripting of opener failed to make them a real part of the gang's wacky doings — an omission which should be remedied in future airings. There should be no outsiders at a *Duffy's Tavern* party. The program's outstanding newcomer, however, is Florence Halop, who won out over 150 auditioned aspirants for the role of the slightly moronic Miss Duffy. It's a tough assignment to follow Shirley Booth in a part which she personalized into something of a national figure, but Miss Halop is more than equal to the job. It would take an expert to detect a difference of inflection in the two Miss Duffy's dumb-Dora chatter. Session is written and paced up to previous *Tavern* standards, with a plug apiece for two of Bristol-Myers brands cleverly injected by Harry Von Zell without slowing up the comedy continuity. All indications would seem to tag *Duffy's* to provide another session of amusing Tuesday night half-hours for armchair nitery addicts."

Ed Gardner's Archie character, the male Jane Ace with the Ebbets Field accent, returned to radio with slight changes in his entourage. Johnny Johnston now provided the vocal embellishment, Paramount's singing-acting sensation, who was contracted for 26 weeks on *Duffy's Tavern* — the first 13 in Hollywood, the second half in New York.

In November 1943, Walter MacEwen and Lester Fuller,

respectively the producer and director of Paramount's *You Can't Ration Love*, were faced with a real problem during filming of the picture. Johnny Johnston, one of two co-stars, had to be off all day Tuesday for rehearsals and broadcast of *Duffy's Tavern*. Meanwhile his co-star, Betty Rhodes, could not work Saturday because she had her own radio program on that day. Marie Wilson, prominent in the cast, had to be excused on Saturday because of her appearance in Ken Murray's *Blackouts* and work had to be completed with musician D'Artega and the gal band within two weeks due to contract commitments elsewhere. Inasmuch as the film did not carry a heavy budget and had a limited schedule, the makers of the picture made every moment count. (To help alleviate some of Johnston's duties, Joan Davis appeared as a guest singer on December 14 and Bing Crosby sang vocals the week prior.

Bing Crosby and Ed Gardner

143

New Miss Duffy

As earlier, another member of the staff who made their debut on *Duffy's Tavern* was Florence Halop, replacing Shirley Booth as Miss Duffy. Duffy's daughter, although more modern-minded than her imaginary father, was not particularly bright. Quick to defend Duffy's beliefs against Archie, she had a complete disregard of logic that usually defeated his loftiest arguments. As Archie explained it, "She's the sort of girl that comes in from left-field in her approach to anything." Miss Duffy was a very proper lady, however, and her presence on the program, apart from providing a willing foil for Archie's wit, indicated that *Duffy's Tavern* was a thoroughly respectable establishment. In fact, prices, it was mentioned in an early fourth season episode, were increased to 20 cents a drink "to keep out the riffraff," as Archie explained. In one radio broadcast, the barkeep dubbed her "Mother Nature's revenge on Peeping Toms."

Throughout the first three seasons, Miss Duffy tottered back and forth with boring boyfriends, was a constant shopper of "daddy's money" and lived the night life: dancing, dining and movies. Weeks after the third season concluded, the July 25, 1943, issue of the *New York Times* broke the news: "Shirley Booth, a major feature these past seasons in *Duffy's Tavern* says she does not expect to return to the show in the fall. In the first place, she noted, she is now divorced from Ed Gardner, the head man in the tavern. Even more important, she adds, the program has become 'sort of a Frankenstein' for her."

In the June 20, 1943, issue of the *Brooklyn Eagle*, Shirley Booth took the high road when she confessed she was not going to return to the show. "I've enjoyed every minute of it," she told columnist Robert Francis. "She's apt to overshadow anything else I may try to do. The trouble is that a radio audience builds up a conception of you on the air and then, when they come to see you on the stage, they're disappointed. I figure it's apt to injure the plays that I'm in. After all, I'm for the theater, first and last. I want to die with my boots on, right on the stage. Anything else has got to run second. And there's another angle I have to consider. I've been getting tagged too much as a comedian. I want to do everything. So when this play [*Tomorrow the World*] came along, I thought it was smart

144

to go off in the other direction and do a serious part for a change... I've had grand times on the program with Tallulah Bankhead and Roland Young. I think he's had more influence on my career than anyone else in the theater."

For Shirley Booth, her primary radio credits before *Duffy's Tavern* included radio interviews such as the Bide Dudley program (January 3, 1937), multiple guest appearances on the Rudy Vallee and other Sealtest programs, as well as recurring supporting roles on soap operas such as *Central City* and *Strictly Business.** Booth replaced June Walker for the final broadcast of *Guess Where?*, a radio quiz program. (By coincidence, Charlie Cantor was also a guest panelist on the same broadcast.) She appeared on *Gotham Nights* on the evening of April 21, 1939, appearing in a scene from *The Philadelphia Story* along with Van Heflin, the pair reprising the same roles they were then presently performing on Broadway.

The cause of Shirley's departure from *Duffy's Tavern* was strictly professional. They say opposites attract... but there is no security when it comes to romance. With each drop of a calendar, the relationship between Shirley Booth and Ed Gardner grew tempestuous. Her first love was the stage; his was radio. Shirley enjoyed a quiet night at home. Ed loved hosting cocktail parties and going out for drinks. Shirley avoided alcohol; Ed drank too much (although a CBS press release once fibbed that he drank only milk). They each tried their hand with both professions but neither of them were successful except in their own field. Ed Gardner moved to California to work out deals involving a potential *Duffy's Tavern* motion picture. Booth was presently performing in *Tomorrow the World* at the Barrymore Theater in New York.

During the last week of June 1943, Jessie Fordyce, one of the three women known as The Three X Sisters, best known on NBC radio as "radio's foremost harmony and novelty trio," was up for consideration for the part of Miss Duffy. Their popularity faded

---

* Shirley Booth played the role of Ruby Ward for two weeks on Procter & Gamble's *Central City*, from June 15 to June 30, 1939. She played the role of Mary Patton on *Strictly Business* from May 31 to August 30, 1940.

The Three X Sisters

in the late thirties as other all-girl groups came along. Uncertain whether she would fit the bill, Gardner took a few days longer to make up his mind. When he decided in favor of Fordyce, she had to decline because The Three X Sisters had signed for a reunion that summer for a USO concert benefit. Her future uncertain, no commitment could be made.

Duffy's Tavern was only a few weeks away from the fall premiere when the solution of finding a replacement came in the form of Florence Halop, sister of Billy Halop, one of the Dead End Kids, and already a radio veteran at the age of 20. Halop apparently had auditioned by record. (A press release issued by the Blue Network claimed Gardner interviewed 150 actresses before deciding on Florence Halop, but we know today that was nothing but mere publicity hype.) Supposedly, Simone Hegeman, Ed Gardner's new wife, listened to the recording and thought she was hearing Shirley Booth. As a result of Simone's statement, Ed signed Halop to a short-term contract. This story could be partially true

146

but instead of an audition recording, Ed Gardner and/or Simone Hegeman may have been listening to Colonel Stoopnagle's radio comedy, *Meet the Colonel*,* on which Halop was a regular, and it was then that her voice was first heard. Halop signed her contract on September 22, 1943.

Halop spent the summer of 1943 keeping busy as a supporting performer on other radio programs including Garry Moore's daytime musical variety series, *Everything Goes* (March 29 to November 19, 1943). To Gardner's surprise, Halop had grown up not in Brooklyn but on Long Island, attending the private Professional Children's School in Manhattan. She had been in radio since an appearance at the age of five on the *Children's Hour*. When asked how she became a natural for radio dialect, she remarked, "I watched, I listened and I did. That is how I learned to act."

The Move to New York

During the summer of 1943, Sam Fuller (not the famous film director), who had directed the past two seasons of *Duffy's Tavern*, received a call from the Navy to serve as a lieutenant. Joseph Hill took over the directing reins. After thirteen weeks on the West Coast, *Duffy's Tavern* moved back to the sixth floor of NBC in New York. Hill hauled East one week in advance to make the necessary preparations. Walter Bunker handled the directing for the last *Duffy's* broadcast in California, December 28, before the eastern trek. The scriptwriters, Florence Halop and Eddie Green

---

* *Meet the Colonel* lasted a mere eight broadcasts, from July 6 to August 24, 1943, as a CBS sustainer. Jack Roche, Ken Lyons and Larry Marks wrote the scripts. Eddie Green was in the supporting cast. The program stemmed from two business arrangements. The first was an April 1943 contract between Stoopnagle and CBS, guaranteeing employment on the network for 26 weeks out of each year, for seven years. The second was Larry Burns, a CBS staff announcer upped to producer status in June, who that same month produced two audition recordings: one was *The Colonel* (the initial title proposal).

made the move. Charles Cantor decided to remain in Hollywood as a result of professional commitments but rejoined the cast in New York a few weeks later. Filling in for the absent Finnegan was John Brown, who played the role of Crackpot O'Toole, and Alan Reed as Clancy the Cop. Singer Johnny Johnston chose to remain on the West Coast in an effort to appear in more motion pictures. Benay Venuta, a radio comedienne-vocalist best known for her stage role on Broadway's *By Jupiter*, became the new singer (at a discounted salary fee which Gardner soon made good on by guesting on the premiere broadcast of her *Money-Go-Round* radio program which premiered a few weeks later). Paul Weston would not agree to move his entire orchestra to the East Coast. He was replaced by Peter Van Steeden, returning to *Duffy's Tavern* in the same capacity he had held in prior seasons.

Fred Allen and Ed Gardner.

The premiere episode of the New York broadcasts, January 4, 1944*, featured Fred Allen, known for his barbs and wit, giving Archie a chance to sharpen his with "why did the chicken cross the road" one-liners and "Why is a street car like a woman?" When Fred Allen paid a visit to the tavern, the jokes started flying, including Duffy's phone call with Archie answering, "Yeah, Allen's here... the bags? Yep, he's got 'em, Duffy... looks like his eyes is waiting for a Red Cap." Duffy wants Allen to emcee a pig roast but when Allen learns the fee is five bucks, he declines. The show closes with Allen answering a questionnaire for Archie in true Allen-wit style. Five days later, Ed Gardner, in the guise of Archie, made a guest appearance on *The Texaco Star Theater*, starring Fred Allen. Besides taking a trip to Allen's Alley, Fred Allen once again visits Duffy's Tavern... this time feet first. He later sues a brewery.

Variety reviewed: "Fred Allen and Ed Gardner—wotta parlay! It couldn't be bad. It was terrif when Allen guested on *Duffy's Tavern*, and it was socko when 'Archie' (Gardner) reciped on the Allen show Sunday night. That's comedy writing and if *Leave Us Face It* makes the *Hit Parade* the boys better start putting a musical setting to Lindy's menu—anything can be plugged into hitdom. But when the plugs for the mock ballad run the gamut from Dinah Shore to Hedda Hopper, who could resist?"

"At that time, among the few radio comedians who were thought of as real wits, Fred Allen was the fastest gun in the business," recalled Abe Burrows. "Fred shocked us by telling us he didn't want to do any of his own stuff on his *Duffy's Tavern* appearance; he would do whatever we wrote for him. That was a scary assignment, writing funny stuff for Fred Allen. It was wanton arrogance. Perhaps the best word is the Jewish chutzpah. All of us who worked on the show were nervous, but I think I suffered most. Not only did I admire Fred as a comedian and as a writer, but I loved him as a friend. I had met him and his wife, Portland,

---

* The broadcast of January 4, 1944, presented a minor bit of confusion to the radio listeners. The first minute of *The Ginny Simms Show* was heard over the network instead of *Duffy's Tavern*, due to a recording mistake made by a sound engineer!

a few years before at a party that Frank Loesser gave. I sang some of my songs for Fred and he was a marvelous audience."

"When it came time for Fred to come in and read the *Duffy's Tavern* script, all of the people who worked on the show were tense, but I out-tensed them all," continued Burrows. "Then came the moment for our first reading of the script. When Fred and Ed Gardner and the rest of the cast started, I felt not unlike the way I felt years later when *Guys and Dolls* first opened in Philadelphia. Even Gardner was nervous, because Fred was one of his idols, too. As they read on, Fred occasionally chuckled. Professional comedians seldom roar with laughter at jokes they like. The biggest reaction they will give you for a good line is an admiring chuckle. Usually they will just give you a small nod of approval with a little wave of the index finger. That first reading went well. And when it was finished, everybody looked at Fred for his reaction. After a moment he tossed the script on the table and quietly said, 'Okay.' Then he turned to Ed Gardner and said, 'Well, Ed, what do we do now? Kick hell out of Abe?' Then he looked at me and he gave me a big grin. I mentally said, 'Bingo.' I felt a bit cocky. Just before Fred saw the script, Ed Gardner was worried. He told me that a few things in it weren't good enough for Fred and would eventually have to be rewritten before we went on the air. However, Fred himself liked everything he read, and when Fred Allen said he liked something, it stayed the way it was. Two days later the show went on the air practically unchanged."

The exchange between Fred Allen and Ed Gardner might not have appealed to the advertising agencies but since neither sponsor was competing against each other, the cross-promotion was accepted with open arms. Especially since the fees involved were minimized. The guest star problem on radio shows, long a headache to sponsors because of the increasingly mounting fees, was being eased considerably through swapping arrangements among radio and film names in which the monetary aspect was relegated to minor importance. As a result, movie stars who usually commanded $3,000 and upwards for a guest shot fling were accepting less than half the usual asking fee through the reciprocal arrangement whereby he would do the hosting job on his own show under similar conditions.

Sponsors made no bones about being overjoyed at the Alphonse and Gaston act for, aside from the coin saving angle, the double-barrel hype given the show through the presence of the guest was a welcome factor. On *Texaco Star Theater*, closing billing included: "Ed Gardner appeared courtesy of Bristol-Myers" and on *Duffy's Tavern*, vice versa. Almost equally as important to the sponsor, as well, was the policy of usually working in a plug for his product on the guest shot. Many of the guest shots were also predicated on a friendship basis and even embraced a radio exchange in talent. Thus James Cagney, in the $3,000-$5,000 guest shot bracket, did a stint on the *Duffy's Tavern* program on January 11 for a reduced fee of $1,200, with the understanding that Ed Gardner reciprocate in a forthcoming Cagney picture or radio show. During that broadcast, the homely Katrinka Yarbotz obsessively pesters Archie with the request of marriage. Meanwhile, Archie asks James Cagney to act in a radio program he wrote entitled "Joyce Cagney, Girl Steamfitter." It's the story of a dame who, though "tribulated by life" and married to a worthless "ginglo," still searches for the "Bluebeard of Happiness." By the time the radio farce is done, Cagney, always the tough guy, threatens to beat up Archie.

The calendar year of 1943 marked an increase in Hollywood's use of radio for advertising exploitations. RKO was always a key player; Warner Bros. and MGM often jumped into the act. Twentieth Century Fox, which often disregarded radio as a major advertising venue, changed studio policy that year to maximize promotion. Martin Starr, with very limited resources at his disposal at United Artists, made perhaps the most important showing of the year with his handling of James Cagney and other stars for radio appearances at high figures. After all, Cagney only received a percentage of the fee — the movie studio received the majority. Cagney was in New York, by the way, spending the holidays with brother William and sister Jeannie, and was awaiting orders to go abroad and entertain the armed forces. Up until the last hour, Cagney's appearance on *Duffy's* was questionable.

Taking a page from the Paul Whiteman experience a few weeks back, Gardner began striking similar deals with other celebrities. Gracie Fields was a guest on *Duffy's Tavern* on the evening of February 29, 1944. Gardner made a guest appearance

151

on her summer radio series a few months later. In late March, Fred Allen and Ed Gardner swapped guest appearances on each other's radio programs again, in the same manner accomplished in January. Gardner, having appeared as a guest on the premiere of Dinah Shore's *Birdseye Open House* in September, received a favor in return when Dinah Shore made a guest appearance on his program two months later.

Dinah Shore at the mike.

Under contract with Paramount, Ed Gardner returned to the West Coast after the thirteen weeks back in New York. The remaining 13 of 39 weeks would once again originate from the West Coast. The *Duffy's Tavern* movie was scheduled for production in July (even though the movie didn't go before the cameras until a few months later.) Charles Cantor, who had remained in Hollywood, returned to the program as Finnegan, replacing the character of Crackpot O'Toole. A new band was added: Joe Venuti and his orchestra. Paul Weston would have taken back the old spot but while Gardner and the cast were away, he accepted a position in the newly created office of musical director for Paramount Pictures. Benay Venuta chose to remain in New York. The weekly singer was not replaced immediately (at one time Gardner considered the vocal talents of June Barton, a war worker), allowing Venuti and his men an extra turn on stage. Director Joseph Hill chose to remain in New York. Hill was replaced by Jack Roche, a producer/director under employment by Young & Rubicam.

Most importantly, Florence Halop chose to remain in New York. Halop was bitten with the patriotic bug and her contribution on a number of war-time radio programs was urgently needed. Among these was *Now is the Time*, a series of four half-hour programs saluting women in the armed forces. The production marked a milestone in radio — the first network show put on by an all-woman crew, including writers, producers, directors, narrators and actors. This put Ed Gardner in a spot to find someone who could play the role of Miss Duffy. And it is here that historians have had conflicting information regarding who played the role of Miss Duffy for the remainder of the 1943-44 season. Miss Duffy was not heard on the program of April 4 (the first broadcast of the season to originate from California) and Helen Lynd, wife of Al Melick, the agent, played the role beginning on April 11, in what *Variety* originally reported was "a one-shot trial." During that broadcast, it was mentioned that Miss Duffy had been away for a short while due to the flu. But anyone with an I.Q. higher than room temperature and half a deaf ear could realize the role was played by someone other than Florence Halop or Shirley Booth. Lynd, a screen actress who usually played the role of giggling blondes, was not well versed in radio and had no sense of timing whatsoever. Throughout the broadcasts of April 11 to May 2, Lynd sounds as if she was reading from the script and did not possess much of a New Yorker accent.

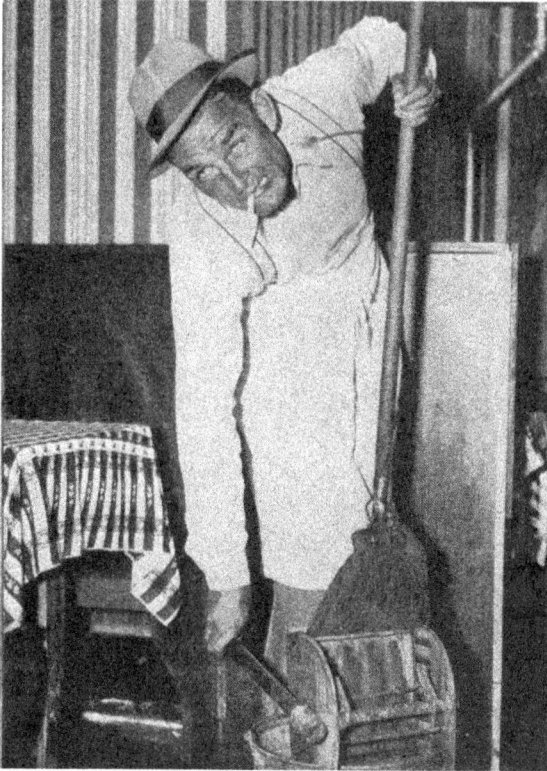

The Scriptwriters

The jump back and forth to New York and Hollywood created a change in scriptwriters throughout the season. According to a press release in April 1944: "*Duffy's Tavern*, Ed Gardner's opus, has an unusual writing set-up. For each episode six or more scripters submit individual shows which are complete in themselves. These are mulled over by Ed Gardner and a "committee" who select a bit here and a tidbit there and finally concoct a program. It's the process week after week. Each writer gets the fee set for his script no matter if a single gag or the entire program is used. If you see six sick scripters listening to Archie on Tuesdays you'll know the answer. Not one of the six will admit that the gags of the other five are worth airing."*

Most of the writers were paid $50 a week for their contributions, required to create a new script within five days, attend a meeting every Sunday with Ed Gardner to review the script, and spend two days leading up to the broadcast revising material and adding more comedy.** Most of those meetings were held at Ed Gardner's house, as Simone, his second wife, later recalled. "At one point the had about ten writers all sitting around the pool and they all had to be served lunch. And I always used to say that if anybody ever walked into the house at one o'clock in the afternoon, somebody would ask if they could have some coffee or tea." She also recalled how the writers would laugh themselves silly feeding each other with jokes.

"Ed and I worked best when we would bounce. That is, we would try to best the other with biting sarcasm, feeding each other one joke followed by another," Abe Burrows later recalled. Burrows was the head writer, paid more than any other writer, but remained in Hollywood during the 13 weeks *Duffy's Tavern* originated from the East Coast. (Burrows got a short-term movie job in Hollywood.) He returned to his post when Gardner and crew returned. The comedians were very close both personally and professionally. When Abe Burrows had a son, James (who

---

* On March 21, 1946, it was reported that *Duffy's Tavern* was cooked up by 11 writers!

** For comparison, it was reported in 1946 that Al Lewis was paid $1,000 a week for comedy writing for *Pabst Blue Ribbon Town*, starring Danny Kaye. In November 1952, Abe Burrows testified before the House Un-American Activities Committee. When asked if he was a Communist, Burrows told the committee that he had paid no dues, either as flat assessments or as deductions from his salary, to any Communist organization, and had not carried a party card. The period under investigation was from 1943 to 1945, during which time the witness was writing and directing the radio show, *Duffy's Tavern* and "doctoring" other shows for a salary ranging from $40,000 and $50,000 annually.

Edgar Bergen and his wife Frances chat with Ed Gardner.

would later co-create *Cheers*, a long-running comedy people often compare to *Duffy's Tavern*), Ed Gardner and Shirley Booth were named godparents.

Gardner, meanwhile, was striking deals with companies on both coasts in return for product placement. When he wanted a watch or a discount on a fur coat, Gardner requested Burrows (not the other scriptwriters) to work into his program a mention of the manufacturer or distributor of those items... even if the reference was the butt of a joke. Somehow these references, though observed by NBC's continuity department during a review of each script, were never changed and went over the air without Bristol-Myers being aware of the paid advertisements. For the broadcast of

February 15, 1944, Ed Gardner was paid a rumored $500 from Gillette to have his scriptwriters incorporate their product and name in the script. His opening monologue with Duffy included the following: "Oh, hello Duffy. Tonight? Laird Cregar. The horror guy from the movies. Huh? Well, he's sort of a king-size Peter Lorre... He's in that picture, *The Lodger*. A guy that walks around with a knife in his hand all the time. Yeah, he's slash-happy. But he's very polite. He walks up to a beautiful dame, removes his hat and bows. Then he removes her hat, head and all. What? He uses a Gillette." At the conclusion of the February 22, 1944, broadcast, Crackpot O'Toole makes reference to the "Eversharp fountain pen."

Publicly, Gardner was quick to take praise for writing most of the scripts for the series, even though it was known that he had scriptwriters on payroll. According to Murray Schumach of the *New York Times*, he did not endear himself with radio writers when he disparaged their abilities. "He concedes that writers make 'some' contributions to his show." Yet, when pressed, he admitted he dreaded appearing anywhere without a script prepared by writers. Last minute requests for guest appearances meant another repeat of the "Two-Top Gruskin" sketch. (Arthur Daley of the *New York Times* once wrote about Two-Top Gruskin in his May 7, 1944, column titled "The Sad Story of Three-Mitt and Two-Top.")

Simone Hegeman

Leave us face it, Ed Gardner was in love. His recent divorce from Shirley Booth was not just the result of "irreconcilable differences." He met a New York radio and stage actress, Simone Hegeman, and wanted to marry her. "My mother was sunbathing at the Hamptons on Wyborg Beach in New York," recalled Ed Gardner, Jr. "It's been decades since I heard the story so if I am mistaken about the exact name of the beach, I can assure you that at the time, Wyborg was the most desolate, romantic part of the Hamptons. My father was renting a house in the Hamptons, a block away from Wyborg. There was a golf course up there and he was probably playing there, too. Anyway, he was walking along the beach and saw my mother and was taken by her beauty. That's how they first met. Soon after that it was goodbye Shirley Booth and hello Simone Hegeman."

It was a fast romance. Ed Gardner went backstage where Shirley Booth was performing the role of Ruth Sherwood in *My Sister Eileen* to break the news. He had fallen in love with another woman and whatever romance he had for Shirley had expired some time ago. In July of 1942, the two flew to Reno and obtained a divorce. On March 25, 1943, Simone and Ed were married. When Ed Gardner was asked by a reporter, "Is she an actress? What does she do?" Ed replied: "She brings out the pipes and slippers." They honeymooned at Lakewood, with the New York Giants. No marriage is a perfect union, but Simone and Ed would remain helpmates until the day he passed away in 1963.

Shirley Booth, meanwhile, continued an active career on both stage and radio, appearing on more radio programs than could possibly be documented, especially since she appeared on numerous talk shows in New York to help publicize the stage plays in which she performed. Looking back today, it is ironic that the actress who turned down a raise in weekly salary to appear in motion pictures, claiming that money was not as important than her love for the stage, found herself appearing on radio to pay the bills. While she attempted to avoid discussion about Miss Duffy because it reminded her of the bitter marriage, on radio Booth played the role of Dottie Mahoney, a resident of Brooklyn, New York, always seeking a man willing to go out on a date with her. A close second to the Miss Duffy character, Dottie Mahoney made guest appearances on the Kate Smith program, *The Raleigh Room With Hildegarde*, *The Victor Borge Show*, *The Vaughn Monroe Show*, *The Danny Kaye Show*, *The Fred Allen Show* and five consecutive appearances (September 2 to September 30, 1945) on *Tommy Dorsey and Company*, among many others. A few years later, she played the role of Phyllis Hogan, a New York working girl (again with a Brooklyn accent) on the situation comedy, *Hogan's Daughter*, a short-run summer series in 1949.

Booth almost had a comeback on radio as Connie Brooks on the long-running *Our Miss Brooks*. In January 1948, freelancer Don Ettlinger was hired by CBS to write the audition script of the then-titled *Our Miss Booth* (Shirley Booth was to be the star).

Ed and Simone on their honeymoon.

When the development of the pilot did not pick up enough speed for Booth, she signed a contract for a new stage production and went East. In May 1948, the lead role in *Meet Miss Brooks* (now re-titled), was again open. Realizing it would take a screen actress to have a flexible schedule for a radio comedy, the second proposal was intended for Joan Blondell but she pulled out of the deal because of plans for film work. In the middle of June, eyes focused on Eve Arden to audition for the lead in what was eventually *Our Miss Brooks*, the CBS situation comedy now being packaged by Hubbell Robinson, the network's programming chief. The audition was cut on Friday the 18th in Hollywood and Arden was not only the third artist to be considered for the role but proved the old adage: "third time's a charm." Years later, Don Ettlinger momentarily borrowed Shirley Booth to help testify that she had, in fact, done an audition recording for his proposed comedy, after having filed a suit in 1951 against CBS when he discovered he never received any piece of the action when the series was taken away. The network claimed it was an in-house production and that Ettlinger had no involvement in the development of the program. Thanks to Booth's testimony, and a recording of the audition, Ettlinger was paid a minor settlement.

Among guest appearances on *The Cavalcade of America* and *I Sustain the Wings*, the highlight of her radio career came on the evening of June 13, 1948, when the Ford Motor Company paid her more money than all of her *Cavalcade* appearances combined, to reprise her stage role of Ruth in a radio production of "My Sister Eileen" on *The Ford Theatre*.

Shirley Booth's career on the stage would culminate with three Tony Awards. Her first was for playing Grace Woods in *Goodbye, My Fancy* (November 17, 1948, 446 performances) and a second for her role as Lola Delaney in *Come Back, Little Sheba* (February 15, 1950, 190 performances). When she reprised her stage role for the latter onscreen in 1953, she received an Oscar for "Best Actress in a Leading Role." She won her third Tony for playing Leona Samish in *The Time of the Cuckoo* (October 15, 1952, 263 performances). From 1961 to 1966, she played the title role for the popular television series, *Hazel*, based on a long-running comic panel by Ted Key about a perfect maid. Shirley Booth received an Emmy nomination for three of the five seasons; she won two Emmy Awards. The actress was interviewed over the years and, naturally, the subject of Ed Gardner and *Duffy's Tavern* came up. Possibly fearing discussion of the show might revisit her stormy marriage, classy woman that she was, Shirley Booth spoke positively about her ex-husband, but very discreetly. "I just couldn't keep up with Ed," she said in 1954. "He loves gaiety and parties and I'm too much of an introvert. I can't bear being around people too long at a time."

Shirley Booth personally admitted that Miss Duffy was an incarnation of the character Mabel from the Broadway play, *Three Men on a Horse*. But her role was so firmly planted in the minds of listeners (and Ed Gardner) that when she left the show in 1943, the part was never filled to his satisfaction. The producer/director/actor had become an expert in the finer points of New York dialect and was convinced that only a true refugee from Flatbush could master it. Press releases and numerous articles in the trade columns reported a nationwide search conducted for a new Miss Duffy. Gardner offered auditions to girls named Duffy as a promotional gimmick; he took the contests to the local level, which appealed in large cities across the country. He even resorted to mass auditions by telephone and transcription. "The part was written around Shirley, originally," Gardner told one columnist. "I've auditioned about a hundred girls in New York and here. If, by the grace of good luck, the right one comes along, fine. But we don't want to sell the part short. We'll probably have to develop a new girl character and write Miss Duffy out of the script." As evident after Florence Halop in 1944, Gardner was never fully satisfied with the actress portraying the role. After listening to a recording of Helen Lynd play the role, Gardner's judgment was justified.

Highlights of the Season

On the evening of January 18, 1944, Lauritz Melchior was the guest celebrity. Archie explains to Duffy that the Metropolitan Opera is the place where society dames with ermine coats and guys with top hats stay while they wait for their limousines to come back for them. Because the Metropolitan is having a special campaign for funds, Archie asked Melchior to come down to the tavern. The barkeep hopes to convince Melchior to take the song back and sing it on stage at the opera.

FINNEGAN: I very rarely attend the opera. What is it?
ARCHIE: Opera? Well, you know what the Ziegfield Follies is….
FINNEGAN: Yeah.
ARCHIE: Well, throw out the dancing dames, throw out the laughs, throw out the entertainment…
FINNEGAN: Yeah?
ARCHIE: Well, what's left is the opera.

Archie verifies with Melchior that the Metropolitan has a brief deficit and offering his services to help raise funds, Archie wants his song incorporated into the next stage performance. To make it easier, Archie wrote his own opera with the song incorporated. Meanwhile, Crackpot O'Toole, the forger, got out of Sing Sing… having written himself a pardon. Archie convinces the forger to write a check in the amount of $300,000, to temporarily help the opera out of debt. But the check is made out for $3,000,000 and Crackpot signed his own name on it!

Ed Gardner, Dinah Shore and Lauritz Melchior.

On the evening of February 8, 1944, Major Edward Bowes, famous for his hosting chores on *Major Bowes' Original Amateur Hour*, was a guest on *Duffy's Tavern*. Archie figures luring Major Bowes to put on his amateur shows at the tavern would mean additional customers and that, in turn, might help quadruple the cash register business. After Finnegan impersonates Katharine Hepburn and Edward G. Robinson, Crackpot O'Toole recites his poem, "Meditation in Solitary." Neither are impressive to Major Bowes, seeking true talent in the contest. After hearing Major Bowes sing "Leave Us Face It, We're In Love," Duffy rejects the idea of a talent contest altogether. In honor of Bowes' appearance for that particular evening, the announcer refers to the program as "Amateur Night at Duffy's."

On the evening of March 14, Archie fancies himself a psychiatrist and tries to psychoanalyze his friends at the bar. When the barkeep learns that musical comedy performer Gertrude Lawrence is going to visit the tavern, he tries to impress her by acting like Noel Coward and writing a play. After the horrible British drama is performed, Lawrence and Archie sing a duet, "This Is It." Jack Gould, writing in his March 19 column for the *New York Times*, remarked: "Gertrude Lawrence's program is scheduled to leave the Blue network after next Sunday, bringing to an end a rather unfortunate venture for the stage star. Her appearance on the air had been regarded as one of the events of the radio season, but from the start her show got bogged down in a lot of chichi and cutie nonsense. It is perhaps ironic that at the close of her radio run Miss Lawrence should prove that she is still a likely broadcasting star. Coming out of the front parlor to appear last Tuesday on *Duffy's Tavern*, she showed that she could dish it out and take it, too, and, given a little fresh material for a change, could no doubt become one of the ether's leading comediennes."

Memorable Line
ARCHIE: Eddie, a cup of tea for Miss Lawrence.
EDDIE: I'm sorry, the tea bag's in use.
ARCHIE: Who's got it?
EDDIE: Moriarity.
LAWRENCE: Well, what's taking him so long?

EDDIE: The bag fell in the cup. He's waiting for it to cool so he can go after it.

On the evening of March 5, 1944, the most complete turnout of the nation's war leaders since Pearl Harbor traded off-the-record political wisecracks with the capital's press at the annual dinner of the White House Correspondents Association. With proceeds going to President Roosevelt's favorite philanthropy, the National Foundation for Infantile Paralysis, the affair drew volunteer entertainment of a headline value on par with the names at the head table. Stars of music, stage, radio and screen took part and, with NBC arranging the show, these included Bob Hope, Gracie Fields, Fred Waring and his singers, opera stars Nan Merriman and Robert Merrill, and Ed Gardner among the guests.

Later that same month, columnist H.I. Phillips remarked in his column how many comedians were trying to rub shoulders with politics, pointing out how Wendell Willkie made a guest appearance on *Information, Please*, a radio quiz program "and it is now up to Governors Bricker and Dewey to get on *Duffy's Tavern* or *Truth or Consequences* if they are to have any chance for the presidency."

Cary Grant and fellow actor Don Barclay, who recently returned from an overseas entertainment tour, teamed up in a comedy routine for a series of guest shots on network shows. Their first appearance was on *Duffy's Tavern* on the evening of April 4, when Archie tries to impress a society woman named Pamela Huntington Smythe by claiming he is a playboy. "I wouldn't dream of learning a trade. The hardest work I'd ever done was to hold a cue stick in a polo game," he explains. Cary Grant stops by and Archie explains how it would impress Pamela if Duffy himself walked through the tavern doors and made a fuss over Archie. Grant playing the role of Duffy, naturally. Don Barclay plays the role of Pamela's father, who expresses concern that Pamela's new interest has no financial responsibility. Grant walks in, with all the mannerisms of Finnegan, ultimately sweeping the heiress off her feet and leaving Archie standing in the sawdust.

Ed Gardner and Cary Grant.

FINNEGAN: I'm Clifton Finnegan. Duh, I'm surprised you don't recognize me.

GRANT: Why should I?

FINNEGAN: Well, I see all your pictures.

GRANT: Well, the film goes so fast that I don't get a chance to look out at the audience.

Grant and Barclay followed on *The Abbott and Costello Show* two days later, on Eddie Cantor's program on April 12 and Dinah Shore's program on April 20.

Beginning with the broadcast of May 9, 1944, songstress Yvette (real name Elsa Harris Silver, an NBC contract vocalist) made her first of two appearances on *Duffy's Tavern*, singing "I'll Be Seeing You." When she left for a three-week performance tour with other talented musicians, Yvette was replaced by Ann Hogan. Best known for her performance in the 1944 Universal Studios movie, *See My Lawyer*, starring Olsen and Johnson, the movie studio promoted her in press releases as "a radio songstress." She was certainly at her peak of fame during the calendar year of 1944 as she was making appearances on other radio programs about the same time she made her *Duffy's Tavern* appearance, including *Command Performance* and *The Charlie McCarthy Show*. In the spring of 1944, she received a letter from a sailor saying he couldn't make her his pin-up girl because there was no way to pin up a picture on a battleship. So he called her his "Strip Up Girl," using adhesive tape to hold the photo. She left *Duffy's Tavern* because of the performance tour but returned just in time to appear in the final broadcast of the season which aired on the evening of June 27, 1944. That broadcast, incidentally, originated not from the NBC studios but from the stage of the Carthay Circle Theater, a famous movie palace in Hollywood on San Vicente Boulevard. This is the same movie theater that hosted official premiere screenings, red carpet events, of such legendary classics as *Snow White and the Seven Dwarfs* (1937) and *Gone With the Wind* (1939).

Leave Us Face It, We're In Love

On the evening of December 14, 1943, songstress Dinah Shore was a guest on *Duffy's Tavern*. Fancying himself a songwriter, Archie tries to convince Dinah to sing his new song, "Leave Us Face It, We're In Love," which she does. Archie flirts with Dinah, unaware that she recently married actor George Montgomery, and quickly turns his attention away when he learns this fact. Joan Davis, another singer, makes a guest appearance on the radio program. Eddie, before hearing the song, remarks how "Leave Us

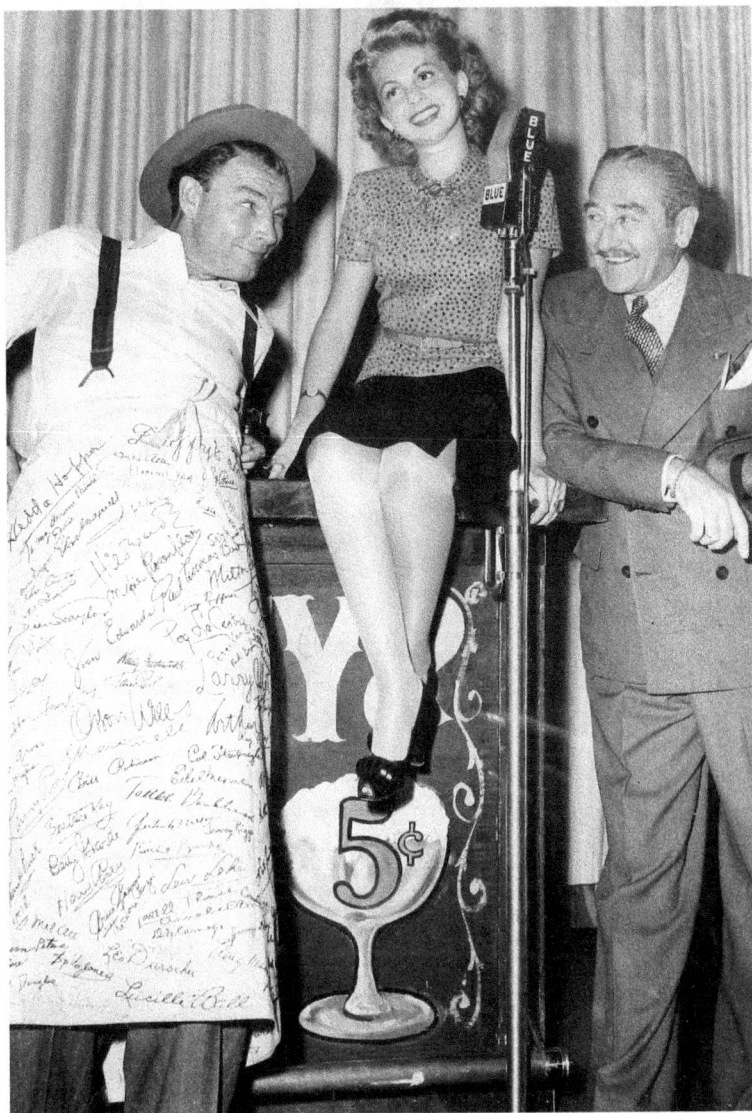

Ed Gardner, singer Yvette and Adolph Menjou.

Face It" will be Archie's start and Dinah's finish. *Variety* reviewed: "Dinah Shore was an ingratiating guest Wednesday night... Highlight of the date was her singing of a satirical number, 'Leave Us Face It, We're in Love,' supposed to be written by Archie (Ed Gardner)... However, her comedy dialog with Gardner and the others on the show was slightly off, mostly a matter of mistiming and slow pickup of cues which should have been corrected by the director."

Duffy's Tavern broadcasts following Dinah Shore's appearance contained the same premise: Archie convincing celebrity guests to sing his song, including celebrities not known for superb vocal chords such as Herbert Marshall and Hedda Hopper. At the conclusion of the January 18, 1944, broadcast, Archie closes the broadcast telling Duffy that his song just got published in sheet music form and is now available on the music stands. While Archie took credit on the air, the true authors of the comedy ditty were Pvt. Frank Loesser (who wrote the famous "Praise the Lord and Pass the Ammunition") and Abe Burrows. The sheet music was published by Famous Music Corp.

A few days after New Year's, Hildegarde recorded her rendition of the song for Decca Records. The record became a big seller. In February, Jan Garber cut six new tracks, one was "Leave Us Face It, We're in Love." In March 1944, Ilka Chase had a new Victor album due soon of Dorothy Parker monologues. Chase recorded her rendition of the same song.

"Ed Gardner suggested that on one of the shows Archie should try to become a big-time songwriter," recalled Burrows. "I thought it was a funny idea and talked it over with Loesser, who liked it, too. He and I went to work and came up with a love song which we wrote using Archie's style and syntax. We gave this song the elegant title of 'Leave Us Face It.' We built a few situations around this song that Archie was supposed to have 'wrote,' and we cast some guest stars who were willing to risk singing it. The first singer brave enough to sing it was Hildegarde. After Hildegarde, we had the gall to invite the late Lauritz Melchior to come on the show and sing it. One of the greatest Wagnerian heldentenors of all time, at the Metropolitan Opera he sang Siegfried, Tannhauser, Lohengrin, and we asked this man to sing 'Leave Us Face It.' He did sing it and seemed to enjoy doing it. Of course, his own English was not perfect, and I suspect that he didn't know why the lyrics got laughs from the audience. Melchior later told me he liked singing the song because he liked Frank Loesser's melody. Frank had the wit to write some very romantic music to our silly lyrics. That made the song even funnier."

On the evening of January 25, 1944, the guest was Deems Taylor, who had recently become the head of the American Society of Composers, Authors and Publishers. Archie makes jokes about his position of authority including making the musicians "put movements in so he'll have a place to talk." The song "Leave Us Face It, We're In Love" is performed while Taylor slyly comments on each section. This particular radio broadcast was transcribed for Decca Records (then planning to release a few *Duffy's Tavern* episodes in a multi-album set) and was also played back over the speaker system during ASCAP's third annual dinner at the Ritz-Carlton Hotel in New York City.

Sheet music promoting Duffy's Tavern.

The novelty eventually got old and executives at Young & Rubicam, representing Bristol-Myers, requested Ed Gardner tame down the solicitations and promotional gimmicks associated with the song. Gardner complied. On the evening of July 20, 1944, *The Callahans* premiered over WMCA in New York. (Spotting of the show on the local station was undertaken with the idea of showcasing the program for national advertisers. Future sessions featured guest stars, but the promising series never went beyond the summer of 1944.) The situation comedy centered at a theatrical boarding house which provided an ideal vehicle for presenting everything including the kitchen sink. One critic compared the program as having "broad humor" with the "same appeal as a *Duffy's Tavern* stanza." Florence Halop played the role of Penelope, the hopeful ingénue from Brooklyn who proved her worth by singing... you guessed it, "Leave Us Face It, We're In Love." Neither the scriptwriter nor director had any prior involvement with *Duffy's Tavern* but her rendition was no doubt a favor to Ed Gardner.

In October and November of 1943, an unpublished polka song titled "Duffy's Tavern" was written by Robert C. Haring (music) and Dick Howard (lyrics). The official pseudonym of Jeanne Granville was listed on the paperwork. Supposedly this song was intended to replace "When Irish Eyes Are Smiling" for the theme song. To date, it appears this polka remains unpublished and unused.

EPISODE GUIDE
October 5, 1943, to June 27, 1944
Sponsor: Bristol-Myers (Sal Hapatica and Minit-Rub)
Series originates from California
from October 5 to December 28, 1943
Series originates from New York
from January 4 to March 28, 1944
Series originates from California from April 4 to June 27, 1944
East Coast broadcast: Tuesday, 8:30 to 9:00 p.m., EST
West Coast broadcast: 8:30 to 9:00 p.m., PST
Director: Joseph Hill (October 5 to December 22, 1943)*
Director: Walter Bunker (December 28, 1943)

---

* Supposedly Abe Burrows took the directing helm for the premiere episode of the season.

Director: Joseph Hill (January 4 to March 28, 1944)
Director: Jack Roche (April 4 to June 27, 1944)
Music: Paul Weston and his Orchestra
(October 5, 1943, to December 28, 1943)
Music: Peter Van Steeden and his Orchestra
(January 4, 1944, to March 28, 1944)
Music: Joe Venuti and his Orchestra (April 4 to June 27, 1944)
Singer: Johnny Johnston (October 5 to December 28, 1943)
Singer: Benay Venuta (January 4 to March 28, 1944)
Singer: Yvette (May 9 and June 27, 1944)
Singer: Ann Hogan (May 16 and 23, 1944)
Singer: Helen Ward (June 13, 1944)
Announcer: Harry Von Zell (October 5 to December 28, 1943)
Announcer: Dan Seymour (January 4 to March 28, 1944)
Announcer: Toby Reed (April 4 to June 27, 1944)
Commercial Spokesman Assistant: Hal Gerard
(October 5 to December 28, 1943)
Commercial Spokesman Assistant: Roland Winters
(January 4 to March 28, 1944)
Commercial Spokesman Assistant: Alan Reed
(April 4 to June 27, 1944)**

Cast
Charles Cantor as Finnegan
(missing for a few weeks as Cantor remained on the Coast)
Eddie Green as Eddie
Florence Halop as Miss Duffy
(October 5, 1943, to March 7, 1944)
Helen Lynd as Miss Duffy (April 4, 1944, to May 2, 1944)
Doris Singleton as Miss Duffy (May 9, 1944)
Sara Berner as Miss Duffy (May 23, 1944)
Connie Manning as Miss Duffy
(May 30, 1944, to June 27, 1944)

** The announcer delivered the commercials but the spokesman assistants supplied the second voice during the weekly commercials, and also supplied brief supporting roles on many of the broadcasts.

Miss Duffy was not featured in the broadcast of May 16. To fill in the void, two celebrities were featured, instead of one, Prince Michael Romanoff and Ann Rutherford.

Episode #98 — Broadcast Tuesday, October 5, 1943
Guest: Veronica Lake
Plot: See page 142.

Episode #99 — Broadcast Tuesday, October 12, 1943
Guest: Orson Welles
Plot: When a rival tavern, Crogan's, lures away Duffy's clientele with a nightly floor show with chorus girls, Archie gets desperate and enlists the help of Orson Welles, actor and professional stage magician, who performs a magic act.

*Ed Gardner shares a laugh
with Franchot Tone and Orson Welles.*

Episode #100 — Broadcast Tuesday, October 19, 1943
Guest: Peter Lorre
Plot: After enjoying seeing Mrs. Carveth Wells do her act with Raffles, the talking mynah bird, creepy-voiced film star Peter Lorre arrives at the tavern and gets caught up in a mystery Archie wrote called "The Case of the Stolen Swami." Johnny Johnston sings "Sunday, Monday, or Always."

Trivia, etc. Mrs. Carveth Wells and her talking bird, "Raffles" was a legit stage act that was a guest on the program!

Episode #101 — Broadcast Tuesday, October 26, 1943
Guest: Ida Lupino
Plot: In an effort to promote the upcoming Paramount motion picture, Archie gets Ida Lupino to be the leading lady in what he predicts to be a film version of his first book, *Duffy's First Reader.* The movie will be called "This is the Archie," spoofing the title of the then-popular motion picture *This is the Army.* Ida is more concerned about who gets top billing. Johnny Johnston sings "Stormy Weather."

Episode #102 — Broadcast Tuesday, November 2, 1943
Guest: Charles Coburn
Plot: Archie thinks that Charles Coburn should give up a 50-year career in acting to become a professional greeter at Duffy's, figuring Coburn an easy mark. Archie challenges him to a game of poker, hoping to put the actor in debt and thereby make good on his dues by working at Duffy's, unaware until it is too late that card shark Coburn is capable of winning every hand.

Episode #103 — Broadcast Tuesday, November 9, 1943
Guest: Lucille Ball
Plot: Archie entertains two friends from the old neighborhood in Brooklyn — Ashley Clinker (also known as Joseph Ashley) and movie star Lucille Ball. When Clinker says he represents "Who's That?," Archie thinks he's going to include him in the book, which will surely impress Lucy, but later finds out he's only selling the book, not editing. Johnny Johnston sings "Paper Doll."

Lucille Ball and Ed Gardner

Memorable Lines
ARCHIE: You remember I always had a talent for writing.
LUCILLE: Yes… I remember those fences in Brooklyn.

Episode #104 — Broadcast Tuesday, November 16, 1943
Guests: Reginald Gardiner and Bill Haines
Plot: William Haines, the interior decorator*, stops by to fix up Archie's apartment, so he can rent out half of the bachelor's pad. While Haines also helps "desecrate" the tavern, Hollywood star Reginald Gardiner arrives and confesses his bags are still at the station. Archie thinks he has found the perfect roommate until Haines cracks jokes about how horrible the conditions are. Gardiner decides to check in at the Waldorf instead.

Trivia, etc. Archie reveals that he lives at 214¼ Third Avenue.

Memorable Lines
MISS DUFFY: (GIGGLES)
GARDINER: What are you giggling about?
MISS DUFFY: You know I have never kissed a man with a mustache… I wonder if… er… What are you going to be doing later? **
GARDINER: Shaving off my mustache.

Episode #105 — Broadcast Tuesday, November 23, 1943
Guest: Marlene Dietrich
Plot: Archie is encouraged to purchase an engagement ring for Marlene Dietrich, thanks to Dave Hossinger's con artist ways of

---

* Guest star William Haines was Hollywood's first openly gay star, losing a major MGM contract in the early thirties after refusing to pretend to be straight. He instead became an extremely successful interior decorator and designer to the stars.
** When Shirley Booth was playing the role of Miss Duffy, her role was listed on the script as Booth, not as Miss Duffy. Following her departure, the scripts reverted to Miss Duffy, signifying the lines the actress was to perform.

Marlene Dietrich and Ed Gardner.

saving 60 percent off all jewelry. When Archie's ideas of inflation are as straight as a bed spring, Harry Von Zell explains how the war has affected inflation and purchasing War Bonds is more important today than ever before. Dietrich visits the tavern to deliver an important Christmas message, encouraging folks like Archie to purchase war bonds instead of trinkets. Miss Duffy is jealous of Marlene Dietrich's legs, believing she can match her legs with the actress anytime. Archie claims it's impossible since Miss Duffy's legs don't match. After being cheated by Hossinger, Archie admits he should have bought a war bond instead.

Memorable Lines
EDDIE: Oh, Marlene Dietrich. That's the gal that thinks you're so handsome that she's absolutely crazy about you.
ARCHIE: Who told you that?
EDDIE: You will in a minute.
ARCHIE: Oh, boy, Eddie. Imagine having a blonde like that around.
EDDIE: Two weeks ago you felt that way about Lucille Ball, a redhead.
ARCHIE: Eddie, two weeks ago you made ham salad, didn't you?
EDDIE: Yep.
ARCHIE: Would you eat it today?
EDDIE: Nope.
ARCHIE: Touche...

Episode #106 — Broadcast Tuesday, November 30, 1943
Guests: Bert Lahr and Dad Crosby (Bing Crosby's father)
Plot: Fed up with abuse from Duffy, Archie decides to quit his job and open up his own tavern, and in order to raise the capital needed for his new venture he hatches a scheme to get adopted by Bing Crosby's father, "Dad Crosby." In order to sell "Dad" that he's a "Crosby at heart," he stages a comedy sketch with guest comic Bert Lahr. After failing to garner laughs, Archie asks Lahr if he remembers getting hit with a tomato in vaudeville. When Crosby agrees to adopt Archie and allow him to open "Crosby's Tavern,"

he is to turn his entire fortune over to him and Archie would receive an allowance… not exactly what Archie had in mind.

Trivia, etc. Bert Lahr subs for Adolphe Menjou, who was promoted at the conclusion of last week's episode but withdrew on account of illness.

Episode #107 — Broadcast Tuesday, December 7, 1943
Guest: Bing Crosby
Plot: Bing Crosby, whom Archie describes as "the straight man in those Bob Hope pictures," drops by the tavern and Archie tries to get the crooner to buy half interest in Duffy's. Archie figures Crosby is a pushover and a cinch because he could help with the present day labor shortage ("Bing grows his own boys"). Crosby, however, explains that he owns two stables but agrees to audition for Duffy in Archie's new floor show, "Duffy's Music Hall" (spoofing Bing's *Kraft Music Hall*). This includes a spoof of *Gone With the Wind*, a southern cotton plantation and Scarlet O'Duffy. Crosby sings "How Sweet You Are."

Trivia, etc. During the close of this broadcast, announcer Harry Von Zell explains that Bing Crosby appeared courtesy of Paramount Pictures, and was soon to be seen in *Going My Way*.

Episode #108 — Broadcast Tuesday, December 14, 1943
Guests: Dinah Shore and Joan Davis
Plot: See pages 166 and 167.

Trivia, etc. A reference to Dinah Shore's marriage to George Montgomery was made in the previous week's show, a tease for the audience to figure out who next week's guest was going to be. Dinah Shore sings "No Love, No Nothing," a current hit at the time.

When Joan Davis appears on the show, she describes Archie as having blue eyes and curly hair.

When Eddie tells Archie that Moriarity won the pinball game, he mis-delivers the score, a slip of the lip during the broadcast!

Episode #109 — Broadcast Tuesday, December 21, 1943
Guest: Herbert Marshall
Plot: In order to impress music publisher Harry Beethoven (played by Bert Gordon), Archie gets guest Herbert Marshall to sing "Leave Us Face It, We're In Love." When the publisher hears the song, he refunds Archie his $15 fee and reveals he is a crook. "If that's the kind of song publishers have to publish, I'm proud I'm a crook," he says, before exiting the tavern. Johnny Johnston sings "I'll Be Home For Christmas." At the conclusion of this broadcast, Harry Von Zell tells the radio audience to pick up this month's issue of *Coronet* magazine, which features a story about the radio program.

Memorable Lines
ARCHIE: Eddie, you remember that song I wrote last week?
EDDIE: Yeah.
ARCHIE: The one Dinah Shore sang?
EDDIE: Yeah.
ARCHIE: Well, it's finally got results.
EDDIE: I was afraid of that — when's the trial?

Episode #110 — Broadcast Tuesday, December 28, 1943
Guest: Hedda Hopper
Plot: Gossip queen Hedda Hopper, whom Archie refers to as "the News Mongress," is stopping by the tavern and Archie hopes to convince her to write about his new song in her syndicated column. He convinces her to sing the lyrics as he plays the piano. Afterwards, Hopper expresses no interest in mentioning the song in her column. It's not big enough news to warrant mention. So Archie convinces Harry Von Zell, Miss Duffy and Finnegan to stage a scene in the tavern, whereupon Miss Duffy sings a few bars and Von Zell pulls a gun and shoots Finnegan to save the idiot from hearing the song. Hopper promptly leaves, not fooled by the scheme, but promises it will be in tomorrow's paper — Louella Parsons' column.

Episode #111 — Broadcast Tuesday, January 4, 1944
Guest: Fred Allen
Plot: See page 149.

Episode #112 — Broadcast Tuesday, January 11, 1944
Guest: James Cagney
Plot: See page 151.

Episode #113 — Broadcast Tuesday, January 18, 1944
Guest: Lauritz Melchior
Plot: See page 161.

Trivia, etc. According to one source, Lauritz Melchior, the Metropolitan Opera singer, was intended to appear as a guest in this episode, but was unable to attend and a completely different script had to be written. No recording is known to exist and the only script found with this date contains the information documented above, found in Ed Gardner's personal bound volumes of radio scripts, suggesting it was broadcast. In the event that Melchior was unable to attend, a lengthier documentation of the intended script is featured.

Episode #114 — Broadcast Tuesday, January 25, 1944
Guest: Deems Taylor
Plot: While Peter Van Steeden is making Archie's song into a symphony, Archie is writing a commentary for Deems Taylor, as Archie explains to Eddie, "one of them things that explains what a composer was thinking about after he's dead." Benay Venuta returns, having been absent the week prior because she was sick, and makes up for it by singing a song. Deems Taylor accepts the task and welcomes all music lovers to Van Steeden's new symphony with the cast playing the leads. After completion, ASCAP calls Taylor to inform him that the symphony is "a slur on the profession" and a "disgrace to music." Taylor decides to leave the tavern... he has a better job on the *Philco Radio Hall of Fame*.

Memorable Lines
ARCHIE: Are you still working at the Philharmonica?
DEEMS: No, I'm now on the Philco Radio Hall of Fame.
ARCHIE: Oh, no more Philharmonica, heh? When'd they can you?
DEEMS: I wasn't canned, Archie... the engagement was terminated by mutual consent.
ARCHIE: Are they still paying ya?
DEEMS: No.
ARCHIE: Don't let them kid you, Deems... you was canned.

Episode #115 — Broadcast Tuesday, February 1, 1944
Supporting Cast: John Brown (Crackpot O'Toole)
Guest: Billie Burke
Plot: Billie Burke, known for playing dumb roles in movies, bumps into Finnegan and the two start a brief romance. While Archie attempts to play Cupid for Crackpot O'Toole and the Hollywood guest, Burke has other notions and prefers only Finnegan. Only when the charade is over, it seems Burke was smarter than she looks and Archie learns a valuable lesson in war bonds and stamps. "It ain't how much as long as it's all you can give."

Memorable Lines
ARCHIE: Just a minute, please ... them tablecloths was turned over last week. Besides, Miss Burke, how is it you remembered the tablecloths and you didn't remember me?
BURKE: I didn't eat off you ...

Episode #116 — Broadcast Tuesday, February 8, 1944
Guest: Major Edward Bowes
Plot: See page 163.

Episode #117 — Broadcast Tuesday, February 15, 1944
Guests: Laird Cregar and Michelle Morgan
Plot: While discussions at the tavern over the recent "Lodger" invite jokes thrown about loosely, Clancy the Cop rejects the notion that little children are exposed to such horror pictures. Eddie won't sign up as an actor in horror pictures in fear of the

real-life monsters, and Miss Duffy is scared because of the movie she saw the night before, "I Married a Werewolf." When Archie relies on Cregar for women advice, the plan for Archie to woo French actress Michelle Morgan backfires.

Episode #118 — Broadcast Tuesday, February 22, 1944
Supporting Cast: John Brown (Crackpot O'Toole)
Guest: Phil Baker
Plot: Once again, a game of *Take It or Leave It* is performed with the tavern crew and guest Phil Baker. "Leave Us Face It, We're In Love" is performed on Baker's accordion. When Crackpot O'Toole offers Archie a stock deal in a fake oil deposit under the Great Salt Lake, Archie takes money out of the cash to pay O'Toole. During the game show, Archie answers the most ridiculous questions, working his way up to the big $64 question: "Where is the largest and richest oil deposit in the United States?" Archie says the bottom of the Great Salt Lake and loses the contest.

Trivia, etc. Archie tries to explain the radio quiz program to Duffy: "They ask you who wrote *Wuthering Heights* and you say *David Copperfield*, and they give you 64 dollars... What? Who pays the 64 dollars? Baker does... It's a bribe so the people will stand there while he tells them crummy jokes. Oh no, he don't only tell jokes, he plays the accordion too. Yeah, that gets him more laughs than the jokes."

Memorable Lines
BAKER: For eight dollars, who's buried in Grant's Tomb?
ARCHIE: Baker, that's insulting. I don't want the money that way. Who's buried in Grant's Tomb? That's an insult... give me a real question.
BAKER: Okay... name the tributary branches of the Mississippi River.
ARCHIE: [PAUSE] General Grant! I accept the insult.

Episode #119 — Broadcast Tuesday, February 29, 1944
Supporting Cast: John Brown (Crackpot O'Toole)
Guest: Gracie Fields

Plot: Because beloved British entertainer Gracie Fields is performing at the Waldorf Astoria in New York City, Archie tries to convince her to sign an exclusive with Duffy's Tavern. Finnegan mistakes Gracie as W.C. Fields. Crackpot O'Toole returns, having swindled Archie in a fake oil deal last week, renting the back room of the tavern. Archie doesn't realize it at first, but O'Toole is paying his rent in counterfeit bills. To convince Archie that she should remain at the Waldorf, Gracie sings "Leave Us Face It We're In Love."

Episode #120 — Broadcast Tuesday, March 7, 1944
Guest: Colonel Stoopnagle
Plot: Archie is trying to figure out his taxes. Finnegan admits he cheated on his — he copied the same from the guy in front of him. In the mold of vintage vaudeville patter, Colonel Stoopnagle and Archie exchange humorous dialogue and Stoopnagle eventually reveals another of his wacky inventions. This one will reduce a person's income tax by 80 percent. Archie uses the new invention to help Duffy afford a mink coat for his wife.

Episode #121 — Broadcast Tuesday, March 14, 1944
Supporting Cast: John Brown (Crackpot O'Toole)
Guest: Gertrude Lawrence
Plot: See page 163.

Episode #122 — Broadcast Tuesday, March 21, 1944
Supporting Cast: John Brown (Crackpot O'Toole)
Guest: Fred Allen
Plot: Archie puts an ad in the newspaper for a tenant in the back room of the tavern, hoping for the additional revenue. When he learns that Fred Allen is having a little spring-cleaning done at his home, forcing him to stay out of his own house for the evening and preventing him from writing the script for his next radio show, Archie attempts to convince Allen to stay in the back room of the tavern for sixty cents rent. The back room comes with the European plan: no bath. No matter how much quiet Archie tries to implement at the tavern so Allen can be undisturbed his efforts fail... including the "Do Not Disturb" sign, which he nails to the

door. When Allen practices with his banjo, the tavern customers start to leave and Archie is forced to shout fire in an effort to vacate the tenant. When all other ideas fail, Duffy himself walks into the tavern. In the back room goes Duffy and out goes Allen, who comments "the pig just came in looking for his feet."

Memorable Line
ALLEN: Yes, Archie, this place draws me like a statue draws a pigeon.

Episode #123 — Broadcast Tuesday, March 28, 1944
Guests: Reginald Gardiner and Leo Durocher
Plot: Archie has dreams of becoming a baseball player with the Brooklyn Dodgers. "I know I'm a Giants fan but after all you gotta start at the bottom," Archie remarks. Durocher won't allow Archie a job but explains how he is looking for a sensational southpaw because he has no left-handed pitcher. If Archie can find one, he can have a contract. When Reginald Gardiner, an actor but also an ex-cricket player, enters the tavern, Archie tries to sign him for Durocher as a left-handed pitcher. When paired together, Archie describes the actor and ballplayer as "Ham and Tongue." Gardiner won't sign but Durocher discovers that beneath the gruff exterior lies a gentleman of culture and from now on the Dodgers will become strictly upper crust... no more bums.

Trivia, etc. "It was a good show and The Lip (Durocher) demonstrated that he is gaining poise and improving his delivery reading lines over the air," reviewed columnist Tommy Holmes.

Memorable Lines
DUROCHER: Stop flapping your yap... if that tongue of yours was a bat, you'd be another Joe DiMaggio.
ARCHIE: Leo... people don't call you Lippy because you are kissable... Anyway, what insults me? I ain't no empire.
DUROCHER: Archie, are you referring that I insult umpires?
ARCHIE: Are you kiddin'? I heard you call him language I wouldn't even use on Duffy.

DUROCHER: I can't imagine what you mean. In the incident you're referring to, it was the last inning, two out and the umpire called the third strike on a ball that was at least ten feet over my head... so I turned to the umpire and I said, "Pardon me, sir, I think you are in error."

ARCHIE: From where I was sittin' it sounded much more colorful.

GARDINER: Archie, cricket is a game something like baseball. Except instead of nine men there are eleven and instead of bases we have wickets.

ARCHIE: Look at that... they copy de game from us and then they louse it up.

GARDINER: Oh, don't be a foop.

ARCHIE: That's twice you called me a foop. What's a foop?

GARDINER: I don't know. It's an insult I invented in your honor. I copied de game from you...

Episode #124 — Broadcast Tuesday, April 4, 1944
Guests: Cary Grant and Don Barclay
Plot: See page 164.

Memorable Lines
ARCHIE: Don't kid me... all them beautiful dames in Hollywood making Kleig-eyes at you... Katharine Hepburn... Ginger Rogers... Rosalind Russell...

GRANT: But Archie... those are just girls I work with... merely business acquaintances.

ARCHIE: You mean they're only... you don't even... hm-mph... maybe I overrated you... maybe you ain't got so much animal maggotism after all.

Episode #125 — Broadcast Tuesday, April 11, 1944
Guest: Carole Landis
Plot: Archie tries to romance Hollywood beauty Carole Landis but falls flat on his feet. The actress shows up at the tavern to deliver a serious wartime message about the necessity of women becoming more assertive and joining the war effort. She accurately

describes the principal opportunities for war work for which women could volunteer. When Duffy decides to replace Archie with Carole Landis as the new manager, the gang decides to salute women by acting like females.

Trivia, etc. Ed Gardner suffers a slip of the lip during this broadcast. He says the words "male hail washer" instead of "male hair washer" and tries not to laugh during the pause and the audience laughter.

Clowning around with Charles Laughton.

Episode #126 — Broadcast Tuesday, April 18, 1944

Guest: Charles Laughton

Plot: Archie intends to turn the joint into an exclusive private club, where only actors can be members. "Like the Lambs Club," Archie explains. "Then we'll get Laughton and we'll call it the Ham's Club." Since larger-than-life actor Charles Laughton is dropping by, Archie tries to make the actor the first member. In an effort to impress him, Archie claims he was a student in England. "The closest you have ever been to an English University was wearing a pair of Oxfords," Laughton jokes.

Episode #127 — Broadcast Tuesday, April 25, 1944
Guests: Bob Crosby and Dolores Hope
Plot: Wanting a radio show to advertise Duffy's Tavern on a national level, Archie invites Dolores Hope, Bob Hope's wife, and Bob Crosby, Bing's brother, to the tavern. For the entire week prior to this radio broadcast, it was advertised that Crosby and Hope would be guests and Archie figures it will bring Bing and Bob to the tavern on the same day. With the two guests in the tavern, a mock radio show is done and told in the style of their famous kin, using hysterical jingles to advertise fake commercials, including triple-soaked pig's feet.

Episode #128 — Broadcast Tuesday, May 2, 1944
Supporting cast: Verna Felton (Dennis Day's mother)
Guest: Dennis Day
Plot: Broadcast shortly before Dennis Day joined the Navy, Jack Benny's stooge-singer shows up and makes plans for a night on the town. Archie digs through his little black book calling up all the women he knows only to suffer one rejection after another. When Dennis' mother shows up at the tavern, hoping to take him back home, the singer is saved by Finnegan, who makes a successful pass at the older lady.

Memorable Lines
ARCHIE: Well, Dennis – greetings to our establishment!
    Whadda ya think of the joint
here?
DENNIS: Gee Arch, I think it's wonderful! Super!
ARCHIE: You really mean it? Gee, that's the first time...
    Honest, I feel like kissin' you.
DENNIS: Go ahead... I only promised my mother about girls.

Trivia, etc. One of the women Archie phones is named Simone, who has to stay home and change diapers. This was an in-joke because Ed Gardner's wife was named Simone and she had given birth on April 28 to Ed Gardner, Jr.

Episode #129 — Broadcast Tuesday, May 9, 1944
Guest: Adolphe Menjou
Plot: Adolphe Menjou gives a lecture on Men's Clothes written by Archie and called "Men's Fashions Through the Ages," for the Policemen's Tuesday Night Footbath and Discussion Club. As the lecture goes from the Fig-Leaf to the B.V.D., the insults to policemen start to come out and when Clancy the Cop asks who the culprit is that wrote the lecture, Archie blames Finnegan.

Episode #130 — Broadcast Tuesday, May 16, 1944
Guests: Prince Michael Romanoff and Ann Rutherford
Plot: After learning that Prince Michael Romanoff owns and runs a restaurant in Beverly Hills and the expensive prices he charges for a meal, Archie is impressed. The way he sees it, a guy could eat in Duffy's for six months and still have enough for the funeral. By trying to convince Romanoff to purchase a half interest in the tavern, Archie figures the new name would legitimately attract Hollywood's elite. Meanwhile, Archie attempts to make MGM star Ann Rutherford fall in love with him by claiming he's royalty, unaware that a Prince is among the guests of the tavern, ready to sweep her back to California.

Memorable Lines
ARCHIE: "And you know who else is coming here tonight, Duffy? Ann Rutherford – from the Mickey Rooney pictures! Mmmm - dish! The kind of girl you could take home to your mother – if you could trust your father."

Trivia, etc. Romanoff's restaurant was a real major eatery for the stars for many years but Romanoff himself was actually a colorful phony, pretending - though everyone knew it - to be a Russian Prince when he was not.

Episode #131 — Broadcast Tuesday, May 23, 1944
Guest: Paul Lukas
Plot: The meeting of the Duffy Film and Cinema Critics comes to order and guest Paul Lukas is chosen as an award recipient. Duffy agrees to give Lukas a year's worth of free meals. When a mishap ties Lukas and Bette Davis, Lukas agrees to split the award and promises to keep away from Duffy's for six months and Davis for the other six months.

Harriet Hilliard and Ozzie Nelson during rehearsals.

Episode #132 — Broadcast Tuesday, May 30, 1944
Guests: Ozzie and Harriet Nelson
Plot: Duffy wants Archie to hire Ozzie and Harriet for his yearly semi-annual boat ride, clambake, weenie-roast and malt-hop of the Men's Auxiliary of the Friendly Sons of Mother Machree. Ozzie can bring his band and Harriet can sing – but Duffy would prefer she do a fan dance (even though she is a married woman).

Trivia, etc. In May of 1944, Ozzie and Harriet did yet not have their own radio program. Together, they formed the weekly musical entertainment on *The Raleigh Cigarette Program*, starring Red Skelton, a position they maintained for a number of years.

Episode #133 — Broadcast Tuesday, June 6, 1944
Guest: Basil Rathbone
Plot: Archie just finished writing a mystery for the radio and wants Basil Rathbone to audition it for the radio moguls as Sherlock Holmes in "Who Done It In Dorset" or "The Murder of the Dead Earl." Archie plays the role of Watson, while Eddie continues to find the solution to the question "Why did Benny Goodman bust up?"

Ed Gardner, Basil Rathbone and Red Skelton.

Episode #134 — Broadcast Tuesday, June 13, 1944
Guest: Joan Bennett
Plot: Archie wants to take Joan Bennett out on the town but since Duffy won't give him a raise, he "borrows" the money from the cash register "like the trains used to lend money to Jesse James." Believing he's a big spender, Joan Bennett asks Archie to find a

date for her friend, Miss Duffy. Not wanting to waste his efforts – or Bennett's – Archie seeks out his close friends (Eddie, Finnegan, etc.) to date Miss Duffy for the evening. Naturally, this fails and the double-date never goes through. Disappointed, Archie returns the cash to the register.

Memorable Lines

ARCHIE: By the way – these flowers are for you. May I token them with your esteem?

JOAN: Well, thank you… oh, I'll bet they were lovely.

ARCHIE: Well they may seem to droop a little… but that, dear lady, is because they are

bowing their petals in deference to thy own far, far greater beauty.

JOAN: A very pretty speech.

ARCHIE: Thank you. Incidentally, their stems don't stack up with yours either.

Episode #135 — Broadcast Tuesday, June 20, 1944

Guest: George Jessel

Plot: Today is Duffy's wedding anniversary and the crew at the tavern has dressed the place up. Toastmaster George Jessel gives a speech entitled "The Wedded Bliss of the Duffys," which is more like a roast than a tribute. Joe Venuti and his orchestra play "In the Good Old Summertime."

Trivia, etc. Actor Pat O'Brien was originally scheduled for this broadcast. When he was forced to bow out, actor Brian Donlevy agreed to substitute. Donlevy, according to *Variety*, bowed out of this episode after taking part in Sunday's rehearsals due to "script differences." Less than a year later, Pat O'Brien would make an appearance on the program. Donlevy, who started his acting career in New York on radio, never made an appearance on *Duffy's Tavern* — just the motion picture released through Paramount.

Opening Monologue

ARCHIE: Sure. All your friends are here to give you their heartfelt condolences. Certainly they're all here – the

Harrigans, the Moriaritys, the Burrows... By the way, the Burrows just had a baby – a baby girl just two days old.

Memorable Lines
ARCHIE: Still with that studio – that I.J. Fox?
JESSEL: That's 20th Century Fox! You're thinking of I.J. Zanuck.
ARCHIE: Yeah, huh. Who they got over there?
JESSEL: Oh, Alice Faye, Gene Tierney, Linda Darnell, Betty Grable...
ARCHIE: And you still find time to make pictures?
JESSEL: Well, Arch, when you work around those girls all day, it gets so that it means nothing... you learn to ignore the Betty Grables... Gene Tierneys...
ARCHIE: Who learned you to ignore them?
JESSEL: Betty Grable... Gene Tierney.

Episode #136 — Broadcast Tuesday, June 27, 1944
Guests: Ransom Sherman and Yvette
Plot: Ransom Sherman, who will have his own radio show this summer filling in the same time slot as *Duffy's Tavern*, is the final guest for the season. Duffy is closing the tavern for the summer and Archie sees a possibility that he will be hired for Sherman's new program. The show will be called the *Nitwit Court* so they put on a mock example of the radio show and Duffy overhears the program through the telephone. Duffy doesn't like it – especially since Archie made a crack about not having a raise.

UNITED STATES VETERANS ADMINISTRATION

Certificate of Appreciation

AWARDED TO

Ed "Archie" Gardner

IN RECOGNITION OF OUTSTANDING SERVICE TO U. S. WAR
VETERANS IN MAKING POSSIBLE THE OFFICIAL RECORDED
RADIO SERIES "HERE'S TO VETERANS" *Third Edition)*

Omar N. Bradley

GENERAL U. S. A.
ADMINISTRATOR OF VETERANS AFFAIRS

*One of many awards bestowed upon Ed Gardner
and* Duffy's Tavern.

CHAPTER SIX
DUFFY'S TAVERN
AND THE HOMEFRONT

THE UNITED STATES, CONCERNED WITH EVENTS in Europe and Asia, attempted to remain neutral by passing the Neutrality Act in August of 1935. As fighting overseas escalated, the threat of U.S. involvement was becoming a reality and, in March of 1941, the same month *Duffy's Tavern* premiered on CBS, the end of the neutrality policy came with the Lend-Lease Act, which allowed the U.S. to sell, lend or give war materials to nations the administration wanted to support. After the U.S. formally declared war on Japan on December 8, 1941, following the attack on Pearl Harbor the previous day, Germany and Italy declared war on the U.S. on December 11, 1941. The U.S. responded with a declaration of war on the same day.

The entertainment industry responded with full support. Hollywood movie studios created propaganda films to help aid in training of U.S. troops. Influential celebrities used their popularity to convince Americans to buy war bonds and stamps. Songwriters such as Irving Berlin, Johnny Mercer and Spike Jones lent their talent to produce a significant number of popular songs ranging from the patriotic to the sentimental. The radio industry donated talent and production staff to help aid the cause, also. The War Department got into the act by producing such radio programs as *Command Performance, Mail Call* and *G.I. Jive.* The major networks donated full use of their facilities to produce recorded transcriptions for direct shortwave transmission to service members, families and troops fighting overseas.

Beginning in November 1942, transcription discs of radio broadcasts, courtesy of the Armed Forces Radio Service, were shipped overseas for shortwave transmission. To accomplish this, exceptions were granted by every union and guild in the broadcasting industry. To avoid legal issues, commercials were cut out of the programs, then new openings and closings with new radio hosts were added. Chilling murder mysteries such as *Inner Sanctum Mystery, The Adventures of Nero Wolfe, The Adventures of Ellery Queen, Creeps by Night* and *The Adventures of the Thin Man* became part of the *Mystery Theater* (later re-titled *Mystery Playhouse* to avoid confusion with *Molle Mystery Theater*). To fill out the remaining time as a result of the editing process, two and three-minute previews of up-coming mysteries were sometimes offered.

Radio comedies were also recorded for the same service. Courtesy of the Special Service Division of the War Department of the United States of America, *Duffy's Tavern* radio broadcasts were included among the AFRS rebroadcasts. Beginning in December 1942, every episode of *Duffy's Tavern* was recorded for the troops overseas.* Because of the commercial deletion, the closing five minutes were usually devoted to "Duffy's Juke Box"

---

* On the March 19, 1942, broadcast of *The Kraft Music Hall,* starring Bing Crosby, the crooner proudly announced that beginning tonight, his radio program would be transmitted via shortwave to military posts around the world.

which featured three songs, "where the feet meet the beat." (In 1944, it was reported that the most popular programs among troops overseas courtesy of transcription discs were Jack Benny and *Duffy's Tavern*.)

In the spring of 1942, radio comedians began taking their programs on the road, with broadcasts originating from military bases across the country. From Camp Cook in California, the Great Lakes Naval Training Center, a U.S. Marine Base in Quantico, Virginia, and Ellington Field, Houston, troops were entertained with live stage performances before and during the scheduled radio broadcast.* Gorgeous beauties such as Rita Hayworth, Frances Langford and Betty Hutton reminded troops what they were fighting for. Radio comedians began cracking jokes about Hitler, Mussolini and Hirohito. On the evening of June 26, 1942, Bob Hope's opening monologue centered on gas rationing. On February 19, 1943, *Amos n' Andy* featured a comical look at volunteer work when Andy pays off his debts and goes to work at a war plant.

During the 1942-43 season of *The Kraft Music Hall*, Bing Crosby began a weekly tradition of conducting brief interviews with war heroes, sergeants, colonels, members of the clergy and other military personnel. For historians who enjoy listening to recordings of war-time radio broadcasts, yesterday's jokes and interviews have become today's history lessons. On *Duffy's Tavern*, such references began as early as the broadcasts of January 8 and 15, 1942. After winning $100 on a horse race on January 8, Archie spends half of his winnings on Defense Bonds, as explained on the broadcast of January 15. The following week, at the conclusion of the January 22 broadcast, a public service announcement was delivered. Dr. John F. Landon explained the baffling nature of infantile paralysis and how every dime donated to the local "Fight Infantile Paralysis" campaign would go marching off to the White House as a vote of confidence and loyalty. The March of Dimes. "The medical profession hopes that despite the National

---

* Radio broadcasts of *Duffy's Tavern* that originated from military bases are noted under their respective episode listings.

Emergency, the public will remain alive to the importance of contributing to the work sponsored by the National Association for the Prevention of Infantile Paralysis," Landon explained. The public service announcement took the place of Schick's usual closing commercial, a gesture on behalf of the sponsor. John Reed King, the announcer, closed the broadcast asking listeners to join the President's Diamond Jubilee Birthday Celebration. "Take your place in his crusade for the children of America. Fight Infantile Paralysis!"

Public service announcements and Government propaganda varied from rationing, volunteer factory work, bond drives, avoiding black market opportunities, and civil defense, often presented in humorous fashion so the message struck close to home. For the broadcast of January 29, Duffy tells Archie that his wife knitted socks for the American Red Cross and they insulted her. She knitted six pair of socks and they sent her a letter thanking her for twelve sweaters. Archie jokes, "She used her foot as a model."

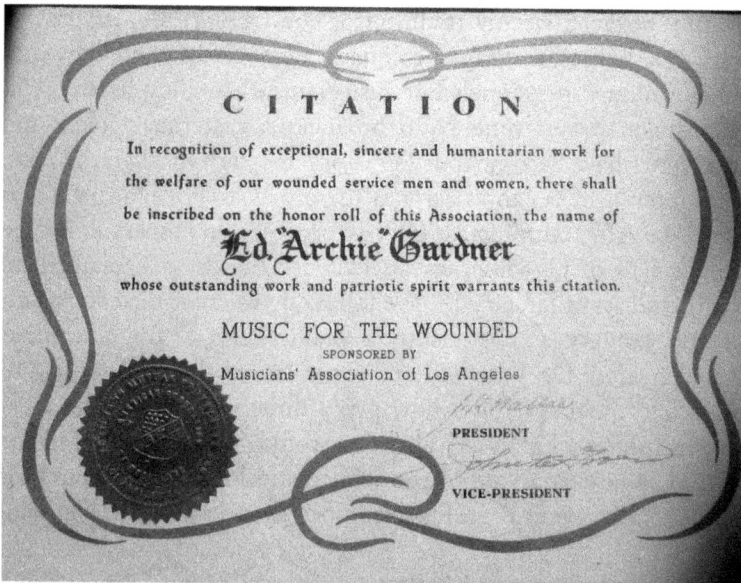

One of many awards bestowed upon Ed Gardner
and *Duffy's Tavern*.

For the broadcast of March 24, 1942, Archie attempts to make a fast buck with a man named Reynolds who is trying to sell black market meat without concern for rationing. On the broadcast of April 21, 1942, one of Miss Duffy's boyfriends, Breckinbridge Hartzempfeloer, is mentioned as being a battleship painter. At the close of one broadcast in May of 1942, Ed Gardner told his employer: "Buy war stamps and bonds. If President Roosevelt could see and talk to you, Duffy [pause without laughing — studio guffaws], he would say, 'I want you to invest ten percent of your wages in stamps and bonds.' A 25-cent stamp will buy 12 bullets. Buy til' it hurts, because it is gonna hurt Hitler more than it is gonna hurt you, Duffy."

During the broadcast of October 6, 1942, Finnegan describes to Archie his latest contribution to the war cause:

ARCHIE: Well, Clifton Finnegan! You're a sight to give a person sore eyes. How are you?

FINNEGAN: Just a second, Arch. (MYSTERIOUS) I got a secret. Are we alone?

ARCHIE: Yeah.

FINNEGAN: Who's that guy standing next to you?

ARCHIE: That's you, Finnegan.

FINNEGAN: Oh, that's okay. I'm all right.

ARCHIE: What's all the mystery about, Finnegan?

FINNEGAN: Arch, I've got the greatest military invention that's ever been invented.

ARCHIE: You have? What is it, Finnegan?

FINNEGAN: A tank that don't need gas.

ARCHIE: A tank that don't need gas? How does it run?

FINNEGAN: It's pulled by a horse.

ARCHIE: But don't the horse get tired?

FINNEGAN: No, he's ridin' in a jeep.

ARCHIE: But don't the jeep need gas?

FINNEGAN: No Arch, I got another horse pullin' the jeep.

ARCHIE: Wait a minute, Finnegan... I can't put my finger on it but there's a fallacy there some place.

FINNEGAN: Go ahead and ask, Arch. Where are you confused?

199

ARCHIE: Don't the horse that pulls the jeep that carries the horse that pulls the tank get tired?

FINNEGAN: But Arch, this is war… somebody has to make the sacrifices.

ARCHIE: Yeah, I guess you're right there. Mechanically it sounds all right, but sometimes these inventions don't work out in theory.

FINNEGAN: No? Take a look at this blueprint.

ARCHIE: Finnegan, I can't see anything. You used blue ink on blue paper.

FINNEGAN: That's to fool the enemy.

ARCHIE: Don't you think they can un-cipher this?

FINNEGAN: No, it's written in German.

ARCHIE: Why did you write it in German?

FINNEGAN: In case it falls in the hands of the Japanese.

ARCHIE: Falls into the hands of the Japanese? Finnegan, why don't you go home and commit suki yaki.

During the broadcast of February 16, 1943, announcer Dan Seymour commented: "Look Archie – do you realize that it only takes four twenty-five cent stamps to buy a hand grenade? A fellow up to his knees in mud with a Jap coming at him can't tell everybody to buy enough stamps to fill the empty spaces in their stamp books – and turn them in for books tomorrow."

An NBC press release dated November 23, 1943, reported: "There won't be any Santa Claus parades this year in Hollywood Boulevard, but the boys and girls are writing their customary letters. Here are three, reported by Ed Gardner, the guy who rings the cash register in *Duffy's Tavern*:

'Dear Santa: Please drop something down Winnie's chimney—you know what.'—Adolph.

'Dear Santa: Please bring me a face—and a better one—to save.'— Tojo.

'Dear Santa: Please send me a chimney and a sock that I can call my own.'—Benito.

For the broadcast of May 26, Eddie recited a limerick for the Lord Byron Ladies' Literary Society.

There once was a man went berserk,
To conquer the world was his quirk.
But Franklin and Joe,
And Winston said NO,
I's referring to Adolph, that jerk.

Marlene Dietrich was a guest on the evening of November 23, 1943, proving Archie's notions about inflation are as straight as a bedspring. Her pep talk to the tavern members and the radio audience was to help with NBC's Christmas campaign to sell War Bonds. Her message was brief, but emphatic. "Ladies and gentlemen, very soon Christmas will be with us again. Many of us will have a sad Christmas this year. All of us will have a heavy heart. For our men will spend Christmas in the front lines, in planes, and ships, on a beach under fire. We can send them our thoughts for this day that should be a day of peace. But our thoughts are not enough. Our prayers are not enough. We can help bring our boys back to our homes. Yes, we can. And we can give our troubled hearts the wonderful feeling that we are doing our duty here at home. We can go to bed on Christmas Eve with a clear conscience if, instead of having bought the many often so useless Christmas presents, we bought War Bonds. Give Christmas War Bonds to your friends and your family. Buy nothing but War Bonds. By doing so, you will make our boys happy. You will help all people to celebrate a real Christmas soon. You will help bring peace to the world." For this broadcast, Marlene Dietrich did not participate much in the comedy part and historians today might wonder if there was a reason. It was later revealed by Simone, Ed Gardner's second wife, that Dietrich was his "dream girl."

At the conclusion of the December 21, 1943, broadcast, Archie tells Duffy that a lot of soldiers are coming home for the holidays and "they ain't supposed to tell us nothin' and we ain't supposed to ask." For the radio listeners, this served as a holiday reminder that "a slip of the lip can sink a ship."

The January 12, 1945, broadcast was dedicated to the U.S. Government War Bond Program.

FINNEGAN: Hey, Arch, what's this inflation?

ARCHIE: Well, Finnegan, that's one of the main things that can happen if guys don't buy bonds and keep them.

FINNEGAN: Oh... Hey, Arch, what's inflation?

ARCHIE: Well, inflation is... Well, do you know what deflation is?

FINNEGAN: No.

ARCHIE: Well, inflation is just the opposite... Y'see, when the output of currency in this country becomes larger than the ingots of gold in Fort Knox... this causes circulation.

FINNEGAN: Well, that's obvious.

ARCHIE: Yes, now on the other hand, money is very sensitive to fluctuations because it's so legally tender, therefore should any demortization cause the gold standard to fall below the 14 karat mark, then consequently the dollar goes up — or rather down... causing prices to sour down — or is it up?

FINNEGAN: But Arch, how could War Bonds stop this inflation?

ARCHIE: Very simple. You see, war bonds is printed on the same kind of paper that money is... therefore, when you buy War Bonds you're taking this paper out of circulation and the government can't get paper to print new money with... ergo... this reduces the amount of out-standing exchequer... which in turn... ergo prevents inflation. See how simple it is?

FINNEGAN: Yeah... all I needed me was for somebody to put it in me own language.

Throughout the war, the scriptwriters also took time to voice public opinion against government propaganda. Throughout the early half of 1945, multiple episodes make reference to paper drives, the blackouts on Broadway and curfews on city streets, expressing an unessential point of view... masqueraded as humor. It was almost impossible for a radio listener not to be preached to, whether it be victory gardens, gasoline rationing or manpower and war production, and *Duffy's Tavern* offered a fresh new approach with an underlying message or moral — perhaps more than most radio comedies that tried to delicately poke fun of the subject matter in fear of reprimand from the Office of War Information.

In October 1944, a vital public service assignment was handed to the advertising and entertainment industry by the U.S. government. It was the campaign to educate the public on the treatment of discharged war veterans, sponsored by the Surgeon General's office of the U.S. Army and undertaken in cooperation with national advertisers both in radio and magazines. The campaign officially started on January 1, 1945, and many in the entertainment industry played an important role with public service announcements after the holiday — including *Duffy's Tavern*. Admitting the importance of past, present and future bond drives and the part played by show biz entertainers and the advertising markets, leaders in both fields considered the veterans rehabilitation campaign even more vital. Bond drives helped finance a fraction of the war and helped contribute to the battle against inflation, but the forthcoming educational campaign was seen as being far more dramatic because of the lasting effect it would have on the lives of thousands of ex-service men and their families.

Spearheading a large percentage of the advertising were drug and cosmetic manufacturers who reportedly gave five percent of their advertising budget to the campaign. This alone figured out to be a million dollar contribution. Subsequently, national advertisers in other industries were called on to do likewise. Bristol-Myers, owning some of the top shows in prime time, took advantage of the peak audiences with messages from the War Department, including Alan Young, Eddie Cantor and *Duffy's Tavern*. By means of the radio-magazine campaign, the War Department hoped to tell the public how to help ease veterans' return to civilian life. The campaign advised people not to comment on or stare at the physically handicapped, nor to make phony comments, which, while aimed at putting the men at their ease, serve to do just the contrary. It also counseled on the handling of psychotic and maladjustment cases. More than three broadcasts of *Duffy's Tavern* in 1945 featured public service announcements about veteran rehabilitation at the close of the program.

For historians of the Second World War, the public service announcements contained on many recordings of vintage radio broadcasts, including *Duffy's Tavern*, have become a living audio document of American history. Sadly, many public service announcements were downgraded as a result of timing. Red Cross announcements were eliminated during rehearsals when the program ran over the allotted 30 minute time frame, as evident when reviewing the original radio scripts. After all, the sponsors footed the bill and unless they forfeited the time devoted to their products, public service announcements were secondary.

Most radio programs were permanently stationed at one studio and, with few exceptions, usually originated from either the West Coast or the East Coast. *Texaco Star Theater* (1938-1940), an hour-long Wednesday night variety series, devoted a half hour for drama from New York and a half hour for music and comedy from Hollywood. *The Cavalcade of America* (1935-1953) originated from New York in the early years, later alternating every week back and forth from the West Coast to the East Coast, giving the sponsor access to more celebrities. Situation comedies, however, remained stationary on one coast or the other. Fred Allen originated from New York City; Jack Benny originated from Los Angeles. Exceptions were made during WWII when comedy programs, on occasion, originated from a military base. For a number of seasons, *Duffy's Tavern* was unique in that the series would switch from East Coast and West Coast in mid-season. This required the actors and scriptwriters to also make the move. Supporting actors often worked on more than one radio program throughout the season and this meant cast changes that often inconvenienced other radio producers. Alan Reed, for example, ceased playing Clancy the Cop when the program switched coasts in mid-season. The solution meant either finding someone else to play Clancy, or not feature the character altogether. The reasons for Gardner's move varied each season, but Gardner obviously had enough clout to force NBC to agree to his terms contractually.

In May of 1945, Ed Gardner and the cast once again made the transition from California to New York. The reason was two-fold. First, Gardner was departing from the Big Apple, days after the season finale concluded on the air, for a USO tour in Italy. Second, he would be able to attend business meetings with his sponsor and their advertising agency in an effort to negotiate next year's budget for the radio program. On May 7, Gardner began his feud with Young & Rubicam and his sponsor Bristol-Myers over the proposed budget for next season. Despite a $1,000 increase which he was certain of getting for the upcoming fall/winter stint, Gardner thought he should get an additional $1,000 on his talent budget to cover the growing cost of writers and actors. The proposed program budget, exclusive of agency commission, Gardner's take, guests and singers, amounted to something around $6,000 per week. He claimed that the expensive talent costs did not prevail when the deal was set. He felt that it would take at least $1,000 to adjust it.

Three weeks later, on May 21, stressed for time because of his overseas departure within two weeks, Gardner decided to re-negotiate and wanted an extra $1,500 a week plus an agreement by the sponsor that they would pay for thirteen guests outside the package price. Again, Gardner cited the increased cost of writers and actors as his reason for the demand.

Referred to by *Billboard* as "a general thorn in the side of Young & Rubicam," Gardner eventually received his $1,000 but Bristol-Myers would not go for the extra guest deal. Gardner then retaliated with a business venture that was certain not to be accepted by the sponsor. He planned to buy a brewery and produce, Bristol-Myers permitting, a new brand of beer called *Duffy's Tavern*. He asked the company for permission to use the name, figuring the whole scheme as a publicity stunt, and wanted the sponsor to angel part of the venture. Gardner indicated he would relinquish his annual demand for increased salary if Bristol-Myers would help him with his new brewery. The company was in the business of drugs, not beer, as verified in a letter addressed to Gardner dated June 3, 1945. In April 1945, Gardner had been telling the press he planned to open a Duffy's Tavern in Hollywood — another business venture that never met fruition because of Bristol-Myers' rejection. By this time executives at the advertising agency were indicating their suspicions of Gardner's promotional gimmicks, fearing the actor would "pocket a percentage of the funds if forfeited to him." Worse, if Gardner profited greatly from such business ventures, he might fund the radio program himself — cutting the sponsor out of the equation, promoting his own product.

Troops stationed overseas often painted their favorites on the sides of bombers.

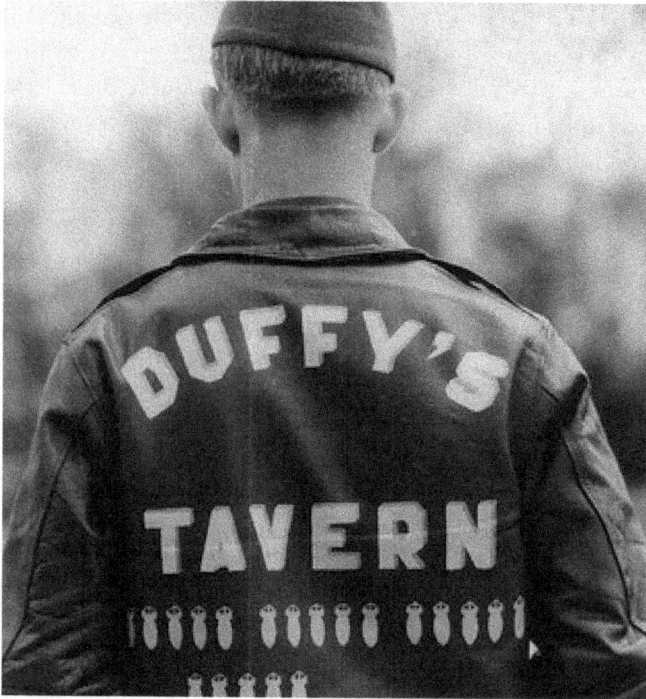

The back of a jacket worn by a serviceman in June 1945.
(Photos courtesy of Roy Bright.)

Solo War Benefits

Charles Cantor and Eddie Green reprised their roles from *Duffy's Tavern*, without the support of Ed Gardner, on many WWII platters recorded for the AFRS. The wartime variety programs were an exclusive treat for troops stationed overseas. For the *Command Performance* broadcast of April 22, 1944, Charles Cantor played the role of Clifton Finnegan in a fake quiz with actress Gene Tierney asking the questions. The answer to each question is George Washington but Finnegan is unable to come up with the correct answer.

On the March 21, 1945, broadcast of *Mail Call*, Cantor played Finnegan when Frank Morgan pretends to be an advisor to the lovelorn and hears Finnegan's recent romantic dilemma. On May 26, 1946, he played the role of Finnegan on *Command Performance*. On March 23, 1947, Cantor reprised the role again on *Command Performance*, offering his take on current events, explaining how he makes 25 cents a week, working 14 hours a day, taking care of a race horse.

Sandra Gould, Charlie Cantor and Eddie Green reprised their respective roles on a broadcast of *Mail Call*, recorded in the summer of 1945, in which Frances Langford paid a visit to Duffy's Tavern. Archie was away on a USO tour but the gang welcomed the singer and actress to the Tavern. Ray Milland also appeared on the same broadcast, while Langford served as the emcee. Harry Von Zell was the announcer. Since the series was exclusive to servicemen overseas, radio audiences in the U.S. never heard Langford as a guest on the *Duffy's Tavern* radio program until 1950.

In 1945, Charlie Cantor made numerous appearances on *Mail Call* and *G.I. Journal* in the role of "Half-Hitch," similar to Mel Blanc's "Private Sad Sack," a voice totally unlike that of Clifton Finnegan.

Request Performance

During the spring of 1945, radio producer Ward Wheelock wanted to create a domestic answer to *Command Performance*, following the same basic formula. Listeners here at home wrote in asking their favorite Hollywood stars to do offbeat routines on the air. During the summer of 1945, Wheelock created a package deal for the Masquers Club of Hollywood, spending a number of months negotiating with the War Department. The resulting series was titled *Request Performance*, figuring that because *Command Performance* was transcribed and played back only for troops overseas, there would be no confusion between the two programs. The idea had huge potential and became a true vaudeville show of the air. Requests for stars to appear on the program came from the home front instead of servicemen and when the idea was submitted to the War Department, the matter was referred to Colonel Tom Lewis, head of the Armed Forces Radio Service. Masquers was to furnish top stars and the program would contain a talent cost of $8,500 weekly. Masquers furnished the American Federation of Radio Artists (AFRA) with a letter assuring the union that Rule 15 guaranteeing a member his standard rate of pay would be adhered to and that there would be no pressure methods to acquire talent for the program.

The premiere episode of *Request Performance*, broadcast October 7, 1945, offered erudite leading man Ronald Colman in a sketch about New Orleans, featuring a duet with Colman and singer Frances Langford, titled "Come Down to New Orleans." Mel Blanc reprised his role as the unhappy postman from the George Burns and Gracie Allen radio show. Charles Cantor reprised his role of Finnegan from *Duffy's Tavern*, sans Ed Gardner. Various cast members from *Duffy's Tavern* would make frequent appearances on *Request Performance*, verifying the popularity of the situation comedy.

The WWII Performance Tour

During the summer of 1945, Ed Gardner spent six to eight weeks in and around Italy, performing his *Duffy's Tavern* act on stage for U.S. troops. Servicemen were treated to live stage performances with musical entertainment from harmonica player Larry Adler, singer Allan Jones, popular pin-up model Jinx Falkenburg, and comedy from Jack Benny. What isn't popularly known was what went on behind the scenes; relations were heated between Gardner and the USO Army Special Service. In early April, Gardner signed an agreement with the USO and, on June 9, the day after the final broadcast of the season aired over NBC, Gardner packed his bags and reported for duty. Frank Sinatra was originally scheduled to go on the same tour but the singer was relocated on a different tour. The highlight of the tour came in July when Ed Gardner, Jinx Falkenburg and the rest of the USO had the privilege of entertaining Pope Pius XII, head of the Catholic Church and sovereign of the Vatican city-state. Gardner later told reporters that he used his very best English "and the Pope understood me completely." The schedule of performances changed throughout the summer and Jack Benny himself later recalled how Post V-E Day shifting of troops caused unusual difficulties for Army officers in charge of arrangements.

Pressured with the knowledge that *Duffy's Tavern* was making a return to radio on September 21 and Paramount was attempting to arrange advance publicity for the motion picture due out in theaters before the end of the month, Gardner spent a good part of August and September publicly venting his disgust toward the USO. On August 3, the United Press International broke the news, quoting Gardner as blaming "a bunch of jerks" in the USO and Army Special Service for "lousing up" overseas performances. "Leave us not blame the poor actors," Gardner was quoted as saying, "It is these characters in the USO and Army officers who should be told a civilian life that is messing up everything for the G.I.'s and everybody else."

Trivia fans take note: As revealed on the broadcast of March 21, 1944, the fictional address for Duffy's Tavern is said to be 222½ Third Avenue.

Gardner claimed that the officials messed up so many shows that his act played to 100,000 men instead of 250,000. Citing an example, Gardner claimed the USO sent a telegram to the Italy Special Service on June 11, mentioning the actors would be available for shows on June 9. Gardner specifically charged that the USO in the Mediterranean theater was run by "a former adagio dancer who didn't know what he was doing and acted like his head was cut off."

"They had us playing *Duffy's Tavern* once to a group of 50 per cent British that let our jokes about Mel Ott fall flatter than a drunk at the tavern," Gardner complained. "I got backing on that, too. Allan Jones got booed by 10,000 troops because he gave a half-hour performance instead of a full hour act. The USO and the Special Service officers told him 30 minutes was the right time. Jack Benny and Larry Adler and 40 of their group were kept waiting in a room for an hour by a USO official who said he had an important message for them. They never did get the message or see the official."

Two days of reflection after returning to the States didn't change Gardner's opinion when, in New York, he was questioned by reporters and remained silent about the ordeal... except to offer one correction to the quotes attributed to him in dispatches. The wire stories had him saying that a Colonel David, whose first name he never found out, "is a very disinterested character who plays politics, so General Clark's headquarters and places like that get four shows a week. I didn't accuse Colonel David, or any specific person, of playing politics," the actor corrected. "Colonel David is in charge of Army Special Service there, and all I said was that there is a lot of politics being played in the Service. The actors play to 600 men instead of 6,000, and the GIs are not even notified ahead of time when some star is coming." Gardner admitted that the Army Special Service booked the acts, but the USO was just as responsible for "making it so a guy feels he should have stayed at home."

Adding to Gardner's complaints was a news bulletin reported by Bill Henry of the *Los Angeles Times* who wrote in his July 27, 1945, column: "Unless Archie had the presence of mind to take

Ed Gardner during the 1945 USO tour.

along a spare bartender's apron on his USO tour of Europe, he's lost the one with the wonderful collection of autographs. Somebody snitched the one he was wearing when he did his show at Fano, in Italy. The apron was priceless." Gardner made no mention publicly about the loss of his apron.

Meanwhile, in Rome, Colonel Leon T. David, chief of U.S. Army Special Services in the Mediterranean theater, declared that Gardner was "talking through his hat" in criticizing the USO and Special Services in Italy. The USO accused Gardner of being "miffed because they didn't roll out the plush carpet for him." Gardner retaliated by declaring that he didn't want "a plush carpet," but that he was interested solely in "bringing entertainment to the fellows who need it." Colonel David asserted that "it is not true that some outfits didn't see a show in two years. What is true, of course, is that some outfits didn't see all the shows they would have liked to see and that we would have liked to give them." He added that some shows, like Gardner's and Frank Sinatra's, were only in Italy a short time "with the result not as many people saw them as wanted." Colonel David also said that Special Service audiences totaling 5,500,000 attended 11,000 movie showings during June, which he declared was "better than three movies per week per man in this theater."

Myron Eicher, USO publicity director, said: "Gardner was always complaining the whole time he was overseas." Eicher also pointed out that the entire unit covered most of Italy, including a private audience with Pope Pius XII, who presented emcee Herb Bruce with a rosary.

Interviewed on arrival at Lockheed Air Terminal on August 4, Gardner said that when he arrived in New York, Lawrence Phillips, head of the New York USO, called him at his hotel and asked for a complete report on the conditions found overseas. Gardner ultimately refused to comply with the request because, he said, Major Schubert, head of the U.S. Special Services Office, had asked that the report be submitted directly to him, with the apparent purpose of investigating the continued derogatory remarks being made by returning USO troupes.

"I'm not doing this for any publicity," Gardner commented, "because I know it's going to leave a bad taste somewhere." Gardner did submit a report to George Murphy, head of the Screen Actors Guild, and included a recommendation that an investigation be initiated. Gardner told reporters that, in his opinion, the entire entertainment setup overseas was a "political football."

Daniel Dare, the associate producer of the upcoming *Duffy's Tavern* movie, sent Ed Gardner a telegram pleading for him to avoid the press, citing that such negativity would only damage relations between the studio and the USO. Ticket sales were important to the studio, Dare explained, having "backed the movie with our actors elite." He reminded Gardner that the studio would only consider a sequel to the film if negative publicity was avoided. It is apparent that Gardner ceased talking to the press (no further complaints appeared in the press after the date on the telegram) and Gardner began focusing on the new season of radio scripts.

BROADWAY RUNAROUND
by Radie Harris

A bon voyage party for Ed "Archie" Gardner (through the courtesy of Young & Rubicam) prior to his USO overseas tour. Ed stalled in California for two days, so that Jinx Falkenburg, who goes along with him, could have a 48-hour honeymoon with her groom, Col. Tex McCrary, before he, too, shoves off in the opposite direction — the Pacific. Both Tex and Jinx dropped in for a few minutes and spent most of those minutes being snapped by the lens hounds, which for Tex proved a tougher chore than anything he faced in the Pacific. He's that kind of a self-effacing guy! Jinx wore her happiness all over her and looked like an ad for Technicolor in a tomato red jersey sports dress. Ed dressed up for the occasion in his white apron with the autographs of every guest who has visited *Duffy's Tavern*. When the drinks were passed around, this "very good Eddie" waved the tray away airily and said, "I never touch the stuff!" His liquid diet now consists solely of Coca-Cola — the reason he was able to pass his physical. Seeing Ed again, I couldn't help but remember the time he was married to Shirley Booth, and they were in the midst of one of their frequent friendly separations. Shirley moved to the Algonquin and one evening Ed came to call. As he framed himself in the doorway, the sight that greeted him was a bevy of girls in various stages of negligee — a process shot from *Girl's Dormitory* (1936 movie). Ed took in the scene and then, turning to Shirley, popped this $64 question: "Tell me, darling, do you prefer marriage — or college?"

In the summer of 1948, Ed Gardner went back to work for the USO and it appears that relations were no longer strained. Gardner even brought back some happy

213

stories from his European tour. He broke up a G.I. show in Germany by walking on stage and saying, "You know, boys, I'm a subtle comedian." With that, his trousers dropped. A woman in Italy walked up to the comedian and congratulated Gardner on his *Duffy's Tavern* air show. "Thanks," said Ed, "and who are you?" Her reply? "My name is Lily Pons." On one particular evening Gardner was talking to Orson Welles, who was crying into his beer, in a Rome saloon. "What's the trouble?" asked the comedian. "It's heart-breaking," wept Welles, "I love this country but the people here don't love me."

War Time Duffy's Taverns

In 1945, Ed Gardner was nominated "the bartender we'd rather have wait on us when we come home" by a group of service men in the 58th Task Force which saw action in the Pacific. Gardner was notified of the nomination by Lieutenant Emil Frank.

During the Second World War, Ed Gardner received hundreds of letters from G.I.s stationed overseas, verifying that *Duffy's Tavern* had become a worldwide institution, with branches operating in Japan, Korea, Germany and Alaska as service clubs. In 1944, *Stars and Stripes* reported: "Replicas of *Duffy's Tavern* are popping up all over the various fighting fronts. The first was a palm-thatched hut on a South Seas island. Now they're everywhere, and Ed Gardner is sending autographed pictures to adorn their walls." Centering momentarily on the home front, according to a news blurb in the March 23, 1945, issue of *Variety*, "Since Ed Gardner debuted his air show, *Duffy's Tavern*, there have been more than three hundred restaurants opened with the name."

For the radio broadcast of November 10, 1948, the building inspector, Joe Moran (played by Marvin Miller), paid the tavern a visit and attempted to condemn the joint. Archie tried to propose to Mary Ann (played by Janet Waldo), a beautiful young girl, and

During the live broadcasts, Archie stood behind this small counter for the benefit of the studio audience, built and designed like one you would find in a real tavern. The phone Gardner used on the program when speaking to Duffy was a real phone, disconnected from the wall. He felt the realism of Archie holding a phone would convince the listeners that what they were listening to was authentic.

stretched the truth about his age, claiming he was much younger than he looked. When it came to providing the birth certificate, he was unable to fulfill the marriage plans. To teach him a lesson, Mary Ann revealed her occupation. She happened to be from the draft board and, courtesy of the Sergeant that accompanied her, Archie was officially drafted. This episode featured a brief behind-the-scenes explanation: the day after the broadcast, Ed Gardner flew to England in order to attend the fifth anniversary of Duffy's Tavern, opened in Bristol in 1943 by U.S. Army officers. His trip took a total of 60 hours travel time and he returned the day before the next broadcast — when it was then revealed that Archie escaped the draft when the U.S. Government discovered just how old he really was.

On January 1, 1945, tragedy struck home when Lieutenant Bernard C. Duffy of the Army Air Forces, whose Duffy's Radio Tavern at 296 West Fortieth Street in New York was supposedly the inspiration for the widely known radio program of similar name, was killed in Burma. On January 3, his widow was informed by the War Department that Lt. Duffy, an aerial photographer, was reported missing. It has since been established that he was killed when an amphibious tractor overturned during a reconnaissance mission through rapids of the Irrawaddy River, according to Arthur Mazzone, then manager of the tavern. A member of the enlisted reserve, Bernard Duffy entered the service soon after the bombing of Pearl Harbor. In 1942, he was stationed in Great Britain, where he escaped death during an airplane crash in Scotland. He was transferred to Burma in 1944.

New York City newspapers throughout the 1980s and 1990s featured a number of articles about a number of Duffy's Taverns that ultimately closed shop, claiming to have been the inspiration for the radio program. One located at Third Avenue and 23rd Street, another at the corner of Third Avenue and West 40th Street. The sources for those articles were never revealed but the fact remains: the radio program was never based on a real tavern. In fact, legal research went into the program before the *Forecast* audition to avoid any connection with a real tavern and risk a lawsuit.

Beginning October 2, 1942, LaHiff's Tavern at 158 West 48th Street in New York City, a famous watering hole during the Roaring 20's for celebrities, journalists, authors and sports figures (especially prize fighters), changed its name to Duffy's Tavern, named for William "Billy" Duffy. William Duffy died in 1934

216

but the new owners wanted to cash in on the rising popularity of the radio program. Ed Gardner sought legal action to prevent the name but because the former owner was actually named "Duffy," Gardner was advised not to pursue an issue that would likely be ruled against him. Years later, the name reverted back to LaHiff's Tavern.

Jinx Falkenburg and Ed Gardner during the USO tour.

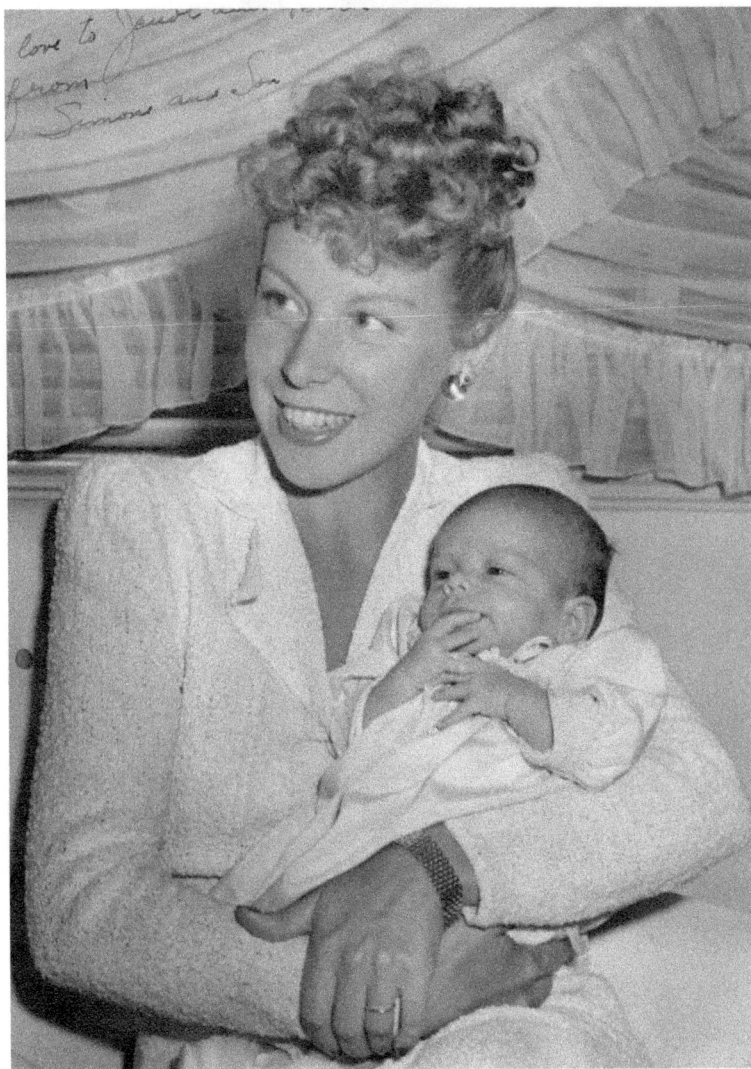

Simone Gardner and her second son, Stephen.

Simone and Ed Gardner, Jr.

Ed Gardner, Jr. spends time with his father.

Ed Gardner, Jr. spends time with his father.

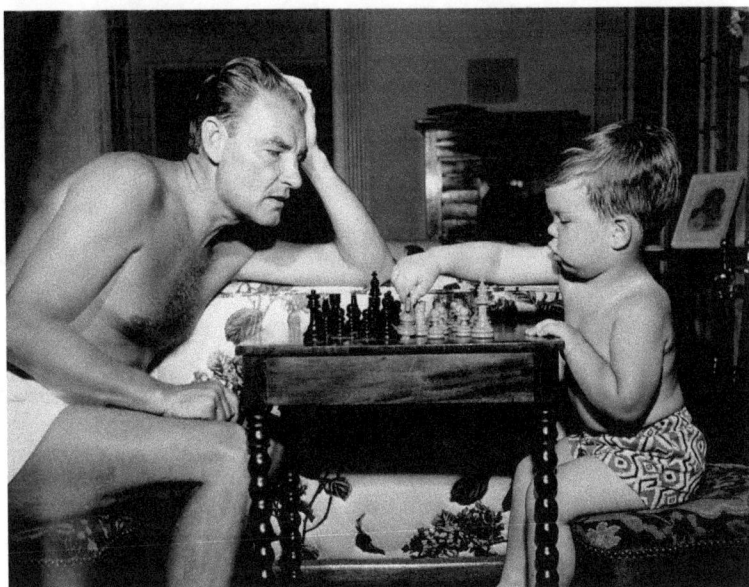

Ed Gardner, Jr. spends time with his father.

Grandma Martha Rogers (Simone's mother) proudly holds Stephen.

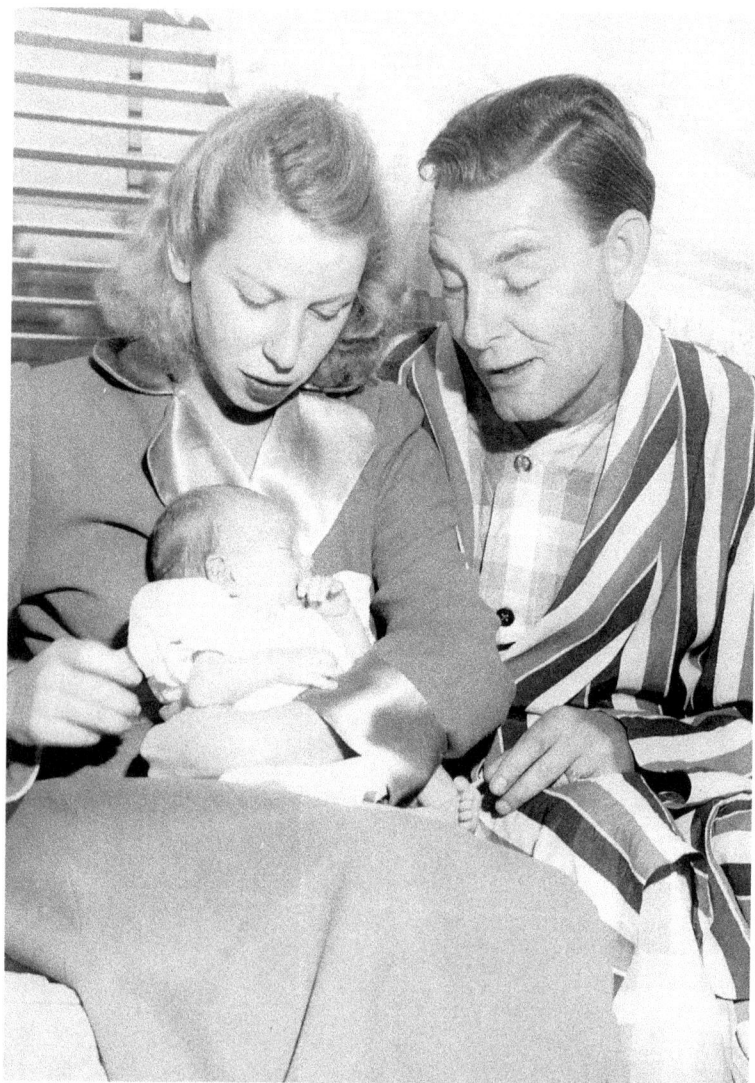

Simone holds Stephen, the Gardners' second son.

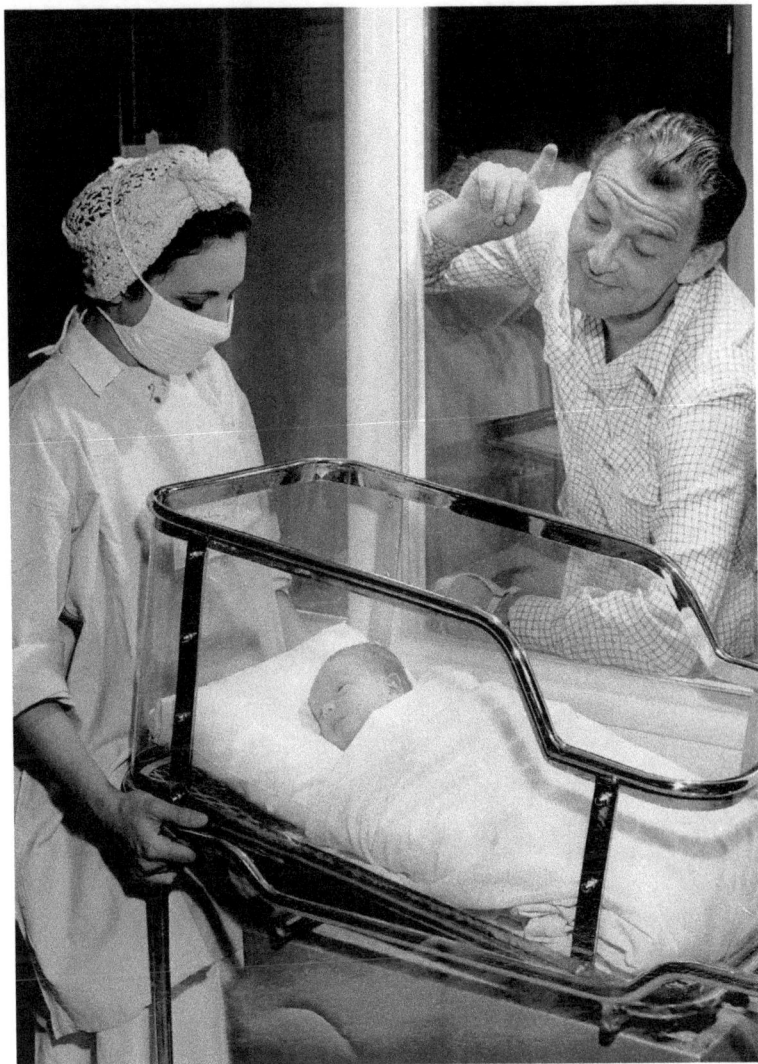

Stephen Gardner on his birthday.

Ed Gardner, Jr. and his father.

Stephen with the family dog, Duffy.

Ed Gardner, Jr. with Anything (the pit bull) and Duffy.

Ed Gardner, Jr. plays with his father.

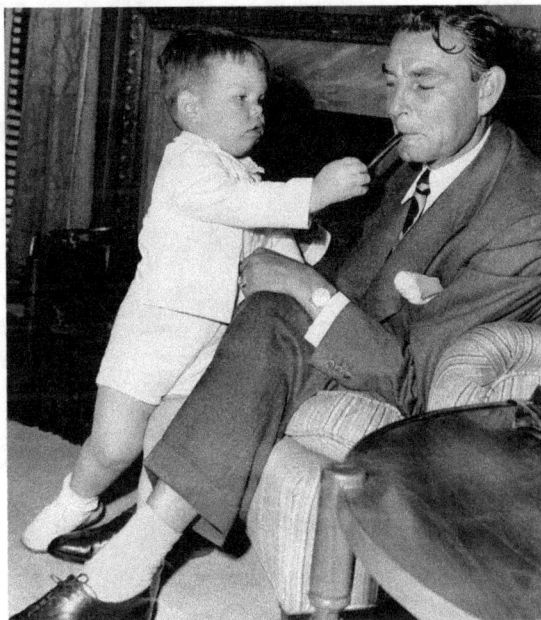

Ed Gardner, Jr. plays with his father.

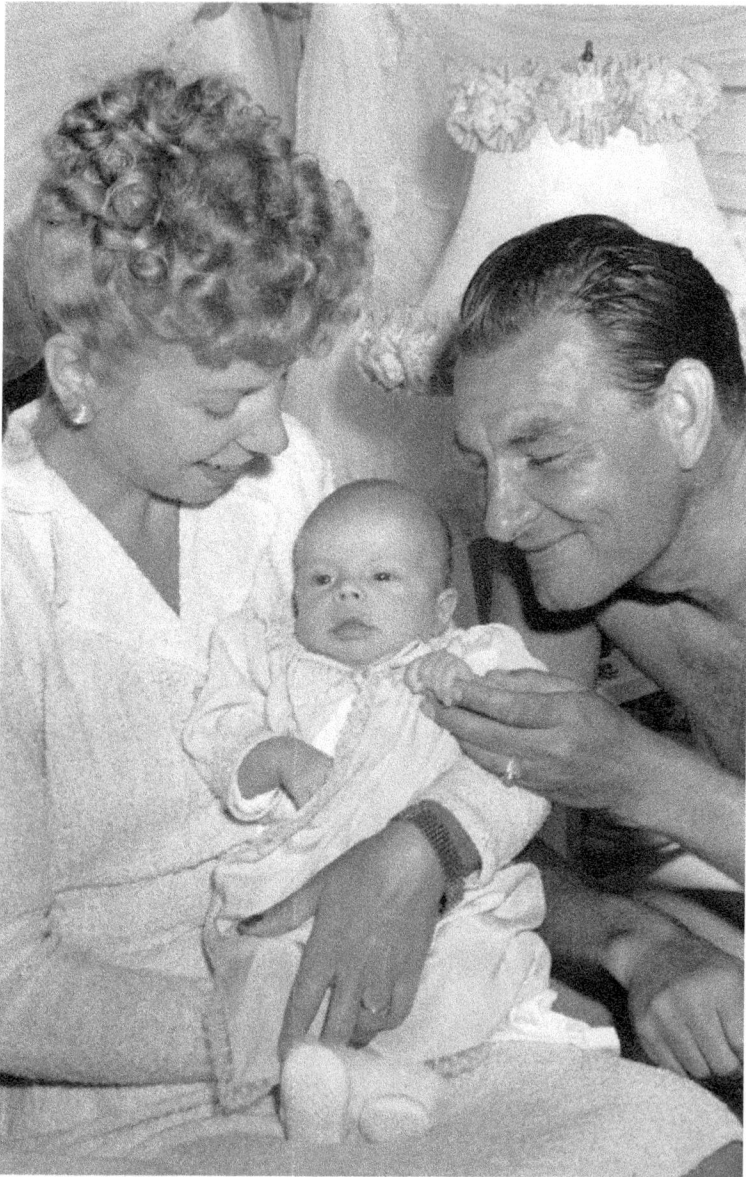

Stephen Gardner and his proud mother.

Ed Gardner, Jr. being introduced to baseball.

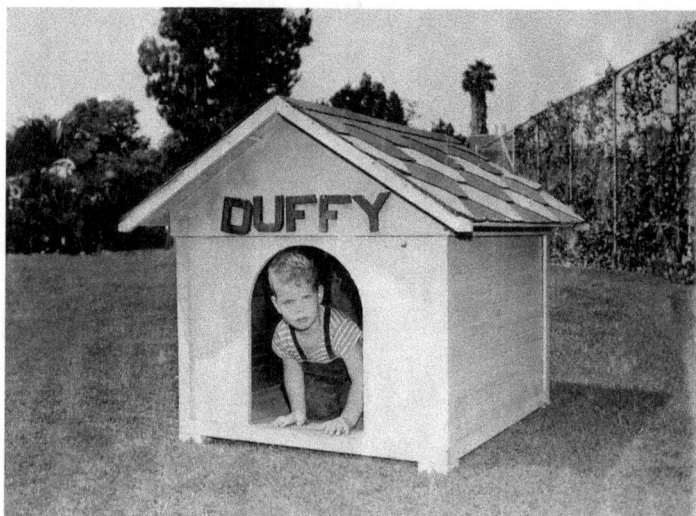

Ed Gardner, Jr. spends time with the family dog, Duffy.

CHAPTER SEVEN
THE FIFTH SEASON
(1944 - 1945)

FOR THE PROGRAM'S FIFTH SEASON, the series moved from the Tuesday night time slot on the Blue Network to Friday nights on NBC, filling the time slot formerly occupied by *The Adventures of the Thin Man*. In its three years under varying sponsorship, *Duffy's Tavern* and its denizens had built a sizable following and since the pattern remained unchanged, a la cookie cutter format, there was no reason why the show wouldn't do well on a different evening and a different network. The ratings remained strong but the principal problem with the show was that it had become too formulaic. The question now was how long that formula could be milked for laughs by Ed Gardner and his writers.

One of the reasons for the move from one network to another was a provision in Ed Gardner's contract which said he would get first crack at available time on NBC or CBS. Gardner, according to the agency, wanted to travel in bigger company than the Blue

Network.* The contract, signed on April 1, 1944, renewed *Duffy's Tavern* with Bristol-Myers for 52 weeks, effective October 1944. It was an unusual proviso that permitted Gardner to cancel at any time he was successful in securing a better spot on another network.

The network switch was the result of Eddie Cantor's radio plans, which were in a state of flux, with Cantor insisting that his sponsor, Bristol-Myers, agree to certain conditions laid down by the comedian (including a $5,000 pay hike). He insisted that the drug firm release him from his contract, which still had a year to run. Cantor had been dissatisfied with the present setup and its $10,000 salary for some time and, in a move to bolster the program, he hired one of Jack Benny's former scriptwriters, paying a reported $2,000 a week! In late March 1944, Cantor publicly admitted he would grab a three year contract, with better coin, now dangled before him by Colgate. The agency representing Eddie Cantor was sweating bullets. If Cantor grabbed the Colgate sponsorship, he would switch from the Sherman Marquette Agency to the William Esty Agency. But there was no loophole that could legalize the switch. Though Cantor would have liked to grab the Colgate offer, his present contract bound him to another year with Bristol-Myers.

By late July, Eddie Cantor reached a compromise agreement with executives at Bristol-Myers. His program remained untouched and unchanged on the Blue Network. *The Alan Young Show*, the summer replacement for Eddie Cantor's time slot, was given a seasonal time slot as a permanent addition to the Bristol-Myers stable, formerly occupied by *Duffy's Tavern*. Gardner successfully made the switch from Wednesday to Friday night as a

---

* The move to NBC was an effort to cover a larger area of the country because NBC offered more radio station coverage. Ironically, *Duffy's Tavern* enjoyed a top rating on the Blue that was not duplicated after the switchover to NBC. Hindsight being clear and effective, Gardner's decision to jump networks sacrificed the top rating for larger coverage.

result of General Foods, who relinquished the NBC Friday night time, which was grabbed by Bristol-Myers.

The new season was scheduled to begin on the evening of October 6. With Paramount insisting that on-air promotion of the *Duffy's Tavern* movie begin immediately on the same radio program, and a New York City premiere on September 5, the radio program took its bow three weeks earlier than initially intended. In mid-August, Dorothy Lamour, Betty Hutton and Ray Milland agreed to appear on the radio comedy to help promote the movie. Ray Milland was unable to attend that season after all. Lamour and Hutton's schedules were so busy that they were unable to appear on the radio show early in the season (Hutton appeared in mid-season). During the closing, the announcer stated that Dorothy Lamour appeared courtesy of Paramount Pictures, but pitched *Rainbow Island*, not *Duffy's Tavern*.

During the summer of 1944, radio actor Alan Reed invested his paychecks in a brewery and successfully signed with an agency to have his own radio program, *The Falstaff Show*, broadcast three times a week. Promoting his own line of beer, the Falstaff Brewing Company, he arranged for guest singers and an orchestra to supply the music. It was here that Matty Malneck and his orchestra caught the attention of Ed Gardner, who arranged for them to appear on *Duffy's Tavern*. Alan Reed had no qualms about Gardner "borrowing" the same orchestra, especially since Reed first caught sight of Malneck through evening band remotes. Hollywood actor Joe E. Brown, however, felt differently. Brown believed he had "discovered" Malneck and his orchestra when he signed them for an "exclusive" deal for his radio program, *Stop or Go*, a radio quiz program. During the first few weeks of the 1944-45 season, while Malneck waved the wand on *Duffy's Tavern*, he underwent different billing as "Don Dugan and his Orchestra" (such as the October 6, 1944 broadcast). The alias was eventually dropped after a number of broadcasts.

Two weeks before the new season began in September, Ed Gardner was feuding with Young & Rubicam about the dough he was to get for the new season of *Duffy's Tavern*. Chief bone of contention was not the agreed upon sum, according to an inter-office memo, but Gardner's feeling that adding more sidemen to the orchestra would mean less dough for him. The advertising agency felt that Matty Malneck's orchestra should have been at least 10 or 12 pieces in order to provide proper musical background, fanfare and arresting opening signature. Gardner's belief was that it would cut his earnings despite the agency's insistence that the orchestra building was for the good of the program. A compromise was ultimately made: the elimination of the as-yet-unsigned-but-planned-upon weekly singer. Malneck's entire band consisted of ten men. An accomplished violinist who supplied musical accompaniment for Charlotte Greenwood and Bob Crosby's radio programs, Malneck proved his worth on the season premiere.

Ever since Ed Gardner produced Rudy Vallee's radio program in 1940, the two had been good friends. It comes as no surprise that Vallee made a guest appearance on the premiere episode which the September 20, 1944, issue of *Variety* reviewed: "...on the debut show with Rudy Vallee as guest, the laughs all stemmed from the same familiar ingredients: Archie's malapropisms, Miss Duffy's perennial man-hunt, Finnegan's boobery, the ever-present proprietor, Duffy and, since Vallee was guesting, his curly hair, Yale and nasology. These have been the laugh-sources since the show became commercial in '41 and since its sameness helped kill vaudeville, somebody on the *Duffy* production staff ought to start thinking about these gimmicks wearing thin. Might be that the film now in the works on the Paramount lot will give the show a shot in the arm along the idea vein. From a performance standpoint, the radio bistro's regulars are tiptop. Gardner, the Canarsie kid, is a natural Archie; Cantor's Finnegan is a boob par excellence, and Eddie Green as the tired, skeptical waiter, is a strong toll for the toughest job in the cast, following Shirley Booth as Miss Duffy. Suffers by comparison."

John K. Hutchens, radio editor for the *New York Times*, felt differently and hailed *Duffy's Tavern* as one of his ten "favorite programs."

In early November, Bob Graham, recently out of the Army, was signed by Ed Gardner to a five-year contract as a featured vocalist on *Duffy's Tavern*. It was Gardner's intention to have the singer make an appearance in the motion picture, but Paramount nixed the idea. Graham made a guest appearance on the October 27 broadcast, and Gardner took to the singer's vocal chords and talents within minutes. When Paramount declined Graham, Gardner went to another movie studio, 20th Century-Fox, and convinced them to sign the snub-nosed handsome singer to a contract. Gardner collected a "finders" fee, provided Graham make a minimum number of appearances on *Duffy's Tavern* to help build up his name. Graham was the first crooner to be signed by 20th Century-Fox after Dick Haymes left the lot and shared honors with David Wayne as Mitzi Gaynor's leading man in *The I Don't Care Girl* (1953). Music director Alfred Newman sent for him to record a duet with Jane Froman for *With a Song in My Heart*.

The Scriptwriters

The third broadcast of the season, September 29, 1944, featured guest Risë Stevens, the famous Metropolitan Opera mezzo-soprano. Jackson Stanley, who put in a couple of years writing for Red Skelton, and worked alongside John Guedel and Art Linkletter in the creation of *People Are Funny*, signed on as a new scriptwriter for Ed Gardner. His first assignment, under the guidance of Abe Burrows, was the Risë Stevens broadcast. As Burrows had guided all of the other scriptwriters before Jackson, he wrote a brief treatment and Jackson was assigned the task of writing the script (including adding jokes throughout). The treatment, dated September 18, 1944, is reprinted below.

Archie tells Duffy that Risë Stevens is coming down to the Tavern and he thinks a dame like Stevens, being a big opera star, will lend a lot of prestige to the joint. When Duffy asks Archie what she looks like, Archie says, "Well, you've seen them opera

237

Risë Stevens

stars" — he's never seen Stevens but she's probably just another one of those big fat dames.

In the first spot Archie is starting to decorate the joint for Stevens — opera style. He tells Eddie that he is going to turn the charm on Stevens, even though the job will be distasteful, because "them big opera dames ain't no joy to look at." But he is willing to do it for the sake of the joint. Eddie asks him slyly if he saw *Going My Way*. Archie says no.

Finnegan comes in and discusses opera with Archie. Then

Miss Duffy arrives. She is anxious to sing for Risë Stevens, and Archie cheerfully offers to break her neck if she does.

After the first commercial, Archie goes out for a moment with Eddie, leaving Miss Duffy alone in the place. This leads into Matty Malneck's number. Following Malneck's number, Risë Stevens walks in and meets Miss Duffy. Miss Duffy tells Risë of her operatic hopes, hits her with a note or two, and then goes out leaving Stevens standing by herself. Archie comes back in, sees Stevens and is very much attracted to her, but he doesn't know who she is. We do this by him going right up and making a quick pass at her, in which pass he lets drop the remark that he wishes Stevens looked like her instead of a big fat opera star. After this, Stevens isn't going to tell him who she is even if he drops dead.

He continues to decorate the joint but he can't get his mind off this girl and he is back with her again. All the time while he is making love to her he is insulting Risë Stevens.

Duffy keeps calling up and asking where is Stevens. Archie says she hasn't shown up yet. Archie asks his lady-love if she is working and she says not regularly and he says gee, if she could only sing he could get her a regular job in Duffy's. He speaks to Duffy and persuades him to give his new girl friend an audition. Duffy agrees. Stevens sings an operatic number. When it is all over, Archie sighs and says too bad — she's so pretty and attractive he could have gotten her the job if she only had a voice.

He asks would she give him her phone number. She says yes, she'll write it out for him. She writes it out for him, hands it to him and walks out and he sees her name written down. (This is one possible payoff.)

Jackson Stanley then proposed a possible angle for the climax. All during the last act, Finnegan thinks he recognizes Stevens. He would swear he has seen her somewhere, but he just can't quite place her. Archie encourages him to identify the dame, as he would like to know her better. After denouncement, Archie is very mad at Finnegan for not having recognized Stevens sooner. Finnegan could have saved him all the embarrassment, particularly since Finnegan comes in all excited after Stevens has left, claiming he has just remembered where he saw her.

ARCHIE: Why didn't you tell me she was Risë Stevens?
FINNEGAN: Risë Stevens, Arch? That ain't Risë Stevens. It's the hatcheck girl at the Bijou Theater.

Stanley wrote six pages of the script, then contacted Burrows saying he couldn't do it. He simply was not capable of writing comedy for a show that required composing witty one-liners within days. After learning that Stanley was unable to complete a single script, Gardner insulted him in front of the other scriptwriters. After one week's service on *Duffy's Tavern*, Stanley quit.

Abe Burrows quickly pounded out a feasible radio script, which pleased Ed Gardner. On the evening of September 29, Archie decides once again to "cuss up the joint," this time with opera and invites Risë Stevens from the Metropolitan Opera. When she shows up, Archie mistakes her for someone else and thinks she's an out-of-work burlesque performer. (He refers to her as "Toots La Shore.") Quite impressed that she can sing opera, Archie ends up embarrassed upon learning her true identity because earlier in the evening he called her "Fatso." Miss Duffy, meanwhile, has taken up singing lessons from Prof. Yasha Panyaslovnik, again, and the teacher suffers a breakdown. The broadcast offered Risë Stevens an opportunity to stretch her vocal chords by singing "Sequidilla" (from Bizet's *Carmen*).

New Miss Duffy

With a new season came a new Miss Duffy, Florence Robinson, who was performing at the Mayan Theater in Los Angeles, a former movie palace, playing the role of a movie-struck small-town kid in Lawrence Riley's *Personal Appearance*, a ten-year-old satire on Hollywood. Ed Gardner and his wife, Simone, went to watch the play and after the performance, at the insistence of his wife, Gardner made his acquaintance with the actress. In early July 1944, Florence Robinson signed a contract to play the role of Miss Duffy. Like others before her, Gardner controlled the option to fire her with the understanding that she was hired on a weekly basis, with no long-term guarantee of employment. During rehearsals, Gardner was unrelenting in his strive to perfect the voice of Miss

Sandra Gould
(Photo courtesy of Steven Thompson)

Duffy. Robinson was supposedly driven to nerves and bowed off the show after ten broadcasts.

Sandra Gould, billed as "one of New York's top comediennes" in New York papers, having recently given birth to a son, and following her short stint as a regular on *The Jack Pepper Show* under the direction of her husband, Larry Berns, a producer/ director at CBS, flew back to California to resume her radio career. The Miss Duffy offspring slot was given grief ever since Shirley Booth (ex-Mrs. Gardner) ducked and according to inter-office memos, executives at Bristol-Myers were certainly getting frustrated. Executives encouraged Gardner to tone down the role in future broadcasts until he finally made up his mind. Married to a producer/director, Sandra Gould was used to moving back and forth from coast to coast, which might have been one of the factoids that appealed to Ed Gardner. Gould not only proved she could pronounce the words in Gardner's favor, she played the role longer than any other actress in the history of the radio program. (From December 25, 1945, to January 4, 1949, during her tenure on *Duffy's Tavern*, Gould played the part of "Mitzi," Judy's friend, on radio's *A Date With Judy*, and occasionally substituted as "Judy" when Louise Erickson was absent.)

Sir Heathcliffe Batterswick

Added to the weekly rotating cast of characters was Sir Heathcliffe Batterswick, an English comedian, played by Alan Mowbray of stage and screen. Mowbray's screen distinction was playing a butler in many movies, but he was known to the Hollywood elite as one of the founding members of the Screen Actors Guild. The two-year deal for *Duffy's Tavern* began when he made his first appearance on the broadcast of February 23, 1945, revealed to be an old friend of Archie's, a comedian who has recently returned from a successful tour. He was residing in New York for a spell so he could write his memoirs of the theater, "the Drury Lane, the Old Vic... and *Command Performance*." Archie hired the comedian to perform at the tavern for five bucks a week and Heathcliffe looked forward to a long engagement. Here, the comedian was able to tell stale and corny jokes for which Gardner's scriptwriters could not find a use. On the program, Archie would later be tricked into paying him ten bucks a week for ten weeks on the evening of March 30, 1945. Mowbray's appearance on the program was cancelled prematurely when the actor signed with producer Scott R. Dunlap to appear in *Sunbonnet Sue* for Monogram Pictures, and began shooting his scenes during the final week of April. His last appearance on *Duffy's Tavern* was on the evening of April 20.

Alan Mowbray and Nigel Bruce pose for the camera during rehearsals.

Robert Benchley

On the evening of November 10, 1944, humorist Robert Benchley drops by the tavern, Archie describes him to Duffy as "the guy's got a great kisser for comedy... looks sorta like a surprised cantaloupe." Archie is putting on a party to officially launch Bob Graham, even though the boy has been singing on the program for a couple of weeks. Archie believes they have another Sinatra. Benchley, helping Archie with the festivities, delivers a lecture on crooning. Graham, meanwhile, asks for a raise. Fifteen dollars a week is not enough. Bob Graham sings "April in Paris."

"One of the biggest moments for me on *Duffy's Tavern* was the time that I actually got to write a monologue for Robert Benchley," recalled Abe Burrows. "When Benchley agreed to be a guest, he startled us by saying he didn't want to do any of his standard material; it was up to us to provide him with something new. I was frightened but excited too. I had begun to tire of the regular weekly routine and the thought of writing a guest spot for Robert Benchley really sparked me. He liked my monologue; when he did it on the air, it went beautifully and it sounded like him. The Hollywood *Variety* reviewed that show and they said something like 'With all the junk we hear on comedy shows, it was a relief to hear Bob Benchley's great humor on *Duffy's Tavern*.' Benchley immediately dashed off a telegram to *Variety*. He told them that he had not written the monologue, that 'it was written by Abe Burrows, America's greatest satirist.' I knew damned well that I wasn't the greatest anything and I also knew that Benchley was being whimsical; but when I read this wire in *Variety*, I began to think that maybe I could be something besides whatever I was. Later on, when I started performing professionally, Benchley worried about me. He told me not to let performing interfere with my writing. He said that once he started acting in movies, he stopped writing. The acting was very demanding and it seemed to use up his creativity. Then, typically, after this confession he quickly told me a story to change the mood. He said that when he started acting he told his friends he was 'throwing away his typewriter.' The word spread and finally the New York *Herald Tribune* had a sad editorial about this. The editorial said it was a tragedy that Robert Benchley was throwing away his typewriter. I said that was a helluva tribute and he said. 'Nonsense, Burrows. The only response was that the *Tribune* got about two hundred letters from people who needed a typewriter."

Larry Gelbart

Beginning with the broadcast of April 27, 1945, Larry Gelbart's initial contribution as a scriptwriter for *Duffy's Tavern* is clearly

The Gardners welcoming the New Year with Hollywood celebrities.

evident. Gelbart's father was a Beverly Hills barber, who trapped Danny Thomas in his chair one afternoon, giving the comic a running account of his 16-year-old son's genius at making wisecracks and gags. Every joke was emphasized with a wild waving of the blade. Thomas lay helpless in the chair, his face splattered with lather. "Send your boy over to see me," he whispered weakly. Thomas was ultimately impressed with Larry's work and turned him over to an agency. The result was that Larry signed to write for *Duffy's Tavern* at $50 a week, a bonanza for a 17-year-old high school senior.* A financial bargain for Ed Gardner. By 1951, at the age of 23, Gelbart was writing for Bob Hope. In 1972, Gelbart was one of the main forces behind the creation and formation of the television series, *M*A*S*H**.

---

* Bill Manhoff, another of Gardner's scriptwriters, began working for Gardner when he was 23 years old.

After finishing a brief time with Danny Thomas and his radio show, Gelbart was signed with an agent, George Gruskin, at the William Morris Agency. Ed Gardner hired Gelbart on an open-ended arrangement. He could hire and fire him at any time. "Owner of the program, able to hire and fire, Ed Gardner did a good deal of both," Gelbart wrote in his autobiography, *Laughing Matters* (1998, Random House, Inc.) "He was most mercurial, to say the least, in his selection of writers. When under the influence, which is where he spent 80 to 90 proof of his time, he went from mercurial to maniacal, creating a revolving door through which writers went after he paid each as near to a pittance as he could manage."

It didn't take the young man long to discover that $50 a week was not sufficient. At the time Gelbart was hired, Abe Burrows departed from *Duffy's Tavern* and Bill Manhoff took his place as the head writer. Gelbart was partnered with Sid Dorfman at the time, learning his craft, creating storylines, loose situations to hook the program's continuing cast of characters for the half hour, and the art of coming up with a script every week and completing it on time. After working for Ed Gardner just over two years, Gelbart received a fan letter from his draft board. It seemed the Army couldn't get along without him. Both Dorfman and Gelbart asked for a jump in salary, at least $100 a week for Gelbart's last two weeks with the program. "I was getting to know very quickly what happens when an agency handles a package. That is, if they are handling a star, they are not likely to ask for more money for the writers that are represented. That rattles relations with the star... I think we both said we wanted $250 a week each. And Ed said, 'No, out of the question.' We said we'd have to quit. He said, 'Okay, no hard feelings.' Later on that same day he went to the reading of the next week's show and when we didn't show up, he said, 'Well, to hell with them. They're fired.' But I am not putting it down. He was one of the best teachers I've had along the way. The biggest lesson was having fun with language."

Larry Gelbart once told a story involving Monty Woolley's appearance behind the microphone. In the three hour span between the first performance (for the East Coast) and the repeat performance (for the West Coast), Woolley and Gardner went to Brittingham's fabled bistro adjacent to the CBS studios at Columbia Square. There the pair consumed, according to one estimate, 20 martinis. During the late show performance (which was regularly done without a live studio audience), Woolley fell down on the floor, the script clutched in his hands. "Ed, the ever-thoughtful host, got down on the floor with him and they finished the program lying on their sides, both smashed." Woolley only made two appearances, June 22, 1943 and December 22, 1944. Considering Gelbart's writing credits start in January 1945, and the holiday festivities would provoke heavy drinking, the latter broadcast seems more credible. The name of the bistro, however, remains questionable since the series was broadcast over NBC at the time, not CBS.

In March 1947, Lee Sterling of NYC wrote to the *New York Post*, "Too many comedians say, 'Leave us follow the *Duffy's Tavern* formula and emphasize ungrammatical remarks. Bad grammar should be clearly labeled a joke. Radio is going to dilute the mother tongue."

Archie, the school teacher

247

Since their stock in trade was verbiage, this fact should have been familiar to Phil Baker and Ed Gardner, but as early as November 1944, it was clear that isolated incidents got both men into trouble. Schoolteachers would, on occasion, submit a letter complaining how the program was destroying the education taught in the classrooms. Those same performers should also have known that the expression "loused up" was not synonymous with "poorly delivered," when applied to a joke. Its use may have been overlooked in private conversation, perhaps, but on the radio it was apparently regarded in extremely bad taste, judging by the number of letters the studio and the sponsor received during any given week. It was enough to warrant public concern.

Columnist Harold Parrott had dinner with Ed Gardner in New York City one evening and later reported the actor spoke just as he did in real life as his radio persona. "Archie's bouts with the English language are wonderful," he remarked. "The other night he said, 'Leave us not brandy woids,' and in talking of Miss Duffy's forthcoming marriage he said the bride had to make up her 'torso.' But I thought you would like to know what happened when Archie (Ed Gardner) was in Brooklyn for one of the early games of the World Series. In a local bar, later, he was introduced as Archie of *Duffy's Tavern*. 'Leave me hear you talk,' said the bartender. Archie spoke, and the bartender said: 'You ain't Archie. You ain't got the same denunciation.'"

Ed Gardner at the Oscars

On the evening of Thursday, March 15, 1945, Hollywood forgot all about the recent strikes, jurisdictions and other dramatic doings for a few hours and galloped through the Oscar derby during the 17th Academy Awards. The show got off to a technical start, which was all right for the technicians but not very hilarious for Joe Public, who did not realize that the technician was the man behind the curtain who made it possible for stars to pay those abnormal income taxes. The show then turned from technicalities to verbal acrobatics when Ed Gardner took over as emcee for the first half of the program in his best Third Avenue dialect and introduced the Andrews Sisters who, in turn, introduced a couple of tunes never heard before except in 1,500,000 juke boxes. The selections were "Don't Fence Me In" and "Rum and Coca-Cola." Next came Danny Kaye, who put on a one-man show illustrating the art of motion picture production in dear old Moscow. During the second half of the program (the half that was broadcast), Bob Hope drew a lifetime membership to the Academy, followed by his emcee job as the awards were handed out. For the radio audience listening in on ABC (then recently renamed from The Blue Network), the first half of the ceremony featuring Ed Gardner was never heard.

Besides his famous apron, Ed Gardner took advantage of his residency in California to solicit autograph requests from his celebrity guests. Charles Coburn, Gene Tierney, Milton Berle and Jennifer Jones, among others, autographed glossy photographs which Gardner collected. Most simply signed their name but when Orson Welles signed a glossy to Gardner, he inscribed, "Dear Ed, Here's looking at you and sometimes unavoidable and always an experience, Orson Welles."

SEASON FIVE
September 15, 1944, to June 8, 1945
National Broadcasting Company
Sponsor: Bristol-Myers
Broadcast from Hollywood, Studio C and B at NBC
East Coast broadcast: Friday, 8:30 to 9:00 p.m., EST
(East Coast performance at 5:30 to 6:00 p.m., Pacific Time)
West Coast broadcast: Friday, 8:30 to 9:00 p.m., EST
Director: John F. Roche
Music: Matty Malneck and his Orchestra
(September 15 to October 6, 1944)
Music: Bert Reeves and his Orchestra
(October 13, 1944, to April 20, 1945)
Music: Matty Malneck and his Orchestra
(April 27 to June 8, 1945)
Singer: Jerry Cooper (October 6, 1944)
Singer: Bob Graham (October 27, 1944, to February 23, 1945)
Singer: Marek Windheim, former grand opera star
(May 18 and May 25, 1945)

Bob Graham was not featured on the broadcast of January 26 to make room for Lauritz Melchior.

Announcer: Jack Bailey
(September 15, 1944, to March 30, 1945)
Announcer: Perry Ward (April 6 and 13, 1945)
Announcer: Michael Roy (April 20, 1945, to June 8, 1945)
Scriptwriters: Abe Burrows, Larry Gelbart, Bill Manhoff
and Jackson Stanley
Producer: John F. Roche

Cast
Charles Cantor as Finnegan
Eddie Green as Eddie
Florence Robinson as Miss Duffy
(September 15, 1944, to November 17, 1944)
Sandra Gould as Miss Duffy
(November 24, 1944, to June 25, 1947)
Alan Mowbray as Sir Heathcliffe Batterswick
(February 23 to April 27, 1945)

Episode #137 — Broadcast Friday, September 15, 1944
Guest: Rudy Vallee
Plot: Back from his summer hiatus, Archie and the gang welcome guest Rudy Vallee, the entertainer who recently returned from his stint in the U.S. Coast Guard. Archie gets the idea of turning Duffy's Tavern into a makeshift nightclub where he and Vallee perform vaudeville patter. Rudy Vallee performs on the saxophone, sings "Time Waits for No One," and Duffy phones to tell Archie he is not impressed. To prove his worth, Vallee attempts a mock radio interview with Archie.

Episode #138 — Broadcast Friday, September 22, 1944
Guest: Gene Tierney
Plot: When Finnegan buys insurance from a shady salesman

named Sam Hancock and names Archie as the beneficiary, the ever flirting and gold digging Archie plans to stage an "accident" so he can raise enough money to take film star guest Gene Tierney out to the Stork Club. Archie figures Finnegan will get food poisoning from the tavern's free lunch but Hancock refuses to pay, citing that since Finnegan ate the food willingly the insurance company would not be able to pay out for an "attempted suicide." Matty Malneck and his orchestra perform "Dance with a Dolly." The closing announcement informed listeners that Gene Tierney appeared courtesy of 20th Century Fox, and could be currently seen in *Laura*.

Episode #139 — Broadcast Friday, September 29, 1944
Guest: Risë Stevens
Plot: See pages 237 and 240. Matty Malneck and his orchestra perform "It Had to Be You."

Memorable Lines
EDDIE: What does that mean in dollars and cents?
ARCHIE: Plenty, Eddie, plenty. The dough's gonna flow like milk and money.
EDDIE: The only thing that flows around here is rain through the roof.

FINNEGAN: Say, Arch, you left the bathmat out.
ARCHIE: Bathmat! Finnegan ... That's the flush carpet!
FINNEGAN: I seen the letters ... B - A - T -

Episode #140 — Broadcast Friday, October 6, 1944
Guest: Nigel Bruce
Plot: When Archie's shady friend Dave Hossinger starts a TV network, "Hossingervision," he cons Archie and guest Nigel Bruce (known for playing Sherlock Holmes' sidekick, Watson, on radio and in films) into writing and performing a mystery play starring Archie as The Purple Dragon (inspired by *The Green Hornet*) and Nigel Bruce playing the role of Dr. Simpson. When a man visits the estate and drops dead of scarlet pimpernels, The Purple Dragon and his sidekick investigate. Jerry Cooper sings "Stardust."

Nigel Bruce and Ed Gardner

Episode #141 — Broadcast Friday, October 13, 1944

Guests: Bill Tilden (tennis player) and Babe Didrikson (famed female athlete)

Plot: When Dave Hossinger sells Archie on the idea of expanding Duffy's Tavern into being an Athletic Club, complete with steam rooms and masseurs for men, Dave is naturally going to defraud Archie, since the expense of shipping athletic equipment to the tavern costs money. Archie tries to get guest stars Bill Tilden and Babe Didrikson to invest in it. Tilden questions the fire codes and Archie tries to impress him with Flash Robinson, the pinball champ of Third Avenue. Jack Stone, Archie explains, unofficially broke the world's record for the pole vault. He was never mentioned in the papers because "when a guy goes over the wall at Sing-Sing, he don't invite the press." Archie's efforts succeed but when he discovers Dave is conning him, Archie laughs. Dave's friend is conning him too. Bert Reeves and his orchestra play "Tico Tico."

Trivia, etc. Due to a line break, the program was partially heard East of Las Vegas, Nevada, from 8:31:36 to 8:55:08. Babe Didrikson was not available to do both the East Coast and West Coast broadcast, so two different scripts were used that evening. Didrikson was not heard on the East Coast version.

Memorable Lines
ARCHIE: Finnegan, this is Big Bill Tilden, the famous tennis champ.
FINNEGAN: I'm quite aware of that, Arch. I once seen Mr. Tilden play in the Forest Hills Stadium.
ARCHIE: Finnegan, how did you happen to go to a tennis match?
FINNEGAN: The word "Stadium" fooled me, Arch… I thought I was sneaking in to see the Tanks.
TILDEN: We get more people that way…

Episode #142 — Broadcast Friday, October 20, 1944
Guest: Dorothy Lamour
Plot: Finnegan comes into money and is willing to give it to Archie if he can arrange for him to get kissed by actress Dorothy Lamour. Breaking continuity by forgetting Finnegan had a romance with other Hollywood starlets in past broadcasts, it is explained that Lamour would be Finnegan's first kiss. This arrangement proves quite convenient when Archie wants Finnegan's money for a down payment on an engagement ring. Archie has plans to propose to the same woman. Naturally, this double-cross backfires. Dorothy Lamour sings "Beloved."

Trivia, etc. This broadcast originated from the San Bernardino Army Base in California.

Episode #143 — Broadcast Friday, October 27, 1944
Guest: Esther Williams
Plot: Finnegan reveals his love for Henrietta, the taxi driver he met on his date with Dorothy Lamour after last week's events. Archie strikes out with swimmer/ MGM star Esther Williams and tries to set Finnegan up with her in the hopes of unloading the cheap engagement ring originally intended for Lamour. But Finnegan

loves only Henrietta and won't even look at Esther Williams or buy the ring for her. Williams, disappointed, gives Finnegan her phone number in the hope that the lovesick puppy turns his eye toward swimming beauties.

Trivia, etc. Charles Laughton was originally scheduled for this broadcast, since it was announced the week prior that he would be the guest. The missing guest star is used as a punch line to a joke. Esther Williams filled in for Laughton, courtesy of MGM, and a plug is given to her next film, *Thrill of a Romance*.

Episode #144 — Broadcast Friday, November 3, 1944
Guest: Maria Montez
Plot: After witnessing Finnegan's string of luck with famous movie actresses, Archie believes he's lost his own sex appeal and "animal maggotism," and invents an outlandish story about the worthless engagement ring and the jewelry having a curse on it, in order to make himself more exotic to guest Maria Montez, Hollywood's hot-blooded Latin seductress featured in many swashbuckling screen adventures. Bob Graham sings "What A Difference A Day Made."

Episode #145 — Broadcast Friday, November 10, 1944
Guest: Robert Benchley
Plot: See pages 243 and 244.

Memorable Line
ARCHIE: What a wit! You know, I love your kind of humor… dry, witty, droll, subtle and yet with that certain somethin' that keeps it from being funny.

Episode #146 — Broadcast Friday, November 17, 1944
Guest: Ida Lupino
Plot: With Archie's legal mind, the manager of Duffy's Tavern tries to draw up a contract to secure the permanent services of Bob Graham, the new singer. When Ida Lupino arrives, Archie and the actress recall their fond days of the theater in England… which were not too fond as Archie recalls. When Lupino hears Bob

Graham sing, she offers the lad more money and a bigger career in Hollywood. To counteract, Finnegan pretends to be Graham's father and Archie tries to negotiate between the two. When she leaves the tavern, Archie tries to change the deal from fifty to six dollars a week.

Trivia, etc. Gracie Fields was originally scheduled as a guest for this broadcast, to help promote a new radio program with a new comedian, Fred Brady. For reasons unknown, she had to pre-empt her appearance and the script was later broadcast in December when Fields was able to appear before the microphone.

Episode #147 — Broadcast Friday, November 24, 1944
Guest: Harold Peary, a.k.a. The Great Gildersleeve
Plot: Archie wants to open a new floor show with Bob Graham as the star... and he hopes to have a revolving stage built. When The Great Gildersleeve arrives, Archie tries to convince the smart businessman to put up some capital. Graham, meanwhile, confesses he is going to college during the day. Archie swears if he can pull the deal off with Gildersleeve, the boy will have enough dough to start his own sorority. Gildersleeve has no interest until Archie mentions the chorus girls. To demonstrate, Archie and the gang put on the "Sawdust Capades of 1944," with Eddie Green singing "Buttercup" and Archie attempting to duplicate Dunninger's mental act. Gildersleeve won't put up the money until he hears Miss Duffy, his new love, sing. When this finally happens, he insists she marry an air raid warden.

Episode #148 — Broadcast Friday, December 1, 1944
Guest: Larry Adler
Plot: With Christmas only 24 days away, Archie questions if Duffy will give them all a bonus... and Archie and Eddie share a good laugh. Dave Hossinger shows up selling Christmas gifts at wholesale prices and, once again, Archie falls for another con game. Larry Adler, the famed harmonica player, drops by the tavern and Archie tries to convince him to perform with Bob Graham for a new floor show. Adler performs "Begin the Beguine." When Archie discovers the stolen goods were fake (most of them made

of candy), he tries to throw the bum out. Bob Graham sings "The Day After Forever."

Episode #149 — Broadcast Friday, December 8, 1944
Guest: Charles Laughton
Plot: Eddie is concerned that he cannot afford a new fur coat for his girlfriend. Archie wants a new Christmas tree for the tavern since the old one is five years old and held up by suspenders. When Archie learns that actor Charles Laughton is coming by to check out the place, he writes a screenplay in the hopes of selling it to Hollywood with a little support from the actor. "The Dutchess and the Pirate," a slur on literacy, crosses an old pirate tale with modern day battle maneuvers. Laughton says he won't buy the script until Archie fleshes the screenplay into a feasible shooting script and "bring it around to me and I'll shoot you." Bob Graham sings "Embraceable You."

Memorable Line
ARCHIE: Well, Charles Laughton! Eddie, get him a turkey leg... make him feel at home.

Episode #150 — Broadcast Friday, December 15, 1944
Guest: Sydney Greenstreet
Plot: Archie describes the large character actor Sydney Greenstreet to Duffy as "sort of like a Mata Hari... only this is a much fatta Mata." Eddie still needs money for a mink coat for Sonia Jones while Miss Duffy hopes her new boyfriend gets her a mink coat. Dave Hossinger shows up, claiming he owns a mink ranch, and Archie discourages Eddie from making a purchase. "There's something Danish in Denmark," Archie remarks. When Greenstreet shows up, jokes about Peter Lorre (the actor's frequent co-star) and "The Malted Falcon" are tossed about liberally. To help clear the air about Hossinger, Greenstreet agrees to work with Archie in a little skullduggery. Greenstreet poses as the biggest criminal in the international underground and, after Hossinger confesses his scheme, Greenstreet decides to rub him out... until he sells the real mink for $25. After Dave Hossinger leaves, Greenstreet discovers it's a cheap imitation rabbit and Archie is down $25.

Episode #151 — Broadcast Friday, December 22, 1944
Guest: Monty Woolley
Plot: Archie receives a package from Duffy marked "Do Not Open Until Christmas." Meanwhile, bearded Monty Woolley stops by the tavern and Archie tries to convince the actor to play the role of Santa Claus for the Christmas Eve party. Woolley isn't accepting of the idea at first until he is placed on the spot in front of a youngster, Wilfrid, Finnegan's kid brother (the black sheep of the family because the young boy has brains). When the youth insults the actor, an explanation is provided: why try to fake Kris Kringle to an educated man of eight? Archie explains to Wilfrid the spirit of Christmas, moments before he opens the package and starts screaming about the cheap gift.

Episode #152 — Broadcast Friday, December 29, 1944
Guest: Gracie Fields
Plot: To prepare for the New Year's party, Archie contemplates hiring a bouncer and Eddie is elected, and then demands a recount. With no girlfriend to take out to the party, Gracie Fields proposes to go with Archie, but he turns her down (he was hoping for Lana Turner or Paulette Goddard). Fields arranges to go out with Finnegan instead. Archie arranges to go out with Peaches La Tour, a striptease artist. Archie is happier when he discovers Peaches hasn't a thing to wear.

Episode #153 — Broadcast Friday, January 5, 1945
Guest: Jinx Falkenburg
Plot: While Duffy's Tavern is entertaining the Navy Construction Batallion, Archie prepares for a visit from Jinx Falkenburg, "the kind of an outdoor girl you want to take indoors." Disappointed from receiving so many rejections, Archie swears a New Year's resolution to remain a spinster... until Jinx Falkenburg arrives and shows interest in Archie. After Jinx talks about her recent tours overseas entertaining U.S. troops, Eddie, Finnegan and Miss Duffy help Archie maintain his New year's resolution by giving the appearance that Archie is already married and has twelve children. When Jinx receives an offer from the Seabees to check out a New York nightclub, she leaves Archie pondering his thoughts.

Jinx Falkenburg during rehearsals.

Trivia, etc. This program was broadcast before an audience of Seabees of the Navy Construction Battalion at Camp Parks, in Pleasanton, California.

Episode #154 — Broadcast Friday, January 12, 1945
Guest: Boris Karloff
Plot: When Clancy the Cop says there is a competition among the taverns in New York to sell more bonds than the others, with a major prize in the wings, Archie writes a horror play in the hope Boris Karloff will star and encourage tavern members to buy war bonds. "Young Monster Malone" tells the story of two mad

scientists, Dr. Frank and Dr. Stein, creating a monster (played by Finnegan) known as inflation.

Trivia, etc. The original title of Archie's play was "A Monster Was Born." The spoof on radio's *Young Doctor Malone* was improvised during rehearsals, as evident on the original scripts, marked in pencil by Ed Gardner himself.

Episode #155 — Broadcast Friday, January 19, 1945
Guest: Linda Darnell
Plot: Archie plans to ask Linda Darnell to the Policeman's Ball. As Archie explains to Finnegan, "Wait'll them bulls see them calves." Photos of the actress in her bathing suit are considered "a beautiful endorsement." Darnell, however, has a crush on singer Bob Graham so Archie masquerades as the 19-year-old. The actress wants to hand deliver an award to Graham and Archie's rendition of "Leave Us Face It" doesn't convince her. When Clancy the Cop tells Archie that he sold a ton of tickets to the Ball because everyone wants to see Linda Darnell, then learns Archie blew his one and only chance, he knocks the manager out.

Trivia, etc. During the broadcast of January 19, 1945, announcer Jack Bailey made the following announcement: "We are pleased to announce that in a poll conducted by the Daily Trojan of the University of Southern California, the editors of over 300 college newspapers have chosen Bob Graham as the outstanding singing discovery of 1944."

This episode features a thoughtful plea to help donate to the March of Dimes.

Memorable Line
EDDIE: Er — Pardon me, but would you people mind moving your conversation to another table? There's a customer trying to sleep under this one!

Episode #156 — Broadcast Friday, January 26, 1945
Guest: Lauritz Melchior
Plot: Archie writes a Western song and believes operatic tenor

Lauritz Melchior is the perfect choice to sing the song... and buy it outright for a hundred bucks. "That Melchior's got a throat like a horse... be great for Westerns," Archie explains. To convince his guest, Archie rigs a series of fake Western Union telegrams to give the appearance that movie studios are clamoring for the rights. Melchior sings "Leave My Heart Ride Tonight on the Prairie" amidst a brief Western sketch, spoofing cowboys and their horses. When a telegram from MGM is signed by Finnegan, Melchior sees past the ruse and leaves.

Episode #157 — Broadcast Friday, February 2, 1945
Guest: Sonny Tufts
Plot: Archie's new song, "Leave My Heart Ride Tonight on the Prairie" is about to be sold to the Million Dollar Publishing Company, as a result of a magazine advertisement Archie answered the other day. He pays the fee from the cash register, against the protests of Eddie. Miss Duffy wants to ask Sonny Tufts to a dance, and tells the actor that her father keeps the tavern for laughs as "a morbid sense of humor." The actor rejects her advances. When Eddie returns from the post office, explaining he never posted the fee or the application because he saw a poster of the president of the publishing company and a $1,000 reward, Miss Duffy tells Archie he can keep the money if he takes her to the dance. He promptly puts the money back in the register.

Trivia, etc. This episode opens with "The following program is being specially recorded to be sent to American servicemen in German prison camps and will be distributed by the War Prisoners Aid of the YMCA."
　　During the closing announcement, the announcer explains that Sonny Tufts appeared courtesy of Paramount Pictures, and Tufts could be currently seen in the Paramount production, *Here Come the Waves*.

Episode #158 — Broadcast Friday, February 9, 1945
Guest: Robert Benchley
Plot: The Lord Byron Ladies' Literary Society is meeting at the tavern and Robert Benchley delivers a lecture. While Finnegan

and Archie debate over Shakespeare and the Encyclopedia Britannica, Mrs. Piddleton arrives and Archie insults her in standard form. Benchley's latest book, *Inside Benchley*, receives a hearty promotion. Archie surprises Benchley when he reveals a lecture he wrote himself, comforting the humorist with the knowledge that there "ain't many big words." The lecture doesn't go off as planned as Benchley, reading Archie's script, talks about the cavemen and their stone books, American literature and the greatest Russian of them all... Ivan Hoe. Benchley proposes to Archie they co-write a book together titled "Outside Benchley," and the humorist promptly leaves.

Trivia, etc. Twice in the broadcast of February 2, Archie made reference to Betty Hutton being guest on next week's broadcast. Her appearance was in conjunction with Sonny Tufts, both of whom were co-stars of *Here Come the Waves*, presently in theaters. She was unable to attend the broadcast and Robert Benchley took her place. Because the script for Hutton was tailor made for her appearance, a last-minute brainstorm involved a re-write of the broadcast of June 15, 1943, with Clifton Fadiman delivering a lecture about American Literature to the same society. In fact, the entire lecture Benchley delivered was verbatim.

At the close of the broadcast, Archie tells Duffy that Betty Hutton came down with a cold and it was hoped she would attend in a week or two. Sadly, this never happened.

Archie closes the broadcast with an important message from the U.S. Government, claiming the Merchant Marine needs more men. "Well, with things cooking the way they are over in Europe, and the tough fight ahead of us in the Pacific, we gotta keep getting supplies over to the guys. That takes ships and to sail them ships you need plenty of guys. The Merchant Marine has got to have about 5,000 new guys every month, especially Mates, Engineers and A.B.'s, so if you know anybody that's a Mate, an Engineer or an A.B., tell 'em to apply at once by wiring collect to Merchant Marine, Washington, D.C., and tell 'em to give their ratings and their addresses. And another thing, Duffy, tell 'em that any of 'em that joins up is fightin' for his country just as any soldier with a gun."

Memorable Lines

ARCHIE: In the meantime, what about having a bite to eat?

MRS. PIDDLETON: No thank you, Archie. I find food unnecessary. Literature provides all the nourishment I need.

ARCHIE: Come, come, Piddy, you didn't get them hips from Longfellow.

Episode #159 — Broadcast Friday, February 16, 1945
Guest: Xavier Cugat
Plot: The Brooklyn atmosphere takes on a Latin-American air when Xavier Cugat, rumba king, arrives at the tavern. Because Cugat is playing out in Hollywood at the famous nightclub, "The Crockadero," Archie does his best to convince "the Latin Spike Jones" to play at Duffy's. Dave Hossinger returns to the tavern and swears he is a new man, having been psychoanalyzed and finding out his crookedness was a neurosis. Archie convinces Hossinger to rig a crooked roulette wheel in the tavern, despite gambling being illegal, and hopes to profit from the scheme. Cugat plays the wheel and wins… forcing Archie to answer the phone, "Cugat's Tavern."

Episode #160 — Broadcast Friday, February 23, 1945
Guest: George Sanders
Plot: Because George Sanders, known for playing "The Saint" in the movies, is stopping by the tavern, Archie digs out an old mystery script about The Purple Dragon, adapting it for the movies, hoping Sanders will participate. Sir Heathcliffe Batterswick, in the meantime, shows up at the tavern and is hired at five bucks a week to be a comedian on stage at Duffy's. During the mystery sketch, The Purple Dragon (George Sanders) is revealed to be an enemy of the underworld who, with his friend and partner, the famous Green Spider (Archie), attempts to thwart a murder schemed by The Pink Death. After the crime is committed, they "grill the dame" (Miss Duffy) and Pierre (Finnegan), the French headwaiter, is revealed to be The Pink Death. Sanders' recommendation? If Archie wants to show off his whodunit, "don't tell them you done it."

Ed Gardner and Joan Blondell

Episode #161 — Broadcast Friday, March 2, 1945
Guest: Joan Blondell
Plot: Grammar school can be a very lonely place for a boy of 18, Archie explains as he goes through an old scrapbook of mementos including a threatening letter from a girl's father and the first valentine he received from Finnegan. Heathcliffe returns to perform comedy on stage, including old, stale jokes such as the customer who asks if they have any frogs' legs and the waiter says, "No, I only walk that way." Archie suspects the jokes are enough

to make Milton Berle want to steal them himself. When Finnegan finds a photo of Archie's old girlfriend, Olga Hammerschlag, he suspects movie star Joan Blondell changed her hair color and went into show biz. Believing he can hypnotize someone, Archie tries to hypnotize Blondell into kissing him and Blondell sees past his scheme and plays along... until Clancy the Cop mistakenly thinks Archie is molesting the young lady and he gets smacked in the head with Clancy's club.

Episode #162 — Broadcast Friday, March 9, 1945
Guest: Ginny Simms
Plot: Eddie discovers that his girlfriend, Sonia Jones, is cheating behind his back. Sir Heathcliffe knights Archie and the barkeep goes from a bum to a duke. When Heathcliffe once again tells horrible standup comedy, Duffy wants Archie to fire him and the barkeep does his best not to fire the comedian. Archie tries to impress band singer Ginny Simms by acting like a Duke and Finnegan interferes until Ginny Simms sees past Archie and claims she is the "Fifty-second Duchess of Batter-wacky."

Memorable Lines
MISS DUFFY: By the way, Miss Simms, I love that cigarette program that you do for the servicemen... If I came down some night, could you get me some?
SIMMS: Cigarettes, Miss Duffy?
MISS DUFFY: No, servicemen, Miss Simms.

Episode #163 — Broadcast Friday, March 16, 1945
Supporting Cast: Frank Nelson (Clancy the Cop)
Guest: Pat O'Brien
Plot: Discussion about how fat Miss Duffy's mother is leads to Archie claiming "you can't make a zephyr out of a heffer." It's Duffy's 35th Anniversary and relations between husband and wife cause Duffy to disappear. This concerns Archie, who spends his time at the tavern trying to impress Hollywood actor Pat O'Brien, who claims he is Irish. The cast deliver eulogies to Duffy, all with hilarious results. When Duffy is found outside the window,

threatening to jump, it takes a while for Archie to remember Duffy lives on the first floor.

Trivia, etc. This same script was restaged with Pat O'Brien and the cast of *Duffy's Tavern* on *Pabst Blue Ribbon Town* on the evening of November 2, 1945.

Memorable Lines

CLANCY: Mr. O'Brien, I envy your wonderful life in Hollywood. That's for me some day when I get too old to go hunting around for crap games… What's it like?

O'BRIEN: Well, I'll tell you, Clancy. During a typical day you'll be floating around in a swimming pool, Ann Sheridan comes up, puts her arms around you, squeezes you, kisses you…

CLANCY: And then?

O'BRIEN: Then the director yells "cut" and you go out and hunt around for a crap game.

Episode #164 — Broadcast Friday, March 23, 1945

Guest: Dame May Whitty

Plot: Phineas T. Stone, a banker, shows up at the tavern to deliver the bad news. The place is always having riots and fights and is patronized by nothing but hoodlums and rowdies. For this reason, the bank will not renew the lease. Archie proposes hiring Dame May Whitty to offer a dignified hostess to keep the peace around the joint. Whitty agrees and forces Eddie to start mopping the cobwebs from the ceiling, demands Miss Duffy stop chewing gum, improves Archie's grammar and smacks Finnegan with a broom handle when he swears. When Clancy arrives at the tavern, Archie takes advantage of a possible solution and claims the old lady is Baby-Faced Whitty and Clancy takes her in.

Episode #165 — Broadcast Friday, March 30, 1945

Plot: Archie promises Duffy an all-star revue after being convinced that his con man friend, Dave Hossinger, has gone straight by becoming a theatrical agent who can bring big stars to Duffy's Tavern. Hossinger promises Eddie Cantor, Dinah Shore, Jimmy Durante, Bing Crosby, Bob Hope and Charlie McCarthy. But after a huge crowd gathers at the tavern and all the celebrities fall through, the only star he can deliver is Harry Hawkins (who turns out to be tavern regular Sir Heathcliffe Batterswick under an alias). Eddie, Finnegan, Miss Duffy and Jack Bailey (the announcer) go on instead. Miss Duffy and Finnegan perform a rendition of the Nelson Eddy/Jeanette MacDonald duet, "Sweetheart."

Episode #166 — Broadcast Friday, April 6, 1945
Supporting Cast: John Brown (Clancy the Cop)
Plot: Archie, tired of loaning money to people, attempts to quit Duffy's Tavern. When Finnegan receives a letter from his late Uncle Byron, who left him gems from the diamond country, presumably his South African diamond mine, Archie tries to latch on to some of Finnegan's money in the hopes of opening "Archie's Inn" (the "inn" partially named after Finnegan). When Sir Heathcliffe attempts to perform at the tavern, Archie pays him not to do so. The gems, however, turn out to be only a book titled "Gems from the Diamond Country."

Memorable Lines
ARCHIE: Hey Arch, can you lend me five until Tuesday? Hey Arch, can you let me have five till Friday?
EDDIE: Yeah, you lose more nickels that way...

Trivia, etc. There was no broadcast on the evening of April 13, due to network coverage of FDR's unexpected death on April 12, 1945. The script originally slated for this date was pushed ahead to next week.

Ed Gardner delivers the wrong line when he's referring to a millionaire's mansion and a yacht, and Miss Duffy covers for him while the audience laughs.

At the conclusion of this broadcast, Archie delivers a vital war message to Duffy: "Well, the war ain't over yet and our guys are still fighting on every front... so the home front has to keep goin', too, and one way we can do it, believe it or not, is with waste paper. Sure... all waste paper is ammunition, Duffy, so save every scrap of it and turn it in to the right agency. I personally am starting the new drive off today by turning in a million dollars worth of waste paper... yep, a book called 'Gems from the Diamond Country.'"

Episode #167 — Broadcast Friday, April 20, 1945
Supporting Cast: John Brown (Clancy the Cop)
Plot: To put a little doubt in people's minds, Finnegan wants to carry around the book he inherited last week. Still wanting to open "Archie's Inn," Archie decides to form a corporation and sell shares in it to raise the needed capital. His latest pigeon is Miss Duffy's new boyfriend, a schoolteacher/rare book collector, Harold Harcleroad. Miss Duffy, desperate, agrees to convince Harold to invest $500 in Archie's scheme if Archie convinces the bookworm to marry her. Only the joke is on Archie, when he gives Harold a gift, "Gems from the Diamond Country," unaware it is worth $500.

Episode #168 — Broadcast Friday, April 27, 1945
Guest: John Garfield
Plot: Duffy's competitor, Grogan's Bar and Grill across the street, added twelve chorus girls that are stealing the customers. Back from entertaining G.I.s, Hollywood actor John Garfield drops by and Archie counteracts Grogan by launching the "Duffy Repertory Company" and Archie's production of "Fish and Fantasy," a witty drama set on a shabby waterfront dive along the coast of Mexico. The love story ends in death and a twist of fate... but the customers prefer the naked dames at Grogan's and when Garfield learns what is across the street, he joins them.

Memorable Lines
ARCHIE: What d'ya think of the place?
GARFIELD: Were there any survivors?
ARCHIE: Gee, John, you ain't been here five minutes and already you've insulted the joint.
GARFIELD: What's the record?

Episode #169 — Broadcast Friday, May 4, 1945
Supporting Cast: John Brown (Clancy the Cop)
Plot: Someone busted into the bank last night and the police are

asking people to keep an eye out for brand new ten dollar bills. After reading how South American diplomats have lots of money, Archie attempts to become a diplomat himself through the services of Slippery McGuire. Only problem is that Archie hasn't decided what country he wants to be an ambassador of. When Clancy heralds the news that he caught the bank robber, Slippery McGuire, he claims Judge Stevens wrote him a letter to establish an alibi... a letter Archie wrote in return for his diplomatic status. Thanks to Finnegan's lack of thoughts, the letter wasn't mailed and Archie is saved.

Episode #170 — Broadcast Friday, May 11, 1945
Guest: Art Linkletter
Plot: Archie is in love with a woman named Dolly Snaffle. All things compared, Ida Lupino, Madeleine Carroll, Esther Williams and Jinx Falkenburg were simply playthings. Archie met Dolly at a coming-out party given for Rubber-Hose Dugan, the extortionist. When Art Linkletter from *People Are Funny* shows up at the tavern, Archie encourages the radio host to put on a show and work in a stunt in which Archie can have a chance to propose to her "with the full persuasive powers of me eloquence." Finnegan becomes a contestant and proposes to the woman... but neither Archie nor Finnegan wins the prize. Linkletter leaves with Dolly in hand.

Memorable Line
LINKLETTER: We will now observe a two-minute silence in memory of the English language.

Episode #171 — Broadcast Friday, May 18, 1945
Plot: Duffy finally gives Archie a raise (now paying $20 a week) and Archie thinks he and his bride-to-be, Dolly Snaffle, will live like queen and king. When Dolly says it's impossible because she spends $15 a week at the beauty parlor, and shows an interest in any single man including Michael Roy, the sponsor spokesman, and Marek Windheim, opera star (who sings "Mother Machree"). Duffy loves Windheim so much that he asks Archie to hire him

(the $5 a week salary to come out of Archie's raise. At least Archie has his job…

Episode #172 — Broadcast Friday, May 25, 1945
Plot: Archie still cannot get the two-timing Dolly Snaffle out of his mind. Discovering she's in love with the new singer, Marek Windheim, who sings "Vesti La Giubba," Archie tricks her into thinking he is destined for opera by lip-synching to Windheim's music… until he slips and insults the woman. Duffy, upset because this week's song is not Irish, wants Archie to fire him.

Trivia, etc. This episode was broadcast from the San Diego Naval Training Station. The special location was at the request of Mac Benoff, a former scriptwriter on the show, who asked that the troupe appear there so that his fellow seamen could see Ed Gardner before they took off for Europe in June.

During the broadcast, Miss Duffy tells Vera Fogarty how the sailors are all attractive in uniform, including those that just got back from sea duty. In the original draft, Archie overhears the conversation and contemplates becoming a veteran who sailed the seven seas, in an effort to impress Dolly. The scriptwriters, for reasons unknown, decided to have Archie attempt to mimic opera instead.

Episode #173 — Broadcast Friday, June 1, 1945
Plot: Archie, believing "a man'll eat anything if he knows that the next day he can see his name in the paper," creates a promotional stunt for the sake of publicity. Archie hires Dave Hossinger as the advertising man, but Eddie disapproves the idea. "With him, the error comes first… then the trial." Calling in his friend Charlie, another con man, Hossinger rigs an old roulette wheel in the back room, sets up a gambling casino, the opera star plays the wheel, goes broke and kills himself. Charlie takes the picture and it will make front page headlines. Archie questions whether this would attract customers. "Arch," Hossinger defends, "do you have any idea what the annual gate receipts are at Grant's tomb?" Ultimately, the scheme fails and Archie is out fifty bucks.

Trivia, etc. The opening announcement explains that this broadcast was dedicated to the United States Government's Veterans' Readjustment Program. The program also features two messages on the treatment and concern of veterans returning to the States.

Memorable Lines

ARCHIE: Eddie, we may not have the most gastorial food in the world, but we do serve a wholesome, balanced diet.

EDDIE: Balanced is right... they got a fifty-fifty chance of recovering.

Episode #174 — Broadcast Friday, June 8, 1945

Guest: Jinx Falkenberg

Plot: Archie plans to leave for a USO tour and promises he won't return. Finnegan asks to have his job because his credentials including being a panhandler. When Jinx Falkenberg arrives, she reveals the fact that she is also spending the summer on a USO tour. To demonstrate what he can do overseas (since Archie cannot sing or dance), Archie demonstrates corny vaudeville comedy and Eddie joins in with a rendition of "Candy." Finnegan and Miss Duffy sing "Indian Love Call." Jinx finds the performance hilarious (in the wrong context) and as the entire cast sings "Auld Lang Syne" to Archie, the phone rings. Duffy asks the manager to please return in the fall.

Summer Replacements

Contractually, Bristol-Myers owned the time slot 52 weeks a year. When *Duffy's Tavern* went on a hiatus for the summer, a short-run substitute had to be produced (often referred to as a "summer replacement"). For the summer of 1943, Young & Rubicam convinced Bristol-Myers to buy *Noah Webster Says*, an NBC sustainer (a program not sponsored) that had premiered in April 1942. The radio quiz program was similar to *Information, Please*, allowing radio listeners to submit lists of words and contestants had to define them. Awards included prize money. The commercials tried to convince listeners to rush out to the stores and buy Minit-Rub. Haven MacQuarrie's quiz program was the subject of

Ed Gardner and Ransom Sherman

momentary business affairs that turned sour when NBC insisted the series should be sponsored on their other network, instead of the Blue. For a brief time in June, NBC convinced Bristol-Myers to sponsor a different program in the same time slot, *Perpetual Emotion*, a situation comedy co-starring Otto Kruger and Binnie Barnes. The ad agency held their ground and *Noah Webster Says* was heard instead. *Perpetual Emotion* aired in a different time slot. During the summer of 1944, *Nitwit Court* entertained radio audiences with a satire of *The Goodwill Hour* with Ransom Sherman as the judge who dispensed personal advice to any nitwit who came before the microphone. A panel gave equally ridiculous suggestions; it was composed of Sara Berner as Bubbles Lowbridge, Mel Blanc as Mr. Hornblower and Arthur Q. Bryan as Mr. Willow. To promote the new program, airing the week after, Bristol-Myers made sure Ransom Sherman was a guest on the final broadcast of the season.

Jay C. Flippen was originally scheduled to be the guest for the final episode of the 1944-45 season to promote *Correction, Please,* a radio quiz show he hosted based on misinformation. Contestants from the radio audience were given $10 each. They bid against each other to see who could spot mistakes in a series of questions, and then bid again for a chance to correct the mistakes. Wrong answers were penalized; correct ones could increase bankrolls tenfold. Ipana toothpaste was pitched in the commercials. Flippen was unable to make the broadcast and Jinx Falkenberg substituted. Willard Waterman was the guest on the final broadcast of the 1945-46 season to promote his own program, *Easy Money,* a radio program exposing rackets preying on unsuspecting people. *Easy Money* was an NBC sustainer since January as a Saturday afternoon filler, moving to Friday evening under sponsorship of Bristol-Myers. This is one of many examples where the network looked favorably at a sustainer and aired the program long enough to successfully gain a sponsor. Originally, Bristol-Myers was considering dropping sponsorship of the time slot at the conclusion of the 1945-46 season and an announcement was made by the network, prematurely, that *Duffy's Tavern* would be dropped from the lineup in June 1946.

For the summer of 1947 and 1948, *The Tex and Jinx Show,* an informal talk program featuring celebrities ranging from newspaper comic artists to silver screen actors, was hosted by Tex McCrary and Jinx Falkenburg. Originally Young & Rubicam took an option on a quiz program, *Comedy of Errors,* as a possible summer replacement. *Tex and Jinx* was apparently a great decision, successful enough in 1947 to warrant a second summer run in 1948. For the broadcast of July 2, 1947, Billy Rose, the showman who turned out numerous hit songs, recalled to guest Mary Martin how, while staging the Casa Maana in Fort Worth, Texas, he turned down Mary Martin who asked him for a job. He told her she might as well go back to "raising watermelons in Texas because she was not the show type." On August 20, 1947, Clarence Nash told how he created the voice of Donald Duck and how he got the job with Walt Disney. On August 4, 1948, guest Paul Winchell told how his mother created the name of Jerry Mahoney, his wooden dummy. On September 1, 1948, Tex and Jinx interviewed Steve

Bykowsky, one of the 31 men who washed the 16,000 windows of Rockefeller Center.

Young & Rubicam was instrumental in finding a summer replacement for *Duffy's Tavern* for their client, Bristol-Myers, with a preference for quiz programs and informal talk shows instead of situation comedies in fear of audience comparison. That policy changed in the summer of 1949 when the ad agency, suspecting *Duffy's Tavern* was going to part ways with them, offered *The Henry Morgan Show* which featured — you guessed it — Henry Morgan, who was known for "kidding the sponsor." On the program, Morgan always gave Gerard (played by Arnold Stang) a job because once when Henry was a young and hungry lad, Gerard's mother fed him Fig Newtons. Various characters appeared such as Daphne, "the dumb girl," who got her subjects and her modifiers in the wrong places. Guests turned up from time to time, including Kenny Delmar and Mae Questel. Bristol-Myers only sponsored the program for 13 weeks. Camel Cigarettes picked up the show for the fall of 1945.

The

War and Navy
Department Department

express to

Ed Gardner

their appreciation for patriotic service
in recognition of outstanding devotion and distinguished
performance rendered servicemen overseas in cooperation with the Armed Forces Radio Service.

Secretary of War   Secretary of the Navy

Washington, D. C.,

One of many awards bestowed upon Ed Gardner
and Duffy's Tavern.

CHAPTER EIGHT
DUFFY'S TAVERN: THE MOVIE

THE 1945 MOVIE

"Hollywood is where a phony can get fast faster than any other place in the world. If you wear spats and a cane, you're a genius. People just look askance at guys like me."
— Ed Gardner

THE EARLIEST INDICATION THAT *DUFFY'S TAVERN* would make a transition to the silver screen was in February of 1943 when gossip columns broke the news that MGM was buying the screen rights to the radio program. In March 1943, Jack Skirball, independent film producer and sponsor of the then-current Alfred Hitchcock melodrama, *Shadow of a Doubt*, was enlarging his picture production program and planned to make four films during the next 12 months. The producer acquired a new partner, Leo Spitz, former president of RKO Pictures and the Keith-

Albee-Orpheum and B.F. Keith Corporation — and at the same time let it be known to the press that their first project would be a comedy starring radio's Fred Allen. The movie would ultimately become *It's in the Bag* and feature Fred Allen and his radio rival, Jack Benny. It was the only movie the duo would assemble. (Spitz went off on his own to co-found International Pictures, a major production firm that would later merge with Universal Studios.) In the movie, wealthy Frederick Trumble makes an eccentric new will and hides much of his wealth in a chair, moments before he is murdered. The new heir, Fred Floogle (Fred Allen), runs a flea circus. The only things he inherits, however, are five chairs which the disgusted Floogle sells… just before discovering their secret. Packed with wisecracks, strange cameos, and nothing sacred, anything-goes digressions, the film was witty enough to attract Fred Allen back to the silver screen after not having appeared before movie cameras for five years.

On April 11, the *New York Times* reported: "The producers also have their eyes on another popular radio personality — Ed Gardner of *Duffy's Tavern* — and are at this moment negotiating for both Mr. Gardner and his program, around which the film would be built." On April 15, the *Los Angeles Times* reported that the screen rights had been sold, contractually securing both Gardner and Shirley Booth for the roles of Archie and Miss Duffy for the movie. Jack Moss would act as producer. On May 15, *Billboard* reported plans to shoot the film at MGM and the Samuel Goldwyn Studios. Two weeks later, the same trio of writers who wrote scripts for the radio program were engaged for the film. Al Glickman, Parke Levy and Max [sic] Benoff were contracted to complete a feasible screenplay before the end of summer. Besides starring in the film, Gardner was supposedly contracted to delve into the screenplay, just as he did in setting up the scripts for the weekly radio broadcasts. *Billboard*, however, reported the sale prematurely. Gardner never signed a contract. He was merely interested in the offer that was being made. *Duffy's Tavern* was open to the highest bidder and he made sure other producers in Hollywood knew this. Relations between Gardner and the producers fell flat when Spitz and Skirball discovered that the radio star was negotiating with the major movie studios.

Among Spitz and Skirball's intentions was the signing of baritone Vaughn Monroe in July 1943, supposedly a definite for the movie, which was to be released through United Artists. Monroe was the first to be signed. The second signing was The Revuers, a quartet of satirists known for their New York nightclub acts, supplying musical talent as vocalists. In July 1943, the quartet left for the West Coast. This would have been their first motion picture and first time in California. To supplement income during their stay, the boys performed at the new reopening of the Trocadero in Hollywood.

A press release dated July 21, 1943, reported: "Unusual arrangements for the screenplay, the first Skirball-Spitz presentation to be released through United Artists, have been announced with the signing of the three writers responsible for the radio show to write the scenario. One of the few times that the radio scriptwriters have gone along with their broadcast achievements, the deal involved the services of Abe Burrows, Mac Benoff and Parke Levy. Eddie Green who plays the waiter on the show, has been signed by producer Moss to portray the same for the screen."

Many years later, on March 24, 1953, when Mac Benoff was called in to testify before the House Un-American Activities Committee, he recalled his involvement with radio and Hollywood.* "I began writing cartoon stuff for *Ballyhoo Magazine* and for such cartoonists as Peter Arno and Otto Soglow. Then I did a few weeks for Eddie Cantor. Then *This is New York* with Ed Gardner and then I wrote for Phil Baker. I don't know how long that was. As long as he was around and that wasn't long. Then I wrote for Tommy Riggs... I came out here to do a picture of *Duffy's Tavern* for Paramount. But I didn't do it. I guess they read the script I wrote." Mac Benoff did in fact write a screenplay scenario dated November 22, 1943. It was never used. (See Appendix C.)

In early August 1943, when Jack Moss joined Columbia as

---

* Benoff, incidentally, never took his testimony very seriously and his wisecracks and witty responses created smiles and laughter, which even committee members acknowledged. Benoff told the Committee that he was in the party about four months, although later testimony indicated he never actually became a member. "I wasn't recruited and I didn't have any indoctrination," he said. "I'm not a political person. I'm a comedy writer. I'm not much interested in politics. Oh, I guess I shouldn't say that."

a producer, his alignment with Leo Spitz to produce a *Duffy's Tavern* movie fell through when Gardner relinquished ownership for failure to convince Columbia to ink a deal. On August 17, Paramount closed a deal for the film rights, for which several major producers had been outbid. According to the terms of the contract, Paramount was allowed to use the title and personnel of the radio program for one picture, with options for four additional films over a five-year period. Ed Gardner had flown to California not just to close the deal with Paramount, but remained in Hollywood for a week and a half following to confer with Paramount executives on the selection of screenwriters and producer for the picture. Joel Moss was not among Gardner's producer candidates. The reported price for the rights to the initial picture was $150,000 (It is understood that Leo Spitz and Jack Skirball put in an offer of $250,000, when first reported they would make a picture.) This included the services of Ed Gardner as an actor playing the role of Archie. Initial plans called for the spotting of many of Paramount's contract players as guest stars in the first picture, which, it was stated, would go into production in early 1944.

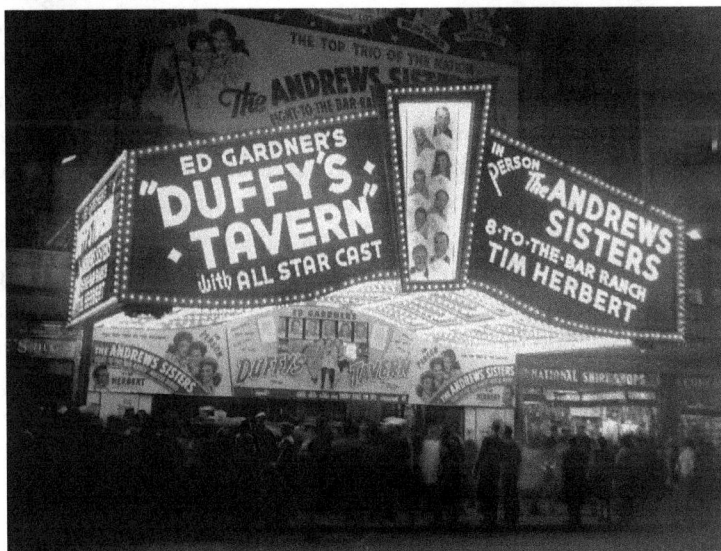

Photo of the Duffy's Tavern *movie promoted at the Paramount in New York City.*

In late August, because of the Paramount deal, the *New York Times* reported Jack Skirball reshuffling his film production plans for the coming season. Dropped from his schedule was the Ed Gardner picture. The producer had also shelved the comedy which Sally Benson was writing around incidents in the Michael Innes novel, *Appleby on Ararat*, originally meant for Fred Allen. Instead, Skirball planned for Allen to star in a comedy penned by Ben Hecht that went by the title *Mating Call*. Those plans also fell through but the film was ultimately produced and released as *It's in the Bag* and would be partially scripted by Hitchcock's wife, Alma Reville.

Because Ed Gardner made Hollywood his permanent home, did his radio show from the West Coast throughout the first half of the 1944-45 season (going back East to "keep his Brooklyn accent"), the radio cast also made the move to the West Coast. In April 1944, Charlie Cantor was signed to reprise his role as Finnegan. Supposedly, when the brass hats got a look at Charlie Cantor three weeks after filming began, they wrote a bigger part for him. Eddie Green reprised his role as Eddie, the waiter. Abe Burrows, the same writer who contributed to the radio program, worked on the screenplay of the forthcoming Paramount picture but only his suggestions and scenarios were used (hence why the opening of the movie credits Melvin Frank and Norman Panama writing the screenplay, and credits Abe Burrows among a list of people providing comedy sketches). Paramount ultimately signed Burrows to a writer-producer contract at the studio.

While the cast for *Duffy's Tavern* may have been large, the roles were brief. Filming was intended to begin in the spring of 1944. Instead, the film was spliced together throughout the summer and fall of 1944, the reason why the movie features various burlesque bits and gag sequences. Billy De Wolfe, having received his honorable discharge from the U.S. Navy, returned to Paramount to fulfill his contract after a comparatively short lapse. As a starter, he made a guest star appearance on *Duffy's Tavern* as a doctor. The studio never made use of his talents as a dancer or impersonator. Maurice Rocco, a Negro pianist, was supposed to perform a specialty number in the movie. His role was minimized greatly. Ann Dorn portrayed the mother of Bing Crosby in screen time lasting less than five seconds. Early in the picture, Freddie Steele, one-time boxing champ, played the role of a waiter at the tavern. Supposedly director William Wellman chose Steele to play a part in *Story of G.I. Joe* (1945) after seeing him work in the movie. Bobby Watson, the Adolph Hitler of *The Hitler Gang* (1944), appeared as the Masseur in the comedy sketch with Betty Hutton.

Brian Donlevy and Paulette Goddard in Duffy's Tavern *(1945).*

Betty Hutton's appearance in the movie was filmed in November 1944, after her personal appearance tour in the East. She was also on tour entertaining troops before filming. Her patriotic duty was demonstrated more than once in *Duffy's Tavern*, when she referred to Ed Gardner and Victor Moore as "commandos" and taking time to listen to Marjorie Reynolds when she explained the benefit was to help employ war veterans. Paramount had announced plans to star Betty Hutton in a musical, *Too Good to be True*, to be based on a story by Harry Tugend, dealing with the romantic comedy adventures of a modern business girl. That film never came to be. Hutton performed "Doing It the Hard Way" as only Hutton could sing it. The new song was also recorded by Hutton for Capitol Records and was available in the stores.

Because of the way the movie was pieced together as it was being produced, a number of intended plans for the picture fell through. After reviewing numerous trade magazines, including Hedda Hopper's syndicated column, it can be verified that in the spring of 1944, Stan Kenton and his orchestra had signed on to supply music for the movie. Kenton and his orchestra never appeared in the film. Sammy Cahn and Jules Styne were going to write the music for the movie but had to go to New York in August 1944 for David Wolper's musical, *Glad to See You*, starring Lupe Velez and Jane Withers. In the same month, Bill Sheehan, who was second assistant to Mark Sandrich on *Here Come the Waves* (1944), wanted to be an actor so Sandrich made a screen test of him with Sonny Tufts and, as a result, Bill had a contract and the promise of a good part in *Duffy's Tavern*. Sheehan never appeared in the film.

Beginning November 30, Paramount put two units at work on *Duffy's Tavern*. Director Hal Walker guided the unit filming scenes with Betty Hutton, Ed Gardner and Victor Moore. On the other unit, producer Danny Dare and dance director Billy Daniel handled the filming of the *Johnny Comes Marching Home* ballet number, featuring Johnny Coy and Miriam Franklin. Sidney Lansfield signed a new deal with Paramount back in July which contracted him to direct six pictures during the next three years. His first was supposed to be *Duffy's Tavern*, filming originally planned to begin August 26. Because filming did not begin until

Ed Gardner admires Betty Gardner's assets.

the first week of October, Lansfield was rescheduled for another picture.

Susan Hayward's suspension at Paramount, which had started over a loan-out to producer Charles R. Rogers, ended in October of 1944. Her first assignment back was to play the female needing to be rescued during the Western cowboy sequence with Eddie

Bracken and Walter Abel. The sequence was filmed, but Olga San Juan played the role. Hayward did not.

In April 1944, it was announced that Bob Hope would make a guest spot in the *Duffy's Tavern* movie. Film fans today still wonder why the comedian never appeared in the movie. The explanation stems from Hope's determination to show Paramount who could enforce more authority behind the cameras, as well as in front of them. Filming began in August and before Bob Hope's scenes could be lensed, the actor took the position that he wanted more time to tour army camps and service hospitals for broadcasts of his weekly radio program rather than be tied down in Hollywood making the three or four films a year his contract presently called for. In November, while preparations were made to start filming *My Favorite Brunette* and his scheduled appearance for *Duffy's Tavern*, the dispute went under fire at Paramount. *Brunette* was held back a few days in production as Bob Hope went on strike. Hope, having provided talents on stage for the USO over the summer, showed intentions to slow down on picture assignments. An adjustment was eventually made between the studio and the actor before Thanksgiving, but filming for *Duffy's Tavern* was completed by that time.

In September 1944, Buddy DeSylva signed Yehudi Menuhin, just a half-hour before the latter took off for overseas, to do a spot in the movie. Menuhin went to England to help with Red Cross benefits and camp shows. He was scheduled to return to Hollywood in early January, and would get in his work at Paramount around contracted appearances with the Los Angeles Philharmonic. This was to be his second appearance on the screen. The studio referred to his planned violin solo appearance in the movie as a "specialty." Plans were to whisk him from the train to Paramount on his arrival January 16, 1945. The orchestra, with Hal Walker directing, was to be ready and waiting, and Menuhin would therefore plunge right into a rendition of "Gypsy Airs" by Sarasate. Reason for the haste was his engagements with the Los Angeles Philharmonic in a series of concerts which were going to take up practically all of his time. His arrival in Los Angeles was late and the studio decided the violin solo was not worth the added expense. Menuhin never appears in the movie.

According to the November 4, 1944 issue of the *Los Angeles Times*, "Bob Graham, that new singing discovery signed by Paramount and immediately borrowed by MGM for *Weekend at the Waldorf*, will make his debut for his own studio in *Duffy's Tavern*. He's talked of now as a cross between Bing Crosby and Frank Sinatra, so that should really put him in the middle."

In late October of 1944, the first specialty number for the movie was completed and in the can, with Sonny Tufts, Brian Donlevy and Paulette Goddard as the leads. It started off with Paulette in a bubble bath when Ed Gardner walked in. Just how Sonny and Brian were to fit into the scene wrinkled the writers' brows, according to one trade column, "but they figure they can't go wrong with an opening like that." All three actors ultimately appeared together in a scene involving a dream sequence and a romance, but no bubble bath. Goddard, however, did appear taking a shower in a brief scene, earlier in the picture.

According to an NBC press release: "Ed Gardner's search for a girl with a Brooklyn accent to play the part of Miss Duffy in the film version of *Duffy's Tavern* has reached such proportions that he's now calling her Scarlet O'Duffy." Playing the role of Miss Duffy was Ann Thomas, who played successfully in *Chicken Every Sunday* on the New York stage and was well-known in the radio world playing supporting roles on *Gang Busters* and *The Cavalcade of America*. Test footage was shot on September 27, which Ed Gardner had to sign off on and agree to since his contract stipulated he had final approval of the actress to play the role of Miss Duffy. *Duffy's Tavern* would be her motion picture debut. Sadly, the studio never made any use of her after the movie. During her time in Hollywood, Thomas wrote a book about the New York professional children's school. She was never hired to play Miss Duffy on radio, and ventured back to New York just a few months after filming was completed. She continued to play supporting roles on radio programs such as *The Adventures of Archie Andrews* and *X Minus One*.

Paul Luther in his "Inside Radio" column remarked: "Ann is without question supreme in the art of delivering dese, dem and dose characterizations in a voice which seems to have been permanently affected by laryngitis. She'd win any poll hands down as the perfect scatter-brained daughter of Archie's employer." Luther, having had the opportunity to share a radio microphone with the actress in November or December 1948, sat down and asked her for a candid explanation, asking why she did not appear on the radio show. According to the actress, it seems that Ed Gardner felt she too would be a natural for the role and tried on numerous occasions to talk her into becoming a *Tavern* regular. One small detail, however, stood in the way. Ann, while agreeing to salary terms, insisted on a one-year contract and Gardner, for reasons of his own, said the deal would have to be on a short-term agreement. For this, the two could not meet eye-to-eye.

William Bendix, with a breath of Brooklyn, was originally planned for the role of Danny Murphy and agreed in May of 1944 to play the role. His role was downplayed to a minor one, standing in the background for a few brief scenes, when Barry Sullivan signed in September to play the role initially intended for Bendix. The downsizing may have been the studio's decision not to associate another radio comedy in the same picture. Bendix had recently signed on for playing Chester A. Riley on radio's *The Life of Riley* back in January. Just a few days after Sullivan signed on to play Danny Murphy, Cass Daley, who had secured a leave of absence from Paramount for a year to concentrate on a career in radio, kept the cinema alive for herself by agreeing to appear in two scenes in *Duffy's Tavern*.

Robert Benchley appears on screen towards the end of the movie, applying his expected style of humor and wit when telling a humorous rendition of Bing Crosby's life, including childhood, schooling and singing career. Having just finished appearing before the cameras for Fred Allen's movie, Benchley helped establish the climax of big-leaguers in the picture, sparked by none other than Bing Crosby, who sang a new version of *Swinging on a Star*, taken from *Going My Way* (1944). Paramount surrounded Crosby with 16 name players, among them Arturo De Cordova, Gail Russell, Cass Daley, Joan Caulfield, James Brown, Helen Walker, Olga San Juan and Jean Heather.

Ann Doran played what was perhaps the shortest role for any of the stars. She appears in the Crosby babyhood period of the sketch and when she sees the future one and only Bing, which the stork has just delivered, she opens her mouth and screams.

Barry Fitzgerald played the role of Crosby's father with his hand in a cast; he broke a finger the night before he started work on the picture. Ed Gardner also suffered an injury during filming. The scene in which Archie seeks Moore's consent to marry his daughter with quantities of brandy was painstaking for Gardner. He had recently injured his back during a game of tennis, revisiting an old injury he suffered when he was a child. Months before the movie was filmed, Gardner also had serious dental work done for his screen debut.

Paramount attempted to make one of their young starlets, Julie Gibson, who played the role of a nurse in the movie, a feature attraction for movie goers. According to paperwork in Paramount archives, there was a plan to shape Gibson into a new blonde bombshell to replace Veronica Lake, who was, at that time, starting to become troublesome behind the cameras. A native of Lewiston, Idaho, her real name was Camille Soray but the studio would not let her use it because it sounded so phony. She started her show business career singing with bands. She went to drama school, did singing bits in pictures and sang on the radio. Eventually, she joined the cast of *Meet the People*. From there, dance director Danny Dare asked her over to Paramount, where she began appearing in unbilled bit parts. "Between scenes I sang the Lamour numbers for my own education — loud and lusty," she recalled. "An executive happened to pass by, and just as you hear in the press agent stories — only this time it was true — he said, 'find out who that girl is and sign her up.'"

Gibson's attitude behind the cameras, however, was not accepted by the director, who complained to the chiefs. He claimed she was more difficult to work with than Veronica Lake, the latter of whom appeared on the set without any reservations and was "the ideal actress" for any motion picture assignment. After the completion of *Duffy's Tavern*, Gibson was put on leave by the studio. "They thought it would be a very good idea, prior to a USO camp tour, for me to see New York for the first time. But they didn't get the idea until after I'd already arrived on my own, and couldn't get any kind of hotel accommodations befitting a glamour-girl build up." Described as a prima donna, Gibson, who was slated to play the co-starring lead in a Technicolor production of "Frankie and Johnny," and signed to report at the Pine-Thomas outfit (a Paramount unit) for the starring role of "Tokyo Rose," was taken off the projects. Gibson then jumped from studio to studio, getting little more than bit parts in movies at Columbia, Universal and Monogram and ending up working mainly behind the scenes on television. Years later, she married director Charles Barton.

Promotion on the radio for the motion picture began as early as the summer of 1945. On July 2, Robert Benchley co-starred with Ray Milland in a performance of "Standing Room Only," on *The Lady Esther Screen Guild Theater*. At the conclusion of the broadcast the announcer explained that both Milland and Benchley appeared courtesy of Paramount Pictures, and the actors could be seen in the up-coming *Duffy's Tavern* motion picture. Cass Daley did a turn on *The Ray Bolger Show* on August 8. The following week, Ed Gardner appeared on the same show. Diana Lynn enhanced the Tommy Dorsey program on August 26. Two days later, Marjorie Reynolds was a guest on *Hollywood Preview*. Mention of the movie was made on all of these broadcasts. By late September 1945, a record number of more than 40 coast-to-coast network broadcasts had been lined up in the exploitation campaign for the motion picture.

Beginning November 9, 1944, Ann Thomas, Miss Duffy of the movie version, appeared on *The Lifebuoy Show*, starring Bob Burns. She played the recurring role of Sharon O'Shaughnessy for thirteen consecutive broadcasts. A magazine article in the 1980s, concerning the Bob Burns radio program, reported Ann Thomas' appearance as Paramount Pictures' attempt to promote the upcoming *Duffy's Tavern* movie. This is simply not true. The movie was not even before the cameras at the time she appeared on the radio show.

Photo of the Duffy's Tavern *movie promoted at the Paramount in New York City.*

On Wednesday, September 5, 1945, *Duffy's Tavern* made its screen debut, appropriately enough, at the Times Square Paramount in New York on the same bill with such "live" entertainment as The Andrews Sisters, movie actor Tim Herbert, Charles Leighton ("New King of Harmonica"), Foy Willing's "Riders of the Purple Sage" and Vic Schoen and his recording orchestra. Management

289

at the Paramount reported that by 1 p.m., *Duffy's Tavern* had generated 7,959 admissions, breaking all opening-day marks for the year. The movie ultimately played for nine weeks at the Paramount. To prove just how profitable the venture was, the film's run at the Paramount is surpassed only by *Going My Way* (1944) and *Lady in the Dark* (1944), both of which ran a record ten weeks.

The day after the New York premiere, the *New York Times* reviewed: "Take it for what it is, a hodgepodge of spare-time clowning by the gang, including a large hunk of Archie, and you'll find *Duffy's Tavern* fair enough... The best way to take *Duffy's Tavern* is as it comes. Some of it clicks into place and some of it doesn't." The plot concerned Archie learning that his tee-totaling customer Victor Moore is going broke and has to lay off a bunch of ex-servicemen. Fearing the worst, Archie goes into action, persuading a truckload of movie stars to pitch in, perform their bits, and help raise enough money for Moore's record company to go back into business. It's a flimsy excuse for a film but the entertainment is nonstop, with some truly memorable numbers performed by Betty Hutton, who whirlwinds through *Doin' It the Hard Way* (written by Johnny Burke, Jimmy Van Heusen), and Cass Daley performing an equally frenetic *You Can't Blame a Gal for Trying* (written by Ben Raleigh and Bernie Wayne). Bing Crosby and Hutton also do an unusual rendition of *Swinging on a Star*. (The lyrics were eliminated. The stars submitted new lines which kid the daylights out of themselves.) Sprinkled throughout are various burlesque bits, gag sequences, and even an oddball radio murder skit performed by Alan Ladd, Veronica Lake and Howard Da Silva, stars of *The Blue Dahlia* (1946), released theatrically earlier in the year. As the lights go out, Da Silva seems to be punching Lake silly, with Ladd daring him to continue. When the lights go on, Ladd gives Lake an arch look and says: "Lady, you'd better get out of here before you get your teeth kicked in!"

Archer Winston, columnist for the *New York Post*, reviewed: "The movie report on Ed 'Archie' Gardner of the radio is entirely favorable. His personality transfers so successfully to the screen that repetitions of the experiment, even on a smaller scale, are in order. Charles Cantor (Finnegan) and Ann Thomas (Miss Duffy) are also assets in the field of moron characterization... Most of the fun comes directly out of the famous big mouth of Ed 'Archie' Gardner, while the smooth Victor Moore holds up his end of the partnership with a good characterization... There are old gags and new, ancient sketches and tired tricks of the movie game. There's abundant humor of a very simple sort but occasionally it's spiced with very original touches good for a guffaw no matter how strict the standard."

Not everyone was impressed. Columnist Erskine Johnson referred to the movie as: "It wasn't funny." Eileen Creelman, columnist for the *New York Sun*, reviewed: "*Duffy's Tavern* is a jumble, sometimes funny, more often dull. It drags along at first, with Mr. Gardner's lines better than his acting. He delivers the comedy lines well, as he does on radio. Perhaps it is too much makeup, perhaps it is too much inexperience, that spoils Mr. Gardner's movie debut. He is funnier to the ear than to the eye. In this first film he has not yet mastered screen technique. As for the vaudeville, a giant and incredible show built up by a giant and quite incredible script, this also alternates between fair and tedious. Mr. Crosby winds up the proceedings with a satire funnier by far to studio workers than to movie spectators. Some of the bits are good. They would have seemed funnier had the sketch been briefer."

During the September 28, 1945, broadcast, Deems Taylor, music critic, made an appearance at the tavern and Ed Gardner, in the character of Archie, slyly promoted the celebrities that appeared in his movie.

TAYLOR: That's simply wonderful. Who was in the picture with you?

ARCHIE: Oh, I had a little support. Betty Hutton, Paulette Goddard, Alan Ladd, Bing Crosby... guys like that. But enough of me, Deems. What have you being doin'?

TAYLOR: Well I've been doing some commentaries on the symphonies with a little support from Tchaikovsky, Damrosch, Toscanini... and guys like that.

ARCHIE: Well, you gotta have a little help.

Throughout 1945 and 1946, jokes about the movie were

291

incorporated into the radio broadcasts. Ed Gardner milked the joke on and off for three years, including the broadcast of February 11, 1948, when Marlene Dietrich was a guest.

MARLENE: I understand M-G-M was very happy with your performance.
ARCHIE: But I made the picture for Paramount!
MARLENE: Yes - I know.

Throughout the forties, Hollywood studios were purchasing the screen rights to many radio programs, hoping to capitalize on the Hooper ratings. Paramount had already made a profit from a series of Henry Aldrich movies. While pre-production was underway for the *Duffy's Tavern* movie, Columbia was moving full speed ahead by casting Nina Foch and Carole Matthews in principal parts in *I Love A Mystery*, an adaptation of the radio program of that title. Columbia also began theatrically releasing a series of mysteries based on *The Whistler*, a CBS crime anthology program. Sam White, a producer at Columbia for the past three years, was signed by Pine & Thomas to produce and direct the screen adaptation of the radio program *People Are Funny*, in which Jack Haley would star.

Paramount was hoping to put *Duffy's Tavern* into the same category as its *Big Broadcasts* of a few years prior. There was some intention of making the *Tavern* an annual event and, consequently, an optional contract had been arranged with Ed Gardner. It was Paramount's first multi-star affair since the studio crowded almost all of its luminaries into *Star Spangled Rhythm* in 1942. The studio would do it again two years later, not in the *Duffy's Tavern* vein, but as *Variety Girl* (1947).

The multi-star situation was currently prevalent on other lots. In January 1945, Warner Bros. released *Hollywood Canteen*, for which the studio's whole acting contract roster did its bit. A month after the release of *Duffy's Tavern*, MGM released its all-star *Weekend at the Waldorf* (1945), which would become the studio's sixth largest grossing film of the year. Meanwhile, Fred Allen was playing host in his United Artists picture, *It's in the Bag*, to a dozen or so top screen and radio personalities.

Advertisement promoting Paulette Goddard's appearance in the
Duffy's Tavern *movie.*

What placed *Duffy's Tavern* apart from most of the other movies being released theatrically at the time was how the post-war phase was being worked into a broad comedy. The plot structure of finding employment for former tavern patrons who

293

have returned from military service was not a common theme with theatergoers in 1945.

Almost every motion picture released through a major studio featured a press book: Paramount was no exception. In the hopes that local theater managers would promote the movie on a local level, a number of snappy spots were composed for local broadcasting should the movie studios want to promote the movie on local airwaves. In certain areas of the country, following the broadcast of *Duffy's Tavern*, a local announcer might have advertised the movie used the following script:

(50 words, 25 seconds)
ANNOUNCER: *Duffy's Tavern* is on the screen! With twenty-eight of Hollywood's greatest stars including Bing Crosby, Betty Hutton, Dorothy Lamour, Paulette Goddard, Eddie Bracken and Alan Ladd, plus Ed (Archie himself) Gardner and the gang! Don't miss the screen's greatest star-spangled laugh hit, *Duffy's Tavern* opening _____ at the _____ Theater.

(75 words, 37 seconds)
ANNOUNCER: Ladies and gentlemen, there are thirty-two Hollywood stars over in *Duffy's Tavern* and as Archie would say, "The joint's jumpin' with piscatorial talent." Yes sir, the funniest show on the air is now the funniest show on the screen with, among others, Bing Crosby, Dorothy Lamour, Betty Hutton, Alan Ladd, Paulette Goddard and, of course, Ed (Archie himself) Gardner and the *Duffy's Tavern* gang. Don't miss *Duffy's Tavern* opening _____ at the _____ Theater.

(100 words; 50 seconds)
ANNOUNCER: Archie's seein' stars — because the stars are crowding *Duffy's Tavern* to the rafters! Yes sir, *Duffy's Tavern* has gone Hollywood with the gayest, swingiest, funniest, star-studded musicomedy ever screened and get this, folks, there are exactly twenty-eight headliners in *Duffy's Tavern* including Bing Crosby, Dorothy Lamour, Paulette Goddard, Betty Hutton, Alan Ladd and, besides, Ed (Archie himself) Gardner and the whole *Duffy's Tavern* air-show. In fact, everybody's in *Duffy's Tavern* except

Duffy and *Duffy's Tavern* is in the _____ Theater! Don't miss *Duffy's Tavern* because, leave us face it, it's the funniest motion picture of the year!

MOVIE STATISTICS
Produced by Danny Dare.
Directed by Hal Walker.
Screenplay written by Melvin Frank and Norman Panama, based on the characters created by Ed Gardner.
Sketches were written by Melvin Frank, Norman Panama, Matt Brooks, Eddie Davis, George White, Barney Dean, and Abram S. (Abe) Burrows.

Cast: Walter Abel (the director); Grace Albertson (telephone operator #2); Valmere Barman (girl at the soda fountain); William Bendix (as himself); Eddie Bracken (as himself); James Brown (as himself); Charles Cane (the cop with Mr. Smith); Charles Cantor (Finnegan); George M. Carleton (Mr. Richardson); Joan Caulfield (as herself); Davidson Clark (the guard); Catherine Craig (nurse #2); Kernan Cripps (Regan's Assistant); Bing Crosby (as himself); Dennis Crosby (as himself); Gary Crosby (as himself); Lindsay Crosby (as himself); Philip Crosby (as himself); Arturo De Cordova (as himself); Cass Daley (as herself); Howard da Silva (the heavy); Barney Dean (himself); Billy De Wolfe (the doctor); Brian Donlevy (as himself); Lester Dorr (painter #1); Phil Dunham (customer #2); Bill Edwards (soda fountain clerk); Betty Farrington (woman with the baby); Frank Faylen (customer #3); Barry Fitzgerald (Bing Crosby's Father); James Flavin (cop #2); Ed Gardner (Archie); Julie Gibson (nurse #1); Paulette Goddard (as herself); Eddie Green (Eddie the Waiter); Buck Harrington (customer #1); Jean Heather (as herself); Len Hendry (waiter #6); Tony Hughes (the manager of the Green Star Shipping); Betty Hutton (as herself); John Indrisano (waiter #7); Roberta Jonay (telephone operator #3); Billy Jones (waiter #2); Audrey Korn (school kid #3); Alan Ladd (as himself); Veronica Lake (as herself); Dorothy Lamour (as herself); Diana Lynn (as herself); Jerry Maren (the midget); Charles Mayon (the stork); Matt McHugh (the man following Miss Duffy); George McKay

(Regan); Victor Moore (Michael O'Malley); Frances Morris (woman who screams); Al Murphy (waiter #9); Noel Neill (school kid #2); Jack Perrin (cop #1); Charles Quigley (Ronald); Theodore Rand (the stage hand); Marjorie Reynolds (Peggy O'Malley); Addison Richards (Mr. Smith, the C.P.A.); Cyril Ring (waiter #1); Maurice Rocco (as himself); Albert Ruiz (the station master*); Gail Russell (as herself); Olga San Juan (Gloria); Fred Steele (waiter #8); Barry Sullivan (Danny Murphy); Charles Sullivan (painter #2); Ann Thomas (Miss Duffy); Beverly Thompson (school kid #1); Sonny Tufts (as himself); George Turner (waiter #3); Ray Turner (the hotel porter); Harry Tyler (the man in bookie joint); Emmett Vogan (the makeup man); Robert Watson (Masseur); Helen Walker (as herself); Crane Whitley (the plainclothesman); Frank Wayne (waiter #4); Stephen Wayne (waiter #5); Charles B. Williams (Mr. Smith's Assistant); and Audrey Young (telephone operator #1).

Production Credits
Art Direction by Hans Dreier and William Flannery **
Dances were staged and choreographed by Billy Daniel
Director of Photography by Lionel Lindon
Editorial Supervision by Arthur Schmidt
Makeup by Wally Westmore
Music Associate was Arthur Franklin
Music Direction was supplied by Robert Emmett Dolan
Process Photography by Farciot Edouart
Set Decorator was Stephen Seymour
Sound Recording by John Cope and Wallace Nogle
Special Photographic Effects by Gordon Jennings
Vocal Arrangements supplied by Joseph J. Lilly

---

* Albert Ruiz played two roles in this movie. Not just as the station master but as the soda clerk!
** William Flannery was also the man responsible for the visual design of Duffy's Tavern.

Dorothy Lamour and Betty Hutton's gowns were designed
by Edith Head.
Paulette Goddard's gowns were designed by Mary Kay Dodson.

Did you ever wonder what was said over the telephone
in those press box-to-bench calls during a football game?
In late 1945, Henry J. McCormick, in his "Playing the
Game" column, recounted what supposedly happened in
a recent game. A team was deep in its own territory and
trying desperately to hang onto the ball until the time
expired. The "spotter" in the press box rang furiously to
get the attention of the harried assistant coach handling
calls on the bench. The latter picked up the receiver and
here's what the "spotter" heard: "Duffy's Tavern, Archie
speaking."

On the evening of February 18, 1945, Bob Hope was
the master of ceremonies for the *Hall Of Fame* program, also
referred to as *The Philco Radio Hall of Fame*. The program
originated from The Earl Carroll Theater Restaurant in
Hollywood, California. Judy Canova, Janet Blair and a trio
from *Duffy's Tavern* including Charlie [Finnegan] Cantor,
Eddie [the waiter] Green and Robert Graham, the
present baritone on *Duffy's*, were heard on the program.
Jimmy Wallington, who temporarily replaced Harry Von
Zell for a few weeks in spring of 1942 and would later
be the regular announcer beginning in the fall of 1946,
was the announcer for *Hall of Fame*. After a catchy tune,
"How Deep Is The Ocean?," a "Duffy's Tavern" sketch was
presented, with not only Duffy missing, but Ed Gardner
as well!

*Ed Gardner and Victor Moore treat Betty Grable with disrespect,
respectfully.*

*Bing Crosby sings with Jean Heather, Helen Walker
and Gail Russell.*

CHAPTER NINE

THE BUSINESS OF BRISTOL-MYERS
THE NBC YEARS
(1945 - 1946)

WHEN ED GARDNER INSISTED THAT he and his cast could support *Duffy's Tavern* without the need of Hollywood celebrities, especially during the second season, he proved his statement was fairly accurate. The scripts in the early years were witty, sharp and hilariously funny. As John Dunning so accurately described the program in his book, *On the Air* (1998, Oxford University Press, Inc.), "*Duffy's Tavern* was a state of mind." Abe Burrows, who was the guiding light behind the scriptwriting for the first four seasons, departed for greener pastures (namely, Hollywood). "It was painful to leave *Duffy's Tavern* and Ed Gardner, a friend and the man who really got me started in radio," recalled Abe Burrows. "I felt very close to him… On a Saturday night I said goodbye to *Duffy's Tavern* and the following Monday, early in the morning, I drove to Paramount."

From artist Lew Landsman from 1946.

Gardner found himself hiring a staff of comics who were guided not by the principles established by Burrows, but instead the strict enforcement of Ed Gardner.* Rather than hire scriptwriters with experience, knowing they would ask for more money than he was willing to pay, Gardner hired people who had little or no experience and could be taught the craft by Bill Manhoff, now promoted to head writer. During the 1945-46 season, for example,

---

* During the summer of 1946, Burrows signed up with the J. Walter Thompson agency and began scripting for the Dinah Shore-Peter Lind Hayes program, sponsored by Ford Motors.

Sid Dorfman and Larry Gelbart would usually compose the first draft. Hy Freedman's specialty was creating Archie's opening monologue. Rik Vollaerts and Vincent Bogert would polish the script with minor rewrites and the rest of the scriptwriters contributed one-liners and jokes. Manhoff would supervise the entire production, with Ed Gardner looking over the script two days before broadcast to provide his own input.

The one-liners were still funny, but the novelty was starting to get old. The program's saving grace from 1945 to 1949 was the celebrities who, each week, appeared before the microphone for 30 minutes of laughs. Celebrities included Hollywood and Broadway actors, famous authors, Metropolitan Opera singers, sports legends, newspaper columnists and radio stars from every major network. The longer Gardner's monologue with Duffy in the beginning of each episode, insulting the evening's guests, the better the program.

The new season of *Duffy's Tavern* was up against stiff competition. CBS chose to move the high-rated and popular Kate Smith program from Sunday to Friday, believing the songstress would smash the competition — NBC's *Duffy's Tavern* and ABC's *The FBI in Peace and War*. To counteract, a new cast member was added: Falstaff Openshaw, a wacky poet played by Alan Reed. Reed, who had already been appearing on the series in the occasional role of as Clancy the Cop used to be a brass polisher on a transatlantic liner. From the passengers he picked up his dialects. Born Herbert Theodore Bergman, he portrayed a gangster in his first radio audition in 1927 - and failed. By later putting the director on the spot, via the phone in the best gangster idiom, he got the job.

Reed got his big break in radio in 1926. Obsessed with the urge to get any kind of hold in radio, someone told him about Charles Schenck, who was then involved with the production of *True Detective Crime Dramas*. Reed strolled into Schenck's office and was told by a too-efficient secretary that the boss was busy and was not to be disturbed. Time was precious so Reed raced down to the corner drugstore and called Schenck. Pretending to be a gangster muscling an actor into an audition, Reed ordered Schenck to see the actor or..."

"Who is this?" exploded Schenck.

"An actor," said Reed. "May I come up?"

"You certainly may," laughed Schenck. "I'll wait for you."

This began Reed's career on radio that paid off with appearances on Rudy Vallee's program, the *Joe Palooka* series, Fred Allen's show and the role of Pasquale on the popular CBS comedy *Life With Luigi*.

Ed Gardner and executives at Young & Rubicam created a deal to take on Alan Reed's Falstaff Oppenshaw character as a permanent member of the *Duffy's Tavern* cast when the show returned to the airwaves on September 21. When the deal was consummated, it meant Reed would cease his weekly appearance on Fred Allen's radio show. It was a perfect union, considering the poet laureate of Allen's Alley could best be described in the *Variety* review of the season premiere: "Alan Reed came equipped with his Falstaffian doggerel. His rhymed nonsense fits the show like a cap on a bottle of beer."

"Falstaff became a household word during the wartime period," Reed later recalled to Chuck Schaden in 1975. "On the strength of Falstaff, I did an awful lot of work in hospitals and canteens and things like that."

For reasons unknown, Reed withdrew his character of Falstaff from *Duffy's Tavern* after five broadcasts. He did remain on the show for a few additional broadcasts in other roles including Archie's Uncle Morton. Reed found himself in demand to make guest shots on radio programs and executives at Don Lee-Mutual made Reed an offer that meant larger paychecks. By late October, Alan Reed and Irene Tedrow teamed up for *The Nebbs*, taking over the Knox Company-sponsored Sunday series starring Gene and Kathleen Lockhart. *The Nebbs* aired only a few weeks until early January when Alan Reed flew back to the East Coast to once again become a regular on the Fred Allen program.

Old to the program was the incorporation of solicitations. In celebration of the *Duffy's Tavern* movie, now in theaters nationwide, the premiere episode centered on Archie putting on a party to celebrate, inviting the entire studio cast down to the tavern — Bing Crosby, Betty Hutton, Alan Ladd and Dorothy Lamour included. While the tavern residents crack jokes about the movie and the stars, no one shows up. Having spent the money on the food and drinks, Archie tells Duffy at the end of the episode, "I'll pay for the stuff. Believe me, the friendship of swell friends like Miss Duffy and Finnegan and Eddie is worth eight bucks." The promotional plugs for the movie might have been a tad overbearing. According to *Variety*, "It was certainly ample reverse lend-lease payment. Had it not been for Bristol-Myers' insistence on plugging not only Ipana and Vitalis, but hitchhiking Ingram shaving-cream as well, one might have been in doubt for this stanza as to the sponsor's identity. Not that the plugs—except for the hitchhike—were bad: in fact, they were well integrated with the humor at hand."

To help publicize the movie, the marketing at Paramount started a "grammar feud" between Smith and Wellesley colleges over Ed Gardner's English heard in *Duffy's Tavern*. The resulting flack spurred a Smith coed critic to do a flattering review in a college sheet, emphasizing entertainment merits of the comic's style of speech. Wellesley critics were up in arms, condemning the use of poor grammar in the movie. In the meantime, Boston papers had been giving considerable space to the "controversy," which could only increase ticket sales to those curious to know what the hubbub was.

The September 26, 1945, issue of *Variety* reviewed the season premiere: "It seems that some people have been worrying for about five years lest the gold-vein would run thin in that mine of uncertain wit known as *Duffy's Tavern*. Well, *Duffy's* came back last week from its summer rest, its wit still largely unclassifiable—ranging as it does from the homey to the slum-going and depending so much on Ed Gardner's malapropisms. But somehow it seems to continue clicking. Certainly the gimmick is no longer new. But moving the bistro uptown would do the joint no good. One might as well settle down right now, consider *Duffy's* in business to stay, and disguise one's desire to be natural when highbrow friends happen to drop in on Friday evenings."

Island Venture

From November 22, 1945, to June 20, 1946, Wrigley Gum sponsored a weekly adventure program titled *Island Venture*, emphasizing that experience in the U.S. Navy has prepared men for achievements in peacetime. Gil Berry, played by Jerry Walter, was a former Naval pilot on a South Sea island for the purpose of establishing an air-freight line among islands in the Pacific. He forms a partnership with "Trigger" Bret, another ex-Navy man, who competes over the affections of Mendoza's daughter, and combats against the villainous Chula. The commercials, kept to a minimum, stressed the shortage of materials to make chewing gum as Wrigley wanted to make it. The scripts were written by Ken Robinson, co-created by Ken Robinson and Ed Gardner Jr. Even the copyright registration card at the Library of Congress verifies this.

One of many copyright cards filed away at the Copyright Office of the Library of Congress.

Recognition

On a personal note, Ed Gardner was enjoying the success that came from his radio program and the upcoming motion picture. On December 13, 1944, Veronica Lake married film director André de Toth; the wedding ceremony was held at Ed Gardner's house. Judge Charles J. Griffin of Beverly Hills performed the ceremony. In March of 1945, film producer and songwriter Buddy DeSylva, a painter in his spare moments, completed a portrait of Ed Gardner. Amidst the motion picture's release and the largest Hollywood clientele to appear before the microphone compared to previous seasons, Gardner was endowed with boundless energy, quick thinking and determination to make *Duffy's Tavern* the best comedy on the air. He credited his assets with putting him in a mansion in Bel Air, California, an accompanying swimming pool to match and a 55 foot yacht. His income from radio alone was estimated at $200,000 that year. Ed and Simone had their first child, Edward Junior, months prior (April 28, 1944). Appropriately, they also got an Irish setter named "Duffy" in honor of the program that generated the family's revenue. To a lot of people it was probably a surprise that Ed Gardner never lived in a sort of residential version of *Duffy's Tavern* – that broken-down beer barrel CBS and NBC had so successfully wired for sound. Some people felt that a guy would have to live in the stale-beery atmosphere of *Duffy's* to be able to get it across on the air so well. Of course, the magic of radio created the illusion of reality. It was 1945 and Ed Gardner was at the top of his game.

When Gardner returned from the summer 1945 USO tour, he discovered his radio program had won a number of awards. Editor Michael G. Ames of *PIC Magazine* presented a published award for Ed Gardner because "this 40-year-old guy is one of radio's outstanding comedians and should be the recipient of a epithet – the PIC Double E for Ether Excellence."

In early September, *Duffy's Tavern* received an honor more unique in the entertainment industry. The program was named to the Honor Roll of Race Relations by the Schomberg Collection of Negro Literature (which was affiliated with the New York Public Library) for featuring Negro actors "without the use of jokes that are offensive to any racial group." Thus *Duffy's Tavern* joined Lester B. Granger, executive secretary of the National Urban League and Lieutenant General John C.H. Lee, General Eisenhower's deputy commander and supply chief, as recipients of this distinguished award. While some theorize that Paul Robeson was the catalyst who sparked a black artistic reappraisal, "colored" performers on

The Gardner family at the swimming pool.

radio found a platform to respectfully demonstrate their talents. Eddie Green, for example, played an important staple on Jack Benny's program before Eddie "Rochester" Anderson became a permanent fixture. Green brought his vaudeville sketches to the airwaves on many occasional guest spots until *Duffy's Tavern* became popular enough to warrant him reprising his Eddie the waiter foil. No one — from midgets to religion — was immune to the verbal punches heard on *Duffy's Tavern*... except one taboo subject: African Americans. "I am educated and I speak perfect English. So perfect, as a matter of clarification, that I have to dumb down my role for *Duffy's Tavern*," Eddie Green later recalled circa 1949 in an interview with actor Lionel Barrymore (who then had a three-a-week interview radio program). "Contrary to what the listeners think, I have to speak Negro in order to assume the stereotype. Folks stop me on the street and ask me about *Duffy's Tavern* and once a fellow walked away believing I was trying to pass myself off as Eddie Green. 'You don't sound like Eddie Green,' he told me. 'I don't sound like myself, either,' I told him."

Ed Gardner taking tennis lessons during his down time.

307

The Alan Young Connection

Radio was not exactly famed for developing its own talent, but rather known for discovering (or borrowing from the stage) existing talent. Case in point: Alan Young, who wisely abjured the school which would have invited microphone homicide by invading Bob Hope's domain of the rapid-fire gag. Having received a medical discharge from the Canadian Navy, and served his apprenticeship on the networks emanating from Toronto, Young made his American radio debut in January of 1944 on *The Radio Hall of Fame*. He was quickly signed for the starring lead in a situation comedy developed by the crew at Young & Rubicam.

The advertising agency was presently representing Bristol-Myers, the sponsor of Eddie Cantor's radio program, *Time to Smile*, which was hawking Sal Hepatica between songs and jokes. Seeking a summer replacement for the sponsor's contracted time slot for the summer of 1944, Young & Rubicam hired Alan Young to portray himself, with a knack for becoming ensnarled in major complications, such as buying a railroad ticket and wandering through Brenbracker's department store. "While not always enjoying an evenness of presentation, his adventures in the store were fresh and bright and should prove one of the more diverting running gags on the kilocycles," remarked a critic for the *New York Times*.

Ironically, an executive at Young & Rubicam discovered Alan Young through a fluke. They were tuning in for *Duffy's* but instead heard Young on *The Radio Hall of Fame*. When Young's summer show proved to be a success, he received his own prime time program, *The Alan Young Show*, in the spot on the Blue Network formerly occupied by *Duffy's Tavern*.

Young was granted the aid of a good supporting cast, including Jim Backus, portraying an engaging stooge, singer Bea Wain (late of *Hit Parade*), and orchestral music conducted by Peter Van Steeden. Steeden was not the only party Young & Rubicam borrowed from the *Duffy's* program. Writer Will Glickman assisted with the scripts. Critics loved Alan Young and the actor received a rating that could rival the Alps. Cantor's substitute lasted a mere thirteen weeks but Bristol-Myers agreed to sponsor the series in the fall, provided it replace *Duffy's* former time slot of Tuesday evening since the *Tavern* was moving to Friday night.

Young & Rubicam was responsible for cross-promoting all of their programs, which explains Alan Young's guest appearance on Eddie Cantor's program on the evenings of June 13, 1945, and December 19, 1945. Ed Gardner, playing the role of Archie, also made a guest appearance on Cantor's comedy on December 5, 1946. Gardner played Archie on Alan Young's program on the evening of January 29, 1946. For the November 15, 1946, broadcast of *The Alan Young Show*, Alan attempts to impress Mr. Dittenfeffer by masquerading Veola Vonn as Madammoiseppe Yvette, a Paris fashion expert who creates fancy French cooking. Alan's big mistake was catering the dinner down at Duffy's Tavern with guests Archie and Finnegan. Charlie Cantor, *Duffy's* Finnegan, would become a regular on Alan Young's program during the 1946-47 season in the character of Zero, Alan's pal. (Adding another connection, Gardner even played the role of a professional forger in "The Palmer Method" on radio's *Suspense*, sponsored by the Schenley Distillers Corporation, a client of Young & Rubicam's, pitching Roma Wines.)

In January 1946, Ed Gardner suffered a severe infection that was quickly diagnosed as acute tonsillitis. A doctor broke the news: Gardner had to have the surgical procedure known as a tonsillectomy. The comedian immediately notified executives at Young & Rubicam. One solution was to hire a Hollywood celebrity to replace the character of Archie for a few weeks in February of 1946. Instead, via shrewd cross-promotion, they chose Alan Young. According to a press release dated February 2: "Ed Gardner of 'Archie' fame will not be on hand when *Duffy's Tavern* opens for business on Feb. 15. Right after this Friday's broadcast, Mr. G will go to the hospital for a tonsillectomy and is expected to miss at least one show. Alan Young will be substitute Boniface in the interim." At the time, no one could predict how long Gardner's recovery would take, so a total of three different scripts (primary writer credit by this time was to Larry Gelbart) were written with Alan Young in mind.

Unwilling to accept medical leave, Gardner was only vacant for the broadcast of February 15. On that particular evening,

FIFTEEN YEARS   JANUARY 7, 1946

TIME

S.Q's WEEKLY NEWSMAGAZINE

CLINT DUFFY'S "ARCHIE"
"...and I seen 3OOO Bum Beefs!"
(Crime News)

VOLUME J.C.!!!   REG. ALL STATES & FBI   NUMBER 70-837

*Artist conception from 1946 of Archie on the cover
of* Time *magazine.*

Eddie answered the phone for Archie, and exchanged the initial dialog with Duffy, almost immediately establishing the reason for Archie's departure. If Ed Gardner was having his tonsils removed, so was Archie. Alan Young dropped by, admired the tavern and unlike most of the weekly guests, found the place to his liking. The main attraction was Miss Duffy, whom Alan Young falls head over heels with. Recording artist Peggy Lee drops by the tavern in the usual fashion and, before her departure, sings a song for the radio audience.

For the broadcast of February 22, the entire crew at Duffy's Tavern is planning a welcome home party for Archie. Eddie again answers the phone but minutes later Archie walks through the doors and everyone breaks out in song. Miss Duffy attempted to have the bakery create a cake in the shape of tonsils but when the bakery discovered they had no such mold they asked if an appendix would be sufficient. Archie describes his hospital visit and compares anesthetic with the effects from drinking rye. Finnegan asks Archie to describe what it is like to be unconscious. Archie cracks jokes about the nurses (even with his arms in a cast the nurses still had to approach his bed in threes). During the party, Archie delivers a testimonial but no one has anything to add as the gang is busy eating… and eating… and eating… and a closing burp.

Murder in Duffy's Tavern

Four weeks after the theatrical release of the *Duffy's Tavern* movie, Ed Gardner decided to venture on his own as an independent producer. He began negotiating with investors to finance a series of *Duffy's Tavern* motion picture sequels. How Paramount agreed to sign a release or grant Ed Gardner first right of refusal for sequels remains unclear but a newspaper columnist reported that Gardner and the company "could not get together on a continuation." Before Halloween of 1945, Frank Gruber, who scripted *Johnny Angel*, verbally agreed to write the story scenario for *Murder in Duffy's Tavern*. Gardner, however, would not agree to Gruber's fee, and decided to write the story synopsis himself, which he promised the *Los Angeles Times* would feature "a murder a minute," supposedly writing eight murders into the first eight minutes of the script. The November 16 issue of the *Times* reported: "Ed Gardner gets *Murder in Duffy's Tavern* before the cameras around Jan. 1. He says there'll be as many gags as murders but in Duffy's language they're both the same."

In December 1945, Danny Winkler, representing Ed Gardner, huddled with executives of RKO, United Artists and Paramount

311

Ed Gardner getting lost in a good book.

over arrangements for the theatrical release of Gardner's first independent production. During the same month Norman Foster, known for helming series entries like Mr. Moto and Charlie Chan pictures and recently returned from Mexico, was named director of the proposed independent production. Frances Hyland, under contract to Republic, was borrowed for writing the shooting script. In January 1946, however, it was reported that Ed Gardner signed an agreement with Eliot Paul, author of *The Last Time I Saw Paris*, to use Paul's forthcoming novel, *Murder in Duffy's Tavern*, as the basis for the picture Gardner would make independently under the same title as the book. Paul would also write the shooting script. Random House was contracted to publish the Paul novel and it was anticipated that the book would be on the stands at the same time that the picture hit the screen. While one columnist reported "*Murder in Duffy's Tavern* was shaping up speedily," the April 29, 1946, issue of the *Los Angeles Times*, for reasons unknown, reported: "Ed Gardner's postponing *Murder in Duffy's Tavern* until fall so he can get caught up with his fishing. He'll spend the summer off the coast of Canada."

For the motion picture, a new character was created as part of the troupe hanging out at the tavern: "Pierre, the French Poodle." According to all accounts, the dog was not only added to supply comic appeal, but would ultimately solve the crime towards the end of the picture. This would explain why, in May 1946, Pierre was incorporated into two *Duffy's* radio broadcasts. For the radio broadcast of May 10, 1946, Finnegan's discovery, "Pierre" the talking dog, made his debut. The role of Pierre, the growling, singing, yodeling dog that wants a part in the tavern floor show, was played by Charles Cantor. Eddie Marr also had a part in this broadcast, acting as the representative of the Ringling Brothers and Barnum and Bailey Circus, called in by Archie to witness the singing dog, "Pierre the Poodle." Marr would play small bit parts of various roles in every *Duffy's Tavern* episode, beginning with this broadcast, until the end of the season. For the broadcast of May 17, the crew at Duffy's Tavern was trying to come up with ideas (some of them corny) on how to get Pierre the Poodle the starring lead on his own radio show. Had the movie been put into production, Gardner explained to one journalist, Pierre, the French Poodle, would have been played by a midget in a dog costume. When Edgar Bergen heard Ed Gardner added a dog to *Duffy's Tavern*, he remarked, "What's radio coming to?" (That from a man who had been making money off a dummy for years.) Pierre's appearance on the radio program was short-lived. He was dropped after two broadcasts, never to return (probably because that was about the time Gardner dropped the idea of the motion picture sequel.)

In March of 1947, Gardner revived his idea for continuing his *Duffy's Tavern* motion pictures. Vincent Bogert, a staff writer for the radio program, went to work on the script. To date, nothing else has been unearthed about the second proposed movie sequel except for a brief mention in the April 9, 1947 issue of the *Los Angeles Times* which reported, "Ed Gardner is talking to Irving Berlin about writing the music for a *Duffy's Tavern* movie." Paramount continued to profit from the movie when *Duffy's Tavern* was reissued to theaters on a limited number of screens across the country in the spring and summer of 1948.*

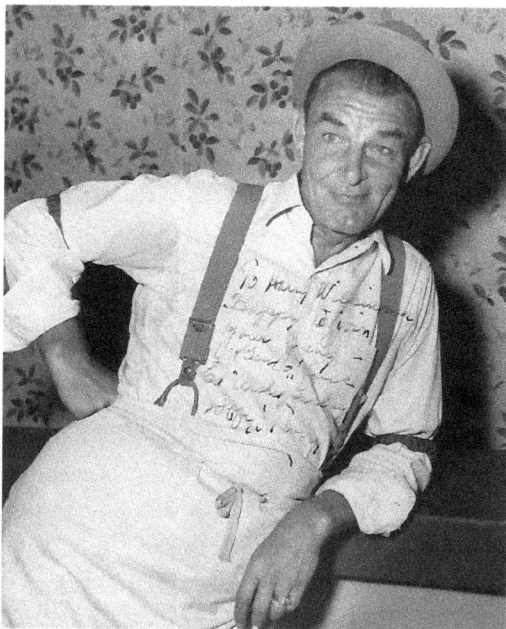

(Photo courtesy of Mike Bennett.)

---

* Newspapers in May 1946 reported "Gardner is now in Hollywood filming *Murder in Duffy's Tavern*." Knowing how gossip columnists ran with a story they felt was from credible sources, and knowing today how the movie never went into production, this is another case in which news blurbs in old newspapers cannot be counted on for accuracy.

Highlights of the Season

The broadcast of November 23, 1945, was regarded as one of Ed Gardner's favorites of the season according to one of his letters dated April 14, 1946. Among the jokes Gardner admired was this one about Wardheeler McGinnis who hung out at Duffy's: "Is he charging?" Archie asks Eddie. "Like the Light Brigade," is the reply. Later, Archie seeks a good slogan and comes up with "Remember the Maine." Eddie's suggestion is "How about 'Remember the Ptomaine'?" Just weeks prior, Gardner also admired a number of political jokes. Miss Duffy opposes the poll tax because she doesn't think people should have to pay a special tax just because they're from Poland. Meanwhile, Finnegan urges the use of blank campaign buttons because "you can't afford to ignore the illiterate vote."

In January 1946, night club comic Dave Barry performed his ever-popular stage show in New York with an impersonation bit for the finale which included Ned Sparks, Winston Churchill and Archie of *Duffy's Tavern*. (Other comedians successfully impersonated characters from *Duffy's Tavern*, including Archie, such as Ollie O'Toole on the Horace Heidt radio program three years earlier.) Larry Storch, another impressionist, received a quick rise to fame as a result of his stage and radio work. Elon Packard and Stanley Davis, scriptwriters for *The Kraft Music Hall*, starring Frank Morgan, won Storch's gratitude when they learned he was being released from the navy and had ambitions to be an impressionist. A demonstration was asked for and given. Packard and Davis couldn't get to Norman Blackburn at the J. Walter Thompson agency fast enough with the glowing report of their new discovery. He was signed pronto for Kraft and the Elgin-sponsored Christmas show and when the word got around, Ed Gardner booked him for a guest shot on *Duffy's Tavern*. Thompson had a contractual hold on him and considered giving Storch a weekly program on radio station KMH. The December 6, 1945, broadcast of *The Kraft Music Hall* proved Storch could handle his own before the radio mike. Within weeks, comedian Larry Storch was making his own mark at the Copacabana in New York City.

With mimics available in glut quantities, to make a real mark took exceptional ability and exceptional material. Storch scored moderately in both departments. He offered a long list of standard characterizations, including a few very good ones. His best (according to columnists in trade papers) were Winston Churchill, Ray Milland, Frank Morgan and Archie of *Duffy's Tavern*. Each bit was provided with an O. Henry finish, which became Storch's stage trademark. Storch had been around for some years and was performing at Ciro's on the West Coast but he never caught on in New York until 1946. On the evening of January 11, 1946, Archie tries to get Duffy's backing for his movie production. Larry Storch is looking for a job and stops by the tavern to offer his services. Storch is referred to as "a kid" by Archie throughout the broadcast. While finishing a rendition of "The Life of Archie," Storch offers a stupendous drama that features none other than the leading stars: Hedy Lamar, Frank Morgan, Ronald Colman, Peter Lorre, Humphrey Bogart, Clark Gable, Barry Fitzgerald, "Finnegan," and Storch played all of the roles in a murder story that took place in Hollywood.

Duffy's Tavern *art by Sam Berman.*

During the broadcast of April 5, 1946, in the middle of broadcasting *Duffy's Tavern*, Larry Bern, husband of Sandra Gould, was stricken with a heart attack and had to be rushed from the control booth to the Cedars of Lebanon Hospital. Bern was a radio celeb himself, being producer of the Jack Carson shows. Because this episode is not known to exist in recorded form, at the time this book went to print, it remained uncertain whether the Miss Duffy character was featured on the program that evening.

On May 4, 1946, Warner Bros. theatrically released their latest Looney Tunes cartoon, *Hush My Mouse*. Directed by Chuck Jones, with voice characterizations by Mel Blanc, Sniffles the Mouse made his last of 12 Warner Brothers cartoon appearances in a spoof of the radio show *Duffy's Tavern*. At Tuffy's Tavern, tough guy Edward G. Robincat comes in for today's special, mouse knuckles. Artie the manager sends his moronic flunky Filligan to catch the over-talkative little Sniffles Mouse. After a few chase gags, Sniffles turns the tables by putting his little hat on a bulldog's bone. Filligan brings the bone to the Tavern, where the bulldog retrieves his bone by beating up Robincat and Artie. Filligan tells Tuffy over the phone, "No, he doesn't need mouse knuckles, but he can sure use some brass knuckles!" (Coincidentally, Sara Berner, the one-time Miss Duffy in 1944, supplied the voice of Sniffles the Mouse for this cartoon.)

Hoping to tie in his show with the Helldorado Rodeo Celebration in Las Vegas, Ed Gardner requested permission of his sponsor, Bristol-Myers, to air *Duffy's Tavern* from Nevada. The May 24, 1946, broadcast originated from the USO Building. The celebrity guest was Roy Rogers. On that particular evening, Archie's uncle left him a saloon in Las Vegas so Archie, Finnegan and Eddie set out to find the place and meet Roy Rogers. Two-Gun Archie, as he calls himself, tries to impress the King of the Cowboys, who discusses one of his movies and sings a song. After pressure from Archie, Roy finally agrees to introduce the barkeep to a casting director over at Republic Pictures.

Ed Gardner and the King of the Cowboys.

SEASON SIX
September 21, 1945, to June 14, 1946
National Broadcasting Company
Sponsor: Bristol-Myers
Day and Time: Friday, 8:30 to 9:00 p.m.
Broadcast from Hollywood, alternating between
Studio A and C at NBC
East Coast broadcast: Friday, 8:30 to 9:00 p.m., EST
(East Coast performance at 5:30 to 6:00 p.m., Pacific Time)
West Coast broadcast: Friday, 8:30 to 9:00 p.m., EST
Complete season originates from Hollywood.
Sponsored by the Bristol-Myers Company
Advertising Agency: Young & Rubicam
Director: David Titus
Assistant Director: Karl Gruener
Music: Matty Malneck and his Orchestra
Sound: Vic Liveti
Sound Mixer: Ralph Reid
Announcer: Marvin Miller
Scriptwriters: Tom Adair, Vincent Bogert, Sid Dorfman, Ray
Ellis, Hy Freedman, Larry Gelbart, Ray Glazer, Bill Manhoff,
Larry Marks, Bill Wagner
Producer for Young & Rubicam: David Titus
Commercial Writer: Sylvia Dowling
Commercial Supervisor: Innes Harris (Hollywood)
Commercial Supervisor: John Swayze (New York)

Cast
Charles Cantor as Finnegan
Eddie Green as Eddie
Sandra Gould as Miss Duffy
Alan Reed as Falstaff Openshaw (September 21 to
October 19, 1945)

Episode #175 — Broadcast Friday, September 21, 1945
Plot: See page 302.

Episode #176 — Broadcast Friday, September 28, 1945
Guest: Deems Taylor
Plot: Falstaff Openshaw wants to propose to Miss Duffy but her father won't allow the poet into the house. Meanwhile, Deems Taylor, music composer and critic, drops by the tavern and Finnegan mistakes him for Spike Jones. Archie has written an opera and wants the cast to put it on so Deems Taylor can provide a professional opinion. Miss Duffy cannot hit the high notes while characters Ipso and Facto clearly rip off a Romeo and Juliet premise. Falstaff adds to the mayhem by playing the role of a referee at a prize fight. Naturally, Taylor thinks the opera stinks.

Trivia, etc. Ed Gardner slips a lip when he makes reference to how much box office his new movie is doing.

Episode #177 — Broadcast Friday, October 5, 1945
Plot: Archie gets a book from the Eagle Eye School of Crime Detection and, after reading it, wants to be the next Bulldog Drummond or "Fido Vance." After learning what a shady criminal looks like, he starts accusing people in the tavern of lifting money from the till... only to reveal in the end that Archie took the money himself so he could pay for the detective course. Falstaff dedicates one of his poems to the boys who will be spending Christmas overseas. He reads his poem as part of the program and includes a plea to mail overseas Christmas gifts early.

Episode #178 — Broadcast Friday, October 12, 1945
Guest: Monty Woolley
Plot: The cultured and dignified actor Monty Woolley arrives at Duffy's Tavern and Archie convinces him to participate in a rendition of his original production, a historical documentary about Falstaff Openshaw. During the program, Archie imitates Fred Allen.

Episode #179 — Broadcast Friday, October 19, 1945
Plot: Tonight's program is announced as being "presented in cooperation with the Drug, Cosmetic, and Allied Industries by the Bristol-Myers Company in behalf of the Veterans Information

Program." The entire show concerns welcoming home the veteran and how to assist him in both personal and business rehabilitation. The reconversion problem receives attention and the proprietor of Duffy's Tavern pledges — via telephone to Archie — that welcoming returning servicemen, rearranging the tavern if necessary to hasten reconversion, and checking all tavern transactions to avoid inflation, will be the future policy of the business. (This same message was delivered, modestly, in the *Duffy's Tavern* motion picture which was presently being shown in movie theaters at the time this episode was broadcast.) Along with the serious message, Archie wants to get a pilot's license so he can fly a helicopter. Falstaff thinks he knows all about romance and tries to assist Miss Duffy. This was also the last of a number of consecutive appearances of Falstaff Openshaw, the poet, played by Alan Reed.

Episode #180 — Broadcast Friday, October 26, 1945

Plot: Archie's Uncle Morton Q. Poggenburg shows up at the tavern and, knowing he's very wealthy and hasn't seen him since he was knee high, Archie tries to impress the uncle with his stupid intelligence. Since the uncle has always wanted to be on *Information Please*, the cast sets up their own version. Archie's plan fails when his super-intelligent nephew pays a visit.

Trivia: Poggenburg was Ed Gardner's birth name.

Episode #181 — Broadcast Friday, November 2, 1945

Plot: Tavern talk about the recent Halloween party momentarily overshadows Uncle Morton, who still hangs out at the tavern. Archie's old school teacher, Miss Dinwhitty, is coming to visit and Archie once again tries to impress someone with his inferior intelligence.

Episode #182 — Broadcast Friday, November 9, 1945

Guest: Maxie Rosenbloom

Plot: When Archie verifies Eddie is working for the opposition, now employed at Grogan's Grill, he sees no other alternative than to call the employment agency and hire a new waiter. "Slapsie"

Maxie Rosenbloom, the prize fighter, shows up and Archie mistakes him for someone else. He didn't recognize Rosenbloom standing up. Rosenbloom, however, takes a bullying approach by using customers to mop up spills, mistakes payments for tips and creates too many problems. When Archie discovers Eddie never quit, he is forced to fire Rosenbloom... which causes Archie to witness his own knockout.

Trivia, etc. The repeat broadcast (11:30 to midnight) was broadcast from the Fox Beverly Theater in Beverly Hills, California. At one point during the broadcast, Rosenbloom accidentally makes a slip of the lip when he says "appointment" instead of "opponent" and tries to cover his mistake over the air.

Episode #183 — Broadcast Friday, November 16, 1945
Plot: Archie, having met a fortune teller named Madame Zooma at Bullethead Branigan's, hires her to help double the business at Duffy's Tavern. When Archie's mysterious (and anonymous) uncle leaves him his entire fortune, Eddie suspects this is part of a post war racket. Madame Zooma, however, attempts a séance to contact the uncle... Archie refers to the séance as "Information Please." Only after it is too late does Archie discover the woman is a con artist and emptied the cash register before leaving. It was she who sent the letter.

Memorable Lines:
MISS DUFFY: It's men like you that make it a pleasure for a
    girl to be an old maid.
ARCHIE: Glad to be of service.

Episode #184 — Broadcast Friday, November 23, 1945
Plot: Archie puts on an essay contest so the tavern can have a slogan. Archie creates the rules of the contest, open to employees and customers of Duffy's Tavern, with a five dollar prize. Eddie comes up with "I like to eat at Duffy's Tavern because they have had the same quality and the same food since time in memoriam." Later he comes up with "Mealtime adventures at Duffy's Tavern - Staring Death in the face three times a day." But no one seems to

care once Grogan's Bar and Grill across the street adds fan dancers to their stage show.

Episode #185 — Broadcast Friday, November 30, 1945
Plot: Dave Hossinger believes he has harnessed the secret of splitting the atom and wants to let Archie in on the scheme. He wants Archie to invest in an "expedition" to the Balkans. There is a professor there, Dave explains, who is really a secret agent on the trail of another atom-bomb secret. Dave even phones the War Department in Washington D.C. in an effort to aid the cause. A professor shows up and is surprised to find that the folks involved are crackpots and Archie loses his percentage of the profits.

Episode #186 — Broadcast Friday, December 7, 1945
Plot: Archie plans a date with his Christmas bonus. Archie is spellbound with a new girl, Amber McNulty, who finds Archie a bore when it comes to romance and, in the end, picks up Finnegan for a good movie and sits in the balcony.

Episode #187 — Broadcast Friday, December 14, 1945
Supporting Cast: Ed Monroe
Plot: Archie hires a lawyer to go after Duffy, claiming he deserves a raise, is seriously underpaid, and works at a tavern with deplorable working conditions. Sneaky business methods are exposed such as fake bottoms in the mugs, but the lawyer phones Duffy to get permission to take five bucks out of the till for his fee and leaves, knowing his five dollar fee from Duffy to turn and look the other way is more money than he's being paid to represent Archie!

Episode #188 — Broadcast Friday, December 21, 1945
Guest: Robert Maxwell plays the harp.
Plot: Archie and Eddie plan to put on a Christmas pageant at the tavern. Archie describes this show as the "Centennial Christmas Show." Eddie and Archie discuss the Christmas season and spirit in general, how to bring joy to the tavern guests, etc. Finnegan starts to doubt whether there is a Santa Claus, having seen the beard come off the one in the department store. Miss Duffy has been doing her last minute Christmas shopping. Eddie Green

does a solo number and vocals on "Santa Claus is Coming to Town." The crew then rehearses by imitating certain actors like Boyer and Laughton. The cast does their own inane version of "A Christmas Carol" with Archie playing the role of Ebenezer Scrooge, who finished eating at Ye Olde Duffy's Tavern and thinks Christmas is a "humbug." Scrooge is a miser, having bankrupted three widows, talked six babies out of their candy and started an anti-Santa Claus rumor at the orphanage. An angel (played by Eddie) visits Scrooge and takes him on a trip through time to see the errors of his ways. Finnegan plays the role of Tiny Tim and Miss Duffy plays Cratchit's wife.

Episode #189 — Broadcast Friday, December 28, 1945

Plot: The bookkeeper is coming and Archie, having lifted a few dollars here and there, is worried about his job (and Duffy's heart) when the discovery is made and word reaches the tavern owner. In an effort to balance the books, Archie starts to call in the tavern debts. When Miss Duffy gives Archie an idea how to pad the figures (making 3 look like an 8), Archie finds partial success. But bribing the bookkeeper isn't possible and, as a last resort, Archie gets Miss Duffy to flirt with the married man and Finnegan, the jealous husband, pulls out a knife and creates a scene. The bookkeeper quickly flees through the front door.

Trivia, etc. According to the NBC Files, there is no closing commercial presented on this program. There was a Christmas theme throughout the program.

Episode #190 — Broadcast Friday, January 4, 1946

Guest: Alan Ladd

Plot: Archie reminds Duffy that tough guy leading man Alan Ladd, who is stopping by the tavern, was in his motion picture. Finnegan keeps mistaking Ladd for an actor from the Hope and Crosby pictures… Bing Crosby. Miss Duffy doesn't care if Ladd is married so she attempts to take him out on a night about town. Archie comments, "When this dame says 'hubba hubba,' what she's thinking is hubby hubby." Ladd is subjected to playing a role in Archie's new movie script, a take on Hitchcock's *Spellbound*.

Memorable Lines
ARCHIE: Well Alan, welcome to Duffy's Tavern.
LADD: Duffy's Tavern - as I live and breathe.
ARCHIE: Well, take your choice, Mr. Ladd — around here you can't do both.

Episode #191 — Broadcast Friday, January 11, 1946
Guest: Larry Storch
Plot: See page 315.

Episode #192 — Broadcast Friday, January 18, 1946
Plot: This was an "educational" program. Archie invites his former school teacher to visit his "Tea Tavern," where he will serve her tea and ask her to take part in a forum discussion on "Contemporary Affairs." He refers to his teacher as "Miss Henrietta Riblet." Archie recalls with fondness how they used to call her "piano legs." He creates a scheme in an attempt to impress her, so she will have high hopes for a former student, but he fails miserably.

Memorable Lines
ARCHIE: Don't you remember Clara Shultz?
TEACHER: (trying to remember) Clara Shultz…
ARCHIE: Remember the redhead that was always showin' off?
TEACHER: Oh yes. I saw Clara about a year ago. She's married and has 12 children.
ARCHIE: Well, once a show-off, always a show-off.

Episode #193 — Broadcast Friday, January 25, 1946
Plot: Archie considers his future investments, dreaming of the day he can retire. When a "March of Dimes" poster is put on display in the tavern, Archie decides to invest in someone else's future. Eddie talks about what a good cause the March of Dimes drive is: "A good cause? Well, it should be," he explains. "It was started by a pretty good man — that Mr. F.D.R!"

Episode #194 — Broadcast Friday, February 1, 1946
Guest: Peggy Lee
Plot: Peggy Lee makes her first of three consecutive appearances

on the program. Having spent a lot of nickels to hear Peggy Lee's voice from the jukebox, Archie has fallen in love with the singer. After renting a new suit from the Duke of Windsor Clothing Company, he tries to impress her. "What a stack of *Esquires*" and "No wonder your voice comes out so good. Look where it's been," Archie remarks. When Duffy wants to come down to the tavern to check out Peggy Lee's curves, Archie, jealous, phones Duffy's wife anonymously, keeping his boss at home. When he discovers that Peggy Lee won't stay at the tavern 'til she meets the employer, Archie disguises Finnegan as Duffy. His plan backfires when Peggy falls in love with Finnegan.

Episode #195 — Broadcast Friday, February 8, 1946
Guest: Peggy Lee
Plot: Archie spends the entire day preparing his farewell. The tavern manager will be visiting the hospital to undergo a tonsillectomy. Finnegan and Miss Duffy frighten Archie into thinking he will not survive the operation so he creates his last will and testament. At the close of the show, an announcement is made that "Archie" really will go to the hospital for a tonsillectomy and that he will be away from the program for one week and return the week after.

Memorable Lines
MISS DUFFY: What's the matter? You look a little green around the gills.

ARCHIE: I ain't being around the gills at all. In fact, I was just having a laugh. Finnegan was telling me how his Uncle Willy died from having his tonsils out.

MISS DUFFY: And what's so funny about that? Thousands of people die every day from having their tonsils out.

ARCHIE: Now Miss Duffy, don't exaggerate. It's just a simple little operation. Besides, what do you know about it?

MISS DUFFY: What do I know about? Well, I had my tonsils out when I was a little girl.

ARCHIE: Well, in those days science was still gropin'. They probably tied a string around your tonsils and slammed the door.

326

MISS DUFFY: I know what I'm talkin' about. Listen, Archie. I knew a girl once, whose brother had a friend that worked for a man that sold old magazines to a doctor. And this doctor told him…

ARCHIE: Now wait just a second. You lost me in the reception room. Who told who what?

MISS DUFFY: Well, he told the boss of the boy whose friend was my girlfriend's brother. That's who.

ARCHIE: Oh.

Episode #196 — Broadcast Friday, February 15, 1946
Guests: Peggy Lee and Alan Young
Plot: See pages 309 to 311. Peggy Lee makes her third and final appearance on the program and sings a song.

Episode #197 — Broadcast Friday, February 22, 1946
Plot: See page 311.

Trivia, etc. One of the unused drafts for February 22 featured a variation of what really was broadcast. Eddie again answers the phone in place of Archie, who is reported to be home from the hospital, recovering from the surgery. Clancy the Cop drops by and talks about his own experience with a tonsillectomy. Before leaving, Clancy manages to sell tickets to the policeman's ball to Alan Young, who dropped by the tavern again to catch another glimpse of Miss Duffy. The tavern owner's daughter, meanwhile, composes a poem in homage to her good friend, named after Archie. Actor Reginald Gardiner shows up at the Tavern and exchanges the usual jabs about the joint. Alan Young, still unable to see the tavern's flaws, defends the place — and Miss Duffy's honor. To everyone's surprise, Archie shows up at the end for a brief few lines to thank everyone for the get well cards and, out of friendship, buy a ticket from Clancy.

Towards the end of the broadcast, there were six seconds of line noise and breaking up of the program which began at 8:55:25. NBC apologized to executives at Young & Rubicam for the technical error.

327

Episode #198 — Broadcast Friday, March 1, 1946
Plot: With Archie back, everything resumes to normal and Archie now answers the phone to address his employer. One of the nurses from the hospital sent Archie a plant and the tavern manager is touched, especially when he disregarded the nurse during his entire stay. This germs an idea to grow a garden in the back of the tavern and Archie tricks Finnegan into removing all the junk so they can plant soil and seeds. Only in the end, after it is too late, does Archie discover what kind of a plant it is — poison ivy.

Trivia, etc. This program concluded thirty seconds earlier than normal, with a Red Cross announcement. March 1 was American Red Cross Day at NBC.

With radio scripts written two to three weeks in advance, it was originally intended to have Alan Young make a total of three consecutive guest appearances (substantiated by a new blurb in the *New York Times*.) The following is a summary of the alternate script that featured Alan Young and Ed Gardner. It would later be re-written for the same March 1 broadcast date, sans Young. Archie is back and answers the phone as usual, cracking jokes about the horrible nurse he had in the hospital. Alan Young shows up with a plant, which he wanted to give as a welcome back gift. Meanwhile, the tavern crew try to learn more about vegetables and farms, and Archie uses a book from the library to discover what kind of a plant it is — until he learns at the end it's poison ivy.

Memorable Lines
MISS DUFFY: Wait a second Archie, just what are you insinuating?
ARCHIE: I am merely insinuating that you are the only dame that I know who, when you're getting ready for bed, the guy across the street pulls his shades down.

Episode #199 — Broadcast Friday, March 8, 1946
Guest: Reginald Gardiner
Plot: Reginald Gardiner plays the part of Sir Heathcliffe Batterswick, Englishman. The program featured a take-off on the "United Nations Organizations" meetings in the United States.

Archie spends his time planning to have the United Nations re-hold their meetings at Duffy's Tavern. Gardiner was currently appearing in the 20th Century Fox production of *The Dolly Sisters*.

Trivia, etc. Reginald Gardiner was originally scheduled for the broadcast of February 22 but, due to Gardner's tonsillectomy, his appearance was postponed a few weeks.

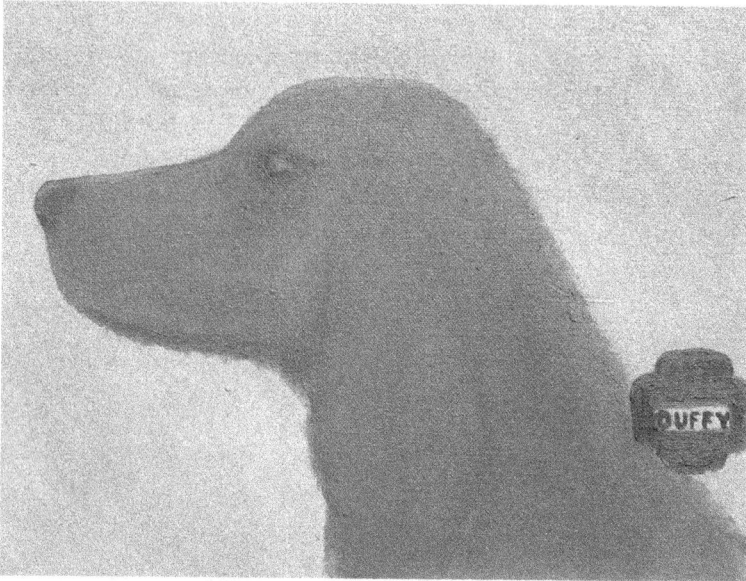

Ed Gardner's painting of Duffy, the dog.

Episode #200 — Broadcast Friday, March 15, 1946
Guest: Morton Downey, singer
Plot: Popular singer Morton Downey, who spent a large amount of time in 1945 and early 1946 performing for troops courtesy of overseas tours, made a few guest appearances on radio programs in the spring of 1946, *The Fitch Bandwagon* (starring Cass Daley) among them. Downey was in California for a short spell in the hopes of finding a job at the Hollywood studios. Days after this *Duffy's Tavern* radio broadcast, Downey went back to New York to perform on stage with Jimmy Walker at the Copacabana. At the time this book was completed, details about this particular radio broadcast remain unknown.

Episode #201 — Broadcast Friday, March 22, 1946
Guest: Diana Lynn
Plot: Archie attempts to offer a piano course and expensive lessons, and actress (and former piano prodigy) Diana Lynn might be his first customer. Archie refers to Lynn as "so fully packed,"

referencing a popular cigarette commercial slogan. Lynn cracks jokes about Gardner and how Paramount is still laughing at him. When she proves to Archie that she is a better student on the piano than her teacher, he gives up.

Episode #202 — Broadcast Friday, March 29, 1946
Guest: Harry Von Zell
Plot: Harry Von Zell, former announcer of *Duffy's Tavern* and present announcer on Eddie Cantor's show (both shows were represented by the same advertising agency), is coming down to visit the tavern and Archie tosses about the idea of renovating the place into a hotel and calling it Duffy's Hotel. His ideas about decorating the rooms are beyond silly and Von Zell simply will not invest. He will, however, participate in Archie's radio program proposal, "John's Other Hopkins, subtitled Stella Fefnik - Girl Woman." The murder story is funny but at the end the potential sponsor phones the tavern and tells Archie there were problems. The fake radio script does not meet with their approval.

Episode #203 — Broadcast Friday, April 5, 1946
Guests: James Dunn and Benay Venuta, actress and vocalist
Plot: The guest spot includes reference to the fact that James Dunn is the Motion Picture Academy Award winner for his performance in *A Tree Grows in Brooklyn*. Archie reminds the audience that he was really born in Brooklyn. Duffy's Tavern has a new Oscar room in recognition of Dunn recently receiving the Oscar. Archie conspires with Finnegan to swipe Dunn's Oscar statuette when the actor is not looking. Dunn catches them in the act, gets it back and, upset, Dunn tells them he won't refer anyone to this stable.

Episode #204 — Broadcast Friday, April 12, 1946
Guest: Marie McDonald
Plot: Archie tries to get singer/actress/pin-up girl Marie McDonald ("The Body") to marry him, claiming he is a millionaire (and refers to himself as "The Wallet.") Pretending to buy and sell stock, Archie succeeds when McDonald agrees to marriage. But when Archie is forced to buy an engagement ring

with money he doesn't have, and McDonald wants a honeymoon on his non-existing yacht, Archie has Miss Duffy pretend to be his wife and Finnegan pretend to be his son.

Trivia, etc. McDonald replaced June Haver, who was unable to appear because of illness.

Episode #205 — Broadcast Friday, April 19, 1946
Plot: Archie believes he can make a quick buck by arranging for a boxing match in the tavern and selling tickets. He matches the inexperienced Finnegan against an experienced prizefighter like the Gorilla. Archie makes excuses for putting on the gloves himself, claiming he's no athlete. They hold the contest in the tavern, complete with ring and gloves.

Trivia, etc. This broadcast includes a plea for food saved here at home to send to the children of war-stricken and famished lands. Archie talks with Duffy in one of the usual telephone conversations but makes the subject of the closing conversation about the importance of saving food. He refers to appeals made to the nation by President Truman and by Herbert Hoover in a broadcast about Europe's food crisis heard earlier on the same evening.

Episode #206 — Broadcast Friday, April 26, 1946
Guest: Esther Williams
Plot: Swimming movie star Esther Williams models clothes for Archie's fashion show. When she expresses her own style of clothing to wear, Archie is forced to accommodate with his own fashion improvements. Disguised as a fashion expert, Finnegan attempts to convince Williams that the rag Archie wants her to wear is a masterpiece of modern day fashion.

Episode #207 — Broadcast Friday, May 3, 1946
Plot: Duffy decides to take up reading. In conjunction with the special broadcast from April 19, the entire program was on the subject of sending food to the starving people of war-stricken areas such as India, Italy and Greece. The script departed from its

usual comedy style and gave a dramatization of the story of John Frederick Muehl, who went to India as a reporter and who wrote about the famine that existed in that land. The story was used with permission of the magazine *Asia and America*. In order to present the dramatization without interruption, the sponsor tonight gave up the use of the middle commercial.

Episode #208 — Broadcast Friday, May 10, 1946
Plot: See page 313.

Episode #209 — Broadcast Friday, May 17, 1946
Plot: See page 313.

Episode #210 — Broadcast Friday, May 24, 1946
Guest: Roy Rogers
Plot: See page 317.

Episode #211 — Broadcast Friday, May 31, 1946
Guest: Lena Horne
Plot: Eddie's new girlfriend is planning to show up at the tavern. He lied about his occupation and is afraid she will discover the truth. Hoping to avoid a confrontation with a hired muscle from the wrong end of the tracks, Archie believes he's solved Eddie's problem when he promotes the waiter to manager. The unsuspecting Eddie, hoping to impress Lena Horne, is unaware that someone is out gunning for the manager of Duffy's Tavern. Eddie treats Archie in a derogatory manner, adding insult to injury. Lena Horne sings "You Go To My Head." When the big guy arrives at the Tavern, it turns out he was hunting the manager to thank him for a favor and pays Eddie fifty dollars.

Episode #212 — Broadcast Friday, June 7, 1946
Plot: Archie meets a woman at the Lonely Hearts Club and she turns out to be a society dame. Miss Van Schnook plans the wedding and Archie gets cold feet, deciding not to marry her when he discovers her apples fell far from the tree. Archie dons a disguise and pretends to be an employee when she arrives at the tavern, telling her that Archie left town to go back home to his

wife and 12 children. She leaves, disgusted, and he wishes her luck in future endeavors. "And if you have any children, name them after - duh - Gargantua."

Trivia, etc. Due to a network error, only the "Broadcasting Company" portion of NBC was heard at the conclusion of the program.

Episode #213 — Broadcast Friday, June 14, 1946
Guest: Willard Waterman
Plot: The tavern is closing its doors for the summer and the cast discusses the various places they plan to visit while they are on vacation. Willard Waterman, a few years before becoming radio's second "Great Gildersleeve," was a guest to promote his weekly appearance on *Easy Money*, a radio program exposing rackets preying on unsuspecting people, which would fill the same time slot over the summer.

LANE vs. *DUFFY'S TAVERN*

Washington, D.C., Thursday, June 13, 1946. With worries over coming elections and pending bills that were considered politically dynamic, Congress gave little attention to a blast against NBC's program, *Duffy's Tavern*, delivered on the floor of the House this week by Rep. Thomas Lane. The Massachusetts Congressman inserted into the Congressional Record an editorial from *The Pilot*, the official organ of the Catholic Archdiocese of Boston, which accused Vitalis and Minit-Rub humorists of "bad taste in dragging the revered name of St. Patrick into the whiskey-soaked atmosphere of Duffy's saloon." The Catholic paper also objected to Archie's recent recital on the same program on a wake he attended which *The Pilot* charged was described as a "rowdy, disreputable affair." Lane complained that on two separate occasions, the program "referred to St. Patrick with unbecoming levity and has ridiculed those of Catholic faith." Lane also declared that the air belonged to the people who controlled it by a turn of the dial and that radio must accept "a greater responsibility to the people." The congressman read a letter from a Boston Catholic paper which called *Duffy's Tavern* a "direct insult" to the people of the Catholic faith.

Distinguished Achievement Award

Whereas Radio Life is dedicated to improvement in the arts of Radio, and Whereas the publishers are desirous of giving recognition to performances and accomplishments of outstanding merit, Now therefore be it known that

"Duffy's Tavern"

is cited for Distinguished Achievement during the Radio Season of 1946-47 as

Outstanding Scripter, Comedy
Honorable Mention

Done in Radio Life's 8th year of publication this 2nd day of Feb. 1947.

Radio Life

Evelyn A. Bigly
PUBLISHER

*One of many awards bestowed upon Ed Gardner
and* Duffy's Tavern.

335

CHAPTER TEN
THE VICE PRESIDENT OF NBC
VS.
RADIO COMEDIANS
(1946 - 1947)

IN JUNE 1946, MARK WOODS, THE PRESIDENT of the American Broadcasting Company, had a gab session with Ed Gardner concerning moving *Duffy's Tavern* to ABC in return for ABC stock. A partnership plan, which had been presented to Bing Crosby (and which, incidentally, Crosby accepted), indicated one of two ways the network was trying to lure listener-pulling personalities and to build up its nighttime ratings. The other was the promise of transcriptions — which Bing Crosby threw into his deal. Gardner had switched to NBC in an effort to boost his ratings and it succeeded for a time. When asked by a reporter, Gardner indicated that his chances of returning to ABC were slim, "unless Woods had an out-of-the-ordinary offer." Gardner, however, negated the latter implication by saying he would not consider a stock exchange deal. On Friday, June 21, Eddie Cantor's pact with Bristol-Myers and Young & Rubicam was torn up by mutual agreement of all involved. This paved the way for Cantor to start his stint for Pabst in the fall. Bristol-Myers stuck by its promise to Ed Gardner in giving him Cantor's Wednesday time slot at 9 p.m., EST on NBC. Two weeks later, the agency moved *The Alan Young Show* to fill the spot vacated by Gardner. It was here on Wednesday night that *Duffy's Tavern* remained for the next three seasons.

Ed Gardner, satisfied with NBC versus ABC regarding the number of radio stations on which *Duffy's Tavern* was broadcast, wanted the Wednesday night 9 p.m. time slot — considered most coveted by the comedian who spent the past two seasons on Friday evenings. Bristol-Myers owned the time slot but it was occupied by Eddie Cantor, who quietly requested the move to 8:30, occupied by Hildegarde's radio program. Young & Rubicam juggled the schedule in order to please all of their top stars... an adjustment that took almost four months in the summer of 1946. Joan Davis, in the meantime, took center stage on CBS for Swan Soap and when she expressed an interest in Eddie Cantor's former night and time slot, already promised to Ed Gardner and specified it in a term in the contract, Young & Rubicam was put in a tight spot. Executives at the ad agency attempted to please Davis, hoping to induce Gardner to relinquish first rights of refusal.

For every radio program that moved into a new time slot, another program was affected. Without spending fifteen pages documenting the entire affair, NBC wrapped up a number of deals that affected a number of radio programs. Eddie Cantor left Bristol-Myers for Pabst. Bristol-Myers released Danny Kaye from his contract instead of waiting until September 1947. Procter & Gamble, which had Rudy Vallee, gave up the time slot. Originally, a deal was being maneuvered for Ralph Edwards' *Truth or Consequences* to get into the Sunday period but that program stayed put on Saturday night. Alan Young moved into Ed Gardner's time slot, with Bristol-Myers currently shopping around for a new show to put into the Friday night ABC segment being vacated by Young. All of which left Cantor's Wednesday night 9 p.m.

From a 1946 issue of Radio Mirror: *(Standing) Ed Gardner with Don Wilson, Parkyakarkus, (sitting) Anthony Smythe, Bernice Berwyn and Michael Raffeto.*

spot open for Ed Gardner's *Duffy's Tavern*. Throughout all of the negotiations, there was a temporary offer on the table whereby Gardner, for a $200,000 asking price, would have relinquished his hold on the Wednesday night NBC time to permit Joan Davis to move in for Bristol-Myers. Gardner wanted the time slot bad enough to turn down $200,000 (equivalent to more than ten times that at the time of this book's writing) and Davis stayed on CBS for another semester for Swan Soap on Monday nights.

With *Duffy's Tavern* on Wednesday evening at 9 p.m., competition took the form of Frank Sinatra on CBS and *The Affairs of Ann Scotland* on ABC. The latter was a new crime drama starring Arlene Francis as a private detective. Bing Crosby was originally slated for the 9 p.m. time slot, but the crooner's contract with the network involved an option to eliminate the transcription disc format which Crosby so valiantly advocated. Under the contract, if Der Bingle could not catch at least 12 in the Hooper rating, Philco had the right of cancellation or going live within 26 weeks of notice. Just where to put Bing Crosby and his record pals was a tougher nut to crack than getting his autograph. ABC wanted him on Wednesday night but Crosby voiced his disgust over the time slot, over which he had no control, because some of Sinatra's fans might cut into the ratings. Crosby, who wanted radio money he could keep without losing most in taxes, received protection on the Philco deal from a capital gains setup. The solution was to schedule Crosby at 10 p.m. and leave the newly-developed female private eye scheduled to combat musical and comedy entertainment.

"Though in a different spot, and while there's no doubt that the malaprop Archie, played by Gardner, will garner a neat share of listeners, there was no doubt that this comedy show too frequently missed fire at the debut," remarked *Variety*. "The opening airer of the new series, which has moved into the ex-Eddie Cantor spot for Bristol-Myers Wednesday nights on NBC, had some laughs in Archie's telephonic conversation with Duffy, his boss, 'the little man who wasn't there,' and in the mangling of the King's English with Finnegan (Charlie Cantor), Miss Duffy (Sandra Gould), and Eddie the waiter (Eddie Green). But it certainly was a lot of talk to take for a half-hour, particularly when the comedy was as far-spaced as it was on the opening show." It was here that *Duffy's Tavern* began a slow and downward slump in the ratings. If Frank Sinatra's vocal chords could be blamed for the ratings slump, the novelty and comedy on *Duffy's Tavern* was half the blame. Faithful followers of both programs had to make a choice and the program enjoyed more reaped the rewards. The Wednesday night time slot was a gamble, to be sure, but a couple of muscles pushed against by Frank Sinatra, the opposition CBS tenant, went a number of rounds.

Over the summer of 1946, Ed Gardner and the family went on an ocean cruise aboard his yacht, the *Duffy's Tavern*, feeling comfortable knowing a strong season was ahead of him, regardless of the competition. In early September, Danny Winkler completed 24 comic strips featuring Ed Gardner's *Duffy's Tavern*; the intention was to syndicate a newspaper comic strip featuring

Ed Gardner woos Carmen Miranda.

the cast of the radio show and Winkler already had two syndicates interested. Gardner, returning from his trip, looked over the strips and approved the artwork. His price, however, was too steep and neither syndicate would pay more than their initial offer. The newspaper comic strip never went to press.

The October 3, 1946, issue of *Variety* reviewed the season

premiere: "The Tavern was jumpin' last night and that augurs well for Ed Gardner and his troupe of trained buffoons. Given a script built on solid laugh lines and spiced by the guesting of Carmen Miranda, the net result was a hilarious session at comedy, malapropism and general bawdiness. If the Tavern help can maintain the tempo of its first night it won't be lacking in customers the rest of the season. Gardner had more than the usual help from Charlie Cantor, Eddie Green, Sandra Gould and John Brown, and there was plenty of hop to the bedlam. Archie rocked the sitters with his play on words such as 'I know which side my Bristol is Myered on, or 'I'm a polygamist, I speak seven languages.' They're sure-fire and never lack for belly laughs and hand-pounding... the gag writers were in top form and the cast made every line ring with applause. Gardner should hope they do as well every week."

Added to Bristol-Myers' accomplishment was the fact that, so far as talent budgets went, the company account concentrated on low-cost shows. The biggest slab of its air talent budget was assigned to *Duffy's Tavern*, (then with a 22 Hooperating), and carried a $10,000 weekly tab for talent (cast, musicians and scriptwriters). Added to the talent was the fictional character Dave Hossinger (or Hosinger depending on which script you consult), who appeared frequently in the 1946-47 season, played by actor John Brown. The character of Hossinger made his first appearance on *Duffy's Tavern* with the broadcast of November 23, 1943, as an old friend of Archie's. Described best as a con man, Hossinger found Archie an easy victim of his schemes. Hossinger appeared on the program often enough that *Variety* columnists actually thought Hossinger was a real person, twice listing him among the cast credits for the show!

On the broadcast of October 2, a patron named Mary Meade, from Shreveport, Louisiana, with a thick southern accent, happens to be at the tavern (described as the new singer Duffy hired for vocal attraction) when guest Victor Mature arrives. She sings Irving Berlin's "Blue Skies," causing Mature to seek an interest in the beauty while Archie is forced to fight the macho actor for her affections. In an effort to calm the situation down, Archie palms off Clancy's niece as a blind date on Mature. She turns out to

Mary Meade

be a pip and Mary remains with the tavern. Mary Meade was tall, blonde and 22 years old at the time she made six appearances on the radio program from October 2 to November 6. She really was born in Louisiana and had a gifted voice which earned her numerous stage work in nightclubs. She was under contract with 20th Century-Fox but the movie studio failed to utilize her skills and she appeared in dozens of un-credited roles as showgirls, cigarette girls, stand-ins and chorus girls in musical numbers.

343

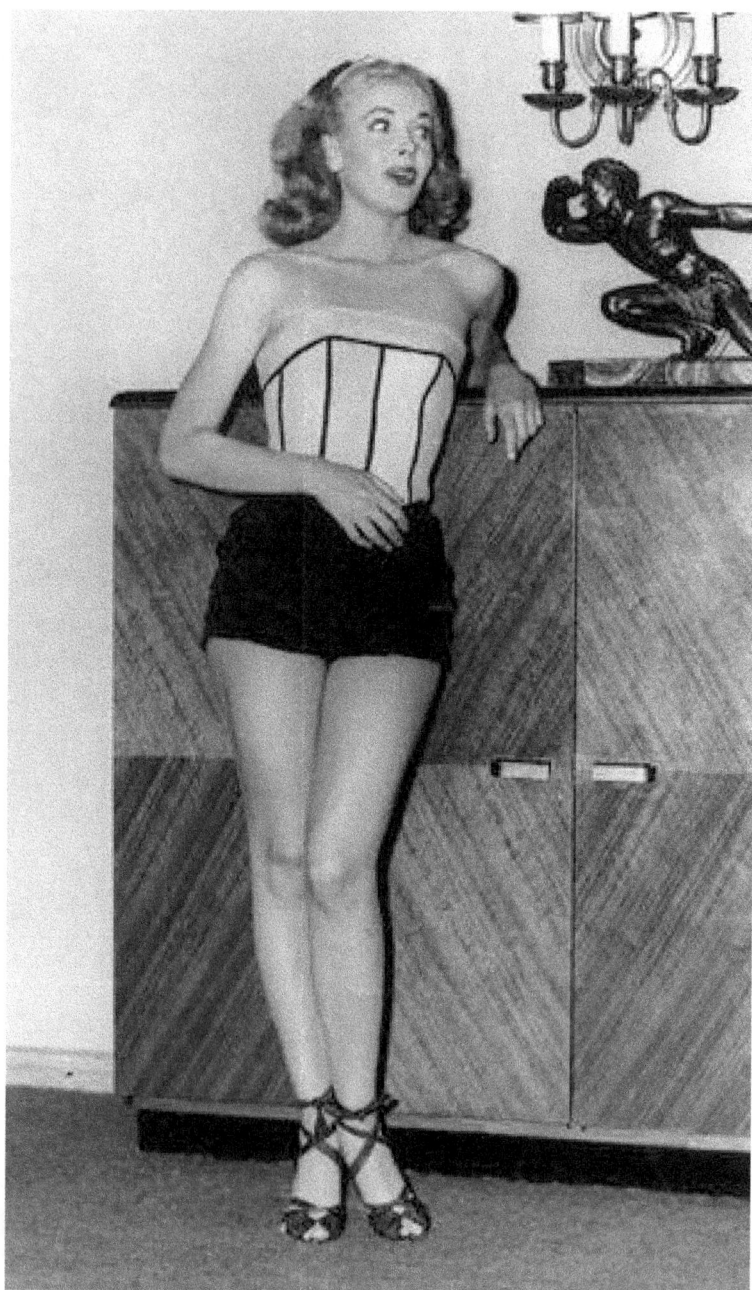

Mary Meade

During her brief stint on *Duffy's Tavern*, Mary could be seen in an uncredited role as a showgirl in *The Thrill of Brazil* (Columbia Pictures, 1946), but the movie was never mentioned or promoted at any time on the radio program. After *Duffy's*, she entertained GIs in the Philippines and Iwo Jima and went on to an exclusive short-lived contract with Eagle-Lion Studios. There, she costarred with Dennis O'Keefe in the independent film noir classic, *T-Men* (Edward Small Productions, 1947), released through Eagle-Lion. She later made the tabloids in 1959 when, for a short spell, she was dating Joe DiMaggio.

Two days before Thanksgiving 1946, Walter Winchell, in his own column, expressed how the *Duffy's Tavern* show was starting to drag. Perhaps he should have refrained from offering his opinion for columnist Paul Dennis published his own take on January 6, 1947, having attended a rehearsal for *Duffy's Tavern* at NBC in New York City. The New Year's broadcast had been the final episode to originate from the Hollywood studios. On January 2, the cast migrated to the Big Apple. Fred Allen was the celebrity guest. Archie wrote a radio script for Fred Allen titled "Dial in the Sun," a takeoff on *The Hucksters*. Archie plays the role of a business tycoon and Allen plays a new advertising man from the agency of Omar, Rudy and Khayam. Allen tries to convince the tycoon to sign up a singer, played by Miss Duffy, who sings a few bars from "To Each His Own." After the reenactment, Archie offers the script as a motion picture for Fred Allen, who rejects it.

According to Dennis' column, Allen's writer, Nat Hiken, was in the studio to write and help ad-lib Allen's lines. Tony Stanford, the director, spoke from the control room. "Hear me now?"

"Yes," said Gardner.

"Unfortunately," muttered Allen as a side remark.

Someone in the studio then told Dennis that a censor wouldn't allow a joke in the script, referring to a business tycoon as B.S. Archie, and Gardner suggested the joke be changed to B.O. Archie. Still no dice, as the censor suggested a safer route: S.B. Archie, but Gardner decided to skip the joke and the initials were changed to C.B. Jokes being censored by the network happened every day. While the network was nothing more than a conduit for the sponsor and the performers, it was also subjected to potential

345

legal action from listeners who took a dislike to offensive jokes. Comedians often tried varied ways of slipping jokes past the censors and in the months that followed, this culminated into a firestorm.

Archie's Little Love Song

Attempting to follow up on the success of "Leave Us Face It," the broadcast of October 23, 1946, featured the world premiere of "Archie's Little Love Song." With lyrics by Ed Gardner and music by Hoagy Carmichael, it came as no surprise that Carmichael himself appeared as a guest that evening, with Archie trying to trick the tavern guest to plug the song. When Gardner convinced Lotte Lehmann, the Metropolitan Opera star, to sing the song on his radio program, her appearance of October 9 was pushed forward to November 13. Mayfair Music distributed sheet music during the final week of November, hitting store shelves in time for the shopping holiday. It was about that same time that Dinah Shore, Frank Sinatra and Bing Crosby were supposedly considering singing their own renditions for record release. By the first week of December, Gardner announced his intentions of following up with another, this time a theme song for the entire cast to perform each week on the program. By Christmas, his attempts were extinguished when both Cantor and Gould expressed a concern; the actors would not sing a song unless they received additional payment. Nothing else has been found to follow up with the facts, leaving the impression that a third musical number was never completed.

"Archie's Little Love Song" was highlighted on a number of radio broadcasts as late as April 9, 1947, when Irving Berlin and Imogen Carpenter paid a visit to the tavern. Archie wants to collaborate in song writing with Berlin. Imogen Carpenter says she was sent by Toots Shor, who says she is a great singer. To test her vocal chords, Archie asks her to plug "Archie's Little Love Song" and play the piano. Berlin's appearance on the program was also in conjunction with 20th Century-Fox's rerelease of *Alexander's Ragtime Band* (1938) in movie theaters.

Miracle in Manhattan

At the suggestion of Ed Gardner, *Duffy's Tavern* decided to partially forego the usual comedy format on the evening of December 25, 1946, to offer the serious Christmas allegory "Miracle in Manhattan." The broadcast opens with Archie and the entire cast decking the tavern with mistletoe. Archie gets ready to lock up the tavern on Christmas Eve, grumpy because he's so tired of hearing the same old *Silent Night* music.

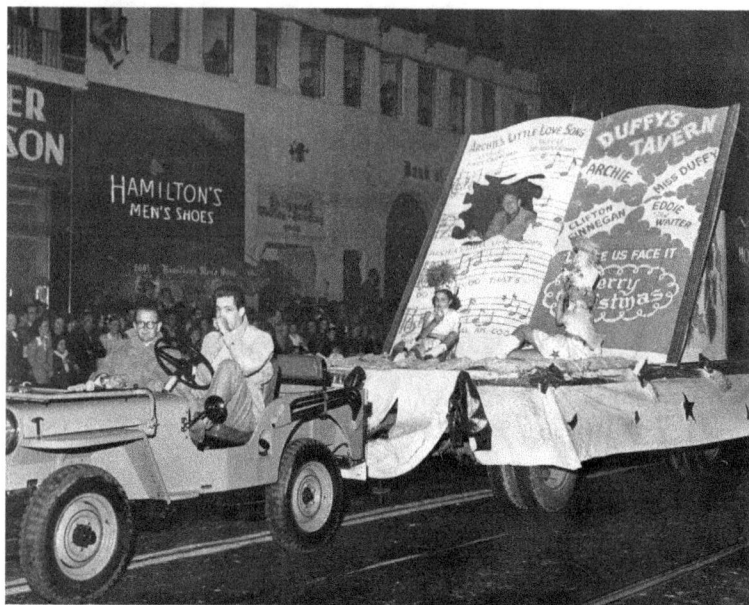

*"Archie's Little Love Song" promoted in a parade.
Location and year unknown.*

ARCHIE: Did you ever listen to the words of that song? All is
calm, all is bright. How do you like that? The world is a mess,
everybody has his hand in the other guy's pocket but it don't
make no difference to the guy who wrote that song. To him,
all is bright.

STRANGER: Well maybe the guy who wrote that song was
thinking of something in men's hearts. Something that shines
a little bit brighter on a day like this.

When a Stranger wanders into the tavern and calmly mystifies
Archie (the stranger says he comes from the East, near Bethlehem),
he encourages Archie to join him on a tour of familiar Manhattan
sights. Throughout the evening, Archie witnesses a number of
spectacles. He sees a crippled boy on the corner walk for the first
time in six years; a blind man regain his sight after being struck by
a taxicab; Joe DiMaggio shake hands with the urchins who admire
him; and he sees a young wife return to save her husband from

suicide. The Stranger explains the rationale to Archie, "That's the trouble with a lot of us. Maybe we're not growing up. Maybe we're just losing track of things that matter. Faith, tolerance and human kindness... You don't find them... you give them." And when the miracles have ended, Archie finds himself back in the tavern with the radio still playing *Silent Night* — only now Archie thinks the music is more than beautiful... it means something. Both Archie and the radio listeners are reminded of the spirit of Christmas, summed up by the Stranger moments before he vanishes.

STRANGER: Well, we all have our troubles, Archie. We all get off the track once in a while. We just need something bigger than ourselves to steer us straight.
ARCHIE: You mean something like... religion?
STRANGER: You can call it that. Call it human kindness... tolerance... understanding.

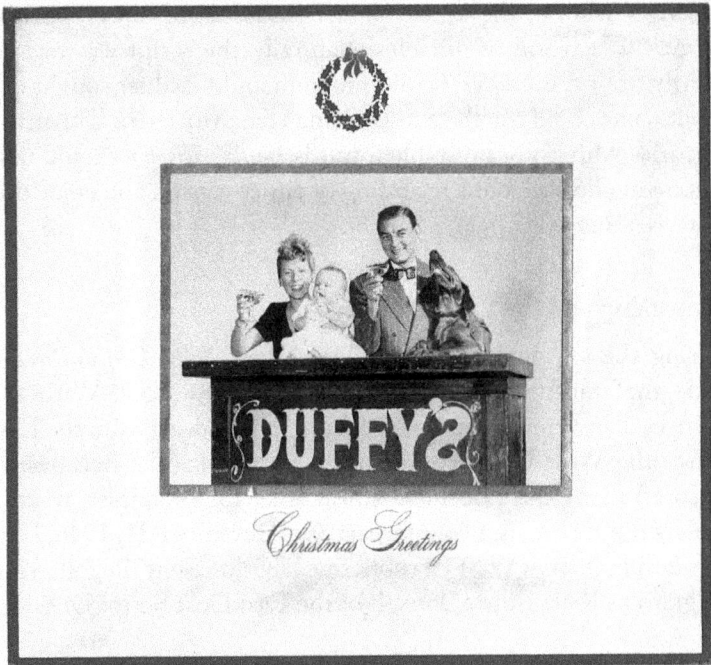

The Gardners' Christmas Card

This holiday offering was repeated on the *Duffy's Tavern* program for the Christmas of 1947, 1948 and 1949, becoming (although short-lived) an annual tradition. Playing the role of "The Stranger" for each rendition on *Duffy's* was Ira Grossel, also known as Jeff Chandler. Chandler would soon enough become a major screen star but would continue to double as a radio actor, sometimes under his birth name of Ira Grossel, supposedly to prevent the movie studios from discovering he was making additional money. For *Duffy's*, neither the name of Grossel or Chandler was mentioned during the opening or closing credits.

The assumption that Ed Gardner wrote "Miracle in Manhattan" originates with the numerous performances on *Duffy's Tavern* during the 1940s. The radio play was originally broadcast on *The Columbia Workshop* on the evening of December 21, 1941. The Christmas play was the creation of Charles Vanda, then the western division program director for CBS. Gardner played the role of a grumpy cab driver who received a strange Christmas Eve passenger who, in the same manner as described above, opened his eyes to a world of miracles. Naturally, the script was revised slightly to fit the *Duffy's Tavern* program and Gardner sought out Vanda so he could pay the author a small fee. Any fan of Christmas allegories who is not favorable towards *Duffy's Tavern* should take a moment and seek out a recording of either version and enjoy this heartwarming tale.

Censorship and the Vice-Presidents

During the seasonal holiday of December 1946, *Duffy's Tavern* made the transition from Hollywood to New York. With the entire cast and crew flying to New York to broadcast from the East Coast, the West Coast censorship department of NBC, having censored many lines deemed "unsuitable" for broadcast, wanted to alert the East Coast counterpart. On December 31, 1946, Don Honrath in NBC's West Coast Script Division, sent the following telegram to Richard McDonagh of the East Cost Script Division:

LAST DUFFY SHOW HERE THIS WEEK. GARDNER AND WRITERS

HAVE FEELING THEY ARE GOING TO
HAVE A GREAT TIME DURING THEIR
SOJURN IN NY. AM LEAVING IT UP TO
YOU TO DISILLUSION HIM. AS YOU
KNOW, GARDNER IS THE SLICKEST
OPERATOR WE HAVE AND I WOULD
LIKE TO MAINTAIN CONSISTENCY
WITHIN OUR RANKS BY SENDING
YOU CUTS WE HAVE REMOVED
FROM HIS SCRIPTS HERE. A LOT OF
DIRT IN HIS SHOW IS BURIED DEEP
AND IF ANY OF OUR MATERIAL WILL
BE OF ASSISTANCE TO YOU, YOU'RE
WELCOME TO IT. OBVIOUSLY HE'LL
TRY THE SAME IN THE EAST THAT HE
HAS HERE. BEST REGARDS AND NEW
YEARS GREETINGS.

On January 2, 1947, McDonagh sent a reply, accepting Honrath's offer. "I am notifying all concerned at this end and you may be assured that the show will stay clean or else." The reason behind the network's intense scrutiny was the result of Rep. Thomas Lane's recent public argument over two of the jokes that, he felt, insulted the Catholic church. The radio program was singled out by name and the network felt this was bad publicity. The other reason was prompted by radio comedians, who were attempting to slip jokes of a taboo nature past the network censors who reviewed each script before broadcast. For years radio comedians were upset that even the mildest joke was deleted from their scripts for reasons that seemed inane. In retaliation, scriptwriters began slipping in jokes about the network and the executives in charge. When the vice-president of NBC initiated a new policy that said radio comedians would not kid radio on the air, the comedians took action.

The debate about comic censorship came to a pinnacle on the evening of Sunday, April 20, 1947, when NBC cut Fred Allen off the air briefly during a wisecrack about a mythical network vice-president in charge of overtime, who received his vacation by accumulating seconds from the ends of overtime broadcasts. NBC, days prior to the broadcast, had ordered to "fade" any jokes directed at the network. When Fred Allen discovered his program was momentarily faded off the air for a few seconds, he spoke to reporters. "Last week, we ran over our time and the last part of the program was cut off," Allen explained. "I decided to use this in the program and build a joke around it. But NBC told me I couldn't kid radio on the air. I don't mind suggested changes in my script if it will improve the show any. But this didn't offer any improvement. Of course, I refused to make the change. I've been on the air for 15 years and this is the first time anything like this has happened to me."

J. Walter Thompson, the advertising agency representing Fred Allen's sponsor, demanded the network reimburse money for the dead air time. "We buy and pay for half an hour's time from NBC for this program. And that's what we expect to get. Allen was cut off the air for about 35 seconds. So NBC is going to get a bill for the time we didn't get. And, oddly enough, on that Sunday night spot, it's a nice little chunk of dough." NBC counterattacked by claiming they estimated the time at 25 seconds. Under contract, if the network had technical issues beyond their control, the sponsor was not obligated to receive a partial refund for dead air. What NBC did not realize until it was too late was their counterattack was also an admission of deliberate dead air and this mistake cost them.

Two days after Fred Allen's censorship, comedians Bob Hope and Red Skelton both had their radio shows censored on the air. Radio's hypersensitive vice-presidents drew more public laughs than either of the gold-plated comedians. Hope was cut off for about 15 seconds following his reference to comedian Fred Allen's experience. During a discussion of Las Vegas, Nevada, Hope remarked, "You can get tanned and faded at the same time." The fading reference was to dice, but Hope added, "Of course, Fred Allen can get faded any time..." and there the audience got the best of radio. The show faded from the air.

On the Red Skelton program, in the early minutes, Red said, "We might ad lib something to hurt the dignity of an NBC vice-president. Did you hear 'em cut Fred Allen off Sunday..." Silence struck again. What the audience did not hear was, "You know what NBC means, don't you? Nothing but confusion, nothing but cuts." Then he came back on with, "…well, now we've joined the parade of stars." Hope and Skelton were said to have referred their scripts to NBC censors, and both were reminded that ad-libbed material would not be acceptable. NBC had only the remark that the cut-out material was "objectionable."

Red Skelton clowning around with Ed Gardner.

The silence was not by accident, because someone in the control room opened a push-button offensive, directed by Clarence L. Menser, vice-president of NBC in charge of programming. Local offices of the broadcasting company issued the following statement: "Two of NBC's comedians decided to have a little fun with the network tonight and both were cut off the air for about 20 seconds. Bob Hope and Red Skelton decided they would make some remarks about Fred Allen, and were told that if they did not delete objectionable material they would be cut off. But Hope and Skelton ignored the NBC order and, like Allen, they were cut off for a few seconds."

The advertising agencies representing Bob Hope and Red Skelton followed the avenue of J. Walter Thompson and NBC issued credits to the sponsor accounts. On the evening of April 23, four comedians defended Fred Allen and his comrades. When Dennis Day's radio girlfriend, Mildred, coming into the room, asked: "What are you doing?"

"I'm listening to the radio," Dennis replied.

"But I don't hear anything," she said.

"I know it," Dennis replied. "I'm listening to the Fred Allen program."

Later that evening, Henry Morgan, on his radio program, said he had seen a movie, "Smash Up, the Story of a Woman." He claimed it gave him an idea for a movie he'd like to make. "Cut-Off, the Story of Fred Allen."

Kay Kyser claimed the whole controversy was a build-up for his new show, a new type of quiz program and wanted to thank Allen, Hope and Skelton for the big send-off. "They were faded for their errors and that's my new show — 'Comedy of Errors'."

Information, Please also got in a jibe on the rival CBS. Ed Gardner jumped the bandwagon on *Duffy's Tavern*, presenting a show based on a political campaign by Archie and the barkeep remarked: "I think I'll get Fred Allen to make my campaign speeches for me during the times he is cut off the air. And then again — I don't think I will. I might want to be vice-president."

None of these comedians faced censorship because, hours before prime time programming, NBC announced that it had a change of heart in what the *New York Times* referred to as "its running feud with Fred Allen on the subject of vacation-minded vice-presidents in radio." It wanted, said NBC, to forgive and, especially, to forget. Harried officials of the network sat around a long table in their office at 30 Rockefeller Plaza most of the day and, in a complete reversal of form, decided to try to ring down the curtain on what Radio Row generally agreed was, at best, only a sustaining comic opera. An executive at NBC reported the network considered encouraging other comedians to make wisecracks about the matter, presumably on the well-substantiated theory that repetition was the quickest way to kill a joke on the radio. The four day skirmish between NBC and its radio comics came to a temporary end when the network agreed to turn the other cheek and invite the comics to say anything they wanted to about the network.

It was later discovered that NBC's decision was swayed because of a substantial number of letters from listeners, mostly favorable to the comedian, including a protest from the American Civil Liberties Union charging that Mr. Allen's rights under the Constitution had been placed in jeopardy, as well as reports that Fred Allen made the front pages of the London press. Late that evening, Kenneth Banghart, while delivering the 11 o'clock news, mentioned Fred Allen. The program continued, loud and clear. He mentioned Bob Hope and Red Skelton, saying that he understood that all three comedians had been offered honorary vice-presidencies, without duties and without vacations. To wit, the program continued uninterrupted until its scheduled close at 11:15.

"Seldom has the futility and silliness of unnecessary censorship been more vividly illustrated," columnist John Crosby remarked. "The deluge of criticism which NBC had to take in twenty-four hours was far worse than anything Mr. Allen by himself could have done."

The bizarre series of events reflected a situation which had been brewing for some months, if not years. Because, for better or worse, popular programs on the air were subject to varying forms of censorship on a pretty regular basis and the issue was neither as black nor as white as it might have seemed offhand. The most prevalent form of censorship was almost as old as commercial radio itself. Comedians on the air had been circumscribed in what they said because of the perennial fear of broadcasters and sponsors that some substantial group of potential customers might be offended. Ed Gardner discovered this with the two jokes that shocked a number of orthodox Catholics. Fred Allen got the last laugh when, one week after the initial fade out, his half-hour radio show was broadcast without interruption. Allen closed his broadcast with, "Well, we got it all on tonight."

When NBC thought that repetition was the quickest way to kill a joke on the radio, they soon discovered they were dead wrong. The jokes kept coming and comedians Jack Benny, Victor Borge, Milton Berle, and George Burns and Gracie Allen took advantage. The network kept its promise and avoided censoring the industry reaction to spoofing radio on the radio. This was, however, only a temporary solution. One year later, it was known that several top comedians were fed up to a point of seeking a shift to another network rather than continue under NBC's strict and allegedly stuffy code. (CBS succeeded by purchasing the *Jack Benny* and *Amos 'n' Andy* radio programs.) The network had begun another form of censorship: thou shalt not make reference to a rival network. Because Bing Crosby succeeded where no other comedian had before, transcribing his programs instead of a "live" broadcast, the network took offense when Crosby, formerly an NBC product, was now on ABC. The network once again nixed all mention of Bing Crosby's rival network show and references to ABC became another sore spot for the network.

If any blame can be placed on the CBS raid against NBC comedians, it was the executives at NBC who chose not to allow pre-recorded radio broadcasts. Bing Crosby's success was a recipe for success with CBS and ABC, offering the luxury of pre-recorded radio broadcasts to any NBC comedian who sought greener pastures. "Once the NBC Television Network became more than just a dream, it must have been difficult to rationalize the use of recorded programs on television while discouraging them on the radio network. This was especially a problem because films and kinescope film recordings were noticeably inferior in picture quality to a live telecast, while electrical transcriptions had long been virtually indistinguishable in quality from a live radiocast."

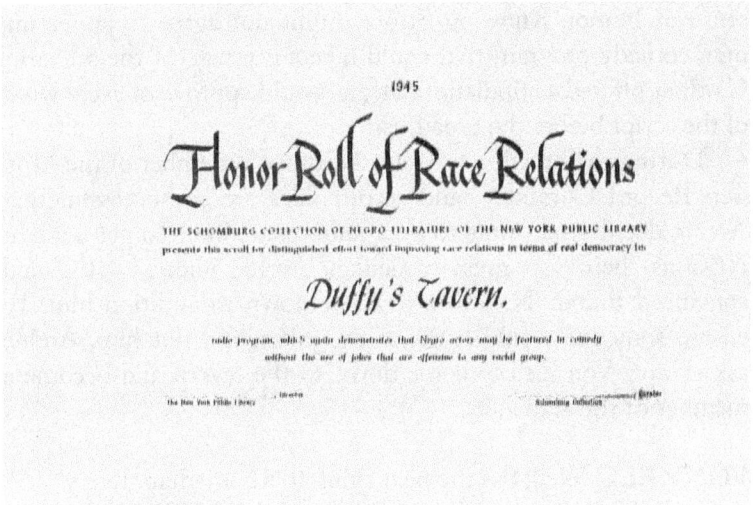

One of many awards bestowed upon Ed Gardner
and Duffy's Tavern.

(Biel, Michael J., *The Making and Use of Recordings in Broadcasting Before 1936*. Ph.D. Dissertation, Northwestern University, 1977) The policy of never using pre-recorded radio broadcasts would eventually be lifted but not until severe damage was done at the cost of NBC's long-established comedians jumping ship. The vice-president's stance against jokes on the air about network executives was a minor concern — but the bad press probably started the gears grinding at CBS, attempting to decipher which comedians were distraught.

In May of 1947, Ed Gardner came up with a gimmick that might have closed the door to vice-president gags. The "gimmick" required an appointment with Sidney N. Strotz (pronounced like throats), West Coast vice-president of NBC, where Gardner proposed to Strotz, in person, that the executive appear on a future broadcast of *Duffy's Tavern*. A few months prior, at a special party for Jack Benny given by Edgar Bergen with assistance of NBC and Standard Brands at the Beverly Hills Hotel, Strotz was among the guests. He mingled, cracked jokes and won the hearts of the comedians in attendance. Since then, Strotz was known among the circles as the only vice-president of the company to have a sense of humor. Knowing Strotz might not agree to appearing on a comedy program that could take advantage of the scenario, Gardner offered a stipulation. Strotz would approve of every word of the script before the broadcast.*

During the broadcast, Archie becomes a member of the "Top Ten Record Company" and record sales are so successful that Archie decides he wants to be a radio comedian. To get a job at NBC as their next great comedian, Archie phoned NBC and convinced Sidney N. Strotz to come down to audition him. To ensure someone would laugh at the jokes, and not him, Archie asks Harry Von Zell to come down to the tavern and become a member of the audience.

VON ZELL: Well, I'm the next thing to a comedian. Every week I stand next to Eddie Cantor. [LAUGHS] Oh, I popped a corny!

ARCHIE: There you are, Harry — a perfect example of what's wrong with radio. You put a guy that ain't funny in front of a microphone and what have you got?

EDDIE: Mr. Archie…

ARCHIE: Eddie! Watch your timing!

EDDIE: Sorry. I just wanted to tell you that Mr. Strotz is here.

ARCHIE: Oh, Von Zell, get up off your knees. Well, good evening, Mr. Strotz. Welcome to Duffy's Tavern. I hope you'll pardon the appearance of the joint.

STROTZ: Don't apologize, Archie… I like the place. [BREATHES DEEPLY] Ahhh… this dead air… just like NBC.

ARCHIE: Yeah, huh? Well, we've all been waitin' for you.

STROTZ: Yes, I'm sorry I was held up but I had trouble selecting my new office furniture.

ARCHIE: Trouble?

---

* Jack Benny once commented that he wished his writers would have come up with the idea, acknowledging Gardner's idea as "brilliant." Surprisingly, Sidney Strotz was a guest on George Burns and Gracie Allen's radio program a year prior.

STROTZ: Yes. We vice-presidents have quite a bit of trouble getting desks to fit our feet.

ARCHIE: Well, big job — big feet. Say, how does a guy get to be an NBC vice-president anyhow?

STROTZ: Very simple. You start out as an NBC guide and then you wander into an empty office and stay there until a little man comes along and puts gold letters on the door.

ARCHIE: Hey, you really got a sense of humor. You don't seem like the kind of a guy that would be annoyed by comedians.

To prove he is as funny as Jack Benny and Charlie McCarthy, Archie hands Strotz a list of questions and Archie delivers the punch lines. Old vaudeville jokes referring to "Mr. Bones" and asking Archie if he likes bathing beauties. "I don't know," Archie responds. "I never bathed any." Strotz is not convinced so he decides to trade places: Archie will be a vice-president while Mr. Strotz becomes a comedian.

STROTZ: Wait a minute... I just thought of a joke.

ARCHIE: You did, huh? Is it clean?

STROTZ: Of course it's clean. It seems that there was a traveling salesman who stopped at a farmhouse and he knocked at the door... [LONG PAUSE] ...so the following summer, the farmer's daughter showed up with a gold bracelet.

EDDIE: What happened to the middle of the joke?

STROTZ: Yeah.

ARCHIE: Sorry, Sid, but as vice-president I had to fade you off the air. We have to do those things, old man, even if it means cutting our own Strotz.

This broadcast may have also resolved the bout between comedians and NBC. During the first week of November, weeks after the new season of comedies premiered on the network, top comedians on the NBC roster were reportedly happy with the new attitude of management toward censorship of script material. The consensus of NBC comedians was that the network had at long last adopted a healthy approach toward censorship in which arbitrary rulings of the blue pencil boys were to be avoided in favor of a more reasonable policy of giving jokesters the benefit of the doubt.

Reaction of gagsters was brought into the open during the good-will mission of NBC programming vice-president Ken Dyke, whose Hollywood junket was made primarily to consult with comic stars and hear their gripes. After a series of confidential talks with Eddie Cantor, Red Skelton, Art Linkletter, Ed Gardner and Jack Benny, it was learned that Dyke assured them that the web was operating under a new policy which would prevent recurrence of incidents similar to last season. Dyke reassured gagsters, however, that there would be no attempt to muzzle jokesters if material used is funny and free from dirt. Although none of the comedians divulged to reporters any details of their talks with Dyke, it was evident that the executive's visit had done much to clear the air and erase ill feeling which existed prior.

Closing chapter to this story: In November, conferences were held with NBC talent, sponsors and agencies for the purpose of developing new methods to eliminate objectionable broadcast material which "might be offensive to American families listening to NBC programs." NBC was receiving enthusiastic cooperation from all of the principal commercial shows and the new policy would be applied should it become necessary to fade a program because of objectionable script. First, NBC will inform both agency and client if any part of a script was found objectionable. Failing to obtain cooperation in the elimination of objectionable phrases, both client and agency will be informed that the program would be faded for at least 30 seconds and the following announcement made on the network: "The National Broadcasting Company regrets the necessity of interrupting this program in order to delete that which, in its opinion, would be objectionable to listeners in many American homes." This cut and announcement would become standard, and NBC executives expressed the hope that with the better understanding now existing between NBC clients, agencies and talent, there would be few, if any, cases where it would be necessary to use it.

Original oil portrait commissioned by Ed Gardner.

Larry Rhine

Beginning May 1947, Nate Monaster and Bob Singer resigned from *Duffy's Tavern*. The scriptwriters had a dispute with Ed Gardner over a raise in salary. Gardner defended his decision based on the fact that the sponsor would not give him a raise and therefore, he could not afford it. Gardner, however, was the producer and it was his job to write the paychecks. The sponsor merely footed the bill. Any money remaining at the end of every billing cycle was often pocketed by the producer. The cheaper he could produce the series, the more the producer profited. Between Monaster and Singer, the scribes agreed to hold their ground, after disputing Gardner's claim, and sought other ventures.

Replacing the scribes was Larry Rhine, who would remain with Gardner until the very end. Rhine's writing career began at the age of eleven when his father threatened to banish "Sport," their dog, from the house if Larry didn't stop pulling his sister's pigtails. Threatened with the loss, Rhine raced to the typewriter and wrote a diplomatic verse debating how much fun the dog is. The poem hit the local newspaper that reported: "Daddy Rhine didn't know he had a poet in the family."

Rhine specialized in English literature at the University of California, which gave him a background for his radio writing, while his experience as head of the varsity debate team developed his resonant speaking voice — a combination valuable around a broadcasting station. Rhine was employed at KGB as a producer, writer and announcer. There, he played the quizzical Baron Gonkerdonk, wrote dramatic monologues as read by Patia Power on *To the Ladies*, contributed scripts for *Public Enemies*, and created the popular *Seven O'Clock Club*. When Rhine resigned unexpectedly in 1933, Arthur Linkletter (yes, *the* Art Linkletter) discovered he had his hands full when, overnight, he stepped in as the new program director.

Rhine went on to write radio scripts for Ben Bernie and co-write a 1940 Universal comedy *The Leather Pushers*, reviewed by *The Hollywood Reporter* as a "thoroughly enjoyable screenplay." Just days after the bombing of Pearl Harbor, the Hollywood screen and radio writer began operations at the Office of War Information end of the Filipino radio activities. On December 15, 1941, he

362

began operations with two programs covering a half-hour daily, enlisting the aid of Filipinos in the San Francisco community.

After the war, in early 1947, Rhine went back to network radio and asked Gardner for a job. Gardner handed Rhine one-page synopsis copies of the radio broadcasts for December 21, 1945, and January 4 and 11, 1946, and encouraged him to listen to a few broadcasts to get a feel for the format. Mentored by Hy Freedman, another scriptwriter, Rhine's contribution to the series began in May of 1947.

Scriptwriters were often fired or "relieved of duty," according to multiple sources and confirmed by three scriptwriters over the years. In 1991, scriptwriter Bob Schiller recalled at a convention held by SPERDVAC (The Society to Preserve and Encourage Radio Drama, Variety and Comedy): "He did that purposely, to keep us on our toes. He always felt that if we were making a lot of money – which he didn't want to pay – we would get lazy and not write as well. He would team people together. He'd say, 'OK, you write with him, and you write with him, and *you* – there's nobody for you to write with so you're fired.' We were mortally afraid of losing our jobs. Most of us were beginners and we were afraid to go home. We'd stay up all night working. I can remember many times taking my sleeping bag to the office. We worked around the clock. Had there been a canary in the room it would have died."[*]

Each week the writers gathered on Friday to begin a work session that lasted until Sunday afternoon, when Gardner arrived to read their "roughs." Once, a writer, looking for some guilt on Gardner's part, told him of their rough working conditions. "Ed," he said, "do you realize that no food has passed my lips for 24 hours?" Writer Larry Rhine jumped in. "You mean you haven't even vomited?"

The scriptwriters for *Duffy's Tavern* were never given contracts like the majority of the radio programs. Gardner's attitude

---

[*] Having signed up to become a member of the Radio Writers Guild in March of 1947, *Duffy's Tavern* scribe Bob Schiller received a pay hike from Ed Gardner. With the extra income, Schiller married Joyce Harris, a radio actress, on July 20.

toward his writers' welfare was apparent when, at the end of each season, he left town without telling them if they were going to be employed again in September. The writers were also required to sit in the audience during the broadcast and laugh loudly at the jokes. "Gardner used to have a postmortem after each show," Bob Schiller explained. "Once he said to me, 'Schiller, I looked down and I saw that you weren't laughing.' And I said, 'Well, Ed, that may have been the joke I didn't write.'"

"We were so underpaid in those days," Schiller continued, "that we'd take the jokes we wrote for *Duffy's Tavern* and send them to *Reader's Digest* and put them in the mouths of our guests and we'd get five dollars. One of the jokes I wrote when Henry Morgan was on the show was 'In Hollywood, if you look hard enough, underneath the false tinsel is the real tinsel.' It's subsequently been credited to Groucho, Fred Allen, and everybody else. But it was in Henry Morgan's mouth as a guest on that show."

One of many awards bestowed upon Ed Gardner and Duffy's Tavern.

McGarry and his Mouse

McGarry and His Mouse was a short-run radio program concerning Detective Dan McGarry (originally played by Wendell Corey, later Ted de Corsia), who solved crimes with his faithful assistant, Kitty Archer (played by a number of actresses at different times). The series originated from New York City and aired as summer replacement for the Eddie Cantor show, also sponsored by Bristol-Myers. Young & Rubicam purchased the program from General Amusement in January 1946, allowing the drug company to sponsor the program during the summer of 1946 (June 26, 1946, to September 25, 1946). Bristol-Myers saw no interest in a weekly program beyond the summer so General Foods picked up sponsorship for a short run in 1947 (January 6, 1947, to March 31, 1947).

The final episode of the summer run, the broadcast of September 25, 1946, featured a *Duffy's Tavern* connection. At 9:26 p.m., the program switched to Hollywood where Ed Gardner did a one-minute spot with the imaginary Duffy during a phone conversation, purposely done as a build-up for the return of the *Duffy's Tavern* program next week in the same time slot. At 9:27 p.m., the program switched back to New York for the conclusion of the program, featuring a second plug (courtesy of the announcer) for the return of *Duffy's Tavern*.

Season Seven
October 2, 1946, to June 25, 1947
National Broadcasting Company
Sponsor: Bristol-Myers
Day and Time: Wednesday, 9:00 to 9:30 p.m., EST
Originated from Hollywood, Studio D
(October 2, 1946, to January 1, 1947)
Originated from New York, Studio 6A
(January 8, 1947, to February 5, 1947)
Originated from Hollywood, Studio D
(February 12, 1947, to June 25, 1947)
Complete season originates from Hollywood
Sponsored by the Bristol-Myers Company

Advertising Agency: Young and Rubicam

Commercial announcer: Jimmy Wallington
(October 2, 1946, to January 1, 1947)
Commercial announcer: Dan Seymour
(January 8, 1947, to February 5, 1947)
Commercial announcer: Jimmy Wallington
(February 12, 1947, to June 25, 1947)
Producer/Director for the Network: John Morris
(October 2, 1946, to January 1, 1947)
Producer/Director for the Network: Walter McGraw
(January 8, 1947, to February 5, 1947)
Producer/Director for the Network: John Morris
(February 12, 1947, to June 25, 1947)
Sound Mixer: Charles Norman
(October 2, 1946, to January 1, 1947)
Sound Mixer: Clarence Westover
(January 8, 1947, to February 5, 1947)
Sound Mixer: Charles Norman
(February 12, 1947, to June 25, 1947)
Producer for the Agency: Anthony Stanford
(October 2, 1946, to January 1, 1947)
Sound: Bob Grapperhaus
Music: Matty Malneck and his Orchestra
Commercial Writer: Sylvia Dowling
Commercial Supervisor: Innes Harris (Hollywood)
Commercial Supervisor: John Swayze (New York)

Scriptwriters: Vincent Bogert, Sid Dorfman, Herbert Finn, Bill Freedman, Morris Freedman, Larry Gelbart, Al Johansen, Lew Landsman, Elroy Schwartz and Anthony Stafford.*

---

* In addition to the names above, the script for November 13, 1946, features additional names: Mel Diamond, Lee Karson and Bill Norman. The December 25, 1946, script features Lou Lasco. The March 5, 1947, script also features Nate Monaster and Bob Singer.

Cast
Charles Cantor as Finnegan
Sandra Gould as Miss Duffy
Eddie Green as Eddie
Cliff Clark as Clancy the Cop
(October 2 to November 20, 1946)
Alan Reed as Clancy the Cop
(November 27, 1946, to June 25, 1947)
All other actors and known roles are listed under the respective
episodes.

Episode #214 — Broadcast Wednesday, October 2, 1946
Rehearsal on September 30 in Studio L. Broadcast live from
Studio D.
Supporting Cast: John Brown (Dave Hossinger)
Guest: Carmen Miranda
Plot: Taking a Latin turn, Archie tries to sign musical performer
Carmen Miranda, pegged as "a South American Cass Daley," to a
contract with the tavern so he can attract the Brazilian millionaires.
After spending a few minutes at the tavern, she admits that while
she likes neighborly relations, all the crazy new gyrations try her
patience. Archie is eventually lampooned as "chili con corny."
Dave Hossinger, meanwhile, sells Archie a recording machine and
Carmen Miranda sings "South America, Take It Away."

Trivia, etc. *Variety* reviewed the season premiere: "Carmen
Miranda was a guest on the initialer, and the script dwelt largely
on the too-obvious buildup to her final emergence, which was
much too late in the layout. Her warbling of *South America, Take
It Away* lost particularly the value it might have had if she had
sung it straight, but the script has the other denizens of the *Tavern*
chorusing at inopportune moments in what was a brutal treatment
of a hit song."

Episode #215 — Broadcast Wednesday, October 9, 1946
Rehearsal on October 7 in Studio L. Broadcast live from
Studio D.

Supporting Cast: Cliff Clark (Clancy the Cop)
Guest: Victor Mature
Plot: Archie describes handsome actor and guest Victor Mature as "a Roman radiator." A patron named Mary Meade, from Shreveport, Louisiana and with a thick southern accent, happens to be at the tavern when Mature arrives. She sings "Blue Skies," causing Mature to have an interest in her, while Archie is forced to defend himself for her affections. In an effort to calm the situation down, Archie palms off Clancy's niece as a blind-date on Mature. She turns out to be a pip.

Episode #216 — Broadcast Wednesday, October 16, 1946
Rehearsal on October 14 in Studio L. Broadcast live from Studio D.
Supporting Cast: Pat C. Flick (Slotterback)
Guest: Martha Raye
Plot: When comedienne Martha Raye puts in an appearance at the tavern, Archie convinces her to help him do a stage act on Friday night at the Bijou Theater. They decide to perform an old-fashioned vaudeville act together and rehearse at the Tavern. The act is beyond corny and by the time he tells the "brother selling his doughnut business because he's sick of the 'hole' business" joke, she makes a steady exit. Pat C. Flick plays the role of "Slotterback" (S.B.) Weisbord, "the most important man in radio."

Trivia, etc. This program has a spot about giving to the Community Chest. Archie called Duffy over the telephone and talks about the many children and grownups who are depending upon Community Chest funds in order to have enough food and clothing. Duffy promises a personal contribution.

The October 19, 1946, issue of *Billboard* reviewed: "One bright spot on the Wednesday night NBC programming is *Duffy's Tavern*. Ed Gardner segment continues as a sprightly piece of Americana. Wednesday show had, in addition to Gardner's curious accent, Martha Raye in the guest spot. Very socko."

Episode #217 — Broadcast Wednesday, October 23, 1946

Rehearsal on October 21 in Studio L. Broadcast live from Studio D.

Guest: Hoagy Carmichael

Plot: Archie wrote a new song, "Archie's Little Love Song," and against the protests of the tavern regulars, will not let them hear it until he has the song "patented." Since no one wants to publish the piece, Archie sings it himself. When Hoagy Carmichael shows up at the tavern, Archie tries to convince him to write a song about Duffy's Tavern, but Carmichael says he doubts it. "I don't think the notes on the piano go that low." Archie convinces Carmichael to sing his song and afterwards the musician says he won't sing it on his radio program… he won't even steal it. Mary Meade sings Carmichael's "Stardust."

Memorable Lines

ARCHIE: You three worked great together in that picture. That scene where she sings and you sit at the piano. Y'know, with that lock of hair hanging over your eyes, you could hardly tell you two apart. Remember when you sat there with that match stick in your mouth?

HOAGY: Yep, we had to shoot that scene seven times.

ARCHIE: How come?

HOAGY: Every time Bacall got close to me, the match would light up.

ARCHIE: Holy Smoke! Boy, that Bacall must be something, huh?

HOAGY: Yeah… but the trouble was that Bogart wound up with her.

ARCHIE: Well, it figures… You had that match stick in your mouth. You couldn't whistle.

Episode #218 — Broadcast Wednesday, October 30, 1946

Rehearsal on October 28 in Studio L. Broadcast live from Studio D.

Supporting Cast: Tommy Bernard (Morton)
Guests: Ozzie and Harriet Nelson
Plot: Ozzie and Harriet celebrate their eleventh anniversary with an intimate dinner at the tavern. Trying to make the place more presentable than an undertaker's parlor, Archie and the crew fail when Harriet wonders if the place is haunted and Ozzie admits it doesn't look much like a tea room. Mary Meade sings "Archie's Little Love Song" for the musicians, who will not agree to plug the song on their radio show. To play on their sympathy, and convince them to change their mind, Archie gets his young nephew, Morton Q. Poggenburg (Tommy Bernard), to fake being ill and claims the boy is suffering from malnutrition. Archie sets Finnegan up as a doctor, who arrives in the guise of Doctor Clifton Cramafrance, M.D. (and mistakenly calls himself Doctor Kildare).

Episode #219 — Broadcast Wednesday, November 6, 1946
Rehearsal on November 4 in Studio L. Broadcast live from Studio D.
Supporting Cast: Hans Conried (the engineer)
Guest: Louella Parsons
Plot: Archie wants to get into Hollywood by impressing columnist Louella Parsons, who disagrees with the lack of class in the tavern. On the way out she sprains her ankle and has to do her radio show from the tavern. Taking advantage of the scenario, Archie writes the script, with a chance for him to sing "Archie's Little Love Song." Parsons sees right through him and will not agree to publicize the tavern or the song. She does, however, insult the tavern by describing a coming-out party for Machine-Gun Van Smythe and those who attended: Second-story Jackson, Crackpot O'Toole, Crudface Clifford, Dame May Fagen, Willie the Slob, One-Eyed Goldberg and his daughter, Cyclops, and a host of others. "Many old friendships were cemented."

Episode #220 — Broadcast Wednesday, November 13, 1946
Rehearsal on November 11 in Studio L. Broadcast live from Studio D.
Guest: Lotte Lehmann, opera singer
Plot: When a limousine crashes in front of the tavern, Eddie and

Louella Parsons and Maurice Chevalier with Ed Gardner.

Archie rescue the woman driver, who turns out to be Madame Lotte Lehmann of the Metropolitan Opera Company. She's looking for some rare, old musical manuscripts and because her chauffeur was off today, she took the liberty of driving herself. Because she crashed into their garbage can, Archie threatens to sue... unless she sings the new song he wrote, "Archie's Little Love Song." Lehmann sings "Last Rose of Summer" and then Archie convinces her to perform his song in a version of "Rigoletto."

Episode #221 — Broadcast Wednesday, November 20, 1946
Rehearsal on November 18 in Studio L. Broadcast live from Studio D.
Supporting Cast: Cliff Clark (Clancy the Cop)
Guest: George Raft
Plot: Archie and actor George Raft used to go to school together and Raft was always a bully, pushing young Archie around. He recalls how Raft would be asked by the school teacher what is six

plus six, and he would answer "boxcars!" Raft insists he is an actor, not a gangster, and to prove it he agrees to run through a radio script written by Archie, inspired by an episode of a radio mystery, *Mr. and Mrs. North*. Archie entitles it "Archie's Little Love Song Murder Case" starring George Raft as "Trigger" Mortis, and you can guess who star as sleuths Mr. and Mrs. South.

Episode #222 — Broadcast Wednesday, November 27, 1946
Rehearsal on November 25 in Studio L. Broadcast live from Studio D.
Script Title: "THANKSGIVING"
Supporting Cast: Alan Reed (Clancy the Cop)
Plot: Archie writes a historical pageant showing how the Pilgrims "thunk up Thanksgiving." Jokes about Pocahontas and how the Indians will get back at the white man by offering them cigarettes and cashing in on the sale of tobacco provide plenty of laughs. It's clearly a take-off on the Priscilla Mullins and John Alden story ("Why don't you speak for yourself, John?"). To remind the radio audience of the seriousness of the holiday, Archie gives a turkey to a poor family.

Trivia, etc. This was the first radio script of the series to feature a script title.

Episode #223 — Broadcast Wednesday, December 4, 1946
Rehearsal on December 2 in Studio L. Broadcast live from Studio D.
Guest: Leo Durocher
Plot: Archie needs money to buy Christmas presents, so he phones Ebbets Field and asks the proprietor if he can get a job as their next pitcher. They won't hire him but Leo Durocher shows up and jokes about baseball, America's pastime. Trying to sign up Durocher to a Mexican ball game so a vacant spot will open at the stadium, Archie disguises Finnegan as Señor Gonzales Valdez, a Mexican baseball magnate, to bid the price up so Durocher will plead to have Archie on the team.

Trivia, etc. Historically, this episode was a take-off on the Mexican ball leagues and the way American players had signed with the Mexican teams.

Episode #224 — Broadcast Wednesday, December 11, 1946
Rehearsal on December 9 in Studio L. Broadcast live from Studio D.
Script Title: "DIAMOND TARARA"
Supporting Cast: Alan Reed (N.G. Tiflis *and* Falstaff Openshaw) and Cyril Smith (Sir Charles).
Plot: Once again Christmas is at their throats and Archie is desperate for the right Christmas gift. He spends much of the time trying to convince N.G. Tiflis, Dave Hossinger's partner, to sell him a diamond "tarara," and only after he succeeds does he discover that it was a nickel-and-dime fake. There is also a comedy sketch about Christmas shopping for furs and jewels.

Trivia, etc. This was the second radio script of the series to feature a script title.

Episode #225 — Broadcast Wednesday, December 18, 1946
Rehearsal on December 16 in Studio L. Broadcast live from Studio D.
Supporting Cast: Alan Reed (Clancy the Cop)
Guest: Joan Bennett
Plot: Joan Bennett agrees to help Archie raffle off the hunk of ice "diamond tarara" from the previous episode. The money is supposed to help the Third Avenue poor people during Christmas time and Archie persuades Joan to give a kiss to the winner in an effort to sell more tickets. Fearing some hoodlum or lowlife might win the contest, Archie rigs the contest so only he can win. But the winner turns out to be Finnegan and after his kiss, he cries, "This is terrible! To think of all the years I've wasted my lips blowin' on soup!" Archie receives a consolation prize, a kiss from Joan herself.

Trivia, etc. Hollywood actress Joan Bennett, then secretary-treasurer of Diana Productions, recently arrived back in the United States to complete filming for *The Woman on the Beach* for RKO, and co-star with Michael Redgrave in *Secret Beyond the Door*, a Freudian version of the Bluebeard tale. She was in England for a few weeks to participate in a "Command Performance" in London with more than 30 top American and British motion picture personalities, all to help raise money for the British Cinematograph Trade Benevolent Fund.

Episode #226 — Broadcast Wednesday, December 25, 1946
Rehearsal on December 23 in Studio L. Broadcast live from Studio D.
Supporting Cast: Helen Andrews (Ann); Robert Bruce (man at accident scene); Ira Grossel (the stranger); Jerry Hausner (the taxi driver); Jack Kruschen (voice at accident scene); Tyler McVey (Paul); Jimmy Ogg (Jimmy Turner, the boy); Franklin "Pinky" Parker (the cop); Ken Peters (Joe DiMaggio); Herb Vigran (the hotel cop); and Bud Widom (the blind man).
Plot: See pages 347 to 350.

Trivia, etc. Charles Cantor was originally slated to double for both Finnegan and the taxi driver.

Episode #227 — Broadcast Wednesday, January 1, 1947
Rehearsal on December 30 in Studio L. Broadcast live from Studio D.
Supporting Cast: Jerry Hausner (the cabbie) and Alan Reed (Happy).
Guest: Benay Venuta
Plot: Welcoming in the New Year, Archie attempts to revive vaudeville by convincing Benay Venuta to stay at the tavern as a regular and yes, he fails. But not before exchanging stale vaudeville jokes that are certain to make the radio audience cry with laughter or be reminded why vaudeville died. Archie also finds himself in an awkward position. It seems his events with Fifi the night before are recounted with her explaining his remarkable drinking skills. Why? Because Archie was so drunk that he cannot remember what he did at the party and it turns out that he promised jobs to everybody in sight. And Fifi wants a job.

Singer Benay Venuta signed a photo to Ed Gardner, her admirer.

Trivia, etc. This script recycles material from the January 1, 1942, script, only the name of the woman demanding a job was Rosa Rita, not Fifi. According to a copy of Vincent Bogert's radio and television scripts at the UCLA Archives, this script actually had a title: "New Year's."

The actress in the role of Fifi remains unknown. Two different scripts have been found with different actresses credited for the role: Rose King and Elvia Allman.

Memorable Lines
ARCHIE: How do you make anti-freeze?
HAPPY: I don't know... How do you make anti-freeze?
ARCHIE: Hide her nightgown.

ARCHIE: You know me, Benay... I always have an eye for the ladies (clicks tongue)
BENAY: Well, put it back in its socket! (clicks tongue)

Episode #228 — Broadcast Wednesday, January 8, 1947
Rehearsal on January 6 in Conference Room 793. Broadcast live from Studio 6A and 8H.
Guest: Fred Allen
Plot: See page 345.

Trivia, etc. According to *Broadcasting* magazine, "When Fred Allen, asked by Archie, on whose *Duffy's Tavern* program he was a guest, how long he had been in radio, replied 'so long that I lent Hooper the nickel to make his first call,' C.E. Hooper promptly sent him a five-cent piece with the message, 'All right. All right. Here it is'."

Episode #229 — Broadcast Wednesday, January 15, 1947
Rehearsal on January 13 in Studio 6B. Broadcast live from Studio 6A.
Guest: Toots Shor
Plot: Toots Shor is the owner of the famous Toots Shor's Restaurant, one of the famous sights of New York City, known for its excellent food and its reputation as a gathering place for celebrities. Since Archie considers his establishment competition, the men brag about their clients and Archie attempts to humiliate Toots. To impress him, Finnegan claims he's a French waiter who speaks Spanish. In desperation, Archie becomes a restaurant-help agent and tries to sell Finnegan to Toots to be his French chef.

Memorable Lines
FINNEGAN: I am insult! In France I am famous for my lemon chiffon pie.

Ed Gardner socializes with Walter Huston and Edward G. Robinson.

TOOTS: How do you make it?
FINNEGAN: Three lemons to each yard of chiffon.

Episode #230 — Broadcast Wednesday, January 22, 1947
Rehearsal on January 20 in Studio 6B. Broadcast live from Studio 6A.
Guests: Minerva Pious and John J. Anthony
Plot: Guests include Minerva Pious, radio actress famous for her role of Mrs. Nussbaum on the Fred Allen radio show and Lester Kroll aka John J. Anthony, famous for his role as radio's "Mr. Anthony," in which he answers questions about the troubles which his listeners seem to have. Anthony plays the presider of *The Court of Human Relations*, listening to the concerns of Eddie Green and then Mrs. Nussbaum. Mrs. Nussbaum falls in love with Finnegan and Mr. Anthony straightens everything out.

Trivia, etc. It was between this week's episode and the following one when Ed Gardner first dipped his foot into television with an ill-fated fifteen minute audition show that aired live on January

26, 1947, from WNBT in New York City. See the chapter on *Duffy's Tavern* on television for details.

Episode #231 — Broadcast Wednesday, January 29, 1947
Rehearsal on January 27 in Studio 6B. Broadcast live from Studio 6A.
Guest: Edward G. Robinson
Plot: Movie star Edward G. Robinson puts in an appearance at the tavern and Archie tells him "just because you quit playin' them gangster parts, you don't have to be a coward." They joke about *Scarlet Street* and painting (he played a painter in the movie) and Archie tries to sell one of his paintings to Robinson in a take-off on the actor's hobby of collecting works of art. Archie even sets up Finnegan as an art critic but the actor isn't fooled and, after meeting Finnegan, Robinson decides he's had enough and leaves.

Episode #232 — Broadcast Wednesday, February 5, 1947
Rehearsal on February 3 in Studio 6B. Broadcast live from Studio 6A.
Guest: Hildegarde
Plot: To attract the international set, Archie wants to hire the guest singer to an exclusive contract that has one too many lines mistakenly written to be considered legal. Archie claims he speaks French and learned it from the underground - the tavern. Hildegarde sings "If This Isn't Love" and Archie and Hildegarde play the leads in his version of "Mademoiselle From Armentieres," a French farce that includes the intro to "Archie's Little Love Song."

Episode #233 — Broadcast Wednesday, February 12, 1947
Rehearsal on February 10 in Studio L. Broadcast live from Studio D.
Guest: Gene Autry
Plot: Archie wrote a cowboy yarn and wants Gene Autry (who sings a song) to play the lead in his new Western. There is no title to the play, but the characters are named Dangerous Dan McArchie and Autry plays... well, he plays himself. Dangerous

Dan robs a bank and the men have to shoot it out. Will Autry jump back in the saddle again and come to the rescue?

Memorable Lines
GENE: What's new, Dangerous Dan?
ARCHIE: Nothing much. Just killed four guys down at the bank.
GENE: Why?
ARCHIE: That's all there was.

Trivia, etc. Walter Winchell, after listening to this broadcast, remarked unfavorably: "Ed Gardner's horseplay with Gene Autry via *Duffy's Tavern* didn't run in the money."

Gene Autry recently arrived from a rodeo tour in Houston, Texas, on February 11 and was unable to participate in the rehearsals until a few hours before the actual broadcast. Autry had recently made a shift from Republic Pictures to Columbia to produce a series of cowboy westerns under his newly-formed Gene Autry Productions. Hence why Archie is trying to break into screenwriting his own western pictures.

Episode #234 — Broadcast Wednesday, February 19, 1947
Rehearsal on February 17 in Studio C. Broadcast live from Studio D.
Script Title: "LAZYBONES"
Supporting Cast: Alan Reed (Clancy the Cop), Leo Cleary (J. Preston Finchley)
Plot: Duffy is sending down an accountant to look over the books. Eddie and Archie look over the books personally and Archie discovers he has not paid his own IOUs. Clancy the Cop, meanwhile, just arrested Benny Hogan, an ex-jockey who was phoning tips on the horse races and was calling the wrong station. J. Preston Finchley, the accountant, arrives and, inspired by Clancy, Archie bets money on the races, a horse named Lazybones, to make the money back in time before the accountant realizes the discrepancy. Tony Barrett makes one of his few appearances on the *Duffy's Tavern* program, playing the part of the radio announcer who delivers the horse race.

Episode #235 — Broadcast Wednesday, February 26, 1947
Rehearsal on February 24 in Studio L. Broadcast live from Studio D.
Guest: Andy Russell, vocalist
Plot: Archie falls in love with Phoebe, a society dame known for her "filthiness"... she supposedly has two million dollars. When Archie tells Miss Duffy that Andy Russell is dropping by the tavern tonight, she screams and faints. Russell arrives and explains how difficult it was to find the place because when he asked a little boy on the streets where Duffy's Tavern was, and the boy gave directions, the little boy's mother arrived and washed the boy's mouth out with soap. Archie tricks Phoebe into thinking he is singing to her over the phone, having Russell sing a few bars of "Amour Amour." She ultimately falls for Andy, who promptly leaves the tavern to meet up with her.

Trivia, etc. Andy Russell, star of the popular *Hit Parade* radio program, performed double-duty on the same evening. After the *Duffy's Tavern* radio broadcast, Russell headed over to the Knickerbocker Hotel to team up with Skitch Henderson to supply entertainment for a women's advertising club dinner.

Episode #236 — Broadcast Wednesday, March 5, 1947
Rehearsal on March 3 in Studio C. Broadcast live from Studio D.
Script Title: "PHOEBE"
Supporting Cast: Jacqueline DeWitt (Phoebe) and Alan Reed (Clancy the Cop).
Plot: Archie has a fiancee named Phoebe De Pyster he wants to impress because she has two million dollars and he figures a marriage of convenience is the quickest way to get rich. Archie sets up Finnegan and Miss Duffy to play the role of as his rich aunt and uncle. Phoebe arrives and it is clearly evident that the girl is truly in love with him, but his friends don't impress her, and when Lord Beaverstream, a noted big game hunter, arrives from England, Archie's chances walk out through the tavern doors.

Memorable Lines
PHOEBE: We'll have them to dinner tonight.

I think it'd be nice if my relatives met your relatives.
EDDIE: A case of the in-laws meeting the outlaws.

Episode #237 — Broadcast Wednesday, March 12, 1947
Rehearsal on March 10 in Studio C. Broadcast live from Studio D.
Guest: Reginald Gardiner
Plot: Archie is still trying to woo the rich girl named Phoebe, "with the light brown checkbook." He wants to take her away to another country and esmploys help from Reginald Gardiner who shows up to offer Archie some advice on etiquette. Finnegan, however, is dressed up like the IRS tax man to see how Archie reacts to a similar situation. When Archie suspects he's Finnegan, he asks a complex question and Finnegan answers incorrectly so Archie figures he's the real thing. "Even Finnegan wouldn't get a wrong answer that fast." In a funny dream sequence, Archie is married to Phoebe and enjoys being a millionaire, with Reginald Gardiner as his butler.

Episode #238 — Broadcast Wednesday, March 19, 1947
Rehearsal on March 17 in Studio L. Broadcast live from Studio D.
Script Title: "GANGSTERS"
Supporting Cast: John Brown (Butch, the tough guy) and Eddie Marr (Knuckles McGurk).
Plot: The gangster routine starts when a brick flies through a window of the tavern. A note addressed to Archie tells him that a new café is opening across the street, and that he will go out of business immediately, "or else." Following this, a rough character named "Knuckles McGurk" enters the tavern with the announced intention of rubbing out Archie. Archie discovers that Knuckles was a grammar school chum and persuades him to call off the killing. Afterwards, two members of the "Purple Punk" gang come on the scene, imply that Knuckles has been put out of the way and that they are going to bump off Archie. Finnegan walks out of the back room, toying with a revolver that Archie had given him to keep him occupied, is introduced as "Bugsy the Brain," and frightens the thugs into a hasty departure. All of this was liberally sprinkled with the usual argot, "dese" and "dose."

Trivia, etc. This episode appeared to have sparked momentary concern with the network, after a number of people wrote in to their local affiliates with complaints. Ray O'Connell of NBC reviewed the script and found that the gangster sequence was handled pretty much in Damon Runyan style and, "in my opinion, harmless enough for adults. It isn't a show for children, but my question is, was it ever?"

Episode #239 — Broadcast Wednesday, March 26, 1947
Rehearsal on March 24 in Studio L. Broadcast live from Studio D.
Script Title: "PETER STUYVESANT"
Supporting Cast: Rolfe Sedan (the professor)
Plot: Archie believes he has found the original Peter Stuyvesant diary. He tries to sell it for a cheap price, then gets the brainstorm of an idea to write a fake copy to sell to the curator of a museum. In an effort to make the fake look authentic, Archie has Eddie throw the book into the oven for a few minutes. A professor representing the museum shows up, discovers many inaccurate facts within the contents and suspects fraud. When a phone call from a local bookshop verifies the real diary is safe and sound and available for $10,000, the professor promptly leaves.

Trivia, etc. The program featured a fade out when Ed Gardner, as Archie, said, "You can take the fountain pen..." The fade was from 9:04:35 to 9:04:53, on orders from the Hollywood producer on censorship of the script.

Episode #240 — Broadcast Wednesday, April 2, 1947
Rehearsal on March 31 in Studio L. Broadcast live from Studio D.
Script Title: "NEWSPAPER"
Supporting Cast: Joe Forte (Scoop)
Plot: Archie uses a printing press to create new menus for the tavern with new prices. When Grogan's across the street prints circulars to attract business, Archie figures better circulation would involve a neighborhood newspaper and begins hiring a staff of volunteers to supply the news. Finnegan serves as a roving reporter. A stranger named Scoop comes into the tavern to seek a job, having worked formerly for the *Chicago Tribune*. When

Duffy's Daily Dipper circulates among the streets, he fears the worst when Scoop turns out to be an inmate from the State Home for the Mentally Defected.

Episode #241 — Broadcast Wednesday, April 9, 1947
Rehearsal on April 7 in Studio L. Broadcast live from Studio D.
Guests: Irving Berlin and Imogen Carpenter
Plot: Archie believes it's possible to collaborate with Irving Berlin in the songwriting business. Imogen Carpenter also pays a visit to the tavern, looking for a singing job, with Toots Shor as a reliable reference. To test her vocal chords, Archie asks her to plug "Archie's Little Love Song," and play the piano. To convince Berlin that Archie is a professional songwriter, Finnegan masquerades as a professor and criticizes "Archie's Little Love Song." Imogen tries to sing the song a second time and purposely messes it up so she can sing "Say So," a song of her own, thus winning the accolades of Berlin.

Memorable Lines
ARCHIE: Carpenter, huh? I didn't know carpenters was gettin' things built so solid these days. What have I got on me... I mean, what have you got on your mind?
IMOGEN: Toots Shor sent me down... he said you might use a singer.
ARCHIE: Honey, you're hired! That is, providin' your vocal is as good as your physical.
IMOGEN: You mean I have to take a physical?
ARCHIE: You already have. Okay, we'll pay you eight bucks a week.
IMOGEN: Eight dollars a week!
ARCHIE: Don't forget, there will be frequent advances!

Episode #242 — Broadcast Wednesday, April 16, 1947
Rehearsal on April 14 in Studio E. Broadcast live from Studio D.
Script Title: "UNCLE HOMER"
Supporting Cast: Jack Mather (Uncle Homer)
Plot: Recycling material from the April 7, 1942, broadcast, Archie gets a letter from his "rich" Uncle Homer who wants Archie to go

into partnership. Uncle Homer from Alaska visits Archie and the tavern, dressed up like a bum, and brags about having prospected for gold, and is now in new York to invest his fortune on Wall Street — but he needs an honest partner. Archie attempts to become that partner.

Trivia, etc. This script was originally slated for broadcast on April 9.

Episode #243 — Broadcast Wednesday, April 23, 1947
Rehearsal on April 21 in Studio L. Broadcast live from Studio D.
Script Title: "FISH AND GAME WARDEN"
Supporting Cast: John Brown (McGinnis) and Alan Reed (Clancy the Cop).
Plot: Inflamed ulcers is one of the complaints that incite a health inspector to pay a visit to the tavern. But that's the least of Archie's problems. It seems Archie is attempting to get into politics and foils every word in the English language to prove he knows more. His hopes of getting elected are extremely slim, even if his reforms might help save the tavern from lawsuits from customers. His solution comes in the form of Ward Heeler McGinnis (played by John Brown) who nominates Archie for Third Avenue Fish and Game Warden. There is an election but Archie soon learns that McGinnis controls the local politics.

Trivia, etc. This script was originally slated for broadcast on April 16.

Memorable Lines
ARCHIE: Gentlemen and mark me well, four score and seven years ago..."
EDDIE: It ain't original.
ARCHIE: Eddie, if it was good enough for George Washington, it's good enough for me.

Episode #244 — Broadcast Wednesday, April 30, 1947
Rehearsal on April 28 in Studio L. Broadcast live from Studio D.
Script Title: "LION TAMER"

Supporting Cast: Ken Christy (Spiegel Hegeman)
Plot: After a number of visitors to the tavern recently have been circus performers and tent show variety acts, Archie gets the yen to be a lion tamer and decides to put on his own circus - forcing Finnegan to play the role of all the animals — including a dog with intelligence. He performs for Mr. Spiegel Hegeman, who actually has a financial interest in the act — until Archie discovers he is the operator of a flea circus.

Episode #245 — Broadcast Wednesday, May 7, 1947
Rehearsal on May 5 in Studio M. Broadcast live from Studio D.
Script Title: "YACHT"
Supporting Cast: Hy Averback (Mr. Hotchkiss, the lawyer)
Plot: The cast and crew talk about where they will be going during their upcoming vacation. Archie wants to travel the world by boat and cracks jokes about sea legs and seagulls. Archie's aunt dies and leaves him a yacht... from which he envisions high seas adventures until the episode concludes with a surprise — the yacht turns out to be in a bottle.

Episode #246 — Broadcast Wednesday, May 14, 1947
Rehearsal on May 12 in Studio L. Broadcast live from Studio D.
Script Title: "PRICE CUTTING"
Plot: With business down since the day the tavern had its grand opening, Archie decides to take a page from President Truman's retail merchant request and cuts prices ten percent. This naturally means cutting the overhead — and salaries. In trying to convince the competition to lower their prices as well, Finnegan is disguised as an ambassador and sent across the street to Grogan's to encourage him to lower his prices... but the scheme fails. Grogan's takes in more customers because the place is always spick and span, the food is good and fresh, the kitchen nice and clean. "That's the trouble with business these days," Archie grumbles. "dirty competition." Matty Malneck and his orchestra play "Deep Down in Your Heart."

Episode #247 — Broadcast Wednesday, May 21, 1947
Rehearsal on May 19 in Studio L. Broadcast live from Studio D.

Supporting Cast: Earl Lee (Mr. S. Crow)
Guest: Boris Karloff
Plot: Duffy is selling the tavern and sends a real estate man to assess the value of the property. To deter any chance of having the tavern sold to private investors, Archie, with bats in his belfry, hires Hollywood's Boris Karloff (offering free zombie drinks as payment) to give the impression that the place is haunted. Archie discovers he has a grave problem when the horror star's theatrics fail to scare the real estate man. Thankfully, Finnegan enters the room and does the job without any effort.

Memorable Lines
ARCHIE: I feel sick! A real estate guy is on his way down here. Duffy is selling the tavern.
EDDIE: You mean we're liberated!?
ARCHIE: Eddie, I think you fail to grasp the gravidity of the situation. A move like this might force us to go to work.

Episode #248 — Broadcast Wednesday, May 28, 1947
Rehearsal on May 26 in Studio L. Broadcast live from Studio D.
Script Title: "MAD RUSSIAN"
Supporting Cast: Alan Reed (Clancy the Cop)
Guest: Bert Gordon, a.k.a. The Mad Russian
Plot: Miss Duffy's coming-out party is being held at the tavern and a lot of society members with deep pockets are invited. Hoping to make Miss Duffy enjoy the evening, Archie gets her a Russian Prince from an escort service, who turns out to be Bert Gordon, known on radio as the Mad Russian. Miss Duffy is taken with the man. During the party, Eddie sing "Volga Boatman" and the entire cast performs a musical. Gordon explains, "Beautiful! We Russians love to suffer." Duffy himself comes into the tavern and, discovering this is his father-in-law to be, the prince races back to Siberia.

Episode #249 — Broadcast Wednesday, June 4, 1947
Rehearsal on June 2 in Studio L. Broadcast live from Studio D.
Guests: Sidney N. Strotz (NBC vice-president in the Hollywood offices) and Harry Von Zell

Actor Bert Gordon

Plot: See pages 357 to 360.

Trivia, etc. This episode also publicizes the LP record set, with Archie describing the various celebrity guests and the Two-Top Gruskin routine.

Episode #250 — Broadcast Wednesday, June 11, 1947
Rehearsal on June 9 in Studio M. Broadcast live from Studio D.
Script Title: "FATHER'S DAY"
Supporting Cast: Alan Reed (Clancy the Cop) and Walter Tetley (Cecil).
Plot: Father's day is coming up and since women expect a gift on

every holiday, Archie complains to Duffy that he needs a raise. This idea doesn't jibe with Duffy, and the request is turned down. Miss Duffy found something for her father and Archie gets to thinking… if he could adopt a kid first, attracting a wife would be easy. He even calls up the Baby Department of a store and asks how their 1947 models are. Archie ultimately adopts a young boy, Cecil. Cecil recites a poem "To Fadda." Archie remarks, "Gee, ain't that sweet! A poet, too! Already the kid has inherited me talent." Archie is no role model for the youth, however, and the kid double-crosses him by telling Clancy the Cop that Archie has kidnapped him.

Episode #251 — Broadcast Wednesday, June 18, 1947

Rehearsal on June 16 in Studio M. Broadcast live from Studio D.
Guest: Rudy Vallee
Plot: Archie is decorating the tavern to remind Rudy Vallee (whom he describes as "a sober Phil Harris") of his old college days. Believing Vallee's appearance will attract a lot of female customers, Archie convinces Vallee to be the star in a private-eye play as "The Hummer, the singing detective," described as a combination of *The Thin Man* and Bobby Breen. Vallee opens up the mystery play with his trademark song, "My Time is Your Time." Rhett the butler calls The Hummer and his faithful sidekick to investigate the murder of his master, Mr. Throckmorton. His widow, Ice Pick Nellie, hated her husband and had all the motive in the world. Having learned nothing at Yale, the detective solves the crime and deduces the obvious.

Episode #252 — Broadcast Wednesday, June 25, 1947

Rehearsal on June 23 in Studio M. Broadcast live from Studio D.
Guest: Burton Holmes
Plot: Burton Holmes, the world famous traveler and lecturer, drops by the tavern and Archie convinces him to talk about his world travels in South America. Burton Holmes has advertised for an interpreter to go with him to Africa. This starts up a series of jokes about pygmies and the proper pronunciation of "Portuguese." Archie attempts to get a position traveling with Holmes during his summer vacation.

Tex and Jinx, 1947

As a summer replacement for *Duffy's Tavern*, Bristol-Myers continued sponsoring the same time slot for *The Tex and Jinx Program*, starring Tex McCrary and Jinx Falkenberg.

June 9, 1947. A major tennis match to launch pro Pauline Betz and Sarah Palfrey Cooke's tennis tour was held at the Beverly Wilshire Hotel. Mickey Rooney opened the afternoon's festivities by scoring a one-set 6-2 victory over Ed Gardner of *Duffy's Tavern*. Gardner chose to take up tennis lessons in the spring of 1945. He publicly criticized the flossy high-priced instructors, crying how they charged seven dollars an hour. "Do you know all he teaches in the first lesson? He teaches you how to leap over the net with your right hand out-stretched so you can be a good loser!"

There's Got To Be A Story Behind This...

The July 7, 1947, issue of *Variety* featured the following advertisement: "CONGRATULATIONS! Jack, Bernard and the rest of the Schwab's on the opening of your new and beautiful Beverly Hills store. (Signed) Bill and Morris Freedman, pharmacists." The bottom of the advertisement cited the scriptwriters, not just as pharmacists, but as "Chess challengers to the radio industry, 39 weeks on writing staff *Duffy's Tavern* 1946-47 season." Why did the scriptwriters do this?

One Apron or Two?

The famed apron worn by Ed Gardner during all of the performances and rehearsals is now considered a Hollywood novelty. Having collected autographed photos from celebrities during the early years of radio broadcasting (*Good News*, *Rudy Vallee*, etc.), Gardner had many of the celebrity guests who appeared on the program sign the apron. Roy Rogers, Lucille Ball, Jinx Falkenburg, Paul Winchell, Ginny Simms, Ray Milland and Oscar Levant were just a few. Even the sponsor once signed it as a joke. Every few weeks, when the opportunity arose, Gardner would take the signed apron to have his mother embroider the famous names into the apron by hand. In July of 1947, Gardner flew from Hollywood to New York to attend the funeral of his mother, Mrs. Emily Poggenburg, who died at the age of 65. Burial was in St. Michael's Cemetery in Woodside, Queens. Following his mother's death, his wife, Simone, embroidered the signatures.

Dinah Shore and Nelson Eddy signing the apron during rehearsals of Duffy's Tavern.

All of the publicity photographs verify the one and only apron, worn by Ed Gardner. Yet, there appears to be a mystery surrounding the possibility of a second. During the summer of 1945, Ed Gardner spent six to eight weeks in and around Italy, performing his *Duffy's Tavern* act for the troops. Bill Henry of the *Los Angeles Times* made a reference to the USO tour in his July 27, 1945, column: "Unless Archie had the presence of mind to take along a spare bartender's apron on his USO tour of Europe, he's lost the one

During the rehearsals of Duffy's Tavern, *Ed Gardner asked every celebrity guest to sign their name on his prop apron. Afterwards, his mother would embroider the signatures to ensure they would remain permanent. Obscure celebrities included Joseph Allen, advertising manager of General Foods.*

with the wonderful collection of autographs. Somebody snitched the one he was wearing when he did his show at Fano, in Italy. The apron was priceless." Nothing has been found since to substantiate whether this was true or not. It is a fact that Gardner and the USO did not get along during that summer and it remains possible the radio actor/producer might have added the theft of the apron on his list of disgruntles.

On April 20, 1949, a columnist for *The Lock Haven Express* reported: "A church benefit in Lock Haven, Pennsylvania, garnered attention when over fifty stars of radio, movies and baseball, loaned their names, photographs and personalized items for the bazaar, a money-raising project for the Junior Service Guild at St. Paul's, held Friday evening, April 22, in the parish house. Golf balls from Bing Crosby, with Bob Hope's name on them, were donated. Autographed baseballs from various players, including Eddie Stanky of the Boston Braves, were up for auction. Gregory Peck sent a linen handkerchief and autographed photo. Shirley Temple sent an autographed photo. James Cagney's gift was a Yankee Doodle bow tie, designed for him during the production of *Yankee Doodle Dandy*. Ed Gardner sent a bar apron with the signatures of many famous people."

"I never heard anything of a second apron," Ed Gardner, Jr. later recalled. "My mother had the only apron that I knew of and she commissioned Christie's Auction House in the 1970s to sell the apron for her. I don't know who bought the apron or how much it went for, but her take was $15,000 for the sale." The apron, verified to be the same one pictured in all of the publicity photos, has since been framed in glass, rectangle shape, and now resides in private collector hands. An educated guess is that the two news briefs were not accurate. To date, with the exception of the two news items, no such evidence has been found to verify a second apron ever existed.

The apron still exists today in collector hands. It has since been framed in glass, hanging on the wall. A recent photograph was compared to photos of the past to verify its authentication and the apron was proven legit. To date, there has only been one apron known to exist.

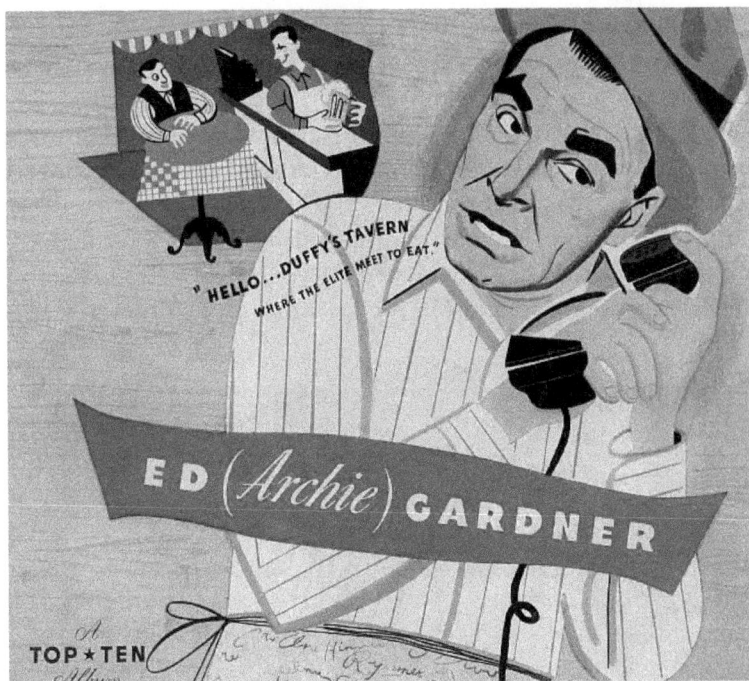

The 1947 Decca Records release. (Photo courtesy of Michael Biel.)

Decca Records

During the summer of 1947, Decca Records released a series of seven "Top Ten Records," a collection of phonograph records featuring excerpts from various radio comedies. Jack Benny, George Burns and Gracie Allen, Amos n' Andy, Edgar Bergen and Charlie McCarthy, Fibber McGee and Molly, Eddie Cantor and *Duffy's Tavern*. For the latter, three episodes from prior *Duffy's Tavern* radio broadcasts were now available for commercial resale, with celebrity guests Deems Taylor (September 28, 1945), George Raft (November 20, 1946) and Nigel Bruce (October 6, 1944). Gardner also recorded his "Two-Top Gruskin" sketch, while the remaining episodes featured the "Deems, Dem and Dose" sketch, and a rendition of "Leave Us Face It, We're In Love."

Gardner had already been copyrighting the radio scripts since the broadcast of March 1, 1941 (Copyright registration D.U.

74149), in care of the William Morris Agency, but for the purpose of protecting his ownership for the various sketches contained in this phonograph album set, each record was individually copyrighted. The Two-Top Gruskin sketch was submitted in script form, copyrighted May 24, 1947. Ed Gardner and Vincent Bogert were listed as the authors.

The "Top Ten Records" did not sell well and not only were plans for other albums abandoned, they were sold off in stores in the late forties for $5 and $10 for the entire group of seven sets.

ED (ARCHIE) GARDNER the Word Mashing, Gag Crashing Manager of "Duffy's Tavern," presents for the first time on special phonograph records for home use his additions to the American slanguage.

Yours
Edw. F. Gardner

CHAPTER ELEVEN
DUFFY'S TAVERN:
THE STAGE PLAY
(1947 - 1948)

IN THE SUMMER OF 1947, A NUMBER OF DOINGS took place that warrant mention. On June 13, Ed Gardner was a guest at the convention of the New York State Pharmaceutical association. Gardner claimed he attended medical school before he turned to less scientific fields. "I didn't finish medical school because my handwriting was too plain," he joked. Charles Cantor (Finnegan) and Gardner cut a specially-slanted transcription of *Duffy's Tavern* for the scientific edification of the apothecary ladies.

From June 20 to September 12, a radio comedy starring Arthur Moore, titled *Arthur's Place*, aired over CBS and was described by listeners and critics as a poor man's *Duffy's Tavern*. The program had such characters as Norville, a dumb straight man, played by Clarence Hartzell, a dialect comedian and a prissy fem known as Mrs. Gossip. As an added attraction a clarinet (a member of Benny Goodman's band; he was a guest star for the premiere episode), was worked in. *Arthur's Place* invited the public in for food and fun, with a Dixieland combination headed by Jeff Alexander that gave the customers jive with their hamburgers. Arthur Moore, who plays the name role, went into a dream routine in the second episode of the series, reminiscent of Ed Gardner-Miss Duffy, with a waitress named Dreamboat, played by Sara Berner*. Even Walter Winchell was not fooled. In his July 9, 1947, column, he remarked: "A new program, *Arthur's Place*, made a clumsy attempt to ape *Duffy's Tavern*." There was no question about it. Anthony Stanford, one of the scriptwriters for *Duffy's Tavern*, also scripted for *Arthur's Place*.

Sponsored by the Borden Company, *Arthur's Place* lasted only a mere 13 weeks. The sponsor, according to one trade column, was unhappy with the show and the ratings, even with a change in cast. A few weeks after the program premiered, Arthur Moore was replaced by Jack Kirkwood, so he could concentrate on production. Ironically, the series was created for Young & Rubicam, who sold the series to Kenyon & Eckhardt, based on the strength of its pitch with an audition record.

Ed Gardner, however, spent much of the summer on vacation with his family. He tinkered with ideas to profit from *Duffy's Tavern*, including a comic strip for the newspapers based on the fictional characters. The same proposal also included *The Adventures of Ozzie and Harriet*, for which Ozzie Nelson was appreciative of

---

* Sara Berner has been indirectly connected with *Duffy's Tavern* multiple times (as evident in this book). She was a talented actress who could not live up to Ed Gardner's expectations when she played Miss Duffy for only one broadcast, May 23, 1944. She was currently playing the role of Mary's girlfriend on the Jack Benny program. She returned to the program as a Greek cook in the broadcast of June 8, 1949. Berner received national exposure when she appeared on Major Bowes' *Original Amateur Hour* and later appeared on numerous radio comedies, best known today as Jack Benny's girlfriend, Gladys, and as telephone operator Mabel on Benny's program. NBC and General Mills tried to star-build Berner through a short-run summer program, *Sara's Private Caper*.

The Gardners at a party with Ralph Edwards, Ann Miller,
Anna May Wong and Gracie Allen.

Gardner facilitating the deal. Neither met fruition but *The Adventures of Ozzie and Harriet* did become a short-run series of comic books in 1949. Evidence has been found that Gardner tinkered with the idea of a comic strip based on *Duffy's Tavern* as early as spring 1946.

Goodbye Sandra Gould

At the conclusion of her third season on *Duffy's Tavern*, Sandra Gould was told she would not receive the raise in salary she was promised. Her devotion to her husband, Larry Berns, became almost legendary in Hollywood during the seven years of his illness, during which he was in and out of the hospital an estimated 48 times. According to a July 1970 article in *TV Guide*, Ed Gardner took her to lunch at the Brown Derby to break the news. When she told him she would quit if the raise were not forthcoming, he said, "Don't be hasty, Sandy. Remember, you have a sick husband." Gould picked up a plate of spaghetti, pushed it in Gardner's face, then stood up, knocked over the table and stalked out of the restaurant. (Soon after the *Duffy's Tavern* imbroglio, Gould was offered a regular berth with the Jack Carson show, *The Sealtest Village Show.*) The parting was as bitter as a divorce court and Gould was one of the few actresses who quit, rather than be fired.

"In interviews, Ed Gardner often told reporters that he wrote most of the story outlines and jokes," Gould recalled to SPERDVAC in 1991. "Then he got a couple of the guys to put it into shape for radio form. I, knowing the list of illustrious 'guys' who put *Duffy's Tavern* into shape, always resented his blatant disregard for the work those 'guys' did. After I left the show, I took an ad in *Daily Variety* and *The Hollywood Reporter* and on the whole back page I listed 378 writers plus one writer who unfortunately was incarcerated in San Quentin and sent in his gags under the number 3987! Ed Gardner was no slouch. After all, a joke was a joke! Hence the ad! Naturally, it was the talk of Hollywood." For crediting writers who supplied her with material while she was on *Duffy's Tavern*, Sandra Gould was presented with a certificate of appreciation by the Radio Writers Guild. On the motion of Phil Leslie and seconded by Don Quinn, a resolution "Expressing official appreciation for her expression of appreciation" was passed unanimously at a membership meeting. The Writers Guild (of which she later became a member) gave her an honorary plaque which said, "To Sandra Gould, a.k.a. Miss Duffy, for meritorious conduct above and beyond the call of duty for defending all the unsung writers of the Writers Guild in Hollywood."

Following her departure from the tavern, Sandra Gould found her services to be in constant demand. She played Minerva, Babs' girlfriend, on a number of *Life of Riley* broadcasts from September 6, 1947, to June 26, 1948. She played supporting roles in many of the *Sealtest Village Store* broadcasts, beginning September 18, 1947. From October 29, 1949, to the end of the run, she played the recurring role of Henrietta on *A Day in the Life of Dennis Day*. In the spring of 1948, Gould found herself employed at Warner Bros. with a role in *June Bride* (1948), *Romance on the High Seas* (1948), and *My Dream is Yours* (1949). She acted on the stage in

The Amboy Dukes (1948) and had a leading role in John Claar's *The Big Shot* (1949).

On the afternoon of September 15, 1947, auditions were held for a new Miss Duffy to replace Sandra Gould. Helen Eley, wife of Sam "Schlepperman" Hearn and a West Coast radio actress who recently appeared as a semi-regular on *The Kenny Baker Show*, a five-a-week musical variety program in the noon time slot, auditioned. Kenny Baker's program expired in June and Eley hoped to start the fall season with a new weekly assignment. Eley was picked over two dozen candidates.

Crosby, Hope and Sinatra

It wasn't until early August that Gardner began planning the new season of *Duffy's Tavern*. Though his brilliance to have the vice-president of NBC appear as a guest towards the conclusion of last season wasn't admired by radio comedians, the premiere of the 1947-48 season certainly sparked admiration. Studio publicity (and a heavy advertising campaign from the advertising agency) announced that Crosby, Sinatra and Hope would all be guests on the same broadcast. On the evening of October 1, 1947, audiences tuned in to hear the whole gang at *Duffy's* returning from summer break. Dave Hossinger promises Archie three major stars for a new floor show: Crosby, Hope and Sinatra. The entire episode was one large buildup for the celebrities. Archie invests in the stars but will not pay Hossinger the amount he claims is worth their value, so Archie gets just what he paid for — Larry Crosby (brother of Bing Crosby), Jim Hope (brother of Bob Hope) and Ray Sinatra (bandleader cousin of Frank Sinatra).* The guests supply corny vaudevillian routines. As Archie explains to Duffy by phone at the end of the broadcast, "Well, maybe, Duffy, but you'll have to admit — at least it was fresh and different!"

---

* In addition to being relatives of "famous people," the guests have prestige in their own right: Larry Crosby as head of the Crosby Foundation; Ray Sinatra was a notable bandleader and arranger; and Jim Hope was executive secretary of the Denver office of the American Guild of Variety Artists.

HELP WANTED

We have an opening for a trade paper radio critic, who can write comedy funny enough to please another trade paper critic. Salary no object. This is an opportunity for some enterprising critic to double his salary.* See Ed Gardner, Duffy's Tavern.

*Up to and including $100 per week.

Advertisement in the October 3, 1947, issue of Variety.

The October 2, 1947, issue of *Variety* featured the following review: "Radio's Mr. Malaprop is back at his old stand again in *Duffy's Tavern* and another of NBC's top comedy entries is off and running. Not that Ed Gardner won't have better shows as the season progresses, but last night's opener had all the ingredients and they were well enough compounded to keep the laughs coming at a reasonable pace. The garbled wit of Archie, whose play on words cues most of the comedy lines, is still his main prop but the other characters indigenous to the tavern managed to get in their share of the raucous reception. There's a new Miss Duffy this semester in the high-pitched Helen Eley and she came through with the Flatbush flavor required of the role. Her bit with the boyfriend, an ersatz cowboy with a voice to match, was a hilarious interlude—to the studio audience, at least. Hard-put for a floor show, Archie went for a fast hustle and came up with Crosby, Hope and Sinatra, but they proved to be two brothers and a cousin, respectively. 'They're here,' Arch tells Duffy, 'relatively speaking.' Which proved a bigger laugh than when the trio went into a song and patter routine. It seemed a good gag but didn't pay off too well. Gardner's 10 scripters just didn't come through with enough funny material. Few of the season's shows have hit their stride on the getaway and Gardner can take some consolation from this occupational lapse. Curtain-raiser had passable quality but was short of par for the tavern."

The last few sentences obviously did not digest well with Ed Gardner. The October 3 issue of *Variety* featured an advertisement, challenging the columnist to do better.

Hoping to improve the laughter on the studio's Richter scale, beginning with the second episode, October 8, Gardner implemented a new warm up device for the studio audience at NBC. He played a record of last week's *Duffy's Tavern*, just before going on the air. To help along the laughs and condition the sitters for the ensuing program, Gardner and his cast were out front mugging as their bits were played. According to plan, if it met the anticipated response, Gardner would continue the mechanical warm up through the season. (No information has been found to verify that he continued this beyond the October 8 broadcast.)

Among the highlights of the new season was a guest appearance by soprano Helen Traubel who performed on radio as early as 1936 and made her first Metropolitan Opera performance on radio in 1941. During the broadcast of October 22, 1947, Archie tries to figure the criminal mind when Clancy the Cop informs him that the police force is offering a $1,000 reward for the capture of Nellie, a female bandit and safe-cracker who blew up a bank, escaped via the rooftops and crashed a car on the Brooklyn Bridge. When Helen Traubel of the Metropolitan Opera makes an appearance, Archie sees that the woman fits the description in the newspaper and suspects Traubel of being "Nellie the safecracker." Archie explained to his guest, hoping to keep her busy long enough to fetch Clancy, that in the tavern visitors had a choice of their one-dish menu. "And judging by appearances," he remarked, "I think you've been taking it when you should have been leaving it." While the opera star sings *Oh, What a Beautiful Morning*, Archie successfully fetches Clancy, who then informs Archie that Nellie was arrested three hours ago.

Having made her debut at the Metropolitan Opera in 1937, her natural flare for comedy was spotlighted here for the first time. When Jimmy Durante heard an air check of the *Duffy's* show that evening and decided "dis Traubel doll's for me," he arranged for her to guest on his program. One week after the broadcast, on October 29, Helen Traubel was "arrested" by Sheriff Falby in El Paso, Texas, an hour before her concert was scheduled to begin at Liberty Hall. Sheriff Falby clamped handcuffs on the singer and placed her behind bars — all for the camera, of course. Traubel posed for the picture which was then sent to Ed Gardner. Pictures of Miss Traubel's "arrest" were snapped by her husband and business manager, William Bass and Charles Drake of Columbia Concerts, Inc.

When offered the opportunity to feature Humphrey Bogart and Lauren Bacall for his radio program, courtesy of Warner Bros., to promote their next motion picture, *Key Largo* (1948), Gardner accepted the lovebirds with open arms. To make the most of the two guests, Gardner arranged for the actors to appear separately on two consecutive weeks. For the broadcast of March 10, 1948, Archie is trying to figure out his income tax when Lauren Bacall arrives at the tavern and confesses that her husband is on his boat today. Realizing he has no chance of muscle-bound interference, Archie attempts to impress her with his manly skills; the actress quickly gives him the brush-off. When comparing the screen star to Miss Duffy, Archie refers to Laurel Bacall as "the look," and Miss Duffy as "the sight." The U.S. Collector of Revenue, Mr. Harry C. Westover, also makes a guest appearance at the tavern and Archie tries to put one over on him by demonstrating how good he is with figuring out his income tax.

The entire program featured an underlying message: the importance of submitting income tax returns by the deadline. The comedy angle is sheer entertainment but the program also served to call attention of listeners to the March 15 deadline for filing their 1947 returns. To present the NBC cue on time, the closing announcement for guest Lauren Bacall was faded at 9:29:25 on the words, "...through the courtesy of Warner Brothers Studios, producers of..." The radio audience, including movie studio executives, never heard the pitch for the up-coming motion picture, *Key Largo*. Ed Gardner received a notice from NBC that the fault lay in the fact that the program ran overtime. A studio executive expressed his disappointment.

Humphrey Bogart and Ed Gardner

For the broadcast of March 17, Humphrey Bogart paid a visit to the tavern. From "The Look" to "The Crook," the second broadcast succeeded where the first did not. A pitch for *Key Largo* was successfully delivered at the end of the broadcast. At first, having heard Archie, Bogart suspected the barkeep was trying to mimic tough guy slang from the silver screen. Finnegan, however, mistakes Bogart for the real thing and hilarious situations ensue. To compensate and show he really wasn't as tough as they made

The October 15, 1947, broadcast poked fun at the Community Chest benefit, but also served to remind radio listeners that the Community Chest was a worthy cause and that current drives were being conducted in many small towns. Donations were encouraged.

him out to be, Bogart did a comedic skit with Miss Duffy where he woos her, a role (described on the program) much like *Key Largo* — an informal product placement for pitching the movie. In a press release promoting Bogart's appearance on the program, Ed Gardner cracked, "Warner's paroled him for one evening so he could do this show."

Fred Astaire, who announced retirement from the screen after filming completed with Irving Berlin's *Blue Skies*, came back in circulation for a radio appearance on *Duffy's Tavern*, following an appearance on *Tex and Jinx* in September. Astaire was still making appearances on radio, but on a limited basis. He preferred to concentrate his time on a new venture, the Fred Astaire Dance Studios. "I quit pictures," Astaire explained, "because I got to the point that I couldn't do another one unless I knew it was the last. There just wasn't any kick in it any longer." On January 15, 1947, he spoke on behalf of the March of Dimes Campaign from Rockefeller Center in New York City, broadcast on radio airwaves. He was a guest on the *Kraft Music Hall* on October 3, 1946, and *Maggi's Private Wire* on March 20, 1947. The dancer, who had had two years of so-called retirement, was announced to replace the broken-limbed Gene Kelly in *Easter Parade* and folks wondered if his return to the screen would be a one-shot affair. Columnist Bob Thomas remarked, "When I saw him at a *Duffy's Tavern* broadcast, he assured me his 'retirement' is over." The news was official, direct from the Tavern itself.

Described as the All-America type, Van Johnson, the MGM star, paid a visit to the tavern on the evening of March 3, 1948. Archie decided to play the gangster type to impress the actor. Miss Duffy swoons over the red-headed star (whom Archie refers to as "carrot top"), but the actor brushes her off in the mold of a screen tough guy. To teach the screen-star and idol of the bobby-soxers a lesson, Finnegan comes in, pretending to be her husband. In order to avoid a nasty confrontation, Van Johnson pays Archie fifty bucks to make Finnegan disappear. Archie seeks to give Van Johnson advice about the real heartthrob technique, the "Archie technique." Adding to the hilarious situation is actor Eddie Marr in the role of the gangster, "Baby Face Pagano," representing the "Third Avenue Protective Association." On March 18, a columnist for the *Los Angeles Times* remarked: "If you think Van Johnson is slipping, you should have been one of the policemen trying to save him from being torn apart on the *Duffy's Tavern* program."

Clearly evident during the 1947-48 season was Gardner's staff of scriptwriters attempting to inject a number of public service announcements into the scripts. For the broadcast of April 14, 1948, a young kid accidentally hits a baseball through the window of the tavern and makes his acquaintance with Finnegan, Miss Duffy and Archie. The kid apologizes for the broken window, blame shifting the existing need for proper recreational places for growing boys. The kid then plays with "A Pocket Encyclopedia of Useful Knowledge" and uses it to quiz the bar patrons, only to receive the most ridiculous answers — especially from Archie. A bigger problem comes along when a young baby is found on the steps of the tavern. Archie falls in love with the baby and suddenly becomes tolerant toward children. Especially when he falls in love with the infant's mother, a rich widow. In the next two episodes that follow, April 21 and 28, Archie organizes a "Boys Club" for the kids who broke the tavern window while they were playing baseball. To raise funds for the club, Archie stages a boxing match... with hilarious results.

Hunk of My Heart

There was irony in humor when Abe Burrows appeared as a guest on the December 31, 1947, broadcast of *Duffy's Tavern*. For years, he fretted in anonymity as the author of numerous *Duffy's Tavern* scripts. Burrows had by this time become known in circles as the life of Hollywood parties, introduced to the general public as "a wit's wit, a clown's clown." In the summer of 1947, Burrows' fans included notables in the world of humor in both New York and Hollywood. He brought his popular song satires to CBS' audience in a new radio series, *The Abe Burrows Show*, sponsored by Listerine on CBS. Burrows and a piano comprised the cast of the show, during which he dissected, with malice aforethought, the various "song types" into which the products of Tin Pan Alley fall. During the broadcast, Burrows was able to display his wit with a number of ad-libs that were not scripted. He discussed Hollywood with Archie, admitting he served a brief spell as a producer at Paramount. "I prefer not to stub my toes at the outset on a new picture," I told the board of directors. "Won't you let me get into my stride by doing a good remake first?"

"That's very modest of you and very wise," said the chairman. "What picture would you like to remake?"

"*Going My Way*," said Burrows. The studio did not understand his brand of humor.

Having achieved a radio program of his own, Burrows remarked: "All I need now is sex appeal. Mine is the only show women turn off to listen to hockey games."

During the *Duffy's Tavern* broadcast, Burrows sang a torch song he wrote called, "You Ate Up a Hunk of my Heart," which declared that the singer's heart was wrapped up in his sweetheart's intestines. "I thought this was the real thing, but you were only jesting," the lyrics read. "Now my heart and my love and my memories, are wrapped up in your large intestine." This prompted a number of letters from listeners, including Everett W. Oglevee of Bloomington, Illinois, who submitted a written complaint on January 2. Fourteen days later, after reviewing the script, including the lyrics of Abe Burrows' song, Ken R. Dyke, the vice-president at NBC, sent the following replay to Oglevee: "We sincerely apologize to you and our other listeners for broadcasting that objectionable portion of the lyrics. Our system of checking lyrics and scripts before broadcast is generally foolproof and airtight, and our faces are really quite red over the slip that was made in this particular instance. I personally checked the matter and found the error was due to the unusual amount of work to which our Continuity Acceptance Department was subjected over the holiday season. I can assure you that this particular lyric is contrary to our policy and we make a constant effort to prevent the broadcast of material of this sort."

What makes this story ironic is that Abe Burrows sang the same song on his radio program, four months prior, on the evening of August 23. CBS never received a single letter of complaint. In October of 1947, Abe Burrows began scripting for *The Joan Davis Show*. Jack Gould, columnist and radio critic, remarked: "It is suspected that Abe Burrows, who is in charge of Miss Davis' scripts, and who worked on *Duffy's Tavern* back in the days when it was an amusing show, primarily is responsible for the welcome change of events."

Beginning in mid-season with the broadcast of January 28, 1948, five additional stations began broadcasting *Duffy's Tavern* for Bristol-Myers.
WJBO — Baton Rouge, Louisiana
WINR — Binghamton, New York
WTCB — Flint, Michigan
WEEK — Peoria, Illinois
KOH — Reno, Nevada

A Sign of Success

They say in Hollywood a sign of financial success is when you don't have to cut your own grass. During the calendar years of 1947 and 1948, the estimated talent cost per episode was $12,500. Ed Gardner, as producer, was able to convince some of the Hollywood celebrities to accept less than usual fees, and thus was able to pocket the difference. Business aside, Gardner and his troupe received a number of salutations... another sure sign of success. In August of 1947, a committee of top radio performers was set up in Hollywood by the American Federation of Radio Artists (AFRA) to co-operate with the Sullivan, Stauffer, Colwell & Bayles Agency of New York in production of the agency's new proposed radio program, *Show of the Year*. Jack Benny, Edgar Bergen, Burns and Allen, Eddie Cantor and Ed Gardner agreed to work with SSC&B's new show, which would rebroadcast what one agency official called a star's "best show of the season" on its weekly outing.

By September, the title of the proposed program changed to *Best Show of the Year* and a firm offer with a two-week stop clause was delivered to American Tobacco, who sought interest. Behind-the-scenes, several advertising agencies were said to have been opposed to their stars under contract appearing on a program under another sponsorship. The charity angle was secured, with the American Federation of Radio Artists cut in for a percentage to set up a welfare fund. By the end of the month, American Tobacco cooled on the idea and decided to continue sponsoring *The Big Story*. In mid-October, Sullivan, Stauffer, Colwell & Bayles withdrew their attempts to sell the program and MCA signed on, believing they could make a sale. Sadly, the series never came to be.

In December 1947, *Ebony*, a Negro monthly picture magazine with a circulation of over 400,000 and an estimated readership of about 1,500,000, released results of its first annual awards for promotion of interracial understanding in the fields of theater, radio, movies and books. The awards were highlighted in the magazine's January issue. Walter Winchell took first place in the radio division, with Arthur Godfrey, *Superman* and *Duffy's Tavern* also getting high rankings.

In January 1948, appeals by top radio artists on behalf of the Salvation Army's Annual Maintenance Fund were recorded on one platter by Amos n' Andy, Mary Margaret McBride, John Gielgud, Lillian Gish, Wendy Hiller, Bob Hope, Robert Montgomery, Kate Smith and Ed Gardner. Local radio stations across the country were booked to carry the record starting January 19 through February 21. The Salvation Army was seeking $1,000,000 to maintain 60 institutions and services in New York.

In May and June of 1948, the Candy Corporation of America, located in Los Angeles, of which Edgar Bergen was vice-president, entered the confection field with Bergen's Better Bubble Gum. The product was a market tie-in with the radio program and additional planned products included items to be tied in with the names of Jack Benny (Benny's Penny Pinchers) and Ed Gardner (*Duffy's Tavern* items).

"He was very popular in New York," Simone Hegeman later recalled. "He was a big hero to any taxi driver who heard his voice."

A Case for Miss Duffy

The replacement of Miss Duffy was a strange phenomenon, since in radio, practically nobody moved around after settling down into a primary role. Gardner's decision to move the series from

Ed and Simone at one of the many Hollywood parties.

Simone and Ed greet Jean Hersholt and Via Hersholt.

Hollywood to New York (or vice versa) in mid-season was only part of the problem. In this respect, Miss Duffy was the Camille of radio. Actresses were either broken on the wheel of Miss Duffy or else went on to greater things. For more than two decades, old-time radio fanzines attempted to offer a list of all the actresses to play Miss Duffy, and the exact dates they played the role. Thanks to a review of existing recordings from the program and the radio scripts housed in numerous archives across the country, the exact dates have been pinpointed.

Shirley Booth (March 1, 1941, to June 30, 1942)
Florence Halop (October 5, 1943, to March 21, 1944)
Helen Lynd (April 11, 1944, to May 2, 1944)*
Doris Singleton (May 9, 1944)
Sara Berner (May 23, 1944)
Connie Manning (May 30, 1944, to June 27, 1944)
Florence Robinson
(September 15, 1944, to November 17, 1944)
Sandra Gould (November 24, 1944, to June 25, 1947)
Helen Eley (October 1 and 8, 1947)
Margie Liszt (October 15 to November 19, 1947)
Florence Halop (November 26, 1947, to June 29, 1949)
Gloria Erlanger
(September 29, 1949, to November 17, 1949)
Pauline Drake (November 24, 1949, to December 15, 1949)
Florence Halop subs for Drake (December 22, 1949)
Pauline Drake (December 29, 1949, to March 2, 1950)
Hazel Shermet (March 9, 1950, to December 28, 1951)

Pauline Drake was added to the cast for November 17, 1949, in a supporting role of Margo, then took over as Miss Duffy beginning November 24. Scripts indicate her last show was February 23, 1950, but scripts were written a week or two before broadcast and for this reason hindsight has proven that scripts

---

* Miss Duffy was not featured in the broadcasts of March 28 and April 4, 1944.

are not always historically accurate. Two sources, including NBC files at the Library of Congress, verify her last appearance as Miss Duffy was March 2, 1950.

Realizing that you cannot believe everything you read in the newspapers, the October 29, 1947, issue of *The* (Massillon, Ohio) *Evening Independent* remarked: "Marjorie Liszt has taken over the Miss Duffy role, with Helen Eley stepping down to a minor part." In truth, Eley left the program for good as verified in the cast lists on the cover of each radio script. According to press releases (if they can be believed), both Liszt and Gardner were born in Astoria, Long Island, and both attended Bryant High School. Liszt became a notable singer and dancer in her early teens. She tried her hand at Broadway before switching to radio in 1935. "A red-headed descendant of Franz Liszt, the composer and pianist would be greatly surprised to hear that the family name has reached such eminence," quoted the press release. The new Miss Duffy was tall, slender, brown-eyed and, as a hobby, made hats for fun. When the war broke out, she was the star of her own radio program over a Detroit radio station, then joined a USO unit to entertain troops, which took her to Alaska and the Aleutians.

Florence Halop Trivia

Throughout 1948, Florence Halop played the recurring role of Hotbreath Houlihan on *The Jimmy Durante Show*. In February 1948, Halop received an offer to audition for *Life's Ambition*, a situation comedy set in a boarding house in which she would play a variety of characterizations and even sing funny songs. *Life's Ambition* was recorded in late March 1948. Dick Mack, the producer/director of the series, was unable to sell the series and, in early 1950, auditioned another talented female for the lead, changing the title to *The Henn House*. Halop lost to Mitzi Green who, in the second audition show, sang and imitated Al Jolson, Mae West and Sophie Tucker. Halop was good friends with the Gardners; her daughter's nickname was "Duffy." Ed Gardner was also godfather to Florence Halop's daughter.

Renee and Veola Vonn

Veola Vonn, who played supporting roles on *The Alan Young Show*, made her first appearance on *Duffy's Tavern* with the broadcast of October 29, 1947. On that broadcast, Archie wants to have Fred Astaire teach him about ballroom dancing and attempts to use this to impress his girlfriend, Renee, only to discover she herself is a French dancing teacher and a sensation in "French circles." As expected, Archie strikes out and she takes a liking to Astaire. Archie gets Fred to dance in the dark with Renee and pretend he's Archie, but Renee is not fooled. Veola Vonn would play the recurring role of Renee in less than a dozen episode of *Duffy's Tavern* from 1947 to 1949. Her initial appearances were touchy because she was playing the role of widow Dahlrymple on *The Great Gildersleeve* on the same evening, broadcast at NBC in the time slot before *Duffy's Tavern*. For the broadcast of October 29, 1947, for example, Vonn had to go from one studio to the next to successfully make two appearances on two separate radio programs on one evening. Vonn faced the same scenario from October 1948 to June 1949, when she played supporting roles in numerous episodes of *Blondie*, which aired one hour before *Duffy's Tavern* on the same network. Had the series not moved to Puerto Rico in 1949, the character of Renee would have probably appeared in additional *Duffy's Tavern* episodes. (Vonn eventually won the recurring role of Dolores Darling, Alan Young's new girlfriend, beginning with the broadcast of December 27, 1946 on *The Alan Young Show*.) Vonn chose to stay in Hollywood and played the recurring role of Babette on *The Dennis Day Show* from 1950 to 1951.

NBC Promotional Gimmick

In November of 1947, authoritative miniatures and dioramas depicting Hollywood's coast-to-coast network radio shows were created and put on display in El Paso, Texas. They were displayed in a 10-ton mobile trailer unit which was parked in the downtown business area for four days. The shows included in the exhibit were *Duffy's Tavern*, Kay Kyser's *Kollege of Musical Knowledge*, Amos n' Andy's "Lodge Hall and Taxi Stand," the Jimmy Durante show, and the Red Skelton show. The construction of the miniatures and dioramas involved the labor of many skilled artists and craftsmen over a period of one year. The exhibit toured the country courtesy of The Marine Corps League, a non-profit organization, offering free admission. Funds from contributions were disbursed by the League and used for their national welfare program.

The *Duffy's Tavern* Stage Play

In late May of 1946, Ed Gardner decided to take *Duffy's Tavern* to a new level in what he described as "a musical comedy with Duffy's as the locale." By the fall of 1946, Hoagy Carmichael, then in New York, was sought for the composer's slot and, according to Gardner, if all went well it would be tested in California that winter in preparation for Broadway come August. "Meet Me at Duffy's" was the tentative title while Gardner and his writers, Vincent Bogert, Stanley Davis and Elon Packard, wrote the book (completed in July of 1946). They also toyed with the idea of adding a new character in the script — Mrs. Duffy, the wife of the elusive proprietor of the tavern. In early January 1947, Gardner traveled from Hollywood to New York. Among business matters and broadcasting the radio program from New York, he made further arrangements for the planned Broadway presentation by meeting with Carmichael, who agreed to write the music. Talk of an early spring production, with most of the *Duffy's Tavern* troupe appearing in the musical, included Sandra Gould, Eddie Green and Charles Cantor. On June 8, Lewis Funke of the *New York Times* sarcastically reported: "Ed Gardner, who was wildly beating the drum last winter about his musical, 'Meet Me at Duffy's,' and telling of Hoagy Carmichael's interest therein, says it's all off. Seems (a) Mr. Carmichael wasn't interested, (b) Mr. Gardner has

413

bought a yacht and (c) Mr. Gardner didn't prefer New York to California." It seems Funke overlooked another reason. Gardner, even with his experience in producing stage plays in New York, was unable to acquire backing for his venture.*

Flash forward to May of 1948. Thanks to the effortless tasks of his scriptwriters, Ed Gardner succeeded in putting together the stage show. Dismissing the notion of a musical, outside of a few introductory minutes, the stage show followed the radio format pretty closely. Tavern regulars Eddie Green, Charles Cantor and Florence Halop were each given an opportunity to trade insults with Archie. Green was even given an opportunity to take the spotlight for a deftly contrived pantomime routine about poker playing. Matty Malneck and his orchestra supplied the music.

The featured guest for the stage show, presented in the same manner as guest stars on the radio counterpart, was Jane Russell. Attired in a strapless evening gown and performing two vocal solos, she and Gardner closed the show with a duet. Then a dead-panned announcer walked out to the the center mike with script in hand and intoned: "Are your hands rough? Well, try Sal Hepatica." Gardner then informed the audience, "We'd better go; the show must be over." This attitude toward the sponsor won critics over and was approved in advance with the radio sponsor who was thankful their product was mentioned by name since they had no involvement with the stage play.

Billboard Magazine reviewed: "This is far and away one of the funniest stage shows to hit this house in a long time. Carrying the format of Ed Gardner's radio package, *Duffy's Tavern*, plus a couple of bits for sight values, on stage is often a risky business. The illusion built up on air shots is frequently destroyed on personal appearances. There is no danger to Gardner's Hooper in

---

* At one time, Irving Berlin may have been consulted for this stage musical. The April 9, 1947, issue of the *Los Angeles Times* reported: "Ed Gardner is talking to Irving Berlin about writing the music for a *Duffy's Tavern* movie." The newspaper columnist may have made an error and mistook this venture for another motion picture.

his current package. It is as hilarious in the flesh as it has often been on the air... Jane Russell's no singer, tho she has a pleasant enough voice. But what she lacks in voice she more than makes up for with looks and an ease that is refreshing to watch. Besides that, the gal is also quite an actress. She straightened for Gardner like a trouper, getting plenty out of the lines and feeding them for maximum effects."

The June 14, 1948, issue of the *New York Morning Telegraph* reported: "Ed 'Archie' Gardner has brought his *Duffy's Tavern* radio show to the New York Strand Theater virtually intact, giving the theater one of its best stage offerings in some time. Gardner makes but slight concession to the visual medium, appearing behind a prop bar equipped with microphone and the ever-present telephone. His delightfully wry humor is, if anything, more effective in its new setting, as he casually murders the king's English – 'that famous German opera, 'Die Meisterstinker' – or comments on cooking 'crepes suzette, those little drunken pancakes.' ... Jane Russell, of movie fame, sings several songs in a surprisingly adequate voice and displays her tall, buxom frame to eye-filling effect."

Taking the stage play on tour during the radio season was a different matter and through the understanding of the advertising agency, Young & Rubicam, and executives at NBC, Gardner convinced them to broadcast the radio program on location, while on tour. Preparing and scheduling in advance, Gardner and the gang left Hollywood for the personal appearance tour to Cleveland, where the June 2 and 9 radio broadcasts originated. According to a telegram at NBC, the local radio station, NBC affiliate WTAM, did not have the space to accommodate the entire cast and crew for the radio broadcast, which meant finding a theater that could seat an audience and supply ample hookup. The theater where the stage play was performed, the RKO Palace, was not the same used for the remote broadcast. Originally, the network considered broadcasting from the Civic Auditorium, but another event was booked for the two dates. Thanks to an employee at WTAM, a suitable location was found: the Rainbow Room of the Carter Hotel, with seating for 1,300. The charge for renting the facilities was $150 per day. However, this included a full day for rehearsal. "Have originated other network shows from there in the past very successfully," the telegram explained. "It does not have a stage, but can be built up for a successful presentation. Have written Stanford Y&R producer about our studio facilities and will see him in Hollywood next week."

The theater was approved and 1,000 tickets were sent to Bristol-Myers for public distribution and for clients (authorized retailers) who were driving distance from the theater. Only 300 were sent to Cleveland for local promotional gimmicks. Ed Gardner requested 50 tickets for himself and Anthony Stanford, an executive at Young & Rubicam who produced and directed the two Cleveland broadcasts, requested 10 for personal reasons. Later, it was discovered that without using a single ticket for newspapers (to gain free publicity), the agency had given away more tickets than hall seats. Thankfully, a figure for the number of seats was underestimated and the problem was avoided.

The tour required the crating and expressing of the prop bar from NBC New York to the Carter Hotel, care of the *Duffy's Tavern* program. It was done on the belief that it would be cheaper to ship the existing bar rather than have carpenters erect a substitute bar.

Courtesy of affiliate WTAM in Cleveland, the June 2, 1948, broadcast went coast-to-coast without a hitch... except for the first three minutes of the program which had very poor quality due to the Cleveland engineer not having the public address system properly adjusted. Jack Payne was the engineer and Chuck Kebbe was the production man. The commercials were delivered by Innes Harris from Hollywood. Afterward, Archie opened the broadcast by telling Duffy that he's "shoving" off tonight to the Palace Theater in Cleveland, "to star in me own stage presentation. A stage presentation? That's an act they put on between the movies to make the audience forget how bad the picture was." Usually the audience would assume that Archie and the gang were at Duffy's Tavern. Breaking the fourth wall, most of the evening's broadcast took place at the theater and the radio audience received a taste of the rehearsals. Eddie Green's rendition of "Nature Boy" was followed by Finnegan and Miss Duffy singing "Rancho Grande." Archie, meanwhile, cracked jokes about Jane Russell, while failing to reach her by phone. Getting nervous because his guest star is not available, Archie and the gang rehearse a corny scene — until the stage manager kicks them off and out. The episode closes with Archie back at the tavern, talking to Duffy by phone and asking his opinion.

Obviously, the entire broadcast was one long commercial to promote the stage play, complete with Gardner naming the day, time and location where the play was being performed. Jane Russell did make an appearance in the second broadcast, June 9. Still in Cleveland, the cast cracked jokes about the local restaurants, no doubt as part of Ed Gardner's free-publicity-in-exchange-for-free-food deal to the local eateries. Archie tried to dictate to a newly hired secretary that he was going to make $20,000 a week in Broadway salary. Jane Russell appears and a reporter wants to interview her but Archie gets in the way, much to her dismay. Later, when Archie buys sweets and flowers for a local hat check girl, the merchants get tough. It turns out that Russell was merely trying to deflate Archie's swelled head.

After the conclusion of the June 9 radio broadcast, the cast left the Midwestern city for the Big Apple. Things must have been a bit hectic with the cast and crew because they opened at The Strand Theater in New York on June 11. The radio broadcast of June 16 and 23 obviously originated from the East Coast, where the program wound up for the season. *Duffy's Tavern* had been renewed next fall and would resume in Hollywood at the usual time.

Without a filmed performance caught on camera, the only way we can get an idea of the staged proceedings is through reviews, mostly from theater critics in New York. "The one drawback is the dull pacing, which can be improved by better choice of numbers by Matty Malneck's band. Ed Gardner, Florence Halop, Eddie Green, Charlie Cantor and Jane Russell are all skilled performers but show workers. Their brand of comedy calls for deliberate pacing. So, by the same token, the band should give the zip to the show and it doesn't. Malneck's opening with a *William Tell Overture* and following with a medley of his own tunes, in which nothing happened, was obviously bad. Inasmuch as the band is costumed in brown derbies and green jerseys with big *Duffy's* across the chest, it would seem appropriate to have them open with *East Side, West Side; Down by the Vinegar Works* or something similar... Charlie Cantor's Finnegan with the characteristic 'du-h,' was a masterpiece and sneakers make-up gave him the sight values; his moronic delivery of lines gave him the ear appeal. Florence Halop's Miss Duffy was all of a piece. She was funny and believable. Eddie Green's waiter was equally amusing. His chatter with Gardner on the new menu was a new high in hilarity. Lad's Harlem poker game panto was okay and well done, but it can stand judicious pruning. Cantor's and Miss Halop's opera act, a bit corny perhaps, was ludicrous. But because the crowd was slow on the take, it took this bit very easy and howled."

A candid photo of the cast during the stage play.

Judging from the box office receipts, the *Duffy's Tavern* stage production was a financial success. The show played four times daily, five on Saturday. The cost for a ticket ranged from 75 cents to $1.50. The Strand Theater had a seating capacity of 2,700. With a successful stage career under his belt, Gardner and his wife rounded out the remainder of the summer with a trip to Europe. The final two broadcasts in New York originated live from The

418

Strand Theater, where the stage performances were conducted. Commercials still originated from Hollywood. For the broadcast of June 16, Archie, on tour for the performance, has decided to take a tour of New York City and Rockefeller Plaza. Once again, the broadcast plays like a commercial. This, of course, makes no sense since Duffy's Tavern was supposedly located in New York City to begin with. After the first seven minutes, logic returns when Eddie did not show up for the stage rehearsal because he was visiting family in town. He apologizes when he returns to the tavern on Third Avenue, only to find it has been condemned by the city. To commemorate a new grand opening, before the city can do anything about it, the crew puts on a benefit dinner. High-hats and old friends attend and Duffy creates a surprise by making it a testimonial dinner for Archie. Duffy himself attends the final moment (but speaks no words as Eddie and Archie speak for him). Before the episode concludes, the cast manages to sing "My Bonnie Lies Over the Ocean."

The final broadcast of the season, June 23, originated from New York and returned the series to the usual format. Archie thinks he's smarter than the contestants of the radio programs he hears on the radio so he tries his wits at a radio contest called "Are You a Genius?" while the folks at the tavern listen to the program over the radio. His competition on the contest is Finnegan, who happens to answer all the questions correctly, while Archie is unable to answer a single one. In the end, Finnegan wins a ticket to Europe and kind-hearted as he is, gives it to Archie.

Ed Gardner never reproduced or sold script copies of the summer 1948 stage production but, within months, grade schools across the country began putting on their own stage productions. In Pennsylvania, a variety program displaying talent from grades 7 to 12 was presented at the Bloomfield school auditorium on December 7, 1948, to aid in the purchase of new stage scenery. Junior and High School grades participated. Among the numbers, the juniors presented their interpretation of the radio program, *Duffy's Tavern*. One week prior, in Virginia, the French and Spanish classes at Dublin High School, organized as El Club de Espanola y Francais, presented an original play on *Duffy's Tavern* which was presented with the newest members of the club taking part. On December 4, previews of the Fort Hill Players productions were presented in the Fort Hill High School auditorium. Among the list of dramatic skits was *Duffy's Tavern*. In March of 1954, two performances by members of the community, most of them amateurs, offered their own rendition of *Duffy's Tavern*, presented by the Brotherhood of Temple Israel at Temple Israel, Long Beach, California.

Perhaps the biggest compliment came in April of 1951. To speak with a Brooklyn accent was one of the problems facing the cast of *Cuckoos on the Hearth*, a three-act mystery comedy under the direction of Helen Thomas. David Egloff, a student at the local high school in Mason City, Iowa, solved the problem by recording an episode of *Duffy's Tavern* on a tape recorder and replaying it until his "dese" and "dose" were perfect. When asked the time, he replied, "one -toity-five."

Ed Gardner takes down his *Duffy's Tavern* sign over his Beverly Hills office. Too many drunks try to get in and buy liquor.
— Press Release dated October 30, 1947

Season Eight
October 1, 1947, to June 23, 1948
National Broadcasting Company
Sponsor: Bristol-Myers
East Coast Broadcast Time: Wednesday, 9:00 to 9:30 p.m., EST
West Coast Broadcast Time: Wednesday, 6:00 to 6:30 p.m., EST
(October 1, 1947, to March 10, 1948)
West Coast Broadcast Time: Wednesday, 7:00 to 7:30 p.m., EST
(March 17 to April 21, 1948)
West Coast Broadcast Time: Wednesday, 6:00 to 6:30 p.m., EST
(April 28 to June 23, 1948)
Complete season originates from Hollywood.
Advertising Agency: Young & Rubicam

Commercial announcer: Jay Stewart
(October 1, 1947, to December 3, 1947)
Commercial announcer: Rod O'Conner
(December 10, 1947, to May 26, 1948)
Commercial announcer: Charles Benjamin
(June 2 and June 9, 1948)
Commercial announcer: Jay Jackson (June 16 and 23, 1948)
Producer for the Agency (a.k.a. Director of Program):
Anthony Stanford
Producer/Director for the Network (a.k.a. Assistant Director):
John Morris (except March 24 and 31, 1948)
Producer/Director for the Network: Bill Karn
(March 24 and 31, 1948)
Producer/Director for the Network: Bob Spencer
(June 2 and 9, 1948)
Producer/Director for the Network: Chuck Kebe
(June 16 and 23, 1948)
Engineer: Charles Norman
(solo for all dates except March 17, 24, 31 and May 3, 1948)
Engineers: Charles Norman and Bob Brooke
(March 17, 24, 31 and May 3, 1948)
Engineer: Harry Caskey (June 2 and 9, 1948)
Engineer: Jack Paine (June 16 and 23, 1948)
Sound: Bob Grapperhaus (October 1, 1947, to May 26, 1948)
Sound: John Shutleff (June 2 and 9, 1948)
Sound: A.G. Horine (June 16 and 23, 1948)
Music: Matty Malneck and his Orchestra
Commercial Writer: Sylvia Dowling
Commercial Supervisor: Innes Harris (Hollywood)
Commercial Supervisor: John Swayze (New York)
Scriptwriters: Vincent Bogert, Herbert Finn, Bill Freedman,
Morris Freedman, Lou Grant, Al Johansen, Lee Karson, Larry
Rhine, Robert Schiller, Phil Sharp and Anthony Stafford.

Cast
Charles Cantor as Finnegan
Florence Halop as Miss Duffy
Eddie Green as Eddie

All other actors and known roles are listed under the respective episodes.

Episode #253 — Broadcast Wednesday, October 1, 1947
Rehearsal on June 16 in Studio F. Broadcast live from Studio D.
Supporting Cast: John Brown (Dave Hossinger); Alan Reed (Mr. Tremens); and guitarist Frank Saputo (as himself).
Guests: Larry Crosby, Jim Hope and Ray Sinatra
Plot: See page 399.

Episode #254 — Broadcast Wednesday, October 8, 1947
Rehearsal on October 6 in Studio E. Broadcast live from Studio D.
Supporting Cast: Alan Reed (Clancy the Cop) and Jay Stewart (as himself).
Guest: Sophie Tucker
Plot: Archie describes Sophie Tucker as "one of the grand old singers of show business ... Sort of a Hildegarde under gas light . .. The last of the Red Hot Mammas!" After having seen *The Jolson Story*, Archie decided to write "The Sophie Tucker Story" for a movie scenario. Sophie Tucker sings "Some of These Days" and then participates in a funny rendition that turns out to be "The Archie Story" which causes Sophie to walk out. Perhaps Archie could do one for Greer Garson?

Trivia, etc. In October of 1944, the singing spot on *Song of the Week* was taken over by Ray Eberle, who replaced singer Jerry Stewart. According to more than one newspaper, a deal was underway for Stewart to become a weekly singer for a number of *Duffy's Tavern* broadcasts. It never happened but Stewart did make an appearance in this episode, three years later.

Episode #255 — Broadcast Wednesday, October 15, 1947
Rehearsal on October 13 in Studio E. Broadcast live from Studio D.
Supporting Cast: Alan Reed (Clancy the Cop)

Guests: The Harry James Band
Plot: When bandleader Harry James stops by the tavern, everyone is excited. Finnegan wants to play the kazoo in his band and Miss Duffy tries to woo him, fully aware he's already married to Betty Grable. James and his band perform "Cottontail" and then agree to Archie's terms to perform for a Community Chest block party. There, the band performs a few bars of "St. Louis Blues," each time eliminating a musical instrument to help cut the costs for Archie, who is too cheap to pay for the entire band. Ultimately, Archie settles for Finnegan's kazoo.

Memorable Lines
JAMES: Shake. You owe us $240.
ARCHIE: For What?
JAMES: That's the minimum scale.
ARCHIE: $240! Harry, for that kind of dough I can get Spike Jones ... And with that washboard he'd probably do me laundry, too.

Episode #256 — Broadcast Wednesday, October 22, 1947
Rehearsal on October 20 in Studio E. Broadcast live from Studio D.
Supporting Cast: Alan Reed (Clancy the Cop)
Guest: Helen Traubel
Plot: See page 401.

Trivia, etc. Margie Liszt not only played the role of Miss Duffy in this episode, but doubled for the role of the little girl.

Episode #257 — Broadcast Wednesday, October 29, 1947
Rehearsal on October 27 in Studio C. Broadcast live from Studio D.
Supporting Cast: Alan Reed (Clancy the Cop) and Veola Vonn (Renee).
Guest: Fred Astaire
Plot: See page 404.

Episode #258 — Broadcast Wednesday, November 5, 1947
Rehearsal on November 3 in Studio C. Broadcast live from Studio D.
Supporting Cast: Alan Reed (Clancy the Cop) and Veola Vonn (Renee).
Guests: Rudy Vallee and George Jessel
Plot: Archie throws a testimonial dinner for himself. Rudy Vallee and George Jessel come down to the tavern to emcee the biggest testimonial dinner Third Avenue has ever had. Jessel refers to Vallee as a "prehistoric Perry Como," starting a momentary rivalry. The dinner goes off as planned, after everyone gets acquainted with each other, and Vallee's speech is more motivational, plugging the Pick-A Note. Jessel, in competition, invites everyone to a special showing of *Nightmare Alley* around the corner at the Fox Theater, a film noir classic he himself produced.

Episode #259 — Broadcast Wednesday, November 12, 1947
Rehearsal on November 10 in Studio E. Broadcast live from Studio D.
Supporting Cast: John Brown (Dave Hossinger) and Alan Reed (Clancy the Cop).
Guest: Dinah Shore
Plot: Dinah Shore plans to drop by the tavern and Archie makes plans to build his own radio station. Dave Hossinger uses eighteen bucks to build a transmitter and then starts successfully broadcasting. Archie buys the station and Dinah agrees to be on his program. To help him out, she pretends to have callers during the interview. Dinah never gets a chance to sing "Embraceable You," due to many distractions, and Clancy the Cop arrives asking to see Dave's broadcasting license. Dave makes an excuse, saying he would never do something to get Archie in jail... and the station is promptly shut down. But not before the cast plugs a number of local merchants. This broadcast was a take-off on radio programs and the way radio stations operated. The take-off especially focused on ridiculous commercials featured on children's programs.

Trivia, etc. The character of Miss Duffy was not featured in this broadcast.

Episode #260 — Broadcast Wednesday, November 19, 1947
Rehearsal on November 17 in Studio E. Broadcast live from Studio D.
Supporting Cast: Alan Reed (Clancy the Cop)
Guest: Henry Morgan
Plot: Henry Morgan pays a visit and Archie tries to get him to invest an interest in the tavern and abandon a Hollywood career. Archie, you see, makes plans to go to the Riviera. To compensate, he plays the role of Morgan's manager and attempts to get Duffy to sponsor Morgan's radio program. Morgan does a skit playing a Russian composer.

Episode #261 — Broadcast Wednesday, November 26, 1947
Rehearsal on November 24 in Studio E. Broadcast live from Studio D.
Script Title: "THANKSGIVING"
Supporting Cast: Alan Reed (The Magic Chef) and Luis Van Rooten (the sports-radio announcer).
Plot: Archie and Eddie are cooking a turkey. While they prepare the bird, the boys think they are listening to "The Magic Chef" on the radio and are not aware they are actually listening to a wrestling match. Afterwards, Archie finishes writing a play for the annual Thanksgiving pageant about the pilgrims, John Smith and Pocahontas. He convinces the gang to stop making the holiday dinner and rehearse his Mayflower play.

Trivia, etc. French singer Jean Sablon was originally scheduled for this broadcast, but was postponed until the following week.

Memorable lines
ARCHIE: Oh... You like the way I steer?
MISS DUFFY: You're magnificent, Miles. That steady, strong
     arm! Such skill! Such assurance!
ARCHIE: Thou hast seen nothin' yet. Look! No hands!
SOUND: TERRIFIC CRASH
ARCHIE: And thus we landed on Plymouth Rock.

Episode #262 — Broadcast Wednesday, December 3, 1947
Rehearsal on December 1 in Studio E. Broadcast live from Studio D.

Guest: Jean Sablon

Plot: When Archie is upset because his girlfriend, Renee, has fallen head over heels in love with Jean Sablon, he plots to have Sablon visit the tavern and insult Renee. Sablon became one of the most widely acclaimed French singers, considered second only in overall lifetime popularity to Maurice Chevalier. After tricking Sablon into visiting the tavern to help settle "foreign relations" (which means Archie's "personal relations"), Archie discovers the singer is wooing Renee, not insulting her. After Archie insults him personally, the Frenchman challenges the barkeep to a duel. Sablon asks: swords or pistols? Sablon chooses a sword... Archie then tries to choose a pistol. Before blood is spilled, Miss Duffy enters the tavern and Archie, tricking Sablon into thinking she is Renee, succeeds in convincing the Frenchman that they were fighting over something other than a beauty.

Trivia, etc. The character of Renee is referenced in this episode, but not heard from, when Archie talks to her over the phone.

This has to be one of the worst radio broadcasts of the season. Comparing a recording of the broadcast with the radio script, it appears the sound effects men couldn't get the sound of the phone ringing at the beginning of the broadcast. After a brief pause, Ed Gardner and Eddie Green ad-lib a reason why Duffy was not calling on the phone and Eddie immediately jumps to the second page. As a result, the entire cast slows their delivery. The high-paced standard often heard on the program is clearly missing.

Memorable Lines
MISS DUFFY: Do you think I've got time to go to the beauty parlor before he gets here?
ARCHIE: Well, do they do spot welding?

Episode #263 — Broadcast Wednesday, December 10, 1947
Rehearsal on December 8 in Studio E. Broadcast live from Studio D.

426

Supporting Cast: Alan Reed (Clancy the Cop *and* the radio announcer)
Guest: Esther Williams
Plot: Archie tricks Esther Williams into coming down to the tavern, believing she is going to give him swimming lessons. When she arrives at the tavern, Archie introduces Esther Williams as "the Seabiscuit of MGM" and then spoofs, in *Meet John Doe* fashion, his romance with the actress. Archie falls in love with Williams and encourages her to jump off the Brooklyn Bridge together, and Finnegan decides to let the newspaper reporters know. The publicity will be tremendous for Duffy's Tavern, and Archie just wants to see her swim in action... but it appears Archie is a coward when it comes to water.

Episode #264 — Broadcast Wednesday, December 17, 1947
Rehearsal on December 15 in Studio E. Broadcast live from Studio D.
Script Title: "FINNEGAN FAMILY"
Supporting Cast: Howard Jeffries (Wilfrid Finnegan); Alan Reed (Father Finnegan *and* Uncle Louie); and Doris Singleton (Hazel Finnegan).
Plot: Finnegan's family comes down to the tavern for the holiday. Eddie and Finnegan cannot solve the problem of what to hang on the tavern's Christmas tree. They soon start an argument about whether there is or is not a Santa Claus so Archie tells Finnegan's family, Hazel Finnegan (the sister), Wilfrid Finnegan (the kid brother who is a "book worm, highly educated"), Father Finnegan and Uncle Louie, a rendition of "The Christmas Carol," "Twas the Night Before Christmas" and "St. Nicholas" all mixed together. Archie fills their heads with Christmas cheer when he dresses up like Santa Claus.

Episode #265 — Broadcast Wednesday, December 24, 1947
Rehearsal on December 22 in Studio E. Broadcast live from Studio D.
Script Title: "THE STRANGER"
Supporting Cast: Helen Andrews (Ann); Robert Bruce (man at accident scene); Ira Grossel, a.k.a. Jeff Chandler (the stranger);

Bobby Ellis (Jimmy Turner, the boy); Jerry Hausner (the taxi driver); Tyler McVey (Paul); Franklin "Pinky" Parker (the cop); Ken Peters (Joe DiMaggio); Alan Reed (the hotel cop); Eric Rolfe (voice at accident scene); and Bud Widom (the blind man).
Plot: Same script from December 25, 1946.

Episode #266 — Broadcast Wednesday, December 31, 1947
Rehearsal on December 29 in Studio C. Broadcast live from Studio D.
Guests: Miss Jackie Van and Abe Burrows
Plot: Archie has two tickets to the Bartender's Ball on New Year's Eve. He spends the afternoon calling all the girls he knows, trying and failing to get a date. Abe Burrows introduces him to Jackie Van, winner of the *Chicago Sun-Times* Harvest Moon Festival Song contest, but even then Archie strikes out — and is surprised at the end when Abe and Jackie announce they are working the Bartender's Ball. Miss Van sings "Lady from 29 Palms."

Memorable Line
ARCHIE: Guess who that was, Eddie - Abe Burrows! Remember - the guy that always used to be around moochin' drinks and telling' them crummy jokes?

Episode #267 — Broadcast Wednesday, January 7, 1948
Rehearsal on January 5 in Studio D. Broadcast live from Studio D.
Supporting Cast: Alan Reed (Elmer Waterprice)
Guest: Garry Moore, emcee of the *Take It or Leave It* radio show
Plot: When Duffy sends an accountant to the tavern to inspect the books, Archie fears the shortage will be caught. In the hopes to leverage the loss, Archie attempts to play a game of *Take It or Leave It* with guest Garry Morre. "What do you have to know on them quiz programs?" Archie asks. "If the question is 'Who invented something,' the answer is Edison. If it's a quotation, the answer is Shakespeare. If it's mathematics, the answer is Einstein." Wanting to help his friend, Garry Moore accepts any answer Archie provides, regardless of how ridiculous the answer is. After winning $64 dollars, Archie decides not to balance the books but to call up Peaches La Toor at the Stork Club for a night on the

town. Eddie will just have to remind Archie to win the Miss Hush contest next year so he can then balance the books.

Memorable Lines
EDDIE: What makes you so sure this auditor's gonna find a shortage?
ARCHIE: Did you ever hear of an auditor findin' a longage?
EDDIE: How much do you figure the books are short? Is it Petty Larceny or Grand Larceny?
ARCHIE: What do you mean?
EDDIE: Well, is it rent money or grain market?
ARCHIE: Grain market? Eddie, it's bad enough that I'm a crook! You don't have to infer that I have friends in Washington.

Episode #268 — Broadcast Wednesday, January 14, 1948
Rehearsal on January 12 in Studio A. Broadcast live from Studio E.
Supporting Cast: Donald Morrison (Señor Gonzales)
Guest: Olga San Juan
Plot: Duffy just celebrated his 13th wedding Anniversary. Archie calls Paramount to get Puerto Rican actress Olga San Juan invited to the tavern to add some class. The studio, recalling his picture, hangs up on him. Archie's second attempt is a success and he convinces her to perform for a rich South American customer with a bulging wallet. Donald Morrison appears in the role of Tyrone Gonzales, South American gold mine operator. The two hit it off fine until Gonzales makes a crack about the Dodgers, forcing Olga into a windstorm.

Trivia, etc. According to the radio script, Finnegan enters the Tavern while Archie and Eddie are finishing a conversation and Archie remarks: "Hell, Finnegan. You're just in time to contribute nothing to the conversation." Because a recording does not exist for this broadcast, the use of the word "hell" cannot be verified. It may well have been a simple typo for "hello."

This episode was not broadcast over WGAL in Lancaster,

Pennsylvania, due to a broadcast of a local basketball game considered to be in the public interest.

Episode #269 — Broadcast Wednesday, January 21, 1948
Rehearsal on January 19 in Studio A. Broadcast live from Studio D.
Supporting Cast: Alan Reed (Giuseppe Vermicelli)
Plot: Deciding that insurance is a sweet racket, Archie opens his own business. He subjects Finnegan to a series of tests to see if he's healthy enough to pass an exam. When a customer named Giuseppe Vermicelli appears, Archie attempts to make him another client, unaware that "the Ezio Pinza of Third Avenue" will need to cash in on the policy very shortly when he loses his voice.

Trivia, etc. This episode was not broadcast over WTAR due to a broadcast of a speech delivered by the Governor of North Carolina which was considered to be in the public interest.

Memorable Lines
ARCHIE: Eddie, modern insurance companies don't make their money off of prospects, they make it off of sadistics.

Episode #270 — Broadcast Wednesday, January 28, 1948
Rehearsal on January 26 in Studio A. Broadcast live from Studio D.
Supporting Cast: Isabel Randolph (Mrs. Piddleton)
Guest: Clifton Webb
Plot: Prissy actor Clifton Webb visits the tavern, as does, once again, the Lord Byron Ladies' Literary Society wanting to hold one of their "tea formations" at the tavern. Webb attempts to discuss Shakespeare, but is subjected to reading a manuscript written by Archie — with hilarious results.

Episode #271 — Broadcast Wednesday, February 4, 1948
Rehearsal on February 2 in Studio A. Broadcast live from Studio D.
Guest: Gertrude Lawrence
Plot: Having seen Gertrude Lawrence as a twisted mental woman in *Lady in the Dark* on Broadway, Archie writes a play, hoping she

will participate. She agrees in a reading and the play turns into a musical with Archie and Lawrence performing together. After the play, he asks how she liked it and she agrees to do it — in the year 1998.

Episode #272 — Broadcast Wednesday, February 11, 1948
Rehearsal on February 9 in Studio A. Broadcast live from Studio D.
Supporting Cast: Alan Reed (Clancy the Cop) and Veola Vonn (Renee).
Guest: Marlene Dietrich
Plot: Romance blooms early for the Valentine holiday. The ice starts melting when Marlene Dietrich visits the tavern. Jokes about the movie studios and entertaining troops are highlighted and Archie proposes marriage to the beautiful actress. He asks if they could have yachts together, his and hers, and, in the end, she admits he is not her valentine.

Episode #273 — Broadcast Wednesday, February 18, 1948
Rehearsal on February 16 in Studio A. Broadcast live from Studio D.
Supporting Cast: Alan Reed (Clancy the Cop) and Veola Vonn (Renee).
Guest: Tom Breneman
Plot: Archie tries to push Tom Breneman into revealing his secrets for kissing ladies on his radio program. Breneman is a radio personality who hosts a daily talk program called *Breakfast in Hollywood*. To help, Tom agrees to broadcast his next show from Duffy's. Dave Hossinger, however, shows up at the tavern, selling "Atomic Orchid" seeds — the seeds are dipped in uranium and orchids grow overnight.

Episode #274 — Broadcast Wednesday, February 25, 1948
Rehearsal on February 23 in Studio A. Broadcast live from Studio D.
Supporting Cast: Alan Reed (Uncle Rodney)
Plot: Duffy attempts to short-change Archie by offering less pay if he accepts payment in cash instead of a check, but Archie isn't

stupid. Uncle Rodney shows up and together they all listen to the radio, a serial called "The Life of John and Mary, also known as the story of Herman and Gladys!" The cast of *Duffy's Tavern* plays all the parts, offering the radio audience a spoof on soap operas.

Episode #275 — Broadcast Wednesday, March 3, 1948
Rehearsal on March 1 in Studio A. Broadcast live from Studio D.
Supporting Cast: Eddie Marr (Baby Face Pagano) and Alan Reed (Clancy the Cop)
Guest: Van Johnson
Plot: See page 404.

Episode #276 — Broadcast Wednesday, March 10, 1948
Rehearsal on March 8 in Studio F. Broadcast live from Studio D.
Guests: Lauren Bacall and Harry C. Westover
Plot: See page 402.

Episode #277 — Broadcast Wednesday, March 17, 1948
Rehearsal on March 15 in Studio F. Broadcast live from Studio D.
Supporting Cast: Alan Reed (Clancy the Cop)
Guest: Humphrey Bogart
Plot: See pages 403 and 404.

Trivia, etc. According to an inter-office memo at NBC, it appears the March 17 episode wasn't broadcast over a number of stations in order to carry an address by Governor Thurmond which was considered to be in the public interest.

Episode #278 — Broadcast Wednesday, March 24, 1948
Rehearsal on March 22 in Studio F. Broadcast live from Studio D.
Supporting Cast: Alan Reed (the voice)
Guest: Dorothy Lamour
Plot: Dorothy Lamour pays a return visit to the tavern and Archie thinks lightning will strike for the third time when he throws his charm on the beautiful actress. When he offers her a meal, she won't eat the food. Finnegan proposes and she turns him down. Archie places money on a horse race and listens on the radio. When he discovers he is broke, he expects her to pick up the tab.

Episode #279 — Broadcast Wednesday, March 31, 1948
Rehearsal on March 29 in Studio F. Broadcast live from Studio D.
Supporting Cast: Alan Reed (Clancy the Cop)
Guest: Malú Gatica
Plot: Duffy declares tonight as "Good Neighbor Nite" at the tavern. Riding on the heels of Carmen Miranda and Maria Montez, actress and singer Malú Gatica was a Chilean performer noted for being a dramatic actress in her native country, but publicized in Hollywood as a singer. She was preparing for her first Hollywood movie role. Archie, wanting to beat the movie studios to the punch, pretends to be a manager so he can sign her up as his client. He arranges for her to sing "Peanut Vendor," but when he pulls out the contracts, Archie isn't able to put one over on her. One phone call is all is takes to lure the actress away from Archie, who promptly gives up any chance of becoming an agent for the new South American singer.

Trivia, etc. The script for this broadcast was originally planned for the broadcast of March 24, 1948.

Episode #280 — Broadcast Wednesday, April 7, 1948
Rehearsal on April 5 in Studio F. Broadcast live from Studio D.
Supporting Cast: Alan Reed (Mr. Stipple)
Guest: Arthur Treacher
Plot: Duffy's Tavern has been quarantined and Archie has to share his apartment with someone in order to save money. He tries with Mr. Stipple, a bar patron and interior decorator, but Arthur Treacher has his own opinions of the layout. Archie describes Treacher as "compared to him, Buster Keaton is the Smilin' Irishman." Archie rents half of his room to Treacher and they promptly redecorate the place.

Trivia, etc. From April 7 to 28, the program commercials pitched Trushay and Vitalis Hair Oil, and a trailer for Ingram. From May 5 to June 30, commercials for Vitalis and Ipana, with trailer for Ingram.

Episode #281 — Broadcast Wednesday, April 14, 1948
Rehearsal on April 12 in Studio F. Broadcast live from Studio D. Two Script Titles: "FOUNDLING / BABY FOUND ON DOORSTEP"
Supporting Cast: Howard Jeffries (the kid); Peggy Knudsen (Mrs. Rodgers); Leone Ledoux (the infant); and Alan Reed (Clancy the Cop).
Plot: See page 405.

Memorable Lines
ARCHIE: Eddie, did you get rid of them kids?
EDDIE: Yeah, I tricked 'em.
ARCHIE: How?
EDDIE: I asked them why they wasn't down at the schoolhouse watchin' the fire.

Episode #282 — Broadcast Wednesday, April 21, 1948
Rehearsal on April 19 in Studio F. Broadcast live from Studio D.
Script Title: "MOOSE McGARRITY"
Supporting Cast: Tommy Cook (Moose McGarrity) and Peggy Knudsen (Mrs. Rodgers).
Plot: Picking up where last week's episode left off, to impress the baby's mother, who turns out to be a rich widow, Archie organizes a "Boys Club" for the kids who broke the tavern window while they were playing baseball. To raise funds for the club, Archie stages a boxing match. He then sets up a boxing ring in the tavern, complete with gloves and ropes. But when Archie goes up against Moose McGarrity, he wimps out, ducks, and loses the woman's affections and interest — especially when she discovers the prizefight was initially a set-up, now exposed for what it really is.

Episode #283 — Broadcast Wednesday, April 28, 1948
Rehearsal on April 26 in Studio F. Broadcast live from Studio D.
Supporting Cast: Lester Jay (Moose McGarrity) and Alan Reed (Clancy the Cop).
Guest: Ray Milland
Plot: Archie continues his work on the "Archie Boys' Society," a boys club idea with a recreation room in the back of the tavern.

One of the boys happens to be boxing champ Moose McGarrity and Archie attempts to become the boy's professional prize fight manager. Actor Ray Milland shows up at the tavern and Archie sets up a fight between the two, realizing a fix could net him a nice profit if the bets were placed the right direction. Archie tries to get Ray to impersonate Moose and the actor and Finnegan spar. A manager in the tavern decides to buy Finnegan. Before the bout can be set, Milland wants to buy a piece of McGarrity after seeing him in action.

Episode #284 — Broadcast Wednesday, May 5, 1948
Rehearsal on May 3 in Studio F. Broadcast live from Studio D.
Supporting Cast: Alan Reed (Clancy the Cop) and Veola Vonn (Renee).
Guest: Gregory Peck
Plot: Archie buys two tickets to the Policeman's Ball and wants to take Renee, his French girlfriend, as his date. After multiple jokes and references about Gregory Peck losing his recent chance at an Oscar, Archie overhears Peck mention how he'd like to have his job for one night. Archie takes advantage and the two switch places. When Renee shows up at the tavern, she notices Gregory Peck's bad leg and he notices her two good ones. Slipping Archie a mickey, the Hollywood star takes Renee to the ball.

Trivia, etc. For the broadcast of April 7, 1948, Arthur Treacher subbed for Gregory Peck. The actor was laid up at his home with a broken leg, having recently been thrown from a horse. During this broadcast, Archie remarks, "Well, Greg, so you finally got here. Just think — that broken leg of yours has kept you away from Duffy's Tavern for a whole month."

Memorable Lines
PECK: Archie, what is it?
ARCHIE: It's called a Finnegan. Finnegan, shake hands with Gregory Peck.
FINNEGAN: Gregory Peck! The famous movie star? Shake!
PECK: Put 'er there, Mr. Finnegan.

FINNEGAN: Gee... Gregory Peck himself! And he shook hands with me. Mr. Peck, I'll never wash this hand again.

ARCHIE: The very thing that he said to Calvin Coolidge... and he kept his word, too.

Beginning with the broadcast of May 5, 1948, *Duffy's Tavern* was heard over an additional 19 stations on the NBC network.

WTRC — Elkhart
WCOA — Pensacola
WMIS — Natchez
KODY — North Platte
KVOL — Lafayette
WGRM — Greenwood
WCRS — Greenwood
KPLC — Lake Charles
KNOE — Monroe
WTNT — Augusta
WFOR — Hattiesburg
KIST — Santa Barbara
WORZ — Orlando
KSYL — Alexandria
KERO - Bakersfield
WLAX — Lakeland
WAML — Laurel
KCRA — Sacramento
WMVA — Martinville

Episode #285 — Broadcast Wednesday, May 12, 1948
Rehearsal on May 10 in Studio F. Broadcast live from Studio D.
Supporting Cast: Alan Reed (Mr. Jackson)
Guest: Frank Sinatra
Plot: During the tavern's spring cleaning, Frank Sinatra arrives and Archie describes the singer as "where Bing bulges out, Sinatra bulges in." Sinatra's visit to the tavern comes to a climax when a

bucket hits him on the head and the famed singer gets amnesia. In a flash of brilliance, Archie calls Mr. Jackson of the Bijou Theater and offers to sell Sinatra for $75 for a single singing performance. When his memory starts coming back, Archie encourages Finnegan to drop a bucket on Sinatra's head again. Sinatra sings "I've Got a Crush on You."

Episode #286 — Broadcast Wednesday, May 19, 1948
Rehearsal on May 17 in Studio F. Broadcast live from Studio D.
Script Title: "SUES DUFFY"
Supporting Cast: Alan Reed (Clancy the Cop and the lawyer named Loophole)
Plot: A customer at the tavern threatens to sue Archie because of an accident that happened "on the premises" of the tavern. Duffy decides to go legal for the occasion and to handle matters himself. Duffy won't give Archie a raise so Archie fakes an accident of his own. Duffy's lawyer comes down and calamity ensues. In the end, Archie is tricked into another lawsuit… this one from Duffy.

Episode #287 — Broadcast Wednesday, May 26, 1948
Rehearsal on May 24 in Studio F. Broadcast live from Studio D.
Supporting Cast: John Brown (Dave Hossinger); Alan Reed (Clancy the Cop); and Irene Winston (Barbara Maxwell).
Guest: Rex Harrison
Plot: Archie meets an intellectual girl named Barbara and to impress her, he poses classy stage and film star Rex Harrison as his intelligent uncle. Jokes about *Information, Please* and John Kieran and the population of Earth are exchanged between Archie and Harrison. After telling the magna cum laude tomato that his entire family are intellectuals, she finds the British actor stimulating and they leave to go for a walk in the park.

Episode #288 — Broadcast Wednesday, June 2, 1948
Rehearsal from WTAM Cleveland on May 31. Broadcast live from the Rainbow Room at the Carter Hotel.
Script Title: "FIRST CLEVELAND"
Supporting Cast: George Roberts (the stage manager)
Plot: This program featured the cast of *Duffy's Tavern* in the role

of vaudevillians in a take-off on the old-time vaudeville routines. Archie played the role of the emcee, Miss Duffy and Finnegan did a romantic Latin duet, Eddie Green did a song-and-dance routine and band-leader Matty Malneck performed on his "soulful violin."

Trivia, etc. Jane Stevens and John Price supplied the voices for the commercial for this episode and next week's episode.

The June 2 broadcast was not aired over WSN because of a political broadcast that was in the public interest.

Episode #289 — Broadcast Wednesday, June 9, 1948
Rehearsal from WTAM Cleveland on June 7. Broadcast live from the Rainbow Room at the Carter Hotel.
Guest: Jane Russell
Plot: See pages 414 and 415.

Trivia, etc. Jane Stevens and John Price supplied the voices for the commercial for this episode and last week's episode.

Episode #290 — Broadcast Wednesday, June 16, 1948
Rehearsal at The Strand Theater in New York on June 14. Broadcast live from The Strand Theater.
Script Title: "BIG HEAD"
Supporting Cast: Arthur Q. Bryan (Clancy the Cop) and Milton Herman (Colucci, the fruit peddler).
Plot: See page 419.

Episode #291 — Broadcast Wednesday, June 23, 1948
Rehearsal at The Strand Theater in New York on June 21. Broadcast live from The Strand Theater.
Script Title: "QUIZ SHOW"
Supporting Cast: Jack Arthur (the quizmaster)
Guests: Tex McCrary and Jinx Falkenburg
Plot: This program was a take-off on the radio quiz show with Jack Arthur in the role of the quizmaster. The guests of the night were Tex McCrary and Jinx Falkenburg whose show would be the summer replacement for *Duffy's Tavern*.

Trivia, etc. The June 23 broadcast was not heard over WHIS due to the Joe Louis - Jersey Joe Walcott fight.

Louis Armstrong and Ed Gardner

CHAPTER TWELVE
THE DOROTHY LAMOUR DISASTER
(1948 - 1949)

CONSIDERING HE WAS UP AGAINST FRANK SINATRA on CBS, Ed Gardner kept a solid percentage of radio dialers according to the Hooper ratings, leaving CBS as the apparent loser. In a show of force, NBC had more muscle and CBS moved Sinatra to a new day and time slot, replacing his show with *Your Song and Mine*, starring Thomas L. Thomas, for Borden. It remained to be seen whether Milton Berle on ABC's *Texaco Star Theater* proved tougher competition and, once again, the network was all eyes on the Hooper ratings. The funny factor for *Duffy's Tavern* was reflective not from fan letters, but from the Hooper ratings which were printed weekly in trade columns. *Duffy's Tavern* continued to follow a cookie-cutter format. By this time, the only highlight of the program was the ribbing that celebrities took from Archie, exchanging insults and getting away with it. Celebrity guests were not featured on Milton Berle's Wednesday night radio program

Ed Gardner and Florence Halop, circa 1948.
(Photo courtesy of Bryan Hendrickson.)

(but were on his Tuesday night television program), and the comedian would ultimately win over audiences of a new medium, television.

A wonderful summary that best describes the 1948-49 season can be found in the October 13, 1948, issue of *Variety*, reviewing the season opener: "Ed Gardner is one of those perennials who still finds his format good and isn't tampering with it. He returned last Wednesday for another go-round in his now pat characterization as Archie, major domo of *Duffy's Tavern*. Listeners found the same other denizens around, too – Charlie Cantor as Finnegan, Eddie Green as the waiter and Florence Halop as Miss Duffy. That the contrived situations built around the guest star of the week and the gags built upon Archie's loose understanding of the King's English come off as happily as they do is not too surprising, in view of Gardner's imposing stable of writers. Gardner got his chow-joint shenanigans off to a par start last week. He was an 'expectant millionaire' and Clifton Webb, guesting, was his 'bum's gentleman' in a plot to woo and win a rich (he thought), if homely femme he met at a summer resort. Sequence was good for a nice quota of laughs, despite some reliance on old jokes and obvious payoff lines."

Bristol-Myers pitched a variety of products during their final season of sponsorship on *Duffy's Tavern*. Trushay, Vitalis and Bufferin were promoted on the first broadcast of the season. Beginning with the next episode, Benex brushless shave cream was added to the list of products. Beginning with the broadcast of May 11, 1949, commercials for MUM deodorant were added to the program.

Among the new scriptwriters for the 1948-49 season was Bob Schiller. "When I got out of the Army, I was told that Ed Gardner would give anybody a week's trial if they could show him some comedy material," Schiller recalled, "so I showed him some of the newspaper columns I had written. I stayed up three nights in a row trying to write what they call a 'spot.' It was not easy. When I brought it in, I was still in my uniform. The head writers read it and they liked it. They called up Gardner, who at the time was living in a palatial mansion in Bel Air, and said, 'I think we've found a writer.' We'd go out to Ed's house every Sunday. 'How are you at pitching?' one writer inquired. I said, 'I used to play first base.' They relayed this information to Ed and he said, 'Hire the son of a bitch.' They thought I was making a joke. I didn't know 'pitching' means pitching jokes. He doubles my salary to $100 the next week and four weeks later he fired me. I was fired four times from *Duffy's Tavern*. I was on the show for four years."

Among the highlights of the 1948-49 season was the "Singing Contest," broadcast December 15, 1948. Having spent an evening at Carnegie Hall, Archie once again wants to bring culture to the tavern. Mrs. Piddleton's Lord Byron Ladies' Literary Society returns and together they agree to put on a singing contest. Delores Marshall plays the role of the Harvest Moon Girl who sings "I Cover the Waterfront," which instigates verbal disputes between tavern members. The field eventually narrows down to Mrs. Piddleton's niece, Bertha, and the Harvest Moon Girl. Finnegan acts as a judge. Delores Marshall, a new singing discovery and recent winner of the Chicago Harvest Moon Festival song competition, made her professional radio debut with this radio broadcast, following an engagement at the Chicago Theater as part of her recognition in winning the contest.

Pointing up the need for strong public relation activity on behalf of the jukebox industry was the skit heard on the broadcast of October 20, 1948. Tending to "make a joke" of public abuse of jukeboxes, the skit revolved around the placing of a slug in a juke. When the mythical machine did not respond with a tune, the customer was advised to "kick it," thereupon the juke burst into song.

In November 1948, Ed Gardner was negotiating with Simon & Schuster to publish a collection of numerous anecdotes, tentatively entitled *Duffy's Tavern Tales*. No such book was ever published.

Because the stage play took up most of his time in New York through the summer of 1948, Ed Gardner and his family never had an opportunity to take a vacation until September, a quick trip to Europe. To make up for this, he took a week's vacation from *Duffy's Tavern* in late March, with approval from the sponsors. Thus, for the broadcast of March 30, 1949, Jimmy Durante pinch hit for Ed Gardner.

For the broadcast of June 8, 1949, the old cook of the tavern is relieved of his job and Archie is forced to find and hire a new one. Cook wanted: College Graduate Preferred. His problem is resolved when a young lady, a Greek cook, shows up and admits she can make Irish stew. But he soon suspects that the cook is a nut, an escaped lunatic who is poisoning the corned beef. When

Baby-Face McGurk and his whole gang arrive at the tavern, the cook offers ample solution. The role of the gangster was none other than Hollywood actor Marc Lawrence. He was typecast as a shady underworld character such as a hoodlum or gangster in many motion pictures, including *This Gun for Hire* (1942), *Dillinger* (1945) and *Cloak and Dagger* (1946). Lawrence also played numerous supporting roles as a tough guy on radio's *Let George Do It*, *Under Arrest* and *The Adventures of Philip Marlowe*. Lawrence was not a featured guest star for this broadcast, nor was he promoted as such. He appeared in the same manner as Alan Reed (playing Clancy the Cop) and Sara Berner (playing the Greek Cook), unbilled even at the close of the broadcast. Columbia Pictures chief Harry Cohn once told Lawrence that Johnny Roselli, a notorious real-life gangster, had remarked how the actor was the best hoodlum in motion pictures.

Joe Kaufman artwork from Variety, *May 21, 1947.*

The Ratings

Of considerable interest was a report in October 1948 revealing the number of radio shows now in the top 15 which did not show there last year, indicating that the program schedule benefited rank and file shows. The newcomers to the list included *Duffy's Tavern*, which had showed a slow and steady decline since 1946.

In competition, beginning January 5, 1949, CBS moved *County Fair*, bankrolled by the Borden Company, to the same time slot opposite *Duffy's Tavern*. The spot was formerly occupied by Thomas L. Thomas' *Your Song and Mine* but the sponsor wanted to drop the musical program for *County Fair*, a game show staging celebrity guests and audience members in competitions ranging from darts to apple-dunking. *County Fair* held strong ratings for three years. Both CBS and Borden agreed in early December 1948 to compete against *Duffy's Tavern*. Best remembered today for the "Elsie the cow" commercials with the signature "moo" that sold a lot of dairy products, *County Fair* earned a fair 6.9 on the Hooper ratings in early March. Milton Berle, in the same time slot, won 10.0. *Duffy's Tavern* earned 19.7.

The Railroad Hour

For reasons unknown, Ed Gardner's name was mistakenly listed among the scriptwriters for a new ABC radio program, *The Railroad Hour*. Sponsored by the Association of American Railroads, the program offered time-honored musical presentations with more of an emphasis on music than drama. From Gilbert and Sullivan to Rodgers and Hammerstein, each production was star-studded and lavish. Ed Gardner was credited for four episodes, "Good News" (October 4, 1948), "Roberta" (November 1, 1948), "Rio Rita" (November 8, 1948), and "Hit the Deck" (November 22, 1948). Recent research verifies the true author was Earl Gardner. The source of the error originates from a number of ABC press releases that inaccurately listed Earl as Ed.

Cutting on Time

Due to a late cast cue, the broadcast of October 20, 1948, opened the microphone without Gardner's knowledge and the radio audience overheard him ad libbing, "skip de commoicials." The program then started and continued normally, until the show had to be clipped on comedy dialog in order to present the closing commercial and cue on time. During rehearsals, lines would not only be revised and improvised, but deleted for the sake of timing. But no matter how much preparation, it was always possible that the program would run over. NBC insisted on fading the mike and cutting to the studio announcer. For the broadcast of March 2, 1949, the program ran overly long and the commercial announcer was faded on the closing credits in order to end on time. The scheduled electrical transcription cross plug for *Mr. District Attorney*, which followed *Duffy's Tavern* on most of the NBC stations, was not presented at all.

Other examples include the December 31, 1947, broadcast, which was supposed to feature an announcement reminding the audience of *Mr. District Attorney*, but was cut at 9:29:25 to present the NBC cue and end the program on time. (The same announcement was cut prematurely in the middle for the March 3, 1948, broadcast.) According to an inter-office memo in the NBC files at the Wisconsin Historical Society, in order to present the NBC cue and end the program on time for the January 28, 1948, broadcast, the Minit-Rub trailer announcement was faded at 9:29:25, near the close of the program, on the following words, "...so get a tube of..." The sponsor was not happy and requested a partial refund for the network's failure to allow the entire commercial to air. NBC claimed the fault was on the director who handled the timing of the program, but the director insisted it was a network decision to fade the mike and therefore, NBC should pay the reimbursement.

The March 17, 1948, program ended almost perfectly with the closing Freedom Announcement (a public service announcement) cut on the words, "...the right to vote..." in order to present the NBC cue and end the program on time. On the evening of April 28, 1948, at 9:28:55, the program was cut for a commercial on the words, "...where did a guy ever get a punch like that?" The commercial ended slightly early at 9:29:23 and two seconds of the program comedy dialogue was heard at low level before the closing cue was presented. It was the network's responsibility to cut a program off on time so the next one would begin on time. It was the director's responsibility to ensure the program concluded on time and did not run over. Oversights like the ones just described were fairly common on all the networks, CBS, ABC and Mutual included, ever since the earliest dates of network broadcasting.* (Adding a humorous note, the March 3, 1948, broadcast had studio P.A. feedback three minutes into the program from the Hollywood studio, due to the engineer trying to bring up the applause mike in order to pickup laughs.)

The Business End of It

Local station affiliates, provided they gave advance notice to the network, were allowed to broadcast regional events in place of national broadcasts. WOC in Davenport, Iowa, for example, chose to carry the finals of the High School and State basketball games on the evening of March 23, 1950. The station manager offered the solution of presenting *Duffy's Tavern* as a delayed broadcast, to be aired at a later time slot, but the network had rights of refusal and chose not to do so. Contractually, the sponsor, Bristol-Myers, did not approve of delayed broadcasts with the belief that the size of the listening audience would not be as large and, therefore, not worth the money vested toward sponsorship. NBC, like all the major networks, kept meticulous records of the number of stations broadcasting the program, on a week-to-week basis. With various reasons for local stations to preempt national programs, the cost of sponsorship varied by week. A flat rate was paid for the total number of stations agreed upon, and the network billed the sponsor for the difference, or issued a credit. Billing was applied monthly.

Just one week prior, the March 16 broadcast was cancelled in Eau Claire, Wisconsin. WEAU chose to broadcast a basketball game which the station considered in the public interest. This meant that General Foods' *Father Knows Best*, R.J. Reynolds' *Screen*

---

* The examples described are not meant to give the appearance that *Duffy's Tavern* had its share of timing problems, but used merely as an example of all network programming as a whole. Many radio programs suffered the same fate. Any observant listener of the April 26, 1942, broadcast of *The Jell-O Program*, starring Jack Benny, would notice how the cast and the skit titled "Jack's Revenge" ran over and is cut off the air.

Guild and Blatz's *Duffy's Tavern* were all cancelled during the time slot required for the game. WTAC in Flint, Michigan, had a local basketball schedule for which the station felt it necessary to cancel Blatz's *Duffy's Tavern* on June 1, 8, and July 13, 1950.

Delayed broadcasts were common under certain arrangements. While under sponsorship of Bristol-Myers, delayed broadcasts were made each Tuesday in Canada, six days late, with the first delayed broadcast October 7, 1947, for CBM in Montreal, at the rate of $144.00 per broadcast (paid for by the sponsor). The October 1 broadcast was recorded for airing on October 7, and so on. The last broadcast recorded was supposed to be June 23, 1948, for Montreal. Arrangements were made by the Ronalds Advertising Agency for Bristol-Myers. According to one trade periodical, the series was canceled over CKEY in Toronto and CBM in Montreal, with the final broadcast on December 24, 1947. The reason given was changed product sponsor allocation in the States, necessitating too many cut-in complications to carry in Canada.*

The cast sharing a laugh during rehearsals.

---

* Delayed broadcasts meant transcription and tape recordings – a blessing for collectors today who are grateful that any of the pre-1948 recordings of *Duffy's Tavern* exist today.

Daylight Savings Time

Not all areas of the country recognized the practice of Daylight Savings Time, causing complications with the network when it came to promotional gimmicks, such as the announcer reminding the listeners of the broadcast time next week to hear the radio program. This meant rewrites for announcer sheets, often referring to "same time next week," avoiding any mention of a specific time. Broadcast times in printed ads were the responsibility of the local station. National magazines, however, stated which day of the week and the network. If the ad provided to the magazine had to indicate a set time, usually New York City was considered the standard.

Because certain areas of the country did not recognize Daylight Savings Time, this meant that the *Duffy's Tavern* broadcasts of March 14 through April 24, 1948, were broadcast on California and Nevada stations an hour later in terms of local time, whereas in Washington and Arizona they were not. Starting April 15, Seattle and Spokane and the Arizona Group would operate an hour earlier in terms of local time. KXLF in Butte, Montana, KGHL in Billings, Montana, and KILO in Boise, Idaho, aired the show at 7 p.m., MST, while KYUM in Yuma, Arizona, KTAR in Phoenix, Arizona and KVOA in Tucson aired the show at 6 p.m., MST. The program was heard live at the same time, but ads in newspapers, for researchers and fans who fail to acknowledge the fact that certain areas of the country did not recognize Daylight Savings Time, might make the mistake of assuming the show was broadcast at different times, with possibly more than one performance of the cast.

Mr. Adam's Bomb

Hoping to invest some of his *Duffy's Tavern* earnings and venture into independent filmmaking, Eddie Green spent much of March 1949 producing, directing and starring in his own comedy two-reeler, *Mr. Adam's Bomb.* He spent most of April and May attempting to book the comedy into Negro film houses, hoping for a positive rate of return on his investment. The entire production set the comedian back $5,000. Suspecting the upstairs boarder,

Mr. Adam Jones, is putting together a lethal weapon (hence the title), the Johnson family calls on the local police to investigate. Law authority in the form of Abbott and Costello impersonators (one played by Eddie Green) ultimately discover Mr. Adam is not creating a bomb but rather hiding a surprise for his niece. Meanwhile, more than half of the short plays are host to a series of vaudeville performances including magic, patter routines, song and dance. Green receives top billing as well as on-screen credit as production supervisor.

The Dorothy Lamour Disaster

Ghost voices, technical difficulties and an overenthusiastic opening night crowd bedeviled a radio broadcast featuring Dorothy Lamour as the "femcee" at the premiere opening of oilman Glenn McCarthy's Shamrock Hotel in Houston, Texas. On the evening of March 17, 1949, Glenhall Taylor, producer of *The Sealtest Variety Theater*, agreed to allow the program to originate from the Herald Room of the new Shamrock Hotel. The usual format of the program involved two guest spots each week: one performed a comedy sketch, the other a dramatic sketch in which Lamour herself usually took part with the guest star. Music was provided by Henry Russell and his Orchestra with vocals by the Crew Chiefs Male Quartet. For the evening of March 17, Hollywood screen actor Van Heflin and comedian Ed Gardner were in attendance to appear on the broadcast. What followed was a scrambled program which faded several times and was off the air completely at others, now considered one of the biggest disasters for NBC in the calendar year of 1947. Thankfully for Glenn McCarthy, Dorothy Lamour's nation-wide radio broadcast was the only "casualty" of the glittering formal opening of his twenty million dollar Shamrock Hotel. While Lamour told the press the whole thing was "unavoidable," her name was briefly tarnished in newspapers across the country that week.

Between 2,000 and 3,000 people jammed into the 18-story hotel's dining rooms for a $42-per-plate dinner marking the formal opening. The confusion was too much for Lamour's radio broadcast which was scheduled at 9:30 p.m. Eastern. As the radio show began, many guests were still hunting for their seats and the hubub was so great that Lamour and her guest stars, Heflin and Gardner, had to shout over the microphone to be heard. "The crowd was still entering the room at the start of the program and we had trouble getting started," Lamour explained. "Later the public address system failed and we departed somewhat from our script."

The program suffered numerous line breaks and was of low quality with the actors' conversation repeated when they obviously thought they were off the air. The continuity of the program suffered most with ad-libbing in an attempt to keep the show moving. At approximately 9:32:42, a telephone conversation going on at the source of the program came over the air and, although muffled, was intelligible. Radio listeners might have wondered if they had bad frequency on their own radios. Because the attendees arrived late, instructions were never given to prevent the high background noise that was picked up by the microphones. Lamour herself made several attempts to get the cast back on the script but to little avail. Gardner ad-libbed freely after an attempt to tell his "Two-Top Gruskin" routine failed. Instead, Gardner announced the names of prominent guests in the ballroom for the benefit of the radio listeners. The dramatic spot between Van Heflin and Dorothy Lamour suffered most with little of the actual script broadcast.

At Chicago, NBC officials said line failure, "probably at the Shamrock Hotel," forced piano standby music to be used during most of the first 12 minutes of the show. The direct cause of the error was never reported publicly, to avoid pointing full blame toward the correct source. In Hollywood, it was an NBC spokesman who blamed the whole thing on an "over-enthusiastic opening night crowd," adding that, "at one point, two diners seized the microphone and shouted into it."

In New York, another spokesman said network executives were conducting an investigation to determine whether any profanity went out over the air. Dorothy Lamour insisted no profanity was involved.

The network at Chicago, the controlling point of the broadcast, stayed with the show for the first five minutes, during line breaks and low quality, in the hope that difficulties would clear momentarily. NBC delivered multiple "One Moment, Please" announcements, then cut to the piano music as filler until 9:43:15 when NBC brought the chaos back to the air.

Ed Gardner had flown to Houston early that morning to participate in the broadcast. He flew back to New York City the morning after and, a week later, took his entire family on a probably much-needed vacation (Honolulu or Miami, depending on varied sources). Ironically, this was not the first time the Sealtest radio program suffered technical difficulties. For the broadcast of October 3, 1946, similar technical difficulties occurred on the same program. AT&T trouble between Denver and Omaha prevented the first two and a half minutes from being broadcast nationwide. Meanwhile, due to Chicago operating error, an announcer apologized to the listening audience and music filled the remaining minute and a half. The WEAF program portion failed to go through for the same reasons, resulting in a standby announcer apologizing and introducing a transcribed orchestra which failed to go out due to engineering trouble. WEAF also had dead air for the first minute and a half.

Season Nine
October 6, 1948, to June 29, 1949
National Broadcasting Company
Sponsor: Bristol-Myers
Day and Time: Wednesday, 9:00 to 9:30 p.m., EST
Entire season originates from Hollywood
Advertising Agency: Young & Rubicam
Commercial announcer: Rod O'Conner
(October 6 to November 10, 1948)
Commercial announcer: Ken Peters
(November 17, 1948, to June 29, 1949)
Producer for the Agency: Anthony Stanford
Producer/Director for the Network: John Morris
Engineer: Charles Norman
Sound: Bob Grapperhaus
Music: Matty Malneck and his Orchestra
Commercial Writer: Sylvia Dowling

Commercial Supervisor: Innes Harris
Scriptwriters: Vincent Bogert, Bill Freedman, Morris Freedman,
Lou Grant, Seymour Kapetansky*, Larry Rhine, Bob Schiller,
Phil Sharp and Anthony Stafford.

Cast
Charles Cantor as Finnegan
Florence Halop as Miss Duffy
Eddie Green as Eddie
Marvin Miller as Joe Moran
(November 3, 1948, to February 9, 1949)
Eddie Stanley as Joe Moran (February 16, 1949)
Howard Petrie as Joe Moran (February 23 to April 20, 1949)
Carleton Young as Joe Moran (April 27, 1949)
Mike Foy as Joe Moran (May 4, 1949)
Ken Peters as Joe Moran (May 11 to June 29, 1949)

All other actors and known roles are listed under the respective
episodes.

Episode #292 — Broadcast Wednesday, October 6, 1948
Rehearsal on October 4 in Studio G. Broadcast live from
Studio D.
Supporting Cast: Elvia Allman (Miss Hortense)
Guest: Clifton Webb
Plot: Clifton Webb, whom Archie refers to as "a Diaper Dan,"
is dropping by the tavern again today. Archie, meanwhile, plans
to woo a woman he knows has two million dollars. To impress
Miss Hortense, Archie convinces Webb to pose as his valet and to
help perform Shakespeare — only the play is a rendition Archie
wrote — with hilarious results. What Archie doesn't know is that

---

* According to one source, Seymour Kapetansky was credited as a
scriptwriter for one or two scripts during this season. Kapetansky wrote
skits for Red Skelton and other comedians. His exact contribution for
Duffy's Tavern remains unknown but was (apparently) very brief.

Hortense is a golddigger herself, hoping to marry Archie for his money!

Episode #293 — Broadcast Wednesday, October 13, 1948
Rehearsal on October 11 in Studio G. Broadcast live from Studio D.
Script Title: "GUILTY CONSCIENCE"
Supporting Cast: John Brown (Dave Hossinger)
Plot: This episode doesn't open with the usual format where Archie answers the phone to take Duffy's call, because his employer doesn't even place a call to the tavern. While Eddie is listening to *Mr. District Attorney* (which usually aired on the same network after this show), Archie gets worried. Duffy hasn't called and Archie is trying to figure out why while the cast plays around with a bottle of champagne at the tavern. Dave Hossinger sold Archie the stolen champagne that almost leads to an international situation with the FBI and everyone else on the trail. It seems the bottle was lifted from a battleship for commissioning and when Archie learns the truth, this scares him into getting rid of it.

Episode #294 — Broadcast Wednesday, October 20, 1948
Rehearsal on October 18 in Studio G. Broadcast live from Studio D.
Guest: Frank Sinatra
Plot: Frank Sinatra makes another return trip to the tavern and sings "Every Day I Love You." When Archie explains that he re-wrote *The Barber of Seville*, he asks Sinatra to play Don Frankie, a Don Juan character, in Archie's own version of the opera.

Trivia, etc. The October 20 broadcast was not aired over a number of radio stations across the country. A special political broadcast for the Republican Party offered political speeches by Senator Robert A. Taft and Thomas E. Dewey. KPRC in Houston, Texas; KRIS in Corpus Christi, Texas; WOAI in San Antonio, Texas; KTBS in Shreveport, Louisiana; and WFAA in Dallas-Forth Worth, Texas. WTRC in Elkhart, Indiana, elected not to broadcast *Duffy's Tavern* on the same evening in order to carry a local football broadcast.

The broadcast of October 27, 1948, was preempted due to Governor Thomas E. Dewey speaking from Cleveland. The Republican National Committee purchased time on both NBC and Mutual, causing the networks to cancel regular commercial accounts for that time period. It was the network's policy (always protected under a contractual clause) not to cut one of the presidential candidates during election year. Under contract, Young & Rubicam would received a commission on the full network time cost.

Episode #295 — Broadcast Wednesday, November 3, 1948
Rehearsal on November 1 in Studio G. Broadcast live from Studio D.
Supporting Cast: Alan Reed (Dave Hossinger and Clancy the Cop)
Guest: Hildegarde
Plot: Just when the Tavern's entertainment license has expired, Hildergarde drops by and tries to entertain the tavern guests. Clancy the Cop is on the lookout for a reason to shut down the tavern and a comedy of errors ensues to keep the flatfoot away.

Episode #296 — Broadcast Wednesday, November 10, 1948
Rehearsal on November 8 in Studio G. Broadcast live from Studio D.
Script Title: "DRAFT BOARD"
Supporting Cast: Eddie Marr (the Sergeant) and Janet Waldo (Mary Ann).
Archie explains that he has no guests tonight because "business is always lousy between elections." Today Archie's draft board sends around Army Recruiting Sergeant Mulvaney to find out why Archie did not report to register. Janet Waldo plays Mary Ann, the girl who checks on Archie's record and then gives the information to the recruiting sergeant.

Episode #297 — Broadcast Wednesday, November 17, 1948
Rehearsal on November 15 in Studio G. Broadcast live from Studio D.
Guest: Jane Wyman
Plot: Archie writes a radio mystery called "Who Did It" with "a dame of the opposite neuter." Jane Wyman plays female detective Ellery Jane in the private-eye mystery that comes complete with Chinese Gong and squeaking door. Archie comments at the end of the show that next week's guest will probably read about him in the December issue of *Radio and Television Mirror*.

Episode #298 — Broadcast Wednesday, November 24, 1948
Rehearsal on November 22 in Studio G. Broadcast live from Studio D.
Guest: Dick Powell
Plot: While Archie is in the process of killing a turkey for Thanksgiving, singer turned tough guy actor Dick Powell drops by the tavern. Archie tries to clip Powell with some info on stocks, bonds, government securities, etc. He then tries to convince Powell to contribute $20 to a program that invests in the turkey farm business for the annual holiday... the partnership of new turkey tycoons.

Memorable Lines
ARCHIE: The Pilgrims was our founding fathers - the inventors of Thanksgiving. And when they sailed for this country, they brought it along with them.
FINNEGAN: How did they ever get it through the Panama Canal?
ARCHIE: A very good question.
FINNEGAN: Thank you. I rather liked it myself.
ARCHIE: Shall I answer it?
FINNEGAN: No. Suppose we just let it stand on its own merits.

Episode #299 — Broadcast Wednesday, December 1, 1948
Rehearsal on November 29 in Studio G. Broadcast live from Studio D.

Script Title: "HYPNOTIST"
Supporting Cast: Veola Vonn (Renee) and Carleton Young (the Professor).
Plot: After witnessing a superb hypnotist at work on stage the night before, Archie gets a book about hypnotism and uses the power of the mind on Renee, his girlfriend. It is Archie's hope that he'll hypnotize her into agreeing she'll marry him. He tries it on Eddie first and, after that fails, he tries it on Renee, who actually falls for it and thinks Gardner is Charles Boyer... Until the real Professor Zodiac (Carleton Young) arrives and takes her lead.

Memorable Lines
ARCHIE: A hypnotist... Professor Zodiac. Terrific! Y'know what he did?
EDDIE: What?
ARCHIE: He got a guy up on the stage and just by hypnotism he had the guy make violent love to a dame.
EDDIE: What's so wonderful about that?
ARCHIE: It was the guy's own wife!

Episode #300 — Broadcast Wednesday, December 8, 1948
Rehearsal on December 6 in Studio G. Broadcast live from Studio D.
Supporting Cast: Alan Reed (Dave Hossinger)
Guest: Carmen Miranda
Plot: Archie only has fourteen dollars to his name and wants to take Carmen Miranda out on a date. She stops by the tavern to say hello and sings "South America, Take it Away," with lyrics changed by Archie. She hesitates at first but finds herself forced to sing. Afterwards, she informs him, "This is the end of the Good Neighbor Policy." Dave Hossinger sells Archie a television station and, mishandling the controls, Archie beams Miranda to South America. Archie himself admits that he wanted to "cement good neighbor relations."

Episode #301 — Broadcast Wednesday, December 15, 1948
Rehearsal on December 13 in Studio G. Broadcast live from Studio D.

Script Title: "SINGING CONTEST"
Supporting Cast: Aileen Carlyle (Bertha) and Isabel Randolph (Mrs. Piddleton).
Guest: Delores Marshall
Plot: Having gone to Carnegie Hall, Archie once again wants to bring culture to the tavern. Mrs. Piddleton's Lord Byron Ladies' Literary Society returns and together they put on a singing contest. Delores Marshall plays the role of the Harvest Moon Girl and sings "I Cover the Waterfront," which starts verbal disputes between tavern members. The field eventually narrows down to Mrs. Piddleton's niece and the Harvest Moon Girl. Finnegan acts as a judge.

Trivia, etc. Delores Marshall was a new singing discovery, a recent winner of the Chicago Harvest Moon Festival song competition. This broadcast marked her radio debut, following an engagement at the Chicago Theater as part of her recognition in winning the contest.

Episode #302 — Broadcast Wednesday, December 22, 1948
Rehearsal time and date unknown. Broadcast live from Studio D.
Supporting Cast: Florence Baker (woman at hotel); Robert Bruce (Joe Di Maggio and man at accident); Charlie Cantor (Finnegan); Jeff Chandler (the stranger); Scott Elliott (the blind man); Bobby Ellis (Jimmy Turner, the boy); Frank Gerstle (taxi driver); Eddie Green (Eddie); Florence Halop (Miss Duffy); Betty Lou Gerson (Ann); Marvin Miller (cop at hotel scene); Franklin Parker (cop at accident); and Donald Woods (Paul).
Plot: Same script from December 25, 1946.

Episode #303 — Broadcast Wednesday, December 29, 1948
Rehearsal on December 27 in Studio G. Broadcast live from Studio D.
Guest: Dorothy Shay, the "Park Avenue Hillbilly"
Plot: During the holiday festivities, Archie spends his time complaining about who didn't get him a Christmas Card. Miss Duffy and Dorothy Shay get along well, sharing the same complaints about men. Shay can't perk Archie up, no matter what

she does, and Archie stays gloomy and cranky at everyone. Shay woos Finnegan, who is a cold fish. She eventually puts one and one together and discovers the two are sore at each other thinking the other hasn't sent him a Christmas card. Shay discovers that Finnegan put all of Archie's cards in his pocket and forgot to mail them. This is why Archie got no Christmas cards in the mail. With the matter cleared up, the barkeep turns his eyes on Dorothy Shay.

Trivia, etc. Throughout December 1948, Dorothy Shay had a four-week engagement at the Cocoanut Grove where she topped the record set by her previous appearance four months prior. To help promote her stage performance, she made a guest appearance on *Duffy's Tavern*.

Episode #304 — Broadcast Wednesday, January 5, 1949
Rehearsal on January 3 in Studio G. Broadcast live from Studio D.
Supporting Cast: Isabel Randolph (Mrs. Piddleton)
Guest: Desi Arnaz
Plot: Archie is engaged to (of all people) Mrs. Piddleton. When Archie learns that her former husbands all died under mysterious circumstances and that she is only wealthy because of their life insurance policies, Archie wants out of the engagement. Desi Arnaz helps Archie by holding a séance to convince her not to marry the tavern keeper.

Episode #305 — Broadcast Wednesday, January 12, 1949
Rehearsal on January 10 in Studio G. Broadcast live from Studio D.
Script Title: "FUR COAT"
Supporting Cast: Isabel Randolph (Mrs. Piddleton) and Veola Vonn (Renee).
Plot: Archie gets engaged to Mrs. Piddleton again and everyone cracks jokes about the bad pairing. "The coroner gives the bride away," Eddie remarks. Archie attempts to get a fur coat off his girlfriend Renee so he can impress Mrs. Piddleton and succeeds. To get the coat back from Mrs. Piddleton before she can leave the tavern with it, he has "Killer" Finnegan play the role of the head

of the Mink Mob. Renee returns, though, before Piddleton leaves, and the plot is exposed.

Episode #306 — Broadcast Wednesday, January 19, 1949
Rehearsal on January 17 in Studio G. Broadcast live from Studio D.
Script Title: "SIGHTSEEING TOUR"
Supporting Cast: Ken Christy (the man) and Eddie Marr (the bus driver).
Plot: Duffy promises Archie a bonus if he can collect on all the IOUs in the register. To give the place more class and attract customers, Archie tries to get a sightseeing tour to go through the tavern on the grounds that George Washington once slept there. He attempts to make the place a historical location with framed counterfeits of letters from George Washington and other colonial founders. Customers are not fooled by the letter — even the "P.S.- Next to Martha's home cooking, I like Duffy's Tavern best."

Trivia, etc. The reason no Hollywood celebrity appeared on the January 19 broadcast was because the script did not call for it. It was proposed to originate this episode from either the Statler Hotel or Lisner Auditorium in Washington D.C., and knowing a celebrity guest would not have been possible, the script was written to avoid any use of a Hollywood star. Broadcasting on location never happened, and the script was not revised to include a star.

Episode #307 — Broadcast Wednesday, January 26, 1949
Rehearsal on January 24 in Studio G. Broadcast live from Studio D.
Guests: Shirley Temple and Judy Canova
Plot: Shirley Temple is coming to the tavern and Archie feels the little girl should be escorted home — a tavern is not a place for a little girl. When she arrives, he does not recognize her, expecting the little girl who appeared in those early Fox pictures. Shirley portrays a "gal of the underworld during the crime wave on Third Avenue" as she "strings Archie along" because he thinks the Shirley Temple he has invited to the tavern is still the curly-haired child actress. He phones Shirley's house but discovers she already

left for the tavern. While Finnegan keeps her busy showing her his collection of stuffed lizards and cigar butts, Archie gets the notion that Shirley Temple has been kidnapped. Comedienne Judy Canova appears near the end of the program to make an appeal on behalf of the March of Dimes.

Episode #308 — Broadcast Wednesday, February 2, 1949
Rehearsal on January 31 in Studio G. Broadcast live from Studio D.
Supporting Cast: Hal March (the lawyer)
Guest: Clifton Webb
Plot: Archie's Uncle Fleischacker visits the tavern, as does Clifton Webb. The actor not only appeared on the show for the premiere episode of the season, but makes a return visit with this broadcast. Archie tries to get Webb to insult him so that he can sue him, and relies on lawyer S. Quentin Fleischacker.

Episode #309 — Broadcast Wednesday, February 9, 1949
Rehearsal on February 7 in Studio G. Broadcast live from Studio D.
Script Title: "24 HOURS TO LIVE"
Supporting Cast: Marvin Miller (Doctor Konkle).
Plot: When a doctor phones Archie to inform him that he is perfectly well and is nothing more than a hypochondriac, but has three days to pay his bill or the patient will face charges, Miss Duffy overhears part of the conversation and thinks that Archie has only three days to live. Hoping to leave on vacation, Archie's intentions are misunderstood and the gang thinks he wants to retire and spend his remaining time relaxing. Archie, however, makes a mistake when Eddie explains why people are concerned and decides to skip his vacation — he'd rather be with his friends instead. The doctor arrives and demands to have the bills paid... leading to the true facts and Archie's embarrassment.

Trivia, etc. The script for this episode was originally planned for broadcast on February 2, 1949.

Episode #310 — Broadcast Wednesday, February 16, 1949
Rehearsal on February 14 in Studio G. Broadcast live from Studio D.
Script Title: "WILLIE GUNDIG"
Supporting Cast: Ken Christy (Willie Gundig) and Alan Reed (the salesman).
Plot: Archie's old schoolmate from P.S. 4, Willie Gundig, is going to pay a visit to the tavern. Reminiscing about his old school days, Archie discovers he was voted "most likely to be a failure." Archie asks Eddie, "When Willie Gundig gets here, what can I do to impress him that I'm also a big success?" Eddie replies, "You could hide." Hoping to impress his old school chum, Archie wants to buy a brand new 1949 Cadillac and convinces the car dealer to leave it by the curb for a few hours. When Willie arrives, Archie discovers his rich old schoolmate is now a bum.

Episode #311 — Broadcast Wednesday, February 23, 1949
Rehearsal on February 21 in Studio G. Broadcast live from Studio D.
Script Title: "ELECTRICITY"
Supporting Cast: Alan Reed (Slippery McGuire)
Plot: Archie is firmly convinced that he owns the patent on electricity, when Slippery McGuire convinces him to file for a patent… because no one else has done it yet. The application costs Archie ten dollars… which goes into Slippery's pocket. Finnegan, however, doesn't comprehend what electricity is and Archie tries to explain it so even a third grader can comprehend. The Patent Office won't accept the application, however, after Slippery explains that they applied for A.C. and overlooked D.C. To do so will cost an additional five bucks… When Slippery explains that Benjamin Franklin never applied for a patent for a kite, Archie smells additional revenue… especially in a windy city like Chicago… but that will cost a few more dollars.

Episode #312 — Broadcast Wednesday, March 2, 1949
Rehearsal on February 28 in Studio G. Broadcast live from Studio D.

Guest: Mickey Rooney
Plot: Archie hopes to break ground in television and writes a play for guest Mickey Rooney, who impersonates actor Edward G. Robinson. The entire cast performs a drama about "Lovable Ol' John" and "Lovable Ol' Mary." John returns from the office to find his wife in the arms of the ice man. The relationship is strained and the lovers quarrel. Twenty years later, now divorced, John is a doctor and Mickey Rooney impersonates Lionel Barrymore in the role of Dr. Gillespie. John discovers the man who stole his wife is on the operating table. Will he save the man's life? Only in a comedy can you expect results never found in a Hollywood movie.

Trivia, etc. Moments after Eddie Green makes his introduction in the beginning of the episode, Ed Gardner accidentally reads Miss Duffy's line and the two share a laugh on the air.

Episode #313 — Broadcast Wednesday, March 9, 1949
Rehearsal on March 7 in Studio G. Broadcast live from Studio D.
Guest: Marlene Dietrich
Plot: Archie writes a television play of historical nature, with spies and intrigue. Marlene Dietrich stops by the tavern and helps Archie with the script. Near the end of the broadcast, Ed Gardner (Archie) makes a plea in behalf of the American Red Cross.

Episode #314 — Broadcast Wednesday, March 16, 1949
Rehearsal on March 14 in Studio G. Broadcast live from Studio D.
Script Title: "CHRISTMAS CLUB"
Supporting Cast: Jerry Hausner (Max); Frank Richards (the customer); Rolfe Sedan (J.B. MacIntosh) and Veola Vonn (Renee).
Plot: Archie goes to the bank to open a Christmas Club account. He tries to take money out right away, unaware of how the Christmas Club works. Even though he started his account with an initial deposit of $10 dollars, he wants to put the money on a race horse.

Trivia, etc. Having browsed many scripts in various archives, two different copies of this same script were found, each with a different title. The other title for this episode is apparently "Archie Saves Money."

Episode #315 — Broadcast Wednesday, March 23, 1949

Rehearsal on March 21 in Studio G. Broadcast live from Studio D.

Script Title: "SPIKE McGURK"

Supporting Cast: Sheldon Leonard (Spike McGurk)

Plot: After a brawl in the tavern, Archie must take inventory of the damages for an insurance company. After a bad confrontation in the tavern, Archie finds himself set to fight Spike McGurk, a shady character who offers Archie the "privilege" of indulging in fisticuffs with him! Archie, bragging, accepts the challenge. Fighting against Archie's luck, McGurk turns out to be an ex-champ.

Episode #316 — Broadcast Wednesday, March 30, 1949

Rehearsal on March 28 in Studio G. Broadcast live from Studio D.

Supporting Cast: Alan Reed (Slippery McGuire)

Guests: Jimmy Durante and Ann Sothern

Plot: Jimmy Durante pinch hits for Ed Gardner tonight while Archie is on a brief vacation. The script continuity concerns Archie being "locked in his room upstairs above the tavern" because he is writing a private-eye play, "The Private Nose," in which Durante will essay the starring role. The celebrity guest is Ann Sothern who receives a phone call from Archie inviting her to "come up and read the play." Will she trust the sly womanizer?

Episode #317 — Broadcast Wednesday, April 6, 1949

Rehearsal on April 4 in Studio G. Broadcast live from Studio D.

Supporting Cast: Elvia Allman (Gertrude) and Veola Vonn (Myrtle).

Guest: Gypsy Rose Lee

Plot: Gardner returns after his one-night absence. Archie refers to Gypsy Rose Lee as "sort of a George Bernard Shaw with air-conditioning." Believing she would like a man with speed, Archie contemplates getting a car for five bucks...only what he gets is

Ann Sothern

a 1914 model. Lee pitches the novel she wrote, *The G-String Murders*, and falls for Finnegan by the end of the episode — she'll pay the down payment for the car so they can have a night out — and she'll perform on the stage just for Finnegan.

Episode #318 — Broadcast Wednesday, April 13, 1949
Rehearsal on April 11 in Studio G. Broadcast live from Studio D. **Supporting Cast:** Ken Christy (the first bum); Jerry Hausner (the third bum) and Alan Reed (the second bum).

Plot: Duffy instructs Archie to conduct an all-cash business hereafter — no more credit. Three bums appear to demand food, creating a comical situation for Archie. Archie discovers one of the tavern guests is J. Everett Poindexter, who Archie suspects isn't really a bum, but a disguised millionaire.

Memorable Lines
MISS DUFFY: (naively) Archie, what's the difference between a bum and you?
EDDIE: He gets paid!

Episode #319 — Broadcast Wednesday, April 20, 1949
Rehearsal on April 18 in Studio G. Broadcast live from Studio D.
Supporting Cast: Sam Hearn (Elmer)
Guest: Cass Daley
Plot: Elmer, a farm boy whom Archie hopes to snare into marriage with Miss Duffy, is new to the tavern and unaware of the barkeep's shenanigans. Could Comedienne Cass Daley actually make Miss Duffy look good to Elmer as a possible bride?

Memorable Lines
ARCHIE: Tonight? Cass Daley. Well, she's sort of a Martha Raye, a Betty Hutton and a Judy Canova, all rolled up into a Marjorie Main.

Episode #320 — Broadcast Wednesday, April 27, 1949
Rehearsal on April 25 in Studio G. Broadcast live from Studio D.
Supporting Cast: Doris Singleton (Milly Van Schnook)
Plot: Archie tries to get married to Milly Van Schnook, a "dame" Archie contacted through the Lonely Hearts Club of the Police Gazette. Archie goes so far as to create a wedding invitation: "I, Archie, hereby announce the engagement to the former Miss Van Schnook, nee Millicent. The Bride and Groom hereby request your presents. Clothes will be optional but we prefer black tie." Milly is drop dead gorgeous but she speaks like Finnegan and Archie is forced to call off the engagement. Finnegan, however, finds her perfect and the two walk out of the Tavern together.

Episode #321 — Broadcast Wednesday, May 4, 1949
Rehearsal on April 25 and 27 in Studio G. Taped on April 28, 1949, in Studio D.
Guest: Charles Coburn
Archie brushes off Duffy's phone calls so he can play gin rummy with the boys. After discovering the hard way that Finnegan and Eddie are pros with the cards, Archie convinces the boys to con Charles Coburn, who happens to drop by the tavern, into losing some money in a high-stakes poker game. But it turns out that Coburn happens to be a pro at the game and cleans the house.

Trivia, etc. This script was originally intended for broadcast on April 27. Coburn's schedule made that impossible so the script and its star were rescheduled for May 4.
This episode featured recycled material from the broadcast of February 26, 1942.

Episode #322 — Broadcast Wednesday, May 11, 1949
Rehearsal on April 25 and 27 in Studio G. Taped on April 28, 1949, in Studio D.
Supporting Cast: Sheldon Leonard (Sam) and Alan Reed (Clancy the Cop)
Guest: Chester Morris
Plot: Chester Morris appears in the role of "Whistling Sam," a desperate criminal who carries a violin case filled with a Winchester. "He's the terror of Third Avenue and is known as 'Whistling Sam' because he whistles *Comin' Thro' the Rye* as he perpetrates his crime." Detective Archie is on the trail.

Episode #323 — Broadcast Wednesday, May 18, 1949
Rehearsal on May 16 in Studio G. Broadcast live from Studio D.
Guest: Bert Gordon as "The Mad Russian"
Plot: Archie decides to enter a contest for "Most Popular Bartender." Duffy makes a phony will which Archie reads, making the barkeep think he will inherit the tavern if Duffy dies prematurely so Archie gets to work to make "the joint pay."

Episode #324 — Broadcast Wednesday, May 25, 1949
Rehearsal unknown. Taped on May 21, 1949, in Studio D.
Supporting Cast: Alan Reed (Vermicelli)
Guest: Ed Wynn
Plot: Archie is on another opera kick and guest Ed Wynn participates in Archie's version of "Carmen." Opera opens at a cigarette company and jokes such as C-A-R-M-E-N (like C-A-M-E-L) are given.

Episode #325 — Broadcast Wednesday, June 1, 1949
Rehearsal on May 30 in Studio G. Broadcast live from Studio D.
Supporting Cast: Bea Benaderet (Agatha Pitts) and Tommy Bernard (the kid).
Plot: Archie is still trying to get married to a wealthy widow. Tonight he finds one with loads of cash — Agatha Pitts — and a child who outwits Archie. The manager's excuse is rational: "I'm not going to get any younger… and you ain't goin' to get any richer." The woman is not attractive and when she asks for a kiss, Archie hesitates claiming it is bad luck before a marriage. (After marriage, it's pot luck.) Proving he knows child psychology, Archie tries to impress Egbert, her son, only the boy is not impressed. Egbert cries when Archie tries to strangle the boy and the manager explains he loved the boy so much that he almost squeezed him to death. His unnecessary roughness causes the wealthy widow to call off the engagement.

Episode #326 — Broadcast Wednesday, June 8, 1949
Rehearsal unknown. Taped on June 4, 1949, in Studio D.
Supporting Cast: Marc Lawrence (the gangster)
Plot: See page 445.

Memorable Lines:
FINNEGAN: I guess I must be goin'. I'm beginnin' to hear voices.
ARCHIE: Finnegan, that's the radio next door!

469

Episode #327 — Broadcast Wednesday, June 15, 1949
Rehearsal unknown. Taped on June 11, 1949, in Studio D.
Supporting Cast: Betty Lou Gerson (Gwen) and Alan Reed (Clancy the Cop).
Guest: Bob Crosby
Plot: Archie refers to Bob Crosby as a radio crooner, defined as "static set to money." Having seen a Broadway musical the other night, Archie aspires to become a talented singer. Bob Crosby drops by the tavern and sings "Bali Hai" while Archie attempts to impress Gwendolyn, his new fiance, during the song. Crosby tries to impress the woman by revealing his position at Crosby Enterprises. "I take care of the petty cash... anything under a million." Bob's song also put her into a romantic mood and Archie ultimately finds himself single again.

Trivia, etc. Archie makes reference to "Some Enchanted Evening" being a song from a show he saw the night before called *South Pacific*. While his reference to Mary Martin being in the show might have been acknowledgement to her appearance on *Duffy's Tavern* years ago, it was more than likely a purposeful plug in return for free tickets to the show.

Episode #328 — Broadcast Wednesday, June 22, 1949
Rehearsal unknown. Taped on June 13, 1949, in Studio D.
Supporting Cast: Rolfe Sedan (Professor Wagner)
Plot: Archie receives a letter in the mail informing him that he has been selected as "Genius of the Week" and a representative will call on him. After testing his mental marvel, Archie receives the third degree from the representative with trivial questions from an encyclopedia. When asked what is man's best friend, Archie's response is "woman." Question after question, Archie attempts to answer one correctly. What he ultimately wins is a set of encyclopedias... for the low fee of $49 dollars. Discovering he has been duped, Archie uses the books to solve a plumbing problem... and gets water on the brain.

Episode #329 — Broadcast Wednesday, June 29, 1949
Rehearsal unknown. Taped on June 13, 1949, in Studio D.

Supporting Cast: Alan Reed (Clancy the Cop).
Plot: With the summer vacation approaching, Duffy plans to take his daughter to Niagara Falls. As Archie jokes, "That's nice. You'll be the first guy that ever brought his own barrel." The cast starts closing up the tavern for the summer and Eddie is taking inventory — including noting five soiled dinner napkins marked "Waldorf-Astoria." By the end of the episode, Henry Morgan never appears as scheduled but Archie makes a plea for the radio listeners to listen to the same time slot during the summer for Morgan's show and thanks everyone for keeping them there for seven years.

Trivia, etc. Henry Morgan was supposed to make a brief appearance at the conclusion of this broadcast to pitch his summer replacement for *Duffy's Tavern*, *The Henry Morgan Show*, sponsored by Bristol-Myers, taking over the same time slot. The July 6, 1949, broadcast offered a special guest, Lee Bristol, president of the Bristol-Myers Company, doing a comedy take-off on his own commercials. He insisted on reading the commercial word for word, comma for comma, exclamation points and so on. "...that comma cost me five bucks and I'm going to read it and every one like it..."

Goodbye Bristol-Myers, Hello Blatz Beer

In February 1949, Ed Gardner, with a year remaining on his Bristol-Myers contract, told reporters that he was in Hollywood talking to CBS about the possibility of moving the series to that network. Reportedly, the company was concerned over the competition it faced in the fall. On CBS, Bing Crosby was going to be moved into the 9 p.m. spot against *Duffy's Tavern*. Eddie Cantor, it was reported, was actively urging Pabst to shift to CBS. CBS had already purchased *The Jack Benny Program* and *Amos 'n' Andy*. J.M. Allen, the Bristol-Myers advertising vice-president, was hoping in early February to renew the comedy on CBS because the network posed a threat as possible competition against their program. Allen asked both CBS and ABC to submit time presentations in connection with the company's two shows, *Duffy's Tavern* and *Mr. District Attorney*.

471

Simone and Ed promoting Blatz Beer.

Two weeks later, Bristol-Myers was in for a surprise. Although the contract had another year to run, Ed Gardner, through attorney Martin Gang, began negotiations for release in order to become a free agent. Release was understood to have been worked out personally by Gardner with no aid from the William Morris Agency who usually represented him in such matters. Gardner's insistence on breaking with Bristol-Myers centered on his demand for a long-term deal, a minimum three-year pact and more money, with the bankroller reluctant on both counts. Bristol-Myers was content with the program... they merely sought the possibility of leaving NBC in fear CBS competition would harm their investment.

Gardner, of course, was looking at the Puerto Rico deal and needed a guarantee of three years for the radio program to meet the qualifications of being tax exempt. Bristol-Myers wanted to play it safe and did not want to agree to a three-year guarantee.

Gardner was granted his release from Bristol-Myers on May 6, 1949. After reviewing inter-office memos exchanged between the sponsor and the advertising agency, Young & Rubicam, to say Bristol-Myers was "disappointed" is describing the sponsor's feelings mildly. Almost immediately, Gardner was mulling offers from all three networks and a number of sponsors and was seeking the best deal — provided they met the terms that Bristol-Myers would not. Several possibilities rumored included a new pact with NBC which would contain capital gains benefits. It was also reported that Pabst Beer was interested in *Duffy's Tavern* only as a radio show, with Eddie Cantor, then currently bankrolled by Pabst, switching exclusively to television. The rumor proved fact and Gardner succeeded in what could be described as one of the shrewdest deals in broadcast history.

Although trade reports say Gardner was anxious to break the Bristol-Myers pact, the release was unexpected inasmuch as the sponsor had already indicated Gardner's option would be lifted for next season. Another root of the trouble was said to be the bankroller's insistence that Gardner make a definite commitment for television in 1950, which he refused to do. The 1947 television audition attempt had flopped critically and left Gardner with a bad impression of the new medium. In his eyes, *Duffy's Tavern* was not yet ready for television. In view of the uncertainty of his television plans, the sponsor chose to give Gardner his requested release rather than continue with a no video guarantee.*

To celebrate his release, Gardner went on vacation to Honolulu for a week. So how could *Duffy's Tavern* have been broadcast with Gardner on vacation and away from the microphone? Simple. Weeks prior, he convinced Bristol-Myers to pay an additional expense and allow the series to be taped in advance for later playback. The May 4, 1949, broadcast was the first to purposely be recorded for the network for later playback. (The second was

---

* When a deal collapsed to give Eddie Cantor his own television program in the middle of May 1949, with Pabst Beer as the sponsor, this gave rise to rumors that Pabst would buy a separate television show, with Ed Gardner's *Duffy's Tavern* mentioned.

May 11 and Gardner returned from vacation on May 15 in time for rehearsals for the live May 18 broadcast.)* The consideration of taping episodes in advance for later playback had begun four months prior. Bristol-Myers considered sponsoring *Duffy's Tavern* during the summer months, rather than seek a summer replacement, under one condition: that a handful of broadcasts were taped and those recordings used during the 13 summer weeks. This would provide the cast a much-needed vacation. Gardner assured Bristol-Myers that the cost factor would be minimal and the sponsor felt the expense justified the per-1,000 listener cost ratio.

AFRA raised objections to the idea of repeating programs through the use of recordings. They feared actors would be paid less if they had to do the program once, not twice. When Bristol-Myers considered recording four new episodes, thus not considering repeating shows already broadcast, AFRA found they had no grounds for objecting to the proposal. In a letter dated January 26, 1949, Chester MacCracken at the advertising agency wrote to Ed Hitz of NBC. "There are still a couple of points to be checked before definite arrangements are made to carry out this plan. Obviously, it all rests on securing permission from NBC... I know the network's policy in the past against such a practice but the indications are that a revision of this policy is seriously being considered."

This consideration became a reality on February 8, 1949, when Ken R. Dyke of NBC wrote in a letter to all NBC vice-presidents, department heads, and division heads: "As a further step towards promoting program flexibility and improving service to the listeners, NBC will immediately discontinue the network recording ban and will permit the use of tape or disc transcriptions on the network."

The question for Gardner was how to convince the advertising agency and the network to agree on recording the broadcasts.

---

* The April 27 broadcast was originally planned as the first episode to be recorded but plans pushed the date to May 4.

Initially, Gardner proposed the final 13 broadcasts of the season be recorded and repeated during the summer hiatus. On March 20, 1949, Ed Hite wrote back to the agency. "It now appears that the plan of using recorded repeat *Duffy's Tavern* programs during Gardner's 13-week vacation is out of the question because of the high union charges, therefore it is rather certain that they will be in search of a summer replacement." The network offered the agency and the sponsor a comedy variety program, *The Henry Morgan Show*, for a price of $4,000 net. The sponsor agreed on $3,500 tops. A few weeks later, the deal was inked. Gardner did succeed in convincing both the network and the advertising agency to allow a total of seven radio broadcasts to be recorded.

COST OF RECORDED PROGRAMS

COST OF RECORDED PROGRAMS				
Date	Show Charge	Pre-Cuts	Editing	Total
May 4	$35.50	$54.50	25 ½ hours $318.75	$408.75 net
May 11	$35.50	$26.50	18 ¼ hours $228.25	$290.25 net
May 18 (live)	xxxxxx	xxxxxx	Xxxxxx	xxxxxx
May 25	$35.50	$26.50	9 ¾ hours $26.50	$184.00 net
June 1* (live)	xxxxxx	xxxxxx	Xxxxxx	xxxxxx
June 8	$35.50	$26.50	9 ¾ hours $26.50	$184.00 net
June 15	$35.50	$31.75	11 ¾ hours $147.00	$214.25 net
June 22	$35.50	*none*	26 ¾ hours $334.50	$370.00 net
June 29	$35.50	$21.25	13 ¾ hours $172.00	$228.75 net

The additional cost of recording programs was, naturally, submitted to the station's accounting department and paid by the sponsor. Raising the cost of radio production was always a concern of any sponsor and this was no exception, especially when NBC

During the June 1, 1949, broadcast, Ed Gardner and Eddie Green both read their lines wrong by accident during the show and Gardner muttered over the air, "Oh, if only we were on that tape!"

informed the advertising agency of the possibility that next season might be entirely taped. When Bristol-Myers lodged a complaint and it appeared negotiations for a renewal in the spring were not possible, NBC attempted to justify the expenses by explaining the free publicity that went into *Duffy's Tavern*, additional on-the-air spot advertising. During the year of 1948, the total number of station break announcements broadcast on behalf of *Duffy's Tavern* was valued at $5,400, based on commercial rates. WMAQ in Chicago, during the same calendar year, aired a total of 178 promotional announcements, valued at the rate of $8,170. The sponsor was not contractually obligated to pay for these announcements. The network simply fulfilled an obligation to promote the program to the best of their ability. It was one of the services designed to help make Bristol-Myers' advertising campaign a success.

The justification was not necessary, however, considering the fact that NBC compiled an "Audience Promotion Report" every four months, reporting the total number of stations carrying the program, transcribed announcements, special announcements and mentions on other radio programs, newspaper advertisements, direct mail promotion, displays, billboards and car cards, and the overall value of air time and newspaper space in both circulation and dollar signs. The Promotion Report also delivered the results of an announcement made on four consecutive radio broadcasts, beginning June 1, 1949, offering free samples of "MUM," a deodorant manufactured by Bristol-Myers, for any radio listener who mailed their name and address to Box 888 in New York City. Executives at the drug firm wanted to gauge the size of the listening audience based on an expectation number. (The number of submissions may not have met with satisfaction, which might be another of the many reasons why Bristol-Myers did not renew the contract for next season.)

In December 1946, NBC initiated a new policy that all copy related to premium offers would be counted as commercial time. It had become a practice by certain advertisers to refer to an item, similar to or identical with the proposed premium, in the script proper before the premium offer is actually made. This practice would be permitted only during a one-week period preceding the start of of the offer itself, and was subject to NBC approval in advance of the exact reference in the script to the premium build-up. During that period only, the references in the script would not be counted as commercial time. During the offer and subsequent to the offer all script references would be counted as commercial time.

The announcement of sponsorship was clarified in detail with the new policy. On the Abbott and Costello show, the opening device was "C-for Comedy, A-for Abbott, M-for Maxwell, E-for Ernie, L-for Lou Costello" was not considered commercial time. One of the constructive developments in commercial radio had been the integration of the commercial message into the structure of the program itself.

Except for the free samples of "MUM," there doesn't appear to have been any promotional giveaways on *Duffy's Tavern* during the years Bristol-Myers sponsored the program. Part of this may have been the attitude of NBC. In January 1947, NBC prepared a "long range sales strategy" and, according to the report, the various rating services were useful as they called attention to the popularity of NBC programs. The weakness of those indexes of popularity was the readiness with which advertisers were prone to accept them as measures of "circulation." It was in 1947 that NBC decided to revive some of the old techniques and originate new ones to measure the selling effectiveness of specific programs. These included pantry-shelf surveys, box-tops, mass-audience participation, free sample offers and other methods to sell the effectiveness as a medium.

During the first week of May 1949, Gardner had a blow-up over the agency's interest in his integration of a commercial for MUM into his show and, as described by Stockton Helffrich at NBC, Gardner "did a great deal of talking about betrayal by the agency and Mr. Trammell." Gardner prevented the commercial from being integrated into the scripts, claiming there was a strict separation between the situation comedy and the commercial time. Bristol-Myers ultimately won out, however, with a special offer made on the *Duffy's Tavern* program starting June 1 and continuing for four weeks through June 22. The offer was for a free sample-size package of MUM. The instructions asked listeners to mail a three-cent stamp (to cover mailing costs) with their name and address. Gardner knew that a special offer for a free product meant one thing: the sponsor wanted to gauge the size of the listening audience based on their giveaway expectation. An expectation was established and the number of responses would dictate whether or not *Duffy's Tavern* truly garnered large enough listenership to justify sponsoring another season. Indications in letters found at the same agency suggest the response for free MUM was only half of what they had expected. The same promotion was offered on the same four weeks of *Mister District Attorney* and the result was, according to statistics at Young & Rubicam, a third larger than *Duffy's*. Gardner, however, had a hidden agenda of his own. The seven recorded broadcasts were to convince a skeptical network that recordings could be used in place of "live" broadcasts. If he was to make the planned move to Puerto Rico, pre-recorded episodes would be essential. And who paid for those test recordings? Bristol-Myers.

CHAPTER THIRTEEN
THE MOVE TO PUERTO RICO
(1949)

WHEN ED GARDNER PACKED HIS BAGS, left his Bel Air home in California and made the move to King's Court, San Juan, Puerto Rico, the U.S. Treasury charged he wasn't living there solely because he liked the aroma of the roses climbing on his bedroom wall. Gardner discovered a gimmick which apparently exempted him from paying taxes to anybody on an income of more than $400,000 a year. Under Section 251 of the Internal Revenue Act, American citizens residing on our island possessions need pay no federal income tax on earnings in the islands. Beginning September 1949, Gardner moved into a rented house on Millionaire's Row, overlooking the sea, and began producing *Duffy's Tavern* on transcription discs for shipment to New York. His guest stars were flown in by airplane to the islands, lured with the promise of a few days vacation and gathering a little sun on the beach.

479

The Gardners and their California home.

In the first year alone, over a dozen Hollywood celebrities took Gardner up on the vacation. Basil Rathbone, Hildegarde, Don Ameche, Gloria Swanson, Shelley Winters, Gypsy Rose Lee, Helen Traubel (always a Tavern favorite), Ray Milland, Hollywood couple Jon Hall and Frances Langford, and Rudy Vallee — the latter of whom loved Puerto Rico so much he made a return trip a year later.

In late April, Hedda Hopper was flown in to Puerto Rico for a vacation... and a guest appearance on the program. Upon her return, she wrote in her syndicated newspaper column, "He has a wonderful setup down there. Every chance he gets, Ed flies to the Virgin Islands to live on his boat. It sleeps six and the skipper comes from California. The sailing is divine; the fish are shy." Treated like a queen, Hopper had nothing but praise for *Duffy's Tavern* in her columns. Any criticisms from the Hollywood elite for his decision to move to a warmer climate were, for the most part, put on ice.

Mixing business with pleasure, Gardner signed a contract with the local government exempting him from payment of island income taxes in return for establishing a new industry there. To date, nothing has been found to suggest NBC was aware of this arrangement but the tale of Ed Gardner and the tax collector is more complicated than the plot which unfolded on his weekly radio program.

In the late forties, radio in Puerto Rico temporarily faced a threat in government ownership. Since government stations were naturally subsidized and did not have to worry about making money, the private stations felt that it would be unfair competition for the Puerto Rican government to accept advertising on their own stations. By 1949, private station owners were able to block the government's attempts to go into the broadcast advertising business. A Federal investigation turned up some unsavory messes, "inspired campaigns" and a lot of other conditions which halted their plans. The biggest moment came on the gala opening day of WIPR, the big government 10,000-watt transmitter, when there was a short circuit. The station wasn't gala that day, or for sometime thereafter.

At that time, radio stations seemed to have been multiplying far too rapidly in Puerto Rico. Officially, there were seven transmitters on the Island in 1947 but there were 28 stations currently opening or authorized by June 1949, the same time Ed Gardner decided to bring *Duffy's Tavern* from Hollywood, California, and Third Avenue in New York City, to a warmer climate.

Puerto Rico had already established its own version of American radio programs including the *Lux Radio Theater*, and U.S. Sponsors such as Ford, Firestone, Alka-Seltzer, Colgate-Palmolive-Peet, Sterling Drug, Coca-Cola and Sears were already sponsoring broadcasts originating from Puerto Rico. But these were local productions and were never transmitted or freighted to the U.S. for broadcast in the States.

Gardner, in an interview for a Puerto Rican newspaper, claimed he gathered more than his share of the world's wealth during the forties and handed most of it over to the Federal Government. In Puerto Rico, he opted to take advantage of a twelve-year tax holiday, which was declared by the government in order to attract industry to the island. While it wasn't precisely what they had in mind, instead of industry, the island got Ed Gardner.

Puerto Rican officials looked the other way when the decision to rate *Duffy's Tavern* as a tax-free new industry was made by president Luis Munoz Martin and his cabinet, in return for a pledge by Gardner to make $250,000 worth of color movies for television in the first year. Theoretically, Gardner would provide enough jobs for Puerto Rican laborers and technicians to justify forgiving him his income taxes. The October 28, 1949, issue of *The El Paso Herald-Post* reported: "Puerto Rico representatives say other big-name American entertainers are free to follow Gardner's example." Most of Hollywood remained stationed on the West Coast.

The Gardners enjoy the Puerto Rican climate and locale.

Under a 1947 law, Puerto Rico promised not to tax new industries until 1959 and, after that, to raise them in three annual installments to the level of existing business. The tax exemption applied to single-owner businesses, partnerships and corporations, both as to corporate earnings and dividends paid to Americans living in Puerto Rico. Through a law made by Congress, Americans living in Puerto Rico came under the island's tax laws if they satisfied two conditions. (1)— Half their income had to come from the "active conduct" of a local trade or business. (2) — 80 percent of their income was paid to them on the island. By the time Gardner made the move, it was reported that more than 50 U.S. concerns had located to Puerto Rico, creating jobs for 7,500 to 8,000 on the islands. Summed up, the new Puerto Rican law and an old U.S. law combined to give U.S. businesses in Puerto Rico exemption from all taxes on income earned on the island. This applied not only to business taxes but also to personal incomes of people working in a transplanted business.

On November 10, 1948, Ed Gardner, who owned *Duffy's Tavern* as a package show, powwowed late at night with Niles Trammell, president of NBC, and Sidney Strotz, NBC's western regional chief. The network offered a capital gains deal to the comedian to keep the star and his program from heeding a similar offer pitched by CBS. NBC wanted to buy Gardner and his show, both as a property. Trammell stressed to Gardner the plans NBC had not only for *Duffy's Tavern* as a major network attraction, but also mapped an outline for the future: television. Weeks later, Edgar Bergen, another NBC performer being eyed by CBS, was offered a similar capital gains deal. Gardner did not agree to the sale right away. Instead, he began researching the pros and cons of such a decision.

Weeks later, in December, Ed Gardner learned of the tax loopholes and approached both NBC and Young & Rubicam with a proposal of his own. Gardner wanted to sell NBC a proposition with a guarantee of services for three years. Essentially the proposal required NBC to: (1) "invest" $350,000 in a contemplated motion picture venture and (2), contract to pay Gardner $15,000 per week for his services during the next three years, representing a total of $1,695,000. In return, NBC would be assured of holding the *Duffy's Tavern* show as valuable property – at least for three years. With CBS recently luring Jack Benny and *Amos n' Andy* away from NBC, and numerous NBC affiliates expressing concern, the studio in March of 1949 sent a letter to all of their affiliates explaining the details that led to the loss of Jack Benny, and reassured them that Dennis Day and Phil Harris would remain on NBC.* From the motion picture investment, the only prospective recovery was contingent upon the film being successfully marketed to the extent that it produced more than $550,000 of revenue to Gardner. If the film earned more than $550,000, NBC received half of such excess but no more than $290,000. Accordingly, the prospective loss on the NBC "investment" was a maximum of $350,000 and a minimum of $60,000. And, Gardner explained in his proposal, production would be moved in Puerto Rico. Would NBC accept a motion picture investment certain to give them a financial loss, but a three-year security on the *Duffy's Tavern* radio program which could net them a sure profit?**

The decades-old practice usually concerned the advertising agencies creating the program, then selling the programs to sponsors. Under this arrangement, the networks rarely owned the shows and the networks made their money by selling airtime to the sponsors. Radio stations were viewed as stand-alone outlets. The only controlling interest the ad agencies had was the commercial time. Because the purchase of *Jack Benny* and *Amos n' Andy* by

---

* It is amusing to see how CBS, purchasing two NBC programs, *Jack Benny* and *Amos n' Andy*, launched a powerful show of force, what NBC referred to at a management committee meeting as "a highly intensified competitive situation." Just months prior, in the fall of 1948, NBC succeeded in their "long range sales strategy" implemented in 1947 with a powerful lineup of their own when they premiered five popular programs that were all using CBS facilities last spring. These substantial additions to the NBC roster meant increased popularity for their affiliates. Among the programs, *Screen Guild Theatre*, *Blondie*, *The Adventures of Ozzie and Harriet* and two Pet Milk programs.

** It was not uncommon for a major network to invest in a motion picture, stage play or Broadway musical. In June and July 1950, NBC invested $200,000 in a musical show titled *Call Me Madam* to be produced on Broadway the coming season, with Ethel Merman as the star of the show. NBC received 35 percent of the net profits of the venture.

The Gardners enjoying the life in Puerto Rico.

CBS involved millions of dollars, and with television on the horizon, executives at NBC realized that the rules of engagement had changed. If this was a game of chess, CBS called a check. William S. Paley, the chief executive at CBS, felt that moving the biggest names on rival networks to CBS would ensure dominance of television. Raiding the opposition and purchasing programs and owning actors as property, rather than try to encourage them to make a network transition, offered strong security. At first, NBC attempted to counter attack with new programming. Eventually, the network reconsidered their stance against transcribed programs, which celebrities and comedians insisted was essential and, in growing numbers, the dealbreaker.

By the end of 1948, Al Jolson, Eddie Cantor, Jimmy Durante and Ozzie and Harriet all set up a hue and cry against the verboten on pre-recordings. Days after ringing in the new year, NBC lifted the ban against tape recording only in cases where both the ad agency and the program's star concur in the use of recordings. As reported in *Variety*, NBC was "setting up a defense against the CBS raiders that is hoped to forestall any further defections by its star comics and singers." Another factor for the change in attitude was because the network, unlike CBS, had no capital gains deals to offer its stars.

Getting back to Ed Gardner... Newspapers and trade columns mentioned in May 1948 that: "*Duffy's Tavern*, reported earlier to be on the verge of a cancellation, has won a 52-week renewal to begin following a short summer layoff." But Ed Gardner understood the power of the press. On October 15, 1948, *The Los Angeles Times* reported the threat of the CBS powerhouse: "Since CBS bought *Amos 'n' Andy* lock, stock and burnt cork for $3,000,000, Ed Gardner offered himself for sale along with *Duffy's Tavern*." In February 1949, the same newspaper reported: "Ed Gardner is in New York preparing a capital gains sale of his *Duffy's Tavern* show. He's waiting for the tax department's final decision on the other capital gains deals in radio before he decides. If the tax department 'closes' the *Amos 'n' Andy* deal, then Gardner will sell his program-characters to CBS." Naturally, this applied pressure to NBC.

In September 1946, NBC's new Radio-Recording facilities, a new Radio City studio, began experimenting with transcription recording and the use of tape, with very good results. The new recording facilities were operating "with reasonable efficiency," according to an inter-office memo, and were anticipated to be fully operating before the end of the year. With the facility completed and RCA having completed their 24th Street plant (then presently under construction), the transcription quality was supposedly the best available. If NBC needed to compete against the other networks and dominate this field, they wanted to get a head start. Sadly, this never happened. On Tuesday, July 10, 1947, during a meeting of the NBC Stations Planning and Advisory Committee, the subject of transcribing programs in advance was addressed. Harry Kopf, vice-president in charge of Sales, made the statement that NBC was receiving considerable pressure as a result of the CBS policy to delay by transcription rather than broadcast live programs.

The Gardners make the move to Puerto Rico.

NBC investigated all facets of the agreement and trade journals began reporting the leak, which resulted in numerous inquiries as to the tax treatment of sales by radio artists. This prompted George J. Schoeneman, Commissioner of Internal Revenue, to issue the following statement on January 3, 1949: "The tax effect of any business transaction is determined by its realities. Accordingly, proposals of radio artists and others to obtain compensation for personal services under the guise of sales of property cannot be regarded as coming within the capital gains provisions of the Internal Revenue Code. Such compensations are taxable at ordinary income tax rates."

Almost immediately, NBC reviewed their policies and Niles Trammell, President of NBC, released an official statement: "Until the United States says that such transactions are lawful, the National Broadcasting Company will continue to refuse to purchase stock in so-called production corporations where the artists who control such corporations are performing on the NBC network. Such arrangements are bound to lead to charges of discrimination between artists who are paying income taxes at the higher rates and those who are paying at the lower rates of only twenty-five percent based on so-called capital gains."

By early March of 1949, rough draft copies of the contract were drawn up and NBC legals reviewed the contracts, fearing Gardner might have a legal right to move to Puerto Rico. A review of Gardner's July 26, 1942, contract with Young & Rubicam, NBC and Bristol-Myers, paragraph 23, stated: "The term 'broadcasts' shall be defined to include both radio broadcasting as it is now being used and/or as it may hereafter be used and through the medium of television throughout the United States, its territories, and all foreign countries or jurisdictions. Nothing herein shall be construed to prevent you or your designee from making feature, non-advertising motion pictures of *Duffy's Tavern*, including material used on the programs hereunder, which motion pictures may be exhibited by means of television."

On March 21, 1949, NBC produced a report documenting all pros and cons regarding Gardner's proposal. "The consensus is that four of the network's top programs are vital to the maintenance of a strong position in the industry. These programs, namely,

Fred Allen, *Fibber McGee*, Bob Hope and *Duffy's Tavern* are of paramount importance not only for their own value, but because it is believed that they have a magnetic influence which attracts and holds other programs in adjacent time positions. In addition, of course, the public's general interest in NBC programming is greatly influenced by the presence of these acknowledged favorites."

In that same month, *Duffy's Tavern* ranked seventh on recent popularity lists.* It followed *Mr. District Attorney*, another high-ranking (eleventh place) program, for a half-hour under the same sponsor, who had the show on NBC since 1940. It was determined that if *Duffy's Tavern* were to move to another network, and strong overtures along this line were being made, that *Mr. District Attorney* would move concurrently. NBC reviewed every possible measure of profit or loss including operating costs, surplus revenue and financial estimates and believed that the network would result in a profit for the three-year term amounting to $133,540, even though NBC made no recovery whatsoever on the motion picture investment.

On March 25, 1949, the *Los Angeles Times* reported: "You can discount rumors about Ed Gardner selling *Duffy's Tavern* to CBS. A Hollywood informant says 'Archie' told NBC last week that he's perfectly happy with the present setup."

Making the Move

While NBC legals were reviewing the contract, a trip was made to San Juan, Puerto Rico, with Ed Gardner, T.H. Phelan of NBC and Ormond Rutheven, formerly of MGM, who was acting as a technical advisor for film production. Having reviewed the broadcasting companies in Puerto Rico, consideration of facilitation was narrowed down to two studios. The first was the auditorium studio of the NBC affiliate, WNEL. The second was

---

* November 22, 1948 — C.E. Hooper organization's bi-weekly computation of popularity among evening radio programs reported *Duffy's Tavern* among the top ten programs. It came in seventh, higher than it had been in 1946 and 1947.

the auditorium studio of WIPR, which belonged to the Insular Government of Puerto Rico. Both were of modern design and contained some equipment that could be used. WIPR won over WNEL because of the modern facilities, including an emergency power supply and more equipment than the other studio, but it had a noisy air conditioner. The solution was to shut off the refrigerator compressors during the broadcasts. Architectural changes would need to be made to provide suitable sound isolation between the studio and adjacent spaces. All communication between the network and Gardner was conducted by telegram, addressed to radio station WIPR in Santurce, Puerto Rico.

On June 23, Ed Gardner, having worked out the technicals with George McElrath of NBC, stipulated the need for two engineers and four tape machines in Puerto Rico to handle the broadcasts. The network chose to send only one engineer, who was flown down to Puerto Rico to help with the recordings. It was Phelan's suggestion that one NBC engineer be sent to San Juan and a local engineer hired to assist him in the production of the broadcast and tape recordings. This was done to satisfy NBC's requirements and also help the local situation by employing one of their own technicians. Under the terms of the contract, Gardner agreed to buy and NBC agreed to sell to him whatever radio, film and television equipment he required in Puerto Rico up to the value of $75,000. Gardner was to pay one-third of the purchase price during the 1949-50 season, the balance during the 1950-51 season. Gardner had the right to return the equipment at the end of the first year and receive credit for the unpaid balance.

The starting date for the new *Duffy's Tavern* season was originally scheduled for September 15, 1949, but in mid-August the season premiere was re-scheduled for September 29. The delay was caused by the preparation of the program. The first two episodes were not recorded until the afternoon of September 22, giving NBC less than a week to prepare for broadcast.

As a general rule, Ed Gardner taped the shows on Thursday evening in Puerto Rico. They were edited and accurately timed the following day or, when the situation deemed possible, as late as Saturday. The recordings were then shipped to NBC in New York via special Pan American Airways courier service (hand-to-

490

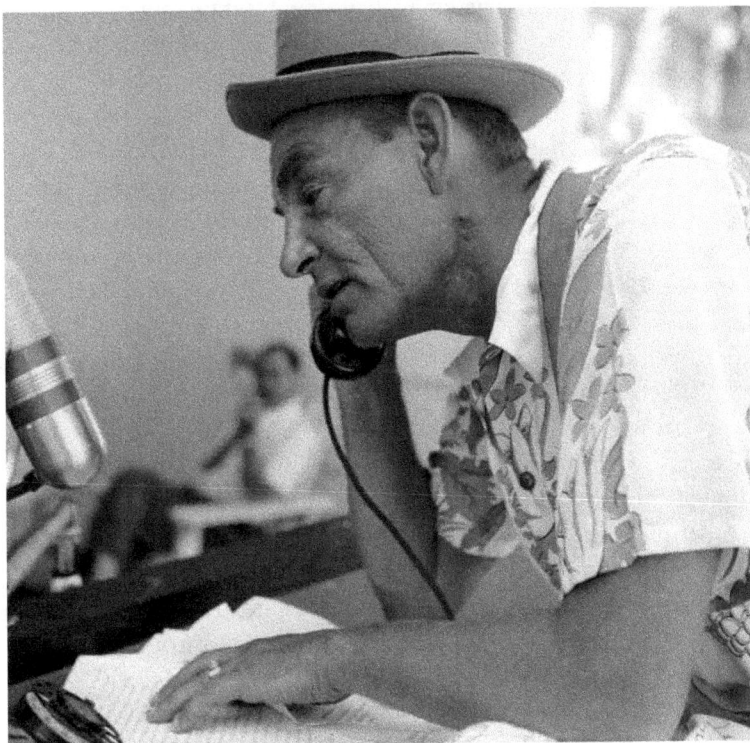

Ed Gardner during the rehearsals in Puerto Rico.

hand). The tape would leave Puerto Rico no later than Sunday and be delivered to New York no later than Monday morning. The tape received on Monday would be played for continuity acceptance sometime during that day. If there was something the network objected to, they notified Gardner immediately. There, they produced a replacement tape (re-editing from the original masters) which could be shipped to New York well in advance of broadcast time. The re-editing rarely happened because of the expenses involved, and because NBC had approval of the written scripts beforehand. The recording that arrived on Monday would be broadcast Thursday, ten days later. Three acetate platters were made of each episode. Two for the advertising agency and the third to Mr. Schmitz, advertising director of the Blatz Brewing Company. After the broadcast, on Friday morning, NBC sent their tape to the advertising agency, which retained a copy for its records. Naturally, as enough episodes were recorded in advance, the recordings were not aired over NBC in the order they were recorded.

The preliminary radio scripts were written three to four weeks in advance of production. Fourteen mimeographed copies of each script were made and distributed to client personnel and Schenley's public relations council. The network, the agency and the sponsor reviewed the scripts and submitted suggested changes and addressed all concerns to Jack Cleary, the producer in Puerto Rico, well in advance of Ed Gardner's re-writing schedule.

Effective September 29, 1949, the entire *Duffy's Tavern* program was broadcast via tape, with the exception of the Cresta Blanca Wine trailer at the conclusion, plus the sign-off, which was done live by the announcer.

While the listening audience continued to listen to *Duffy's Tavern* as usual, with a new sponsor now promoting Blatz Beer, behind-the-scenes there were initial complications. Evelyn Dodd was Ed Gardner's secretary and she handled most of the business and communication between Gardner's office and NBC. In an exchange of letters beginning October 24, 1949, it appears Dodd did not know all of the aspects regarding radio production, seeking to ensure clearance for copyrighted music, unaware there was also the matter of mechanical rights clearance, which meant the payment of a fee to the person who recorded the music on tape.

The advertising agency presenting the Blatz Brewing Company was Kastor, Farrell, Chesley & Clifford, Inc., located in New York. The agency representative who handled the account was Van Amburgh. The initial contract was for a 52 week sponsorship (including the summer months), starting September 29, 1949, and concluding on September 21, 1950. Under contract, specific NBC affiliates across the country could air the program on a delay (later playback that same evening). While Gardner and his crew produced the *Duffy's Tavern* episodes, the announcer's opening and closing was not included. Those were done "live" from New York, due to union policies.

In a letter from Peter Zalantis at NBC, he addressed a concern that had occurred at the network but would become minor when compared to the freight costs of the *Duffy's Tavern* tapes. "We received a cable from Mr. Gardner requesting clearance of 'Sweet Adeline' for the program of October 27," he explained. "The cable came collect at a cost of $4.69 which was paid out of pocket by Mr. Van Amburgh of Network Sales. Since it is not our custom to receive or assume costs or collect wires, will you be good enough to continue sending your music clearance requests via air-mail?"

Evelyn Dodd's query came at an unusual time since a number of broadcasts had already gone into production in Puerto Rico, and been broadcast over NBC. The question of a mechanical charge on "When Irish Eyes Are Smiling" was discussed and cleared before Ed Gardner left the States. He had a letter from Nat Lefkowitz, who quoted Herman Starr, Head of the Music Publishers Holding Corporation, stating that Gardner could continue to use the song and that there would be no problems regarding rights or royalties. However, Starr himself did not put his statement in writing. On October 24, W.S. Chesley Jr. of Kastor, Farrell, Chesley and Clifford, Inc., explained to NBC that "there seems to be no question in anyone's mind about the legality of this thing. There is a possibility, at a future date, when the music publishers have come to an agreement on their Television situation with the network that they will then take up the matter of fees for use and establish uniform rates."

After the issue of music clearance was resolved, the matter of sound quality and timing had to be ironed out. The air conditioning system played a role in the production of two episodes in late November or early December, when a noticeable fuzzy quality was discovered on two recordings, both copies of tapes — both air and protection. Other technical mistakes as a result of the use of tape are in evidence on the November 24, 1949, broadcast. Due to the NBC engineer accidentally jumping cue and starting the Cresta-Blanca recorded trailer on the closing applause, instead of waiting until completion of the transcribed credit, words lost were "Tune in again next week for *Duffy's Tavern*, transcribed over most of these same stations."

The length of time was supposed to be 29 minutes and

20 seconds per broadcast. For the broadcast of October 27, 1949, the show ran short. But not because of the recording — because of the machines. "It is my firm belief, after my experience with *Duffy's* tonight, that those tape machines still cannot be counted on for accuracy in timing," engineer Bob Sosman wrote in an inter-office memo. "On the two times that I listened to and timed the show this week, I clocked Archie's 'Goodnight everybody' at 28:08. Tonight on the air it came at 28:01." This meant that one machine played the tape seven seconds slower than the other. But since the show itself came up short, a total of three, five-second dead spots turned up during the broadcast. Months later, the problem resurfaced when the program of March 9, 1950, came up 15 seconds short, and NBC staff improvised by filling in an American Red Cross announcement after the program close.

The November 16, 1949, issue of *Radio Daily* reported: "Petrillo's demands that *Duffy's Tavern* employ AFM musicians for their tape recordings in Puerto Rico may result in Ed Gardner altering his plans to continue production of his show down in San Juan." This caused executives at NBC to investigate and they found there were no demands being made by Petrillo, an example of how today, historians should not accept everything they read in the trade columns as fact, without secondary verification.

The Battle Begins

In Washington, D.C., Gardner's Puerto Rican adventure drew a bleat of anguish from at least one Congressman, Representative Noah M. Mason (R- Ill.), who included Gardner among a number of "tax dodgers who are continuing their raids on the Treasury," and asked Congress to close the loopholes in the tax laws. Mason was a close student of social and economic affairs and was a member of the tax-writing House Ways and Means Committee. "The fast-growing racket of doing business without paying income taxes must be stopped by Congress next year or the national economy will be destroyed," he spoke publicly.

On October 8, spurred by a handful of congressmen, the Bureau of Internal Revenue made a quiet investigation of radio's newest tax gimmick. A spokesman at the Revenue Bureau and the agency was closely examining the long and complicated Puerto Rican law to determine whether it was possible for U.S. radio shows to skip taxes by broadcasting from the island. One official said he was "afraid that if there is such a loophole, a number of other programs may do the same thing." His fears were substantiated when, just a few days later, a Broadway columnist stated that "Hollywood moguls are working out a plan to set up film companies as co-operatives to escape many taxes." Meanwhile, Mason made plans to introduce a new bill of his to add a provision ruling out the Puerto Rican moratorium as far as radio broadcasts to the U.S. were concerned. The bill would close several loopholes in the present tax laws. Mason's bill had the backing of a number of congressmen.

On the morning of Friday, November 11, with the strong backing of the Treasury Department, Congress took fast steps to plug the tax loophole. A special group from the House Ways and Means Committee booked airline flights for the island to study Social Security in Puerto Rico and include an on-the-air spot study of the 53 U.S. businesses that jumped to Puerto Rico in the preceding year to take advantage of the loophole.

One newspaper headlined: "U.S. PLANNING 'ANTI-GARDNER' TAX ALTERATION." But, as usual, with any bills that don't directly affect those who write them, the hope to plug up the apparent loophole in tax legislation, proposing to eliminate or at least reduce tax liabilities for those who move their business to Puerto Rico, was only a proposal. Throughout the month of December and January, newspapers and trade columns across the country were quoting individuals at the U.S. Treasury stating the bill was being written. But on February 4, the House Ways and Means Committee admitted to not even writing a single word of the general tax revision bill, let alone a clause to include the closing of the loophole. One trade paper, upon learning of this fact, claimed Ed Gardner was "an odds-on choice to escape taxes."

On February 8, 1950, Thomas J. Lynch, the general counsel of the U.S. Treasury, discussed the details of the bill to newspaper reporters, claiming the individual responsible for their motivation: "A radio entertainer recently entered into an arrangement with the Puerto Rican government under which he agreed to produce all his radio and television transcriptions and films on that island in return for exception from U.S. tax even though he may stay in Puerto Rico for only a short period each year." If this sounded repetitive, it was because weeks prior, Lynch instructed employees of the Treasury not to single Gardner out by name, in fear he would have grounds to fight back, citing the matter as personal, rather than professional.

The uncertainty expressed by Snyder as to whether the "entertainer," was out of reach to the U.S. tax was not cleared up even after the comedian filed his 1949 tax return. Internal Revenue Bureau experts explained that the exemption took effect if 80 percent of Gardner's gross income for 1949 came from Puerto Rico and if half of it was derived from a trade or business or the rendition of personal services. Gardner publicly fought back by bringing to the public's attention that exempt from U.S. taxes were federal employees, as well as private employees, in the Canal Zone, Samoa, Wake Island, Guam, Midway and Puerto Rico.

By June, the House Ways and Means Committee had written into the new excise tax bill a provision putting Puerto Rico on the same basis for taxation purposes as foreign nations. To qualify for an exemption from federal income tax, a U.S. citizen would have to become a "bona fide" resident of Puerto Rico, according to the terms of the committee provision. Ed Gardner would remain free of income tax if he exiled himself in Puerto Rico, an Internal Revenue Bureau official told *Billboard*, in giving an informal interpretation of the loophole-plugging action. Because Gardner moved "bag and baggage" to the island, the comedian qualified for a continued exemption even under the committee amendment. Gardner was able to travel State-side whenever he liked without affecting his Puerto Rican residence. The chief effect of the committee provision, if enacted, would be to prevent any income tax avoidance by persons commuting regularly to the island, earning their pay there and still maintaining U.S. residence.

Under present law it was possible to do exactly that and be free of taxes on income from Puerto Rican sources if such sums amount to the greater part of an individual's annual income. To fulfill the requirement of the proposed law, upon first learning of the proposed provisions, Gardner put his $85,000 Holmby Hills colonial mansion up for sale in April of 1950, and established permanent residence in Puerto Rico.

"It's a funny sort of government that makes it profitable for anyone to go elsewhere and do business," remarked a columnist for the *Wisconsin State Journal.* "When federal income taxes are as high as they are now, every citizen looks over his personal affairs carefully, in order to secure all the deductions possible. Most of us would like to retain as large a share of our earnings as Uncle Sam will permit us to keep. It becomes sort of a game. Along about income tax time, friends exchange helpful hints on the deductions that they 'got away with' last year. We buy books and pay out money to tax lawyers, because the thing is getting pretty complicated. It's getting so that if a citizen gets anything back out of the week-by-week "take" that the government collects, he has won a moral victory. Workers in the entertainment industry would have tried all sorts of weird schemes to cut down taxes. Authors, artists, musicians, comedians and others who have high earnings for a comparatively few years but earn nothing when they lose public favor have resorted to every trick in the book in order to keep bigger shares of their paychecks. Take Archie Gardner [sic], star of the *Duffy's Tavern* radio program. Archie moved his show to Puerto Rico... The Bureau of Internal Revenue is pretty mad about Archie outsmarting its smartest experts but there isn't a great deal the bureau can do about it... It's a strange set-up that encourages a man to leave the United States and live on an island in order to get rich."

Ratings

Throughout October and November 1946, the ratings for *Duffy's Tavern* tumbled from 15th to 39th according to Hooper. Months later, in March 1947, the chart was re-evaluated. *Duffy's Tavern* scored a national Hooper of 21.4 against an East Coast rating of

11.4. In the national ranking, *Duffy's Tavern* grabbed ninth place, whereas on the East Coast it was practically in the cellar — in 52nd place. The time differential might have been a factor. A survey from October 1946 to February 1947 discovered a radical difference in listeners in the Mountain States compared to the National average. No less than five shows of the top 15 evening list nationally did not show among the leaders in the Mountain area. These shows included Bing Crosby, Walter Winchell, *Bandwagon*, *The Great Gildersleeve* and *Duffy's Tavern*. In December 1947, *Duffy's Tavern* took another sizable dive in the ratings when it failed to make the chart. By May 1949, though, *Duffy's Tavern* jumped from 31st to 18th place in the AC Nielsen radio ratings.

FOURTEEN
"HOLLYWOOD"
by Ed "Archie" Gardner
August or September of 1949

Being a man who is loath to give credit where credit is due (by credit I am not inferring to the kind which concerns bill collectors), I will admit that there are independent producers in Hollywood besides meself. There is Wanger and John Ford and Goldwyn among others. But I have advantages over all of them. That is why me first big indie, "Pigsfeet in Paris," is progressing so rapidly toward a beginning. Before I list why I will succeed where others have failed, let me explain that 'Pigsfeet in Paris' is not a story of Ed 'Archie' Gardner on a walking tour of that famous confidential capital. The word 'pigsfeet' has nothing to do with the producer, which is meself.

As a leading independent producer, I have discovered Puerto Rico, and Puerto Rico has discovered me. We are both happy. I intend to broadcast *Duffy's Tavern* from there as well as produce pictures there. Which is a first.

Duffy's Tavern gives me a running start. I will be able to feed actors like they have never been fed before. Thus as a producer I have the food problem licked. I have me own jernt. What other leading motion picture producer can claim likewise? I am also a sweeping success in me Tavern. I'll even sweep out me own studio. I don't think any other producer can make that statement.

There are other problems in producing a picture, but they're too infindismal to bring up. Like money, I can handle money and vice versa. Most indie producers have a money problem. I don't. I can handle this thing through sheer personality.

War Agencies of

THE GOVERNMENT
OF THE
UNITED STATES

award this plaque to

E. A. Gardner

a member of the

WAR ACTIVITIES COMMITTEE
MOTION PICTURE INDUSTRY

for Outstanding Service in
World War II

*One of many awards bestowed upon Ed Gardner
and* Duffy's Tavern.

CHAPTER FOURTEEN
BLATZ BEER
(1949 - 1950)

THE FUTURE OF *DUFFY'S TAVERN*, and Gardner's move to Puerto Rico, was dependent on whether he would be able to sign a new sponsor. The sales force weakened without the backing of an advertising agency, with Gardner representing himself. Having worked for an advertising agency and carrying a program that NBC agreed was valuable, his problem was resolved the day after the final broadcast of the season. On June 30, 1949, the question of whether Blatz Beer (Schenley Industries, Inc.) would buy the George Burns and Gracie Allen radio package, which CBS had been pitching up, or settle for Ed Gardner's *Duffy's Tavern*, resolved itself with the Milwaukee brewery signing a deal with Gardner. The program's format was a natural for beer sponsorship (irony writ large when considering the fact that a few years prior, the word "Tavern" was temporarily dropped from the title). The reported price for the package was $15,000 per episode, representing a hike of about $1,500 over the price Bristol-Myers had been paying. General David Sarnoff, president of RCA, NBC's parent organization, was figured in the sale, a commentary on NBC's "high echelon" sales technique. The negotiations leading up to the Blatz Beer sponsorship took place during Gardner's negotiations with NBC regarding the move to Puerto Rico.

Blatz Beer advertisement.
(Photo courtesy of Steven Thompson.)

502

Initially, Ed Gardner was under contract to Bristol-Myers until June 1950, the sponsor having recently exercised its option for the last year of a three-year pact. The present package price was around $13,000 weekly. During the first week of February 1949, Gardner traveled to New York City to discuss renewal with revised terms. He wanted the weekly cost raised in any new agreement. Supposedly, his proposal involved a five-year deal, during which NBC would guarantee the comic a basic annual income, even if the network was not able to sell the program to a commercial sponsor. At the same time he was negotiating with NBC and talking with CBS, Gardner huddled with executives of ABC with a view to signing a deal, presumably should he fail to work out a renewal with Bristol-Myers.

Paul Luther, in his "Inside Radio" column, reported: "According to one of our Hollywood sleuths, the latest show to join the growing list of available air properties is *Duffy's Tavern*. Here, however, it seems the reason for the cancellation is sponsor's dissatisfaction with the show rather than a desire to reduce expenses which is why so many of the big name features have been given their notices."

In February 1949, the president of NBC made an announcement of a new company policy of accepting recorded programs on the network. Ten RCA magnetic tape recorders were purchased and installed in New York for this purpose, at an estimated cost of $25,000. Gardner's move to Puerto Rico was ensured and Bristol-Myers walked away, leaving NBC to negotiate with a new sponsor: Schenley Distillers, which had purchased Blatz Beer in 1943. During the last week of June 1949, CBS and NBC were in a fight for Ed Gardner and his *Duffy's Tavern* stanza. Gardner took the initiative to sign a contract with Schenley, promising every episode would not only have a commercial spot, but product placement in each script. CBS offered the 10 p.m. Wednesday time slot, following Groucho Marx and Bing Crosby, both of which would start in the fall. NBC offered to retain the 9 p.m. Wednesday time slot occupied by *Duffy's Tavern*. Gardner did not want to compete with Groucho Marx on CBS and NBC counter-offered a different time slot: Thursday at 9:30 p.m.

In late June, *Billboard* reported: "It appears now that Ed Gardner and *Duffy's Tavern* will wind up on CBS next fall under the sponsorship of Blatz Beer. After a long discussion period, attorneys for the sponsor and the William Morris Agency, which represents Gardner, will look over the first draft of the contract." NBC won out, though, by offering Gardner a more promising contract, as detailed in a prior chapter of this book. The sponsorship arrangement was no different than any other in the broadcasting industry except for one unusual feature: it called for a straight 52 weeks of airing, without the traditional summer hiatus. The sponsor also signed up for the television rights to the show, but never planned to put the program on the viewing tube. The sponsor was charged according to the number of radio stations and billed once a month for a set price per station. Quoting F.M. Greene in his telegram: "Probably reference has been made about stations which will not accept beer at an early period and might have to debate it at some period after 9:30, but this is an individual station problem which must be checked with each station."

Almost the entire NBC network was scheduled to air *Duffy's Tavern* under the terms of the contract, a network of 163 stations. For every station that did not air the program on any given week, a credit was reflected on the bill. On August 12, the sponsor, having reviewed the list of stations and territories, requested the cancellation of *Duffy's Tavern* over station KSD in St. Louis, Missouri. The reason for the cancellation was that Blatz had no distribution in St. Louis. The local affiliate found another program to air during that time slot. In September, station KGW in Portland, Oregon, found it necessary to tape the broadcast and air it at a later time slot. Initially, the Oregon State Liquor Law prohibited advertising alcoholic beverages on radio and television before a set time, limiting the exposure of alcoholic beverages to a juvenile audience. The cost of recording each broadcast was $10 and NBC, for a time, debated with Blatz over who should pay the recording charge. Ultimately, the Oregon state law was amended and the station withdrew its request for a later time period.

It was during the same month that an exchange of correspondence occurred between Senator Johnson, who was Chairman of the Senate Interstate Commerce Committee, and the FCC, on the subject of liquor advertising by radio. The Senator wrote to the Commission and to the Alcoholic Tax Unit of the

Treasury Department strongly expressing his views against liquor advertising. The Commission replied saying that its authority over liquor advertising was limited to consideration of a licensee's overall program service at the time of application for a renewal. The Commission's letter also said that the carrying of liquor advertising by stations located in states where either the sale or advertising of liquor was prohibited would be contrary to the public interest; that as to other states programs containing liquor advertising raise the same problems as any program directed toward a limited audience; that the advertising of liquor by radio may raise serious social, economic and political issues in a community and thereby impose an obligation upon a licensee to make comparable facilities available to individuals or groups desiring to promote temperance; and that the Commission was fully cognizant of the seriousness of the matter and would exercise whatever authority it could.

The October 1949 issue of *Sponsor* reported that WGY, General Electric's radio station in Schenectady, reversed the long-standing policy against taking beer and wine advertising, to enable listeners to receive such programs as Blatz's *Duffy's Tavern* and Pabst's *Life of Riley*. This appeared to be a little bright ray of sunshine for both the sponsor and the network, but it was short-lived.

The issue in Oregon resulted in more ulcers for NBC throughout the winter and spring. Efforts had been made to trim the commercials in such a way that they would get by the Liquor Control Board. Unfortunately, the "as broadcast" scripts which KGW was forced to deliver which contained the mutilation of the commercials made executives at Blatz Beer feel the broadcasts were worthless from a selling point of view. In the spring, the Oregon State Liquor Law attempted to prevent Blatz from advertising via radio as long as Blatz continued to have its product endorsed by prominent public people. KGW was then warned by the Liquor Commission and the station manager forwarded the ever-growing problem to the network in both Hollywood and New York. The situation culminated in Jack B. Peters of the advertising agency, Kastor, Farrell, Chesley & Clifford, writing a letter to an executive at NBC on May 10, 1950. "We regret very much that the National Broadcasting Company and the station have been unable to convince the Liquor Control authorities in Oregon that this was national advertising originating outside the state and should not be subject to their local rules. The fact remains, however, that we are getting a broadcast that is of no value to us and we are therefore forced to ask you to cancel the *Duffy's Tavern* program on station KGW in Portland and station KMED in Medford, Oregon."

Left to Right: Larry Rhine, Hazel Shermet, Ed Gardner, Charles Cantor and Eddie Green.

The same letter from Peters also suggested a larger problem for the network. "While the dropping of Portland and Medford would not cause us to lose the full network discount at this time, we feel that these stations should be classed in the same category as Nashville, Raleigh and the others that do not accept beer sponsored programs as far as allowing us credit in the event that the full network discount should ever be placed in jeopardy by some unforeseen circumstances." The network attempted to penalize the sponsor, under a pre-cancellation clause in the contract, for every week the program was not broadcast on affiliates that the network felt was beyond their control. The network consulted both stations and it was eventually resolved to cancel the program over KGW without any penalty to the sponsor. KMED, however, was never cited for not living up to the letter of the law and the sponsor asked the network for an exemption. An inter-office memo at NBC, dated May 29, mentioned Blatz's disappointment in being contractually obligated to pay for two weeks worth of advertising on a station in Oregon that, they felt, should not be paid because of the unusual situation.

In early November 1949, KCMO began broadcasting *Duffy's Tavern*. The reason the station did not feature the program in September was because AT&T was unable to repair a test board that would allow a connection to the station. Blatz wanted sponsorship in the Kansas City area but NBC officials advised they could not guarantee such a feed and that it was the advertising agency's responsibility for said arrangements. The program was heard over KCMO beginning November 10. The program was recorded through the feed and broadcast at a later time.

Effective December 14, WIS stopped carrying the recorded beer cut-in announcement at the end of the *Duffy's Tavern* program. In place of the announcement, the station chose to run a public service message. When Blatz executives discovered this, they again expressed displeasure to the network.

Season Ten

The 1949-50 season marked the beginning of the first radio season when NBC and CBS were not standing fast against the broadcasting of recorded or transcribed programs. The primary step in junking the old policy, which demanded that all programs go on live, was when NBC and CBS joined the two other national networks — ABC and MBS, which never did prohibit recorded programs — in permitting transcribed broadcasts. The most resounding cheer for recorded shows came from the radio stars themselves who were happy for the more leisurely schedule under which they could work, and who felt that recordings made for a better show. Eddie Cantor was quoted as saying, "All shows should be recorded because you get a better performance." What Cantor meant was that taped programs like his, recorded ahead of time, could run for a full hour before a studio audience, then be edited down to a well-paced thirty minutes, leaving only the best portions for air presentation.

The gradual lowering of the ban against transcribed programs had been touched off to a great extent by Bing Crosby. In 1946, the singer ended his contract with *Kraft Music Hall*, a live show, and took leave of radio. Because he was making money which could be spent only with the Internal Revenue Bureau, Crosby refused to be shackled to a rigid radio schedule which bound him to a live performance week after week. Later, however, he was sold on the idea of doing a tape recorded show which allowed him a flexible schedule. He could record several programs ahead of time and then take a vacation. The Crosby case, which precipitated envy amongst other entertainers confined to a rigid schedule, was watched with keen interest by the whole industry. When the show went on the air via ABC, after NBC refused to accept a recorded program, it was announced to listeners as being "transcribed in Hollywood." That kind of announcement seemed to carry enough zing to make the listeners feel fortunate instead of asking questions. Most of them never realized they were hearing a show which, in some cases, had been transcribed six weeks earlier.

While the stars of radio were much in favor of taping their shows, certain industry executives viewed the trend as what one termed "a psychological hazard." It was generally agreed that the average listener was unaware of any difference in tonal quality between a live and recorded broadcast but, according to the NBC

Charles Cantor in Puerto Rico. Unused photo for Life *magazine.*

research department, some listeners felt cheated when they heard the announcement, "This is a transcribed broadcast."

Several sponsors also leaned toward this same theory. Lever Brothers Company sought an arbitration board when it disagreed with Bob Hope over whether his contract allowed him to record his program, which the comedian wanted to do. Lever won out and Hope, unlike his pal Bing, still punched a time clock. It was reported that one reason certain sponsors refrained from recorded shows was because this would not allow the luxury of making changes in their advertising copy at the last minute.

Since a rule of the Federal Communications Commission required transcriptions to be identified at the beginning and end of each program, NBC was experimenting with words to abide by the regulation without emphasizing the fact to the listener.

The idea was to bury the tag "transcribed" among the sparkling verbiage of a slick talking announcer. Whatever the pros and cons of tape recording, such a method sometimes prevented red faces on occasions when a live show opened the door to the unexpected. Ralph Edwards, when transcribing an episode of *This is Your Life*, found this out the hard way. When the taxi driver whose life was being unfolded that night was offered a Philip Morris cigarette, which sponsored the show, he commented: "Oh, no. I always smoke Camels."

In view of Bing Crosby taking over the Wednesday time slot for Chesterfield on CBS, Gardner's program was moved to a later time slot. Soon after, when CBS announced a new time slot for Crosby, 9:30 p.m., NBC moved the program from Wednesday to Thursday, figuring *Duffy* would be happier bucking less formidable opposition.

With a new sponsor came new authority regarding program content. In late July, a plan was made to add several new characters to the show... all of whom would provide a semi-subtle advertising gambit à la product placement. Among those slated to become regular habitués of the tavern was a Sir John Schenley, a Mr. I.W. Harper and a James Pepper, all these being trade names of products turned out by Schenley Distillers. Executives of the bankroller were reported trying to figure out a character named Blatz who could be worked into the proceedings but their suggestions were promptly rejected by Ed Gardner. Under contract, Gardner had final approval of script content. Gardner did approve the use of commercials as a tie-in with the storyline and for a time the programs signed off with the "Quartette" composed of Archie, Eddie, Miss Duffy and Finnegan doing the "Milwaukee Chant." Inter-office memos and telegrams dated August 9, 1949, reveal NBC's offense to on-air promotion, especially considering said product placement constituted an endorsement from a celebrity. Gardner ignored the network and in every broadcast, Archie's opening catch phrase when answering the phone also incorporated a mention of Blatz Beer. When Clancy showed up at the tavern, Archie offered him a Blatz Beer. In every episode, Archie and Eddie talked briefly about Blatz Beer being served in Duffy's

Tavern, a deliberate commercial with celebrity endorsement. As featured in the premiere broadcast of September 29, 1949:

ARCHIE: Let's start by havin' a beer. Incidentally, Eddie, y'know this year we're servin' none other than Blatz.
EDDIE: My, my — Blatz beer!
ARCHIE: Yes sir, this summer I didn't just waste me time fritterin' it. I went out and checked up on all the guys I know that ever lived in Milwaukee — that's the nation's capital for premium beer, y'know — and the consensusness of opinion of guys that lived there is that Blatz is Milwaukee's finest beer. So I made a deal with the Blatz people.

For the October 6, 1949, broadcast, Archie remarked: "Belt me with a Blatz. Finnegan, when one is talking about a high class beer, I think one could find a more couth way of expressing oneself. Okay, Eddie. Belt me with a Blatz."

The biting sarcasm of prophets who protested that such product placement influenced a younger generation into a life of sin received as much attention as Ed Gardner and his move to Puerto Rico. Statistically, after a review of the radio scripts, one journalist debated that tavern food served from the kitchen to a customer was referenced twenty-one times more than the words "beer" or "wine" uttered from the lips of Archie. (The journalist was mistaken. The statistic should have read the other way.)

Regarding new characters, faithful listeners did notice a new persona that appeared from time to time: Archie's "Uncle Fenwick" who, a garbage collector by occupation, somehow managed (repeatedly) to get money from Archie through enchanting stories that he told about the African diamond mines and other vast projects that tempted Archie into making "investments."

F. Chase Taylor, the first celebrity to waltz through the doors or grace through the doors of Duffy's Tavern almost a decade prior, appeared in multiple episodes during the Blatz sponsorship. Once in character as Col. Lemuel Q. Stoopnagle, then in multiple supporting roles including that of Clancy the Cop.

511

Gloria Erlanger

The New Miss Duffy

Relocation to the islands necessitated taking along Charles Cantor and Eddie Green to continue their roles as Finnegan and Eddie. Florence Halop, upon learning of the move, informed Ed Gardner that her roots were planted firmly in American soil. This forced Gardner to find yet another new Miss Duffy. By 1949, Gardner's reputation for firing and hiring women for the role was well-established among casting circles. With the new series (so-to-speak) came a new Miss Duffy discovery that could be considered a Cinderella-like event. Nineteen-year-old Gloria Erlanger of New York burst into a movie producer's office unannounced while Gardner was in conference with the producer, wanting to know about a screen test she had taken. Gardner, who was planning auditions for a new Miss Duffy, was fascinated with the girl's high-pitched, giggly voice. He broke off the conference, took the girl to an audition studio, and she won the job.

Billboard reviewed the season premiere in their October 15, 1949, issue: "Three innovations mark the return to the air of *Duffy's Tavern*: a new sponsor, a new Miss Duffy and a new point of origin (Puerto Rico). The first seems to have latched on to a natural, in terms of working its plugs into the show; Miss Erlanger still sounds strange to ears accustomed to the more strident deliveries of Florence Halop and Shirley Booth, but acquitted herself well; and the value of the island dependency as an originating point still is to be settled. The show caught was pretty much in the old *Duffy's* groove... The show, taped in Puerto Rico, came thru with little perceptible difference in sound quality from the local variety of transcribed airers. The bankroller, however, is reported not completely pleased with results so far. As long as the quality of material retains the level shown on this episode, however, there is little doubt that *Duffy's* will remain a popular favorite."

The *Los Angeles Times* reviewed: "Its rugged individualism still unsullied by the Puerto Rico point of origin, *Duffy's Tavern* is still *Duffy's* with Archie (Ed Gardner), unparalleled master of the malaprop, Miss Duffy's nasal-pure Brooklynese and the rest of the 'elete' character line-up intact."

Miss Duffy, however, had no desire for fresh air, swimming or fishing on the islands. After eight consecutive episodes, Gloria Erlanger packed her bags and flew back to the States. She never did succeed with a career in Hollywood and eventually settled down as a housewife. Pauline Drake, on the other hand, had a minor contribution to Hollywood as Mrs. Kennedy in a number of Edgar Kennedy film shorts and unbilled roles as a secretary, receptionist, telephone and switchboard operator in more than four dozen Hollywood motion pictures. Drake's ability to adapt to the island and an on-again, off-again production schedule was more tolerant. She lasted 14 episodes before returning to the States. Replacing Pauline Drake was Hazel Shermet, a graduate of Carnegie Tech Drama School, who would ultimately become the final aspirant to the role of Miss Duffy.

"I took a girlfriend of mine with me," Hazel Shermet later

recalled. "She said, 'Look, just pack enough clothes for two weeks. I hear he fires everyone.' I did my first show there with Paulette Goddard. After the show he [Gardner] carried me around the stage on his shoulders. I was down there for three seasons. Then I later came back to do some scenes from Duffy's on *Monitor*."

Shermet's continued appearances as "radio's dizziest dame" meant that she had won the approval of Ed Gardner, a notoriously tough critic. She had timing and vocal intonation which was not strongly evident with Erlanger and Drake. She had, before moving to Puerto Rico, appeared with many other top comedians on radio, including Jack "Baron Munchausen" Pearl, Maxie Rosenbloom, Goodman Ace and Arthur Godfrey, and was already a veteran television performer. An attractive young woman who wrote for a hobby, she was unmarried and always willing to let it be known that she was an excellent cook, specializing in "mad dishes" of her own inventions.

"I started in radio when I was seven years old in Philadelphia on WIP doing fairy stories," Shermet recalled. After college, she obtained a job writing commercials for an advertising agency. "I would write them and record them and do all of the parts because I was really writing them more or less for myself. But they would hire somebody else because I was a writer." She considered herself an actress and convinced a director at NBC to arrange an audition for her. "I took the audition and the next day I did *The Henny Youngman Show*, which was a real thrill. The next week I sang in *The Milton Berle Show*. He held my hand. If you've ever worked with Milton, you know you can't lose him. I was trying to sing opera and he was holding my hand."

Shermet had a short-lived career as a writer for *Duffy's Tavern*. Gardner, after hearing her ad-lib jokes during rehearsals, asked her to join the writing staff. For additional pay, she was expected to add jokes during a "pitching" session. Instead, she found the writers in unified silence as they tried to think of situations for the program. Her future husband, Larry Rhine, also a scriptwriter for the series, sent her to another room with a typewriter and paper, with orders to write a Miss Duffy spot. "I sat for two hours," she recalled. "I just wrote 'Duffy's Tavern' at the top of the page. For two or two and one-half hours I sat there. Then I came out and said, 'It's been a wonderful career. I'm going swimming.'"

Months after Shermet's relocation to Puerto Rico, Boxer "Slapsie" Maxie Rosenbloom made not one, but two guest appearances on *Duffy's Tavern*. Shermet had worked with Rosenbloom before when she appeared on his radio program, *The Slapsie Maxie Show*, from September 8 to 29, 1948. The reunion of old friends culminated with a wedding. "I study people," the fighter told writer Larry Rhine. "Gardner is afraid he's going to have to take me out to dinner and pay. Joe (another writer) is a bit of an alcoholic. He can't wait to get out to the bar. And you and Miss Duffy are auditioning – so why don't you get married?" As it turned out, Rosenbloom's instincts were accurate. In New York on May 5, 1951, Hazel Shermet married the head writer on the program, Larry Rhine.

Colonel Stoopnagle, RIP

In another cost-cutting measure, Ed Gardner began recycling scripts from prior broadcasts. Larry Rhine was instructed to review material and rewrite it for feasible scripts. References to war bonds and Hitler were replaced with modern-day con schemes and Russians. While Vincent Bogert, Al Johansen, and Phil Sharp had no involvement with these new versions, they were credited on the covers of each script. Faithful listeners may not have noticed the tavern's relocation based on the production, but it is possible they recognized recycled plot devices such as the frustrated efforts of Archie to attain social prominence, to become a Don Juan, finding a rare diary, trying to sell a fake Stradivarius, and to increase his weekly wage from the penurious sum given him by Duffy, the boss, who is never seen nor heard on the show but who is volubly represented by his daughter, to whom all men are fair game. Literary society meetings were again held at the Tavern. When a Hollywood celebrity made an appearance, such as Rudy Vallee or Boris Karloff, the same script they performed in the States years prior was reused almost verbatim. If radio listeners expected something fresh, the program now failed to deliver.

Somehow, radio critics never caught on. John Crosby, in the *

515

*At the studios in San Juan, with Gloria Swanson
and Colonel Stoopnagle.*

October 11, 1949, issue of the *New York Times*, remarked: "I was fearful Mr. Gardner's characters, a weird assemblage of humanity if ever there was one, might mellow under the Caribbean sun. They haven't, though. The denizens of Duffy's still resemble Third Avenue characters as much as they ever did."

Added to the cast of characters was Ed Gardner's good friend Frederick Chase Taylor, known to the radio world as Colonel Lemuel Q. Stoopnagle, comedian. Stoopnagle was the first guest to walk through the doors of *Duffy's Tavern* and not only did he guest now as Stoopnagle, he was heard every week in a number of supporting roles including Clancy the Cop. Beginning in January 1950, Chase began suffering from shortness of breath and dizziness. Preliminary diagnosis suggested heart failure. His last two contributions were recorded on March 21. He flew back to the United States on March 22. His appearances on *Duffy's Tavern* turned out to be his final contribution to the art of comedy.

In Boston, Massachusetts, on May 29, 1950, F. Chase Taylor died at the New England Baptist Hospital, two weeks after he was admitted for treatment of an internal ailment. He was 52. His obituary in many trade columns credited him for bringing a refreshing new brand of humor to radio in the early thirties when he teamed with announcer Budd Hulick as "Stoopnagle and Bud."

His final appearances on *Duffy's Tavern*, transcribed prior to his death, were broadcast over NBC earlier in the month.

Eddie Green

In October 1949, five weeks after moving to Puerto Rico, newspaper columnists were quick to dismiss the rumor going around Harlem that Eddie Green had died. An official at NBC, however, confessed that he was ill and on the serious list. Even before he left New York for Puerto Rico, Green looked pale and told reporters that the heavy press of work on him in Los Angeles had sapped some of his strength and caused him to give up several lucrative radio shows. Among these was the *Amos n' Andy* show, on which he played the slow-talking lawyer, Stonewall.

Eddie Green continued to play the role of Eddie the waiter until late March when, on the 21st of the month, while recording the next two episodes, Eddie was only able to complete the first episode. Nicodemus Stewart, best remembered in the recurring role as the Negro elevator boy where Alan Young lives on *The Alan Young Show* (exact dates February 1 to July 5, 1949), took over the role as Eddie, the waiter. After a clinical diagnosis, it was discovered that Green was suffering from a heart ailment no doubt brought on by the heat and humidity. He took the next available plane out of the country and returned to Los Angeles for a rest and relaxation. Stewart played the role for two additional episodes, the second of which, script title "Bobby Capo," would never air over NBC.

Juano Hernandez, who was Puerto Rican and resided in Puerto Rico, was among the replacements for Eddie. Moreland, best known as Birmingham Brown in the Charlie Chan film series, flew down to Puerto Rico to play the role of Eddie for almost a dozen episodes. (Green and Moreland worked together on the set of *Mantan Messes Up* in 1946, shortly after the completion of the *Duffy's Tavern* movie.) Whether Gardner did not want to go to the expense of replacing Eddie with actors from the States, or whether he felt Green was best suited for the role, remains inconclusive. Whatever the reason, observant listeners probably noticed how the character of Eddie the waiter was no longer on the program. No explanation on the radio programs was provided for his absence. Eddie Green died on September 19, 1950.

On March 13, 1950, a suit was filed to enjoin the Parnell Company of Cincinnati, Ohio, from using the name "Duffy's Tavern California Sherry" on their whiskies and gin. The suit was filed in Federal Court in Cincinnati by the Bank of America National Trust and Savings Association of California. The bank said it was the trustee for the right to use the name, representing Ed Gardner. It said it had an exclusive agreement to allow Schenley Industries, Inc. the right to use the name for radio and television purposes.

The lawsuit didn't end there. On July 18, 1952, the damage suit, charging infringement of the radio program name by a liquor concern, was dismissed by Federal Judge John H. Druffel on application of the plaintiff. The Parnell Company in Cincinnati sued Schenley Industries, Inc., for $150,000, charging Schenley had used "Duffy's Tavern" as a trade name for a whisky after it had been popularized by a radio program.

Season Ten
September 29, 1949, to September 21, 1950
National Broadcasting Company
Day and Time: Thursday, 9:30 to 10:00 p.m., EST
Complete season originates from Puerto Rico
Sponsored by Schenley Distillers
Advertising Agency: Kastor, Farrell, Chesley & Clifford
Producer/Director for the Network: John Cleary
Sound Engineer: Dudley Connolly
Sound: Kay Taylor (September 29, 1949, to May 18, 1950)
Sound: Joseph Loughery (May 25, 1950)
Sound: Kay Taylor (June 1, 1950)
Sound: Joseph Loughery (June 8, 1950, to September 21, 1950)

Musical Director: César Concepción
(all dates except March 23 to April 27, 1950)
Musical Director: Penya subs for vacationing Concepción
(March 23 to April 27, 1950)
Scriptwriters: Vincent Bogert, Al Johansen, Larry Rhine
and Phil Sharp.

Cast
Charlie Cantor as Finnegan
Gloria Erlanger as Miss Duffy
(September 29, 1949, to November 17, 1949)
Pauline Drake as Miss Duffy
(November 24, 1949, to December 15, 1949)
Florence Halop as Miss Duffy
(via recording from 1948; December 22, 1949)
Pauline Drake as Miss Duffy
(December 29, 1949, to March 2, 1950)*
Hazel Shermet as Miss Duffy
(March 9, 1950, to September 21, 1950)
F. Chase Taylor as Clancy the Cop and other characters
(individually listed)
Anthony Stanford as Clancy the Cop (July 13 and 27, 1950)
John Kane as Clancy the Cop
(August 31 to September 21, 1950)

Eddie Green as Eddie (September 29, 1949, to May 4, 1950)
Hamtree Harrington as Eddie
(October 13, 1949, to November 3, 1949, November 17, 1949)
Juano Hernandez (May 11 and September 7 to 21, 1950)
Nick O'Demus, a.k.a. Nicodemus Stewart as Eddie
(May 18 and June 1, 1950)
Mantan Moreland as Eddie (June 22 to August 31, 1950)

All other actors and known roles are listed under the respective
episodes.

---

* The Miss Duffy character was not featured in the broadcast of
February 23, 1950.

Episode #330 — Broadcast Thursday, September 29, 1949
Taped on September 22, 1949.
Script Title: "UNCLE FENWICK AND THE URANIUM MINE"
Supporting cast: F. Chase Taylor (Uncle Rufus T. Fenwick)
Plot: When the Acme Finance Department comes around looking for Archie, who failed to make his payments, he tries to borrow ten bucks from his friends to make good on his debt. When Archie's Uncle Fenwick stops by the tavern, only Eddie can see past the phony who plans to sell Archie fake stock in an African Uranium mine. Only after he signs the contract does Archie discover he co-signed on a $500 loan for his Uncle… and reads the contract when he answers the phone to tell the Acme Finance Department what he thinks of them.

Memorable Lines
FINNEGAN: What's this Uranium, Arch?
ARCHIE: Uranium? It's what we call in scientific circles as P.U. 235. They use it for atom bombs.
FINNEGAN: Oh. How do they get it, Arch?
ARCHIE: Well, y'see first they make a great big hole in the ground…
FINNEGAN: Yeah.
ARCHIE: Then they take the Uranium out of the hole and they send it to Oak Ridge and chop it into little atoms. Then they stuff these atoms into a bomb and drop it out of an airplane.
FINNEGAN: What for?
ARCHIE: To make a big hole in the ground.
FINNEGAN: But Arch, why do they do all that?
ARCHIE: Progress.

Episode #331 — Broadcast Thursday, October 6, 1949
Taped on September 22, 1949.
Script Title: "RIVER RATS GANG"

The character of Eddie did not appear in the broadcasts of April 13, 20, 27, May 11, 18, 25, and June 8 and 15, 1950.

Supporting cast: Juano Hernandez (McGurk), F. Chase Taylor (the tough guy) and Douglas Warner (the kid)
Plot: When the River Rats Gang, hired by a rival tavern, sends a telegram to Archie threatening hostile action if Duffy's Tavern doesn't close shop, Archie panics. Knuckles McGurk shows up to shoot Archie, but discovering they are old school chums, forgets the whole thing. When a tough guy arrives, hoping the third attempt will succeed in closing Duffy's, Finnegan pretends to be Dopey the Dip and threatens to kill the tough guy with an empty gun.

Trivia, etc. This script was recycled from the broadcast of March 19, 1947.

Episode #332 — Broadcast Thursday, October 13, 1949
Taped on October 6, 1949.
Guest: Colonel Stoopnagle
Plot: Because the tavern hasn't shown a profit in ten years, Archie forms Duffy's Tavern, Incorporated, and hosts the first business meeting of the board of directors. Colonel Stoopnagle suggests the tavern get a better cook. To help with tavern expenses, the Colonel introduces a money-making machine, proposing they turn the tavern into a gas station and add a few floors (fourteen to be exact). Stoopnagle is quickly accepted as an "efficiency expert."

Trivia, etc. Much of the banter exchanged between Colonel Stoopnagle and the gang was reprinted and restaged from the broadcast of March 7, 1944.

Episode #333 — Broadcast Thursday, October 20, 1949
Taped on October 6, 1949.
Script Title: "LOLITA"
Supporting cast: Marta Rodil (Lolita) and F. Chase Taylor (Clancy the Cop)
Plot: Archie intends to hire a girl for the Tavern who can sing. She's from a Latin country and Archie decides to throw into the script one Blatz joke too many to ensure that the girl feels at home. The girl shows up, believing Archie is an honest man, and intends

521

on marrying him. He brushes her off till she gives him a goodbye kiss, then changes his mind because of the way she kisses — but it is too late, she has left.

Trivia, etc. When local actors and actresses like Marta Rodil appeared on the program, under union regulations, a permit fee was required. NBC paid the fee.

Episode #334 — Broadcast Thursday, October 27, 1949
Taped on October 20, 1949.
Script Title: "THE LANDLORD AND THE NEW LEASE"
Supporting cast: F. Chase Taylor (Chisley)
Plot: Duffy's is being evicted by the landlord, Chisley, because the rent on the place has not been paid in full. Archie failed to read the fine print of the contract so he meets Chisley personally. Archie explains the rent is too high under the conditions the building is in. He claims it should be condemned and Finnegan appears as a building inspector to eliminate the problem.

Trivia, etc. The name of Chisley, the man who charges Duffy rent for the plot of ground where the Tavern resides, was originally Grimsby in the first draft of the script.

Episode #335 — Broadcast Thursday, November 3, 1949
Taped on October 20, 1949.
Script Title: "MRS. PIDDLETON AND THE POET PLUMBER"
Supporting cast: Catherine Randolph (Mrs. Piddleton) and F. Chase Taylor (the plumber)
Plot: Mrs. Piddleton and the Lord Byron Ladies' Literary Society, whom Archie refers to as "culture-vultures," are planning to have a meeting at the tavern. Having read Edgar Allen Poe's *The Raven*, Archie wrote to the publishing company to invite the author down to lecture. Finnegan must pose as Poe himself and attempt to recite the poem, referring to the sponsor instead: "We sat at home, drinking Blatz Beery." Meanwhile, the plumber comes by to fix a leak and Archie tricks him into reciting his own poem, "The Sonnet of a Lead Pipe."

Trivia, etc. The November 12, 1949, issue of *The Los Angeles Times* featured a review of this broadcast: "Last Thursday's show moved fast with some sharp lines and smoothly integrated commercials for Blatz Beer. Relying on incongruity for most of its laughs, the script had Archie wrestling with the Muse. He'd promised to find a poet to lecture a group of fem patrons but his bid for Edgar Allen Poe's services was rejected. Archie finally tagged a mad number and, in the process, tangled with a variety of garbled quotations, parodies and puns, i.e. 'Do you know Poe's Raven?'... 'I didn't even know he was dead.'"

Episode #336 — Broadcast Thursday, November 10, 1949
Taped on November 3, 1949.
Supporting Cast: F. Chase Taylor (Uncle Fenwick)
Guest: Cornel Wilde
Plot: Cornel Wilde is supposed to stop by and Miss Duffy admits that her girls club voted him "the one we'd most like to stand next to in a crowded subway." Archie's Uncle Fenwick also shows up and Archie, remembering how he was swindled with the fake mine a few weeks back, keeps his attention turned toward Wilde. Archie comments how much he admires the actor because when Wilde whistles, he gets dames — when Archie whistles, he gets taxis. The actor meets the usual cast of characters and, before he leaves, Archie attempts to make the place as busy as a beehive, only to discover that his Uncle paid for beer with counterfeit currency.

Episode #337 — Broadcast Thursday, November 17, 1949
Taped on November 3, 1949.
Script Title: "MARGO, THE MYSTIC"
Guest: Pauline Drake (Margo)
Plot: Archie met Margo the Mystic, a fortune teller, at a party over at Bullethead Brannigan's and Archie figures to lure her to Duffy's Tavern. As Archie theorizes, she could tip them off when the Health Inspector plans to come down. After receiving a letter stating his uncle passed away and he inherited all of his uncle's wealth, Archie quits his job. Problem is, Archie isn't sure which uncle because they passed away before signing the letter. Margo arrives and conducts a séance in the dark, hoping to communicate

DUFFY'S TAVERN: A HISTORY OF ED GARDNER'S RADIO PROGRAM

with the dead man. Finnegan pretends to be the late relative and when Archie discovers the ruse and turns the lights back on, Margo has vanished and the cash register is empty.

Episode #338 — Broadcast Thursday, November 24, 1949
Taped on November 10, 1949.
Script Title: "THE THANKSGIVING TURKEY AND THE TERRIBLE TURK"
Supporting Cast: F. Chase Taylor (Clancy the Cop, the chef and the radio announcer)
Plot: Archie is throwing a big Thanksgiving dinner at the tavern tonight and attempts to get a small turkey to feed 27 people. Finnegan sets out to find one large enough and he does - 150 pounds and from the zoo. Only this turkey has four legs and isn't a turkey! Archie learns how to cook a duck but messes it up 'til Duffy sends one already prepared as a thanksgiving gift.

Trivia, etc. The sketch with the turkey being prepared courtesy of the chef on the radio was restaged from the broadcast of November 26, 1947.

Memorable Lines
ARCHIE: Did you find the turkey?
FINNEGAN: Yep.
ARCHIE: Where?
FINNEGAN: At the zoo.

Episode #339 — Broadcast Thursday, December 1, 1949
Taped on November 10, 1949.
Guest: Basil Rathbone
Plot: Since Basil Rathbone appears, Archie gets him to play a lead in "The Purple Scorpion," an old radio play he adapted for television. Archie plays Doctor Simpson, the smart one, and Rathbone plays the title character, an English detective. They set out to find who the murderer of a dead corpse is, only to discover after hilarious complications that the master of ceremonies was not shot at all - he swallowed poison.

Episode #340 — Broadcast Thursday, December 8, 1949
Taped on November 17, 1949.
Supporting cast: F. Chase Taylor (Uncle Fenwick)
Guest: Helen Traubel
Plot: Archie finished writing a new song, "The Rajah of Blue-koo" and hopes to convince Helen Traubel to sing it. In an effort to impress the Metropolitan Opera star, Archie claims he's a fan of opera and fakes a letter from Caruso, spelled with a K. After Traubel sings "He's Goin' Away," Archie strikes a deal. With the understanding that the Metropolitan is seeking donations and funds to fix a deficit, Archie will donate his time and services to help raise money in return for her singing his song. Naturally, the sponsor, Blatz, is incorporated into the lyrics. With assistance of Uncle Fenwick, Archie arranges for a three million dollar check (a forgery) to be handed to Traubel.

Trivia, etc. This episode was a basic rewrite of the broadcast of January 18, 1944, which had Lauritz Melchior as the guest.

Episode #341 — Broadcast Thursday, December 15, 1949
Taped on November 17, 1949.
Script Title: "PRE-CHRISTMAS SHOW — A CHRISTMAS CAROL"
Supporting cast: F. Chase Taylor (Clancy the Cop)
Plot: Eddie and Archie are so broke they exchange imaginary Christmas presents. Miss Duffy complains about not finding a present for her boyfriend and men getting fresh in the crowded store elevators. Hoping to spread a little holiday spirit, Archie re-writes Dickens' *A Christmas Carol* and the entire cast acts out the roles, with Archie as Scrooge. Finnegan plays Tiny Tim, who is so hungry he wishes he was dead. Eddie and Miss Duffy play the roles of Mr. and Mrs. Scratchett. After seeing the errors of his ways, Scrooge gives the family fifty thousand pounds and learns that it is better to give than to receive.

Trivia, etc. This episode features music from the chorus of the University of Puerto Rico.
The take-off of Charles Dickens' *Christmas Carol*, and a

number of jokes, including Eddie's Sonia Jones/Gabriel Heatter joke, were restaged from the December 21, 1945, broadcast.

Episode #342 — Broadcast Thursday, December 22, 1949
Cast: Same as December 22, 1948.

Trivia, etc. The annual holiday offering, unlike the past three years, was not a new rendition. Ed Gardner requested permission from the American Federation of Radio Artists to re-broadcast a recording of the *Duffy's Tavern* Christmas episode from December 22, 1948, and AFRA agreed under one strict condition. It would be necessary to pay all performers who appeared on that program "a fee at least equal to that paid for their original appearance." In order to facilitate matters for Gardner, AFRA informed him that he could send checks for the choral singers and other performers who were not presently in Puerto Rico, so they could make the proper distribution. They also advised Gardner to contact AFM direct since their rules and regulations might play a factor.

As a result of reusing the Christmas 1948 recording, this broadcast featured Florence Halop as Miss Duffy and Ken Peters as the announcer. The only difference between this episode and the 1948 version were the Blatz commercials, recorded on November 17, 1949.

Episode #343 — Broadcast Thursday, December 29, 1949
Taped on November 25, 1949.
Script Title: "ARCHIE'S NEW YEAR'S EVE DATE"
Supporting Cast: Marta Rodil (Lolita) and F. Chase Taylor (Clancy the Cop)
Plot: Archie gets out his little red book and starts calling women up for a date to the New Year's Eve ceremonies. After one woman is in a decompression chamber and another threatens to hang herself, Archie chooses Lolita, a Spanish girl.

Episode #344 — Broadcast Thursday, January 5, 1950
Taped on November 25, 1949.
Script Title: "ACCOUNTANT CHECKS ARCHIE'S BOOKS"
Supporting Cast: F. Chase Taylor (Brad Dunstreet)

Plot: When Duffy has a problem with the books, Archie takes on the task of being the CPA for Duffy but finds it no solution when Duffy himself sends an accountant to the tavern. To get the accountant out before he finds out something is wrong with the books, Archie gets Finnegan to pretend to be Miss Duffy's husband and accuse the accountant of cheating behind his back.

Memorable Lines
DUNSTREET: I am the accountant Mr. Duffy sent down.
ARCHIE: Oh - oh... Speak of the debit.
DUNSTREET: My name is Brad Dunstreet... CPA.
ARCHIE: Oh, a man of my own cloth.
DUNSTREET: What?
ARCHIE: I am also a Satisfied Public Accountant.

Episode #345 — Broadcast Thursday, January 12, 1950
Taped on December 8, 1949.
Supporting Cast: F. Chase Taylor (the radio announcer)
Guest: Don Ameche
Plot: To celebrate Duffy's anniversary, Archie puts on a party at the tavern. Duffy is forced to remain home due to the flu. Don Ameche delivers his rendition of "My Wild Irish Rose" and Duffy approves, hoping to make the actor an Irishman. Originally the script called for Ameche to deliver a brief speech to open the party but timing during rehearsals eliminated the speech. Except for the brief musical rendition, Ameche is relegated to standing around and exchanging one-liners with the cast. Finnegan cracks jokes about not seeing any motion pictures with Ameche in the cast since *The Story of Alexander Graham Bell* (1939), then refers to him as Paulette Goddard.

Memorable Line
ARCHIE: Yeah, that's the guy, Duffy. Always smiling and showing off them beautiful white teeth... Yeah, he's famous for 'em... y'know, like they call Frank Sinatra "The Voice" and Jimmy Durante "The Nose"....mmm... they call Don Ameche "The Choppers."

Episode #346 — Broadcast Thursday, January 19, 1950
Taped on December 10, 1949.
Supporting Cast: F. Chase Taylor (Clancy the Cop)
Guest: Gloria Swanson
Plot: Duffy makes an effort to visit the tavern and see Gloria Swanson when he discovers she used to be a Mack Sennett bathing beauty. Archie asks Eddie what they can do to make the tavern look a little more high class. Eddie suggests throwing out the customers. Archie brags that he knows Swanson personally and then asks her to cover for him to prove to Clancy that they really were having a brief romantic fling. She agrees to play along and Archie faints.

Trivia, etc. This script is a re-write of the October 9, 1941, broadcast, which also featured Gloria Swanson as the guest star.

Episode #347 — Broadcast Thursday, January 26, 1950
Taped on January 5, 1950.
Script Title: "FINNEGAN THE MILLIONAIRE"
Supporting Cast: F. Chase Taylor (Clancy the Cop)
Plot: Same plot as the broadcast of April 6, 1945, with a couple noticeable changes: interjection of Blatz beer in the script and the name of the book is "Priceless Pearls from the Pacific: A Collection of Poems by Byron Finnegan."

Episode #348 — Broadcast Thursday, February 2, 1950
Taped on December 15, 1949.
Supporting Cast: F. Chase Taylor (Clancy the Cop)
Guests: Jon Hall and Frances Langford
Plot: Duffy asks Archie to hire Frances Langford and Jon Hall to entertain at the annual Winter Skeet Shoot and Beefsteak of the Friendly Sons of Mother Machree. The couple agrees for a fee of $5,000 and Archie works his way up from $16. To audition and prove their worth, Hall and Langford perform "I Don't Know Why" and Duffy counter-offers. Seeing how they haven't been up in the mountains in a long time, the couple agree for only $6, provided they don't have to mingle with the guests.

25

Trivia, etc. Besides enjoying the beach and scenery, Frances Langford and Jon Hall spent time on Ed Gardner's boat. Langford had a strong passion for fishing and boating. (She and her second husband spent much of their time on their yacht and included the Florida Oceanographic Society among her charitable causes.)

Episode #349 — Broadcast Thursday, February 9, 1950
Taped on January 12, 1950.
Script Title: "PROFESSOR CRABTREE"
Supporting Cast: Martha Sleeper (Miss Farmsworth) and F. Chase Taylor (Professor Crabtree)
Plot: Same plot as the broadcast of October 13, 1942, with a couple of noticeable changes: interjection of Blatz beer in the script and the name of the society girl whom Archie would like to interest in matrimony has been changed to Penelope Farmsworth.

Episode #350 — Broadcast Thursday, February 16, 1950
Taped on January 12, 1950.
Script Title: "EDDIE GETS ENGAGED"
Supporting Cast: Juano Hernandez (Sam Jones) and F. Chase Taylor (Professor Crabtree)
Plot: When Sonia Jones asks Eddie to marry her and he declines, one-round Sonia breaks her umbrella over Eddie's cranium. Forced in a corner, Eddie finds himself engaged to marry the woman on Saturday. When Sam Jones, better known as "Muscles" Jones, visits the tavern to defend his sister, Eddie poses as a fake Swami (per instructions from Archie), and predicts a horrible future for Sonia... until Eddie and Archie discover that Muscles only came to prevent the marriage, not enforce it.

Episode #351 — Broadcast Thursday, February 23, 1950
Taped on January 20, 1950.
Script Title: "THE COLONEL WRITES A PLAY"
Guest: Colonel Stoopnagle
Plot: The Colonel sends a telegram to Archie. He found a wonderful television play in the pockets of an old straight jacket. When he arrives, he admits he tried writing Aesop's Fables, but his work never went anywhere. So the cast is assigned roles for a

drama entitled "Young Dr. Archie, Boy Intern" or "How to Take Out an Appendix."

Episode #352 — Broadcast Thursday, March 2, 1950
Taped on January 20, 1950.
Script Title: "ARCHIE GETS NEW JOB"
Plot: Archie is dissatisfied with no raise so he quits. Archie seeks a new position and decides to answer an ad for a restaurant manager wanted – "high class, refined, hard-working." Archie packs his bartender's manual and his one formal shirt but compassion wins over when Duffy calls back and Archie accepts the same offer as last year's salary.

Trivia, etc. This script was originally planned for broadcast the week before.

Episode #353 — Broadcast Thursday, March 9, 1950
Taped on February 1, 1950.
Supporting Cast: F. Chase Taylor (Mr. Brittlegap)
Guest: Paulette Goddard
Plot: Archie proposes marriage to actress Paulette Goddard, hoping stale jokes he stole from Bob Hope during a USO tour would impress the dame. Same plot as the broadcast of September 22, 1944, with a couple of noticeable changes: interjection of Blatz beer in the script and the name of the insurance agent has been changed to Mr. Brittlegap. A number of jokes from the June 8, 1945, script also creep into this broadcast. Archie describes Paulette Goddard to Duffy as having a face "that would launch a thousand ships and a figure that'll bring 'em right back to port again," a joke that was obviously influenced by WWII.

Episode #354 — Broadcast Thursday, March 16, 1950
Taped on February 1, 1950.
Script Title: "ST. PATRICK'S DAY SHOW"
Supporting Cast: F. Chase Taylor (Clancy the Cop)
Plot: The crew is rehearsing a pageant for the Annual St. Patrick's Day Pig Roast and Musical. Archie wrote it, obviously, and it tells the life story of Patrick Duffy and how his employer grew from

a tadpole to a cocoon, and almost kissed the Blarney Stone. The whole thing backfires as entertainment and Eddie is asked how he liked the play. "I'm not in a position to say," Eddie remarks. "Whattya mean?" asks Archie. "If I say, I won't have no position," Eddie comments. Duffy comments by phone and fires Archie.

Memorable Lines
FINNEGAN: How come the 17th of March always falls on St. Patrick's Day?
ARCHIE: Oh, I dunno... Maybe it's a coincidence.

Trivia, etc. Frank Tooke, program manager of radio station KYW in Philadelphia, sent a letter of complaint to NBC after someone complained about a joke in this episode. An official at NBC agreed that "some of these are overly sensitive," but explained that such criticism justified greater deference to the listener feelings. The NBC official was quick to point out that ABC had a similar experience on their television program, *Stop the Music*, which included a ballet number descriptive of an Irish "revel." Apparently the treatment was highly imaginative and graphic showing the goings on in an Irish saloon.

Episode #355 — Broadcast Thursday, March 23, 1950
Taped on February 3, 1950.
Script Title: "ARCHIE'S FARM IN THE BACK YARD"
Supporting Cast: F. Chase Taylor (Clancy the Cop)
Plot: Same plot as the broadcast of March 1, 1946, with a couple of noticeable changes: interjection of Blatz beer in the script and it was Duffy who sent the potted poison ivy plant to Archie, not Archie's nurse.

Episode #356 — Broadcast Thursday, March 30, 1950
Taped on February 3, 1950.
Supporting Cast: Martha Sleeper (Pamela Smythe) and F. Chase Taylor (the father)
Guest: Tony Martin
Plot: Same script from April 4, 1944.

Episode #357 — Broadcast Thursday, April 6, 1950
Taped on February 17, 1950.
Supporting Cast: F. Chase Taylor (Conolly)
Guest: Gypsy Rose Lee
Plot: Same script from April 6, 1949.

Trivia, etc. The character of Conolly, who appears in a number of consecutive episodes, may have been named after the sound engineer, Dudley Connolly.

Memorable Lines
ARCHIE: The way you talk you'd think this was just some ordinary dump.
GYPSY: On the contrary, I think it's very extraordinary.

Episode #358 — Broadcast Thursday, April 13, 1950
Taped on February 17, 1950.
Script Title: "MRS. PIDDLETON'S MUSICALE"
Supporting Cast: Martha Sleeper (Mrs. Piddelton)
Plot: Same script from April 14, 1942.

Trivia, etc. F. Chase Taylor was originally slated to play the role of Clancy the Cop, but due to timing, Clancy's scene was written out during rehearsals.

Episode #359 — Broadcast Thursday, April 20, 1950
Taped on February 24, 1950.
Script Title: "ARCHIE WANTS A DIPLOMA"
Supporting Cast: Martha Sleeper (J. Twiddle) and F. Chase Taylor (Clancy the Cop)
Plot: Archie wants to receive an honorary degree but Eddie insists he should be a CPA (Chicken Plucker's Assistant). After sending a letter of falsehood to the principal of the public school where he grew up, Archie receives a visit from J. Twiddle. Archie attempts to impress the principal of the school by dressing Finnegan up as a college professor to verify Archie's status as a scholar. Naturally, this attempt fails to impress and Twiddle agrees to hand Archie a

diploma if he comes back to school every day for six months. He doesn't have to study anything… they want to study Archie.

Episode #360 — Broadcast Thursday, April 27, 1950
Taped on February 24, 1950.
Script Title: "ARCHIE SUES DUFFY"
Supporting Cast: F. Chase Taylor (the lawyer named Loophole)
Plot: Same script from May 19, 1948.

Episode #361 — Broadcast Thursday, May 4, 1950
Taped on March 21, 1950.
Supporting Cast: F. Chase Taylor (Clancy the Cop)
Guest: Joan Davis
Plot: After seeing the success of Hopalong Cassidy, Archie writes his own western, with him and Joan Davis in the leads. She plays the part of a shootin' gal from the West, named Fanny Oakley. Archie plays Dangerous Dan McArchie, who killed four guys at the bank because that's all there was. Finnegan mimics the sound effects of horses' hooves and whinnies, as well as doubles for the sheriff. When the sheriff swears he smells a skunk, Oakley shoots her gun and opens another nostril for the sheriff to smell clean. McArchie loses when he draws against Oakley, opening the door for a hilarious death scene.

Trivia, etc. This episode was recycled from the broadcast of February 12, 1947, with Joan Davis playing the part Gene Autry did in the 1947 version.

Episode #362 — Broadcast Thursday, May 11, 1950
Taped on March 10, 1950.
Script Title: "ARCHIE'S SLOGAN CONTEST"
Supporting Cast: F. Chase Taylor (Clancy the Cop)
Plot: Same script from November 23, 1945.

Episode #363 — Broadcast Thursday, May 18, 1950
Taped on March 21, 1950.
Script Title: "ARCHIE THE PRIZEFIGHTER"
Supporting Cast: F. Chase Taylor (H-Bomb Hogan)

Plot: Same script from April 19, 1946. Instead of Finnegan fighting in the ring, Archie puts on the gloves as he goes up against H-Bomb Hogan.

Episode #364 — Broadcast Thursday, May 25, 1950
Taped on March 30, 1950.
Guest: Rudy Vallee
Plot: Same script from March 21, 1944, with Rudy Vallee delivering Fred Allen's lines.

Episode #365 — Broadcast Thursday, June 1, 1950
Taped on March 24, 1950.
Script Title: "ARCHIE THE DETECTIVE"
Plot: Same script from October 5, 1945.

Episode #366 — Broadcast Thursday, June 8, 1950
Taped on April 4, 1950.
Supporting Cast: Martha Sleeper (Miss Gwendolyn)
Guest: Ray Milland
Plot: Archie is dating a society woman named Miss Gwendolyn Van Schuyler, whose feathered friends are fan dancers. Archie polishes up his manners and romantic talk. He tries to keep Miss Duffy away from the likes of Ray Milland, while at the same time preventing Milland from seeing his new girlfriend (God forbid, Milland gets the wrong impression of Archie). Milland, after glancing at Miss Duffy, remarks, "This is one case where even the Russians wouldn't take over." When the fan dancer arrives, he tries to masquerade as a cab driver named Sam Schultz to help steer her away but his sophisticated charms and good looks cause Gwendolyn to fall in love with the actor. "What a bird brain," Archie remarks.

Memorable Lines
MILLAND: You've heard the expression 'build a better
   mouse trap'?
ARCHIE: Yes.
MILLAND: You've done it.

Episode #367 — Broadcast Thursday, June 15, 1950
Taped on April 27, 1950.
Script Title: "FATHER'S DAY"
Supporting Cast: Vilma Carbia (Chiquita Juarez)
Plot: Realizing he is missing out on being a father, never acknowledged on Father's Day, Archie decides to get married to Chiquita Juarez, a singer who tells Archie that her career is her only love. Finnegan poses as Archie's wealthy father in order to give Chiquita a better impression of Archie as a matrimonial prospect. When she catches a glimpse of Finnegan and does a double take, Archie remarks, "Well, don't forget, Chiquita, they don't make parents like they used to."

Episode #368 — Broadcast Thursday, June 22, 1950
Taped on April 21, 1950.
Guest: Hedda Hopper
Supporting Cast: Anthony Stanford (Clancy the Cop)
Plot: By order of Duffy, Archie is putting on another coming out party for Miss Duffy, who has had one every year for the last ten years. Eddie remarks that in groundhog circles it's now known as "Miss Duffy Day." Hedda Hopper accepts an invitation and when she calls Tyrone Power to ask how many pups his pedigree dog delivered, Archie mistakes the good news as human delivery. When he hears she delivered four, Archie remarks, "Well, that's Hollywood for you." When Hedda Hopper discovers only fifteen bucks is spent on the party, she starts racking up the bills for a thousand dollar party. When Clancy asks Archie who the crazy is that is responsible, he tricks Hedda Hopper into doing an impression of Napoleon and Clancy takes her in.

Episode #369 — Broadcast Thursday, June 29, 1950
Taped on April 29, 1950.
Script Title: "PRESS AGENT SHOW"
Supporting Cast: John Cleary (Nick) and Anthony Stanford (Uncle Fenwick)
Plot: Same script from June 1, 1945. Instead of Dave Hossinger creating the ludicrous idea of staging a murder in a gambling room, Archie's Uncle Fenwick does the job.

Episode #370 — Broadcast Thursday, July 6, 1950
Taped on May 6, 1950.
Script Title: "MRS. PIDDLETON — VIOLIN SHOW"
Supporting Cast: Catherine Randolph (Mrs. Piddleton) and Anthony Stanford (Heifetz)
Plot: Heifetz, the great violinist, convinces Archie to pass a "musical aptitude test," proving he's a musical genius. Heifetz tricks Archie into buying a fake Stradivarius. Then Archie tries to sell Mrs. Piddleton the violin, but the truth hurts when she discovers the ruse.

Trivia, etc. This script recycled material from the broadcast of May 5, 1942.

Episode #371 — Broadcast Thursday, July 13, 1950
Taped on May 6, 1950.
Script Title: "PANYASLOVNIK — VIOLIN SHOW"
Supporting Cast: Charles Cantor (Panyaslovnik) and Anthony Stanford (Clancy the Cop)
Plot: Miss Duffy answers the phone instead of Archie, who is still mad because a swindler sold him a fake violin the week before. Archie attempts to pawn the fiddle off to someone else, but no shop or store or respectable person is willing to fall for the same con. Meanwhile, Professor Panyaslovnik is attending the tavern and, after a few more musical depreciation jokes, he buys the fiddle in exchange for a bum check.

Trivia, etc. This script recycled a little material from the broadcast of May 12, 1942, and a lot of material from the broadcast of May 19, 1942.
Charles Cantor plays the role of Finnegan and of Panyaslovnik, the teacher of the man who, before every performance, sprays the throat of opera star Ezio Pinza.

Episode #372 — Broadcast Thursday, July 20, 1950
Taped on May 23, 1950.
Script Title: "ARCHIE'S TWO GIRLFRIENDS"

Supporting Cast: Vilma Carbia (Chiquita) and Martha Sleeper (Renee)
Plot: Archie is engaged to two women at the same time. Renee and Chiquita. Archie blames a split personality for putting himself in that position, so he juggles the game between the two women by finding out who wants to be the perfect housewife. When Renee kisses him on one cheek, and wants to know how he got a second on the other cheek, he comments, "Honey, your kisses are so hot, it burned right through to the other side."

Episode #373 — Broadcast Thursday, July 27, 1950
Taped on May 27, 1950.
Script Title: "NEWSPAPER SHOW"
Supporting Cast: John Kane (Scoop)
Plot: Same script from April 2, 1947.

Episode #374 — Broadcast Thursday, August 3, 1950
Taped on May 27, 1950.
Supporting Cast: John Kane (Clancy the Cop) and Martha Sleeper (Penelope, the society girl).
Script Title: "ARCHIE MEETS SOCIETY GIRL"
Plot: Same plot from February 9, 1950, which recycled material from October 13, 1942.

Episode #375 — Broadcast Thursday, August 10, 1950
Taped on June 3, 1950.
Script Title: "ARCHIE'S INSURANCE COMPANY"
Plot: Same script from January 21, 1948. Instead of Giuseppe Vermicelli as the customer, Panyaslovnik is the Russian client (doubled by Charles Cantor).

Episode #376 — Broadcast Thursday, August 17, 1950
Taped on June 3, 1950.
Script Title: "MISS DUFFY'S NEW BOYFRIEND"
Supporting Cast: John Kane (Homer) and Mary O'Neil (Bubbles, the girlfriend)
Plot: Same script from June 2, 1942.

Episode #377 — Broadcast Thursday, August 24, 1950
Taped on June 9, 1950.
Script Title: "ARCHIE'S WISDOM TOOTH"
Supporting Cast: John Kane (Konkle, the dentist)
Plot: Archie has a wisdom tooth that hurts and he needs to have it extracted. Dr. Konkle, a part-time horse dentist, appears at the tavern and since he promises his price and his cure are quick and painless, after a few frights, Archie is happy.

Episode #378 — Broadcast Thursday, August 31, 1950
Taped on June 9, 1950.
Script Title: "ARCHIE BETS ON WRESTLING MATCH"
Supporting Cast: Harwood Hull (the sports announcer) and John Kane (Dudoff and Clancy the Cop).
Plot: Customers went to a competing tavern because the television set at Duffy's is broken. Assets missing suggest Archie is a petty crook. Pretending to be Duffy, Archie calls the accountants to avoid an audit. To clear his name, Archie bets on a wrestling match but Finnegan cannot recall the name of the man Archie wants to bet on, "Killer Kapetansky."

Episode #379 — Broadcast Thursday, September 7, 1950
Taped on June 21, 1950.
Script Title: "ARCHIE BUYS AN AIRPLANE"
Supporting Cast: Charles Cantor (Slippery McGuire) and John Kane (Clancy the Cop)
Plot: Eddie and Miss Duffy suspect Slippery McGuire plans to pawn off a junky crate when Archie fancies himself a pilot and wants to buy an airplane. If a leopard can change his spots, it'll be stripes for McGuire, who claims he's selling war surplus on the black market. Slippery claims he's purchasing the surplus from Harry Truman, then sells Archie the plane piece by piece... the propeller will cost a dollar. Then there is the need to pay rent for the hangar. Only after Archie is handed a parachute and tire patches is he informed that Clancy is looking for McGuire.

Episode #380 — Broadcast Thursday, September 14, 1950
Taped on June 21, 1950.

Script Title: "PANYASLOVNIK PROPOSES TO MRS. PIDDLETON"
Supporting Cast: Charles Cantor (Panyaslovnik) and Catherine Randolph (Mrs. Piddleton)
Plot: Mrs. Piddleton and her group are coming to the tavern so Archie hires Yasha Dimitri Panyaslovnik to perform in the floor show that night. They rip a new band tune with woodwinds and violins. Panya says it's horrible. Instead, Panya and Miss Duffy sing "Dark Eyes" and the prince woos the woman into a marriage engagement — but he's already married!

Episode #381 — Broadcast Thursday, September 21, 1950
Taped on June 24, 1950.
Supporting Cast: Charles Cantor (Slippery McGuire) and John Kane (Clancy the Cop)
Guest: Barry Nelson
Plot: Slippery McGuire sells Archie a radio station for eighteen dollars. Archie plans to use the equipment and broadcast high-class programs and advertise quality products (like Blatz beer). When Barry Nelson arrives and briefly promotes *The Man With My Face*, Archie encourages the Hollywood actor to participate. The interview doesn't go very well as Barry barely gets a word in edgewise with constant commercials breaking in every minute. Miss Duffy sings "A Heart That's Free." Clancy walks in and threatens to fine Archie for broadcasting without a license, until McGuire saves Archie by saying the equipment doesn't work and Archie wasn't really broadcasting. Archie thanks the crook for cheating him out of eighteen dollars.

Trivia, etc. This script recycled most of the material from the broadcast of November 12, 1947.

Blatz Cancels

Under contract, Schenley was obligated to sponsor the program for two years. In July 1950, when the liquor company notified the network that they were going to option a cancellation clause (subject to average Hooper ratings for the 1949-50 season falling below the rating for the 1948-49 season), NBC contractually had to pay Gardner for another year of broadcasts. Gardner was contracted to produce 52 shows at $14,250 each, and seek a new sponsor to recoup the network's losses. Under the terms of the contract, Schenley had to pay a cancellation fee of $100,000 to NBC for not renewing a second season, a cost much less than if they continued to sponsor the program for the full 52 weeks. Under the terms of the contract, a loophole NBC apparently failed to notice, the $100,000 was to be paid to Gardner. One columnist in the *New York Times* reviewed these facts and remarked: "In the matter of money, Gardner is very, very sharp as well as very, very acquisitive." NBC realized they had no other choice but to reluctantly continue broadcasting *Duffy's Tavern*, regardless of sponsorship.

The show wasn't fetching the kind of ratings Schenley considered commensurate with the money they paid NBC. The notice that it was blitzing out on *Duffy's Tavern* sent Charles (Bud) Barry, NBC vice-president of programming, flying down to Puerto Rico in the same month, in an effort "to come to some understanding." The "understanding" involved cutting down the asking price for the package, with Barry asking Gardner to bring the program to a cheaper figure. The cost per program was between NBC and Ed Gardner. NBC in turn sold the program to a sponsor. It was the network's hope to convince Blatz to agree to another year if the price was lower. Schenley, in turn, agreed to reconsider and pick up the tab for another year. Ed Gardner would not budge on the price. Although there had been criticism in some quarters that the radio comedy wasn't what it used to be since Ed Gardner had been domiciling in Puerto Rico, the series was contracted to renew for one additional season, sponsored or sustained.

NBC was concerned, naturally, because in May 1950, rumors and unconfirmed reports had Schenley virtually set to drop *Duffy's Tavern* after the first 52 week schedule. The firm was said to be prepping entry into television in the fall, based on the results of the roller derby telecasts, which they were sponsoring. *Duffy's Tavern* was not going to be included in their future television ventures. The cancellation of sponsorship was not a bluff. As one newspaper delicately put it, the show was canceled at the end of its current cycle "because of the economic indefensibility of network radio production and time costs."

In August, Ed Gardner flew to the United States to meet with potential sponsors. But hand shaking and smooth talking was not strong enough to convince a company to commit to a 52-week schedule. And Gardner's move to Puerto Rico was looked at negatively in most trade columns. It remains possible that a few advertising agencies wanted to disassociate with *Duffy's Tavern*. By late September, NBC announced that the future of the situation comedy was pending, but "it is expected to become a part of a projected Sunday night 90-minute variety show." This would ultimately become Operation Tandem.

CHAPTER FIFTEEN
THE MAN WITH MY FACE
(1950)

IN JUNE AND JULY OF 1950, FULFILLING HIS obligation to President
Luis Munoz Martin and his cabinet, Gardner went into production
with his first (and only) full-length motion picture. The finished
product ended up being a smart, absorbing film noir titled *The Man
With My Face*, starring Barry Nelson. (Gardner's initial proposal in
January was to produce a series of low-budgeted Spanish films
for distribution in Spanish-speaking countries. Production was
scheduled for April, with a cast of Latin-American players.)

Samuel Taylor's novel was originally serialized in *Liberty*
magazine from February to July 1948. It would be published as a
novel by London Books later that year. According to an August
20, 1948, *Hollywood Reporter* news item, Thomas McGowan and
Ernest Wolfe acquired the screen rights to Taylor's story for an
independent production, but an April 11, 1950, issue of the same
stated that Jesse Smith Productions had also optioned the story. A
short time afterwards, Ed Gardner purchased the rights.

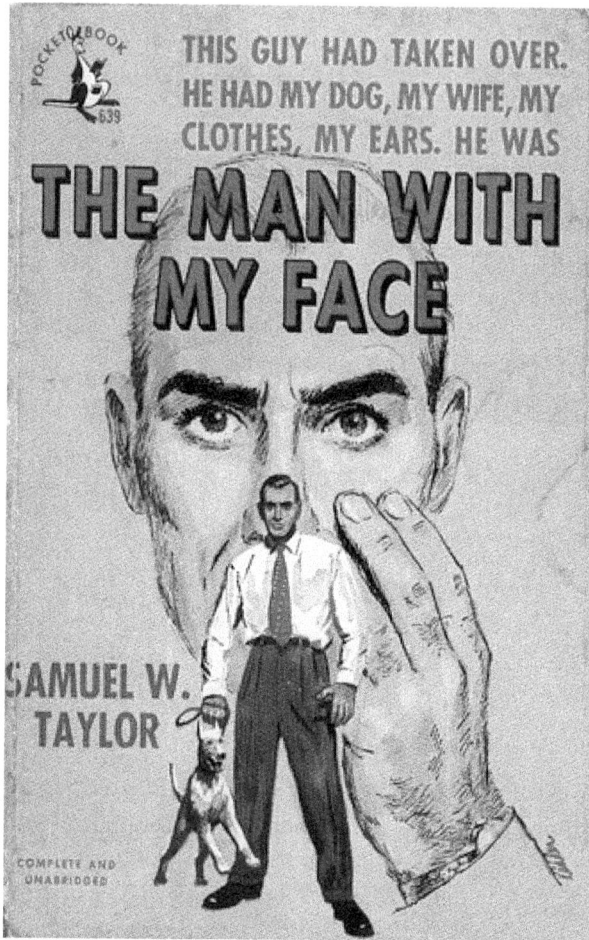

The original dime novel.

Taylor himself had already written a screenplay adaptation, originally with the locale of Redwood, California. Having reviewed locations throughout Puerto Rico, the script was re-written to cater to the new exotic locale of the islands. Vincent Bogert, one of the radio scriptwriters, contributed to the re-writes (hence the jokes exchanged between Happy, the bartender, and Chick). As an in-joke, characters in the movie such as Larry Sharp and Al Grant were named after radio scriptwriters Al Johansen, Lou Grant, Larry Rhine and Phil Sharp.

The story involved "Chick" Graham (played by Barry Nelson), who returns home one day and is shocked to discover his wife and his brother-in-law do not recognize him. When a man with identical features and face walks into the room, "Chick" discovers that the stranger has swapped places with him. The case of mistaken identity blows into a conflict involving the San Juan police, who give pursuit, mistaking him for a murderer. Applying the "wrong man" theme, a notorious embezzler named Al Grant is in league with Chick's wife and brother-in-law. With the assistance of a former love, Chick follows one lead after another, evading the police and foiling the crooks' scheme. During their getaway, Chick outsmarts a vicious Doberman left to guard him and, following an effective chase sequence, manages to expose the plot to the authorities. The final chase sequence was shot on location at the decayed Fort Morro Castle in San Juan. The fort, one of the oldest in the Caribbean, was occupied by the U.S. Army and Gardner was able to secure permission to shoot scenes on location.

The entire film was shot on location. The Café Caribe was located inside the Caribe Hilton, the same place where Charlie Cantor was living in great style and loving it during his stay in Puerto Rico.

A number of radio actors made appearances in the movie, John Kane and John Cleary among them. Hazel Shermet (billed as Hazel Sherman), radio's Miss Duffy, and scriptwriter Vincent Bogert, appear in a brief scene as patrons at the nightclub bar.

Barry Nelson was among a few of the Hollywood actors, radio actress Betty Lou Gerson included (billed as Lynn Ainley in the movie), who flew down to Puerto Rico to appear in the motion picture. During production, two Dobermans were brought in from Hollywood for filming. One of the dogs proved to be vicious when it ended up biting Barry Nelson three times during filming. Gardner later vented to a Hollywood columnist when he complained about Nelson's attitude toward the incident. "That Nelson is a game cuss. The only bite he put on me was on my pocketbook." Filming was completed in 33 days and Nelson returned to the States, vowing to never again return to Puerto Rico and never to work again with Ed Gardner. The actor had signed with Gardner to appear in two

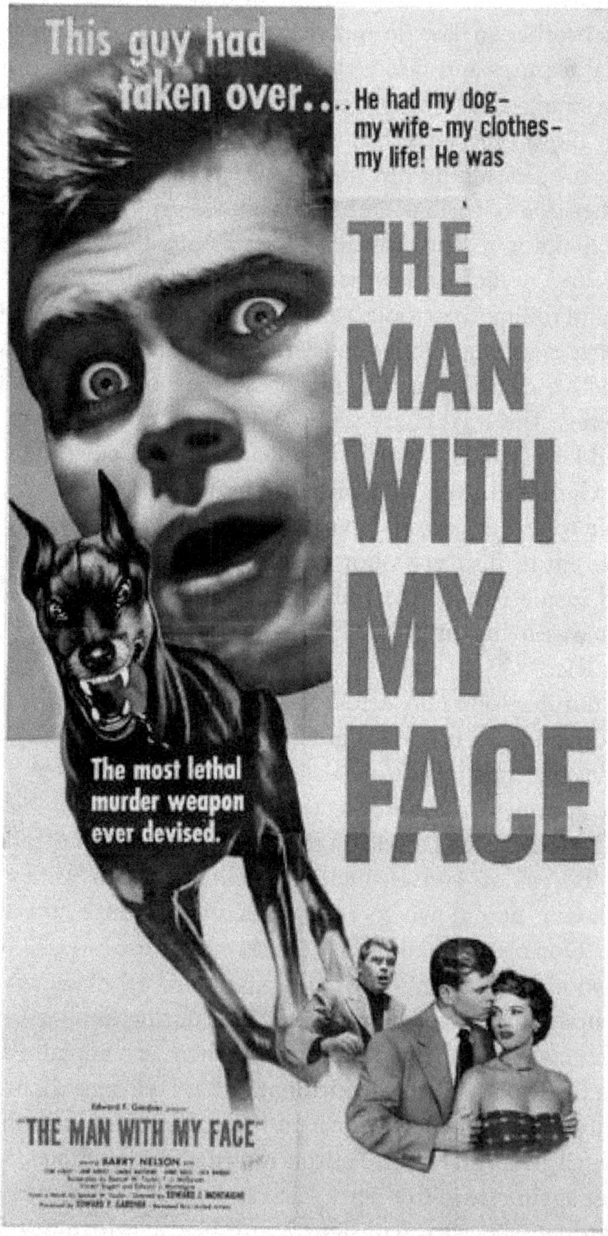
This guy had taken over...
..He had my dog-
my wife-my clothes-
my life! He was
THE MAN WITH MY FACE
The most lethal murder weapon ever devised.
"THE MAN WITH MY FACE"
BARRY NELSON

additional motion pictures but an offer to appear on Broadway, a play titled *The Moon is Blue*, offered more money.

Nelson was the only established "name" in Hollywood that appears in the movie. Gardner chose to hire actors who were second tier and much of the casting was still being contracted during the first week of filming. John Harvey signed for a role four days after production began. He immediately packed his bags to fly south. For the last five years, he had been doing Broadway plays. His last film role was opposite Betty Grable in *Pin Up Girl* (1944).

The music score was completed a few days before Halloween.

In January 1951, Gardner went to New York to negotiate the sale of his movie and attend a preview screening. He then flew to Hollywood for a few days to discuss the deal with a distributor who could handle a theatrical release both abroad and overseas. When Gardner approached Howard Hughes, he discovered the millionaire would not touch the film. Attempting to make a profit on product placement, Pan-American had paid Gardner a fee to insert some shots of Pan-Am planes arriving at and leaving Puerto Rico. Also added were a number of shots of the Pan-American ticket bureau. This affected the sale to Howard Hughes of RKO, who happened to own TWA.

The Man With My Face was eventually released by United Artists, screening in U.S. theaters in May 1951. *Variety* reviewed in their May 16, 1951, column: "The Samuel W. Taylor novel is the basis for a good meller, but story development is too static and seldom reaches a pitch of realism. Only in the final minutes, when there is a lusty chase sequence, does the pic get into full swing. Yarn is about a hard-working accountant who is innocently involved in a $1,000,000 robbery in Florida by having his identity usurped by a crook and his partner in the accountancy biz. This is difficult enough to swallow but the continued slayings, via a trained dog, are kept up right under the eyes of the local gendarmes until, near the close, all characters, including the police, wise up to the conspiracy. Nelson is one of the few actors in the film who emerges unscarred in a dual role. Henry Lascoe carries off his minor part well but the remainder of the supporting cast is

undistinguished. Fred Jackman, Jr.'s, camera gives the production its highest professional touch."

After production of his first independent feature was completed, Ed Gardner began making plans for early shooting of his second motion picture, *Pigsfeet in Paris*. (The screenplay for *Pigsfeet in Paris* was registered for copyright in March 1949.) Prior to *The Man With My Face*, Gardner had intended to make *Paris* his first venture. With a new season of *Duffy's Tavern* around the corner, Gardner decided to focus on the distribution of his first movie. In the summer of 1951, he traveled to Paris, France, to film stock footage in natural settings around Montmartre, Pigalle and other Parisian neighborhoods. According to columnist Mark Barron, "Gardner has not been living a life in Puerto Rico, he assured me. He is building a house there. He has a boat in which he cruises around the Virgin Islands and he has a film studio in San Juan." The character of Archie from *Duffy's Tavern* was going to be incorporated into the movie. For reasons unknown, the film was never produced.

To help promote *The Man With My Face*, references to the movie were made in a few episodes of *Duffy's Tavern*. For the broadcast of October 12, 1951, Archie fancied himself a movie producer.

ARCHIE: The producer. The big so and so. And I do say so myself, I did a magnificent job on that picture. Now tell me, do you remember which part you remembered the most?

MISS DUFFY: Sure. The part right before I had to slap the sailor.

CHAPTER SIXTEEN
OPERATION TANDEM
(1950 - 1951)

IN MID-AUGUST 1950, AN AMBITIOUS advertising program was created by NBC executives, a new method of show-selling, labeled "Operation Tandem," in which six bankrollers would buy participations five nights weekly in a variety of shows, instead of latching on to one single property. As the new system was set up, each sponsor would get plugs from Thursday through Monday on five of seven different programs. This included comedies such as *Duffy's Tavern* and *The Phil Harris and Alice Faye Show*, action and intrigue such as *Dangerous Assignment* and *The Man Called X*, a Hollywood prestige program called *Screen Directors Playhouse* (originally intended to have Cecil B. DeMille as the host), an NBC Symphony and a Sunday evening ambition titled *The Big Show*. This was the network's main priority by a powerful selling team captained by NBC president Niles Trammell. Working with him in the big sales pitch were executive vice-president Charles Denny, who reportedly fathered the plan; the newly acquired

The Man Called X premiered on the evening of October 7, 1942, with Herbert Marshall as Ken Thurston, an Intelligence Agent. After General Motors (promoting its line of Frigidaire products) dropped sponsorship on CBS in September 1948, NBC wanted to revive the series under a slightly revised title, *A Man Called X*, with a new audition recording produced in March 1950. The series was revived on October 13, 1950, but failed to gain sponsors as part of the Operation Tandem program until the broadcast of November 11, 1950.

assistant to the president, John K. Herbert; Maurice B. Mitchell, who came over from directing the Broadcast Advertising Bureau; sales vice-president Harry Kopf, and eastern sales chief Walter Scott. The idea behind the new sales concept was that it would give bankrollers a chance to get their messages aired on a multi-week basis in big-league evening shows. Positions within the shows would be rotated to give each sponsor a fair shake. The initial cost of five participations weekly was a reported $1,250,000 for a 39-week ride. Competing against other networks, NBC believed "Operation Tandem" might be the future way of selling programs to sponsors.

While some advertising agencies were enthusiastic about the proposal, other sectors of the industry were raising questions. For one thing, ABC planned a similar venture, called "drumfire in depth," for its afternoon schedule. In the ABC concept, for the cost of one half-hour across-the-board, a sponsor would get plugs in four shows daily, five days a week. The plan never got off the ground, ABC finding no takers. Another questioned the security of a comedian who might jump ship in mid-season to another network. NBC was already two steps ahead on this potential concern.

During the first week of March 1949, negotiations were completed for the purchase of rights to the *Fibber McGee and Molly* program to protect the network against another loss to CBS. In order to accomplish this, NBC entered into agreement with Jim and Marian Jordan, the stars of the program, and Management Corporation of America, their agents; Don Quinn, the writer of the situation comedy, and his wife, Edythe Quinn; S.C. Johnson & Son, Inc., the sponsor; and Needham, Louis & Brorby, Inc., the agency. The total sum reported was $759,000 for the initial payments to be made under the contracts, plus a fee for each additional broadcast following. NBC was attempting to prevent CBS from purchasing any more of their popular and high-rated radio programs.

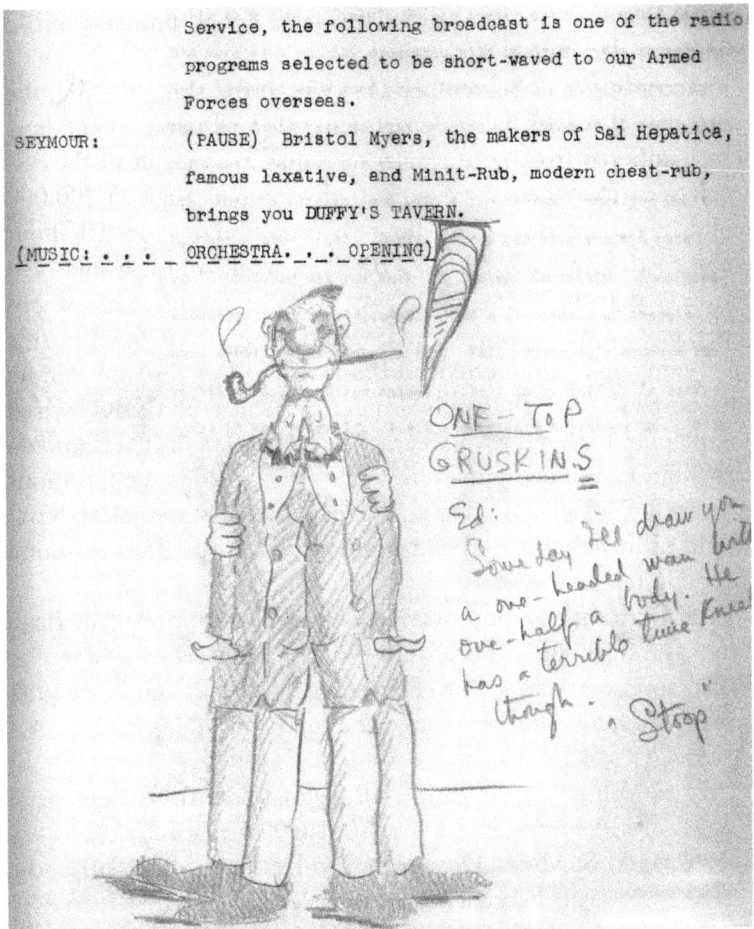

Ed Gardner sketch on a radio script.

In February and March 1950, NBC was able to work out an arrangement for the services of Phil Harris and his wife, Alice Faye, and for their program, under the assurance that the program would not move to another network. NBC contracted with Phil Harris-Alice Faye Enterprises, the stars' partnership, for the services of Harris and Faye for 35 sound broadcasting programs per year for two years beginning in the fall at $4,000 per program. NBC also contracted to furnish all the other elements of the program for the same number of broadcasts for $14,500 per broadcast. Harris' work was exclusive to NBC except for an occasional guest appearance on the Jack Benny program. NBC sold the program to the sponsor.

According to a September 11, 1950, NBC staff meeting, the major activity of the Sales Department was on Operation Tandem, which suffered from stiff agency resistance as a result of the 39-week security. Agency executives also argued that $1,200,000 could buy a sponsor a half-hour of time and a good half-hour show costing from $7,500 to $10,000 a week, and it would be a property that the client would own without sharing with others. The same amount, they argued, would also permit for a terrific spot campaign in preferred positions, instead of the one-minute plug provided on "Operation Tandem." As a result, NBC revised the plan and offered a 13-week cycle at $400,000. It was known that station representatives frowned on the idea, and stations reportedly looked upon it as an encroachment. Nonetheless, NBC would ultimately succeed and it amounted to the most stunning sales coup in radio annals.

By October, two sponsors were willing to commit — American Home Products and Mars Candy — at $400,000 each for 13 weeks. Other sponsors were soon to follow and as a result, the 1950-1951 season of *Duffy's Tavern* featured the following sponsors:

Whitehall, November 10, 1950, to April 27, 1951
RCA Victor, November 10, 1950, to April 27, 1951
Liggett & Myers, December 8 to December 22, 1950, and
February 8 to April 27, 1951
Ford, November 24 to December 15, 1950
Buick, January 19, 1951 only

Ed Gardner's sketch of Vincent Price during rehearsals.

Charlie Cantor, appreciative of the extensive vacation in Puerto Rico, dropped a bombshell in Gardner's lap when he announced he was leaving for New York, hoping to start a new career in the field of television broadcasting. He was offered placement on *The Colgate Comedy Hour*. Sid Raymond signed up to play the role of Finnegan. Raymond, having dropped out of New York University to entertain on stage, quickly established a career on radio and voicing cartoon characters (including Baby Huey). He went on to lead the traveling version of the radio show *Major Bowes Original Amateur Hour*, which scoured America for talent. During World War II, Raymond led a small troupe that performed at the front lines, sometimes under fire. New York radio and television actor Jimmy Stephens was inked to play Clancy the Cop.

Sam Raskin (often mistakenly billed as Sam Raskyn when he made guest appearances on television programs in the sixties) was a virtual unknown in Hollywood and broadcast circles but agreed to play the role of Eddie the waiter. His stint was short lived. He played the role for only two episodes, replaced by Frank L. Wilson, a Negro actor who played supporting roles in dozens of motion pictures dating back during the silent era. The character of Eddie the waiter was then replaced by the character of Yasha Panyaslovnik, a music teacher, beginning with the broadcast of January 19, 1951. The role of Panyaslovnik was played by Bert Gordon, best known for playing "The Mad Russian," a radio character known for his "steel wool" haircut, ears which wiggled and for his famous tag lines, "How dooo you dooo!" and "Do you mean it?" These lines and Gordon's caricature appeared in several Warner Bros. cartoons while Gordon himself became the central comedian in *School for Swing* (1937), *Sing For Your Supper* (1941) and *How Doooo You Do!!!* (1945).

Gardner, finally making headway for producing his first motion picture on the islands and dealing with the casting issues for *Duffy's Tavern*, flew to New York in late August to work out a sponsorship deal. By August 24, Gardner had reached an agreement with NBC radio program chief Charles (Bud) Barry. Gardner agreed to a substantial cut in his hassle with Barry. Instead of $15,000 weekly, it was estimated that NBC would be offering the package for the new season at a figure in the neighborhood of $10,000. The deal was said to include a filmed TV pilot which NBC hoped to pitch to potential sponsors and in which Gardner was obligated to star. This would ultimately become the Jeanette MacDonald pilot that aired on *All Star Revue* (detailed in the next chapter). Regarding the sponsor issue, NBC, as already discussed, slated *Duffy's Tavern* as part of their Operation Tandem plan, which meant the series would have multiple sponsors in any given thirty-minutes.

A radio critic for *Variety* offered a biting review of the season premiere: "Compared with yester-years, *Tavern* is now serving a 3.2 brew. It has lost much of the bite it once had, largely through absence of the cast that originally created its fabulous characters and also because it lacks the scripting savvy that once made it a topflight comedy entry. Ed Gardner, of course, is still Archie the manager, the pugnacious malapropper with the inflated ego, but the material misses the old spark. Additionally, the foils – the moronic Finnegan (minus Charles Cantor), the man-crazy Miss Duffy and the sharp Eddie – aren't as expertly rendered as they were in the airer's heyday."

The lure for getting celebrities to appear on the show came in

Old Time Radio DIGEST

No. 43   January·February 1991 $2.50

ED "ARCHIE" GARDNER

Cover of the January–February 1991 issue of the OTR Digest. *Illustration by Dave Warren.*

the form of an all-expenses-paid vacation and celebrity guests who chose to take advantage of the offer included Margaret O'Brien, Veronica Lake, Michael Romanoff and Sir Cedric Hardwicke. The highlight of the season, however, was the broadcast of February 9, 1951, with Hollywood guest Shelley Winters. Archie opens the mail and among the threatening lawsuits and requests to rendezvous with jail breakers is a valentine with no name on it. Archie is puzzled as to who sent him the love letter and suspects Shelley Winters because the initials "SW" couldn't possibly mean "sweetheart." Suspecting she has ulterior motives, Archie gives the actress the brush off when she arrives at the tavern. However, love strikes the heart and Archie attempts to give the false impression that he is a multi-millionaire. Only after the masquerade is unveiled does Archie discover the valentine was from Finnegan. Archie, commenting about Shelley Winters: "with them legs, she's made more successful crossings than Pan American Airways."

"While there I'm going to get a couple days of sleep, and I want to go swimming," Winters told the Associated Press, when asked what else she planned to do besides appear on *Duffy's Tavern*. Her appearance was in between making a film and a Broadway musical.

For the holiday season, the cast of *Duffy's Tavern* recorded a special 15-minute program in behalf of the Christmas Seal Campaign to help bring public awareness and raise funds for the fight against tuberculosis. This special transcription did not air on any major network, coast-to-coast, but it did circulate to various radio stations across the country that chose to air the program as a public service special and filler between regularly scheduled programs.

Season Eleven
November 10, 1950, to April 27, 1951
National Broadcasting Company
Day and Time: Friday, 9:30 to 10:00 p.m., EST
Producer: Jack Cleary
Writers: Larry Rhine and Al Johansen
Musical Director: César Concepción
(November 10, 1950, to April 13, 1951)

Musical Director: Abraham Pea
(final three episodes of the season)
Engineer: Dudley Connolly
Sound Effects: William R. Anthony
Director: Ed Gardner
Announcer: Harwood Hull

Scriptwriters: James Carhartt, Al Johansen, Larry Rhine
and Nicholas Winter
(Carhartt and Winter went back to the U.S. after the first three
episodes.)

Cast
Hazel Shermet as Miss Duffy
Sam Raskin as Eddie (November 10 and 17, 1950)
Frank Wilson as Eddie
(November 24, 1950, to January 12, 1951)
Bert Gordon as Yasha Panyaslovnik
(January 19, 1951, to April 27, 1951)
Sid Raymond as Clifton Finnegan
James Stevens as Clancy the Cop (*Clancy not on every broadcast.*)

Episode #382 — Broadcast Friday, November 10, 1950
Taped on November 8, 1950.
Supporting Cast: James Stevens (Pierre)
Guest: Sir Cedric Hardwicke
Plot: Same script from November 16, 1943.

Trivia, etc. *Variety* reviewed the season premiere: "Sir Cedric
Hardwicke turned in a neat guest shot, his bored sophistication
providing a comic contrast to the Third Avenue lowbrows peopling
the Tavern... Situation revolved around Archie's trying to get Sir
Cedric to room in his decrepit flat. It involved some moderately
amusing bits as Gardner mangled the art of interior decoration.
Perhaps it's the result of the origination from Puerto Rico, but the
audience seemed too easy to please, enthusiastically applauding

559

some lines that were worth only a chuckle."

Episode #383 — Broadcast Friday, November 17, 1950
Taped on November 14, 1950.
Script Title: "ARCHIE THE AGENT"
Supporting Cast: Sid Raymond (Panyaslovnik and Finnegan)
Plot: Archie thinks he can be a successful theatrical agent and signs Miss Duffy to a contract. Panyaslovnik, the music teacher, tells Archie that he's certain he can provide a song bird more lovely than Miss Duffy, but Archie considers her a blimp and asks, "What is that, a bustle she's wearin' or is she carryin' a beer keg on her hip?" After hearing Miss Duffy sing, Archie cracks jokes and resigns as a theatrical agent.

Episode #384 — Broadcast Friday, November 24, 1950
Taped on November 22, 1950.
Guest: Margaret O'Brien
Plot: Archie writes a television play, and hopes Margaret O'Brien will be able to pronounce long words like "prologue" and "agony." Mistaking the young lady as the little girl he saw in the movies, Archie threatens to feed her castor oil and send her to bed if she doesn't participate in his mock version of Cinderella and her two evil step-sisters, Heffer and Zephyr. After the drama, Archie thinks the script is twenty years ahead of its time but O'Brien thinks a play like this will put her back ten years.

Episode #385 — Broadcast Friday, December 1, 1950
Taped on November 24, 1950.
Script Title: "THE GENEALOGIST"
Supporting Cast: Vilma Carbia (Marquesa Maria Luisa Dolores) and Sid Raymond (Finnegan and Panyaslovnik)
Plot: Same script from November 27, 1941.

Episode #386 — Broadcast Friday, December 8, 1950
Taped on December 4, 1950.
Guest: Prince Michael Romanoff
Plot: After learning that Prince Michael Romanoff owns and runs a restaurant in Beverly Hills, and the expensive prices he charges for a meal, Archie is impressed. The way he sees it, a guy could eat

in Duffy's for six months and still have enough for the funeral. Archie attempts to earn five percent commission by selling the tavern over to Prince Michael Romanoff. Archie makes the mistake of trying to pass off a fake chef and Romanoff rejects the offer.

Trivia, etc. This episode recycled material from the broadcast of Tuesday, May 16, 1944.

Episode #387 — Broadcast Friday, December 15, 1950
Taped on December 9, 1950.
Supporting Cast: Lopez Balaguer (as himself) and Sid Raymond (Finnegan and Panyaslovnik)
Guest: Veronica Lake
Plot: While Lopez Balaguer, a Puerto Rican singer and actor, is outside "lubricatin' his gargle," Archie attempts to entertain Veronica Lake. The picture of Duffy was flipped over so it won't scare the actress, while Miss Duffy and Veronica exchange jokes about *I Married A Witch* and *I Walked With A Zombie*. Archie asks Veronica to swoon over his latest music discovery, Balaguer, but his singing (and that of Finnegan's) isn't doing the trick. Archie kisses her and that still doesn't do the trick. But when Duffy's photo is revealed, the actress faints.

Trivia, etc. This episode recycled material from the broadcast of Tuesday, October 5, 1943.

Memorable Lines
ARCHIE: Veronica is one of the most beautiful dames in this world... Her face beams like a full moon in April... her shoulders have the whiteness of the blossoms in May... her eyes twinkle like little snow flakes in December. What happened to June, July, August, September, October and November? The censors cut them out.

Episode #388 — Broadcast Friday, December 22, 1950
Taped on December 15, 1950.
Supporting Cast: Johnny Zerbi (Wilfrid)

Guest: Charles Coburn
Plot: Same script from December 22, 1944, with Charles Coburn reciting Monty Woolley's lines.

Episode #389 — Broadcast Friday, December 29, 1950
Taped on December 15, 1950.
Script Title: "CUTTING PRICES SHOW"
Plot: Same script from May 14, 1947.

Episode #390 — Broadcast Friday, January 5, 1951
Taped on December 22, 1950.
Guest: Vincent Price
Plot: When Archie discovers Vincent Price is going to drop by the tavern, he attempts to take advantage by having Price become the first member of the Private Actor's Club. When the actor puts in an appearance, Archie exchanges barbs with the bard. Miss Duffy refers to the barkeep as "man's best friend." To convince Archie that he can earn his membership, Price does a scene from Shakespeare, tells jokes and sings songs.

Trivia, etc. This episode was a rewrite of the April 18, 1944, script, with Charles Laughton as the guest star.

Memorable Lines
FINNEGAN: Okay bud, let's shake hands and be friends.
PRICE: Isn't there a more sanitary way?

Episode #391 — Broadcast Friday, January 12, 1951
Taped on December 22, 1950.
Script Title: "ARCHIE, THE PURE FOOD INSPECTOR"
Supporting Cast: Lopez Balaguer (as himself) and Sid Raymond (Finnegan and Ward Heeler McGinnis)
Plot: Archie is forced to close the books on all customers who want to digest alcohol on credit. This includes Ward Heeler McGinnis, a tavern regular, who prevented the building inspector from shutting the place down... and Archie has trouble telling him he has to pay his debts. McGinnis even convinces Archie that he could be elected as Pure Food Inspector for the entire Third

Avenue district. Archie dreams of the reforms he plans to enact…
until election day when Peaches La Tour, a fan dancer, wins the
majority vote.

Episode #392 — Broadcast Friday, January 19, 1951
Taped on January 16, 1951.
Script Title: "MRS. PIDDLETON'S TOWN HALL
MEETING"
Supporting Cast: Catherine Randolph (Mrs. Piddleton)
Plot: Mrs. Piddleton and the Lord Byron Ladies' Literary Society,
"a club where people who don't know how to read listen to lectures
by people who don't know how to talk," plan another meeting at
the tavern. When H.V. Kaltenborn rejects the offer to participate
in a forum, Yasha Panyaslovnik, the new waiter at Duffy's Tavern,
is drafted. The Duffy Town Hall Meeting of the Air also features
Miss Duffy, an authority on maritime relations and Finnegan, an
"authority on subversive politics." Subjects include solutions to
inflation and what Confederate money is worth in Prussia.

Episode #393 — Broadcast Friday, January 26, 1951
Taped on January 19, 1951.
Guest: Joan Bennett
Plot: Same script from June 13, 1944.

Episode #394 — Broadcast Friday, February 2, 1951
Taped on January 19, 1951.
Script Title: "ARCHIE'S DRAFT BOARD"
Supporting Cast: John Cleary (the sergeant) and Linda White
(the girl)
Plot: Same script from November 10, 1948.

Episode #395 — Broadcast Friday, February 9, 1951
Taped on January 27, 1951.
Guest: Shelley Winters
Plot: See page 558.

Trivia, etc. Lousy jokes about Miss Duffy waiting for a valentine
from Gregory Peck and receiving 40 valentines (from Macy's, they

had a sale) were deleted during the rehearsals and never used on the program when Miss Duffy first enters the episode.

Episode #396 — Broadcast Friday, February 16, 1951
Taped on January 27, 1951.
Script Title: "ARCHIE WRITES AN OPERA"
Supporting Cast: Catherine Randolph (Mrs. Piddleton)
Plot: Archie went to the opera last night (no, he wasn't drunk) and finds himself inspired to write his own. Panyaslovnik believes there is enough suffering in the world already, and Mrs. Piddleton shows up at the tavern to find out if Archie liked the opera. Discovering her literary society plans to visit the Metropolitan tonight, Archie convinces her to pay for cheaper seats and watch his opera, "plus we'll throw in a free lube job for their hearing aids." Miss Duffy sings "The Laughing Song" from *Die Fledermaus*, then Archie and the gang deliver a "condensed and filched" version of *The Barber of Seville*. After hearing the opera, Mrs. Piddleton says she will send money to the Metropolitan Insurance Company. "With operas like that, you'll need protection!"

Episode #397 — Broadcast Friday, February 23, 1951
Taped on February 6, 1951.
Script Title: "ARTHUR TREACHER FASHION LECTURE"
Supporting Cast: John Cleary (Clancy the Cop)
Plot: The policemen are having their annual Footbath and Discussion Club meeting at the tavern and Archie arranges for Arthur Treacher to deliver a lecture on Men's Clothes. Archie wrote the lecture. Treacher describes how primitive man wore loin cloths, the invention of the cotton gin machine, modern fashions and "how to be neat while walking the beat." Clancy and the other officers are insulted by the latter and threatens to jail the man who wrote the lecture. Thinking quickly, Archie blames Treacher and the actor is taken away as Archie advises him, "as we say in fashion circles, when in doubt, wear stripes."

Trivia, etc. John Cleary, the producer, plays the role of Clancy the Cop in this episode.

Memorable Lines
ARCHIE: Well, you know how some guys go around lookin' as though they smelled something bad? Treacher looks like he found it. You've seen him in pictures, Duffy, he's the tall, thin, silent type... sort of an English Gary Cooper... only he says "right-ho" instead of "yup."

Episode #398 — Broadcast Friday, March 2, 1951
Taped on February 6, 1951.
Script Title: "ARTHUR TREACHER CLASSES UP THE JOINT"
Supporting Cast: John Cleary (Clancy the Cop), Father Haskins (the lawyer) and Sid Raymond (Happy Dan)
Plot: Same script from March 23, 1945, with Arthur Treacher filling in the part Dame May Whitty had in the 1945 version.

Episode #399 — Broadcast Friday, March 9, 1951
Taped on February 20, 1951.
Script Title: "ARCHIE THE HYPNOTIST"
Supporting Cast: Martha Sleeper (Renee)
Plot: Same script from December 1, 1948.

Episode #400 — Broadcast Friday, March 16, 1951
Taped on February 20, 1951.
Script Title: "ARCHIE HIRES MAXIE AS WAITER"
Guest: Maxie Rosenbloom
Plot: Same script from November 9, 1945.

Episode #401 — Broadcast Friday, March 23, 1951
Taped on February 28, 1951.
Script Title: "ARCHIE FINDS A DIARY"
Supporting Cast: Harwood Hull (the professor)
Plot: Same script from March 26, 1947.

Episode #402 — Broadcast Friday, March 30, 1951
Taped on February 28, 1951.
Script Title: "ARTIE SHAW BLOCK PARTY"
Guest: Artie Shaw

Plot: Same script from May 28, 1947. Instead of the party being held in Miss Duffy's honor, Artie Shaw is the recipient. Bert Gordon reprises the same role he played in the 1947 version, without the romance he shared with Miss Duffy.

Episode #403 — Broadcast Friday, April 6, 1951
Taped on March 10, 1951.
Script Title: "VALLEE DETECTIVE SKETCH"
Guest: Rudy Vallee
Plot: Same script from June 18, 1947.

Episode #404 — Broadcast Friday, April 13, 1951
Taped on March 10, 1951.
Script Title: "ROSENBLOOM FLOOR SHOW"
Plot: Same script from November 24, 1944. Miss Duffy sings "Kiss Me Again."

Episode #405 — Broadcast Friday, April 20, 1951
Taped on March 21, 1951.
Script Title: "THE CIRCUS COMES TO TOWN"
Supporting Cast: John Cleary (Mr. Flugel)
Plot: Same script from April 30, 1947.

Episode #406 — Broadcast Friday, April 27, 1951
Taped on March 22, 1951.
Script Title: "PHIL BAKER"
Supporting Cast: Harwood Hull (Elmer)
Guest: Phil Baker
Plot: Same script from January 7, 1948, with Phil Baker reading the same lines Garry Moore did in 1948.

Episode #XXX/407
Taped on March 24, 1951.
Script Title: "BOBBY CAPO"
Supporting Cast: Vilma Carbia (the girl)
Guest: Bobby Capo
Plot: Same plot used for November 2, 1951, with a couple of differences. A wealthy heiress from South America spends a

thousand bucks at a local nightclub and when Archie discovers she wants to see a Latin Floor Show, he hires Bobby Capo from the Calderon Studio to sing and perform. Instead of the Brooklyn Dodgers, he hates the Giants.

Trivia, etc. Duffy's Tavern was not broadcast on May 4, 1951, even though May 4 was the date originally scheduled for the final broadcast of the season. Collectors of old-time radio recordings offer an episode about Latin Night with guest Bobby Capo dated May 4, but in reality NBC began broadcasting *A Man Called X* for a two-month summer replacement in that same Friday evening time-slot. Because this episode never aired, the same script was re-used a few months later and broadcast on the evening of November 2, 1951. With Gardner's now-legendary cost-consciousness, it's surprising that a new recording was made rather than simply use the one they already had.

CHAPTER SEVENTEEN
THE FINAL SEASON
(1951)

DURING THE MONTH OF AUGUST 1951, Ed Gardner was in New York City transacting a number of business deals. With an eye to eventually putting his *Duffy's Tavern* show on television (as well as continuing the radio series), he was re-casting virtually the entire program during his current stay in the Big Apple. He was seeking actors who looked the parts of the radio voices, even though the actual transition to video (he believed) would be several years in the future. A business deal with NBC went sour as the network would not meet Gardner's terms. NBC was pitching the program as part of its "Operation Tandem" sales plan but the sponsors involved with Tandem wanted to explore other options before committing.

Charlie Cantor, who teamed with Eddie Cantor (no relation) on a number of television's *Colgate Comedy Hour* episodes, decided to rejoin Ed Gardner in his original role of Finnegan on radio's *Duffy's Tavern*. Honeymooners Hazel Shermet and Larry Rhine were hitting the hot spots in New York but also agreed to return to Puerto Rico for another season of *Duffy's Tavern*. Gardner was also scouting for a replacement for the role of Eddie the waiter and found him performing in a night club. Ed "Fats" Pichon sang and played the piano in a style somewhat reminiscent of the late "Fats" Waller, and Gardner tapped him for the new waiter. His interpolations of "Basin St. Blues" and "Ain't Misbehavin'" added a pleasing musical note to the proceedings. His deadpan delivery was reminiscent of Eddie Green's and the piano player agreed to supply most of the music for the program on top of playing a part. Unfortunately, his timing for delivery when it came to reading radio scripts was awful but improved after the first two episodes. farchie's little

On the business end, a three-way rhubarb developed in September among the participating sponsors on the NBC "Operation Tandem" over the properties chosen for the five-nights-a-week program parlay for the 1951-1952 season. With Whitehall, Chesterfield and RCA investing the majority, which added up to a hefty chunk of money, NBC was anxious to make peace all around by allowing the sponsors a common meeting ground regarding the five shows chosen. A half-hour of *The Big Show*, the Boston Pops Orchestra, *Mr. Keen, Tracer of Lost Persons* (which Whitehall succeeded in maneuvering over from CBS in order to incorporate it into Tandem), *Screen Directors Playhouse* and *Duffy's Tavern* were the initial offerings. All three sponsors initially agreed on the wisdom of continuing with *The Big Show* and *Mr. Keen*. None of them favored the Boston Pops, which was not included with the 1951-52 season. NBC promised delivery of a Dean Martin-Jerry Lewis radio show as a substitute. Chesterfield was opposed to *Duffy's Tavern* and there was a dispute over *Screen Directors Playhouse*, despite the latter parlaying itself into one of the more successful network properties. Ultimately, though, *Duffy's Tavern* would be removed from the equation and NBC was forced to carry the program as a sustainer. Under a new contract, if the network was unable to sell the program within 13 weeks, they would cancel the series. In mid-October, the network planned a second strip of three half-hours as part of a proposed "Tandem Two," which also included the middle half-hour of *The Big Show*. Among the proposals was luring Himan Brown's *Inner Sanctum* series to NBC. This proposal never met fruition and as a result, *Duffy's Tavern* was destined for only another 13 weeks.

The gag writers during the first year in Puerto Rico. Left to right: Larry Rhine, Al Johansen, Vincent Bogert and Phil Sharp.

The first episode of the new series centered on Archie and the gang sharing stories about their summer vacation. Archie's ego swells to the max when he fancies himself as a "darling of the press," believing he is a successful movie producer, having released his latest motion picture, *The Man With My Face*. Critics, according to Archie, were speaking ill of the picture but showing no hard feelings. He plans a big dinner party to celebrate his new movie. Hedda Hopper, Dorothy Kilgallen, Louella Parsons and Walter Winchell have all been invited. The gang even pulls out the best utensils in town (they were stolen from high-class restaurants). As the listeners probably expected by this point, no one attends and Archie learns a valuable lesson: no one should be too good for his friends, especially those who stuck by him through thick and thin.

Archie even asks for forgiveness when he admits his shame. The plugs for the motion picture were so many that the entire half-hour seemed like an infomercial.

The second episode was funnier. Duffy is selling the tavern and sends a real estate man to assess the value of the property. To deter any chance of having the tavern sold to private investors, Archie, with bats in his belfry, hires Hollywood celebrity Boris Karloff (offering free zombie drinks as payment) to give the impression that the place is haunted. Archie discovers he has a grave problem when the horror star's theatrics fail to scare the real estate man... but thankfully, Finnegan enters the room and does the job without any effort. The reason the script was funnier was because the script was from May 21, 1947 (four years earlier), when Boris Karloff made an appearance on the show.

After reviewing the first two broadcasts from Puerto Rico, NBC decided to switch the initial broadcast schedule and against Ed Gardner's wishes, the Boris Karloff episode aired first. Today, anyone listening to both episodes might wonder if the dates are incorrect.

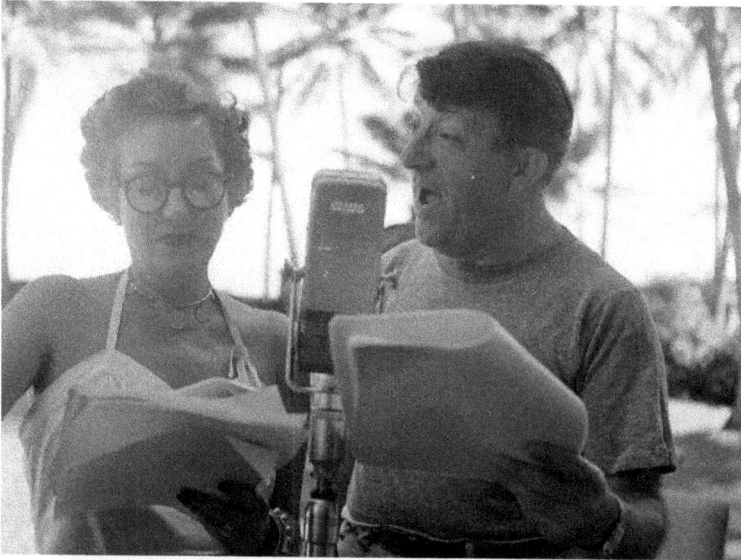

Gloria Swanson and Charles Cantor in Puerto Rico.
Unused photo for Life *magazine.*

Like the last two seasons, the scripts for the final season were nothing but rewrites of previous episodes. The second episode of the season closes with Archie remarking how the $8.00 dinner was worth it for his friends — the same joke that closed a previous episode during the forties. When Deems Taylor made a guest appearance for the broadcast of November 16, the same script from September 28, 1945, was used, with most of the dialogue intact. The only noticeable difference was Archie's motive for writing an opera; Eddie wanted to submit his opera for television.

The production was lackluster. The editing of episodes were oftentimes careless, as lines delivered were obviously cut out, evident when the laughter from the audience cuts dead silent between brief scenes of dialogue. The jokes were sometimes so bad that Ed Gardner allowed his eldest son to act as a judge of merit. "I remember my dad would ask me to read the scripts and I would scratch out lines that were just awful. I remember telling him, 'Dad, these jokes are corny.'"

Variety, on the other hand, enjoyed the season premiere. "*Duffy's Tavern* is back on NBC after its summer hiatus with perhaps the best show since Ed Gardner transferred the operation to Puerto Rico. Gardner has surrounded himself with a cast that more nearly approaches the stanza's heyday of several years ago." Had they known the script was recycled from a broadcast years ago, they might not have thought so highly. To keep NBC from figuring out the recycling of scripts, information supplied to the network for their press releases made no mention of the actual plots. Case in point, the premiere episode when NBC promoted: "*Duffy's Tavern* becomes even more ghastly than usual when Ed (Archie) Gardner plays host to Boris Karloff and attempts to arrange a blind date for Miss Duffy." The audience reaction, according to *Variety*, "was a bit too free-and-easy, some of the lines not meriting the yucks they registered."

According to an NBC Staff Meeting on October 8, 1951, Charles (Bud) Barry commented on the strong fall scheduled which had been developed for the radio network and reviewed a number of new programs, mentioning that *The Dean Martin and Jerry Lewis Show* was outstanding and that *Duffy's Tavern* showed "Ed Gardner at his best."

Duffy's Tavern *tape masters from Puerto Rico.*

"Gardner had been hiring writers from bars and God knows where else," Larry Rhine recalled. "He brought a team of four of us down there." Rhine later recalled how the writers once wrote a script during a hurricane. "Everybody else was running for the highlands and boarding up windows. We were sitting there, as the wind was bending over trees, writing jokes... The second year I wrote the show alone." Actually, Rhine had a little assistance from a then unknown, Budd Grossman, for at least four of the scripts. Grossman would eventually became an established scriptwriter for television including *My Favorite Husband, Dennis the Menace, Gilligan's Island, The Doris Day Show, Maude* and *Three's Company.*

Season Twelve
October 5, 1951, to December 28, 1951
National Broadcasting Company
Sustaining, no sponsor
Day and Time: Friday, 9:00 to 9:30 p.m., EST

Producer and Director: Ed Gardner
Scriptwriters: Larry Rhine and Budd Grossman.
Musical Bridges and Novelty Numbers by Ed "Fats" Pichon and
George Kudirka.

Cast
Charlie Cantor as Finnegan
Hazel Shermet as Miss Duffy
Ed "Fats" Pichon as Fats, the waiter and piano player

Note: The numbering system for the remaining episodes depends on your point of view. Because the Bobby Capo episode was recorded but never broadcast, some believe there should be no official episode number. Others believe the numbering system should remain unchanged. The remaining episodes below have two numbers; the first number represents the actual numbers of broadcast and the second represents the actual numbers of episodes total (non-broadcast included).

Episode #407/408 — Broadcast Friday, October 5, 1951
Supporting cast: Arthur Rieck (Mr. S. Crow)
Guest: Boris Karloff
Plot: Same script used on May 21, 1947.

Trivia, etc. The line delivered by Boris Karloff, "Post Ghosties," was initially rejected by NBC in fear that the word "Post" would have been advertising for a company not sponsoring *Duffy's Tavern*. The line remains unchanged, as verified by the recoding of the broadcast.

Episode #408/409 — Broadcast Friday, October 12, 1951
Plot: See page 549.

Episode #409/410 — Broadcast Friday, October 19, 1951
Supporting cast: Gayle Jones (Morton)
Plot: Archie's little nephew, 11-year-old Morton, proves to be well educated when he visits the tavern and discovers his uncle Archie lied about being a millionaire. When Morton expresses a

desire to be on a radio quiz program, Archie convinces Finnegan and Miss Duffy to be panelists on a mock version of *Information, Please*. Morton delivers the correct answers every time but the others seem to have their doubts. This was the same script from October 26, 1945.

Episode #410/411 — Broadcast Friday, October 26, 1951
Supporting cast: Gayle Jones (Morton) and Martha Sleeper (Miss Dinwiddy)
Plot: Miss Duffy and her girls' club plan a Halloween party. Archie tries to help Morton with his homework. But nothing is more hilarious than when Morton's schoolteacher drops by the tavern and, appalled by the tavern atmosphere, insists on taking the youth away. Archie falls in love with the beautiful woman and tries to impress her, insisting Duffy's Tavern is the only place in the entire city that offers curbside service to drunks on the sidewalk. In an attempt to prove he is a Harvard graduate, Archie disguises Finnegan as an old college professor... which doesn't fool the teacher.

Trivia, etc. This is the second consecutive episode to feature Tootsie Roll candy, an obvious product placement.
Archie closes the episode by telling Duffy that he will be appearing on *The Big Show* on Sunday night. This promotional spot was recorded separately from the rest of the production and inserted by NBC engineers.
This episode was a re-write of the script broadcast on November 2, 1945.

Episode #411/412 — Broadcast Friday, November 2, 1951
Script Title: "JOSITA VISITS THE TAVERN"
Supporting cast: Rafael Beliza (Diego Dinero)
Guest: Josita Hernandez
Plot: Archie invites Diego Dinero, a wealthy South American splashing across newspaper columns for his lavish spending, to Duffy's Tavern for a Spanish floorshow. Archie phones an agency and gets what he describes as "a Maxie Rosenbloom in high heels."

Josita Hernandez, a Brooklyn girl who can mimic a Spanish accent, agrees to the masquerade as part of the tavern's Spanish night club performance. The Brooklyn born tamale proves better than Miss Duffy's stale jokes and Finnegan (billed as the Mongoose of Madrid), until a crack about the Brooklyn Dodgers causes Josita's attitude to come out and give Diego Dinero a chewing out he will never forget.

Memorable Line
JOSITA: I happen to be a Dodger fan. And speaking of baseball, what's Joe DiMaggio doing over there?
MISS DUFFY: I beg your pardon!
ARCHIE: And now, Miss Hernandez, you've made a grave error. DiMaggio occasionally gets to first base.

Episode #412/413 — Broadcast Friday, November 9, 1951
Script Title: "ARCHIE'S SINGING CONTEST"
Supporting cast: Martha Sleeper (Abigail Piddleton)
Guest: Josita Hernandez
Plot: When Mrs. Piddleton agrees to allow Duffy's Tavern to host a cultural singing contest, Archie rigs the contest so his new girlfriend, Josita, is a cinch to win. The tug of war with tonsils gets a bit complicated when Finnegan cannot remember who he is supposed to call the winner and Mrs. Piddleton asks for her new protégé, Miss Duffy, to be the winner. Miss Duffy certainly sings like a bird, Mrs. Piddleton insists, but Archie thinks more like a vulture.

Trivia, etc. The original ending for this episode was recorded without prior approval of NBC. In the original ending, Finnegan asked that they stop the music and proclaimed Miss Duffy the winner. When Archie debated, Finnegan makes a crack about South Americans and NBC disapproved of the line. The episode was ultimately re-edited and instead, as evident with the recording circulating among collectors, Archie abruptly announces Miss Duffy as the winner.

Episode #413/414 — Broadcast Friday, November 16, 1951
Script Title: "THE DEEMS TAYLOR SHOW"
Guest: Deems Taylor
Plot: Same script as September 28, 1945.

Episode #414/415 — Broadcast Friday, November 23, 1951
Script Title: "ARCHIE'S TEA ROOM"
Supporting cast: Gayle Jones (Morton) and Martha Sleeper (Abigail Piddleton)
Plot: Archie opens a tea room in order to marry Mrs. Abigail Piddleton, a wealthy widow, because of her recent acquisition of money. When it's pointed out that her legs need a complete overhaul, Archie is still interested in matrimony, gambling that long skirts will make a comeback. Mrs. Piddleton explains that she is seeking a family man. To help foster the illusion, Archie convinces Morton to play the role of his son, "the result of a distant marriage." When this appears to fail, Archie tries the sick kid scheme, with Finnegan playing the role of a medical doctor. The tea room fails to impress, even when Miss Duffy plays the role of a gypsy fortune teller.

Memorable Line
MISS DUFFY: I am the gypsy... and I know many things for I walk by night...
ARCHIE: Gertie, please stick to the tea leaves. Never mind what you do by night.

Episode #415/416 — Broadcast Friday, November 30, 1951
Script Title: "ARCHIE INHERITS A HORSE"
Supporting cast: Harwood Hull (the voice)
Plot: A weighing machine predicts good luck for Archie, who finds himself the half-owner of a racehorse. When Duffy sends down a side of beef, Archie overhears the conversation and mistakenly believes they plan to cut up the horse. Later, Archie bets two dollars on his horse when it's entered in a race. The 25-year-old horse dies on the track but Archie finds himself extremely lucky when the other half-owner, Duffy, lost $500 on the race.

Episode #416/417 — Broadcast Friday, December 7, 1951
Script Title: "BABY LEFT AT TAVERN"
Supporting cast: Martha Sleeper (the woman)
Plot: Same script broadcast on April 14, 1948.

Episode #417/418 — Broadcast Friday, December 14, 1951
Script Title: "ARCHIE'S TEACHER VISITS THE TAVERN"
Supporting cast: Martha Sleeper (Teresa Tomkins, the school teacher)
Plot: Recycling the same plot from the broadcast of January 18, 1946, Archie's former school teacher is making a tour to see her old pupils and drops by the tavern. Archie tries to impress her until Finnegan refers to her as "ol' turkey neck" multiple times. Archie is no help when he refers to her face as a "road map of Mongolia."

Trivia, etc. Martha Sleeper accidentally delivers Gardner's line instead of hers and, after she correct herself, Gardner tells her to make up her mind which line she wants to read.

Episode #418/419 — Broadcast Friday, December 21, 1951
Script Title: "McGUIRE SPLITS THE ATOM"
Supporting cast: John Brown (the professor) and Harwood Hull (Slippery McGuire)
Plot: In what might be one of the most ridiculous episodes of the season, Slippery McGuire tricks Archie into thinking the government spent two million dollars to split the atom and needs to find a way to put it back together again. Archie, believing he is helping humanity, harbors both Slippery and his colleague, the professor, in the back room so the two can work on the top secret project. Even after Bellevue Hospital calls, looking for one of their inmates, Archie still doesn't figure that he is being conned.

Trivia, etc. This episode was a rewrite of the broadcast of November 30, 1945.

Episode #419/420 — Broadcast Friday, December 28, 1951
Script Title: "ARCHIE WINS A TRIP TO HONOLULU"

Supporting cast: John Brown (the radio voice and Clancy the Cop) and Harwood Hull (Uncle Rodney)
Plot: Archie enters a slogan contest in the hopes of winning a trip to Honolulu. Archie wins but the gang is shocked to learn that the contest was open to children 13 years and younger. In order to claim the prize when Uncle Rodney of the radio program visits the tavern, Archie disguises Finnegan as the boy. The radio host is not impressed, nor amused, and promptly exits.

Regardless of what encyclopedias have been saying for years, and websites repeatedly reprinting the same material, the final episode of *Duffy's Tavern* was on December 28, 1951. There were no 1952 broadcasts. On the evening of January 4, 1952, *NBC Presents: Short Story*, an anthology program, moved into the *Duffy's* time slot.

The Cancellation

If faithful listeners were still listening to *Duffy's Tavern* in late 1951, NBC could not find judicial cause to keep the program on beyond the calendar year. The network was unable to launch "Tandem Two" and all attempts to sell the program to a new sponsor failed. The final season lasted 13 broadcasts. Archie remarked in the season premiere how the tavern had no business. The ratings suffered just as poorly. In an inter-office memo dated November 23, 1951, from Mitchell Benson, radio programming production executive, to Charles (Bud) Barry, the national program manager of NBC, the last nail sealed the coffin with the following words: "In accordance with your instructions, we are canceling the *Duffy's Tavern* program effective with the broadcast of December 28th."

A few weeks before Christmas, Charlie Cantor returned to Beverly Hills, "a fugitive from *Duffy's Tavern*" quoted a columnist for *Variety*. The tax deal was no bargain to him, so he decided to remain in the United States. Should *Duffy's Tavern* return to the air, Cantor wanted no part of it. By this time, Cantor estimated that he appeared on more than 35,000 radio broadcasts in his 25 years as a radio actor. He established his record, which won him the title of "Anonymous the Great," by being ready, willing and able throughout the last quarter of a century, to play the part, in any dialect (except Swedish), and to imitate chickens, birds, dogs, babies, trains, police and factory whistles, and airplanes in good and bad repair. Cantor claimed he once acted on as many as 30 radio shows in one week. It has been verified that he was in seven shows on the same day of the week. Among his credits: *Easy Aces*, *Dick Tracy*, *Dangerous Paradise*, *The Amazing Mr. Smith*, and *The House of Glass*. Living in Puerto Rico severed connections with producers who discovered he was no longer ready, willing or able. Substitutes became the standard and Cantor sought redemption by working his way back up the ladder of success. His Finnegan persona came in handy on the screen, especially in Damon Runyon adaptations such as *Stop, You're Killing Me* (1952) and multiple episodes of television's *Damon Runyon Theater*. Today, pop culture fans recognize Charlie Cantor as the lingerie salesman for the classic Jack Benny Christmas episode.

Larry Rhine and Hazel Shermet also left Puerto Rico (they beat Cantor to California by a few days), after learning the news that *Duffy's Tavern* was not going to be renewed. Ed "Fats" Pichon followed two days after Cantor.

By September 1951, Gardner had just completed a new ranch-style house on a hill overlooking the city. He kept his yacht in St. Thomas and was more relaxed. According to Gardner's press release, he now referred to "we Puerto Ricans." He was healthier than he had been in years but his struggle with alcohol by this time was starting to take a toll. He found more comfort with the bottle as a result of the cancellation of his radio program on NBC. With cast and crew returning to the States, insecurity in the form of desertion might have also been a factor. Gardner spent much of his leisure time playing tennis, swimming, deep sea fishing and sailing. He was fixed to remain permanently behind in Puerto Rico... for a while.

In late 1951, Gardner attempted to blow down the legend that he pocketed millions because of his move to a U.S. possession, to save on his March 13 tax bill. "As it turned out, I'm a little bit ahead financially, but not as much as people think," Gardner

Ed Gardner playing around on his yacht.

explained. "If I come back here now, I might be able to work out as good a tax deal in this country, with capital gains and all. A couple of other comics here have as good a tax deal as I have." When he moved to Puerto Rico, Gardner explained, he agreed to invest $250,000 in the country. He made the movie for $300,000, and had to chalk it up for a loss. At least, that was the "official" cost. A year later, when Gardner was in the U.S., interviewed by Frederick C. Othman of the El Paso, TX *Herald-Post*, he claimed he lost $200,000 as a result of the movie. The figure was quoted as $150,000 in another interview for another newspaper. Regardless of the figure, Gardner's visit to New York was not to satisfy newspaper columnists, but for business.

"I was lunching with Abe Burrows in New York recently," Gardner explained. "Abe was selling paper boxes when I took him on as a writer years ago and now he's a big performer on TV. Three people in a row came over to our table and I looked up hopefully. They all wanted his autograph. I decided it was time to go into television." This inspired Gardner to film a television show for NBC's *All Star Comedy Show*, a contractual obligation Gardner had not yet fulfilled for the network. He attempted to talk with a number of newspaper boys during his trip to New York, only to repeatedly receive a rejection in the form of, "Oh, you're ducking taxes." This was why Gardner decided quickly to discuss his present financial state with reporters who had not already taken a negative stance. "Believe me, I tell 'em. I'm still paying ten times as much as they are. Some taxes are higher in Puerto Rico than they are here. But my income tax is less."

"That criticism isn't good," Gardner defended, when talking to columnist Aline Mosby. "While I used to have four sponsors bidding for my radio show, now I got one. They say they understand. I'm not doing anything wrong living there, but does the public understand? People ask what do I do about passports and how do I get my money out of the country, like I was duckin' to a foreign land. Puerto Rico is part of the U.S. and I'm a good American. As Puerto Rico doesn't have representation in Congress, they have their own tax laws." Gardner cited living expenses as one example. "When I lived in California, it cost me $1,300 a month to pay the servants, not counting the meals. In Puerto Rico, I had six servants for $250 a month. My wife doesn't need any furs there, either," Gardner joked.

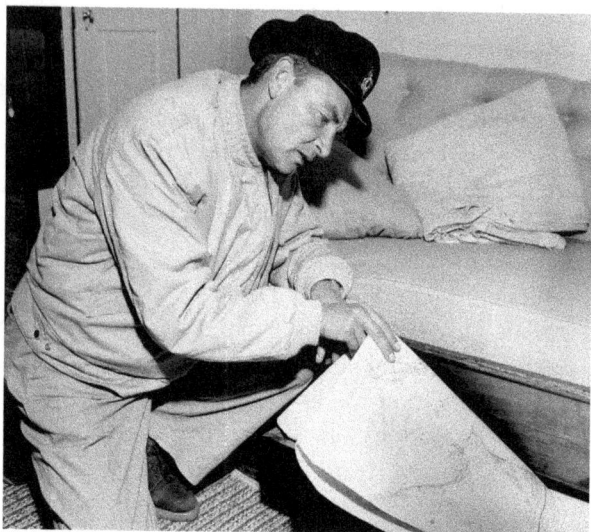

CHAPTER EIGHTEEN
DUFFY'S TAVERN
ON TELEVISION

IN 1947, BRISTOL-MYERS WENT INTO TELEVISION for the primary purpose of learning all it could about television commercial techniques. This phase, according to the company, was the sponsor's biggest problem, secondary to the program itself. On the evening of January 26, 1947, the few who had a television set in their home were treated to a special broadcast over WNBT in New York City. From 8:20 to 8:35 p.m., Ed Gardner participated in an experimental 15-minute telecast of *Duffy's Tavern* featuring a commercial for Minit-Rub. The hour-long program was *Televarities* and every week Bristol-Myers bankrolled talent for comedy routines, news, filmed presentations and musical entertainment. Past entertainment included Eddie Cantor and Alan Young. Because the program was televised "live" and not filmed, it is assumed that a recording of this telecast does not exist. What little is known can be found in the February 8, 1947, issue of *Billboard* magazine. According to the reviewer, Ed Gardner "showed the same lack of interest and effort on the part of the 'manager of *Duffy's Tavern*' as has been shown by other name performers doing video appearances in the past. Gardner, working in front of a decidedly mediocre 'tavern' backdrop and with nothing more in the way of an assist than having a stooge customer come in and order a coke, went thru his by-now standard two-headed pitcher routine. Viewers couldn't possibly have gotten anything more out of seeing Gardner and the gang via tele than they'd gotten in the past having him do it unseen over the air. Perhaps name performers can't very well be blamed for going to no extra pains whatsoever for a TV showing for which they are getting little if anything in the way of remuneration, and on which they figure they are playing to no more than a couple of thousand people at the outside. But the lamentable fact remains that this type of performance, and production effort behind the performance, is doing video no good whatsoever. The viewer can only be left with the impression that television makes little difference with attractions of this type; that they could get the same amount of entertainment, and usually more, by simply tuning in to the attraction's regular radio show. It would seem, however, that some performers would have enough of a sense of responsibility toward the industry of which they are a part, to go to a small measure of extra trouble to add a mite to their routines which might make such routines more interesting as video fare than as straight radio. Gardner certainly didn't do it, nor did Bob Hope and a number of other names the week previous on the West Coast KTLA (Paramount) commercial video station opening. Rest of the show consisted of the Four Vagabonds, who are among radio's and certainly video's top singing quartet... Bristol Myers continues its experiment with inexpensive single-line cartoon drawings (plus still-shot photos of the product) combined with a running script that was slightly on the corny side, resorting to numerous hard-to-take puns to get across the Minit-Rub message."

In the August 26, 1950, issue of *The Los Angeles Times*, a brief news blurb reported: "Ed Gardner will soon announce a video deal for D.T." This never happened. Neither did a 1951 telecast even though the May 26, 1951, issue reported: "NBC this week was reported talking TV deals with Olsen and Johnson and Ed Gardner. O&J may possibly do one or more stints on the *Four Star Revue*. Jimmy Durante this week bowed off the series for the season and the web needs a fill-in, since the series is scheduled to run until mid-July. A deal with Gardner would presumably videoize his *Duffy's Tavern*, which recently wound up a sustaining run on NBC."

The 1952 Pilot Presentation

In what might be considered the most tragic story in the history of the condensed milk business, the 1952 filmed television pilot took a nose dive. With an expired contract with Milwaukee, Gardner was approached by a theatrical agent from New York who flew down to the islands to meet the actor personally. The Pet Milk Company, said he, wanted to start a television series on film in Hollywood and it was interested in Archie for its star. He sold Gardner on the idea and weeks later, at the Hal Roach studios, the first *Duffy's Tavern* television show was put to film.

The story begins in late March 1952. Ed Gardner flew to California to participate in an hour-long filmed version for a one-shot tryout on the *All Star Revue* sometime late in the season. Should the stanza click with television audiences, the National Broadcasting Company had plans to give it a regular TV spot next season. Gardner, however, insisted on permanent residence in Puerto Rico, where he made his home for the last three years and enjoyed a more favorable income. "We're not moving back to Hollywood," he told the press. "We plan to live in Puerto Rico for the rest of our lives. My wife loves it and so do the boys. We pay servants $50 a month and Simone doesn't need her furs. It's wonderful even if my kids (age 4 and 8) do speak Spanish and I don't know what they're talking about." The initial proposal, should the pilot sell, was to do six to ten hour-long productions, televised on a rotating basis with another comedy program. Gardner said he would commute to Hollywood from Puerto Rico to appear as Archie in those productions. He would not consider anyone else for the role.

Ed Gardner

Simone Gardner

The entire production was shot on film, chiefly because Gardner declined the option of a live show. Negotiations with both Filmcraft and the Hal Roach Studios eventually settled with the latter when Ed Gardner was able to own a controlling interest in the package, with the show receiving a minimum budget of $40,000. "I turned down other offers for television because I do not prefer live telecasts," Gardner explained in a letter. "I also don't believe any comedian can be on TV regularly without wearing out his welcome." Leo Morgan was hired to produce the show and the William Morris agency negotiated for the studio space. This would mark the first time a situation comedy show would be televised on *All-Star Revue*.

Very little is known about the filmed television program except for the cast which included Hazel Shermet as Miss Duffy and Ed "Fats" Pichon, from the radio series, and two new actors, Ed Max as Finnegan and Rhys Williams as Clancy the Cop. Columnist Walter Ames visited the set in Hollywood and wrote a brief in his column: "The set is a masterpiece of stage construction. It made me want to sidle up to the bar and order a quick beer."

When an agent called on Ed Gardner to sell him a band for his *Duffy's Tavern* television pilot, Gardner informed him that there would be no band—only a piano. This was a departure from most television production at the time, especially with a singer around the saloon like Jeanette MacDonald. Hoagy Carmichael was originally signed up to play the piano, but backed down when another job came along offering more money.

Rehearsals took place on Thursday, April 24 at Hal Roach Studios, where director Peter Godfrey worked closely with the material, the cast and crew. Filming only took four days, beginning Friday, April 25 and concluding Wednesday, April 30. Before the entire production went before the cameras, two of the three agencies representing the clients (Kellogg's, Pet Milk and Snow Crop) on *All Star Revue* were reportedly unhappy with the way things were going during the filming. Their chief complaints were that the script was sub-par, "more adaptable to radio," and that not once during the hour did they move out of the saloon. Letters of dissatisfaction were sent to NBC.

Hal Roach, Jr. and Simone at the Hoover Dam.

Rudy Vallee went through his entire routine as a guest on *Duffy's Tavern* without saying a single word. Downed by an operation for abscessed throat, ever a pro, Vallee reported to the set for his scenes with Jeanette MacDonald and Ed Gardner, mouthing all of his dialog. A week later, when he regained his voice, he dubbed in those scenes.

The date of the scheduled telecast on *All Star Revue* was moved from May 31 to June 21 because of the delay in getting prints processed. After the reported 91 minutes of footage was edited to its televised length, it would be run off for an audience to dub in the laughs as Hal Roach Studios did with the televised *Amos 'n' Andy* series. The lab technicians explained in a report to the president of NBC that they were not certain that they could turn out the completed footage in time for the original date.

The finished product, without the laugh track, was previewed by a network production executive on the morning of Monday, May 5. The end result was reportedly so disappointing to NBC that an attempt was made to salvage something out of the footage and a fresh start made. To this end, NBC agreed to the postponement of the show from May 31 to June 21. Agency reps were not allowed by Gardner to see the completed film until after the audience laughs were dubbed in. The show was said to be budgeted at $40,000 but it was later reported to have cost $55,000. Reportedly, the finished product reduced Rudy Vallee's scenes to monosyllables. Jeanette MacDonald's lines were cut out, leaving her only as a guest singer. Ultimately, a copy of the pilot was shipped to New York City where Pat Weaver, a top NBC-TV executive, agreed to pass judgment on the completed film.

By way of explanation, the origin of the issue began while Ed Gardner, en route to the West Coast from Puerto Rico, read up on condensed milk. He discovered that Pet Milk was one of the leading brands; that perhaps its chief competitor was known as Carnation Milk. Gardner and his crew had evidently written a skit which semi-kidded the milk company, Pet Milk, one of the bankrollers. Gardner wanted to incorporate the company name in the form of "product placement." It was first approved during a review of the script and then later rejected. The picture was produced in and around Duffy's bar but how can you have a bar without some liquor bottles in sight? Gardner had plenty of bottles on view. Pet Milk wanted milk bottles instead.

The big climax of the performance had Archie functioning as a phony banker in an ascot tie, striped pants and frock coat with boutonnière. Funny it was, too. Even Gardner smiled at the memory of it. The film was previewed for the prospective sponsors. "They were not enthusiastic," Gardner reported. "They were pained by those bottles on the back bar. They wanted condensed milk in 'em. We figured maybe we could fix that by re-shooting, but then we came to the banker sequence. Me with the flower in my buttonhole. That's what flung 'em. My advertising Pet Milk with a carnation on my lapel." Gardner blamed that error on the property department. He claimed he didn't even notice he was wearing the opposition's trademark. But the Pet Milk boys did.

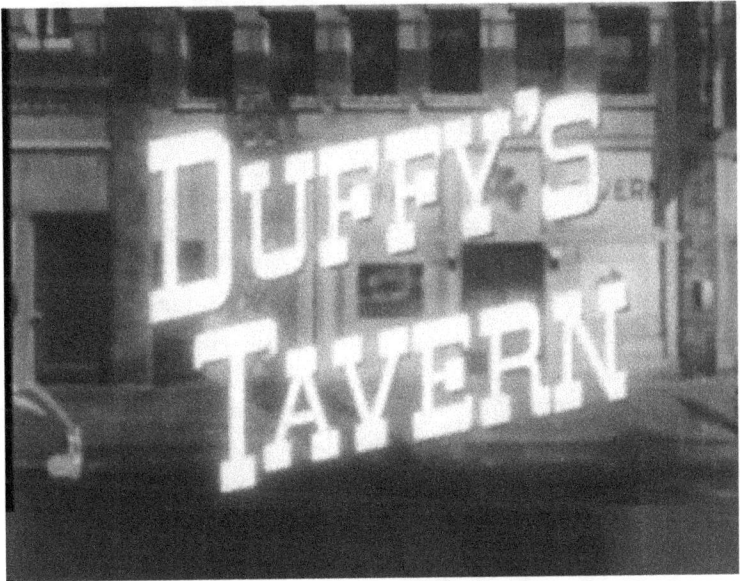

After Pat Weaver reviewed the pilot, he agreed it was beyond satisfactory for telecasting, but was forced to cancel the telecast and instead substitute a variety show, hurriedly put together by Hal Kemp, an NBC executive producer. The reason was that the president of Pet Milk appealed to NBC vice-president Ed Madden, in a reportedly heated session, standing firm that the show would not be acceptable for airing. What no one reckoned with was Pet Milk, whose turn it was to be the main sponsor. (All three sponsors were featured on a rotating basis.) Rather than take a loss of $50,000, the network decided to salvage something from the film and edit the footage to a half-hour show and use it as a pilot for a fall sale.

Gardner, it later came out, conspired with director Peter Godfrey to film 91 minutes of footage on purpose. Should the pilot not air over NBC, Gardner owned the rights to the unsold film itself and had a weather eye on theatrical distribution. Another alternative was to cut the film into two individual television episodes. Gardner, meanwhile, told the advertising agencies that it was unfair to pass judgment on the uncut version, until the laugh track was added to the hour-long version. "Working on *Duffy's Tavern* was an exciting experience," Jeanette MacDonald publicly defended. "There have been rumors about the show falling far short of the humor expected from it but they're untrue. They came from people who saw the film in its rough form, before it was edited and cleaned up. I think video audiences will really enjoy Gardner's efforts."

In late June, Gardner jumped to a different network, attempting to lure interest from the producers of CBS' *Colgate Comedy Hour*. John Lester of the *Long Island Star-Journal*, without viewing the pilot himself, reviewed the facts behind the production and attempted telecast. "I feel I'm doing the show no injustice in advance when I submit the possibility that the parade has already passed by, that any degree of success it may have had will be minor compared to its radio glory, and will be based on re-capturing that following…; being great on radio and being great on television are two entirely different and far removed things."

The Hal Roach Studios

Keeping in mind that the networks, sponsors, agencies and actors had the same radio mentality when it came to telecasting programs "live," more than half of television broadcasts in 1953 were not pre-recorded on film. In the summer of 1953, Ed Gardner signed a contract with Hal Roach Studios, licensing the *Duffy's Tavern* radio program for a series of 39 half-hour shows filmed directly for syndication. The William Morris agency assured Gardner that pre-mapping syndication plans was the best route to ensure the largest profits. This marked the first time that a name show had been produced for syndication at the outset, with Hal Roach Studios continuing with *Amos n' Andy* soon after.

Originally, Gardner agreed to allow Official Films to syndicate the series, but the company felt the asking price for the series was too expensive and Official thumbed down the offer. Instead, Matty Fox, president of Motion Pictures of Television (MPT), financed and syndicated the series, with an estimated budget of $40,000 per episode. This was considerably high, when you realize that a filmed situation comedy in 1953 (reusing the same living room and office sets week after week) cost an estimated $20,000 per episode. Gardner received a flat fee just for the licensing agreement: $30,000. Hal Roach, Jr., personally oversaw the production. Casting began in August and September of 1953, with cameras rolling during the last week of September.

Most of the material was adapted from radio scripts, but a handful of episodes did feature original plot material. The first scriptwriters to sign up included Larry Rhine and Ben Starr. Almost before shooting began, the Women's Christian Temperance Union and other groups began protesting against the series, believing the program would be aimed to younger viewers and a plethora of liquor bottles would be prominently displayed. To reassure the groups, Gardner personally explained that the scripts were being written so a lot of action was taken away from the tavern. "It's supposed to be a Third Avenue bar in New York but we can't make it too low-down," Gardner complained. "If I had all the money in the world, I'd say I'd do it my way and be arty, but these groups might pressure the sponsor..."

MPT, meanwhile, was investing an estimated thirty million dollars in television production and syndication, including the acquisition of ten-year rights to *Flash Gordon*, a King Features Syndicate property, contract signed in late September. The television series was produced in Berlin with an all-American cast supervised by Edward Gruskin.

Casting for the video *Duffy's Tavern* took only three weeks.

Brown-eyed Pattee Chapman was 27 years old when she signed for the role of Miss Duffy, in a role that critic John Crosby remarked "sometimes seems to go all the way back to the McKinley Administration." She had been idling around New York doing stage productions a couple of years earlier when the thought came that she might do better in Hollywood. Her finances were at a low ebb so she posed as a 12-year-old and traveled half-fare on an airliner. "I didn't have much money," Pattee later explained, "so I dressed as a little girl. The stewardess combed my curls in the morning before we landed and saw that I drank my milk and even had me change seats with a grownup passenger so that I could talk to a little boy my own age." When Chapman signed up for *Duffy's Tavern*, she lied about her age and reported she was 23.

Pattee Chapman as Miss Duffy

When Ed Gardner wandered into Will Wright's ice cream parlor in Beverly Hills, Pattee was working there nights and playing occasional television roles in the daytime, including *Our Miss Brooks* and *I Married Joan*. Having been a fan of *Duffy's Tavern* from the radio (or so she told Ed Gardner), she knew how the girl who filled the Miss Duffy role talked. When Gardner ordered pistachio ice cream she knew just what to do. "We ain't got no pistachio," sing-songed Pattee. "How's about some tutti-frutti?"

"Change your clothes," said Gardner. "We're gonna see a man about an acting job." Two days later, Pattee became Miss Duffy.

The new role of Charley the waiter, who usually tempered Archie's rash actions, was played by Jimmy Conlin, a veteran of over 50 years in the entertainment business who built his reputation on the Keith-Orpheum vaudeville circuit. Conlin was no spring chicken by the time he accepted the role and his New York accent was not laid thick for the television program, but what appealed more to Gardner was Conlin's comedic timing. Some theorize that having Charley instead of Eddie was a more "politically correct" approach, but had an African-American played the role, like Rochester on *The Jack Benny Program* and Eddie Green himself on radio's *Duffy's Tavern*, the role would have undoubtedly been portrayed in good taste.

On the publicity front, Michael O'Shea, an independent New York press agent, was signed to handle the publicity for *Duffy's Tavern*, an important role in the future success of the program. Under his spearhead, full-page advertisements for the television series began appearing in trade papers during the first week of November, including *Variety* and *Broadcasting Telecasting*. It remains difficult today to verify whether his efforts to sell the series to local television stations were successful. Two weeks before O'Shea signed with MPT, on October 16, *Duffy's Tavern* was sold nationally on television to the Scott Paper Company for NBC, a coast-to-coast telecast for all 39 weeks. The program was not ready for station use before January 1, but selling the program in advance began almost as soon as the series went before the cameras.

A few days before Christmas, MPT's new Film Syndication Division used the Schwerin Research Corporation to pretest the audience reaction, hoping the reports would help sell their television programs. By this time, the pilot for *Janet Dean, Registered Nurse* had already been completed, the third of six programs in which MPT was investing. Adults previewed *Duffy's Tavern* and *Janet Dean*, while juveniles watched *Flash Gordon*. *Duffy's* attained an average "liking score" of 76, *Janet Dean* achieved an average of

80 and *Flash Gordon* received better than an 85. Had the results proven negative, the company would have re-shot the films with the objectionable factors eliminated or corrected. Such surveys, however, only served one purpose: to convince a sponsor to buy a product. Comedian George Jessel, two weeks later, criticized surveys and ratings and did a little fact checking on his own. "First of all, they always listen to me on CBS, which I'm not on; second, they like Johnny Burke who's been dead several years," Jessel wrote. "I made a dozen calls this past week and asked people what program they listen to on Thursday night on NBC. Four people said Jackie Gleason, who's on CBS, 8 p.m. on Saturdays. I asked the next four what they listen to on CBS on Saturday night. One fellow hung up on me; the other three said the *Colgate Hour*. I asked the next two people what program they enjoyed most and they answered George Jessel's *This Is Your Life*. And the other said, *Duffy's Tavern*, which is not on."

Duffy's Tavern was still fresh on everyone's mind because sales for sponsorship were strong in February of 1954. Roma Wines agreed to pick up the tab on an alternating week basis for 26 weeks (13 episodes total), over KTLA in Los Angeles, beginning February 23. Just a few days prior, Arizona Brewing purchased 26 episodes of *Duffy's Tavern* for eight markets, seen in El Paso, Texas; Albuquerque and Roswell, New Mexico; Las Vegas, Nevada; Phoenix, Tucson and Yuma, Arizona and San Diego, California. In early March, 26 episodes of the series were sold to WTVI in St. Louis, sponsored by Old Judge Coffee. In late March, Arnold Bakeries signed for 26 episodes over WNBT in New York City.* In late April 1954, the Gulf Brewing Company, through its agency, Foote, Cone & Belding, purchased *Duffy's Tavern* to be shown on WOAI in San Antonio, Texas.

---

* Simone and Ed Gardner flew in to New York to attend a party commemorating the premiere of the television program, and watch the premiere episode as it aired over WNBT, but Ed Gardner was bedded down at the St. Regis because of a minor surgery and they had to reluctantly cancel their appearance.

To break even on production costs, MPT had to get the program into at least 70 markets, a third of them major ones. MPT eventually made it but with little to spare. Certainly not enough to warrant a second or third season. As one columnist explained in the April 24, 1954, issue of *Cue* magazine: "When an old favorite like *Duffy's Tavern* shows up in a new medium, it starts out with millions of pre-sold rooters. But unless succeeding films in this series are a distinct improvement over the first couple of episodes, we won't even be left with our memories. For the televersion of *Duffy's* is bad enough to make us wonder whether the 14-year-old radio series was really as smart as we once thought."

The cast of the television series.

Gardner's three-year contract with Matthew Fox, board chairman of Motion Pictures for Television, Inc., called for 39 episodes a year and a budget set at $45,000 per episode for a total outlay of $5,265,000 for the 117 films. Every half-hour film was shot in both black and white and in color. It was about this time that trade columns were predicting that stations would be showing syndicated film shows in color by the fall of 1955 and pointing out that color set circulation was expected to be large enough in key markets for stations to introduce color-originating equipment.

By the end of the calendar year, 65 stations pledged to purchase network color pickup equipment and MPT expected public demand to grow for color telecasts. The firm went deeply into color when it entered syndication a year before with the first 26 episodes of *Duffy's Tavern* tinted via Eastman color. The company quickly switched ground after it was discovered that the color productions were coming out fuzzy on the air. Compared to the technology of today such color prints, if they were made available, would appear faded at best. When production for the remaining 13 episodes of the season began in late April 1954, they were shot in monochrome (black and white). For television stations that complained about the color, black and white prints were shipped to replace them. *Janet Dean* suffered the same and quickly shifted to monochrome. (*Flash Gordon*, shooting in Germany, never went to color, since there were no color facilities currently available in West Berlin.)

The first 26 episodes were shot under the direction of Harve Foster, who proved very efficient in completing a television drama on time and on budget. The May 15, 1954, issue of *Billboard* reported: "Motion Pictures for Television, Inc. is pulling back on its color plans for syndicated series, having decided not to shoot further *Duffy's Tavern* segments in color after the first 26." Ed Gardner would later be interviewed by a columnist for *TV Guide* who failed to go into details about the switchover, only to quote Gardner saying that the second season would be shot entirely in color.

Reviews poured in; split on both sides. Critics either criticized the program in comparison to the radio program or accepted the show for what it was and suggested promise. Walter Ames, after watching the first episode, wrote a review for the February 25, 1954, issue of the *Los Angeles Times*, claiming *Duffy's Tavern* "seems to have the kick to stick around awhile this time. I say this despite expected protests from some mothers that the language used on the show might tend to influence their offspring. Any youngster of influenceable age should be in bed by the time this comes on the screens. Ed Gardner as Archie proved he hasn't lost his zip in the role but the real find was Alan Reed as Finnegan. If I didn't know Alan, I'd say he was born for the role of the stupe."

Ed Gardner cross-promoting the TV series in a beer advertisement.

One reviewer remarked in the April 7, 1954, issue of *Variety*: "Show isn't going to break any records, though, for the simple reason that sight doesn't add to much to the show. On the radio, it was basically very funny dialog, adequate situation and good voice parts. On television, it's still dialog, voices and situation, with the latter suffering because little's left to the imagination. Restaurant setting, on-screen actors and some sight gags don't add very much. As a result, what convulsed 'em at home 10 years ago is only mildly amusing today. Big redeeming feature of the segment caught was some crisp dialog and some classic Gardner malaprops ('gargoyle, bring me a maggot of champagne' and 'Pate de paux pas')."

"The old zest and flavor seem to be strangely missing, in this cleaned-up, spick-and-span *Duffy's Tavern*," remarked columnist Leo Mishkin for *Sight and Sound*. In his April 15, 1954, column, Mishkin wrote: "Remember the times when Clifton Fadiman, or Tallulah Bankhead, or maybe even Noel Coward would visit the place? Remember the smell of the stale beer, the sawdust, and the ripe old cheese on the free lunch counter down at the end of the bar? Remember some of those parties held by the friends and neighbors, with a couple of friends and neighbors occasionally found a day or two later, still sleeping off the effects of same? The old *Duffy's Tavern* is no more, torn down, no doubt, like so many other landmarks around town, making way for progress and advancement, and the cause of higher civilization. Archie and Finnegan and Miss Duffy have moved to a new location. But it just isn't the same any more."

The plots were pretty much in line with the radio program. Each week, Archie found himself the central character in an attempt to impress a wealthy widow or beautiful girlfriend, always falling victim to his own scheme. In the episode "Archie, the Chef," Archie made a play for the richest girl in the world, who also happened to be a patron of the tavern, and tried to persuade her father, a gentleman who likes fine food, that he, Archie, was a first-class chef. The first class chef was actually out in the kitchen, hired solely to attract more wealthy patrons, and proved a big hit. The chef, however, was bewailing a broken romance, and it was up to Archie to keep the chef happy on one hand, and the father of the richest girl in the world well fed on the other.

In the episode, "A Date for Miss Duffy," Archie faced the problem of how to get Miss Duffy married to a former classmate of Archie's, Egghead Anderson, who reportedly came up in the world since both he and Archie had flunked out of kindergarten and was now established in an elegant apartment in a swank hotel.

To impress Egghead with his own affluence and social standing, Archie paid a call dressed in a polo helmet and polo coat.

"Do you play polo?" inquired Egghead.

"Doesn't everyone?" returned Archie, with his eyebrows raised. A good question.

To further to impress Egghead, Archie took over a Long Island mansion – through the courtesy of some skeleton keys owned by Second Story Jackson – and installed Miss Duffy as its owner and heiress. Anyone with an I.Q. higher than room temperature would have seen it coming a mile away that eventually Egghead himself would turn out to be nothing more than a fortune hunter, that the real owners of the Long Island mansion would return home unexpectedly, and that Archie would wind up, at the finish, trying to explain to Duffy what happened.

In an interview for *TV Guide*, Ed Gardner expressed his dissatisfaction for working long hours but a new respect for television actors. "In radio," Gardner explained, "I was the producer and director, and half the time the writer, and also Archie. I was goin' all the time. It was an awful mental strain. But here it's different. Hal Roach, Jr. does the producing and Harve Foster directs and they bring the scripts in and they're in pretty good shape. All I have to do is memorize the lines and I'm not so sharp at it. But it's them hot lights and all that standin' around that gets me. We're shootin' in color so they gotta light the place up like it was the third degree and five in the afternoon I tell ya I'm shot. We figured to make only twenty-six films, but just this morning they tell me we're set for thirteen more and I should bust my head against a wall or something."

While filming commenced for the thirteen additional episodes throughout the spring of 1954, sales were given a boost by another company. The Fortune Merchandising Corporation, an operation headed by Leonard Schain which held a virtual monopoly on promotion-merchandising servicing to sponsors and television outfits, best known as the merchandising arm for Gene Autry's television program, began a campaign in July 1954 attempting to sell the *Duffy's Tavern* program to potential sponsors, primarily for breweries, and to additional television outlets that did not already carry the program. Proposed premiums and giveaways included glassware and bar devices. Fortune was able to sell the program on additional stations, helping MPT recover their costs. A few days after being notified that the *Duffy's Tavern* television program would not be renewed for a second season due to lackluster sales, Ed Gardner told columnists in July 1954 that he had decided to hang up his hat for good. "I'm quitting as an actor and comedian. I've had it," he said. "Fifteen years is long enough to be a clown. I'd rather do something else now. I'm going back to my original racket — writing, producing and directing." Gardner told reporters that *Duffy's Tavern* would never be resurrected for TV unless Art Carney agreed to play the role of Archie, whom he felt was the best (and only) person qualified for the role.

Another reviewer in the February 25, 1954, issue of *Variety* remarked: "Some shows lend themselves better to radio than television and the transition to the sight medium generally comes off lumpy. So it is with *Duffy's Tavern*, one of the real vets of the sound waves, which is going to take a lot of doing to make it palatable at the tubes. The main fault is Ed Gardner's lack of acting savvy. Standing in front of a mike reading from a script is one thing; acting like one on a stage is another. 'Archie,' who is Gardner, bridged it with awkward difficulty and his efforts at best were clumsy. He just hasn't become an actor overnight just because television is here and he wants in."

"Ed was really terrified. He was absolutely in a panic," Simone later recalled to Carl Amari on his radio program. "He was not an actor and suddenly he had to act in front of a camera and he would panic. It made him seem wooden. He didn't have the spontaneity that he had when he was hiding behind the bar with the funny hat."

Another contributing factor might have been the disillusioned shock from faithful radio listeners, who for many years, had a mental vision of what the tavern looked like. The television counterpart was as nice a place as you could want to take your own grandmother. The silverware and napery gleamed in the light and out in the kitchen there was even a French chef (for one episode, anyway). There wasn't a single speck of sawdust on the floor, there didn't seem to be any bar at all, and even Archie the manager kept his hat on all the while he was on duty. Clifton Finnegan, new for

TV waiter Charley and the ineffable Miss Duffy herself were also on hand but seemed to be much more gentle, cultured folk than radio listeners had every reason to expect them to be. There was a good deal less of the atmosphere and quaint charm that once permeated the place. As a result of all these contributing factors, a business decision was made not to renew the comedy for a second or third season. The program continued in syndication throughout the fifties. In 1955, the series was telecast over the airwaves in Hamilton, Ontario; Seattle, Washington; and a second run in New York City. In 1956, the series was telecast in Plattsburgh, New York and Kansas City, Missouri. In 1957, folks in Chicago, Illinois watched the program before prime time programming. In 1958, *Duffy's Tavern* opened for business in Atlanta, Georgia. In 1959, the comedy was seen on the small screen in Oklahoma City, Oklahoma and Green Bay, Wisconsin.

In the fall of 1957, Gardner scripted a new television series titled *Inside McManus* and started looking for a young "Archie" to play the title role. Supplementing additional income, Gardner began appearing in guest spots on other television programs such as *Alfred Hitchcock Presents*. Television viewers who looked closely at the Elgin watch commercials on Perry Como's show in 1956 and 1957 might not have realized it at the time, but Santa Claus bore a striking resemblance to the comic.

Television Episode Guide

Producer: Hal Roach Jr.
Production Supervisor: Manuel Goldstein
Director: Harve Foster
Camera: Lathrop Worth
Art Director: McClure Capps
Film Editor: Gene Fowler, Jr.
Assistant Directors: Bill Forsyth and Jimmie Lane
Scriptwriters: Morris Freedman, Frank Gill Jr., Larry Rhine and Ben Starr

Cast
Ed Gardner as Archie
Pattee Chapman as Miss Duffy
Alan Reed as Finnegan
Jimmy Conlin as Charley, the waiter
James Burke as Clancy the Cop

Episode #1 "The Grand Opening"
Plot: Duffy's Tavern re-opens with a grand gala but none of the tavern regulars care to walk through the door. Archie investigates and discovers a gambling hall next door is luring the customers away. To counteract the competition, Archie makes it known that he dropped one of Miss Duffy's valuable rings in the chicken fricassee.

Episode #2 "The Gypsy Princess"
Plot: Archie promises a real gypsy fortune teller when Mrs. Piddleton and her Lord Byron Ladies' Literary Society drop by the tavern. When a fortune teller is nowhere to be found, Archie convinces Finnegan to dress up as a gypsy fortune teller. This episode was a remake of the November 23, 1951, radio broadcast. The cast includes Lizz Slifer as Mrs. Piddleton.

Episode #3 "Archie Gets Engaged"
Plot: Archie's girlfriend, a striptease artist named Peaches La Tour, dumps him, Archie proposes to the wealthy Mrs. Van Clyde instead. When Mrs. Van Clyde gives Archie a credit card, he uses it to buy expensive gifts in the attempt to win back Peaches' affection. The cast includes Veda Ann Borg as Peaches and Barbara Morrison as Mrs. Van Clyde.

Episode #4 "Honesty is the Best Policy"
Plot: Archie tries to marry a wealthy widow (played by Elvia Allman) to get the money to pay off a gambling debt before a gangster named "Sweet Sue" (played by John Doucette) can carry out his threats. Also in the cast are Lillian Culver, Grace Hayle and Jack Lomas.

Episode #5 "A Date for Miss Duffy"
Plot: Archie learns that an old school chum who struck it rich as an oil millionaire is dropping by the tavern. In an effort to get Miss Duffy a date and impress the millionaire, Archie pawns the woman off as a wealthy heiress. Also in the cast is Francis Bavier, Larry Dobkin, Thurston Hall and Herb Vigran.

Episode #6 "Archie the Hero"
Plot: Mistakenly believing he has only three days to live, Archie decides to perform a dangerous heroic act in an effort to win a romantic evening with Peaches La Tour, the burlesque stripper (played by Veda Ann Borg).

Episode #7 "Archie, the Hypnotist"
Plot: Danzo the hypnotist (played by Trevor Bardette) encourages Archie to go on vacation. While Duffy is under the influence of the hypnotist, Archie convinces the tavern's owner to give him three days off, his first vacation in years. Archie then hires a ne'er-do-well to take his place, thinking the vagrant can only make his work look good in comparison. This episode borrows elements from the December 1, 1948, radio broadcast.

Episode #8 "Archie's Roommate"
Plot: To get enough money to take Peaches to an expensive nightclub, Archie takes in a roommate, played by Prince Michael Romanoff, but the plan backfires when the new roommate refuses to pay the rent in advance. This episode borrows a plot device from the April 7, 1948, radio broadcast. After the episode aired, critics raved about Romanoff's performance and he received an offer to star in his own television series.

Episode #9 "Archie, the Father"
Plot: Archie's dream of fatherhood is recognized when an apparently abandoned baby is found on the doorstep of the tavern and Finnegan brings the basket inside. The youth completely captivates Archie and his pals. This episode is a remake of the April 14, 1948, radio broadcast.

Episode #10 "Archie's Landmark"
Plot: Archie tries to raise money to repair the tavern before a city inspector condemns the crumbling building. Then he gets an idea and tries to make a historical landmark out of *Duffy's Tavern* by formally asking the Historical Society to confirm the rumor that George Washington slept there. This episode is a remake of the January 19, 1949, radio broadcast.

Episode #11 "Archie's Newspaper"
Plot: When a rival tavern creates new matchbooks that are the talk of the street, Archie decides Duffy's Tavern needs their own publicity and begins printing his own newspaper. This episode is a remake of the April 2, 1947, radio broadcast.

Episode #12 "Archie Buys a Dog"
Plot: Archie uses tavern money to buy a dog and then tries to resell it for what appears to be a profit, unaware the dog is a nothing but a mutt. Only then does Archie learn that the auditors are coming to look over the books.

Episode #13 "Archie's Double Date"
Plot: Archie and Finnegan agree to go on a double date, but fight over which one of them gets stuck escorting horrible Hannah.

Episode #14 "Archie's Singing Contest"
Plot: Archie's plan to court a beautiful actress, Daphne Drake (played by Mary Beth Hughes), by holding a fake singing contest backfires when he selects Finnegan to be the judge of the "contest." This episode is a remake of the November 9, 1951, radio broadcast. Cast includes Aileen Carlyle, Fritz Feld, Kathryn Sheldon and Lizz Slifer.

Episode #15 "A Trip to Florida"
Archie goes on a quiz program to win money so he can give presents to his girl and to win an all-expense paid trip for two to Florida. What no one knows is the contest is open only to children. Archie's girlfriend, Peaches La Tour, is played by Veda

Ann Borg. This episode was a remake of the December 28, 1951, radio broadcast. Also in the cast is June Whitley and Carlton G. Young. The original title of this episode was "Archie Goes to Florida" during production.

Episode #16 "Archie, the Genial Host"
Plot: Archie enters a contest in the hopes of winning the title of "Most Popular Bartender on Third Avenue" and attempts to swing the election by serving free food and beer to gain popularity.

Episode #17 "Gems from the Diamond Country"
Plot: Archie hopes to use gems that Finnegan has inherited to pay off a gambling debt. The role of Coloucci is played by Fortunio Bonanova. This episode is a remake of the April 6, 1945, radio broadcast.

Episode #18 "Archie Buys a Racehorse"
Plot: Archie goes into partnership with a friend, Slippery McGuire (played by Jesse White), to buy a racehorse. When the horse wins, Archie doesn't collect because, "the contract says you're the party of the second part and the first part (of the nag) won." This episode is a remake of the November 30, 1951, radio broadcast. Also in the cast was Veda Ann Borg as Peaches La Tour, Charles Lane and Vernon Rich.

Episode #19 "Miss Duffy's Coming Out Party"
Plot: When none of the tavern's denizens will serve as Miss Duffy's date at her coming-out party, Archie is forced to hire an escort service. What she gets is Prince Igor, played by Benny Rubin. This episode is a remake of the May 28, 1947, radio broadcast. Also in the cast are Bill Arnold, Veda Ann Berg, Don Brodie and Valerie Vernon.

Episode #20 "Archie Faces Marriage"
Plot: A beautiful woman (played by Lola Albright) rents the use of the tavern's back room to print "greeting cards" and convinces Archie to propose to her… in order to cover up her illegal activities.

It turns out she's a counterfeiter of U.S. currency. Mrs. Magruder, her associate, is played by Sarah Padden. This episode is a remake of the February 29, 1944, radio broadcast.

Episode #21 "Archie's Publicity Stunt"
Plot: When a pearl is found in an oyster served at a rival tavern, Archie tries to counteract the attention with a publicity stunt... which ultimately backfires on Archie and his pals.

Episode #22 "Archie's Floor Show"
Plot: Archie tries to hire the beautiful star of a rival tavern's floor show.

Episode #23 "Archie, the Politician"
Plot: Archie decides to enter the election race and run for city council as alderman. Peaches La Tour, his girlfriend, is played by Veda Ann Borg. The original title of this episode was "Archie, the Alderman" during production. Mary Beth Hughes was originally slated to play the role of Archie's girlfriend.

Episode #24 "Archie, the Chef"
Plot: In order to attract more wealthy patrons, Archie hires a French chef, Pierre (played by Maurice Marsac) and keeps him in the kitchen sight-unseen. The chef is a big hit and soon wealthy patrons are lining up to sample the fine cuisine. When a beautiful and wealthy woman falls in love with the food, Archie tries to make her fall in love with him by claiming he is the chef. This episode was partly adapted from the January 26, 1943, radio broadcast. Also in the cast was Hal Baylor, Myrna Dell and Lou Leonard.

Episode #25 "Archie's Yacht"
Plot: Archie inherits a yacht and decides to join a yacht club to enter the social set. Only after all the calamity does Archie discover the yacht is nothing more than a ship in a bottle. This episode was a remake of the May 7, 1947, radio broadcast. Also in the cast is Joyce Holden.

Episode #26 "Archie's Insurance Company"
Plot: Archie decides to open an insurance company and soon sells his first policy — to a mobster (played by John Harmon) who is marked for death by a rival mobster.

Episode #27 "Archie the Bluebeard"
Plot: Archie tries to juggle dating two beautiful, hot-tempered women at the same time. This only gets Archie into trouble. The role of Chiquita, the Spanish singer, is played by Charlita, and Renee, the French model, is played by Renee Godfrey.

Episode #28 "Archie the Ambassador"
Plot: Archie is intrigued when a tavern patron, Slippery McGuire (played by Jesse White) exploits his vanity and offers to make him an ambassador in an exotic foreign country. This episode is a remake of the May 5, 1945, radio broadcast.

Episode #29 "Archie, the Ex-Coward"
Plot: After Archie accidentally knocks out two burglars, he decides his true calling is in the boxing ring so Finnegan arranges for a bout with a professional boxer, Spike McGurk, played by Mike Mazurki. This episode is a remake of the April 21, 1948, radio broadcast.

Episode #30 "Archie Buys a Fiddle"
Plot: Archie buys an original Stradivarius for $15 and then discovers he cannot sell it for a profit. The role of Heitelz is played by Sig Ruman. This episode is a remake of two radio broadcasts, May 5 and 12, 1942.

Episode #31 "Archie, the Heir"
Plot: Archie tries to convince the executor of an estate that he's really the family's long-lost heir, unaware that the Fenston family prefers to eliminate any chance of losing the inheritance by attempting to poison him. The role of Fenston is played by Pierre Watkins and Mrs. Fenston by Kathryn Gard.

Episode #32 "Damage Suit"
Plot: Archie decides he wants to become a lawyer but, not having enough money to pay for school, he persuades Finnegan to have an accident in the tavern. He intends to collect from the insurance company enough money to study law, not realizing he's breaking the law! This episode was a remake of the January 21, 1948, radio broadcast.

Episode #33 "Archie's Boys Club"
Plot: In order to impress a pretty girl (played by Martha Hyer) whose younger brother is a juvenile delinquent, Archie decides to open a boy's club. This episode is a remake of the April 21, 1948, radio broadcast.

Episode #34 "Wedding in the Tavern"
Plot: Archie is asked to attend a wedding reception and can't get his tuxedo out of the rooming house so he claims to have contracted a rare disease.

Episode #35 "Archie Sells the Tavern"
Plot: Archie's attempt to auction off the tavern brings in two bidders — a sea captain and a Mexican who are determined to outbid each other for ownership of the bar. Archie ultimately ends up dunked in Central Park Lake.

Episode #36 "Claude's Black Bag"
Plot: Claude brings a time bomb into the tavern, hidden in a mysterious black bag, which is set to explode when his girl Gladys marries someone else.

Episode #37 "Archie, the Detective"
Plot: Archie gets mixed up in a case of mistaken identity and attempted bank robbery. To clear his name, Archie helps Clancy the Cop apprehend Saloomi Sam, the safe cracker. The role of Sam is played by Joe Vitali.

Episode #38 "Archie's Rich Uncle"
Plot: Archie receives a letter from his wealthy uncle, a gold miner,

and thinks he's coming into a fortune. This episode is a remake of the April 7, 1942, radio broadcast.

Episode #39 "Archie, the Actor"
Plot: Archie wangles a part in a play and takes a fling at the theater to prove to a girl, Daphne (played by Mary Beth Hughes) that he is an actor. John Hubbard is also in the cast.

Scriptwriter Bob Schiller once remarked that Duffy never walked into his own tavern. "Ed Gardner always figured that [we should] leave that to the imagination. He thought it would spoil everything if suddenly Duffy would show up. One of the wonderful things about radio was that you couldn't see it. In one of the shows, for example, Archie says, 'What's our new waiter doing?' 'He's mopping the floor' is the reply. 'What's wrong with that?' he says, 'he's mopping it with a customer!' Try to do that on television."

CHAPTER NINETEEN
AFTER DUFFY'S TAVERN

IN FEBRUARY OR MARCH 1954, Ed Gardner acknowledged he had a serious drinking problem and, with the help of his family, went to Alcoholics Anonymous. His two sons, Stephen and Ed Jr., and his wife, Simone Hegemann, were very supportive. Years prior, Gardner was known for taking more than a few drinks between the East Coast and West Coast broadcasts. Applying hindsight, it remains possible that Gardner found comfort with the bottle when he lost two good friends as a result of the heat in Puerto Rico (Green and Taylor), pressured with the fact that his radio program was a closed book and a potential television series was not looking promising. In early September, Ed Gardner and wife celebrated a party in Cannes, having been on the wagon for six months. "My dad did have a drinking problem," Ed Gardner, Jr. later recalled. "It got so bad he took a swing at someone without thinking twice. He eventually went to AA and became clean and sober. He was that way for the last nine years of his life."

"He had a very big problem with drinking," recalled Simone Hegeman. "I didn't realize when we were first married and it became difficult over the years. I didn't see any hope of changing his pattern of drinking which I recognized. He didn't drink regularly. But if he had a beer, he would have to go on a bender. He would go weeks and months sometimes without drinking but it didn't help. And finally, by some miracle, he joined AA. He cut it out cold. That was after ten years of marriage. I know that on our fifteenth wedding anniversary we were in Hawaii and we had about 12 people and we were sitting around and everyone making toasts. I stood up and I said I wanted to make a toast and I said, 'I want to drink to our fifteenth wedding anniversary. Five of the happiest years of my life.' It gives people hope that they can beat it."

Ed Gardner and family in Hawaii.

During that same year, according to two trade columns, Gardner seriously considered getting into politics. Nothing else has been found beyond that brief mention but by Christmas 1954, the Gardner family returned to California and moved into a new home in Benedict Canyon. Reporters often brought up the subject

of Puerto Rico with derogatory insinuations that the comedian purposely attempted to evade paying taxes. Gardner preferred the term "tax avoidance." The subject was ultimately dropped over time, especially in 1955, when the Virgin Islands began attracting Hollywood elite because of the tax break they would receive, just as Puerto Rico once drew Ed Gardner and others seeking to escape high tax rates. Bob Ellis who, a decade prior, was a deejay on radio station KNX after having been under contract to MGM, was president of his own company. Bob Ellis Enterprises, which planned production of motion pictures and audio platters turned out under the Ellector Records brand, justified his actions from Saint Thomas. "The Virgin Islands have provided us residents with tax advantages which have given us tremendous incentive to go into preproduction." His first album was *Great Songs of Love* and the net gains were more substantial than if he was a resident of the United States. When asked by a reporter why he pulled up stakes in Puerto Rico, Gardner explained: "We took the two kids and moved to Spain and I was gonna retire. But then the dukes kept getting all the good tables in the restaurants and like I said there was nobody to talk shop with."

Hoping to break into Broadway with his own musical, *The Petunia Peddler*, Ed Gardner wrote the book while Jay Livingston and Ray Evans supplied the songs (at least two of the songs, "You're My Guy" and "Caribbean Tango," were written by Ed Gardner). In August, Gardner flew to New York City from the West Coast to have discussions with Courtney Burr about funding the production. The deal was never closed because Burr felt the music needed work. Gardner flew back to the Coast to rewrite many of the songs. By September, Gardner had secured Alan Young and Harold Peary for the cast but, in the end, the show never opened.

In September 1956, Ed Gardner joined the J. Walter Thompson Agency in an executive capacity on the program creation level. He operated in the agency's New York headquarters in the radio-television department. It was Gardner's hope that he would create a new comedy program that would launch a new phase in his career. The Agency, however, had changed since his pre-*Duffy* days, when he had started with the Thompson agency in

Ed Gardner's personal bound volumes of radio scripts.

a creative post in the radio department. Gardner was not satisfied with employment and quit just weeks later.

In the spring of 1957, after he read a blurb in the trade papers, Ed Gardner threatened to sue ZIV-TV for planning to produce a television series called *Harbor Patrol*. Gardner claimed he had a similar idea and felt he had prior rights. The attorney at ZIV reviewed all possible angles and could not find any evidence of ZIV being informed prior about *Harbor Patrol*, nor any communication between ZIV and Gardner. The actor/producer ultimately dropped his complaint when he could not prove his claim. "If you ever gave a thought to license my *Duffy's Tavern* property, do not bother to ask," Gardner wrote in a letter to John L. Sinn, president of ZIV Television Programs. "The ideas I conceive are proprietary. I guess there is nothing too small you would not consider stealing. What happened to honor among thieves?"

Beginning in June 1955, NBC premiered a magazine of the air, *Monitor*, heard in full weekend slates of four-hour blocks. Old radio stars such as Bob Hope and Fibber McGee and Molly appeared in new skits. Besides comedy, *Monitor* took listeners to

619

the boulevards of Paris, an assault on the sound barrier with an Air Force jet pilot... and Ed Gardner. The program managed to convince agencies to invest more than one million in ad revenue with the first program, a month before the premiere. Where Operation Tandem attempted to excel, *Monitor* succeeded. A few weeks before Christmas of 1957, Steve Gardner, then age nine, joined his dad for a series of three-minute radio vignettes for NBC's *Stardust* program, a copy of the successful *Monitor*. The series was so successful that weeks later, Pabst Brewing paid $750,000 for new George Gobel and Ed Gardner/*Duffy's Tavern* vignettes. Under the Pabst deal, the brewery would bankroll a total of 20 Gobel and Gardner five-minute *Stardust* capsules per week for 42 weekends. *Stardust* was a program where advertisers wanting to return to radio could be encouraged by "name-glamour appeal," and would pick up an additional 10 nighttime participations a week for the same 42 weeks and 12 *Stardust* participations a week for the 10-week stand not occupied by Gobel and Gardner. Backing up Pabst, RCA also purchased a total of 20 Gobel and Gardner segments a week on *Stardust* for a 20-week stand. The Pabst and RCA deals, together with a 52-week renewal on *News on the Hour* from Brown & Williamson and Bristol-Myers, comprised the bulk of the business. The balance of the business comprised short term saturation campaigns and long running tidbit sponsorships from some 15 advertisers.

In November 1955, with the success of the commercial records from years prior, Gardner signed a contract with Sunset Records to release a 12-inch LP featuring recordings of the four episodes, now edited down and re-spun as a platter. The package would be tagged "Duffy's Tavern Revisited."

In 1955 and 1956, Ed Gardner appeared as a guest on television's *Toast of the Town*, hosted by Ed Sullivan. Gardner appeared on the 1955 telecast in the form of a video clip. The April 15, 1956, telecast, however, gave Gardner the opportunity to perform before the cameras.

Although living in semi-retirement, Gardner never rejected an offer that financially reimbursed his time. During the first week of January 1961, Gardner reported to Revue Studios to make a guest appearance on television's *Alfred Hitchcock Presents*, co-starring with Claude Rains. Father Amian's church isn't in very good shape and needs an expensive new roof. At a mid-week service, a stranger leaves a ten dollar bill in the collection plate. The stranger becomes a regular attendee and continues to make generous donations. The stranger, Mr. Sheridan (played by Ed Gardner), has taken to praying for winners and since doing so has had nothing but success at the track, winning bet after bet. Sheridan convinces Father Amian (Claude Rains) to place a bet on a sure thing and Amian regrets his rash act as soon as it's done. Feeling guilty, he prays for the horse not to win and still profits in the venture. This was one of the few episodes of the series directed by Alfred Hitchcock. "I recall a special gulp of joy upon seeing Ed Gardner speaking my words," recalled author Henry Slesar, whose story was featured on the program.

The Gardners went on tour across the globe, including Egypt.

One year later, Ed Gardner made a second appearance on the program — this time under the direction of Leonard Horn. Amos Duff (played by John Fiedler) is a mortician whose business is failing. The bills are piling up and Amos laments the fact that he has never sold his top of the line class A funeral. He does finally get a client when Marvin Foley (Ed Gardner) makes arrangements for his business partner's funeral. Supposedly, the partner was killed in a car accident but Amos discovers a bullet wound. Foley agrees to buy the class A funeral provided Amos cremates the body. Several months later, Foley has yet to settle his final account for the funeral. With the body cremated, Foley refuses to pay but Amos reports the case to the police with a convincing piece of evidence. Not everything goes up in smoke during cremation.

In the spring of 1957, Ed Gardner made a guest appearance on an NBC special saluting the sport of baseball. Gardner told the same Two-Top Gruskin story he told so often many times in the past.

During the holiday season of 1957, Ed Gardner and writer-director Jerry Devine formed a new independent film company, Gardner-Devine Productions, to co-produce a series of motion pictures. The pair purchased the screen rights to *The Hidden Persuaders*, a novel written by Vance Packard, intending to film the book as an exposé in documentary form, possibly for a sale to television. The book explored the introduction of professional psychologists' motivational research into the advertising industry in the 1950s and its powerful effects. Brand name association for symbolic significance was exploited and a study of how Americans developed consumption for consumption's sake. But even more accurately, and ominously, consumption for the sake of the economy. In the late 1950s, it appeared we might reach a "saturation point" at which people, having everything they needed, might foster a serious sales slump and trigger a recession. The documentary was never produced.

Throughout 1957 and 1958, Gardner and his wife went on a lot of tours through Tangiers and Europe. In Madrid, locals used to mistake the comedian for actor Gary Cooper and want his autograph. In California, Gardner loved to play golf and participated in a number of golf tournaments with radio and television celebrities, raising money for charity. Some of those tournaments were also televised.

In February 1961, UPA, which currently had *Mr. Magoo* and *Dick Tracy* in syndication, was prepping a pair of half-hour animated series for the next television season, one of them based

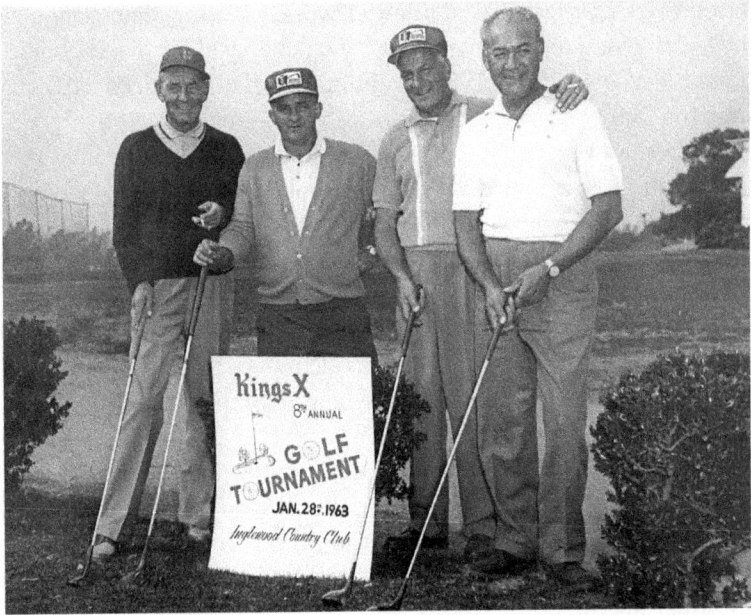

Ed Gardner during a golf tournament.

on *Duffy's Tavern* and the other to be a cartoon mystery thriller, tentatively titled *Boo!* Henry G. Saperstein, president of UPA, had approached Gardner in late 1960 to produce a series of five-minute *Duffy's Tavern* cartoons and a proposed pilot for "Two Headed Gruskin." According to the contract proposal, Ed Gardner would supply the voice of Archie (for $250 per cartoon) as well as supply 200 premises adapted from the original radio scripts. Gardner requested he be the story consultant, and be paid $250 for every premise adapted into an animated cartoon. Gardner, after looking over the contract, questioned the company's assets and wanted a clause stipulating he be paid within ten days after each vocal performance. Nothing more has been found following the contract negotiations. The cartoon series, for reasons yet unknown, never came to be.

At that same time, however, Ed Gardner's "Archie" voice was being introduced to a whole new generation who had never heard of Duffy's Tavern via a different cartoon series. Cartoon producers Bill Hanna and Joe Barbera had successfully switched to television after years of theatrical animation work, creating many popular new characters such as Yogi Bear, Huckleberry Hound and Quick-Draw McGraw. From 1959 to 1962, they also produced cartoons starring Snooper and Blabber, a cat and mouse detective team. Radio veteran Daws Butler voiced Snooper in an unofficial direct imitation of Archie the Manager's Brooklynese.

During his later years, Gardner spent time with a number of Hollywood celebrities. "My dad was well loved by everyone in Hollywood," Ed Gardner Jr. recalled. "He was the life of the party. I think the only person my father never liked was John Wayne." Sid Caesar and Jonathan Winters celebrated Thanksgiving at the Gardner home. Esther Williams taught Stephen and Eddie Jr. how to swim.

When the boys had a loud party at the house one day, the judge across the street called the police. Upon learning what had happened, Ed Gardner paid a visit to his neighbor and threatened the judge if he phoned the police again. Consult the father first, Gardner justified.

Towards the end of his life, Ed Gardner was a friend of Edward G. Robinson and the two spent a lot of time together. Robinson later confessed that he would have died poor if it was not for the financial advice of his friend, Ed Gardner.

In the summer of 1963, Ed Gardner's health took a downward turn. "My father got sick on a friend's boat when they went out on the water and they had to turn around," Ed Gardner, Jr. recalled. "That was not a happy day in the Gardner home. He was in the hospital for two weeks and I remember nurses in white surrounding the bed." Ed Gardner died on August 17, 1963, at the age of 62, leaving behind a wife of 21 years and two sons. The official release sent to the press (and printed in the papers) reported the cause of death as liver ailment. In reality, Gardner was suffering from pancreatic cancer, cirrhosis of the liver, and an impacted colon. Among the Hollywood elite to visit Gardner on his death bed was Edward G. Robinson.

Ed Gardner's life can be summed up by revisiting part of the eulogy delivered by the Rev. Kermit Castellanos, D.D. at the All Saints' Church on August 20, 1963. "This is a special kind of community in which we live. There are justifiable criticisms of

Family photo with Ed Gardner towards the end of his life.

Funeral services for Ed Gardner. Ed Junior (left), Simone and Stephen (right).

it, there are deep needs of all kinds, there are often questionable business practices – BUT – this community has a great heart. When a member suffers loss and sorrow there are many who feel it – who reach out to offer love and affection and concern. And today we are here to try and say thank you to God for a man with a unique gift of humor. This was a special kind of ministry – the ministry of laughter. And the world needs to laugh. Countless millions enjoyed him as Archie of *Duffy's Tavern*. They laughed, they relaxed, they were refreshed. Life became happy and enjoyable in innumerable ways for millions that no one can ever tabulate or evaluate. But there was far more to Ed than Archie. This was just one facet of his life and a small part of his wit – perhaps the smallest of his talents. He was above all else a writer, and he had a great understanding of life, with a sense of proportion and a sense

626

of values. He saw humor in every situation because he saw beyond the external. He was never caustic or bitter. He will be recognized and appreciated as one of the great humorists of all time."

In January 1964, Shirley Booth was a guest on *The Jack Paar Show*. With knowledge of her late-husband's passing months prior, the actress had an opportunity to speak candidly about her rocky marriage with Ed Gardner. She did reminisce about her work on *Duffy's Tavern* and, a high-class woman all the way, spoke highly of Gardner and how talented he was.

One of many commercial releases of Duffy's Tavern.

627

Today, collectors of retro radio broadcasts are on the prowl for recordings of *Duffy's Tavern* both for collectability and enjoyment. Episodes existing in collector hands vary in audio formats, but the best sound quality still exists as a result of first-generation transfers from the original masters, distributed on CD format. The majority of the earliest broadcasts of the series (the live broadcasts) do not exist in recorded form. Virtually all of the later broadcasts (the pre-recorded broadcasts from the Puerto Rico years) do exist. Many from 1942 to 1944 were recorded for troops overseas, via the Armed Forces Radio Service. "Lost" recordings still surface from time to time, the majority being AFRS Transcription discs. No one during the forties had the foresight to predict a commercial market for the recordings and contracts between the network, the sponsors and the advertising agency never dictated the necessity of recording the broadcasts, or the cost factor involved. Today, each and every episode of the series is still Federally protected under the Copyright Law, because Gardner did register the radio scripts for copyright. Companies like Radio Spirits have licensed the programs for commercial release. eBay, old-time radio newsletters, monthly antique periodicals, and private collectors across the globe, have kept the door open that "lost" radio broadcasts will continue to be discovered and made available to collectors.

APPENDIX A
THIS IS NEW YORK
EPISODE GUIDE

This is New York ROAMED FREELY AMONG CELEBRITIES and cab drivers alike. The show of January 29 took a look at the city's Yiddish theater, with an appearance by actress Molly Picon. Lyn Murray and his Chorus supplied the vocals for most of the episodes. Leith Stevens and his orchestra provided background accompaniment.

Episode #1, Broadcast December 11, 1938
Guests: Louis Armstrong, Ed Gardner, Fats Waller and Alexander Woollcott.

Episode #2, Broadcast December 18, 1938
Guests: Former New York Mayor Walker, Deems Taylor and Sophie Tucker.

Episode #3, Broadcast December 25, 1938
A Christmas concert with the Bowery Mission Carols, the Raymond Scott Quintet, the Harlem Abyssinian Baptist Church Spirituals, and the Liederkranz Singers. Script written by Russell Crouse and Alexander Woollcott.

Episode #4, Broadcast January 1, 1939
Guests: Eddie Duchin, comedians Howard and Shelton, Elsa Maxwell, Cornelia Otis Skinner, Deems Taylor, Grover Whalen (President of the New York World's Fair), and Barry Wood.

Episode #5, Broadcast January 8, 1939
Guests: Shirley Booth, George Jessel, Ted Peckham, Otto Saylow and Hiram Sherman.

Episode #6, Broadcast January 15, 1939
Guests: George Abbott (a producer), Sheila Barrett (a professional mimic), Lucius Beebe (a producer), Rosa Cinda (a piano player), José Ferrer, Fredi Washington, and Ethel Waters.

Episode #7, Broadcast January 22, 1939
Guests: Margaret Bourke-White (a photographer), Morton Downey, Samuel Leibowitz (an attorney), Jack Pearl, Sigmund Spaeth and Deems Taylor.

Episode #8, Broadcast January 29, 1939
Guests: Frank Fay, Bill Harrington, Marjorie Hills, Arthur Murray (a dance instructor), Gertrude Niesen, and Molly Picon.

Episode #9, Broadcast February 5, 1939
Guests: Irène Bordoni, Theresa Helburn of the Theater Guild Board of Managers, Lucy Monroe, Jane Peerce, Bill Robinson, and the Philharmonic Symphony Ensemble.

Episode #10, Broadcast February 12, 1939
Guests: The Andrews Sisters, Jane Froman, Clyde Hagar, Raymond Massey, Billy Rose and Erna Rubinstein (a violinist).

Episode #11, Broadcast February 19, 1939
Guests: Elaine Barrymore, John Barrymore, Hildegarde, Raymond Paige, and Deems Taylor.

Episode #12, Broadcast February 26, 1939
Guests: Frank Crumit, Fred Dannay (co-creator of *Ellery Queen*), Ella Fitzgerald, Manny Lee (co-creator of *Ellery Queen*), Julia Sanderson, and Chick Webb.

Episode #13, Broadcast March 5, 1939
Guests: Lionel Barrymore, Connee Boswell, Walter Huston, Casper Reardon (a harpist), and Hope Williams. Deems Taylor is master of ceremonies on this broadcast.

Episode #14, Broadcast March 12, 1939
Guests: Marc Connelly (a playwright), James Melton, Jane Pickens and Kate Smith.

Episode #15, Broadcast March 19, 1939
Guests: The Dunbar Bell Singers, Nancy Hamilton, Walter Huston, Ethel Merman, and the Hall Johnson Choir.

APPENDIX B
RHYME INSPIRED BY THE OPENING OF A PLACE OF REFINEMENT

The enclosed poem was a publicity feature released by CBS, issued in September 1941.

I ain't no poet, like the Bard of Avon
But welcome, folks to "Duffy's Tavern."
Ladies 'n' gents . . . an' kiddies too,
We run our joint for the likes of you.
An' anyone who gets too noisy,
Will wake up in some town in Joisey.
Each Thursday night we take the air.
An' we'll be heard most everywhere.
The network? Only take one guess,
It's coast-to-coast on CBS.

As time goes on, we'll bring you guests,
To entertain with tunes an' jests.
And Old Man Duffy'll squawk an' moan
About the show, by telephone.
We aim to please an' treat you well,
We have a high-class clientele.
If fun an' music you are havin'
Just tune in on "Duffy's Tavern.".
- (signed) Archie

APPENDIX C
DUFFY'S TAVERN: MOVIE SCENARIO
BY MAC BENOFF

Dated November 22, 1943

Note: The original movie scenario had a number of grammatical errors. For accuracy, we retained the original text as it was in the scenario.

DUFFY'S TAVERN

If you've ever been to New York you've seen Duffy's Tavern. Possibly you saw it in Brooklyn or in the Bronx or right here in Manhattan where our story takes place. You may have seen it as Tim's Bar and Grill or Mac's Chophouse, but whatever their names, they all have in common the time-worn bar, the customary juke box, the shaky floor, the peeling plaster, the quiet beery dignity.

The sign on the door reads: DUFFY'S TAVERN, age having overtaken the "r," and down on the right side of the window the gold letters proclaim: "Tables Reserved For Ladies." But now new sounds are reverberating within its hallowed walls. A miracle of entertainment has reached Duffy's Tavern, and the sign on its dirty window proclaims boldly: "Tonight Only — Betty Hutton, Dorothy Lamour, Dick Powell, Bing Crosby."

THE NEIGHBORHOOD

The neighborhood is excited and we see inhabitants making preparations to appear for the gala occasion at Duffy's. Mr. and Mrs. Cavendish, better known as "Everybody's Undertakers," are locking up the doors of their embalming headquarters. Before he closes the door, Mr. Cavendish, as a reflex action, whispers "Good night" — and is quite surprised when a pixie group of voices answers him, "Good night." He locks the door and walks down the street toward the Tavern, from whence Betty Hutton's voice emanates. As he passes Lefty's Poolroom, he waves to Lefty, motioning him to come on down.

Mr. and Mrs. Colucci, popular fruit peddlers, have now joined the Cavendishes. They wave to Mr. Cohn in his candy store. Mr. Cohn will soon be there. Now they enter through the swinging door the sacred confines of Duffy's Tavern. Once again we stop to look at the window sign and note that underneath the big letters which blazes forth the list of famous stars, is written in the smallest possible letters the words — "On Records."

THE TAVERN

Inside the Tavern, a goodly crowd has come. Cheerful noises and whistling happy sounds are heard, muffled only by the sawdust on the floor. At the bar, the ubiquitous Archie is drawing beers, directing customers to favored seats, and engaging in his perennial duty, talking to Duffy on the telephone. As usual, he is having an argument with Duffy. This time it's about a raise. A lot of new business is coming in tonight, and he is threatening Duffy that he may leave him for a better job at, perhaps, the Stork Club or El Morocco. Eddie, the waiter, chimes in. He'd like a raise, too. Archie relays Duffy's question, "What's the matter, Eddie, have the tips been getting lighter?"

"Either the tips has been getting lighter, or they're putting less silver in the dimes," says Eddie.

Running true to form, Duffy refuses both requests, which causes Archie to flare up in an angry outburst at him, ending with "Duffy, it's a lucky thing for you that I can't crawl through this phone and get you."

Miss Duffy, who is sitting at the cash register reading "True Trash," takes exception to Archie's remark, because, after all, she is her father's daughter.

Archie, of course, never pays much attention to her and advises her to kindly clean out her cash register of stockings, lipsticks, powder base, hair pins, etc., and prepare for the night's take which, for the first time in months, may amount to something.

Miss Duffy advises Archie to go about his own business, to do something about the stuffiness in the place — the broken windows aren't providing enough air. Archie, assuming his managerial role with the pompousness he ofttimes loves to affect, says, "Eddie, perhaps with all the people in here, the joint should be air-conditioned." But Eddie, who always brings Archie down to earth, merely shakes his head and says, "You can't condition this air — you gotta get rid of it." Archie agrees.

A breathless figure darts through the swinging doors and approaches Archie. It is Clifton Finnegan, the dimwitted answer to a madman's prayer. In his dulcet, dropsy voice he is scarcely able to contain himself as he pours out the fact that Mr. Flyshacker, the landlord, is coming up the street. He tells Archie to hide. Mr. Flyshacker is very angry. Archie quietly jumps into an empty pickle barrel.

Mr. Flyshacker, senior member of the firm of Flyshacker, Bushwacker, Millstone and Briggs, enters. Peremptorily he surveys the Tavern, takes a second to make a formal demand for six months' back rent and, knowing that there is none forthcoming, proceeds to place the dispossess notice on the door.

Miss Duffy, rising to the situation, stands on what she imagines are her legal rights and says to Mr. Flyshacker: "You can't hang up a dispossess notice except for the party for whom it's intended. Why don't you wait for Archie?" This stumps Mr. Flyschaker for a moment and he says: "All right, when will he be here?" Miss Duffy says: "it's no use waiting — he's left for the evening." Whereupon Mr. Flyshacker flies into a rage.

Now the gang is all excited and Finnegan, in a lame-brain effort to pacify Flyshacker, casts around for an opening. Seeing the pickle barrel he says, "Uh, uh — Flyshacker, why don't you sit down. Here, have a pickle." Flyshacker says: "All right, don't mind if I do." The gang is mortified as Flyshacker looks at the pickle barrel. Finnegan stands there stunned when Archie comes to the rescue and we see his thumb come up out of the barrel. Finnegan, alert to the situation, says: "How about this one?"

Flyshacker does a take, realizing what has happened, and rushes over to the barrel, exposing Archie. In a fury, Flyshacker again begins to paste up the dispossess notice. Everyone is terrified — Duffy's Tavern closing! They beg him not to hang it up. Archie points out to Flyshacker the crowd that is in the Tavern, saying that this is a sign of new business. He pleads with him. Flyshacker is impressed. Archie promises to have the money for him by the end of the week. After many entreaties by all, Flyshacker gives him the few days and says that is final. He leaves but not before he has a beer which Archie serves him from a glass with an extra special false bottom.

By this time the crowd is getting impatient for all the guest stars that are advertised on the window. Archie says to them: "Okay, now for the festivities." He walks to the jukebox, looks at the numbers, drops a slug in and says to the crowd: "And now folks, we are going to be treated by them golden tones of Dorothy Lamour."

As Dorothy Lamour's voice comes out of the jukebox, the crowd gets into a violent argument with Archie as they discover that none of the stars they expected are going to be there in person. In an attempt to pacify them with live entertainment, Archie offers them a song by Eddie Green. Eddie does "Tit Willow" but, as good as it is, it is not enough to appease a crowd waiting for big Hollywood stars. They all leave, angrily denouncing Archie as a fraud.

THE BACK ROOM
The little group now holds an anxious meeting in the back room. What to do? The money must be raised by Saturday and they have just been dealt a tremendous blow. All have various suggestions for

raising the money quickly. Finnegan knows where he can get his hands on a phony roulette wheel. Archie suggests perhaps a fake raffle. Eddie suggests selling Duffy as fat for the salvage drive.

The phone rings. It is Miss Duffy's boyfriend, Breckenridge Hartenpfelder. Yes, Miss Duffy will meet him at the movies even though she has a date with Ernest Deifendorfer. Before she leaves for the movies Miss Duffy discusses with them whether she shouldn't marry Breckenridge Hartenpfelder, the battleship painter, for his money and in that way save the Tavern. If only Ernest Deifendorfer, the window cleaner, could get a steady salary instead of washing windows on commission then she could marry for love and money at the same time.

As they are talking, Archie happens to notice an item in the paper. It shows the arrival of the Hollywood Bond Cavalcade which is in New York for week. Under the item there is a picture of Betty Hutton standing in front of her hotel. Archie suddenly gets an idea. He interrupts the conference to say that he is leaving. He doesn't tell them where and goes, saying he'll be back later and may have the solution to their problems.

ARCHIE'S APARTMENT

Back at his one room apartment, Archie begins to dress up. He rolls out his bed four or five times and extracts from under the mattress a freshly pressed pair of pants. He puts on a clean pair of socks that are hanging on the stove, dons his jazz bow and, all duded up, leaves.

ARCHIE AT THE HOTEL

We see Archie entering the hotel lobby where Betty Hutton is staying and as he does so somebody handing out cards advertising a dentist hands him one. Archie puts it in his pants' pocket without looking at it. He gets on the house phone and asks for Betty Hutton. Hutton's maid answers and we see that Betty is about to leave. When the maid asks who it is, Archie draws himself up and says that he has called in reference to a very important job and that he is Archie of 'Chez' Duffy's. Hutton is busy and says that if Archie wants to he may try her later — right now she has to leave.

Undaunted, Archie tries to go up the elevator where he is

stopped by the chief operator and thrown out. Going around by the back entrance he gets in the way of a group of men unloading a truck with produce. Archie gets an idea. He takes off his coat, grabs a package and gets into the building. Just as he imagines he is safely inside, someone takes the package from him, sending him back for more. He begins helping the men with the packages, much to his chagrin. When the truck leaves Archie sees a valet take a suit on a hanger out of a small delivery car into the hotel.

Furtively, Archie backs up to the truck and seeing a tray of dresses picks one up without looking. Unbeknown to him it is a child's size. When the inspector again stops him, asking where to, Archie says: "Betty Hutton."

The agent looks at the small sized dress in wonderment. Archie does a take when he sees what he has and says, 'it shrunk.' Having passed the agent, Archie gets into the hotel and goes up the freight elevator, alighting on Hutton's floor.

A chambermaid steps out of a closet, taking a vacuum cleaner as Archie makes for Hutton's room. Just then someone opens a door and says to Archie: "Valet?" Archie says, "Yes," and the party beckons him in and hands him an armful of clothes to be cleaned as soon as possible. Naturally Archie has to take them and carries the big load aside.

Just as he makes for Hutton's room, clothes and all, he sees the same chief operator who threw him out coming toward him. He grabs all the clothes, covers himself up and ducks into the maid's closet. The operator, having made his inspection, goes back into the elevator, but nobody comes out of the closet.

The chambermaid, having seen all this, goes up to the closet and opens the door. Archie falls out, hitting the floor with an awful thud. The maid screams. She uncovers Archie's face — he is out cold. The freight elevator operator comes out and, seeing what has happened, runs for assistance. Amidst all this to-do, Hutton comes out of her room and passes Archie, but it's too late now — he is too dead to the world to communicate with her.

MISS DUFFY AND HER BOYFRIENDS
Miss Duffy is at the movies, flanked by Breckenbridge Hartenpfelder and Ernest Deifendorfer. Both are throwing each

other dirty looks as they interfere with each other's passes. Both ply her with candy and, as she favors one or the other, they burn. The picture over, they leave. Breckenbridge asks if he may be alone with Miss Duffy — he has something important he wants to ask her. It is obvious there is love in the battleship painter's eyes. Miss Duffy looks at Ernest helplessly. Little does Ernest know what trouble she now has.

Ernest leaves, cursing the day he ever studied to be a window cleaner, and on commission yet. Breckenbridge tries to propose to Miss Duffy but each time is interrupted. The train is too crowded or the taxi driver interferes with him. In desperation he escorts her to the top of a Fifth Avenue bus in order to get some privacy. Building up to the grand climax, he is a just about to propose to her when a stilt walker advertising a restaurant sidles up to the bus. In a playful mood he looks over at Breckenbridge just as he is about to say, "Miss Duffy, will you marry me." Breckenbridge looks around him and, unbelieving, does a triple take. This is too much for him. He leaves in a huff.

BACK AT THE TAVERN
Eddie and Finnegan ask Miss Duffy whether she has seen Archie. She hasn't. They wonder what happened to him. Miss Duffy sends Finnegan out to look for him and tells him: "Don't come back without him."

THE HOSPITAL
Archie is lying in a private ward, having been brought to the Eastside Hospital by the hotel. His case is diagnosed as a coma produced by a fall. Evidently he suffocated with all the clothes around him in that small closet and would have been killed by the fall if he hadn't been protected by these same clothes.

Now he lies there in a clean white bed, an enigma to all. There are no marks of identification on him and the hotel authorities have tried every tailor shop in town but nobody knows him. The only other clue they have is the dentist card and they have already contacted this dentist's office.

The coma, however, doesn't look bad on Archie. A smile is playing about his face as he is sandwiched between the cleanest sheets he ever slept in. And there is a reason for his smile, for Archie is dreaming the most beautiful dream he ever had.

THE DREAM

We see the biggest, most colossal Duffy's Tavern anybody ever saw. As we come close to the beautiful entrance and read the gorgeous six foot high neon sign we see that even here the "R" is left out of the Tavern — just as the lettering over the windows and on the window itself, the beautiful English scroll, lacks the same letters that they did originally in "Tables Reserved for Ladies."

The swinging doors swing musically, two trumpeters welcoming customers. And similar adjustments — only on a larger scale. But inside. A bar at least three thousand feet long that runs all the way up one side of the Tavern to the second tier. A jukebox of tremendous proportions, but not with records. No sir! The orchestra is right in this jukebox and Benny Goodman, big as life, is leading it. And when one of the customers puts in a nickel, Benny Goodman's orchestra slides out of view and Tommy Dorsey slides right in. Beautiful, expensive beer glasses with false bottoms right up to the top! The same pictures that were on the wall in the old Duffy's Tavern are here, too, but in lavishly gilded frames. And why here's Archie wearing a tuxedo coat and under it his apron. Standing next to the gold phone, pressing spigots marked champagne, he surveys the packed house, filled with righteous pomposity. This is indeed a gathering deserving of the attention of such as "Mine Host," Archie.

Paulette Goddard is here and she is sitting at the same table with the Coluccis! And here is Fred MacMurray bottoms-upping with the Cavendishes!

Everybody is there. Archie is now faced with a problem. Dorothy Lamour and Betty Hutton both want to sing. He tosses a gigantic penny and when it stands up on edge, they sing a duet.

Such a place is Duffy's! All are wearing evening gowns and tuxedoes, and, why here's Finnegan in a tuxedo and, as he proudly shows Archie, brand new sneakers!

And look, here's Miss Duffy! She looks quite pretty sitting at not one, but three cash registers. One for change, one for dollar bills and one for the trash she usually keeps in the register. Again she has a problem and she cannot make up her mind, but this time it's between Ray Milland and Fred MacMurray. And what do you know — in Fred MacMurray's latest picture he plays the part of a window cleaner, and in Ray Milland's picture he is a battleship painter. If only Fred made as much as Ray. As she reads the super-duper issue of "True Trash" we can see that she has her worries.

Duffy calls up and Archie tells him they have taken in forty-six thousand dollars for the day. But Duffy, as usual, is disgruntled. What a guy! Everything is wonderful but Duffy is never satisfied and the conversation winds up in the same way with Archie telling Duffy, "Duffy, it's lucky for you I can't crawl through this phone and get you."

As he munches from the free lunch which consists of everything from pressed duck to caviar, Bing Crosby and Bob Hope enter. Archie immediately offers them jobs which they accept.

Everything is swell and even when the terrible looking landlord enters, looking like the devil, it doesn't worry Archie. He tells the landlord he'll have the rent in a few days. Eddie Green, resplendent in his uniform, enters the scene, and for some reason he is troubled, but Archie pooh-poohs him as he dreams on.

THE GANG IS WORRIED

Miss Duffy and Eddie are holding a conference. Nobody has seen Archie. Clancy the Cop comes in with Finnegan. They ask Finnegan why he didn't return. Finnegan says to Miss Duffy, "You told me not to come back without him." He adds, "But don't worry, we'll get him. I put an ad in the 'Lost and Found'."

They pay no attention to Clifton and we can see that they are all really worried — a horrible word playing about their lips: the morgue! The morgue! Well, if they have to, they have to.

They go down to the morgue and give the officer a description of Archie and he says, "Yes, go right inside." But when they go inside, they don't find Archie. It seems that from the description they gave him, all the mugs in the morgue look like Archie.

The landlord, having come back to see how they are making out with the rent money, thinks that a trick is being played on him. He tells them he won't stand for any of their monkey business — the money or the dispossess and that's final!

AT THE HOSPITAL
The dentist is there and of course he doesn't know Archie. He looks at the bridgework and maintains that no dentist would claim it — it must be homemade.

The authorities are puzzled. Archie shows no signs of coming out of his coma, but is physically as perfect as ever. He just lies there not hurt in any way. Nothing disturbs him — not even pin pricks, and why?

THE DREAM
Because in his dream the pin pricks are represented to be Veronica Lake, Paulette Goddard, Claudette Colbert and Barbara Stanwyck pinching his cheeks. Finally, one of them hurts him and he chases them all away. What tenacious girls — how they fight over him! Fist fights almost. And Archie is keeping each one of them on a string, giving each one of them a line — but not loving any one of them. What a playboy! What a success! What a Tavern and what a one-room apartment! A dozen pairs of trousers under the mattress! Two dozen socks on the stove! An automatic dumbwaiter! That's living!

When Goddard sees this swellegant layout, she confesses her love for him, saying she would like to take care of this place for him. Archie knows it's breaking her heart, but sadly turns her down. His life must be devoted to his career, not marriage, and he couldn't stand to have his wife work for him. After all, isn't he the finest night club impressario in the world? Who ever thought that Crosby and Hope would turn out to be such a great pair of bartenders? But only Archie saw their possibilities and now everyone is dying to work for him, even gratis, because it's such an honor.

Alan Ladd pleads with Archie to let him be a bouncer but Archie says no, enough is enough. He can't afford to make Hope and Crosby jealous. As Archie turns Ladd down, Duffy calls and again is disturbed. When Archie says, "Duffy, it's a good thing I can't crawl through this phone and get you," the phone miraculously begins to enlarge and Archie starts to crawl through.

AT ARCHIE'S BEDSIDE

The hospital nurses and two attendants restrain Archie as he starts to crawl under the pillows. He is getting violent. They call for help. The doctor comes running in and they all listen to Archie as he hollers, "Duffy! Duffy!" As he quiets down they realize they now have the first important clue.

Contact Duffy. But how? One of the interns gets a bright idea — he's got the problem solved. He turns to the phone book and looks up the name Duffy, but falls back in consternation as he sees five pages of Duffys. "Well, there's only one thing to do — start phoning all of them."

THE END OF ARCHIE

The gang is heartbroken. No sign of Archie anywhere and they've investigated all over. Even Lefty offered two free hours of pool to anybody who would bring him back dead or alive but nothing came of it.

The gang sits around and reminisces. "Poor Archie! And he was a swell guy, too." Miss Duffy says she fought with him like a brother. Eddie reveals that he owed him thirty dollars and even Finnegan admits that Archie was the only one he ever considered his equal.

As they sit around considering, the phone rings and Finnegan answers it. Very impatiently he listens and then hangs up. They pay no attention to him because Cavendish is outlining his estimate on a plot of ground in Long Island. As they wait for Duffy to come down and make the final arrangements, Miss Duffy confesses that it looks as though she is going to have to marry Breckenbridge Hartenpfelder to save the Tavern. Poor Ernest is heartbroken as he leaves. He says he doesn't even care if his window belt breaks.

The landlord drops in for a minute to see how things are going. He doesn't care how he gets his money as long as he gets it.

Eddie Green asks Finnegan who that was on the phone. Finnegan thinks a moment and says if he remembers correctly it was a hospital. They all look at him. "A hospital? What do they want?" He says, "They wanted to find out if anybody we know is missing." They all leap on him and say, "Didn't you tell them that

Archie is missing?" Finnegan says, "Is Archie missing? I thought he was dead."

With an effort they restrain themselves and ask him what was the name of the hospital. Finnegan says, "The — the — gee, I forgot." They say, "Try to remember." Suddenly, Finnegan gives a whoop of excitement. "I got it," he says, lifting up the short leg of the table and taking out the phone book. "We'll look up the hospital in the book." They turn to hospitals and now it's their turn to be dismayed. There are four pages of hospitals in the book. Well, the only thing they can do is call all of them.

AT THE HOSPITAL
Having exhausted all the Duffy clues, the hospital now has decided to give up the search. As the doctor makes out his final report it is decided that Archie will be shipped to a public hospital. Archie shows no signs of awakening. He dreams on.

THE DREAM
A big number is taking place in Duffy's Tavern. It's a gala evening again. Miss Duffy coyly noises it around that she has an announcement to make. Fred and Ray both wait with bated breath. Miss Duffy stands up and says that she is going to marry Breckenbridge MacMurray. The guests at Duffy's look at each other in amazement. Who is Breckenbridge MacMurray? Miss Duffy stammers, "No, no. I made a mistake — it's Ernest Milland." She breaks into tears. She doesn't know who she means.

Fred and Ray leave, disgruntled. This is a bad incident for the Tavern. Finnegan suddenly comes in, throwing pickles around. Archie says to him, "Get out, Finnegan!" and points his finger at him. He looks at his finger and it turns into a pickle.

Eddie keeps looking at Archie, all the time saying, "I told you so! I told you so!" Archie goes to bandage his finger when the Colluccis come up to him and say they never will come to the Tavern again — the prices are too cheap. They only got a bill for eighty dollars for dinner. Archie doesn't know what to make of all this — he's got to stop it some way.

Hope and Crosby resign. They have discovered the false bottoms in the glasses.

Suddenly the landlord comes in. He asks for the rent. A hundred thousand dollars for the month. Archie says, "Well, at least I won't have any trouble here." With a laugh and a leer, Archie begins to count it out for him. He says, "Here, you money grubbing Flyshacker! Ten thousand, twenty thousand, thirty thousands, fifty, sixty, ninety thousand dollars, ninety-five thousand dollars, ninety-eight, ninety-nine, ninety-nine hundred and ninety-nine dollars and the rest in change. Forty, fifty, sixty, seventy — ninety-five cents." A nickel short.

Archie counts again. "Yep, ninety-nine hundred and ninety-nine dollars and ninety-five cents." Archie looks in the cash register for a nickel — nothing there. Miss Duffy hasn't got it. Nobody else has — not even Crosby, not even Hope. Archie sticks a finger in the phone slot — nothing there. Nobody has a nickel. Archie can't get one. In a last desperate attempt he goes to the jukebox — nothing but slugs.

Flyshacker hollers, 'Come across with the dough!" But this is no joke. Archie just hasn't got that other nickel and the landlord won't take less, saying he gave him enough time to get the money and that now he is going to foreclose. He tells everybody to get out — he is dispossessing the joint.

Archie says, "You can't do that for a nickel." The landlord says, "Oh, no?" He whistles and a gang of huskies enter. They briskly begin to move everything out, speeding it up as they do so. Archie tries to stop one of them but they grab him. Excitedly he shouts, "Let me go! Lay off me! Let go! Let go!"

AT ARCHIE'S BEDSIDE

As Archie struggles to release himself from the imaginary Flyshacker and his gang, Finnegan, Eddie Green, Miss Duffy and Clancy all hold him down.

Shaken out of the coma, Archie comes to and looks around him bewilderedly. "Where am I?" he asked. "What happened to me?"

They tell him what has happened to him but he hasn't yet quite come to and doesn't fully understand what they are saying.

The doctor, after a quick diagnosis, pronounces him as fit as he ever was and he leaves the hospital with the gang. They proceed back to Duffy's Tavern. Happily, they pat Archie on the back and tell him how happy they are to find him. But Archie doesn't quite understand their talk. He is still filled with his dream thoughts, imagining Duffy's Tavern to be a tremendous place.

The gang look at each other, nodding wisely. They realize that Archie hasn't quite gotten over everything. Miss Duffy begins to tell him that she is going to marry Breckenbridge and save the place. When she mentioned the landlord he quickly asks them if they have a nickel. "Sure, they have." He grabs it and tells them not to worry — everything is now going to be settled.

THE DECLINE OF ARCHIE

Back they go to the Tavern and when they get there, Archie really comes to. As he sees the crummy exterior, the dirty windows, the broken sidewalk, he realizes that it all really has been a dream. Dejectedly, he gives Eddie back the nickel.

Duffy's is as dingy as it ever was — much dingier, in fact, by contrast with the Tavern he has just been dreaming of. He is crestfallen, and a bitter smile comes to his lips when he hears Betty Hutton's voice float out into the street. His eye catches the "Tonight only" sign on the window which has been left there.

The gang is caught by Archie's dejected spirit but in a lame effort to cheer him up they say, "Buck up, pal! Make the best of it." After all, Miss Duffy is going to pull them all out of the jam.

INSIDE THE TAVERN

When they all go in they see quite a crowd and a lot of merriment and are very much surprised. Archie rubs his eyes a dozen times when he sees what looks like Paulette Goddard and Veronica Lake sitting at a table with the Cavendishes.

They all holler, "Surprise!" He looks around and sees Alan Ladd and Fred MacMurray and a lot of other people that he met in his dream.

What is this — another dream? But no! It's really them. And that voice. He looks at the juke box — it's not coming from there. He looks around. It's really Hutton. Sure enough, there is Betty Hutton up on a chair — she's really singing.

There's Bob Hope! Even Miss Duffy and the rest of the gang

are amazed. What is this? How did this happen? Before they are able to get an explanation, Ernest Deifendorfer comes up with a mouthful of smiles. Well, how do they like all this? He asks. They love it. But how?

Crosby butts in and puts his arm around Deifendorfer. The kid told them all about Archie and before he left for Hollywood he thought he has to put in an appearance at the Tavern and he had brought Bob Hope, too. Miss Duffy beams. Archie loves him. But Archie says, "How did you get to these stars? I couldn't even get to one of them. They threw me out of the hotel."

"Simple," says Ernest. As a window cleaner he just climbed up the building and knocked on the window and came in. He told one — one brought the other and that's how they all came down.

The landlord comes in, but there is more than enough money in the cash register to pay the rent. Flyshacker gets paid off, and is unceremoniously thrown out.

Miss Duffy kisses Ernest. How could she ever have through of marrying Breckenbridge?

Archie stands there jubilantly — happy as a lark. He even begins to survey everything with that old pompous stance of his. He gets a thought. Who took care of the Tavern while they were all gone? "Duffy did," says Ernest. "Duffy? Where is he?" they all ask. Ernest says he went home. He couldn't stand the noise when all the stars came down.

As they all join in song and dance, Duffy phones. Sure enough, the old crank is still unhappy. He walked all the way up from the Tavern and is now soaking his feet in a tub of hot water. Archie is about to have a fight with him, but the good fortune is too much and he just smiles and holds the ear piece away from him as Duffy rants and raves and Archie joins in the song.

THE END

APPENDIX D
ETIKET FOR THE ELITE
BY ED GARDNER

Reprinted from the June 1944 issue of *Tune In*.

Leave us not brandy words. This is a right and a wrong way to disport one's self under all occasions, even when visiting one's in-laws. If one perspires to success in this bale of tears, his manners must be such that he will help to make any high-class socialistic gathering a real fiasco.

That is why we should all have etiket, a phrase which means simply the proper forms of behavior under all circumstances, especially if someone is looking. I have wrote these hints on etiket after years of practicing up on me own manners, whether at home, abroad or in the company of the elite who meet to eat at *Duffy's*. Nowadays, when they see me coming, folks murmur prettily behind their hands: "Here comes Archie, the churl." Which of course, makes me feel that me efforts to learn etiket and pay me debt to society has not all been wasted.

We will take up one subject at a time — in a cavalrycade, so to speak. The first item on the menu is:

Dining Out Formal

Dining out formal is just like in a restaurant except more should go in the mouth than upon one's tie. When finally at table, it is protocol for the guest of honor to be sat on either the right or the left of mine host, depending upon which side of mine guest mine host is sitting.

Introductions come right after stuffing of napkins into the waistcoat (prenounced "westkut"). Always introduce the lady first, thus: "Mr. Jones, shake hands with the wife."

However, if the girl is not a wife but just a ordinary fiancé, and you present her to several people, the form is thus: "Miss Brown, Mr. Jones, Mr. Smith, Miss Brown, Mr. Jones, Mr. Smith, Mr. Doe, Miss Brown, Mr. Smith, Mr. Williams, etc."

When meeting the nobility, it is proper to address them as "Your Grace" or "Your Duchess." If meeting royalty, however, it is better form to use "Your Majesty" or "Your Majestess," depending — of course — upon whether it is a king or a queen. In case of a earl, I have found it good policy to just say "How do you do."

Throughout the evening's regalia, it is of primitive importance to watch to every request of mine hostess. Per example, if she says, "Please pass the nutcracker," it is very bad form to hand her a beer bottle. If you drop your napkin, don't go under the table after it unless you are sure you can find your way back again. Tongues will wag freely if you fail to return to your chair by the time the party breaks up.

When leaving table at a private dinner party, resist the temptation to slip some monastery consideration such as a dime under the plate for the waitress. Unless you can make it a quarter, a winning smile will suffice.

This now arrives us at:

Dining Out Unformal

When dining al fresco (extra for soup and desert), one is behooved to watch carefully to his manners — even, perish forbid, if one must go so far as to take off his hat. First off, when calling for service, it is considered *de trop* to whistle for the waiters. It is preference to tap a spoon on one's water glass. As to eating, it is considered *rigor mortis* to pick up boiled potatoes with the fingers. Spearing them with the fork is the correct way to handle this always puzzling point of gastromic procedure. This does not apply if the potatoes are mashed. In that case, one spears with one's spoon.

When the cordials are served, it is considered bad form, no matter what the occasion, to attempt to open a beer bottle with your teeth.

When dining in French restaurants, it is best to do as the Romans do. In calling for the check — or *"addicion"* — I have found it good politics to use the proper French, which is, "Waiter, the *garcon*, if you please." It is surprising the results you get. A common mistake is when you reach for the check and get it. The proper form here is to get one's hand stuck in one's water glass until the crisis is past, not neglecting to murmur, "Well, next time, old chap."

Getting down to the finer points of etiket, we finally come to:

Love Making

When asking a girl for a kiss, one has the choice of two methods — of, if those involved are inclusive, the two may have the choice of one method. I am speaking of an approach. This, to be pacific, may be the "Darling, isn't it a lovely moonlit night — may I hold your hand?" method or the "How about it, kid?" method. These both have their points and are often interchangeable, such as times when the "How about it, kid?" method works even better in the moonlight.

Always be fair to the other guy. At parties or siestas, suggest kissing games. This is a sporting gesture to give the other fellow a chance — which, of course, in my case, he ain't got.

The well-appointed lover is usually well dressed. The most effective forms of dress I have encountered in my own behalf has been a quiet tie with a loud shirt or versa visa and a formal tuxedo with optional dinner jacket (same number of buttons and buttonholes and a carnation in the boutonear). If a appropriate chapeau is not to be found, a hat makes a good substitution. Dames are very noticeable of this.

If you are going to be a successful swane, you have got to spend money. Tightwads never caught no molasses. Unless you are prepared to spend some 60 cents for orchids, another 2 bits for bom-boms and at least a buck and a half (what the English call a "moon and six pence") for the opera, you might just as well stay home. It is not that the opposition sex is golddiggers, it is just that people who do not spend money is repugnizant to dames.

Last Words on Love

Do not let romance blot out business out of your mind. If you must kiss a dame goodnight in a hallway, at least have the presence of mind to stuff a few circulars in her letter box. Most men are all alike dazzled by the first pair of plucked eyebrows, false eyelashes and painted toe-nails that wink at them. The man of perspicacity will take as much care in choosing his mate as in choosing his underwear. Remember the old adagio that opposites attract. Blondes attract brunettes and brunettes blondes. So keep in mind that if you are stupid enough you will go out with an intellectual.

The wise lover will learn to dance well. He will not be a wallpaper. "Tripping the light bombastic," as it is sometimes called, is the easiest of the social graces it you are graceful. If not, it is best to "sit this one out," which is more fun, anyway.

It is smart to think of little presents occasionally. They need not be expensable if chosen wisely. I have gotten some very good results with such trinkets as a potted lilac, mother-of-pearl snuff box, horse-hair ring, ivory back-scratcher (Chinese, if possible, with the long nails) and a combination jackknife and bottle opener. Of course, any kind of diamonds is always permissible and in good form.

If you are a gentleman at heart, these hints on etiket will come easily and naturally to you. If you are a bum, you may have to work at it a little harder, but it is worth it. Believe me, I know.

APPENDIX E
ED GARDNER'S
RADIO APPEARANCES

All broadcast times are Eastern Standard unless otherwise noted.

Battle of the Sexes (December 5, 1938)
Series Regulars: Singers Frank Crumit and Julia Sanderson; **Network:** NBC; **Sponsor:** Cummer Products Company (Molle Shaving Cream); **Broadcast Time:** Tuesday, 9:00 p.m.; **Running Time:** 30 minutes; **Content:** Ed Gardner was among the guests on a quiz program with a staunch male-female competition.

The Adventures of Ellery Queen (June 25, 1939)
Series Regular: Hugh Marlowe; **Performers Included:** Deems Taylor; **Network:** CBS; **Sponsor:** sustained; **Broadcast Time:** Sunday, 8:00 p.m.; **Running Time:** 60 minutes; **Content:** Ed Gardner and Deems Taylor were guest panelists, referred to as "armchair detectives," who attempt to solve the mystery of "The Last Man Club" before the conclusion of the murder sketch is revealed. This was the second episode of the series.

The Magic Key of RCA (July 24, 1939)
Series Regular: Colonel Lemuel Q. Stoopnagle; **Performers Included:** Jane and Virginia Rogers, Nathaniel Shilkret and the Victor Concert Orchestra; **Network:** NBC Blue; **Sponsor:** RCA; **Broadcast Time:** Monday, 8:30 p.m.; **Running Time:** 60 minutes; **Content:** This was the second broadcast in a summer series featuring series regular Colonel Lemuel Q. Stoopnagle. Ed Gardner was the guest comedian for this broadcast, billed as "the native New Yorker," his first of two appearances on the program. (Script excerpt reprinted in Appendix H.)

The Magic Key of RCA (August 14, 1939)
Series Regular: Colonel Lemuel Q. Stoopnagle; **Performers Included:** Bea Wain, Nathaniel Skilkret and the Victor Concert Orchestra, and Jane and Virginia Rogers; **Network:** NBC Blue; **Sponsor:** RCA; **Broadcast Time:** Monday, 9:00 p.m.; **Running Time:** 60 minutes; **Content:** Ed Gardner, billed as "the native New Yorker," made his second of two appearances on the program. (Script excerpt reprinted in Appendix I.)

The Columbia Workshop (August 31, 1939)
Performers Included: Marie Wilson; **Network:** CBS; **Sponsor:** sustained; **Broadcast Time:** Thursday, 10:00 p.m.; **Running Time:** 30 minutes; **Content:** Ed Gardner and Marie Wilson star as a young married couple who find themselves closer to each other after their first big fight in a drama titled "Apartment to Let."

Good News of 1940 (November 9, 1939)
Series Regulars: Fanny Brice and Hanley Stafford; **Performers Included:** Roland Young and Walter Huston; **Network:** NBC; **Sponsor:** Maxwell House Coffee; **Broadcast Time:** Thursday, 9:00 p.m.; **Running Time:** 60 minutes; **Content:** Ed Gardner tells a story of "Duffy's Tavern" and then sings a song about California. Gardner was also producer and director of this radio program at the time it aired on NBC.

The Columbia Workshop (July 7, 1940)
Performers Included: William Bendix and Richard Widmark;

Network: CBS; **Sponsor:** sustained; **Broadcast Time:** Sunday, 8:00 p.m.; **Running Time:** 30 minutes; **Content:** Ed Gardner provides "Archie" dialogue during his narration of a fantasy about a great ballplayer with very fast eyes in a drama titled "The Cockeyed Wonder."

The Columbia Workshop (July 21, 1940)
Performers Included: Walter Kinsella; **Network:** CBS; **Sponsor:** sustained; **Broadcast Time:** Sunday, 8:00 p.m.; **Running Time:** 30 minutes; **Content:** Ed Gardner is a guest in a drama titled "The Canvas Kisser," a comedy about a prize fighting kangaroo who falls in love.

The Columbia Workshop (August 25, 1940)
Performers Included: Ed Gardner and Beatrice Kay; **Network:** CBS; **Sponsor:** sustained; **Broadcast Time:** Sunday, 8:00 p.m.; **Running Time:** 30 minutes; **Content:** A nostalgic look back at the days of vaudeville, scripted by Al Rinker, ex of the footlights. The drama was titled "I Follow the Seals," told in flashback style as two principals discussed old times over a luncheon. In the end, the one who bragged about his terrific work and "important connections with the West Coast" clearly defined the fight and futile hopes of people who no longer find things rosy.

The Columbia Workshop (September 8, 1940)
Performers Included: Vicki Vola and Helen Dumont; **Network:** CBS; **Sponsor:** sustained; **Broadcast Time:** Sunday, 8:00 p.m.; **Running Time:** 30 minutes; **Content:** Ed Gardner is a guest in a drama titled "The Major Goes Over the Hill," about a tough army major who suddenly cannot make a decision, deserts, and becomes a beauty advisor. The script for this broadcast is also known as "Big Boy Blue."

Penthouse Party (June 13, 1941)
Series Regular: Ilka Chase; **Performers Included:** Bert Parks and Yvette Harris; **Network:** CBS; **Sponsor:** sustained; **Broadcast Time:** Friday, 10:30 p.m.; **Running Time:** 30 minutes; **Content:** Ed Gardner and Dick Todd are the celebrity guests.

The Treasury Hour — Millions for Defense (October 7, 1941)
Master of Ceremonies: Graham MacNamee; **Network:** NBC Blue; **Sponsor:** Bendix Aviation Corp.; **Broadcast Time:** Tuesday, 8:00 p.m.; **Running Time:** 60 minutes; **Content:** Celebrity guests included Red Barber, Bill Stern, Gene Autry, William Hillman, and Ed Gardner as Archie. Barry Wood introduces Archie to Red Barber, who encourages the comedian to tell the story of Two-Top Gruskin. (Note full title and exact spelling of this radio program was taken directly from the radio script.)

The Columbia Workshop (December 21, 1941)
Network: CBS; **Sponsor:** sustained; **Broadcast Time:** Sunday, 10:30 p.m.; **Running Time:** 30 minutes; **Content:** A touching Christmas story about a cab driver and his strange Christmas Eve passenger. This is the same script that would be slightly revised and dramatized several times on *Duffy's Tavern*.

The Texaco Star Theater (February 11, 1942)
Series Regular: Fred Allen; **Performers Included:** Portland Hoffa; **Network:** CBS; **Sponsor:** Texaco Oil and Gas; **Broadcast Time:** Wednesday, 9:00 p.m.; **Running Time:** 60 minutes; **Content:** Ed Gardner plays the role of Archie and announcer John Reed King would later acknowledge Archie's appearance on Fred Allen's radio show on the February 12 broadcast of *Duffy's Tavern*.

The Navy Relief Show Preview (March 3, 1942)
Network: CBS; **Sponsor:** unknown; **Broadcast Time:** Tuesday, 11:30 p.m.; **Running Time:** 30 minutes; **Content:** Ed Gardner plays the role of Archie. Other celebrities lending a hand for this patriotic broadcast include George Jessel, Sophie Tucker and Dinah Shore.

The Kate Smith Show (April 10, 1942)
Series Regular: Kate Smith; **Performers Included:** Ted Collins; **Network:** CBS; **Sponsor:** Grape Nuts; **Broadcast Time:** Friday, 8:00 p.m.; **Running Time:** 55 minutes; **Content:** Ed Gardner and Raymond Massey are guests.

Quixie-Doodles (April 24, 1942)
Series Regular: Colonel Stoopnagle; **Performers Included:** Alec Templeton; **Network:** NBC; **Sponsor:** Ontario Travel; **Broadcast Time:** Friday, 7:00 p.m.; **Running Time:** 30 minutes; **Content:** Ed Gardner was a guest, along with Alec Templeton, on Stoopnagle's comedy program.

The Adventures of Ellery Queen (May 2, 1942)
Series Regular: Carleton Young; **Performers Included:** Shirley Booth; **Network:** CBS, West Coast; **Sponsor:** Bromo Seltzer; **Broadcast Time:** Thursday, 9:30 p.m. (P.S.T.); **Running Time:** 30 minutes; **Content:** Ed Gardner and Shirley Booth were guest panelists, referred to as "armchair detectives," who attempt to solve the mystery of "The Living Corpse" before it is revealed. Ed Gardner was originally scheduled to guest on the March 14, 1942, broadcast. He failed to show because he was at a script conference for *Duffy's Tavern*. A friend of announcer Ernest Chappell, who also happened to be in the studio at the time, took Gardner's place. To make up for his error, Gardner delivered Shirley Booth as an added guest for this episode.

The Kate Smith Show (May 15, 1942)
Series Regular: Kate Smith; **Performers Included:** Ted Collins; **Network:** CBS; **Sponsor:** Grape Nuts; **Broadcast Time:** Friday, 8:00 p.m.; **Running Time:** 55 minutes; **Content:** Ed Gardner once again plays the role of Archie.

The Kraft Music Hall (September 17, 1942)
Series Regular: Bob Crosby; **Performers Included:** Robert Benchley, Mary Martin and Igor Gorin; **Network:** NBC; **Sponsor:** Kraft Foods; **Broadcast Time:** Thursday, 9:00 p.m.; **Running Time:** 30 minutes; **Content:** Ed Gardner plays the role of Archie in this episode to promote the new season of *Duffy's Tavern*. This was the summer season with Bob Crosby as the star, while Bing was on vacation.

The Kate Smith Show (December 11, 1942)
Series Regular: Kate Smith; **Performers Included:** Ted Collins;

Network: CBS; **Sponsor:** Jell-O; **Broadcast Time:** Friday, 8:00 p.m.; **Running Time:** 55 minutes; **Content:** Archie attempts to hire Kate Smith to sing at Duffy's Tavern. A network air check recording of this broadcast does not exist, but an AFRS rebroadcast, edited down to 29 minutes and 30 seconds, exists in circulation with the incorrect broadcast date of December 18, 1942. Kate Smith and Ted Collins would return the favor by appearing as guests on the *Duffy's Tavern* program four days later.

The Camel Comedy Caravan (December 25, 1942)
Series Regulars: Xavier Cugat and his Orchestra; **Performers Included:** Lanny Ross and Herb Shriner; **Network:** CBS; **Sponsor:** Camel Cigarettes; **Broadcast Time:** Friday, 10:00 p.m.; **Running Time:** 30 minutes; **Content:** Ed Gardner, Roland Young and Cornelia Otis Skinner are guests on this special hour-long holiday program.

Treasury War Bond Show (December 31, 1942)
Network: NBC Blue; **Broadcast Time:** Thursday, 8:30 p.m.; **Running Time:** 60 minutes; **Content:** Ed Gardner, Ilka Chase, Gladys Swarthout, Herb Shriner and Larry Adler are among the guests of this hour-long war bond show. Al Goodman and his Orchestra supplied the music. Colonel Richard C. Patterson is the guest speaker.

Treasury War Bond Show (January 16, 1943)
Network: NBC Blue; **Broadcast Time:** Saturday, 7:00 p.m.; **Running Time:** 60 minutes; **Content:** Ed Gardner, Lanny Ross, Georgia Gibbs, Charles Laughton, John W. Vandercook and Eddie Cantor are among the guests of this hour-long war bond show.

The Old Gold Program (January 27, 1943)
Series Regulars: Sammy Kaye and his Orchestra; **Performers Included:** Red Barber; **Network:** CBS; **Sponsor:** Old Gold; **Broadcast Time:** Wednesday, 8:00 p.m.; **Running Time:** 30 minutes; **Content:** Ed Gardner plays the role of Archie, trying

to sell Sammy Kaye the idea of leaving the airwaves for a job at Duffy's. His efforts fail so Shirley Booth, the titian-haired "Miss Duffy" will become a guest on Sammy Kaye's radio program on February 17, singing a song, promoting *My Sister Eileen* and representing Archie in a second effort to convince Kaye to visit the tavern.

The Camel Comedy Caravan (February 19, 1943)
Series Regulars: Xavier Cugat and his Orchestra; **Performers Included:** Lanny Ross and Herb Shriner; **Network:** CBS; **Sponsor:** Camel Cigarettes; **Broadcast Time:** Friday, 10:00 p.m.; **Running Time:** 30 minutes; **Content:** Ed Gardner delivers a commencement address at Harvard.

Stage Door Canteen (March 4, 1943)
Series Regulars: Bert Lytell, and Raymond Paige and his Orchestra; **Performers Included:** Yehudi Menuhin and Harry Carey; **Network:** CBS; **Sponsor:** Corn Products; **Broadcast Time:** Thursday, 9:30 p.m.; **Running Time:** 30 minutes; **Content:** Ed Gardner, Shirley Booth and Charlie Cantor reprise their roles as Archie, Miss Duffy and Finnegan from *Duffy's Tavern*.

A Salute to Paul Whiteman (April 10, 1943)
Host: Rudy Vallee; **Performers Included:** Morton Downey, Gracie Fields; The King's Men; **Network:** NBC Blue; **Sponsor:** sustained; **Broadcast Time:** Saturday, 11:15 p.m.; **Running Time:** 1 hour and 42 minutes; **Content:** This late-night program celebrated Paul Whiteman being recently named as "Director of Music" for the NBC Blue network. Ed Gardner plays the role of Archie in a *Duffy's Tavern* routine. Other guest comedians included Lum and Abner. George Burns and Gracie Allen and Dinah Shore were originally scheduled as guests, but were unable to attend. Matty Malneck and his Orchestra appear via hookup from Los Angeles. This program was originally scheduled for 1 hour and 30 minutes, but since the network was scheduled to play music the rest of the night, the program ran a few minutes overtime.

War Bond Drive (May 1, 1943)
Network: NBC; **Sponsor:** sustained; **Broadcast Time:** Saturday, 2:00 p.m.; **Running Time:** 3 hours; **Content:** From Central Park Mall, this special three-hour NBC broadcast featured a number of the station's exclusive celebrities in the hopes of selling war bonds. Ed Gardner plays the role of Archie.

The Old Gold Show (May 5, 1943)
Series Regulars: Sammy Kaye and his Orchestra; **Performers Included:** Red Barber; **Network:** CBS; **Sponsor:** Old Gold; **Broadcast Time:** Wednesday, 8:00 p.m.; **Running Time:** 30 minutes; **Content:** Four months ago, Ed Gardner didn't succeed in selling Sammy Kaye the idea of leaving the airwaves for a job, but here he tries again. Archie's description of the fabulous Duffy's Tavern provoked Sammy's curiosity and Sammy visits the tavern. Said Archie, the "figurehead" of Duffy's: "Picture a place with the smartness of the Savoy-Plaza... the esprit de corpse of El Morocco... the prices of Max's Busy Bee. Ten cents for pigs' feet and sauerkraut... 25 cents for a seven course dinner." Sammy is not convinced that it would be a good business bet.

The Kraft Music Hall (August 12, 1943)
Series Regular: Bing Crosby; **Performers Included:** John Scott Trotter and his Orchestra; **Network:** NBC; **Sponsor:** Kraft Foods; **Broadcast Time:** Thursday, 9:00 p.m.; **Running Time:** 30 minutes; **Content:** After cracking jokes about dancing with Hedy Lamarr, Trotter's attempt to join the Air Force and Duffy's preference of Sinatra over Crosby, Archie interviews Bing for a possible job as a singing waiter at Duffy's Tavern.

Paul Whiteman Presents (August 29, 1943)
Series Regular: Paul Whiteman; **Performers Included:** Jimmy Durante and Dinah Shore; **Network:** NBC; **Sponsor:** Standard Brands, Inc.; **Broadcast Time:** Tuesday, 7:30 p.m.; **Running Time:** 30 minutes; **Content:** Ed "Archie" Gardner attempts to romance Dinah Shore.

What's New? (September 4, 1943)
Series Regular: Don Ameche; **Performers Included:** Cass Daley, Jose Iturbi, and Dinah Shore; **Network:** NBC Blue; **Sponsor:** RCA; **Broadcast Time:** Saturday, 7:00 p.m.; **Running Time:** 60 minutes; **Content:** Gardner used David Sarnoff's preceding remarks about RCA's work in the field of electronics as the springboard for ten minutes of topical fun-poking. Gardner attempts to romance Dinah Shore (again) since he failed a few days ago on Paul Whiteman's radio program.

Birdseye Open House (September 30, 1943)
Series Regular: Dinah Shore; **Performers Included:** Roland Young and Cornelia Otis Skinner; **Network:** CBS; **Sponsor:** Birdseye; **Broadcast Time:** Thursday, 9:30 p.m.; **Running Time:** 30 minutes; **Content:** Ed Gardner plays the role of Archie.

The Kraft Music Hall (October 28, 1943)
Series Regular: Bing Crosby; **Performers Included:** John Scott Trotter and his Orchestra; **Network:** NBC; **Sponsor:** Kraft Foods; **Broadcast Time:** Thursday, 9:00 p.m.; **Running Time:** 30 minutes; **Content:** Ed Gardner plays the role of Archie in this episode. This was the first of five consecutive episodes with Bob Crosby substituting for Bing Crosby.

The Lifebuoy Show (November 18, 1943)
Series Regular: Bob Burns; **Performers Included:** Spike Jones and His City Slickers; **Network:** NBC; **Sponsor:** Lever Bros.; **Broadcast Time:** Thursday, 7:30 p.m.; **Running Time:** 30 minutes; **Content:** Ed Gardner plays the role of Archie, filling in for comedian Bob Burns, who is unable to appear before the microphone during this broadcast. Ida Lupino is also guest on this broadcast.

The Elgin Company's Second Annual Tribute to the Armed Forces (November 25, 1943)
Host: Robert Young; **Performers Included:** Gracie Allen, Edgar Bergen, Jose Iturbi, Frances Langford and Frank Lovejoy;

Network: CBS; **Sponsor:** Elgin Watches; **Broadcast Time:** Thursday, 4:00 p.m.; **Running Time:** 2 hours; **Content:** Special Thanksgiving broadcast. Ed Gardner plays the role of Archie when the radio audience visits Duffy's Tavern, and Two-Top Gruskin joins the Army. Alan Reed reprises his role as Falstaff Openshaw to recite his poem, "Downfall," before stepping out of character to read a serious and moving poem.

The Kraft Music Hall (December 2, 1943)
Series Regular: Bing Crosby; **Performers Included:** Trudy Erwin, John Scott Trotter and his Orchestra; **Network:** NBC; **Sponsor:** Kraft Foods; **Broadcast Time:** Thursday, 9:00 p.m.; **Running Time:** 30 minutes; **Content:** Ed Gardner plays the role of Archie in this episode, who found the Kraft Music Hall quite easily by asking a police officer "where is the most likely place to find Sinatra?" Archie plans to leave Duffy's and open his own "joint," called Crosby's Tavern. Archie explains that Corsby's father was at Duffy's Tavern last Tuesday and gave permission to use the name of Crosby... after he adopts Archie.

Star For a Night (December 15, 1943)
Series Regular: Paul Douglas; **Performers Included:** Hugh James (the commercial spokesman); **Network:** Blue Network; **Sponsor:** Adam Hats; **Broadcast Time:** Wednesday, 10:30 p.m.; **Running Time:** 30 minutes; **Content:** The premiere episode of the series with Wendy Barrie and Ed Gardner in an original comedy sketch designed to embarrass volunteer participants who can win money judged by an applause meter. Gardner's role was so brief the radio audience might not have even known it was him.

The Texaco Star Theater (January 9, 1944)
Series Regular: Fred Allen; **Performers Included:** Portland Hoffa; **Network:** CBS; **Sponsor:** Texaco Oil and Gas; **Broadcast Time:** Sunday, 9:30 p.m.; **Running Time:** 30 minutes; **Content:** Besides taking a trip to Allen's Alley, Fred Allen visits Duffy's Tavern. A barrel falls from the back of a truck and hits Allen in the head. Clancy the cop drags Allen's body into the Tavern, mistaking the comedian for a tavern bum. Finnegan knocks Allen

unconscious twice during the visit and when the comedian wakes to announce his identity, Archie quickly tells Finnegan to "watch the cash register." Allen later sues the brewery for damages with Archie acting as his attorney. The hilarity in the tavern carries over to a court of law.

Radio Hall of Fame (January 30, 1944)
Performers Included: Frances Langford, Johnny Mercer, Colonel Stoopnagle and Deems Taylor (emcee); **Network:** NBC Blue; **Sponsor:** Philco; **Broadcast Time:** Sunday, 6:00 p.m.; **Running Time:** 60 minutes; **Content:** Ed Gardner, as Archie, tells the story of "Two-Top Gruskin." Gardner, Eddie Green and Budd Hulick appear in their Minsky's burlesque sketch, "Western Union."

Note: This broadcast featured a guest, a seaman named William Riley, who was a lad who had falsified his age to enlist at 15, and was by that point a veteran of three major invasions.

What's New? (February 19, 1944)
Series Regular: Don Ameche; **Performers Included:** Perry Como, Laird Cregar and Gladys Swarthout; **Network:** NBC Blue; **Sponsor:** RCA; **Broadcast Time:** Saturday, 7:00 p.m.; **Running Time:** 60 minutes; **Content:** Ed Gardner plays the role of Archie in another *Duffy's Tavern* sketch.

What's New? (February 26, 1944)
Series Regular: Don Ameche; **Performers Included:** Sigrid Gurie, Frances Lederer, and the King Sisters; **Network:** NBC Blue; **Sponsor:** RCA; **Broadcast Time:** Saturday, 7:00 p.m.; **Running Time:** 60 minutes; **Content:** Ed Gardner plays the role of Archie in another *Duffy's Tavern* sketch. This was the final broadcast of the series.

White House Correspondent's Dinner (supposedly March 4, 1944)
Host (emcee): Ben Grauer; **Performers Included:** Gracie Fields and Bob Hope; **Network:** NBC; **Sponsor:** sustained; **Broadcast Time:** unknown; **Running Time:** 1 hour and 45 minutes; **Content:** An all-star show from Washington D.C., honoring

President Roosevelt, held by The White House Correspondents Association. Ed Gardner tells the story of "Two-Top Gruskin," which stops the show. A recording of this dinner exists but whether the entire dinner was broadcast remains unknown. The exact broadcast date has not yet been verified.

Mic About Town (March 12, 1944)
Series Regular: Shirley Eder; **Performers Included:** Ann Rutherford; **Network:** WMCA; **Broadcast Time:** Sunday, 6:03 p.m.; **Running Time:** 27 minutes; **Content:** This variety musical featured Ed Gardner and Ann Rutherford as guests. At the time this book went to print, the skits and songs remain unknown.

Money-Go-Round (March 25, 1944)
Series Regulars: Benay Venuta and Fred Utail; **Performers Included:** Lanny and Ginger Gray; **Network:** NBC Blue Network; **Broadcast Time:** 7:00 p.m. **verify; Running Time:** 30 minutes; **Content:** Second episode of a short-run quiz program with a novel twist. A cash award being determined by contestants' choice of portion of a running jingle sung by the Lanny and Ginger Gray duo. Benay Venuta queried the male contestants while Fred Utail performed the same chore for the distaffers. Allen Funt was the scriptwriter. Ed Gardner made a brief appearance, participating in a brief telephone conversation with one of the contestants.

The Texaco Star Theater (March 26, 1944)
Series Regular: Fred Allen; **Performers Included:** Charlie Cantor and Alan Reed; **Network:** CBS; **Sponsor:** Texaco Oil and Gas; **Broadcast Time:** Sunday, 9:30 p.m.; **Running Time:** 30 minutes; **Content:** Besides taking a trip to Allen's Alley, Fred Allen visits Duffy's Tavern where Archie tries to get Fred's traffic ticket fixed.

Suspense (April 20, 1944)
Performers Included: Hans Conried and John McIntire; **Network:** CBS; **Sponsor:** Schenley Distillers (Roma Wines); **Broadcast Time:** Thursday, 8:00 p.m.; **Running Time:** 30 minutes; **Content:** Ed Gardner breaks away from his Archie

666

character for a dramatic performance as a forger who gets his just deserts in "The Palmer Method."

The Charlie McCarthy Show (May 7, 1944)
Series Regular: Edgar Bergen; **Performers Included:** Ray Noble and His Orchestra; **Network:** NBC; **Sponsor:** Standard Brands, Inc.; **Broadcast Time:** Sunday, 8 p.m.; **Running Time:** 30 minutes; **Content:** Mrs. Van Snort is giving a tea and musicale and doesn't know where to hold it. A woman of her social position needs a place of refinement. Ed Gardner appears in the role of Archie, trying to convince Edgar and Charlie how Duffy's Tavern could resolve the problem.

Your All-Time Hit Parade (June 2, 1944)
Series Regular: Milton Cross; **Performers Included:** Mark Warnow and His Orchestra; **Network:** NBC; **Sponsor:** American Tobacco Co. (Lucky Strike); **Broadcast Time:** Friday, 8:30 p.m.; **Running Time:** 30 minutes; **Content:** In an effort to stimulate interest, beginning with the May 5, 1944, broadcast, radio stars were cut in on the show to build the impression that all the big names in radio were playing the game of "name the song before the gong." Bob Hope and his wife, Eddie Cantor, and Burns and Allen all took turns. On June 2, Ed Gardner and the cast of *Duffy's Tavern* appeared on the program, geared for laughs built around the song-guessing game. The program originated from NBC New York for the musical segments with switchovers to NBC Hollywood for the cast of *Duffy's Tavern*.

The Chase and Sanborn Show (June 18, 1944)
Series Regular: Gracie Fields; **Performers Included:** Lou Bring and His Orchestra; **Network:** NBC; **Sponsor:** Standard Brands, Inc.; **Broadcast Time:** Sunday, 8 p.m.; **Running Time:** 30 minutes; **Content:** Ed Gardner plays the role of Archie, dramatizing in flashback the reason why Duffy's Tavern is closed for the summer so that renovations could be made to the place. On the last day of the year, Archie attempts to muscle himself into a script writing job for Gracie Fields. He scripted a radio serial titled "Life Could

Be Ghastly... Tally-Ho." They perform the sketch with hilarious results.

The Charlie McCarthy Show (September 10, 1944)
Series Regular: Edgar Bergen; **Performers Included:** Ray Noble and His Orchestra; **Network:** NBC; **Sponsor:** Standard Brands, Inc.; **Broadcast Time:** Sunday, 8 p.m.; **Running Time:** 30 minutes; **Content:** Ed Gardner appears in the role of Archie, who informs Bergen that he is the official ambassador of Duffy's Tavern... what he does is ambass. After practicing his Spanish and Bergen disregards Archie's attempt to be respectable, Archie shouts, "what an abdominal trick! What if this gets out? My friends will laugh at me." Charlie remarks, "You should have brought them along tonight."

The Drene Show (September 16, 1944)
Series Regular: Rudy Vallee; **Performers Included:** The Les Paul Trio; **Network:** NBC; **Sponsor:** Proctor and Gamble (Drene); **Broadcast Time:** Saturday, 8 p.m.; **Running Time:** 30 minutes; **Content:** Ed Gardner talks with Rudy about his recent visit to Duffy's Tavern while and Rudy tries to get Miss Duffy to swoon with the "Sinatra" technique, singing "Sweetheart of All My Dreams."*

Everything for the Boys (October 3, 1944)
Series Regular: Dick Haymes; **Performers Included:** Helen Forrest; **Network:** NBC; **Sponsor:** Auto-Lite; **Broadcast Time:** Tuesday, 7:30 p.m.; **Running Time:** 30 minutes; **Content:** Ed Gardner discusses Duffy's post-war plans with Dick Haymes, suggesting opening more Duffy's Taverns across the globe such as France and Mongolia. Archie then sings a new song for Haymes, entitled, "Duffy's," to the old tune of "Mother."

Parade of Stars (October 3, 1944)
Performers Included: Bob Hope; **Network:** NBC; **Sponsor:**

---

* A recording of this broadcast exists in circulation with the incorrect date of September 14.

sustained; **Broadcast Time:** Tuesday, 8:45 p.m.; **Running Time:** 15 minutes; **Content:** Season preview of NBC comedies, broadcast via electrical transcription. This same electrical transcription aired over certain NBC stations on October 6 as a filler between programs. NBC conducted a series of meetings with station managers, clients and agencies in New York, Chicago and Hollywood at which time stations thoroughly discussed all phases of the Parade of Stars operation and planned with the NBC Promotion Department the material for each up-coming Parade of Stars. This was a radio special used to promote the up-coming lineup of programs for the new fall season. Clients and agencies were then asked for their assistance and counsel in building material that stations could and would use. NBC got the jump on the competition with the NBC Parade of Stars, founded in 1942, and the special improved each year. At first the program was nothing but an infomercial but additional and original talent was added to ensure the program was worthy of listener attraction. Columbia soon attempted to meet the competition with the same. NBC went to considerable expense to ensure the success of the Parade of Stars.

The Hollywood Democratic Committee (recorded October 8, 1944) **Performers Included:** Gloria DeHaven, Danny Kaye, Gene Kelly, Phil Silvers, and Jack Warner; **Network:** unknown; **Sponsor:** unknown; **Broadcast Time:** unknown; **Running Time:** 2 hours and 17 minutes; **Content:** A recording of the Hollywood Democratic Committee exists, with the recording date of October 8, 1944, and internal evidence suggests this was broadcast over the radio, but nothing has been found to verify it really aired. Hollywood celebrities honor Harold Ickes, with Judy Garland singing "Over the Rainbow," and Ed Gardner and Charlie Cantor perform a sketch from Duffy's Tavern, where Archie tells the story of "Two-Top Gruskin."

The Elgin Company's Third Annual Tribute to the Armed Forces (November 23, 1944) **Performers Included:** Edgar Bergen, Jimmy Durante and Victor Moore; **Network:** CBS; **Sponsor:** Elgin Watches; **Broadcast**

Time: Thursday, 4:00 p.m.; **Running Time:** 2 hours; **Content:** Special Thanksgiving broadcast. Ed Gardner plays the role of Archie in the same manner he did the previous year. Admiral Chester W. Nimitz is guest speaker.

Bob Hope and Ed Gardner prepare for the Sixth War Loan Drive.

Sixth War Loan Drive: Now Let's Talk Turkey About Japan (November 23, 1944)
Performers Included: Jack Benny, Bob Hope and Dinah Shore; **Network:** NBC; **Sponsor:** sustained; **Broadcast Time:** Thursday, 11:30 p.m.; **Running Time:** 90 minutes; **Content:** "Now Let's Talk Turkey to Japan" was the slogan of NBC's day-long contribution to the Sixth War Loan Drive on Thanksgiving Day. Each program on the air during the entire 19 hours of broadcasting devoted some part of its time to the war bond and Thanksgiving themes. Featured were eminent military leaders, stars of stage, screen and radio (including Ed Gardner, Eddie Cantor, Frank Morgan and Kay Kyser), service chaplains, distinguished clergymen, and war bond salesmen. The ringing of a doorbell, followed by a message from a bond salesman, was heard at intervals throughout the day. Pickups from overseas included our G.I.s from the battle fronts; representatives of the governments of liberated countries paying tribute to the United States; and an address from Winston Churchill. The day-long series of Bond programs was coincidentally highlighted with an announcement by the War Department at midnight of a raid on Tokyo by our B-29 Super-Fortress. To wind up the day of special programs, NBC presented a 90-minute variety program from Hollywood of all known NBC talent.

The Drene Show (February 1, 1945)
Series Regular: Rudy Vallee; **Network:** NBC; **Sponsor:** Procter and Gamble (Drene); **Broadcast Time:** Thursday, 10:30 p.m.; **Running Time:** 30 minutes; **Content:** Ed Gardner plays the role of Archie, as a substitute for Frank Sinatra who was originally scheduled to be the guest star. Anita Boyer was the guest vocalist.

Everything for the Boys (February 20, 1945)
Series Regular: Dick Haymes; **Performers Included:** Helen Forrest; **Network:** NBC; **Sponsor:** Auto-Lite; **Broadcast Time:** Tuesday, 7:30 p.m.; **Running Time:** 30 minutes; **Content:** This episode served as a tribute to Borden General Hospital, Chickasha, Oklahoma. From the Southwest Pacific, an interview with ensign John W. Miller of the U.S. Coast Guard, from Newark, New

Jersey. Archie explains to Dick Haymes how a V-mail letter from a French dame, Cheri O'Brien, gave him the idea of opening sidewalk cafes named after Duffy's, in France.

Radio Hall of Fame (February 25, 1945)
Host (emcee): Frances Langford; **Performers Included:** Nigel Bruce, Johnny Mercer, Alan Reed and Paul Whiteman; **Network:** NBC Blue; **Sponsor:** Auto-Lite; **Broadcast Time:** Sunday, 6:00 p.m.; **Running Time:** 60 minutes; **Content:** The program originated from the Earl Carroll Theater Restaurant in Hollywood. Ed Gardner performs a *Duffy's Tavern* routine.

This is My Best (March 6, 1945)
Performers Included: Joseph Kearns and John McIntire; **Network:** CBS; **Sponsor:** Schenley Liquors (Cresta Blanca); **Broadcast Time:** Tuesday, 9:30 p.m.; **Running Time:** 30 minutes; **Content:** Ed Gardner guest stars in a drama titled "Mademoiselle Irene, the Great." *Variety* claimed Sandra Gould would reprise her role as Miss Duffy for this broadcast.

Tribute to President Roosevelt (April 15, 1945)
Host: Bette Davis; **Network:** NBC; **Sponsor:** sustained; **Broadcast Time:** Sunday evening time slot; **Running Time:** 2 hours; **Content:** A tribute broadcast shortly after the death of President Roosevelt. Many Hollywood celebrities participated: Jack Benny, Edgar Bergen, Ingrid Bergman, James Cagney, Eddie Cantor, Ronald Colman, Bing Crosby, Deanna Durbin, Ed Gardner, Will Hays, Bob Hope, Kay Kyser, Charles Laughton, Harold Peary, Dick Powell, Shirley Ross, Ginny Simms, Ethel Smith, John Charles Thomas and Robert Young. Ed Gardner speaks about how getting the country out of the Depression is what F.D.R. meant to him. Broadcast originated from Hollywood.

The Seventh War Loan Memorial Day Program (May 30, 1945)
Host: Jack Benny; **Network:** NBC; **Sponsor:** sustained; **Broadcast Time:** Wednesday, 11:30 p.m.; **Running Time:** 2 hours; **Content:** NBC devoted Memorial Day to a series of programs in behalf of the 7th War Loan Drive and in memoriam to American servicemen

killed in battle. The theme of the War Bond series was "Buy Bonds to Beat the Japs." Many programs included excerpts from Japanese newspapers and magazines voicing the intent of Japan to destroy America. Climaxing the events was a special 90-minute broadcast titled, "NBC Salutes the Mighty Seventh," a full two-hour show with an all-star cast. The first hour originated from New York with Fred Waring as emcee. At 12:30 a.m. (Eastern) the broadcast originated from Hollywood with a tribute to our fighting men and the lesson is pounded very clearly: how little we are asked to contribute in comparison to any man on the battlefield. Their target is Tokyo. Our target is $14 billion in U.S. War Bonds. To help put a spotlight on that target, the entertainment world of Hollywood contributed. Art Linkletter did a *People Are Funny* spot on the show with two people selected from the audience. Judy Canova sang "One Meatball." Jack Benny and Ronald Colman performed a comedy routine. Joan Davis gave a serious bond plea. Dinah Shore sang "Night and Day." Archie (Ed Gardner) tried to explain inflation with Finnegan (Charlie Cantor), a skit they performed prior on *Duffy's Tavern*.

The Ray Bolger Show, a.k.a. *The Rexall Summer Show* (August 17, 1945)
Series Regular: Ray Bolger; **Performers Included:** Singer Jeri Sullavan, Roy Bargy and his Orchestra; **Network:** CBS; **Sponsor:** Rexall; **Broadcast Time:** Friday, 10:00 p.m.; **Running Time:** 30 minutes; **Content:** Musical variety program starring Ray Bolger. Ed Gardner and Charles Cantor reprise their roles as Archie and Finnegan. Archie needs to come up with extra cash to renovate the tavern. When Ray Bolger drops by, Archie dresses Finnegan up as a blonde in the hopes of tricking Ray into buying half interest in the tavern. Bolger closes the show with the song, *We're Off to See the Wizard*, with lyrics changed to salute Archie and his romantic efforts. The closing announcements mention Ed Gardner appears courtesy of Bristol-Myers and Paramount Pictures, but fail to mention the *Duffy's Tavern* movie.

NBC Parade of Stars (October 8, 1945)
Host: Ralph Edwards; **Performers Included:** Bob Hope,

Raymond Massey and Dinah Shore; **Network:** NBC; **Sponsor:** sustained; **Broadcast Time:** Monday, 10:00 p.m.; **Running Time:** 90 minutes; **Content:** A special preview program offering excerpts and samples of the coming season. Abbott and Costello perform one of their routines, Jack Benny and Don Wilson perform an excerpt from one of their upcoming scripts, George Burns and Gracie Allen do a brief comedy sketch, an excerpt from a prior broadcast of *Meet Me at Parky's* with Parkyakarkus, and Ed Gardner and the cast perform a brief sketch. (Gardner actually appears in two separate spots.) The entire 90 minute broadcast is not known to exist in recorded form. About 30 minutes of excerpts from this program exist in collector hands.

Pabst Blue Ribbon Town (November 2, 1945)
Series Regular: Danny Kaye; **Network:** CBS; **Sponsor:** Pabst Beer; **Broadcast Time:** Friday, 10:30 p.m.; **Running Time:** 30 minutes; **Content:** Ed Gardner and the cast of *Duffy's Tavern* fill in for Danny Kaye, who was presently entertaining troops for the USO. Each week a different comedian substituted for Kaye. It's Duffy's 33rd Anniversary and relations between husband and wife cause Duffy to disappear. This concerns Archie, who spends his time at the tavern trying to impress Hollywood actor Pat O'Brien, who claims he is Irish. The cast deliver eulogies to Duffy, all with hilarious results. When Duffy is found outside the window, threatening to jump, it takes a while for Archie to remember Duffy lives on the first floor. Actor Pat O'Brien was born Irish-American, known throughout Tinseltown as "Hollywood's Irishman in Residence," often playing Irish immigrants in motion pictures. In real life, he bore no discernible accent, but he could pour on the "brogue" when the role called for it — including this radio broadcast. That really is Pat O'Brien singing towards the end of this radio broadcast. O'Brien had great vocal chords, singing "When Irish Eyes Are Smiling" and "To Call You My Own," demonstrated in *In Caliente* (Warner Bros., 1935).

The Ginny Simms Show (November 16, 1945)
Series Regular: Ginny Simms; **Network:** CBS; **Sponsor:** Borden; **Broadcast Time:** Friday, 7:30 p.m.; **Running Time:** 30

minutes; **Content:** Ed Gardner plays the role of Archie when Ginny Simms pays a visit to the Tavern. Re-creating the same sketch done on *Duffy's Tavern* many times before, Archie tries to convince the celebrity to sign an exclusive contract to work at the establishment. His efforts to impress Ginny Simms don't succeed as Archie hopes.

The Alan Young Show (January 29, 1946)
Series Regular: Alan Young; **Performers Included:** Jim Backus and Veola Vonn; **Network:** ABC; **Sponsor:** Bristol-Myers; **Broadcast Time:** Tuesday, 8:30 p.m.; **Running Time:** 30 minutes; **Content:** The plot remains unknown. It is believed that this episode sets the stage for Alan Young's consecutive guest appearances on *Duffy's Tavern* as a result of Gardner having his tonsils removed.

The Dick Haymes Show (March 30, 1946)
Series Regular: Dick Haymes; **Performers Included:** Gordon Jenkins and his Orchestra, and Helen Forrest; **Network:** CBS; **Sponsor:** Auto-Lite; **Broadcast Time:** Saturday, 8:00 p.m.; **Running Time:** 30 minutes; **Content:** Ed Gardner talks about *Duffy's Tavern.*

McGarry and His Mouse (September 25, 1946)
Series Regulars: Ted de Corsia and Betty Garde; **Network:** NBC; **Sponsor:** Bristol-Myers; **Broadcast Time:** Wednesday, 9 p.m.; **Running Time:** 30 minutes; **Content:** *McGarry and His Mouse* was the summer replacement for *Duffy's Tavern*. Ed Gardner was a guest on the final episode of the season, a one minute guest spot, to promote next week's season premiere.

NBC Parade of Stars (October 14, 1946)
Hosts: Ralph Edwards and Red Skelton; **Performers Included:** William Bendix, Bob Burns, Judy Canova, Dennis Day, Bill Stern, Roy Rogers, Lowell Thomas and Rudy Vallee; **Network:** NBC; **Sponsor:** sustained; **Broadcast Time:** Monday, 10:30 p.m.; **Running Time:** 2 hours, 45 minutes; **Content:** A special preview program offering excerpts and samples of the coming season, while also celebrating NBC's 20th anniversary. Perry Como, Phil Harris

and Alice Faye, Alan Young, Jo Stafford and many others perform brief skits and samples from future scripts. Ed Gardner and the cast perform a brief sketch of *Duffy's Tavern*. This broadcast was originally scheduled for two hours, but ran almost three!

The Alan Young Show (November 15, 1946)
Series Regular: Alan Young; **Performers Included:** Jim Backus, Charlie Cantor and Veola Vonn; **Network:** NBC; **Sponsor:** Bristol-Myers; **Broadcast Time:** Friday, 8:30 p.m.; **Running Time:** 30 minutes; **Content:** Alan is planning to impress Mr. Dittenfeffer with French cooking, so he caters a dinner down at Duffy's Tavern. Doris Singleton, who played the recurring role of Betty, Alan Young's girlfriend, made her final appearance on the program with this broadcast. (Nina Klowden replaced Singleton beginning the week after.) Ed Gardner had worked with Doris Singleton in May 1944 when she played Miss Duffy for a one-time broadcast.

The Eddie Cantor Show (December 5, 1946)
Series Regular: Eddie Cantor; **Performers Included:** Margaret Whiting and Harry Von Zell; **Network:** NBC; **Sponsor:** Pabst; **Broadcast Time:** Thursday, 10:30 p.m.; **Running Time:** 30 minutes; **Content:** Eddie Cantor and Harry Von Zell drop in at Duffy's Tavern in the hopes of collecting empty beer bottles for charity. Placing a bet regarding how many letters will be addressed to Eddie Cantor if he sings Archie's song, Cantor and Gardner both sing "Archie's Little Love Song." Archie is not as critical as the lunch counter... the pig's feet got up and walked out.

The Vaughn Monroe Show (January 18, 1947)
Series Regular: Vaughn Monroe; **Network:** CBS; **Sponsor:** Camel Cigarettes; **Broadcast Time:** Saturday, 7:30 p.m.; **Running Time:** 30 minutes; **Content:** Charlie Barnet and Ed Gardner are guests.

The Fred Allen Show (January 19, 1947)
Series Regular: Fred Allen; **Performers Included:** Charlie Cantor and Minerva Pious; **Network:** NBC; **Sponsor:** Standard Brands,

Inc.; **Broadcast Time:** Sunday, 8:30 p.m.; **Running Time:** 30 minutes; **Content:** Because the Board of Health is threatening to shut down Duffy's Tavern, Archie places an ad in the paper in the hopes some wealthy man will seek an interest in buying the place. Fred Allen stops by and both Finnegan (Charlie Cantor) and Archie mistake the comedian for a potential real estate man. Archie fails in his attempts to prove how valuable the tavern is… just when a real potential buyer walks through the door.

Hi! Jinx (February 3, 1947)
Series Regulars: Jinx Falkenburg and Tex McCrary; **Network:** NBC; **Sponsor:** Con Edison and Campbell Soups; **Broadcast Time:** Monday, 8:30 a.m.; **Running Time:** 30 minutes; **Content:** Ed Gardner and his wife, Simone Hegeman, are guests. This is the only known radio appearance of Simone.

Texaco Star Theater (May 11, 1947)
Series Regular: Tony Martin; **Performers Included:** Victor Young and His Orchestra, and Evelyn Knight; **Network:** CBS; **Sponsor:** Texaco Gas and Oil; **Broadcast Time:** Sunday, 9:30 p.m.; **Running Time:** 30 minutes; **Content:** Ed Gardner makes his first of two appearances on the program.

Texaco Star Theater (June 8, 1947)
Series Regular: Tony Martin; **Performers Included:** Victor Young and His Orchestra, and Evelyn Knight; **Network:** CBS; **Sponsor:** Texaco Gas and Oil; **Broadcast Time:** Sunday, 9:30 p.m.; **Running Time:** 30 minutes; **Content:** Ed Gardner makes his second of two appearances on the program. Gardner was also scheduled for the July 20, 1947, broadcast, but had to back out and Cass Daley filled in for him.

The Kraft Music Hall (February 5, 1948)
Series Regular: Al Jolson; **Performers Included:** Lou Bring and His Orchestra; **Network:** NBC; **Sponsor:** Kraft Foods; **Broadcast Time:** Thursday, 9:00 p.m.; **Running Time:** 30 minutes; **Content:** Ed Gardner auditions Al Jolson and Oscar Levant for Duffy's Tavern. Gardner greets Al Jolson as "Asa, your maiden name."

Al Jolson and Ed Gardner on The Kraft Music Hall.

Jolson sings a few bars of "When Irish Eyes Are Smiling." The sound man makes a mistake when the phone does not ring and Archie pretends to be talking to Duffy on the phone. The way he is delivering his lines, Ed Gardner is either drunk or he never attended the rehearsal.

Breakfast in Hollywood (February 19, 1948)
Series Regular: Tom Breneman; **Network:** NBC; **Sponsor:** Kellogg's; **Broadcast Time:** Thursday, 11:00 a.m.; **Running Time:** 30 minutes; **Content:** Ed Gardner is interviewed by Breneman, who was a guest on *Duffy's Tavern* the night before.

Breakfast in Hollywood (April 29, 1948)
Series Regular: Garry Moore; **Network:** NBC; **Sponsor:** Kellogg's; **Broadcast Time:** Thursday, 11:00 a.m.; **Running Time:** 30 minutes; **Content:** Ed Gardner was among the guests to offer a brief tribute to Tom Breneman, who died prematurely on April 28.

Radie Harris Interview (June 14, 1948)
Series Regular: Radie Harris; **Network:** CBS; **Broadcast Time:** Monday, 3:55 p.m.; **Running Time:** 5 minutes; **Content:** Originates from Hollywood. Radie Harris conducts a brief five minute interview with Ed Gardner.

Hi! Jinx (June 24, 1948)
Series Regulars: Jinx Falkenburg and Tex McCrary; **Network:** NBC; **Sponsor:** Consolidated Edison and Campbell Soups; **Broadcast Time:** Monday, 8:30 a.m.; **Running Time:** 30 minutes; **Content:** Ed Gardner makes his second of two appearances on the interview program.

Football Games 1949 (January 1, 1949)
Series Regulars: Dorothy Lamour and the Henry Russell Orchestra; **Performers Included:** Basil Rathbone; **Network:** NBC; **Sponsor:** Sealtest; **Broadcast Time:** Thursday, 9:30 p.m.; **Running Time:** 30 minutes; **Content:** Ed Gardner is interviewed.

The Sealtest Variety Theater (January 6, 1949)
Series Regulars: Dorothy Lamour and the Henry Russell Orchestra; **Performers Included:** Cornel Wilde; **Network:** NBC; **Sponsor:** Sealtest, Inc.; **Broadcast Time:** Thursday, 9:30 p.m.; **Running Time:** 30 minutes; **Content:** Dorothy pays a visit to Duffy's Tavern where she is forced to listen to Archie, calling himself "The Whispering Archie," sing "The Sweetheart of

Sigmund Freud." Lamour would prefer to participate in a beauty contest in the La Brea tar pits. Gayne Whitman and Sarah Berner have supporting roles. The program was presented in cooperation with AFRA (American Federation of Radio Artists) through an agreement between the sponsor and AFRA, whereby AFRA supplied talent for guest stars for each broadcast and Sealtest paid AFRA a certain amount each week, this amount to be used in a Health Insurance Fund for radio artists.

The Jimmy Durante Show (January 7, 1949)
Series Regular: Jimmy Durante; **Performers Included:** Roy Bargy and his Orchestra; **Network:** NBC; **Sponsor:** R.J. Reynolds; **Broadcast Time:** Friday, 8:30 p.m.; **Running Time:** 30 minutes; **Content:** Durante pays a visit to Duffy's Tavern. Florence Halop plays the role of Hotbreath Holliman (not Miss Duffy) in this episode, attempting to impress Durante by pretending to be a fashion expert. Ed Gardner reprises his role of Archie and Jimmy Durante puts in an appearance at the tavern to encourage Archie to go on a date with a woman named McGriffs. Archie, however, has his eyes set on another woman and then cries, "Egad, they start me out with a 'Portrait of Jenny' and I wind up with 'The Snake Pit'." When the wealthy (but homely) woman announces she has eight million dollars, Archie remarks, "I judge you to be twenty-six." Alan Young was also a weekly regular on Durante's program by this time, but due to illness was unable to attend this broadcast.

The Sealtest Variety Theater (March 17, 1949)
Series Regulars: Dorothy Lamour and the Henry Russell Orchestra; **Performers Included:** Basil Rathbone; **Network:** NBC; **Sponsor:** Sealtest, Inc.; **Broadcast Time:** Thursday, 9:30 p.m.; **Running Time:** 30 minutes; **Content:** See the chapter about the Dorothy Lamour disaster for more information.

The Big Show (November 26, 1950)
Series Regular: Tallulah Bankhead; **Performers Included:** Fred Allen and Ed Wynn; **Network:** NBC; **Sponsor:** Ford, RCA Victor and Anacin under Operation Tandem; **Broadcast Time:** Sunday, 6:00 p.m.; **Running Time:** 90 minutes; **Content:** Tallulah

Bankhead takes the entire *Big Show* cast to Duffy's Tavern, where Ed Gardner attempts to impress the guests by charging five dollars at the hat check. This includes Fred Allen, Jack Carson, Mindy Carson, Portland Hoffa, Lauritz Melchior and Ed Wynn. Ed Wynn tries to explain Lauritz Melchior's opera with his usual "Carmen" sketch. Ed Gardner breaks up over the air when he makes a mistake while delivering his lines.

This is New York (May 23, 1951)
Series Regular: Bill Leonard; **Network:** CBS; **Sponsor:** unknown; **Broadcast Time:** Wednesday, 9:00 a.m.; **Running Time:** 45 minutes; **Content:** Radio host Bill Leonard interviews Ed Gardner about his childhood, growing up in New York City, the 1945 *Duffy's Tavern* motion picture and how *Duffy's Tavern* was created. While Gardner avoided the financial and business end of the radio program, he briefly discusses his day-to-day luxury living in Puerto Rico.

The Big Show (October 28, 1951)
Series Regular: Tallulah Bankhead; **Performers Included:** Jimmy Durante, The Ink Spots and Dorothy Sarnoff; **Network:** NBC; **Sponsor:** Ford, RCA Victor and Anacin under Operation Tandem; **Broadcast Time:** Sunday, 6:00 p.m.; **Running Time:** 90 minutes; **Content:** Ed Gardner, playing the role of Archie, cracks jokes with Tallulah Bankhead about Duffy's Tavern and then tries to encourage her to come to work at the "high class dump." The Ink Spots perform "Java Jive." After a performance by The Ink Spots, the following scene was originally slated for the program but deleted during rehearsals to ensure the program ended on time.

Deleted Scene
TALLULAH: Well, what do you say, Archie? Aren't they wonderful? Do you want to use them at Duffy's?
GARDNER: No, they'll be too expensive, Tallulah.
TALLULAH: But they said they'd appear there for nothing.
GARDNER: Yeah, I know. But with them there the laundry bills will be too big.
TALLULAH: Laundry bills!

GARDNER: Yeah. You see we do a big business in spare ribs. When these guys finish singing, everybody's got to put down their spare-ribs and wipe their hands on the table cloth so they can applaud.

TALLULAH: I don't suppose you've ever heard of napkins?

GARDNER: Yeah, I've heard of 'em. What about 'em?

TALLULAH: Well, a good way to keep down your laundry bill is to use paper napkins.

GARDNER: We tried it. The newsprint comes off on your shirt front. But I tell you what I might be interested in, Tallulah. That little musical combo you got back there.

TALLULAH: Oh, Meredith Willson's orchestra?

The Big Show (December 9, 1951)
Series Regular: Tallulah Bankhead; **Performers Included:** Ann Sothern and Robert Cummings; **Network:** NBC; **Sponsor:** Ford, RCA Victor and Anacin under Operation Tandem; **Broadcast Time:** Sunday, 6:00 p.m.; **Running Time:** 90 minutes; **Content:** Ed "Archie" Gardner reminds Bankhead that she has an unpaid bill from when she ran out of Duffy's Tavern the last time she paid a visit. Gardner then told his story about Two-Top Gruskin, the famous baseball player on Duffy's team, Duffy's All-American Irish Yankees usually referred to as the D.A.A.I.Y. (This is the same monologue that Gardner recited on numerous other radio programs many times over.) Gardner later joins Bankhead in a rendition of "Leave Us Face It."

The Big Show (February 24, 1952)
Series Regular: Tallulah Bankhead; **Performers Included:** Kay Armen, Victor Borge and Gertrude Berg; **Network:** NBC; **Sponsor:** various sponsors under Operation Tandem; **Broadcast Time:** Sunday, 6:00 p.m.; **Running Time:** 90 minutes; **Content:** Ed Gardner appears in his Archie characterization, attempting to convince Tallulah Bankhead that they should sing a duet together. "You know opera, Tallulah. Good old opera. That's where a guy walks out on the stage and they stab him, and instead of bleedin' he sings... ah, the opera!" Archie then tries to convince the actress that he is a graduate of Harvard. When Archie answers the phone,

he attempts to convince Duffy that he is a former ball player in the major league... which somehow leads to inventors and their inventions... "And the greatest woman of them all, Tallulah Bankhead, who invented Bette Davis..." Gardner and Bankhead, accompanied by the chorus, sing "A-Round the Corner," an original song with comical lyrics. Before the broadcast, NBC objected to a line spoken by Ed Gardner: "You know when you're sittin' in the parlor in the dark, you like somethin' you can locate in a hurry." NBC requested the line be changed to "You like to be able to locate your girl in a hurry." NBC objected to another of Gardner's lines: "She what? Went to the beauty parlor again? That's the third time this week, Duffy. Wouldn't it be cheaper if you just got drunk?"

AFRS Programs
Produced for troops stationed overseas, these programs were not broadcast in the United States. They were broadcast over the Armed Forces Radio Service with a direct shortwave transmission to the troops overseas. The dates listed for the following programs are the recording dates.

Command Performance (recorded on March 13, 1942)
Master of Ceremonies: Kate Smith; **Performers Included:** Robert Benchley and Henny Youngman; **Network:** AFRS; **Running Time:** 30 minutes; **Content:** Ed Gardner appears as Archie and tells the story of "Two-Top Gruskin" and how he attempted to join the Army.

Command Performance (recorded on March 13, 1942)
Master of Ceremonies: Katharine Hepburn; **Performers Included:** Kathryn Grayson, The Jesters, Ted Lewis and His Orchestra; **Network:** AFRS; **Running Time:** 30 minutes; **Content:** Archie refers to Katharine Hepburn as a "high class tomato." Hepburn was never a guest on *Duffy's Tavern* so this episode marked the only time she was ribbed by the comedian. Archie proposes doing Shakespeare together on the stage... William Randolph Shakespeare, that is.

*Ed Gardner and Katharine Hepburn rehearsing
for* Command Performance.

Command Performance (recorded on August 21, 1943)
Master of Ceremonies: Ginger Rogers; **Performers Included:**
Arthur Q. Bryan and Alice Faye; **Network:** AFRS; **Running
Time:** 30 minutes; **Content:** Ed Gardner offers Frank Sinatra a job
at Duffy's Tavern. Archie refers to Frank Sinatra as "a piccolo with
a bow tie." Because this episode was not broadcast domestically,
there are some risqué jokes about women and their figures.

Command Performance (broadcast on December 25, 1943)
Master of Ceremonies: Bob Hope; **Performers Included:** Fred
Allen, Jack Benny, Jimmy Durante, Nelson Eddy, Spike Jones and
The City Slickers, Frances Langford and Dinah Shore; **Network:**
AFRS; **Running Time:** 90 minutes; **Content:** Special Christmas
broadcast. Ed Gardner plays the role of Archie and once again
performs the "Two-Top Gruskin" routine.

Mail Call (recorded on April 26, 1944)
Performers Included: Ida Lupino and Irene Manning; **Network:** AFRS; **Running Time:** 30 minutes; **Content:** Ed Gardner, Eddie Green and Charlie Cantor participate in "A Tribute to Brooklyn," an original play scripted by Archie himself. The cast also performs an English drawing room drama. Ida Lupino assists with the fun by playing the role of the Duchess, while Archie plays the role of the Dutch.

Command Performance (recorded on October 7, 1944)
Master of Ceremonies: Dinah Shore; **Performers Included:** Connie Haines, Chico Marx and Art Tatum; **Network:** AFRS; **Running Time:** 30 minutes; **Content:** Archie tells Dinah Shore how Duffy's Tavern celebrated when France was liberated. He attempts to speak French until he discovers she speaks the language fluently. When asked how he prepares Duck for serving, Archie admits that Finnegan is the resident cook.

Jubilee (recorded on February 5, 1945)
Master of Ceremonies: Ernest Whitman; **Performers Included:** Eddie Heywood, Lena Horne and Les Paul; **Network:** AFRS; **Running Time:** 30 minutes; **Content:** Ed Gardner, Eddie Green and Charlie Cantor appear in character when they perform a sketch from Duffy's Tavern.

Command Performance (recorded on August 15, 1945)
Master of Ceremonies: Bing Crosby; **Performers Included:** Lucille Ball, Lionel Barrymore, Claudette Colbert, Ronald Colman, Bette Davis, Marlene Dietrich, Greer Garson, Cary Grant, Rita Hayworth, Lena Horne, Danny Kaye, Burgess Meredith, Carmen Miranda, Edward G. Robinson, Ginger Rogers, Dinah Shore, Frank Sinatra, Claire Trevor, Orson Welles and Loretta Young; **Network:** AFRS; **Running Time:** 100 minutes; **Content:** Special "Victory Extra" program to celebrate the end of the war. Ed Gardner appears towards the end of the broadcast and refers to Claudette Colbert as a "high class tomato." Gardner reuses the same script, almost verbatim, he performed with Katharine Hepburn on the same program in 1942.

Greer Garson and unidentified men with Ed Gardner.

Command Performance (broadcast on December 25, 1945)
Master of Ceremonies: Bob Hope; **Performers Included:** Mel Blanc, Bing Crosby, Cass Daley, Jimmy Durante, Judy Garland, Harry James, Kay Kyser, Frances Langford, Dinah Shore and Frank Sinatra; **Network:** AFRS; **Running Time:** 2 hours; **Content:** Special Christmas broadcast with Bob Hope preparing for a big bash at his house. Archie offers his services to get Bing Crosby as musical entertainment at the Hope residence (for a commission, of course). Bing asks how Duffy's Tavern has been and Archie jokes that it's been closed due to "alterations."

Here's To Veterans (recorded on February 20, 1947)
Performers Included: Lotte Lehmann and Jimmy Wallington; **Network:** AFRS; **Running Time:** 15 minutes; **Content:** Ed Gardner plays Archie, who convinces opera singer Lotte Lehmann to sing his newly written love song. This was an excerpt from the November 13, 1946, broadcast of *Duffy's Tavern*.

Symphony Under The Stars (recorded on August 5, 1948)
Master of Ceremonies: Pat McGeehan; **Performers Included:** Gene Autry, Edgar Bergen, Irving Berlin, Jimmy Durante, Ed Gardner, Jack Haley, Danny Kaye, Frances Langford and Virginia O'Brien; **Network:** AFRS; **Running Time:** 2 hours and 10 minutes; **Content:** Presenting musical entertainment, Edgar Bergen and Ed Gardner were perhaps the only non-singers among the cast that participated.

To The Rear March (Undated, Episode #68)
Performers Included: Jim Backus, Arthur Q. Bryan, Eddie Cantor and Harry Von Zell; **Network:** AFRS; **Running Time:** 30 minutes; **Content:** Ed Gardner, Eddie Green and Charlie Cantor are heard in character, courtesy of a recording from April 1946 of *Duffy's Tavern* (probably April 19, 1946). Archie tells the history of boxing and then fights "The Gorilla."

To The Rear March (Undated, Episode #82)
Performers Included: Joan Davis, Bob Hope and Frank Sinatra; **Network:** AFRS; **Running Time:** 30 minutes; **Content:** Ed Gardner, Eddie Green, Alan Reed and Charlie Cantor are heard in character, courtesy of a recording from September 1945 of *Duffy's Tavern*. Archie is disappointed when none of the Hollywood stars he's invited to the Tavern for the dinner show up.

To The Rear March (Undated, Episode #92)
Performers Included: Victor Borge, Henry Morgan and Arnold Stang; **Network:** AFRS; **Running Time:** 30 minutes; **Content:** Features an excerpt from the June 18, 1947, broadcast of *Duffy's Tavern*, with guest Rudy Vallee.

Hi Neighbor (Undated, Episode #38)
Performers Included: Martha Wilkerson; **Network:** AFRS; **Running Time:** 15 minutes; **Content:** The hosts are Jack and Jill. In this episode, "Jill" is visited by Archie of Duffy's Tavern.

The Eyes and Ears of the Air Force (Undated, Episode #13, Second Series)
Narrator: Westbrook Van Voorhis; **Network:** unknown; **Running Time:** 15 minutes; **Content:** Syndicated program sponsored by the Ground Observer Corps Recruitment Department. Ed Gardner guests in a dramatic story about a pilot in trouble. Circa 1947, 1948 or 1949.

APPENDIX F
ASSORTED NEWS BRIEFS

Chuck Riesner, trumpet player, hopes to do an episode of *Duffy's Tavern*.
— columnist Hedda Hopper, July 14, 1943

"The Touchdown Club affair is loaded to the guards with sports personalities such as the irrepressible Jimmy Conzelman, Maj. Gen. Taylor of West Point and so on. The Press Club dinner was headlined by Archie of *Duffy's Tavern*, with Miss Duffy, Clifton Finnegan and Eddie the waiter and with Ben Grauer as emcee."
— columnist Bill Henry, January 16, 1947

"Gardner had monogrammed Duffy's Tavern mugs."
— *The Los Angeles Times*, October 25, 1947

"Last night the 21st annual dinner of the NY baseball writers was held, at the Hotel Commodore, in the grand ballroom. Among the entertainment was Ed Gardner of *Duffy's Tavern* to confuse the

issue a trifle more, and between these two outbursts the writers weighed in with everything they had."
— *The New York Times*, February 7, 1944

"The latest stars to offer their services for the annual all-star show and fashion revue of the Israel Orphan Asylum on March 18 at Madison Square Garden were Milton Berle, Henny Youngman and Ed Gardner."
— *The New York Times*, February 24, 1944

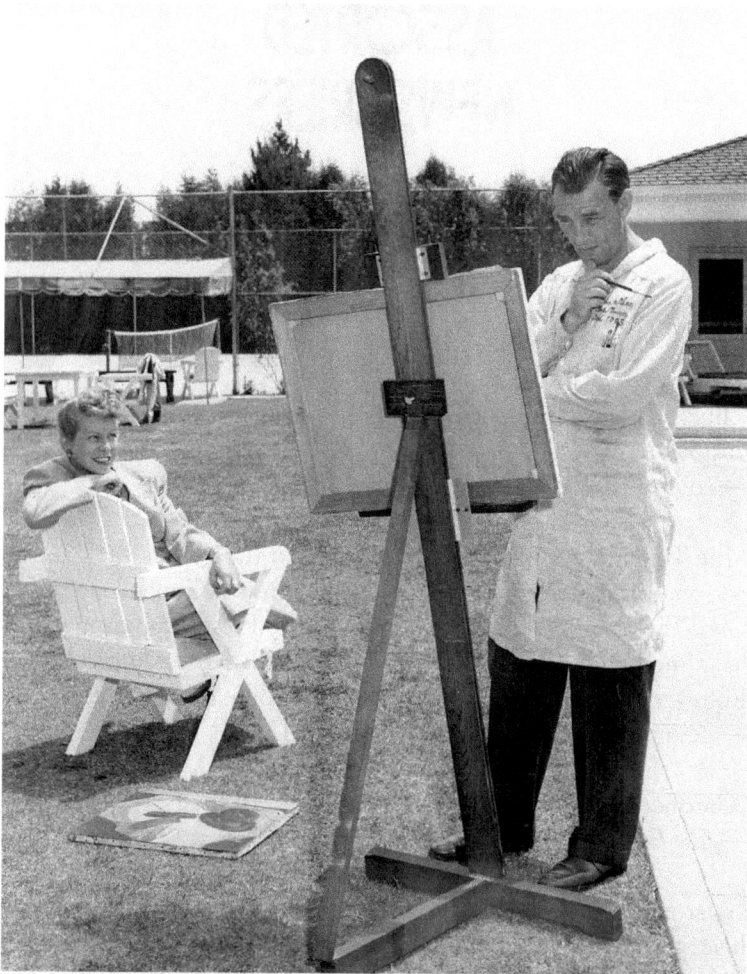

"Ed Gardner is the only radio comedian represented in the current movie stars exhibit at the Los Angeles Hall of Art. His painting of a circus horse is surrounded by pictures by Ella Raines, June Haver, Linda Darnell, Jeanne Crain, Reginald Gardiner, Jane Powell, Marguerite Chapman, Hoagy Carmichael and other stars."
— *The Los Angeles Times*, April 2, 1948

"Warden Clinton T. Duffy, of San Quentin penitentiary, has bought an interest in a cocktail lounge on the peninsula. His associates are Louis Saroni and Merrill Stock. The warden said his business venture will have no effect on his post at San Quentin, but columnists were quick to joke that it was now 'Warden Duffy's Tavern.'"
— *The San Francisco Chronicle*, September 6, 1947

"Things I'd like to see happen in radio during 1943... More comedy programs as good as *Duffy's Tavern*. By the way, the guest spots on *Duffy's* are always most competently filled."
— columnist Jerry Lesser, January 2, 1943

"Emcee for National Press Club's dinner to the President will be Ben Grauer, with Ed Gardner and *Duffy's Tavern* cast supplying comedy."
— NBC Press Release, January 18, 1947

"At first, the sight of an audience terrified me, and when I get out on a stage without a mike in front of me, I get positively sick."
— Ed Gardner, 1943

APPENDIX G
HIGHEST-RATED NBC RADIO SHOWS

According to the Wednesday, September 26, 1951, issue of *Variety*, the following is a twenty-year list of the highest-rated shows broadcast over NBC. (*Variety* did not disclose the source of this information.) The program listed on the top of each list had the highest rating of the year. The programs listed at the bottom of each list had the fifth-highest rating.

1932
Amos 'n' Andy
The Chase & Sanborn Program (Eddie Cantor)
The Fleischmann Hour (Rudy Vallee)
Blackstone Plantation (Crumit & Sanderson)
The Lucky Strike Dance Hour

1933
The Chase & Sanborn Program (Eddie Cantor)
The Texaco Fire Chief (Ed Wynn)

The Lucky Strike Dance Hour
Show Boat (Lanny Ross)
The Fleischmann Hour (Rudy Vallee)

1934
The Chase & Sanborn Program (Eddie Cantor)
Show Boat (Lanny Ross)
The Fleischmann Hour (Rudy Vallee)
The Texaco Fire Chief (Ed Wynn)
Baker's Broadcast (Joe Penner)

1935
The Jell-O Program (Jack Benny)
The Fleischmann Hour (Rudy Vallee)
Show Boat (Lanny Ross)
Baker's Broadcast (Joe Penner)
Town Hall Tonight (Fred Allen)

1936
Major Bowes' Amateur Hour
The Jell-O Program (Jack Benny)
The Fleischmann Hour (Rudy Vallee)
Town Hall Tonight (Fred Allen)
Baker's Broadcast (Joe Penner)

1937
The Jell-O Program (Jack Benny)
Town Hall Tonight (Fred Allen)
Kraft Music Hall (Bing Crosby)
The Fleischmann Hour (Rudy Vallee)

1938
The Chase and Sanborn Program (Edgar Bergen)
The Jell-O Program (Jack Benny)
The George Burns and Gracie Allen Show
Town Hall Tonight (Fred Allen)
Kraft Music Hall (Bing Crosby)

1939
The Chase and Sanborn Program (Edgar Bergen)
The Jell-O Program (Jack Benny)
Kraft Music Hall (Bing Crosby)
The Johnson's Wax Program (Fibber McGee and Molly)
Good News of 1939

1940
The Jell-O Program (Jack Benny)
The Chase and Sanborn Program (Edgar Bergen)
The Johnson's Wax Program (Fibber McGee and Molly)
The Pepsodent Show (Bob Hope)
One Man's Family

1941
The Jell-O Program (Jack Benny)
The Johnson's Wax Program (Fibber McGee and Molly)
The Chase and Sanborn Program (Edgar Bergen)
The Pepsodent Show (Bob Hope)
The Aldrich Family

1942
The Johnson's Wax Program (Fibber McGee and Molly)
The Pepsodent Show (Bob Hope)
The Charlie McCarthy Show (Edgar Bergen)
The Aldrich Family
The Jell-O Program (Jack Benny)

1943
The Pepsodent Show (Bob Hope)
The Raleigh Cigarette Program (Red Skelton)
The Johnson's Wax Program (Fibber McGee and Molly)
The Charlie McCarthy Show (Edgar Bergen)
The Jack Benny Program

1944
The Pepsodent Show (Bob Hope)
The Johnson's Wax Program (Fibber McGee and Molly)

The Raleigh Cigarette Program (Red Skelton)
The Charlie McCarthy Show (Edgar Bergen)
The Jack Benny Program

1945
The Pepsodent Show (Bob Hope)
The Johnson's Wax Program (Fibber McGee and Molly)
The Sealtest Village Store (Joan Davis with Jack Haley)
The Kraft Music Hall (Bing Crosby)
The Charlie McCarthy Show (Edgar Bergen)

1946
The Pepsodent Show (Bob Hope)
The Johnson's Wax Program (Fibber McGee and Molly)
The Charlie McCarthy Show (Edgar Bergen)
The Raleigh Cigarette Program (Red Skelton)
The Lucky Strike Program (Jack Benny)

1947
The Pepsodent Show (Bob Hope)
The Johnson's Wax Program (Fibber McGee and Molly)
The Lucky Strike Program (Jack Benny)
The Fred Allen Show
The Charlie McCarthy Show (Edgar Bergen)

1948
The Johnson's Wax Program (Fibber McGee and Molly)
The Lucky Strike Program (Jack Benny)
The Fred Allen Show
The Pepsodent Show (Bob Hope)
The Amos 'n' Andy Show

1949
The Johnson's Wax Program (Fibber McGee and Molly)
The Bob Hope Swan Show
Duffy's Tavern
Mr. District Attorney
The Great Gildersleeve

1950
The Pet Milk Program (Fibber McGee and Molly)
The Judy Canova Show
Mr. District Attorney
The Bob Hope Show
The Great Gildersleeve

1951
You Bet Your Life (Groucho Marx)
The Pet Milk Program (Fibber McGee and Molly)
People Are Funny (Art Linkletter)
The Big Story
Father Knows Best (Robert Young)

APPENDIX H
THE MAGIC KEY OF RCA
(JULY 24, 1939)

For the broadcast of July 24, 1939, Ed Gardner appeared as Archie, talking to Colonel Stoopnagle, making numerous references to Duffy's Bar and Grill, and telling the story of Two-Top Gruskin. Archie also assisted with the RCA commercial with announcer Ben Grauer. There was originally supposed to be a second sketch, but during rehearsals the sequence was scratched out to ensure the program ended on time. That deleted sequence is included in this book.

ARCHIE: Hello, Colonel Stoopnagle.
STOOP: Hello, Archie.
(APPLAUSE)
STOOP: Say, Ben, this is the fellow I was telling you about.
GRAUER: Oh, Archie, the native New Yorker.
ARCHIE: Hello, Mr. Grauer. You know, listening to you fellows talk about New York made me feel kinda sad. New York just ain't the same no more.

STOOP: What do you mean, New York just ain't the same no more?

ARCHIE: I mean, New York just ain't the same no more. My father used to say, "Archie, New York ain't the same no more." And before him, way back in 1870, my grandfather used to say New York ain't the same no more. Personally, I don't think New York ever was the same no more.

STOOP: Well, I think New York is pretty nice, especially if you want a good time. What do you do for divertissement, Archie?

ARCHIE: For what?

STOOP: Well I mean, where do you hang out?

ARCHIE: Oh. Well, for divertissement, I hang out in an establishment known as Duffy's Bar and Grill.

STOOP: Sounds like a place with that certain air of distinction.

ARCHIE: Yes and no. It has a little distinction, but I guess that's because there ain't any air in the joint.

STOOP: What is the attraction at Duffy's?

ARCHIE: Duffy, himself. You never on your life saw a man who could stand up so straight and look so stupid.

STOOP: Well, how old a man is this Duffy?

ARCHIE: Well, he ain't sure whether he's 38 or 56. All he knows is he was born in 1894.

STOOP: Sounds like a high grade imbecile.

ARCHIE: Yeah. Swell fellow. You ought to see how he runs our ball team, the Duffy Bar and Grill A.C.

STOOP: Duffy is the manager?

ARCHIE: The smartest in baseball on account that he ain't got no brains. Who turned Bow-Legged Harrigan into a second baseman?

STOOP: Duffy?

ARCHIE: Duffy. He figures Harrigan is so bow-legged that if a grounder goes through his legs, the shortstop can go right through after it. And what about Gorilla Hogan, the greatest catcher that ever lived?

STOOP: A Duffy discovery?

ARCHIE: A Duffy discovery. What a man. He runs with the speed of a canteloupe. You ought to see the Gorilla. He looks like he just stepped out of a jungle. A natural born catcher.

Stands six feet fourteen inches high, and squats standing up. The only reason anybody thinks of him as Hogan is because that was his father's name.

STOOP: He sounds pretty terrifying.

ARCHIE: He is. He used to be a fighter, but they had to bar him from the ring; he was too tough. In his last fight he fought a fellow named Battling Cassidy. The first thing happens when they come to the center of the ring to shake hands. The Gorilla shakes Cassidy's hand, and immediately Cassidy goes down for the count of eight. Then when they start to fight, the Gorilla lifts up his fist and brings it down on top of Cassidy's hand so hard that from that day to this the guy is known as Concerting Cassidy.

STOOP: What a powerful man!

ARCHIE: Colonel Stoopnagle, I can safely say that he is the most powerful man, if he is indeed a man, who ever drew the breath of life, if indeed he does draw the breath of life. Let me read you his ring measurements. Gorilla Hogan: ankles - 38. Waist - 53. Biceps - 23. Neck - none. Chest - expanding and 53.

STOOP: And this… this… thing is the catcher on your ball team?

ARCHIE: The only guy in the world who could catch Two-Top Gruskin.

STOOP: Oh, Two-Top Gruskin is your pitcher?

ARCHIE: Well, he used to be. And there's another example of Duffy's genius. One day Duffy says to Dugan the shortstop, "Dugan, we got a great ball team here, but I'm afraid it lacks color. What's the answer?" So Dugan says, "Color, eh?" Well, this may not be it, Duffy, but I think I know where I can lay my hands on a pitcher with two heads." So Duffy says, "A pitcher with two heads? I don't know, Dugan, do you think it'd be a novelty?" So Dugan says, "Well, what if it ain't? You can't pass up a pitcher that can watch first base and third base at the same time." So Duffy says, "It's an angle. And besides, the guy would be a natural for double-headers."

STOOP: Now, Archie, did you actually see his two headed pitcher yourself?

ARCHIE: Certainly. I remember the night he first walked into

Duffy's Bar — dressed up formal — to sign his contract. Everybody in the joint was staring at him.

STOOP: I should think they would.

ARCHIE: Yeah. So Two-Top turns his two heads to the crowd and says, "What are you starin' at? None of you guys ever see a tuxedo before?" Well, Duffy quickly covers his embarrassment. He says, "Waiter, bring two beers for this man." Then he turns to Gruskin and says, "Two-Top, I'm a man of few words. Report tomorrow morning. There's a uniform and two caps waiting for you in the locker room."

STOOP: Well, how did Two-Top get along with Gorilla Hogan?

ARCHIE: Not quite as well as you'd naturally expect.

STOOP: They didn't hit it off, eh?

ARCHIE: Frankly, no. The trouble starts right in the first game. The Gorilla signals for a fast curve, so Two-Top nods one head and shakes the other. Well, this is very confusing to the Gorilla, who ain't so bright anyway, so he throws down his glove and makes a bee-line for Duffy. "Duffy," he says, "I'm getting' good and sick and tired of two headed pitches — I quit." So Duffy says, "Now wait a minute, Gorilla. Don't get hot headed. Go out there and talk it over with the guy. After all, three heads is better than one." But the Gorilla says, "Nope. It's no use. I just can't help feelin' that the guy ain't normal. One of us will have to go, Duffy, and don't forget who owns the baseball."

STOOP: And that was Two-Top's finish, eh?

ARCHIE: Yeah. It was pretty sad, the way the lumps came up in his throats when Duffy told him. Well, I gotta run along Colonel Stoopnagle. The Gorilla's down in the barber shop havin' his chest shampooed and he's waitin' for me. I'll be seein' ya, huh?

STOOP: Wait a minute, Archie, before you go. What finally became of the two headed pitcher?

ARCHIE: Who, Two-Top? Oh, he went back to his old job. Watchin' tennis matches for Pathe News. Well, so long Colonel Stoopnagle.

SOUND: (APPLAUSE)

DELETED SEQUENCE

SOUND: (KNOCK ON DOOR)

STOOP: Come in.

SOUND: (DOOR OPENS, CLOSES)

ARCHIE: Colonel Stoopnagle, my name is Archie. I'm the detective from down the hall.

STOOP: My name is Stoopnagle. I'm the detective from up the hall. Meet Ben Grauer, he's the detective from up the creek.

ARCHIE: How do you do. I just thought I'd drop in to pay a social call, us being neighbors, and both detectives. How's business?

STOOP: Well, it's pretty slow. How can we possibly compete with those low priced Chinese detectives?

ARCHIE: Yeah, it's a tough year in our business. I was talking to a friend of mine the other day, Crudface Clifford, a safe cracker. And you know when those fellows don't work, we don't work. He says to me, "Archie, things certainly are bad in my game. You remember I used to crack safes? I made a good living, drove my own stolen car, was well thought of in the community... now look at me. I'm out picking pockets like a common thief."

STOOP: What a comedown. I have a friend, a fellow who used to make counterfeit fifties and hundreds. Just recently he had to make up a line of phony two dollar bills to retail for 39 cents. So what happens? He works like a dog turning out counterfeit dough, and his wife spends it faster than he can make it.

ARCHIE: Yeah, it's tough. This year us detectives got wallets to match our feet.

SOUND: (PHONE RINGS)

STOOP: The Whodunit Detective Agency, Stoopnagle speaking. Huh? Oh. It's for you, Archie.

ARCHIE: Thanks. Hello? Oh, yes, Mr. B. I'll be right over to your house.

SOUNDS: (HANG UP)

ARCHIE: I have to go right out on a case, Colonel. Could I borrow some dog biscuits from you?

STOOP: Dog biscuits? Whose house are you going to?

ARCHIE: The Baskervilles.

SOUND: (DOOR SLAM)

STOOP: He'll probably be hounded to death.

APPENDIX I
THE MAGIC KEY OF RCA
(AUGUST 14, 1939)

For the broadcast of August 14, 1939, Ed Gardner appeared as Archie, a "typical New Yorker," making his second of two appearances on the program. Duffy's Tavern is referenced as Duffy's Bar and Grill, and Archie once again tells a story of Two-Top Gruskin. A number of lines were deleted from the script during rehearsals. The complete monologue, including the deleted lines, are reprinted below.

STOOP: You talk just like that fellow Archie we had on this program a few weeks ago.

GRAUER: Oh, Archie, is certainly the typical New Yorker.

STOOP: You stone worshippers are all alike. New York is all right, but have you ever had the feeling of walking in your own garden — of knowing every blade of grass by name? Have you ever felt that you could almost talk to your flowers? Why, even the little worm in the ground is my pal. I can walk right up to him and say, "Hi, there, worm!"

ARCHIE: Hello, Colonel Stoopnagle.

STOOP: Well! Hello, Archie!

SOUND: (APPLAUSE)

STOOP: Say Archie, what has been going down at Duffy's Bar and Grill?

ARCHIE: Well, really Colonel that Duffy's gettin' absolutely too stupid to associate myself with. You know what he does last night?

STOOP: What?

ARCHIE: Well, he's ridin' down in the subway readin' a newspaper and he's got all these pigeons on him. One on his shoulder, one on his knee and one on his hat. So the guy sittin' opposite him recognizes him and says, 'Say Duffy, what are you doin' with all them pigeons?' So Duffy says, 'I don't know. They just happened to get on with me at Fiftieth Street.' I swear, Colonel, there's one man could blow his brains out and still live.

STOOP: He sounds like a little on the clever side.

ARCHIE: Duffy's listening in tonight, you know. He thinks maybe you're the man for the job.

STOOP: What job?

ARCHIE: Master of ceremonies at this summer semi-annual pig roast and musicale.

STOOP: You mean that Duffy himself is passing judgment on me tonight?

ARCHIE: Yep. With all ears akimbo. That's one thing Duffy insists on. He personally picks his own pigs and masters of ceremonies.

STOOP: Oh, I don't blame him. I wouldn't expect him to buy a pig in a poke.

ARCHIE: A pig in a poke — ha, ha. That's right up Duffy's sense of humor. Keep it up and I think you're in.

STOOP: Thanks.

ARCHIE: Unless you're nearsighted like that master of ceremonies we had last year.

STOOP: What happened to him?

ARCHIE: Well, you see, Duffy's wife is... shall we say... kind of a big fat tub. So last year she comes to the pig roast in a sleeveless dress and sits right next to this new master of ceremonies. Well, the whistle to start eatin' hardly blows before the near-sighted guy has his knife in the sauerkraut and his fork in Mrs. Duffy's left arm.

STOOP: That must have been embarrassing.

ARCHIE: Well, that only started it. A few minutes later he's at it again. He goes over and bows to a barrel of beer and says, 'May I have this dance, Mrs. Duffy?' Well, that burns Duffy up, so he goes over to the beer barrel and says, 'Ignore him, dear.' So Duffy turns to the guy and says, 'Young man, I may be wrong but I'm not far from it. I think you're fired. How much salary am I payin' you?' The guy says 'Nothin'.' So Duffy says, 'Go get your pay.'

STOOP: I'll have to watch my step if I get the job, eh?

ARCHIE: That's right and here's a tip for you. If you want to get in right with Duffy, buy a couple of chances on the raffle. Second prize is a kiss from Mrs. Duffy.

STOOP: What's first prize?

ARCHIE: A second helping of pig. And another thing, Colonel. See that you meet the right set down at Duffy's.

STOOP: Who are they?

ARCHIE: Oh — Crudface Clifford, Gorilla Hogan...

STOOP: Hogan? Is he the muscle you were talking me about? The fellow you said was an ape.

ARCHIE: No. Hogan's only half ape.

STOOP: What's the other half?

ARCHIE: Ape. And you also want to meet Roast Beef Nicholson and Two-Top Gruskin.

STOOP: Oh yes, Two-Top Gruskin. He's the baseball pitcher with the two heads who watched first and third at the same time.

ARCHIE: Yeah, that's the guy.

STOOP: There's a fellow I'm dying to meet.

ARCHIE: Two-Top? I don't see why. There's nothing outstanding about him. What is he? Just a guy with two heads.

STOOP: Is he gonna be at the pig roast?

ARCHIE: I don't think so.

STOOP: Why not?

ARCHIE: Well, he didn't exactly conduct himself like no gentleman last year. The first thing happens when Duffy serves him a hunk of pig. Two-Top says, 'Is this all I get, Duffy?' So Duffy says, 'What do you want? It's a full portion.' So Two-Top says, 'Yeah, but don't forget. I got another mouth to feed.' That's how the romance started.

STOOP: Two-Top had a romance?

ARCHIE: Yeah. With a girl named Inez Harrigan. She's an ex-chorus girl, you see, so when she hears the word 'food,' she turns around and gives Two-Top a quick glance. Then she turns around again and gives him a second glance to confirm the first glance which she cannot believe, and right away she realizes she's in love. As she later said to me, 'Archie, I can't quite put my finger on it, but there's something different about that man. I guess it's because he's so tall, blond and brunette.' There's only thing Inez didn't like about him. She said whenever she kissed him she always had a feeling that they were not quite alone.

STOOP: And did Two-Top fall in love with Inez?

ARCHIE: Yeah. He nearly went out of his minds about her.

STOOP: He was beside himself, eh?

ARCHIE: Yeah. Duffy'll like that one too — if he gets it.

STOOP: Did Inez and Two-Top ever get married, Archie?

ARCHIE: No. You see Inez turned out to be an old girlfriend of Gorilla Hogan's. The Gorilla caught them one day, just as Two-Top was kissin' Inez and playin' 'I Love You Truly' on a harmonica at the same time. The Gorilla turns to Inez and says, 'Inez, what has Two-Top got that I haven't got? Maybe you'd like me better if I had two heads?' So Inez says, 'Not two heads like the one you got, Gorilla.' Then the Gorilla turns on Two-Top and he says, 'Let's fight it out man to man and the winner gets the girl. If you win, I'll be your best man. But Two-Top says, 'No thank you. I'll be my own best man.'

STOOP: And they really fought it out?

ARCHIE: Sure. And what a fight! No more than it begins the gorilla starts a powerful right from the floor. Two-Top ducks one head to one side and the other head to the other side and the punch goes right between him and knocks Duffy stiff as a merchant. So you can see, Colonel, why Two-Top may not be invited to the Pig Roast this year?

SOUND: (PHONE RINGS)

STOOP: Hello? Oh, just a minute. It's for you, Archie.

ARCHIE: Thanks. Hello? Oh, hello, Duffy. How do you like Stoopnagle, Duffy? Oh. What? Well some people like him, Duffy. Oh. He wants to know what can you do to entertain his friends, Colonel, outside of funny stuff.

STOOP: Well, I can sing a song for him.

ARCHIE: He says he can sing a song, Duffy. What? Oh, you want something with more novelty. Got anything with more novelty, Colonel?

STOOP: How about a talking horse?

ARCHIE: He says how about a talking horse? What could a horse say that would be of any interest? Yeah, I see your point, Duffy. Just a minute. Duffy says, can you do anything unusual yourself?

STOOP: Well, I can walk a tightrope, saw a woman in half, turn cartwheels, sing, dance, recite and play the organ.

ARCHIE: He says he can walk a tightrope, saw a woman in half, turn cartwheels, sing, dance, recite and play the organ. Is he a notary public? Listen, Duffy, don't be a hog — give the fellow a chance. Okay, Duffy. (HANG UP) He says you should sing, Colonel.

STOOP: Fine. (PIANO IN. STOOP SINGS "Oh, give me a ho-o-ome..." PHONE RINGS LOUD. STOOP STOPS.)

ARCHIE: Hello? Now wait a minute. Calm down Duffy! What? Oh, Duffy, I can't tell the man a thing like that. (He says you were pretty good, Colonel.) I know — I know, Duffy! All right, keep your shirt on. G'bye.

STOOP: Well, do I get the job, Archie?

ARCHIE: Well, Duffy hasn't decided yet. However, he says if you get a job for the day of the pageant, take it; but if you don't have a job for that day — get one. In the meantime, he'll let you know. Well, so long, Colonel.

SOUND: (PLAY OFF & APPLAUSE)

JUST LISTENING IN
BY DON FOSTER

Ed Gardner was a guest columnist for Don Foster's "Listening In" column for the July 16, 1945, issue of the *Chicago Daily Times*. Foster was on vacation and Gardner, never one to turn down an opportunity to promote *Duffy's Tavern*, wrote the following piece.

Most men wait until they are dead before starting to write their autobiography, but I feel that now is a better time. More opportune, so to speak, I wish to state that the events as herein under set forth is purely of me own volution and true to the best extent of me liability and knowledge. Any deliberate falsehood is purely a typographical error... I was born. So much for that. For birthplace I had a gaudy but tasteful palace on Park Avenue. My parents were away most of the time as pater was busy at the bank and mater was too busy with politics (at the time she was running for governess). It was pretty tough for me as a boy, walking along the streets in those little Lord Fauntleroy shoes and hearing the other kids holler, "Rich kid! Rich kid! Never earned a nickel in his life!" And I couldn't answer then; I couldn't talk, because being borned with a silver spoon in me mouth, I could only gurgle until I reached three and the installment man came and took the spoon away. The childhood of a rich kid ain't all beer and pretzels. But me childhood began to pass before me very eyes. The bud began to give away to the flower. Education begun to ripen me. From private to prep, from prep to tech, from tech to high, from high to night, and then came the universities — Princeton, Dartsmouth, Oxford and finally Harvard. How well I remember those inter-sorority fights when I stood on the campus and threw rocks at Yale.

Then it happened, like a bolt of blue. Things got bad with pater at the bank and we had to give up everything. Pater even had to sacrifice his three Duesenbergs. This was a great loss to pater. He really loved them three dogs. Finally we lost the house. It was then I set out to make me own way in the world. So that is how I came to take this job at Duffy's. But enough of this. I now has to get back to me job. If Duffy knew I was writing this on his time he would fly into a transom of rage.

THE TYPEWRITER IN THE BACK ROOM AT DUFFY'S TAVERN

BY ABRAM S. BURROWS

In 1944, Essential Books in New York published *Off Mike: Radio Writing by the Nation's Top Radio Writers* (ed. Ed Jerome Lawrence), a collection of essays from men and women responsible for scripting some of the most popular radio programs of the time. Abe Burrows contributed a chapter revealing the process for which a radio script was constructed for the situation comedy, citing the January 4, 1944, broadcast as an example.

Leave us face it, boys. When Ed Gardner sees this chapter, the first thing he's going to say is, "When the hell did Burrows get time to do it?" Because when you write a comedy program, you're chained to your typewriter. Occasionally, when you knock out a good script, the boss gives you another link for the chain. A successful comedy writer is one who can go to the bathroom without having the boss unlock him. But before I start taking bows for terrific industry and stick-to-it-iveness, to say nothing of comedy brilliance, leave me face something. I work for a character

713

who not only is a character but who knows plenty about comedy writing. So take a rule. A guy is only as smart as the comic he works for.

I know there is a lot of loose talk in this book about radio's occupational hazard, the mighty ulcer. But nobody has been thoughtful enough to tell you how to get one of your own. Very well. You can join us on a trip that will end twenty mimeographed pages from now. You will be required to bring along as basic equipment a package of Tums, some Benzedrine, and lots of coffee. And incidentally, if en route you should think of any jokes, for Pete's sake, speak up!

The first thing that happens is a little guy calls you up and says: "Fred Allen is going to be your guest next Tuesday." The little guy who tells you this is now through for the week. He doesn't have to do another thing until the following week when he calls you up and says: "Your guest next week will be Cary Grant." (It is not too late to stop reading this chapter right here and go get his job. He probably never heard of Tums.)

However, there we are. We have Fred Allen as a guest. *Duffy's Tavern*, let us remind you, is a story show. That is, we get one basic plot and stick to it all the way through. Most comedy shows start off with either a monologue by the comic or a scene between the comic and his cast. This is followed by an interview with the guest star, which leads into a third spot, which is a sketch of afterpiece, with the entire cast taking part. But on *Duffy's Tavern* we go on plot from the gun, generally observing the rules which apply to sound farce construction. That is, we plunge Archie into a jam immediately, get him in a little deeper by the time we reach the second spot, and try to get him out before the show goes off the air.

So we call a conference to get a story-line for Fred Allen's appearance. We look under the rugs. No story-line. We look out the windows. No story-line. We go out to lunch. No story-line. But finally somebody remembers that St. Patrick's Day is coming and on St. Patrick's day, Duffy, the unseen proprietor of the Tavern, always holds what he calls his "Spring Semi-Annual St. Patrick's Day Musicale and Pig Roast." So we say, why not let Archie try to hire Fred Allen as the M.C. for the pig roast? Then Duffy won't want Fred, and Fred will have to audition for him. This will give us a splendid opportunity to louse up Allen and have a lot of fun while Duffy is insulting him.

Okay. We have our premise, our springboard, our basic situation. We then lay out a three-page synopsis describing what everybody does and when: Archie, Eddie Green, Finnegan, Miss Duffy. We also decide where to place the commercials (without these, it's futile work), and the musical numbers.

Leave us pause again for a maxim or two. The average comedy show, after you deduct commercials, opening, closing, musical numbers, and musical transitions, contains a grand total of eighteen to twenty minutes of dialogue. Therefore, if you want laughs, you had better keep that plot simple and uncomplicated. Build it so that there is room for plenty of socko comedy bits. You have to know what your comic's strong points are, and in your plot include lots of opportunities for him to parade these strong points before the microphone. For instance, Archie is wonderful when he's lying about his background, literary, social, athletic, or musical, so in our plots we always try to include something in this vein. He's a great comic lover. He's a great one at Malapropisms. (As he once said to Carole Landis: "You are a lovely pale gossamer, who should be placed on a pedestrian and worshipped.")

Well, sir, we're all set now. We have a premise: a nicely typed story-line. Now all we need is a script full of jokes. We have to tell our story and make sure we don't go more than three lines without a belly-laugh. The first question that comes up immediately is: "Don't you have a joke file?" The only answer I can give to this is, I find it easier without one. The drawbacks of joke files are many. First, while you're trying to find a joke that will fit your particular situation and trying to make it fit your dialogue, you could be thinking up half a dozen original gags which flow right out of your dialogue and make your script sound smoother. Another serious drawback is the fact that many comedy writers with natural comedy minds start relying on files as a sort of mental crutch and eventually injure their natural comedy sense. Besides, with priorities, where are you going to get a file anyway?

Okay, forgetting files, the next question is: "How do you set about getting jokes?" Well, if you want to be a comedy writer, no doubt you or your friends or your wife class you as a wit of the first water. No doubt your wife, sitting home with you of a Sunday night listening to the Jack Benny show, has said, "Honey, you say much funnier things than that all the time! Like when I bought that hat and you said it looked just like a victory garden." Well, sir, in every joke the straight line is the hat, and the punch line is your own classic remark about the victory garden. When you're sitting alone writing jokes, you have to keep throwing straight lines at yourself. Keep throwing them until one of them lights a spark. (However, that spark must flame a lot brighter than that victory garden crack, or you'll never get a job on the Jack Benny show.) For instance, when Archie is talking to Eddie Green about being in love with a girl, he says: "Eddie, I'm in love again." Remember when you were a kid and your brother told you he was in love, you always had a wisecrack? Well, we have a wisecrack, too. Eddie Green says to Archie: "So you're in love again. Boy, that love bug must use up all his red points on you!" This joke was actually constructed by someone throwing the straight line ("Eddie, I'm in love again") over and over until a witty answer came up. If you can't think of a funny answer, maybe there's something wrong with the straight line. Keep changing that, until something bubbles. What you do learn after years in the business is how to throw pregnant straight lines. (I use the word "pregnant" advisedly, because the pains are not unlike childbirth.)

So we play this game of put and take until we're cross-eyed, and finally we've assembled a bunch of jokes which we've put together, polished and rewritten. Then we have a preview of the program with an audience present to find out what we've got. Those people out there don't know it, but they're guinea pigs; in this case, however, the guinea pigs are dissecting us. After the preview, Ed Gardner and I sit down to massacre and manicure the script. We rewrite, cut out, chew up, rephrase, shorten, lengthen and sometimes throw the whole thing out and start from scratch. On the next day, which is the day of the show, there is a dress rehearsal, after which there is a shorter version of the above horror bill. But finally it's show time, and you have to go on with what you've got. You are rewarded when the audience laughs, and you go home and sleep contentedly because you have done your job well and have earned the right to get up the next morning and pick up the phone and have the little guy tell you: "Abe, next week your guest is going to be Hedda Hopper."

We've made writing a comedy show sound pretty horrible, but it's really not. It's a stimulating, exciting form of writing, which, when you get the knack out of it, comes fairly easily. Besides, for those of you who are crass materialists (and that includes me), it pays well.

Uh-huh, you're interested. Well, how do you crack the charmed circle? How do you get a job on one of the big comedy shows? Well, you wouldn't ask for a job as a plumber's helper without knowing how to fix a sink. So, before you try to get a job as a comedy writer, make sure you know how to put your material down on paper. Learn something about writing. And the best way to learn something about writing is to write. Put it down on paper until you find it's easy to put it down. Read all the plays you can lay your hands on. Listen to all the radio shows. Don't apply for a job with just a ready wit, figuring you can toss your stuff off verbally. Crystallize your wit on paper. And when you think you're ready, pick out a comedian you think you'd like to write for. Write something that you think is in his style. Then write him and ask him if you can submit it. In most cases, it's smarter to send the material to the comedian or his chief writer directly, instead of the advertising agency or the network. Another way of cracking the comedy racket is through an agent or artist's manager. If you send your stuff to a good agent, and he thinks well of it, he may sell you to the comic. And don't be discouraged. That comic is looking for you as diligently as you're looking for him.

Well, now you know. You have to be a natural wit: i.e., the life of the party. You know that you need twenty pages of jokes. You need a smart comic to write for. You need Benzedrine and coffee. Well, frankly, Butch, if you know all that, all you need is that little guy to call you up.

APPENDIX L
ARCHIE'S NOW
IN HOLLYWOOD

by Frederick C. Othman, United Press Correspondent
September 28, 1944, issue of *PM Magazine*

Leave us now consider a high class saloon patronized only by beautiful blonde society tomatoes. Duffy's joint, that is. The celebrated tavern of the non-visible Duffy came to life today on Paramount's Stage One, with Archie behind the bar and Finnegan making passes at the free lunch and Director Hal Walker trying not to laugh while the cameras were turning.

Archie, who signs his checks Ed Gardner, had on his peach-colored suspenders and it was a pleasure to meet him. You can talk about your Webster and your Funk and Wagnalls all you want, about your Roget and his Thesaurus; this Gardner has done more than anybody else to change the English language. Leave us not get too excited about it, but the fact remains that Gardner has added phrases to the language that cannot be erased. So there was Gardner talking to Finnegan, whose name is Charlie Cantor. The subject was Miss O'Mally, as played by Marjorie Reynolds.

'Leave us not burn our bridges until we come to 'em,' said Archie.

719

'What is that you say Finnegan? A dame? She happens to be a very high class society tomato.' And so on, fat into the afternoon, with Archie slapping down Finnegan every time he tried to move in on the hard-boiled eggs. Archie's pals report that when he was a top-flight radio producer a few years ago, his grammar was as good as anybody's, his accent not even vaguely Brooklynesque. He was producing a radio drama titled *This is New York* and he needed a character from across the river and he had to do it himself. That started Archie. As the years passed, Gardner's grammar became worse and much worser, his accent more strangled, until he sounded as though he were talking with a clothes pin on his nose.

Before Gardner got into the radio business, he was an ordinary young man who couldn't hold a job, no matter what. He tried his hand at piano playing, train dispatching, baseball playing, typewriter selling, miniature golf course building, and WPA play directing. This latter led naturally into radio script writing and first thing Gardner knew he had become Archie. Leave us not sneer. Archie is doing all right.

SELECTED BIBLIOGRAPHY

— Cox, Jim. *American Radio Networks: A History* (McFarland & Company, Inc. 2009)

— Cox, Jim. *Radio Speakers* (McFarland & Company, Inc., 2007)

— Diehl, Lorraine B. *Over Here! New York City During World War II* (Harper Collins, 2010)

— Dunning, John. *On The Air* (Oxford University Press, 1998)

— Gelbart, Larry. *Laughing Matters* (Random House, 1998)

— Ellett, Ryan. *Encyclopedia of Black Radio in the United States, 1921-1955* (McFarland & Company, Inc., 2012)

— French, Jack. *Private Eyelashes: Radio's Lady Detectives* (Bear Manor Media, 2004)

— Grams, Martin. *The History of the Cavalcade of America* (Morris Publishing, 2000)

— Grams, Martin. *The Big Show: Tallulah Bankhead's Radio Career* (Bear Manor Media, 2014)

— Grams, Martin. *Radio Drama: American Programs, 1932-1962* (McFarland & Company, Inc., 2000)

— Hickerson, Jay. *The 4th Revised Ultimate History of Network Radio Programming and Guide to All Circulating Shows* (Presto Print II, Hamden, Connecticut, 2010)

— Kanter, Hal. *So Far, So Funny: My Life in Show Business* (McFarland & Company, Inc., 1999)

— Lake, Veronica. *Veronica: The Autobiography of Veronica Lake* (Bantam Books, 1969)

— Nelson, Ozzie. *Ozzie* (Prentice-Hall, Inc., 1973)

— Ohmart, Ben. *Hold That Joan: The Life, Laughs and Films of Joan Davis* (Bear Manor Media, 2007)

— Reed, Alan and Ohmart, Ben. *Yabba Dabba Doo!* (Bear Manor Media, 2009)

INDEX

Arlen, Richard 6
Armen, Kay 682
Armstrong, F. Wallis 6
Armstrong, Louis 97, 439, 629
Arnaz, Desi 460
Arno, Peter 278
Arnold, Bill 609
Arnold, Edward 21
Arthur, Jack 438
Arthur's Place (radio program) 395, 396
Astaire, Fred 404, 423
Autry, Gene 378, 533, 603, 658, 687
Averback, Hy 385

Bacall, Lauren 402, 432
Bacher, Bill 7-9, 18
Backus, Jim 308, 675, 687
Bailey, Jack 250
Baker, Florence 459
Baker, Kenny 399
Baker, Phil 105, 106, 183, 248, 278, 566
Baker's Broadcast, The (radio program) 6, 8, 694
Balaguer, Kopez 561, 562
Ball, Lucille 174, 175, 389, 685
Banghart, Kenneth 355
Bankhead, Tallulah 47, 48, 60, 145, 602, 680-682
Barber, Red 658, 660, 662
Barbera, Joe 623
Barclay, Don 164, 166, 186
Bardette, Trevor 607
Bargy, Roy 673
Barman, Valmere 295
Barnes, Binnie 271
Barnet, Charlie 676
Baron, Paul 131
Barrett, Sheila 630
Barrett, Tony 379
Barrie, Wendy 664

Franklin, Arthur 296
Franklin, Miriam 282
Fray, Jacques 49
Fred Allen Show, The (radio program) 158, 676, 696
Freedley, Vinton 97
Freedman, Bill 366, 389, 421, 454
Freedman, Hy 301, 319, 363
Freedman, Morris 366, 389, 421, 454, 605
Freeman, Everett 93
Frees, Paul 99
Froman, Jane 237, 630
Fuller, Lester 142
Fuller, Sam 82
Funke, Lewis 413

G-String Murders, The (book) 466
G.I. Jive (radio program) 196
G.I. Journal (radio program) 207
Gabel, Martin 31
Gable, Clark 316
Gaige, Crosby 4
Galen, Frank 16, 18
Gang Busters (radio program) 57, 92, 285
Gang, Martin 472
Garber, Jan 169
Garbo, Greta 7
Gard, Kathryn 611
Garde, Betty 675
Gardiner, Reginald 176, 185, 328, 329, 381, 691
Gardner, Earl 446
Gardner, Ed (Almost every page of the book.)
Gardner, Jr., Ed 304, 392, 615
Gardner, Simone (see Hegeman, Simone)
Garfield, John 267
Garland, Judy 8, 9, 669, 686
Garr, Eddie 16
Garson, Greer 422, 685, 686
Gatica, Malu 433

Hills, Marjorie 630
Hitchcock, Alfred 24, 275, 621
Hite, Ed 475
Hitler Gang, The (movie) 281
Hitz, Ed 474
Hoffa, Portland 658, 664, 681
Hogan, Ann 166, 172
Hogan's Daughter (radio program) 158
Hold Back the Dawn (movie) 136
Holden, Joyce 610
Hollywood Hotel (radio program) 6
Hollywood Preview (radio program) 288
Hollywood Reporter, The (periodical) 362, 398, 543
Holmes, Burton 388
Holmes, Tommy 185
Home Book of Verse, The (book) 48
Honrath, Don 350
Hopalong Cassidy (radio program) 24
Hope for a Harvest (stage play) 58
Hope, Bob 1, 78, 100, 164, 197, 245, 249, 265, 284, 297, 308, 352,
    354, 355, 392, 399, 408, 489, 509, 530, 586, 619, 643, 648,
    649, 665, 667, 668, 670-673, 684, 686, 687, 695-697
Hope, Dolores 188
Hope, Jim 399, 422
Hopper, Hedda 149, 168, 180, 282, 480, 535, 571, 689
Horine, A.G. 421
Horne, Lena 333, 685
Hornet, Green, The (radio program) 251
Hot Mikado, The (stage play) 96, 97
House of Glass, The (radio program) 581
Houseman, John 44
Howard, Bob 58, 64
Howard, Dick 171
Howard, Tom 630
Hubbard, John 613
Hucksters, The (movie) 345
Hughes, Howard 547
Hughes, Mary Beth 608, 610, 613

Manning, Irene 685
Mantan Messes Up (movie) 517
March, Fredric 23
March, Hal 462
Maren, Jerry 295
Marie Antoinette (movie) 11, 12
Marks, Larry 147, 319
Marr, Eddie 313, 381, 432, 456, 461
Marsac, Maurice 610
Marshall, Delores 444, 459
Marshall, Herbert 168, 180, 552
Martin, Mary 22, 95, 115-117, 272, 470, 659
Martin, Tony 531, 677
Martin. Pres. Luis Moniz 543
Marx, Groucho 364, 503, 697
Marx, Harpo 685
Mask and the Face, The (stage play) 4
Mason, Noah M. 494, 495
Massey, Raymond 23, 630, 658, 674
Mather, Jack 383
Matthews, Carole 292
Mature, Victor 342, 368
Maxwell, Elsa 43, 49, 630
Maxwell, Robert 323
Mayer, Louis B. 8, 11
Mayon, Charles 295
Mazurki, Mike 611
McBride, Mary Margaret 408
McCall, George 23
McCarthy, Glenn 451
McCormick, Henry J. 297
McCrary, Tex 213, 389, 438, 677, 679
McDaniel, Hattie 97
McDonagh, Richard 350, 351
McDonald, Marie 331, 332
McElrath, George 490
McFadden, J.A. 31
McGarry and his Mouse (radio program) 365, 675

Monaster, Nate 362, 366
Money-Go-Round (radio program) 148, 666
Monitor (radio program) 619, 620
Monroe, Ed 323
Monroe, Lucy 630
Monroe, Vaughn 277, 676
Montez, Maria 254
Montgomery, George 166
Montgomery, Robert 408
Moon is Blue, The (stage play) 547
Moore, Arthur 395, 396
Moore, Garry 147, 428, 679
Moore, Sam 7
Moore, Victor 282, 287, 290, 291, 296, 669
Moreland, Mantan 517, 519
Morgan, Frank 9, 207, 316
Morgan, Henry 364, 425, 471, 687
Morgan, Leo 590
Morgan, Michelle 182
Morris, Chester 468
Morris, Frances 296
Morris, John 366, 421, 453
Morrison, Barbara 606
Morrison, Donald 429
Mosby, Aline 583
Moss, Jack 276, 278
Movie-Radio Guide (magazine) 69
Mowbray, Alan 242, 243, 250
Mr. Adam's Bomb (film short) 450, 451
Mr. and Mrs. North (radio program) 372
Mr. District Attorney (radio program) 91, 447, 455, 478, 489, 696, 697
Mr. Keen, Tracer of Lost Persons (radio program) 570
Mr. Magoo (cartoons) 622
Murder in Duffy's Tavern (movie) 311-314
Murphy, Al 296
Murphy, George 8, 212
Murray, Arthur 46, 630

Taylor, Deems 12, 13, 44, 60, 119, 137, 169, 181, 182, 291, 320, 393, 573, 578, 629-631, 655, 665
Taylor, F. Chase (see Stoopnagle, Colonel)
Taylor, Glenhall 451
Taylor, Kay 518
Taylor, Robert 9
Taylor, Samuel 543, 547
Taylor, Tommy 140
Temple, Shirley 461, 462
Templeton, Alec 659
Tetley, Walter 387
Tex and Jinx Show, The (radio program) 272, 389, 404
Texaco Fire Chief, The (radio program) 693
Texaco Star Theater, The (radio program) 18, 19, 22, 204, 664, 658, 666, 677
The I Don't Care Girl (movie) 237
There I Stood with My Piccolo (book) 11
This Gun for Hire (movie) 445
This is My Best (radio program) 672
This is New York (radio program) 12-18, 681
This is the Army (movie) 174
This is the Life (radio program) 38
This is Your Life (radio program) 510
This is Your Life (television program) 598
Thomas, Ann 285, 286, 288, 290, 296
Thomas, Danny 245
Thomas, Helen 420
Thomas, John Charles 672
Thomas, Lowell 675
Thomas, Thomas L. 441, 446
Thompson, Beverly 296
Thompson, Rene 2
Thompson, Steven 2, 502
Three Men on a Horse (stage play) 160
Three X Sisters, The 145
Three's Company (television program) 574
Thrill of Brazil, The (movie) 345
Thrills of a Romance (movie) 254

White, Linda 563
White, Sam 292
Whiteman, Paul 135-137, 151, 661, 662, 672
Whiting, Margaret 676
Whitley, Crane 296
Whitley, June 609
Whitman, Ernest 98, 685
Whitty, Dame May 265
Widmark, Richard 656
Widom, Bud 374, 428
Wilde, Cornel 523, 679
Wilkerson, Martha 687
Williams, Charles B. 296
Williams, Esther 253, 332, 427, 624
Williams, Hope 631
Williams, Rhys 590
Willing, Foy 289
Willkie, Wendell 164
Willson, Meredith 11, 12
Wilson, Don 339
Wilson, Frank 555, 559
Wilson, Marie 143, 656
Wilson, Ted 77-79, 82
Wilson, Ward 58
Winchell, Paul 272, 390
Winchell, Walter 345, 379, 396, 408, 498, 571
Windheim, Marek 249
Winkler, Danny 311, 340, 341
Winsella, Walter 657
Winston, Irene 437
Winter, Nicholas 559
Winters, Jonathan 524
Winters, Roland 172
Winters, Shelley 480, 563
Wisconsin State Journal (newspaper) 497
With a Song in My Heart (song) 237
Withers, Jane 282
Wolfe, Ernest 543

ABOUT THE AUTHOR

Martin Grams, Jr. is the award-winning author and co-author of more than twenty books about old-time radio and retro television. *Duffy's Tavern* was a project spanning more than a decade of research and required the author to travel all over the country to various archives. "The decision on what subject to write about stems from the importance and necessity of what needs to be documented and preserved. Very little has been written about *Duffy's Tavern*," Martin explains.

He is also the author and/or co-author of *The Twilight Zone: Unlocking the Door to a Television Classic* (2008), *The Time Tunnel: A History of the Television Program* (2011), *The Green Hornet: A History of Radio, Motion-Pictures, Comics and Television* (2009), *The Shadow: The History and Mystery of the Radio Program* (2010), *The Have Gun-Will Travel Companion* (2000), *Science Fiction Theatre: A History of the Television Program, 1955-57* (2011), *The Sound of Detection: The Radio Adventures of Ellery Queen* (2002), *Car 54, Where Are You?* (2009), and many others.

OTHER BOOKS WRITTEN OR CO-WRITTEN BY MARTIN GRAMS, JR.

THE TIME TUNNEL: A History of the Television Series (2013)

THE SHADOW: The History and Mystery of the Radio Program (2010)

SCIENCE FICTION THEATRE: A History of the Television Program, 1955 - 1957 (2010)

THE GREEN HORNET: A History of Radio, Motion Pictures, Comics and Television (2009)

THE TWILIGHT ZONE: Unlocking the Door to a Television Classic (2009)

CAR 54, WHERE ARE YOU? (2009)

THE "LOST" SAM SPADE SCRIPTS (2009)

THE RAILROAD HOUR: A History of the Radio Series (2007)

I LED THREE LIVES: The True Story of Herbert A. Philbrick's Television Program (2007)

THE RADIO ADVENTURES OF SAM SPADE (2007)

GANG BUSTERS: The Crime Fighters of American Broadcasting (2004)

www.ingramcontent.com/pod-product-compliance
Lightning Source LLC
Chambersburg PA
CBHW060319100426

42812CB00003B/821

*9 7 8 1 6 2 9 3 3 3 5 8 8 *